CREATIVE INTERVEN[...]

TOOLKIT

A PRACTICAL GUIDE TO STOP INTERPERSONAL VIOLENCE

WELCOME TO THE CREATIVE INTERVENTIONS TOOLKIT: A PRACTICAL GUIDE TO STOP INTERPERSONAL VIOLENCE

All content is the same as the toolkit that has been available on www.creative-interventions.org since 2012.

This Toolkit is also available in a shorter Workbook form.
See *Creating Interventions Workbook: A Short and Practical Guide to Stop Interpersonal Violence*

at www.creative-interventions.org.

Creative Interventions
www.creative-interventions.org

HOW ARE YOU USING THIS TOOLKIT?
PLEASE SHARE YOUR EXPERIENCES

As more people continue to use this Toolkit, we are hearing more stories about challenges- and successes - in ending and preventing violence.
Please share your stories on www.creative-interventions.org/stories

We invite you to share back your:

- Suggestions for changes or future tools
- Stories about how you were able to use this Toolkit for study, organizing, or confronting and transforming violence

ISBN 978-1-84935-464-6
Library of Congress Control Number: 2021940216

AK Press
370 Ryan Avenue #100
Chico, CA 95973
USA
www.akpress.org
akpress@akpress.org

AK Press
33 Tower Street
Edinburgh, EH6, 7BN
Scotland
www.akuk.com
akuk@akpress.org

Please contact us to request the latest AK Press distribution catalog, which features books, pamphlets, zines, and stylish apparel published and/or distributed by AK Press. Alternatively, visit our websites for the complete catalog, latest news, and secure ordering.

Cover illustration by Kill Joy (https://justseeds.org/artist/killjoy)
Printed in Canada on acid-free paper

TABLE OF CONTENTS

PREFACE & ACKNOWLEDGMENTS

0.1. Creative Interventions: The Story Behind This Toolkit ---- P-2 | 2
0.2. A Community Effort ---- P-7 | 7

SECTION 1. INTRODUCTION & FAQ

1.1. Welcome ---- S1-2 | 14
1.2. The Community-Based Intervention to Violence: An Introduction ---- S1-4 | 16
1.3. Who Is This Toolkit For? ---- S1-6 | 18
1.4. What Is in This Toolkit? ---- S1-12 | 24
1.5. What Is Our Bigger Vision? ---- S1-16 | 28
1.6. Real Life Stories to Share ---- S1-18 | 30
1.7. This Toolkit as a Work in Progress ---- S1-29 | 41
1.8. FAQ - Frequently Asked Questions about the Toolkit ---- S1-31 | 43

SECTION 2. SOME BASICS EVERYONE SHOULD KNOW

2.0. Introduction ---- S2-2 | 58
2.1. What Is the Community-Based Intervention to Interpersonal Violence? ---- S2-3 | 59
2.2. Interpersonal Violence: Some Basics Everyone Should Know ---- S2-14 | 70
2.3. Violence Intervention: Some Important Lessons ---- S2-37 | 93

SECTION 3. MODEL OVERVIEW: IS IT RIGHT FOR YOU?

103 3.0 Introduction S3-2
104 3.1. Reviewing the Community-Based Intervention to Interpersonal Violence S3-2
110 3.2. What This Model Is NOT S3-8
114 3.3. Building a Model on Generations of Wisdom S3-12
115 3.4. Values to Guide Your Intervention S3-13
117 3.5. What Are We Trying to Achieve: 3 Key Intervention Areas S3-15
121 3.6. Interventions over Time: 4 Phases S3-19
126 3.7. Tools for Interventions: 8 Sets of Tools S3-24
131 3.8. Model at a Glance: Tools across the 4 Phases S3-28
133 3.9. Tools to Use Before You Get Started S3-30
138 3.10. Next Steps S3-35

SECTION 4. TOOLS TO MIX AND MATCH

140 4.0. Introduction S4-1
143 4.A. Getting Clear. What Is Going On? S4A-1
173 4.B. Staying Safe. How Do We Stay Safe? S4B-1
215 4.C. Mapping Allies and Barriers. Who Can Help? S4C-1
245 4.D. Goal Setting. What Do We Want? S4D-1
277 4.E. Supporting Survivors or Victims. How Can We Help? S4E-1
303 4.F. Taking Accountability. How Do We Change Violence? S4F-1
389 4.G. Working Together. How Do We Work Together as a Team? S4G-1
427 4.H. Keeping on Track. How Do We Move Forward? S4H-1

SECTION 5. OTHER RESOURCES

5.1. Key Definitions: Words We Use and What They Mean to Creative Interventions S5-2 450

5.2. Real Life Stories and Examples from the Toolkit S5-8 456

5.3. Creative Interventions Anti-Oppression Policy S5-38 485

5.4. Community-Based Responses to Interpersonal Violence Workshop S5-40 488

5.5. Taking Risks: Implementing Grassroots Community Accountability Strategies, by Communities Against Rape and Abuse (CARA) S5-50 498

5.6. Distinguishing between Violence and Abuse, by Connie Burk, Northwest Network of Bisexual, Trans, Lesbian and Gay Survivors of Abuse S5-68 516

5.7. Portrait of Praxis: An Anatomy of Accountability, by Esteban Kelly and Jenna Peters-Golden of Philly Stands Up (PSU) S5-78 526

5.8. Confronting Sexual Assault: Transformative Justice on the Ground in Philadelphia, by Bench Ansfield and Timothy Colman of Philly Stands Up (PSU) S5-89 537

5.9. Shame, Realisation and Restoration: The Ethics of Restorative Practice, by Alan Jenkins S5-96 544

5.10. Tips for Seeking a Therapist [for People Who Have Done Sexual Harm], by Anonymous S5-106 554

5.11. Resource List S5-116 564

LIST OF TOOLS

SECTION 3. MODEL OVERVIEW: IS IT RIGHT FOR YOU? TOOLS

134 Tool 3.1. Is This Model Right For You? Checklist ---------- S3-31

135 Tool 3.2. Values to Guide Your Intervention. Creative Interventions Checklist ---------- S3-32

136 Tool 3.3. Values to Guide Your Intervention (In Your Own Words). Guiding Questions ---------- S3-33

137 Tool 3.4. Values to Guide Your Intervention (In Your Own Words). Checklist ---------- S3-34

SECTION 4A. *GETTING CLEAR* TOOLS

160 Tool A1. Getting Clear Snapshot: Short Question Guide ---------- S4A-18

163 Tool A2. Getting Clear Worksheet ---------- S4A-21

164 Tool A3. Naming the Harm Chart ---------- S4A-22

168 Tool A4. Harm Statement Worksheet ---------- S4A-26

169 Tool A5. Getting Clear: Intervention Factors At-a-Glance ---------- S4A-27

SECTION 4.B. *STAYING SAFE* TOOLS

191 Tool B1. Risk Assessment Chart ---------- S4B-19

195 Tool B2. Safety Plan and Action Worksheet ---------- S4B-23

201 Tool B3. Safety Plan and Action Chart ---------- S4B-29

204 Tool B4. Escape Safety Checklist ---------- S4B-32

207 Tool B5. Meeting Person Who Did Harm Safety Worksheet ---------- S4B-35

SECTION 4.C. MAPPING ALLIES AND BARRIERS TOOLS

Tool C1. Mapping Allies & Barriers: Snapshot/Quick Guided Questions S4C-16 230

Tool C2. Mapping Allies & Barriers: Worksheet S4C-17 231

Tool C3. Ally Roles Checklist S4C-19 233

Tool C4. Good Ally Checklist S4C-20 234

Tool C5. Allies to Work with the Person Doing Harm Chart S4C-22 236

Tool C6. Barrier Checklist S4C-25 239

Tool C7. Allies and Barriers: Summary S4C-27 241

Tool C8. Invitation to Help with an Intervention S4C-29 243

SECTION 4.D. GOAL SETTING TOOLS

Tool D1. Dealing with Strong Negative Feelings and Fantasy during Goal Setting S4D-20 264

Tool D2. Goal Setting Guided Questions and Chart S4D-21 265

Tool D3. Mapping Combined Goals Chart S4D-24 268

Tool D4. Shared Collective Goals Chart S4D-25 269

Tool D5. Collective Goals Summary Checklist and Next Steps S4D-26 270

Tool D6. Turning Goals into Action S4D-31 275

SECTION 4.E SUPPORTING SURVIVOR OR VICTIMS TOOLS

Tool E1. What Does the Survivor or Victim Need? Checklist S4E-20 296

Tool E2. What Does the Survivor or Victim Need? Guiding Questions S4E-22 298

Tool E3. Survivor or Victim Participation in an Intervention Chart S4E-24 300

SECTION 4.F. TAKING ACCOUNTABILITY TOOLS

354 Tool F1. Staircase of Change S4F-52

365 Tool F2. Level of Participation for Survivors or Victims Chart S4F-63

369 Tool F3. Self-Reflection and Guiding Questions for Survivors or Victims and Allies S4F-67

380 Tool F4. Self-Reflection and Practice for Allies. Practice Questions S4F-78

383 Tool F5. Breaking through Defensiveness. Guiding Questions for Person Doing Harm S4F-81

385 Tool F6. Preparing for Direct Communication. Affirmations and Guided Questions for the Person Doing Harm S4F-83

SECTION 4.G. WORKING TOGETHER TOOLS

407 Tool G1. Working Together Snapshot: Short Question Guide S4G-19

410 Tool G2. Team Roles: Checklist S4G-22

416 Tool G3. Agreements for Sustaining a Team over Time S4G-28

417 Tool G4. Communication Worksheet S4G-29

421 Tool G5. Decision-Making Types and Models S4G-33

SECTION 4.H. KEEPING ON TRACK TOOLS

436 Tool H1. How Are We Doing? End of Meeting: Guiding Questions S4H-10

438 Tool H2. What Are Next Steps: Guiding Questions S4H-12

439 Tool H3. Are We Ready for the Next Step: Guiding Questions S4H-13

440 Tool H4. How Did We Do? Reflecting on an Action: Guiding Questions S4H-14

442 Tool H5. How Are We Doing? Individual Self-Check: Guiding Questions S4H-16

443 Tool H6. How Are We Doing? Group Self-Check: Guiding Questions S4H-17

445 Tool H7. How Are We Doing? Closing an Intervention: Guiding Questions S4H-19

PREFACE & ACKNOWLEDGMENTS

✱ PREFACE & ACKNOWLEDGMENTS

WHAT IS CREATIVE INTERVENTIONS?

Creative Interventions (CI) started in 2004 in Oakland as a national resource center to create and promote community-based interventions to interpersonal violence. Its founders worked with survivors of domestic violence and sexual assault for many years but found limitations in the U.S. approach to working with violence. CI was established as one way in which we could use our experiences and knowledge to equip everyday people to confront, challenge and overcome violence.

The organization was started with the purpose to develop what it and others call a community-based approach to ending interpersonal violence. This approach is an alternative to the more common way that organizations typically deal with interpersonal violence. Organizations that deal with domestic violence and sexual assault generally view violence as an individual problem or rely on the police and criminal justice system as a solution. We wanted to turn back to our communities and strengthen community-based systems to resist violence in all of its forms.

For CI, the community-based approach is one in which everyday people such as family, friends, neighbors, co-workers, members of community organizations such as faith institutions, civic organizations or businesses are the people who take action to intervene in violence.

INCITE! WOMEN OF COLOR AGAINST VIOLENCE

CI was inspired by a social movement that led to the formation of a national organization called Incite! Women of Color against Violence (see www.incite-national.org) in 2000. At that time, over a thousand people, most from communities of color, gathered at the first Color of Violence Conference in Santa Cruz to seek new, alternative responses to violence – a response that turns towards communities and away from policing and prisons to address interpersonal violence.

It is also inspired by a statement that was created by Incite! Women of Color against Violence and another organization, Critical Resistance, that was founded in 1998 at a conference also attended by thousands committed to prison abolition. Together Incite! and Critical Resistance found common ground in their joint statement, Incite! Women of Color against Violence and Critical Resistance Statement on Gender Violence and the Prison Industrial Complex (downloadable at https://incite-national.org/incite-critical-resistance-statement/).

The Incite!-Critical Resistance joint statement opens with the words:

> We call on social justice movements to develop strategies and analysis that address both state AND interpersonal violence, particularly violence against women. Currently, activists/movements that address state violence (such as anti-prison, anti-police brutality groups) often work in isolation from activists/movements that address domestic and sexual violence. The result is that women of color, who suffer disproportionately from both state and interpersonal violence, have become marginalized within these movements. It is critical that we develop responses to gender violence that do not depend on a sexist, racist, classist, and homophobic criminal justice system. It is also important that we develop strategies that challenge the criminal justice system and that also provide safety for survivors of sexual and domestic violence. To live violence free-lives, we must develop holistic strategies for addressing violence that speak to the intersection of all forms of oppression.

In the spirit of this statement and in honor of the many who have resisted violence over the generations, we at CI started what we planned to be an organization that would exist long enough to help create new resources to continue this work. At the end of the distribution of this Toolkit, we also planned to end the organization and rebuild new ways to support a community-based response to violence that would truly rely upon local communities, from informal friendship networks to community institutions such as faith institutions, unions or community organizations – and not upon a single organization such as CI.

The limited time horizon of the organization was deliberate and served the purposes of:

- Keeping focus on the community-based nature of the project rather than on the institutional life of CI; and
- Allowing for risk-taking within the organization (since many of the concepts and practices of CI were and are considered experimental, controversial and risky) due to reduced concern regarding long-term reputation or well-being of the organization

THE WORK LEADING TO THIS TOOLKIT

This Toolkit the result of a 3-year period from 2006 to 2009 during which CI joined with partner organizations in the San Francisco Bay Area including Asian Women's Shelter, Shimtuh, Narika, and La Clinica de la Raza. We also had partnerships with other individuals and organizations such as those listed in Section 0.2: A Community Effort.

Our organizations worked closely together to create a different, alternative approach to issues of domestic violence and sexual assault. All of our organizations have years of experience working in mostly immigrant communities on the issues of domestic violence and sexual assault. And all were interested in coming together to try to create different options for people experiencing violence.

✱ PREFACE & ACKNOWLEDGMENTS

We sought answers to the questions:

- How can family members, friends, neighbors, co-workers and community members get actively involved in ending violence when their own loved ones are experiencing interpersonal violence? These people are what we end up calling *community allies* or what others might call bystanders or social network.
- How can we use our connection and care for people who are victims or survivors of violence to not only provide safety but also opportunities for them to heal and re-connect to healthier relationships?
- How can we all provide greater safety for survivors or victims of violence even if they stay with or need to co-exist in the same community with people who have harmed them?
- How can we get violent or abusive people to stop the harm they have caused, repair it – and change their attitudes and behavior so that they become part of the solution?
- How can we change violent behavior by using our connection and care for people who have caused harm rather than by using threats, punishment or policing?
- How can we change everyday beliefs, practices and skills to address, reduce, end and prevent violence?
- How can we use all of the above to create the safe, respectful and healthy communities that we all seek?

These are challenging questions that called for a new approach and model for addressing interpersonal violence.

The 3-year project that we called the Community-Based Interventions Project brought our team together to create a new vision for violence intervention, to work with people experiencing violence, and to develop a model and tools from our work during that time.

During that time, we answered calls and requests from people facing some form of interpersonal violence who were seeking something different than what they could find from other existing domestic violence or sexual assault services. We partnered with them to find our way towards the concepts, tools and lessons in this Toolkit. We were initially guided by the questions listed above and the values that we had created at the outset of CI (See Section 3.3: Guiding Your Intervention with Values). Our process was open and experimental. Much of it was based upon the knowledge we had about the dynamics of interpersonal violence and the answers we all developed using the key questions found in Section 4. Tools to Mix and Match. Each situation was unique. But these common questions led us to figure out a response that fit the values and needs of those who came to CI. Many times, the people coming to CI found satisfaction in imagining what they truly wanted and needed – without being told what that should be. They found support in asking friends and family members to come together to find a different way to think about their situation of violence and to create strategies that could bring about change. They often considered but did not necessarily follow through with all of the steps of what could be a long, difficult and risky process.

From the beginning, we offered a community-based approach that was different than what is usually available. And it mostly involved asking questions that would help lead those seeking our help to find the resources that they needed among their own friends, family and community and find the answers from what they knew about their own situation of violence, their values and their goals.

Because we helped to ask questions and hold a process that relied upon those facing the situation of violence to come up with their own responses and resources, we call this a facilitated model. We are not the experts. We are there to help people find their own expertise within a situation that is often filled with enough confusion and strong emotions to make it difficult for one to do on one's own. During this period, we encountered about 25 situations of violence and met in person with over 100 people coming together to seek solutions.

Together, with the facilitators at CI and their allies, they were able to think differently about what they needed and what they wanted to do to resolve violence: through self-reflection and clarification (A: Getting Clear); thinking more clearly about safety (B: Staying Safe); finding help among their friends, family and community (C: Mapping Allies and Barriers); coming up with what they really wanted (D: Setting Goals); supporting survivors or victims (E. Supporting Survivors or Victims); thinking about what they wanted from the person doing harm (F: Taking Accountability); finding ways to work collectively with their community (G: Working Together); and moving through what could be a long and winding process towards their goals (H: Keeping on Track).

This Toolkit is the result of this project. It contains the model that we built together with our partners and with those who came to seek our help. It includes any tips and useful information that we were able to gather during this period of time. And we expect that it will be used and then improved upon by all of you who may use it in your own situations of violence and in your own communities.

The Toolkit is available on the website www.creative-interventions.org and also accompanies stories of people who have taken action to end violence, stories that are featured through the Story Telling and Organizing Project (STOP) available at www.stopviolenceeveryday.org. We hope to expand the Toolkit from English to other languages with the help of others who find this Toolkit useful.

✱ PREFACE & ACKNOWLEDGMENTS

THE TOOLKIT AND THE GOALS OF CREATIVE INTERVENTIONS

With this Toolkit on the website, CI has reached its organizational goals:

1. Develop a model and tools to support community-based responses to violence.
2. Document these models, tools and lessons through creating useful and accessible websites, Toolkits, audio clips, stories and so on.
3. Make these models, tools and lessons available to the public.

We Invite You to Build Upon Our Collective Work

With this, we are closing down the other formal operations of CI except for maintaining the website (www.creative-interventions.org) as we had planned from our very beginning, and to make room for you who use this Toolkit to make it your own. Our email at info@creative-interventions.org will also be answered by volunteers who continue to work to keep the Toolkit, accompanying resources and ongoing discussions a living collaborative project for as long as it is useful and viable.

Through the website or whatever other connections we create, we encourage you to add to it, share stories, and develop new approaches for communities to end violence in all of its forms.

The project, StoryTelling & Organizing Project (STOP) (www.stopviolenceeveryday.org), carries on as an independent and companion project to continue to support community-based interventions to violence, collect and share stories as all of us seek to end interpersonal violence, and to grow the movement towards liberation. Your experiences with the Toolkit and improvements can be shared on this website and its volunteers and collaborators, as well.

A COMMUNITY EFFORT

A collective community is behind this community-based response to violence. Many of us as individuals and as organizations are working together to challenge violence in all of its forms. Many have been involved in working both on the Community-Based Interventions Project that has generated this Toolkit.

The key partner organizations towards the creation of this Toolkit are:

Incite! Women of Color against Violence (National). Creative Interventions is an affiliate of this national organization and is a creation of the social movement that Incite! represents.

Creative Interventions (Oakland, CA) (with many, many individual supporters – volunteers, board members, advisory board members, staff, organizational partners, large and small funders)

Asian Women's Shelter (Oakland, CA)

Narika (Oakland, CA)

Shimtuh, a project of Korean Community Center of the East Bay (KCCEB) (Oakland, CA)

La Clinica de la Raza (Oakland, CA)

StoryTelling & Organizing Project (STOP) (National). STOP is a spin-off project of Creative Interventions and is working with a partnership of community organizations to promote community-based responses to violence through story telling and organizing around successful strategies for communities to challenge violence in all of its forms. See www.stopviolenceeveryday.org.

✱ PREFACE & ACKNOWLEDGMENTS

The individuals who made up these teams:

- CI Staff: Rachel Herzing, Mimi Kim, Isaac Ontiveros
- CI Interventions Team: Sutapa Balaji, Leo Bruenn, Juan Cuba, Rachel Herzing, Isabel Kang, Ann Rhee Menzie, Mimi Kim, Orchid Pusey, Poroshat Shekarloo (Kalei Valli Kanuha: Evaluator and Mentor)
- CI Board Members: Crystal Baik, Mimi Kim, Susun Kim, Christine Lipat, Heba Nimr, Jesus Solario
- CI Advisory Committee Members: Trishala Deb (New York, NY), Staci Haines (Oakland, CA), Kalei Valli Kanuha (Honolulu, HI), Kelly Mitchell-Clark (San Francisco, CA and now international), Sue Osthoff (Philadelphia, PA), Julia Perilla (Atlanta, GA), Beth Richie (Chicago, IL), Poroshat Shekarloo (Oakland, CA and national), Kabzuag Vaj (Madison, WI)
- Other advisors and mentors (not represented in the list of key partners and/or influences) including: Rhea Almeida, Colleen Baik, Sujatha Baliga, Morgan Bassichis, Lisa Bates, Connie Burk, Alisa Bierria, Andrea Bible, Margaret Benson-Thompson, Maria Bratko, Mateo Burch, Rose Braz, Ching-In Chen, Eunice Cho, Inhe Choi, Adena Chung, Vicki Coffey, Eboni Colbert, Timothy Colman, Anna Couey, Kuki Cuban, Angela Davis, David Denborough, Ganga Dharmappa, Ejeris Dixon, Alice do Valle, Jai Dulani, Michelle Erai, Mordecai Ettinger, Micah Hobbes Frazier, Catlin Fullwood, Alan Greig, Di Grinnell, Alexis Pauline Gumbs, Ka'iana Halli, Judy Han, Shira Hassan, Elizabeth Hausler, Caprice Haverty, Xandra Ibarra, Ruthie Gilmore, Serena Huang, Vanessa Huang, Gaurav Jashnani, Alan Jenkins, Eungie Joo, Mariame Kaba, Joo-Hyun Kang, Sara Kershnar, Theryn Kigvamasud-Vashti, Helen Kim, Miho Kim, Tina Kim, Kim Klein, Paul Kivel, Thao Le, Leah Lakshmi Piepzna-Samarasinha, Sujin Lee, Chris Lymbertos, RJ Maccani, Sonja Mackenzie, Claude Marks, Teresa Martyny, Beckie Masaki, Johonna McCants, gita mehrotra, Mia Mingus, Vanessa Moses, Soniya Munshi, Susan Murray, Alicia Ohs, Emily Ozer, Grace Nam, Tessie Nam, Sitara Nieves, Julia Oparah, Joan Pennell, James Ptacek, Catherine Pyun, Andrea Ritchie, Clarissa Rojas, Ana Romero, Beth Roy, Manju Rajendran, Ann Russo, Mayseng Saetern, Andy Smith, Nat Smith, Jen Soriano, Theeba Soundararajan, Thenmozhi Soundararajan, Melissa Spatz, Lisa Thomas-Adeyemo, Aimee Thompson, Mary Ann Thompson, Emily Thuma, Aunty Ulu, Saba Waheed, Sujata Warrier, Cheryl White, Janelle White, Tommy Wong, Judith Wrubel, Nina Yusuf

Other key partners and/or influences include:

- Amokura (Whangerei, Aotearoa)
- Audre Lorde Project – Safe OUTside the System (New York, NY)
- Caminar Latino (Atlanta, GA)
- Casa Atabex Ache (Bronx, NY)
- Center for Media Justice (Oakland, CA)
- Challenging Male Supremacy Project (New York, NY)
- Chicago Metropolitan Battered Women's Network (Chicago, IL)
- Close to Home (Dorchester, MA)
- Communities against Rape and Abuse (CARA) (Seattle, WA)
- Community United against Violence (CUAV) (San Francisco, CA)
- CONNECT (New York, NY)
- Critical Resistance (National; Oakland, CA; Los Angeles, CA)
- DataCenter (Oakland, CA)
- Dulwich Center (Adelaide, Australia)
- Eastside Arts Alliance (Oakland, CA)
- Escuela Popular Norteña (Binghamton, NY)
- Females United for Action (FUFA) (Chicago, IL)
- Free Battered Women (San Francisco, CA)
- Freedom, Inc. (Madison, WI)
- Freedom Archives (San Francisco, CA)
- generationFIVE (Oakland, CA)
- Generative Somatics (Oakland, CA)
- Harm Free Zone (Durham, NC)
- Harm Free Zone (New York, NY)

✱ PREFACE & ACKNOWLEDGMENTS

- Institute for Family Services (Somerset, NJ)
- Justice Now (Oakland, CA)
- Ke Ala Lokahi (Hilo, HI)
- Kindred (Atlanta, GA)
- Korean American Women in Need (KAN-WIN) (Chicago, IL)
- Namelehuapono, a project of Parents and Children Together (PACT) (Honolulu, HI)
- Nodutdol (New York, NY)
- The NW Network of Bi, Trans, Lesbian, and Gay Survivors of Abuse (Seattle, WA)
- Philly Stands Up (Philadelphia, PA)
- Project Nia (Chicago, IL)
- Restorative Justice for Oakland Youth (RJOY) (Oakland, CA)
- Revolution Starts at Home Collective (National)
- Beth Roy and Radical Therapy (San Francisco, CA)
- San Francisco Women against Rape (SFWAR) (San Francisco, CA)
- Sista II Sista (Brooklyn, NY)
- Southern California Library (Los Angeles, CA)
- Support New York (New York, NY)
- Third Path (Honolulu, HI)
- Third World Majority (Oakland, CA)
- Transgender, Gender Variant & Intersex Justice Project (TGIP) (San Francisco, CA)
- Ubuntu (Durham, NC)
- Visions to Peace Project (Washington, DC)
- Women and Girl's Collective Action Network (Chicago, IL)
- Young Women's Empowerment Project (YWEP) (Chicago, IL)

Special thanks to those working on this Toolkit:

Writing Team/Interventions Team: Sutapa Balaji, Leo Bruenn, Juan Cuba, Rachel Herzing, Isabel Kang, Mimi Kim, Orchid Pusey

Editing Team: Xandra Ibarra, Eunice Cho, Tina Kim, Catherine Pyun

Graphic Arts/Design: Tania Allen, Judy Han, Sid Jordan, Danbee Deb Kim (final/lead designer), Lala Openi, and Tommy Wong

Reviewers: Crystal Baik, Morgan Bassichis, Alisa Bierria, Eunice Cho, Trishala Deb, Xandra Ibarra, Gaurav Jashnani, Tiloma Jayasinghe, gita mehrotra, Mariame Kaba, Tina Kim, Paul Kivel, RJ Maccani, Beckie Masaki, Soniya Munshi, Heba Nimr, staff of The Northwest Network of BTLG Survivors of Abuse, Leah Lakshmi Piepzna-Samarasinha, Philly Stands Up Collective, Clarissa Rojas, Ann Russo, Aimee Thompson, Mary Anne Thompson

Funders include:

- Many, many individuals donating money, in-kind support, moral support and help of all kinds – your generosity continues to fuel our continued work within and beyond CI
- Aepoch
- Ben & Jerry Foundation
- The California Endowment
- Echoing Green Fellowship
- Echoing Green Accelerator Grant
- Funding Exchange, Beyond Prisons Initiative
- Funding Exchange, Donor Advised Fund
- The Robert Wood Johnson Foundation, Vulnerable Populations, Fresh Ideas
- Ms. Foundation
- Target Foundation
- Women's Foundation–Donor Circle on Race, Gender & Human Rights

✱ PREFACE & ACKNOWLEDGMENTS

NOTES

1 INTRODUCTION & FREQUENTLY ASKED QUESTIONS

1.1 Introduction

1.2 Community-Based Intervention to Interpersonal Violence: An Introduction

1.3. Who Is This Toolkit For?

1.4. What Is in This Toolkit?

1.5. What Is Our Bigger Vision?

1.6. Real Life Stories to Share

1.7. This Toolkit as a Work in Progress

1.8. Frequently Asked Questions about the Toolkit

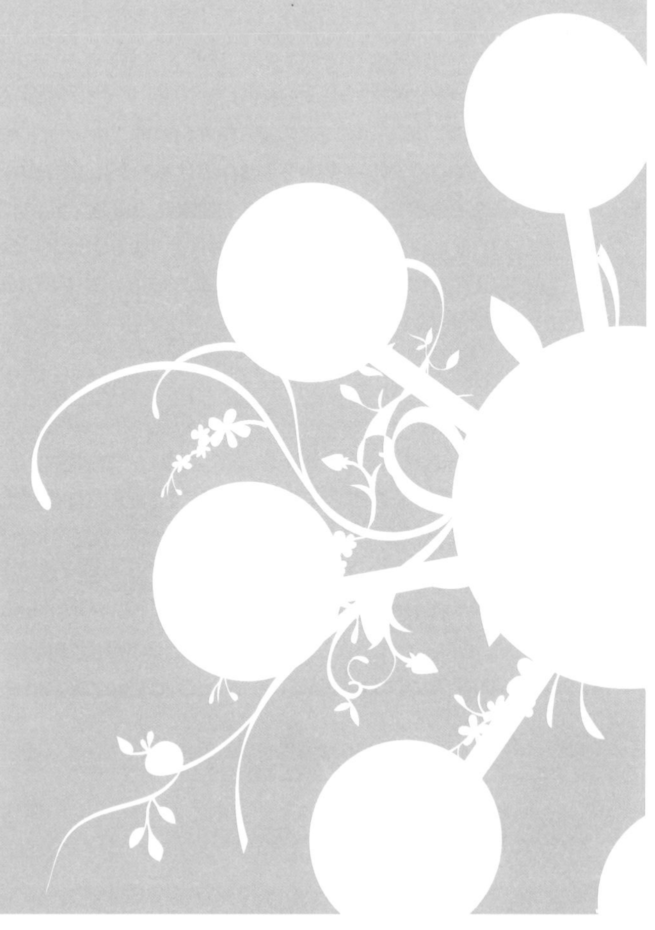

We need to trust people to be the experts on their own lives and have faith in people to set the course for working from harm to transformation.

1.0. INTRODUCTION

If you are reading this, it is likely that your life or that of someone you care about has been impacted by interpersonal violence – domestic violence, sexual abuse or assault or family violence. Perhaps you are in a crisis and you're not sure what to do, but you feel an urgent need to do something. Or maybe you have been trying to address a situation of violence, but you need some more ideas and resources on what to do. Perhaps you heard about this Toolkit because you are seeking safety, but calling the police is not a safe option for you. You may be reading this because you have been abusive or violent and are looking for support on how to change.

This Toolkit helps us figure out what steps we can take to address, reduce, end or even prevent violence—what we call violence intervention.

This Toolkit promotes an approach called community-based interventions to violence or what some call community accountability or transformative justice as a way to break isolation and to create solutions to violence from those who are most affected by violence – survivors and victims of violence, friends, family and community. It asks us to look to those around us to gather together to create grounded, thoughtful community responses. It builds on our connections and caring rather than looking at solutions that rely only on separation and disconnections from our communities. It invites us to involve even those who harm us as potential allies in stopping that harm and as active partners in deeply changing attitudes and behaviors towards a solution to violence. It expands the idea of violence and its solutions from that between individuals to one that includes communities – both close and intimate communities and the broader communities of which we are a part.

This Toolkit is based upon the knowledge that our communities have been carrying out creative responses to end violence for many generations. When faced with someone in need of help, our aunts, uncles, and cousins, our friends and neighbors, our faith leaders and the people of all ages have been figuring out ways to address, reduce, end or prevent violence. We at Creative Interventions are building upon these best efforts and successes as well as lessons from mistakes and failures. These lessons have often been ignored as we look increasingly towards the police and agencies to protect us. Centering what we call community-based interventions reminds us of the importance of our own histories, our own expertise and our important roles in ending violence.

BY INTERPERSONAL VIOLENCE, WE MEAN...

- Domestic violence or intimate partner violence that takes place within an intimate relationship such as marriage, domestic partnership, dating relationship, former relationship.
- Family violence that can include domestic violence between intimate partners, but can also extend to children, parents, grandchildren, grandparents, other family members and others who may be very close to family like family friends, guardians, and caretakers.
- Sexual violence that includes unwanted sexual attitudes, touch or actions such as sexual assault, rape, sexual harassment, molestation, child sexual abuse, and incest.
- Child abuse that is any kind of abuse against children including neglect or emotional, physical or sexual abuse; we consider any form of sexual activity between an adult and a child as abuse.
- Elder abuse that is any kind of abuse against elderly people.
- While CI focuses on the types of violence just listed above, this Toolkit may also be useful for those experiencing violence in other settings such as within neighborhoods, schools, organizations, workplaces, or other employment situations – these forms of violence can also be considered interpersonal.

See Section 2.2: Interpersonal Violence: Some Basics Everyone Should Know for more information about interpersonal violence.

Interpersonal violence is very commonly a way to gain power and control over another person. It often takes advantage of unequal power. This is why interpersonal forms of violence are so often committed by men against women and girls, boys against girls, male-identified over female-identified, adults over youth and children, able-bodied over people with disabilities, citizens over immigrants, legal immigrants over undocumented immigrants, people with high status over people with lower status, rich over poor or those who financially depend on them.

1.2. THE COMMUNITY-BASED INTERVENTION TO INTERPERSONAL VIOLENCE: AN INTRODUCTION

The community-based intervention to interpersonal violence is an approach based upon the ideas and work of many individuals and organizations thinking about and developing similar approaches to violence. It offers the insights, tools and lessons learned from the three years during which Creative Interventions worked with community members seeking a response to their particular situations of violence. It is a work in progress. (See Preface and Acknowledgements for more information on the process leading up to this Toolkit).

This Toolkit focuses specifically on interpersonal violence, or what we might know as domestic violence, sexual abuse or assault or family violence – although it might also be useful with other forms of violence. Therefore, it involves situations of violence in which people often know each other – and may even be very close as intimate partners, family members or people who live or work with or near each other.

The Creative Interventions community-based response to violence is based upon the fact that first responders to interpersonal violence are most often friends, family and community members. It assumes that solutions to violence are most meaningful and effective if they come from those closest to and most impacted by violence. It believes that solutions created by communities affected by violence can strengthen the skills and ability of ordinary community members to keep violence from happening again.

The Creative Interventions community-based approach is:

- **Collective.** The intervention involves the coordinated efforts of a group of people rather than just one individual.

- **Action-Oriented.** A community takes action to address, reduce, end or prevent interpersonal violence.

- **Community-Based.** The intervention is organized and carried out by friends, family, neighbors, co-workers or community members rather than social services, the police, child welfare or governmental institutions.

- **Coordinated.** The intervention links people and actions together to work together in a way that is coordinated towards the same goals – and that makes sure that our individual actions work towards a common purpose. It sees us as a team rather than individual, isolated individuals working as lone heroes or rescuers – or as separated parts, not knowing about or considering what actions others may be taking.

- **Holistic.** The intervention considers the good of everyone involved in the situation of violence – including those harmed (survivors or victims of violence), those who have caused harm, and community members affected by violence. It also builds an approach that can include anyone involved in a situation of violence as a participant in the solution to violence – even the person or people who have caused harm if this is possible.

- **Centers on Those Most Affected by Violence to Create Change.** The intervention centers those most affected by violence. It provides ways for those affected by violence and causing violence to develop new skills, insights and ways to put together a solution to violence – or to form a system that not only addresses violence but reduces the chances that violence will continue.

- **Supports the Sometimes Complex Pathway to Change and Transformation.** Changing violence, repairing from violence, and creating new ways of being free from violence can take time. For the survivor/victim, the intervention relies upon consideration of the best ways to support survivors or victims of harm by sharing the responsibility for addressing, reducing, ending, or preventing violence (breaking isolation and taking accountability), without blaming the survivor/victim for their choices (without victim blaming), and by offering support towards what they define as their own needs and wants (supporting self-determination). For the person doing harm, the intervention relies upon consideration of the best ways to support people doing harm to recognize, end and be responsible for their violence (what we also call accountability), without giving them excuses (without colluding), and without denying their humanity (without demonizing).

- **Facilitated.** The intervention works well if someone in our communities can act as a facilitator, someone who can act as an anchor for the process of intervention, or someone who can help us to walk through different parts of this Toolkit. Therefore, we call this a facilitated model. The facilitator role can be taken on by more than one person or it can rotate among group members as the process continues. The facilitator does not have to be a professional or someone who is an expert on violence intervention. It simply needs to be someone who can be clear-headed, act within the values and guidelines of the group, and who has some distance from the center of violence to be clear of the chaos and confusion that is often a part of a violent situation. See more about the facilitator role in Section 4.C. Mapping Allies and Barriers. If one cannot find a facilitator, then at the very least, this Toolkit and the many people whose experiences it represents may help to guide us through the process of violence intervention.

1.3. WHO IS THIS TOOLKIT FOR?

This Toolkit is meant for anyone interested in using a community-based approach to address, reduce, end or prevent violence (what we call an intervention). Unlike most violence-related resources, it does not assume that those intervening in violence must be trained professionals. It sees any and all of us involved in or affected by violence in our personal lives as potential actors in the solutions to violence.

Below, we introduce different types of relationships that you might have to a situation of violence, with special considerations about what to think about as you read or use this Toolkit. We also include an explanation of our use of certain terms. You may also want to refer to Section 5.1: Key Words — Definitions for a guide to other terms used in this Toolkit.

SURVIVOR

COMMUNITY ALLY

PERSON DOING HARM

FACILITATOR

People Connected to the Situation of Violence

You may be using this Toolkit as a resource to help you or your group to address a situation of violence directly affecting you. The following are some of the basic ways you may be related to the violent situation. This section introduces the language that this Toolkit uses to name the different ways people may be involved in or related to interpersonal violence.

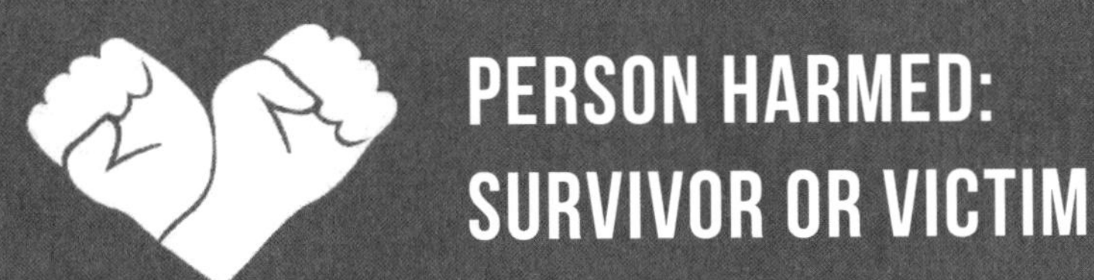

PERSON HARMED: SURVIVOR OR VICTIM

Are you someone who is being directly harmed or has been harmed by violence? The harm can be physical, emotional or verbal, sexual, financial and other.

We often refer to this person as the survivor or victim of violence. This Toolkit usually includes both terms because different people prefer one term over the other. We also know that often you will simply refer to someone's name without having to use these terms, survivor or victim, at all.

Although there may be one or two primary people being directly harmed by violence, it may be important to consider other people who may also be harmed. This harm may be direct violence, indirect harm resulting from violence, or threatened violence. A common list of others who can also be survivors or victims of violence can include:

- Children of all ages
- Family members (mother, father, sister, brother, aunt, uncle, in-laws, etc.)
- Household members (other people living in a violent home such as roommates, boarders)
- Intimate partners including spouse, domestic partner, dating partner, girlfriend, boyfriend, etc.
- Friends
- Neighbors
- Co-workers

If you think you are the survivor or victim or if you want to pay attention to the perspective of the survivor or victim, look at the Special Considerations sections throughout this Toolkit that point to things for survivors or victims to consider.

COMMUNITY ALLY

Are you someone who is a friend, family member, neighbor, co-worker, or community member who is close to or connected to someone being harmed? Are you close to or connected to someone who is causing harm? Were you called in to help deal with a situation of violence?

We often refer to this person as an ally or community ally. In other settings, you might hear this person called the bystander or part of a social network. In this Toolkit, we use the language of ally or community ally. We also know that often you will simply refer to someone's name without having to use these terms, ally or community ally, at all.

Because this Toolkit is geared towards action, the ally or community ally may also become part of a team or become one who is intervening in violence. At times, the language can shift to team member or someone involved in the intervention.

If you think you are the ally or community ally or if you want to pay attention to the perspective of the ally or community ally, look at the Special Considerations sections throughout this Toolkit that point to things for allies or community allies to consider.

PERSON DOING HARM

Are you someone who is harming others or who has harmed others in the past? Or have you been accused of being this person by others?

We often refer to this person as the person or people doing harm. Alternatively, you may see the language person who has caused harm or person who has been violent or abusive. We also know that often you will simply refer to someone's name without having to use the term, person doing harm or similar kind of language at all.

In this Toolkit, we stay away from the language of perpetrator or perps, offenders, abusers, batterers, rapists, predators, criminals and other language of that kind that assumes that someone who has caused harm will always carry that label. We also stay away from the language of the criminal justice system since we are seeking a different approach. Since this Toolkit supports change, including the change of attitudes and behaviors of people who have done harm, we want our language to reflect this possibility for change.

If you think you are the person doing harm, or if you have been accused of being this person, or if you want to pay attention to the perspective of the person doing harm, look at the Special Considerations sections throughout this Toolkit that point to things.

WHAT IF IT IS HARD TO TELL?

Am I a Survivor or Victim, an Ally, or the Person Doing Harm?

In some situations, it can be hard to tell if someone is the survivor or victim, the ally, or the person doing harm – or if people are all of these things. There are many reasons. For example:

- The survivor or victim may blame themselves and feel like they may have caused the abuse. They may be told by the person doing harm and others that they are to blame – and may begin to wonder if this is true. In our experience, this is often the case with women or female-identified people who are taught to blame themselves and take responsibility for problems within relationships.
- This may be a situation where each person has committed acts of violence against the other but where there is a clear difference in power – therefore, one person's violence may either be much less harmful than that of the other or one person's violence may be in self defense. In this case, we will still consider the person most harmed or using violence in self-defense as the survivor or victim. We consider the person most responsible for harm as the person doing harm.
- This may be a situation of what is often called "mutual abuse or violence" – that is, the balance of power is somewhat equal between people in the relationship and one person is as likely as the other to be abusive and as likely to harm the other.

Note that this Toolkit addresses situations in which there is one person or set of people more responsible for violence and with more power to abuse than the other. It is not made for situations of mutual abuse or violence in which there is relative equality of power and vulnerability in the situation of violence. In situations of mutual abuse or violence, mediation or relationship/couple/family /organizational counseling or therapy may be more appropriate. This Toolkit does NOT recommend mediation in situations in which there is a one-sided pattern of abuse or patterns of abuse because mediation is based upon equal power of both sides to negotiate. See Section 3.2 What This Model Is NOT, for more about mediation.

See Section 2.2. Interpersonal Violence: Some Basics Everyone Should Know and Section 5.6. Distinguishing between Violence and Abuse, by Connie Burk of Northwest Network of Bisexual, Trans, Lesbian and Gay Survivors of Abuse for more information.

THE ROLE OF THE FACILITATOR

Since this is a facilitated model, one of the participants in the intervention may take on the role of facilitator, the person who may serve as an anchor or a guide through the intervention process. The facilitator role can be taken on by more than one person or it can rotate among group members as the process continues. This role is unique, and facilitators may have special needs and concerns throughout the intervention. Therefore, Tips for Facilitators also appears throughout the Tools in Section 4. Tools to Mix and Match. See Section 4.C. Mapping Allies and Barriers for more information on the role of the Facilitator.

OTHERS WHO MAY FIND THIS TOOLKIT USEFUL

Anti-Violence Organizations

This Toolkit has been written by people who have a lengthy history of working in the anti-violence movement and are seeking community-based responses to violence. We encourage anti-violence organizations including domestic violence and sexual assault centers and programs, batterer intervention programs and violence prevention programs to consider offering community-based interventions as another option for people seeking help.

Other Types of Organizations, Groups or Businesses

This Toolkit is also for people working in service organizations, faith-based institutions, community centers, political organizations, unions, sports teams, schools, child care centers, businesses or other groups where people live, work, worship, or participate in activities together. People often seek support from their workplace or from community members. This Toolkit can help.

1.4. WHAT IS IN THIS TOOLKIT?

This Toolkit is divided into sections:

Section 1. Introduction. You are now reading the Introduction which provides a general overview of the Toolkit, including definitions, visions, and goals.

Section 2. Some Basics Everyone Should Know. The next section has some information that it is important to know as you think about what you want to do about violence and consider using this Toolkit to help you. Some Basics Everyone Should Know includes:

- **What Is the Community-Based Intervention to Interpersonal Violence?** This section is a more detailed discussion of the fundamentals of the Toolkit's approach to violence intervention.
- **Interpersonal Violence:** Some Basics Everyone Should Know. Our society continues to feed us misinformation about interpersonal violence. This section gives an overview of some key information about the dynamics of interpersonal violence that may help you make a more effective response.
- **Violence Intervention:** Some Important Lessons. In this section, we offer some basic lessons that Creative Interventions has learned about violence intervention over the 3 years of our project. It also builds upon the many lessons shared among other groups who have been creating similar responses to violence, many of which are listed in the Preface and Acknowledgements: A Community Effort.

Section 3. Model Overview: Is It Right for You? This section gives you an opportunity to think more carefully about the violence that you may be facing and helps you consider whether this approach is a good fit. It can spark more reflection on your situation of violence, your values, your resources, and the types of actions you might be willing to take.

Section 4. Tools to Mix and Match. This section has a whole series of tools and examples to help you as you go through different phases of an intervention to violence. Since every situation of violence and every intervention to violence is different and therefore difficult to predict, these tools are meant to be mixed and matched. As you consider and move through an intervention, you may need to revisit the tools as you go through the twists and turns of an intervention process.

THE SETS OF TOOLS INCLUDE:

- **A. Getting Clear.** This set of tools includes questions designed to help you think more clearly about what the situation of violence is (no matter what your role is in the situation), what information to share with other people who are helping, and how to make sure that this reflects the most updated information. It also helps you think about how to safely keep track of and share information without making people have to keep repeating their story again and again.
- **B. Staying Safe.** This set of tools considers the very important issue of risks, dangers and safety. Violence of any form — including physical, emotional, sexual, and financial —can cause harm, which can sometimes be devastating. Taking action to address violence can also cause new sets of risks and dangers. Therefore, this section offers various tools to figure out how best to stay safe or reduce harm as you move through the steps of an intervention.
- **C. Mapping Allies and Barriers.** The community-based approach brings people together to overcome violence – even if it is only a couple of people. This set of tools guides you through a process to consider people to bring along as allies. It helps define what particular roles people can best play. It also helps you identify who might be barriers or pose a danger, and people who might become allies with some additional support.
- **D. Goal Setting.** This set of tools guides you to consider the actual outcomes that you are seeking. Each person in a group may actually have different goals. These tools are designed to help you come up with what the group's goals are so that individuals do not act in conflict with each other. It also helps you to separate goals that might be unrealistic or those that we might wish for, something that is very common, from those that are more realistic and are also in tune with your values.
- **E. Supporting Survivors or Victims.** This set of tools helps to keep your focus on supporting survivors or victims. It helps you develop time, space and skills to support survivors or victims of interpersonal violence. It also explores the different levels and ways that survivors or victims of violence can participate In a process of intervention and accountability.
- **F. Taking Accountability.** This set of tools is particularly useful for those who are directly encountering the person or people who have caused harm or a community that may have contributed to a situation of violence. This includes many tips and guides on how to engage (meaning the many different ways in which a community may communicate with, challenge, make requests of, and also support) a person doing harm through what may be many phases of accountability. This Toolkit supports the process of accountability without relying upon the police. That process may include community pressure, need for safety

measures and possible consequences. At the same time, as much as possible, this Toolkit upholds an approach of compassion and connection rather than shaming, punishment and banning.

- **G. Working Together.** This set of tools helps your group to work well together. Many of us are not taught to work in teams. Rather, we are often taught to value individual thoughts and actions. Working well together can be the most important part of a successful intervention – as well as the most challenging. These tools encourage you to reflect on how the group Is communicating, making decisions and sharing information with one another so you are working in a coordinated way – and not in a way that conflicts with the actions of others.
- **H. Keeping on Track.** This last set of tools helps you to keep moving forward through what may be a long process. It helps to guide your process of reflection, strategizing, thinking ahead, and identifying useful lessons along the way. It includes elements that are helpful for both groups and individuals, such as individual self-checks to keep you on track. Finally, it offers some guides to consider if and when an intervention reaches closure and ways to make sure that changes that you were able to achieve can hold steady in the future.

SECTION 5. OTHER RESOURCES.

This section has some useful resources including developed by Creative Interventions as well as other organizers and projects:

5.1. Key Words – Definitions. This has a list of words and terms that appear in this Toolkit with the definitions that we use.

5.2. Real Life Stories and Examples. This puts together the stories from this Toolkit in one place.

5.3. Creative Interventions Anti-Oppression Policy (Anti-Discrimination/Anti-Harassment). This is an example of the Creative Interventions policy that defines abusive attitudes and behaviors within an organization and states organizational policies about abuse.

5.4. Sample One-Day Workshop on Community-Based Responses to Violence

5.5. Taking Risks: Implementing Grassroots Community Accountability Strategies, by Communities Against Rape and Abuse (CARA). This is a useful piece written by CARA presenting their principles guiding community accountability.

5.6. Distinguishing between Violence and Abuse, by Connie Burk of Northwest Network of Bisexual, Trans, Lesbian and Gay Survivors of Abuse. The Northwest Network has developed a comprehensive process for assessing the dynamics of determining who is using violence. This is an introduction to Northwest Network's analysis about the dynamics of power and how this relates to the difference between violence and abuse.

5.7. Portrait of Praxis: An Anatomy of Accountability, by Esteban Kelly and Jenna Peters-Golden of Philly Stands Up (PSU). This is a piece written by PSU describing their organization and the community accountability process they have developed for people doing harm.

5.8. Confronting Sexual Assault: Transformative Justice on the Ground in Philadelphia, by Bench Ansfield and Timothy Colman of Philly Stands Up (PSU). This is an article written by two members of PSU about a situation of sexual violence in the Philadelphia community and PSU's vision of transformative justice.

5.9. Shame, Realization and Restoration: The Ethics of Restorative Practice, by Alan Jenkins. This article is written by an Australian practitioner with a long-term commitment to restorative practices.

5.10. Tips for Seeking a Therapist [for People Who Have Done Sexual Harm], by Anonymous. This article is written by a person who is two years into an accountability process for doing sexual harm. It gives some tips on finding a therapist from the perspective of one person who went through the process of getting help from therapy.

5.11. Resource List. This is a brief list of resources available on community-based interventions to interpersonal violence, community accountability and transformative justice. It also includes some articles and zines that can be helpful in particular to survivors of violence and people doing harm.

1.5. WHAT IS OUR BIGGER VISION?

> ***Our goal is not ending violence. It is liberation.***
>
> — Beth Richie

This Toolkit brings together vision and practice in a practical model with concrete tools. We hope that the Toolkit may help you consider and carry out ways to address, reduce, end or prevent violence.

Our vision is based on the following assumptions:

1. **Help comes from those closest to you – friends, family, neighbors, co-workers, and community members.** This model does not rely on social services, crisis centers or the police. It can be used alongside any of these forms of help, but it can also be carried out if you do not use these other forms of help or if you do not feel safe to use other types of services. With the help of this Toolkit, you may be able to create a response which is quicker, safer and more effective than professional services or the police.

2. **Recognizes that people experiencing violence may need to or want to remain in their relationships or community.** Most places such as domestic violence services, sexual assault services and so on assume that people being abused should leave those abusing them. They may think that people who have committed violence should be separated – through leaving, arrest and/or restraining orders. If you want violence to stop but also need to or want to consider staying in the same community or even same relationship, it can be difficult to explore these options if you turn to mainstream services. This Toolkit can help guide you towards other possibilities.

3. **Relies on community response.** Most places that help with violence work regularly with the criminal justice system. They may automatically tell you call 911, not thinking about how this might be unwanted or even harmful. Someone may not want to risk arrest. Someone may not want to turn to restraining orders which usually order people to stay away from each other or stop living together. Others may be undocumented and fear that the police could turn them over for deportation. Someone may be of a race or nationality, religion or immigration status, sexual orientation or gender identity that makes them vulnerable as a target for police violence rather than police assistance. There may be other reasons to fear that the police could make the situation worse rather than better.

4 **Helps people prepare for and take actions towards safety, support and transformation.** This Toolkit is oriented towards action —or at least the consideration of action – that moves towards goals of safety, support and transformation from violence. Actions can be immediate or long-term with lots of phases. Every small action can make a difference. What is important is that we are able to do what we can to take more control over our own lives and make decisions which are healthy and positive for ourselves and others. These are the small things that, all together, step by step, can lead towards more options for safety – and a possibility for deeper change and transformation.

- Considers ways to come together to support the sometimes complex pathway to change and transformation. Changing violence, repairing from violence, and creating new ways of being free from violence can take time. This Toolkit helps guide people through the difficult process of repair and change.

  For the survivor/victim, the intervention relies upon consideration of the best ways to support survivors or victims of harm by sharing the responsibility for addressing, reducing, ending, or preventing violence (breaking isolation and taking accountability), without blaming the survivor/victim for their choices (without victim blaming), and by offering support towards what they define as their own needs and wants (supporting self-determination).

  For the person doing harm, the intervention relies upon consideration of the best ways to support people doing harm to recognize, end and be responsible for their violence (what we also call accountability), without giving them excuses (without colluding), and without denying their humanity (without demonizing).

5 **Builds towards long-term community self-determination, health and sustainability.** Although this Toolkit is aimed towards practical, pragmatic responses to individual situations of violence, its larger vision is towards more self-determined, healthier, and sustainable communities. As these new approaches, skills and attitudes become part of everyday community-based responses to violence, we will strengthen the capacity of our communities to resist the devastation of interpersonal violence and to shift our collective energies towards greater self-determination and well-being for all.

1.6. REAL LIFE STORIES TO SHARE

Story from a Survivor: A Community Confronts Domestic Violence

Introduction

This story is a survivor's story of how she faced the violence of her husband through her own courage and the support of a network of friends and family. Married to a police officer, she could not turn to the police for protection. Instead, she overcame her own sense of fear and shame to reach out to a circle of friends. Together, they offer the resources of care and nurturing of her and her children to create a solution to violence that offers protection and compassion. This story is also in Section 4.D. Setting Goals to show how she is able to name her goals – what she calls "wants" – and how her friends and family support her reach her goals.

A Community Confronts Domestic Violence

Two years ago, I was married to a man who I'd been with for ten years prior, and our relationship had troubles. Over the last year of our marriage, my former partner was going through training as a police officer, and at the same time, we had just relocated to a new state. We were struggling with some large issues in the marriage, and things had gotten more difficult. I just became increasingly afraid of someone that I used to feel really safe with.

I have three kids who were 10, 6, and 4, and they were witnessing a lot of arguments, a lot of loud screaming, a lot of doors being slammed, a lot of things that I felt were really unsafe for them to see. My home just felt more and more dangerous. I felt scared to leave the house. I felt scared to come home. I felt scared to sleep in my bed.

The last straw came one night when I had gone to a friend's house and my partner followed me in his car. And when I arrived at my friend's house, he pulled up and got out of the car and was yelling and screaming horrible things at me. I felt very afraid, but I didn't know what to do. I knew wherever I went, he would follow me. So I decided I would go to my office which was nearby, and it was night time so there wouldn't be anybody there. When I finally got inside, I waited for a few minutes and he left.

I called a friend, who came and met me at my office, and she suggested that I call another friend who had a house I could go to while we figured out what to do, so that's what I did. When we got there, everybody sat around in the living room and just reassured me that it was safe for me to be there, that they were welcoming of it, that they understood. I was at this point on the run from someone who was furious and had a gun, and I still felt bad. I felt like I was exposing people to something that I couldn't control, something I was terrified of. But I didn't know what else to do at that point, and they were saying it was where they wanted me to be.

My friends asked me, are there some people that I could gather up, that I could call, that might be support from in this time. I guess I should say that being part of this, this community organization which is committed to ending sexual violence which meant that we had a way of responding that I knew people would come together. I knew if I needed help, people would come and talk to me and we could work it out together. So it didn't feel strange to meet, to call people and say, "Hey, I need help, and this is what's going on."

And at the same time, experiencing these things in my home felt like people would see me differently; people would judge me; people would think I was a hypocrite; people would think I was weak. And I remember being really troubled by that the first few days. But I got reassurances from folks that that was exactly what the point of the organization was, and that experiencing harm is not about being strong or weak, that experiencing harm just is. It's what we choose to do about it that's important.

So we made phone calls, and asked people to come over. We had 7 or 8 people come over and just started talking through what to do. At that point it felt totally overwhelming. I was still on, "Is this really happening to me?" and, "What can I do to make it okay?" rather than thinking of anything beyond tomorrow, or next week.

But I think my wants were something like: I want to be in my home; I want my kids to feel safe; I think I said, "I want him to leave."

I think those were basically it at that moment, and then we just brainstormed what needs to happen right now in the next hour, in the next day, in the next week, for those wants to happen. We walked through it so if I want to be in my home, how do we make that happen? How do we make sure that that's a safe space? And, I think one of the answers to that question was, at least in the near future, having folks be there with me.

So we eventually set up a schedule. We put out an email with a schedule for the week, and blanks for people to fill in, and I was amazed that people did fill it in. And they did come by. They came by every day and they came and sat in my living room, and they brought food, and we just sat together. I was amazed at that. That was how we got home to be a safe space for me again.

When we were thinking about whether to call the police or not, I did feel like I needed some help in calming the situation down, but I didn't know what to do, because if I can't call his friends on the job, and I can't call them in...It doesn't seem right to call them in an unofficial way, because who knows what's going to happen with that. And calling them in an official way doesn't necessarily seem like it's going to produce any certain results either.

So we tried to think about who could talk to him. And we figured out some people in the community that he could talk to, if he was open to doing that. My mom talked to him, and she was willing to deal with him. He was totally raging, and for whatever reason she was not intimidated at all and just was able to talk to him really calmly.

I had people checking on me, people staying during the daytime hours, sometimes overnight for the next week, and it just felt good. It felt so good to have this full house, you know, this busy house of people coming by, and, you know, people were playing with the kids, and we were making art in the kitchen, and someone was always making tea, and it felt not alone.

In terms of talking about successes, I guess the biggest one is that I did get all three things that I wanted, that I identified as wants to happen. That my kids went through that time feeling safe; that he did leave the house; that I was able to return home; and that all that happened in a fairly short amount of time. So in terms of success, I'd say, ultimately for me as a survivor, those were the most meaningful successes.

Another success in terms of communication was that we made a phone list immediately. That was one of the first things we did so I always knew I had someone to call. And people would call and check on me. At that time, I think it was hard. I was worried about people burning out. I was worried about people feeling overwhelmed by me and my stuff.

So I didn't have to constantly, hour by hour, be reaching out for needs to be met because we'd identified them beforehand and there were enough people involved. It felt like no one was carrying all of it, or more than they could. It certainly wasn't that things didn't feel hard. It felt really bad. I think what was helpful was this wasn't an intervention where it was like, "How are we going to get him away from me? It was like, "How are we going to make sure that there's not harm happening in our community? How are we going to make sure that we've done our best to address that? The problem was consistently the harm. The problem was consistently the events or the behaviors, or the things that were harmful that were happening, but not him that was a problem – not that my choice to stay as long as I had was a problem.

That made it possible for me to feel like I could come into the space and say what I needed which at that time really included not being someone who was perpetrating harm against him by engaging the power of the state whether or not it would have benefited me in that moment. It could only have had negative effects on him.

And then I got to make a decision about what do I really need right now to do my work, to take care of my kids, to get through this day, to heal.

We need to trust people to be the experts on their own lives and to take them seriously and have faith in people to set the course for working from harm to transformation. I think that comes best from people who are experiencing harm and have a vision for themselves about what they want. And to give people time to identify what that is and be willing to sit with the discomfort of not being able to rescue somebody in a simple or quick way. I think that those values were ultimately the most healing for me.

Adapted from the Community Responds to Domestic Violence. Full audio and written transcript available from StoryTelling & Organizing Project (STOP) www.stopviolenceeveryday.org.

Story from Community Allies: A Small Story (He Korero Iti)

Introduction

The following story offers one real life example of what we mean by community-based interventions to violence. This story is also featured in Section 4.G. Working Together. This story shows how ordinary people in a family come together to creatively and collectively prevent a situation of violence against a child using the vision and values we discuss the previous Section 1.5.

A Small Story (He Korero Iti)

We live in a town, but many of my husband's extended family (whanau) live in the valley where he grew up about 40 kilometres away. My husband and his brother are renowned for a number of things – one being how they extend the life of their cars and vans using highly technical items like string and wire – another how they share these vehicles for a variety of tasks such as moving furniture or transporting relatives, building materials, tractor parts, traditional herbal medicines (rongoa), eels, vegetables, dogs, and pigs (dead or alive).They are renowned for being people of the people, the ones to call on in times of trouble and death, the ones who will solve the problem and make the plan. They travel to and from town, to the coast to dive for sea food, to endless meetings, to visit extended family (whanau) - along the many kilometres of dirt roads in and around the valley, through flood or dust depending on the season in those patched up, beat up, prized cars.

There are a number of things to know about the valley - one is that the last 33 children in the world of their small sub-tribe (hapu ririki) to grow up and be educated on their own lands go to school here, despite government efforts to close the school. Another is that the valley is known to outsiders and insiders as 'patu wahine' – literally meaning to 'beat women' and this is not said as a joke. The mountain for this valley is named as the doorway spirits pass through on their way to their final departure from this life. This valley is also the valley where my husband and his siblings were beaten at school for speaking their first language. It is the valley their mother sent them to so they would be safe from their father – back to her people. It is where they milked cows, pulled a plough, fed pigs but often went hungry, and were stock whipped, beaten and worse.

My brother-in-law still lives in the valley, in a group of houses next to the school. So it's no surprise that one of our cars would be parked by these houses – right by where the children play. Perhaps also not a surprise that while playing that time old international game of rock throwing our eight year old nephew shattered the back window of the car. If I'd been listening I probably would have heard the 'oh' and 'ah' of the other children that accompanied the sound of glass breaking from town, and if I'd been really tuned in I would have heard the rapid, frightened heart beat of 'that boy' as well.

His mother is my husband's cousin – and she was on the phone to us right away. She was anxious to assure us 'that boy' would get it when his father came home. His father is a big man with a pig hunter's hands who hoists his pigs onto a meat hook unaided. He is man of movement and action, not a man for talking. Those hands would carry all the force of proving that he was a man who knew how to keep his children in their place. Beating 'that boy' would be his way of telling us that he had also learned his own childhood lessons well.

So before he got home we burned up the phone lines – sister to sister, cousin to cousin, brother–in-law to sister-in-law, wife to husband, brother to brother. This was because my husband and his brother know that there are some lessons you are taught as a child that should not be passed on. The sound of calloused hand on tender flesh, the whimpers of watching sisters, the smell of your own fear, the taste of your own blood and sweat as you lie in the dust – useless, useless, better not born. This is a curriculum like no other. A set of lessons destined to repeat unless you are granted the grace of insight and choose to embrace new learning.

So when the father of 'that boy' came home and heard the story of the window 'that boy' was protected by our combined love (aroha) and good humor, by the presence of a senior uncle, by invitations to decide how to get the window fixed in the shortest time for the least money. Once again phone calls were exchanged with an agreement being made on appropriate restitution. How a barrel of diesel turns into a car window is a story for another time.

Next time my husband drove into the valley it was to pick up the car, and 'that boy' was an anxious witness to his arrival. My husband also has very big hands, hands that belong to a man who has spent most of his life outdoors. These were the hands that reached out to 'that boy' to hug not hurt.

A lot of bad things still happen in the valley, but more and more they are being named and resisted. Many adults who learned their early lessons there will never return. For people of the land (tangata whenua) this is profound loss – our first identifiers on meeting are not our own names but those of our mountains, rivers, subtribe (hapu) and tribe (iwi). To be totally separate from these is a dislocation of spirit for the already wounded. This is only a small story that took place in an unknown valley, not marked on many maps. When these small stories are told and repeated so our lives join and connect, when we choose to embrace new learning and use our 'bigness' to heal not hurt then we are growing grace and wisdom on the earth.

By Di Grennell

Whangarei, Aotearoa-New Zealand

Glossary:
Whanau – extended family group
Rongoa – traditional herbal medicines
Hapu ririki – small sub-tribe
Patu – hit, strike, ill treat, subdue
Wahine – woman/women
Aroha – love, concern for
Tangata whenua – people of the land
Hapu – subtribe
Iwi –tribe

Adapted from the Community Responds to Domestic Violence. Full audio and written transcript available from StoryTelling & Organizing Project (STOP) www.stopviolenceeveryday.org.

Story from a Person Doing Harm: A Story of Sexual Harm, Accountability and Compassion

Introduction

The following story offers one real life example of what we mean by accountability. A longer version of this story is also featured in Section 4.F. Taking Accountability. This story shares the process that one person is taking on the road from causing sexual harm to taking accountability for that harm. It also reveals the complexity ties between someone's acts of sexual violence and one's own early victimization, a situation that is common. While this story is from an unusual situation in which someone doing harm initiated their own process of accountability, it is useful in showing that deep change is possible. It also tells us that what can be a long and painful process of accountability can also lead to healing for the person who has done harm. The story teller requests anonymity not only because of confidentiality but also so this story does not become a means for this person to receive public recognition or a sense of heroism. He also asks that if people are able to recognize him or other identities through the details included in this story, that you please have compassion about who you share these identities with. If you recognize him, he asks that you please talk with him about this story, even if only to acknowledge that you know this part of his history.

Surviving and Doing Sexual Harm: A Story of Accountability and Healing

In all of my years trying to find resources, I've only come across three stories of people who've done harm and only one of them had enough information, enough of the person's real story, to actually be helpful to me. I want to tell my story to help people who are trying to work on their sh** and also to help people who are supporting that process or who are mentors to have some idea of what might be going on for that person who still doesn't understand themselves – to help folks be better support for accountability processes.

You know, for most of the harm that I've done, I've never really been called out for it, so I don't really have other people's names for it, just my own names. I consider myself to have sexually assaulted people, also crossed people's boundaries in sexual ways that aren't sexual assault, and just generally had patriarchal behavior. And then the last thing that's always a little more difficult for me to talk about is that I also molested a relative of mine when I was young.

My accountability process started in my early 20's. The violence and harm I had been doing wasn't just a one-time thing where I just messed up once, it was like an ongoing pattern that was chronic, and happening over and over again in my life. There were a couple of moments when I was able to stop myself in the moment when I was doing harm, like when I hurt someone I cared about very much, seeing her weep when I pushed her sexual boundaries, what I see as sexual assault, I said, "Sh**. I need to stop right now." But even then, that kind of like horror wasn't enough to let me intervene in the big, chronic patterns. It took a lot more before I could start changing, even when I was recognizing chronic patterns of harm I was doing in my life and hated that I was doing those things.

By that point in my life, I was a total wreck. For years and years of my life, my mind had been filled almost with nothing but images of doing gruesome violence to myself. I was having trouble just keeping my life together. I was just under huge amounts of stress, having total breakdowns on a fairly regular basis, and was just being ripped apart inside by everything. And also, being ripped apart by trying to keep myself from the knowledge of what I'd done. It was too much for me to even look at. At the same time, I really wanted to talk with people about it. I was just so scared to do it because of the particular sorts of thing that I had done. You know, like, people who sexually abuse are the most evil of all the monsters in our cultural mythology. And everybody is basically on board with doing nothing but straight up violence to them. And so much of my life had been organized around just trying to keep myself safe that it wasn't a risk I could take. It wasn't even a question of choice. It just wasn't a possibility, even though wanted nothing more.

At some point, I started spending more time around people involved in radical politics and feminist politics. And so one person that I knew, I'll call him Griffin (not his real name), one of their friends had been sexually assaulted. So I just happened to be at a table when Griffin was having a conversation about what people were going to do about it. And that was the first time that I had ever heard of Philly Stands Up. Where I was living at the time was really far away from Philly, so it was just basically a name and an idea. But, you know, that one tiny seed of an idea was enough to make me realize that it was possible. That there were people that I could talk to that weren't going to destroy me.

It was a few months later. There was just a lot of stuff going on in my life where my history of doing violence to people and my history of surviving violence, they were coming up over and over and over in my life. But I still refused to acknowledge either of them. And it wasn't like a conscious thing. I don't know exactly what it was, but I hadn't gained the moment of insight yet into understanding that that is my history. I ended up talking with that same friend, Griffin, who had mentioned Philly Stands Up, and just in this one conversation, my whole history came out. It was the first time I talked with anybody about either my history of being molested and raped or my history of doing sexual violence to other people. That was a moment when I stopped running from my past. Those two things in my life, surviving violence and doing violence, are inseparable. I started coming to terms with both of them in the exact same moment. That was the first time I ever broke my own silence. And that's when I started trying to find some way of doing accountability.

Part of what made this possible was the particular relationship with one of the people I had harmed, June (not her real name), a person that I loved tremendously, and somebody who, even though I haven't seen her for years and probably won't see her again in my life, I still love tremendously. And so the pain of hurting somebody that I love that much was part of it. And then I think part of it was that I had had someone to talk to. I'd never been able to communicate with people about anything in my life before. And part of it was that things got so bad at one point that I didn't have the choice anymore of not seeking support. I had a breakdown where somebody came into my life and listened to me, and I couldn't hold it in any more. And so I had started learning how to communicate from that. And then Griffin, the person I had the conversation with, really started off my own accountability process. I think for me, it was about that friend. I didn't feel threatened by them. I had a trust with them that if I talked to them, they would still care about me and see me as a person. But it's all part of this much larger context. It wasn't just something about that one particular friendship that made the difference; it was like this whole arc of all these huge things that were happening in my life, all of these breakdowns and changes and new commitments and new understandings that were all developing together that brought me to that point...

...Now it's been years of seeking support through political groups working on accountability and therapy and staying committed to the process. The things I now understand about healing, in the wholeness of my experience, as both a survivor and a perpetrator, look very different than the ones that I've read about or that people have talked to me about, where it's healing only from surviving abuse or violence.

I think that the three biggest emotions that I've had to contend with in that healing and transformation – and this is something that I've only articulated in the last, like, month of my life – I think the three biggest things that I've had to contend with are guilt, shame and a traumatic response to being vulnerable.

I think those three things – in myself at least – are the sources for the self-hate. It took me a long time trying to figure out even what guilt and shame are. What the emotions are, what they feel like. I would just read those words a lot, but without being able to identify the feeling. One of the things someone told me was that it seems like a lot of my actions are motivated by guilt. And that was strange to me because I never thought that I had felt guilt before. I thought, "Oh, well, I feel remorse but I don't feel guilt." It was years of pondering that before I even understood what guilt was or what it felt like in myself. Once I did, I was like, "Well damn! That's actually just about everything I feel." I just hadn't understood what it felt like before, so I didn't know how to identify it.

Now my understanding of guilt is that it's the feeling of being worthy of punishment. That guiltiness crops up when I become aware of the harm that I've done. I might engage in minimization, trying to make that harm go away, so that I don't feel that guiltiness for it any more, so that I don't feel worthy of being punished. I might try denying it – same sort of thing. Maybe I'm going to try to numb myself so that I don't feel that – so that I don't have that feeling any more. Or maybe I'm going to make that punishment come to me – just being in that place where there's this feeling that the other boot is gonna drop all the time, and that it should drop, trying to bring about a sense of resolution to that sense of impending harm by harming myself.

And another thing that I can see in myself is trying to get out of that sense that harm is gonna come to me by dedicating my life to amending the harm. But the thing is that it's different from compassion, trying to right wrongs because of guilt instead of because of compassion. Doing it through guilt, I notice that I can't assert any boundaries with myself. It's like a compulsion, and it leads me to burnout, Because any time that I stop, that feeling comes back, and it's like, the harm is gonna come. I'm learning how to stay present with that difficult feeling and breathe through it. It helps me a lot.

And then, as far as the shame goes, my understanding of shame is it's like the feeling that I am someone who I cannot stand to be. I was at this workshop where somebody was talking about their experiences with addiction and said, "My whole life, when I was in the middle of this addiction, I had this combination of grandiosity and an inferiority complex." You know, like this sense that I was better than everyone else and that I was the worst scum of the earth. I think when that's the manifestation of shame – that this is who I should be and this is who I really am. When I've seen myself in that kind of place, then usually I'm reacting to the shame either by trying to drown out that awareness of the side of me that's scum, and one of the primary ways that I did that was through finding ways of getting sexual rushes or something like that. And the other thing that I've seen myself do is trying to eradicate that part of me that's the scum. And mostly that happened through fantasies of doing violence to myself, targeted at that part of myself that I hated, that part of myself that I couldn't stand to be, and trying to rip myself into two. I think that's a lot of what was fueling my desire for suicide, too.

One of the things that happened with the accountability process is that once I started talking to people about the things I was most ashamed about, and making it public, then that grandiosity went away. And instead I had to come to terms with this other understanding of myself that wasn't as caught up in illusions of grandeur and instead was this forced humbleness. Like, I'm a person and I'm no better than anybody else. I'm a person and I can also change. So through talking about the things that I'm most ashamed of, that shame became transformative for me. That was a really big aspect of healing for me. And it required a lot of grieving, a lot of loss. And that's something that I was going through during that first year when I was talking with people about it.

As I was talking with other people about it, all these possibilities were closing off in my life. I'll never be able to do this thing now. I'll never be able to have this type of relationship now. The world was less open to me. Like, I can't think of myself in the same way any more. A lot of times I didn't really have the capacity to really face it. But in the moments of insight I had, where I was coming to terms with it, I was really grieving, weeping, over the things that I was losing because of the accountability. That was a big part of healing for me, finding and connecting with and expressing the grief. And also the grief over everything that I had done.

There are still some things that I probably will have to let go of but that I haven't allowed myself to grieve yet, some possibilities that I'm still clinging to. I've found that a lot of time when I get on a power trip and find myself in this controlling sort of attitude, one of the things that resolves that is if I can find a way to grieve. The power trips, the controlling attitudes, tend to happen when I'm trying to control things that are changing. If I can just accept the change and grieve ways that possibilities are changing, then that brings me back. I mean, I've come to terms with a lot of the things that I was grieving when I first started talking with people about it. I'm starting to be able to find ways in my life now of different paths to some of the same things that I wanted for my life, but just paths that have a lot more humility in them. And I think that's one of the really valuable things that accountability has given me. Any time I start that thinking big about myself, then I bring it back to this accountability that I'm doing and It's helped me a lot in just like helping me find ways to stay connected to humility. That's something that I really appreciate about it.

The third one's a traumatic response to vulnerability. And this is one that I still don't understand that well because I'm just now starting to have some understanding of it. But like I was saying before, because of the violence that I've experienced in my own life, a huge portion of my life has been dedicated to keeping me safe. And for me, those behaviors have been enforced in myself through that same type of self-hate and violence. So if I leave an opening where I'm vulnerable, then that self-hate comes to close it down. If I ever mess up in a way that left me vulnerable, then I find that I start having all these fantasies of doing violence to myself. It's a way of enforcing in myself to never let that happen again. I don't really understand it that well. One of the things that I've been working on more recently is learning how to be open to vulnerability. And that's the last part of self-hate that I've healed the least…

…I have a friend that's been involved in a lot of accountability work, and he's insisted to me that what I'm doing isn't accountability because there's not survivors somewhere who are issuing a list of demands or that kind of thing. But for me, that's only one aspect of accountability. There's another aspect that's being accountable to myself, making sure that I'm living the values that are important to me in the world. Ultimately, accountability for me is a commitment to do what I need to do to make sure that I don't repeat those patterns, that they stop with me. Part of that has been the work around creating boundaries for myself. Part of that has been the healing and transformation. And part of it is also engaging with the world, to not see it as an individual thing, but to see myself as part of a social struggle. I need to be engaged with the world to be part of ending all of this sexual violence that's everywhere.

The accountability has this gift of humility. One of the things that is really valuable for me about that humility is the amount of compassion that it's allowed me to have for other people. I still have superiority complexes, but nowhere near like I did. At this point in my life, I'm able to understand myself as being the same kind of human as so many other people. I don't put myself on a different level from them. And so I feel like I have a much greater ability to understand people's struggle and pain, and to learn from it, and to love people, coming out of that compassion and shared struggle.

That ability for real, authentic love is something I never had. I thought that love was this obsessive thing. And when I realized that I needed to stop that, I had this moment of grieving and loss and doubt, because I thought, "Well, if I stop this, will I ever feel love again?" It required this huge shift. Once it quieted down, once I stopped it, then the whole landscape was just silent. It took me awhile to re-tune my hearing so that it wasn't just the roar of this obsession, but that I could hear the birds, and the insects, and the breezes. From there, learn a sort of love that's based in resilience, and shared commitment, and sacrifice. So that's been a real gift that it's given me.

Another thing too, is that I can bear to live with myself. I never could before. Most of the time I'm okay being in my own skin. It's been huge – even though I went through some extremely dark and difficult periods where the basin of depression that I'd lived in for so long in my life dropped into an abyss, Coming out of that abyss, through a continuing commitment to accountability, it's like the first time in my life when I'm starting to feel I'm free of this sort of depression and this crippling anxiety and paranoia. I have emotional capacity now; like I can feel things. I'm still not in a place where joy is a big part of my life, but it seems possible now. Through all this grieving and everything that I've done, I've also had a couple moments of clarity and lightness that I'd never experienced before in my life.

I think something else that has been a real gift for me, in terms of accountability, is the possibility for having lasting intimate relationships with people, whether sexually or not sexually. And having some capacity for pleasure – sexual pleasure, even, because before it was so caught up in shame and guilt and feeling triggered that I only ever felt horrible. Now I don't feel like I'm consigned to that for the rest of my life. I feel that there's a possibility of being liberated from it.

1.7. THIS TOOLKIT AS A WORK IN PROGRESS

This Toolkit is a Guide, Not a Guarantee

While this Toolkit may not always lead all the way to our most ideal goals, it helps us imagine how we want to respond to violence and work towards a vision of healthy communities. It helps increase the possibility of a community-based change away from violence, but it is not a guarantee.

It helps increase the possibility of community-based and directed transformation of violence, but it is not a guarantee. Some of you may not be able to put together enough of the resources including time and energy to move all the way through an intervention. You may not be able to find a group or your group may not be able to work well enough together. You may encounter too many risks and dangers to see this as an approach that will work for you. You may decide to use an approach available in more traditional domestic violence or sexual assault organizations. However, even the process of thoughtfully considering a community-based approach may help others clarify their own understanding of the situation and motivate others to do more preventive work or be better prepared if they encounter violence in the future.

Shifting Our Expectations and Our Definition of Success

The Toolkit has useful information for anyone interested in addressing, reducing, ending or preventing violence. However, we also understand that violence intervention is a difficult and often unpredictable process. Success may not mean reaching every goal we set. You may use this Toolkit to only consider some of your options or to move through part of the process without reaching all of your initial goals. Attempting any part of this process can be useful and valuable. We have learned through our own work that success often takes unexpected forms.

Improving this Toolkit through All of Our Experiences

This Toolkit is a work in progress. It has the best information that CI was able to collect during its years forming the StoryTelling & Organizing Project (www.stopviolenceeveryday.org) and its Community-Based Interventions Project (www.creative-interventions.org). We at CI also see this Toolkit as just a beginning.

We invite you to read through the various sections of this Toolkit and see if it works for you. If you are reading this, then we also ask you to consider how you can help someone else who may benefit from this Toolkit but have a difficult time reading this due to language, difficulty or dislike of reading, or level of emotional crisis. We ask you to contribute to efforts to find ways to offer this information, tools and lessons in forms that are accessible to many people.

Finally, if you use this Toolkit for your own intervention, consider how your experiences and lessons learned can add to and improve this Toolkit. As others pick up this Toolkit and begin to use it, we expect that new lessons will be learned; new tools will be created; and new stories of success as well as failure will add to our collective knowledge of how to end violence.

As you create additional useful knowledge, lessons, and tools, we invite you to contribute this knowledge to others by connecting to our websites www.creative-interventions.org or www.stopviolenceeveryday.org or offering your contributions to other public forums.

1.8. FREQUENTLY ASKED QUESTIONS ABOUT THE TOOLKIT

Below are some frequently asked questions about this Toolkit and about the community-based approach to violence intervention. Look below to see if you may have these same questions or if they can help guide you towards some of the highlights in this Toolkit. Brief answers and suggested sections for further reading follow each question.

FAQ #1: WHAT DO YOU MEAN BY INTERPERSONAL VIOLENCE?

We define interpersonal violence as the types of violence that happen in our interpersonal relationships including:

- Domestic violence or intimate partner violence that takes place within an intimate relationship such as marriage, domestic partnership, dating relationship, or a former relationship.
- Family violence that can include domestic violence between intimate partners, but can also extend to children, parents, grandchildren, grandparents, other family members and others who may be very close to family like family friends, guardians, caretakers and so on.
- Sexual violence that includes unwanted sexual attitudes, touch or actions such as sexual assault, rape, sexual harassment, molestation, child sexual abuse.
- Child abuse that is any kind of abuse against children.
- Elder abuse that is any kind of abuse against elderly people.
- While CI focuses on the types of violence just listed above, this Toolkit may also be useful for those experiencing violence in other settings, including neighborhoods, schools, organizations, workplaces, and employment situations. These forms of violence can also be considered interpersonal.

The violence may be physical, emotional, sexual, economic, or may take some other form.

See Section 2.2. Interpersonal Violence: Some Basics Everyone Should Know for more information.

FAQ #2: WHAT IS A COMMUNITY-BASED INTERVENTION TO INTERPERSONAL VIOLENCE?

In brief, the CI definition of community-based interventions to interpersonal violence is:

- An attempt to address, end, reduce, or prevent interpersonal violence (or what we call intervention),
- Using community resources rather than relying on the police or social services,
- That directly involves friends, family, co-workers, neighbors, or community members (what we mean by community),
- With the possibility of directly dealing with (or engaging) the person or people doing harm.

See Section 2.1. The Community-Based Intervention to Interpersonal Violence and Section 3. Model Overview: Is It Right for You? for more information.

FAQ #3: WHAT DO YOU MEAN BY ACCOUNTABILITY?

In brief, accountability is the ability to recognize, end and take responsibility for violence. We usually think of the person doing harm as the one to be accountable for violence. Community accountability also means that communities are accountable for sometimes ignoring, minimizing or even encouraging violence. Communities must also recognize, end and take responsibility for violence by becoming more knowledgeable, skillful and willing to take action to intervene in violence and to support social norms and conditions that prevent violence from happening in the first place.

Accountability is a process. It involves listening, learning, taking responsibility, and changing. It involves conscientiously creating opportunities in our families and communities for direct communication, understanding and repairing of harm, readjustment of power toward empowerment and equal sharing of power, and rebuilding of relationships and communities toward safety, respect, and happiness.

For Creative Interventions, we are promoting a different way of thinking about accountability. We promote a vision that is more positive, tied to responsibility and change, but not to punishment and revenge, and can be driven by connection and care rather than fear and anger alone. This is not to take away from the fact that violence and abuse cause fear, anger and outrage. It does. And such emotions have their place.

But the change from violence to compassion, safety, respect and health also needs to come from the values that we want to see even if these might be difficult to feel when we are facing violence. And we are promoting accountability as a way to keep our communities whole, safe and healthy, rather than a way to punish, separate and send away.

This does NOT mean that survivors or victims need to forgive the people who do harm, or that we simply ask for an apology and everything is fine, or that relationships and families need to stay together. None of these fit the definition of accountability, although it is possible that forgiveness, apologies and even staying together may be part of what some people decide that they want and may even be able to reach.

Accountability is a process. We see accountability as a pathway to change. Although we use this pathway to show steps towards accountability and a vision of positive and transformative change, an intervention may never reach any of these steps. Intervention goals may only anticipate reaching Step 1 as a measure of success.

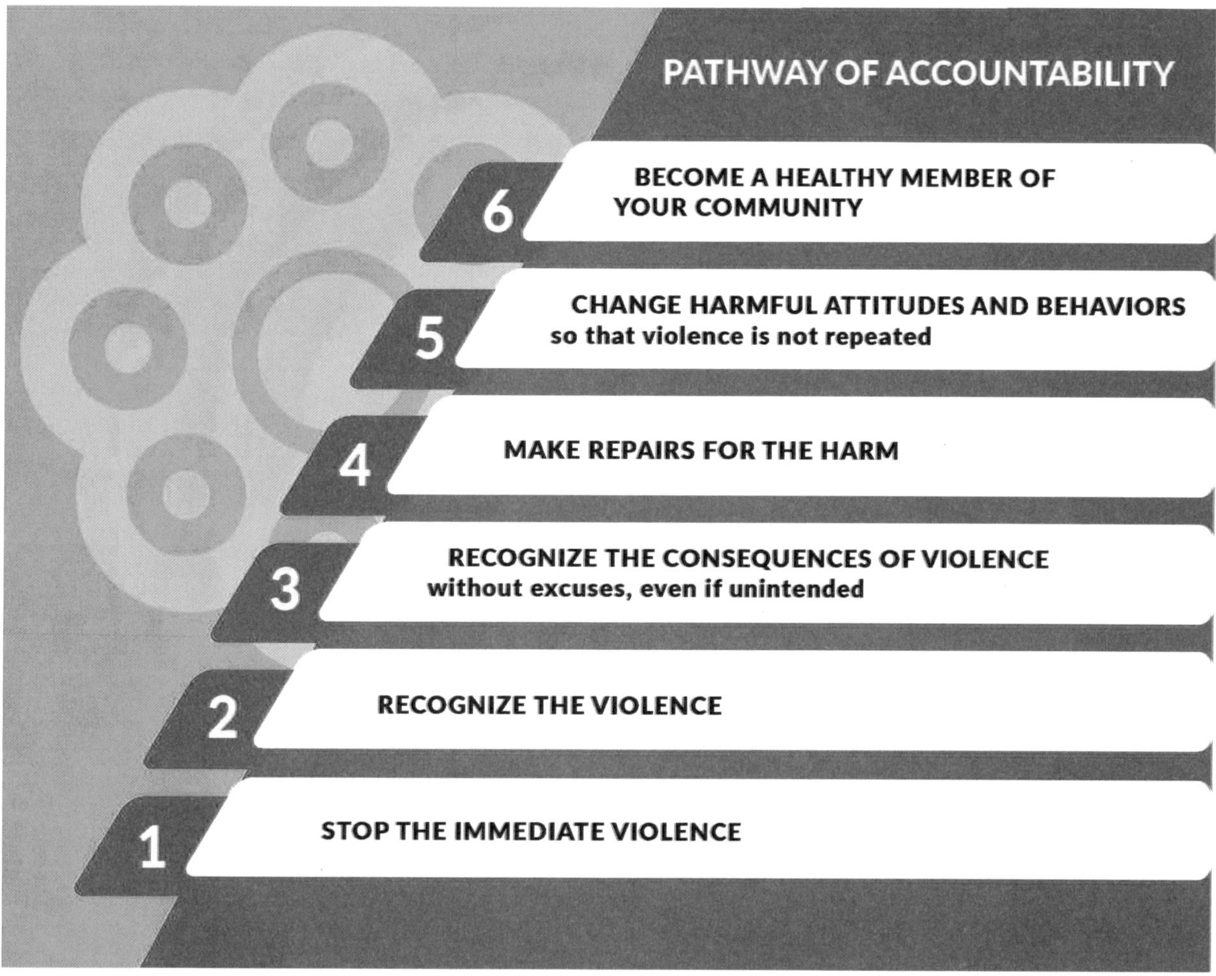

PATHWAY OF ACCOUNTABILITY
6
BECOME A HEALTHY MEMBER OF YOUR COMMUNITY
5
CHANGE HARMFUL ATTITUDES AND BEHAVIORS so that violence is not repeated
4
MAKE REPAIRS FOR THE HARM
3
RECOGNIZE THE CONSEQUENCES OF VIOLENCE without excuses, even if unintended
2
RECOGNIZE THE VIOLENCE
1
STOP THE IMMEDIATE VIOLENCE

FAQ #4: WHY ARE YOU USING LANGUAGE LIKE A PERSON DOING HARM? ISN'T IT JUST EASIER TO SAY BATTERER OR RAPIST?

In this Toolkit, we stay away from the language of perpetrator or perps, offenders, abusers, batterers, rapists, predators, criminals and other language of that kind that assumes that someone who has caused harm will always carry that label. We also stay away from the language of the criminal justice system since we are seeking a different approach. Because this Toolkit supports change, including the change of attitudes and behaviors of people who have done harm, we want our language to reflect this possibility for change.

See Section 5.1. Key Words - Definitions for more about the language that appears in this Toolkit.

FAQ #5: COMMUNITY ACCOUNTABILITY LOOKS LIKE MOB ACTION OR VIGILANTISM TO ME. IS THIS WHAT YOU MEAN?

In this model, collectives or groups of people may be involved in a process of accountability, but we do not condone acts of violence meant as "punishment, vengeance, a way to get even, to let them know how it feels, to hurt them for the sake of making them feel the pain." Our aim is to offer an approach to violence and intervention that relies upon compassion and connection to the person doing harm. We view this approach as a way to invite the person doing harm to participate in the process of accountability and to understand this as ultimately a benefit to them as well as others in their community. The image of "invitation" guides our approach. In balance, some use of force, even if in forms of gentle pressure, may be especially likely at the beginning stages of stopping violence and addressing the harms. We can also think about some form of pressure as a way of "leveraging" our power or influence with the person doing harm.

See Section 4.F. Taking Accountability for much more information on accountability.

FAQ # 6: I WAS HARMED. AND FOR ME ACCOUNTABILITY WOU LOOK LIKE LETTING THIS PERSON BE VERY, VERY SORRY THAT THEY EVER DID WHAT THEY DID. COULDN'T COMMUNITY ACCOUNTABILITY BE USED TO LET THE PERSON DOING HARM REGRET THAT THEY EVER DID WHAT THEY DID?

Feeling sorry, feeling regret or feeling shame may be natural feelings as someone becomes accountable for their harmful attitudes and actions. However, this is different from us "making sure" someone feels sorry through punishment, shaming and inflicting suffering. In our society, we are not taught the difference between making someone feel sorry and creating a process to effectively address and stop violence. Accountability and vengeance are often confused. Seeking justice and revenge are also confused. While the desire for vengeance is very understandable, we ask people to acknowledge these feelings and step back and reflect on them, as well. We also have a set of values underlying our community-based responses that do not support revenge.

See Section 3.4. Values to Guide Your Intervention for a discussion and tools to clarify your values.

See Section 4.D. Goal Setting for more support on thinking about the goals of an intervention and community accountability process.

FAQ # 7: AREN'T THERE CRISIS LINES OR SHELTERS OR POLICE TO DEAL WITH THESE THINGS? WHY ARE YOU ASKING PEOPLE TO GET INVOLVED? ISN'T THIS DANGEROUS?

What we have found is that people who are harmed often turn first to families and friends. They often turn to crisis lines and shelters or police as a last resort – or maybe never at all. For some people, for example, someone who is an undocumented immigrant, someone who is already in legal trouble, or someone who is already the target of the police, they may not feel like they can turn to the police for help.

We believe that we can all do a much better job in increasing our knowledge and skills in addressing, reducing, ending or preventing violence (what we call "violence intervention"). If we as ordinary community members can get better at this, then we are more likely to address violence when it first happens, rather than waiting until it is so serious or after so much harm has already been done. We can act with care and compassion to those we are closest to, including people who are causing harm. We can more immediately come to the assistance of our loved ones or those we understand and share community with. We can address harm directly and firmly without pretending like nothing is happening, blaming the victim or hoping someone else will deal with it. We can make our homes, families and communities the kinds of healthy places that we want to live in.

We also hope that as this approach becomes more known and more resources like this Toolkit are made available, then crisis lines and shelters can also provide more support for those of us who would like to take action to address violence when it is happening in our own families and communities. See Section 4.B. Staying Safe for more about addressing concerns about safety and danger.

FAQ #8: THIS APPROACH LOOKS LIKE THE RIGHT ONE FOR THE SITUATION THAT I KNOW ABOUT, BUT I SEE THAT IT NEEDS A FACILITATOR. HOW CAN I FIND A FACILITATOR? ARE THERE PROFESSIONALS OR EXPERTS OUT THERE WHO CAN DO THIS? WILL I HAVE TO PAY?

Right now, there are very few organizations or "professionals" that are actually familiar with or prepared to assist with this type of approach to violence intervention. What we believe is that many of us have some kind of trusted person or people we are connected to and who, with the help of resources like this Toolkit, can do a pretty good job as a facilitator. They may already know us, be familiar with our culture and our language and be interested in a good outcome. In this approach, the facilitator does not make the decisions nor know everything. The facilitator is someone who is an anchor to a process that can get complicated, emotional and lengthy. They can help ask questions, look to see where this Toolkit and other resources might be helpful, help us remember what we have already decided. Or if we cannot find a facilitator, then this Toolkit can be a helpful guide to help us to lead, organize or take part in a community-based intervention.

Over time, we hope that more people in the community – the "go-to" people, "natural helpers," faith leaders, neighborhood leaders, family leaders, people who are good at this but may never have been leaders before – can build up their skills to be able to act as facilitators, allies and so on. One of our mottos has been "Make ending violence an everyday skill." We hope that the will, the desire and the ability to help end and prevent violence will be one that we all have and that we teach to our communities, our children and future generations. In that way, we will not only be better at addressing and ending violence. We will eventually weave this into our lives so that harm will be addressed and stopped by anyone and everyone. Harm may eventually be prevented from happening in the first place.

See "Tips for Facilitators" throughout Section 4 of the Toolkit for concrete suggestions on how to facilitate various parts of your process.

FAQ #9: THIS TOOLKIT IS SO LONG. HOW CAN YOU EXPECT AN AVERAGE PERSON TO READ THIS?

Yes, this Toolkit is long. Violence intervention, unfortunately, cannot be written into a recipe or be reduced to 10 easy steps. This Toolkit tries to incorporate the types of considerations such as safety, making goals, communicating and working well together that may be relevant in dealing with many situations of violence intervention. Our experience at Creative Interventions showed us that there are so many different types of situations of violence, so many different types of people who may get involved in a violence intervention, so many unexpected things that can happen along the way. We wanted to do the best we could to include many different types of situations that might arise. We also know that we may be dealing with dangerous situations and that it is common that danger increases when people take action to address and end harm.

People who do harm sometimes feel even more threatened and feel that their sense of control is being taken away when they are challenged or when the dynamics of power change. This can sometimes set off a period of heightened danger and uncertainty. This is not to say that we should, therefore, not take action. This means that we need to be especially prepared to deal with these situations and make sure that we take precautions. Much of this information and these tools are geared towards taking action while considering safety and risks.

We know that the written form and length of this Toolkit can make this inaccessible to many people. We tried to keep the language simple, to explain terms that might be unfamiliar to people, and to focus on practical steps more than philosophical or political arguments. We hope that people who can read this or download this from a computer can help to make this knowledge available to those who may have a different way of learning and understanding. We hope that people add to this Toolkit or make new tools that are easy to use and understand and will share them with others through the Creative Interventions website or other means.

We also expect that when people are in danger or have loved ones who are being harmed or who are harming others, this Toolkit will become much more meaningful. We expect that people will be relieved to find a section that addresses their particular situations or needs. They may not need the entire Toolkit but they may be able to find enough useful information to support them to reach their goals.

FAQ # 10: THIS TOOLKIT MAKES AN INTERVENTION LOOK SO LONG AND COMPLICATED. I DON'T KNOW HOW I CAN TAKE THIS ON.

This Toolkit is written to include interventions that may involve lots of people or may try to take on a long-term process of change for the person doing harm. It rests on the belief that patterns of violence are often the result of attitudes and behaviors that are built up over a long time, perhaps even many generations. They are unlikely to change with a single event or action.

We also understand that smaller actions may be significant steps. Working up the courage to tell one person about a situation of violence can be huge. Gathering friends to stay at one's home to provide safety and comfort may not transform the person doing harm, but it may provide a safe and healing environment for a survivor and her children. Safely removing a gun or weapon from someone's house may not stop a pattern of domestic violence, but it may significantly reduce the possibility of serious or deadly harm. Small actions may break the sense of isolation, shame and fear. They may give the message to the person doing harm that people are watching and are standing solidly with the survivor. These actions may give the message that people also care about the person doing harm and can support them to make significant changes.

FAQ # 11: I AM A VICTIM OF VIOLENCE AND WOULD LOVE TO HAVE THE KIND OF SUPPORT THAT I SEE IN THIS TOOLKIT. BUT I DON'T HAVE ANYBODY I CAN TURN TO. I CAN'T THINK OF ANYBODY TO SUPPORT ME.

It is true that the community-based response may not be within everyone's reach. People may need to rely upon the types of help that is available in many communities in the U.S., including crisis lines, shelters, counseling centers, medical centers, and criminal justice system responses.

At the same time, we have seen that once people begin to think in this more community-based way, possibilities can begin to open up. You may begin to look at people as possible allies, and find allies in unexpected places. You may not find people that are involved in a long-term team, but individuals may still serve a useful role even if it is a small or short-term role. We call ourselves Creative Interventions because creativity is often just what is needed. There is no set recipe, but creativity, flexibility and a little help from resources like this Toolkit may make some form of intervention possible: something that may help you reach at least some of your goals.

See Section 4.C. Mapping Allies and Barriers *to help brainstorm about who can help – and what possible roles they may play.*

FAQ #12: I AM INVOLVED IN AN ACCOUNTABILITY PROCESS AS AN ALLY AND SOMETIMES I FIND MYSELF WITH A LOT OF NEGATIVE FEELINGS TOWARDS THE SURVIVOR OF VIOLENCE. I HAVE TO ADMIT THAT I ACTUALLY LIKE THE PERSON DOING HARM MORE THAN THE SURVIVOR. IS THIS NORMAL?

It is possible for us to dislike the survivor of violence. Survivors are not perfect people. They are imperfect like anyone else. Sometimes we expect them to be the "perfect victim" – beyond guilt, always following through with what they say they're going to do, appreciating us if we are helping them. Sometimes we are angry because they have mixed feelings for the person doing harm and may seem to go back and forth between fearing them and defending them, sometimes making it difficult for allies to know what to do. Sometimes the effect of abuse and the difficulties of an intervention can make those who have experienced violence feel afraid, angry, disappointed, frustrated, exhausted, confused and other emotions that can appear unpleasant to the rest of us.

Sometimes people who cause harm have used personal charms or personal power to hide their abusive behavior or to excuse it.

It is important to learn more about common dynamics regarding interpersonal violence like domestic violence and sexual assault so that we can normalize what may look like confusing attitudes or behaviors on the part of the survivor and the person doing harm. It can also help to explain the confusion that allies often feel. And it can help to explain our feelings about the person doing harm. Doing what is right to address, reduce, end or prevent violence does not necessarily mean that we "like" the survivor and "hate/dislike" the person doing harm. It does help to be clear about our goals and to understand the sometimes complicated dynamics about violence and interventions to violence.

See Section 2.2. Interpersonal Violence: Some Basics Everyone Should Know *for more information and support around these types of confusing feelings. They are natural but can mislead us into doubting the survivor or siding with the person doing harm.*

See Section 2.3. Violence Intervention: Some Important Lessons *for more information about the dynamics of interventions.*

See Section 4.E. Supporting Survivors or Victims *for more information about providing support for survivors under many different conditions.*

See Section 4.F. Taking Accountability *for more information about supporting accountability for people doing harm under many different conditions.*

FAQ #13: I AM BEING ASKED TO INVOLVE MYSELF IN A COMMUNITY-BASED INTERVENTION, BUT I'M HONESTLY NOT SURE WHO IS THE VICTIM AND WHO IS PERSON DOING HARM.

Sometimes it is not clear who is the survivor or victim of harm and who is the person doing harm. Someone may be lying; the survivor may also take actions that are harmful; and, in some cases, the harm is "mutual" – that is, the harm can be relatively equal on both sides. Often times interpersonal harm takes place behind closed doors, in private. We may not "see" what happened and may feel like it's one person's word against another's. We do not have a foolproof way to be able to tell who is the survivor or who is the person doing harm. But we also do not expect that the survivor will be a "perfect survivor" – that they may also do things that appear abusive – or they may be doing things that are violent, sometimes in self defense.

We are looking at "patterns" of power and control. We are looking at who may be in a position of power that gives them more control, that may make them more able to manipulate power, that may make their abuse excused, and that may make them more able to hide their abuse. Therefore, male privilege remains a frequent power dynamic in excusing male violence against women or girls. Citizens or people with permanent residency often use their more stable status in the U.S. to control and violate people who may be undocumented or who may be dependent on others for their immigration status or their well-being. People with higher income or status may use this against those with less resources. Same for able-bodied people violating people who have disabilities. People using homophobia and transphobia or the fear or hatred of lesbian, gay, bisexual, transgender or queer (LGBTQ) people may take advantage of this vulnerability to threaten and abuse LGBTQ people.

However, violence does not always go in the directions we just named. It is possible for someone in a more vulnerable position in society is the person who is more abusive within a relationship. Dynamics of power and abuse tend to follow these dynamics, but not in every situation.

These dynamics may play into our confusion about who is the survivor and who is the person doing harm. Understanding these power dynamics may help us to be able to better understand the dynamics of abuse.

See Section 2.2. Interpersonal Violence: Some Basics Everyone Should Know *for more information and tools that might clarify the dynamics of violence including who is the survivor and who is the person doing harm.*

See Section 4.A. Getting Clear *and S***ection 5.6. Distinguishing between Violence and Abuse** *written by the Northwest Network of Bisexual, Trans, Lesbian and Gay Survivors of Abuse that might help clarify confusing dynamics of violence including who is the survivor and who is the person doing harm.*

FAQ # 14: I AM INVOLVED AS AN ALLY IN AN ACCOUNTABILITY PROCESS BUT I FEEL A LOT OF RESERVATION ABOUT WHAT WE ARE DOING AND WHY. I DON'T KNOW IF I CAN SUPPORT THIS PROCESS ANY LONGER.

Although most people involved in violence intervention generally want the violence to end and for people to heal, people often disagree about the best way to achieve this.

This Toolkit tries to take into account the fact that many people enter an intervention thinking that they want the same thing but actually having very different opinions on the details of the goals and the best way to get there. Also, even the smoothest intervention often involves strong emotions, including fear, guilt, and blame, which can make us feel a lot of doubt. We may feel like we're on a rollercoaster of emotions. We may change our mind about what we think.

While this Toolkit supports a collective process, each individual will have their own sense of what is right, what they believe, and their own personal limits about how or if they want to take part in a process. This can be as simple as having time limits – how much time they're willing to spend on a process and times of the day that they have available. This may be deeper in terms of their belief system about how things should be handled.

This Toolkit encourages people to be thoughtful and true to themselves and others about what are their guiding principles, goals for what they want the intervention to achieve, and personal limits or what we call "bottom-lines." It also encourages people to discuss these with each other and find group decisions that may actually change someone's mind and educate them about the dynamics of violence and the positive possibilities of group action. It relies on the belief that group discussion and action can make a better outcome than those of a single person or the chaotic actions of a group that does not communicate with each other. It is best to get these frank discussions out in the open sooner than later so that decisions can be made based on clear communication. It may still be possible that people will decide that they cannot take part in a process because they simply do not have the time or energy or because their disagreements are too deep. It is also possible that people can still take a role but may need to shift and take a role that better suits their abilities or their belief system.

See Section 4.C. Mapping Allies and Barriers. *Who can help? to think more about what kinds of roles might be a good fit.*

See Section 4.D. *Goal Setting to think about the group goals and individual goals, and to see how these can come together into a common set of goals that everyone can support.*

See Section 4.G. Working Together *to identify problems and to help figure out positive ways to work together as a team.*

FAQ # 15: I AM A SURVIVOR OF VIOLENCE AND HAVE ASKED SOME PEOPLE TO HELP ME WITH AN INTERVENTION. BUT I AM SO FRUSTRATED WITH THEM. ISN'T THIS MY INTERVENTION? WHY AREN'T THEY DOING WHAT I WANT THEM TO DO?

There can be many reasons why people end up in disagreement about a community-based intervention. The tools in this Toolkit help with processes to acknowledge disagreements or different points of view and still coordinate efforts behind some agreed-upon goals. This also means that community members may have perspectives and goals that are different than those of the survivor. This may be a healthy set of differences that when discussed can actually lead to a better, more effective process.

On the other hand, this may be a reflection that at least some allies do not understand the dynamics of violence or do not value the unique perspectives of the survivor. While some types of domestic violence or sexual assault resources say that they put the survivor's needs at the center no matter what, this Toolkit promotes a process that puts the perspective and experiences of the survivor at the center of an intervention without necessarily saying that whatever the survivor or victim says or wants is what everyone else must follow. While this may indeed be the dynamic in some interventions, we support processes that can make room for discussions about how decisions will be made. It may be necessary for allies to listen to each other and gain an understanding of each other's perspectives. Allies need to listen particularly well to the perspectives and experiences of the survivor. And the survivor or victim may also need to acknowledge and understand those of the allies. In this approach, there is also a place for people to take into account the perspective of the person doing harm and make room for their perspectives, needs and well-being without supporting or excusing acts of harm.

See Section 4.D. Goal Setting *to think about the group goals and individual goals – and to see how these can come together into a common set of goals that everyone can support.*

See Section 4.E. Supporting Survivors or Victims *for more information about supporting survivors.*

See Section 4.G. *Working Together to help figure out positive ways to work together as a team.*

FAQ #16: I AM THE SURVIVOR OF VIOLENCE. FINALLY, PEOPLE ARE RECOGNIZING AND DOING SOMETHING ABOUT THE VIOLENCE. I'VE HAD ENOUGH OF THE VIOLENCE AND JUST WANT THEM TO CARRY THE BURDEN OF THE INTERVENTION. SHOULDN'T COMMUNITY ACCOUNTABILITY MEAN THAT I CAN TURN IT OVER TO THE COMMUNITY?

In our experience, it is difficult to carry out an intervention without some involvement of the survivor. Exceptions may be in the case where the survivor is a child and it is inappropriate as well as dangerous for adults to put the burdens of an intervention on the child. The balance of how much the survivor is involved can be challenging, especially when the survivor and the community allies don't agree about the level of involvement.

There are many reasons that it may be helpful for the survivor to be involved include the fact that they may best know the harms that have been done. Others may choose directions that unintentionally endanger a survivor or lead to actions that are completely unsatisfactory to a survivor.

We have found that survivors choose many different ways to be involved. Some want to make all the decisions. Some want to be completely left out. Some only want occasional reports about what is going on or may want to make decisions about certain things. Some may completely disagree with the intervention.

See Section 4.E. Supporting Survivors or Victims *for more information about how to think about and plan for different levels of survivor involvement in an intervention.*

FAQ # 17: I AM INVOLVED IN A PROCESS OF COMMUNITY ACCOUNTABILITY AND FEEL LIKE THE PERSON WHO DID HARM KEEPS TRYING TO GET OUT OF ACCOUNTABILITY. AREN'T WE JUST LETTING THIS PERSON MANIPULATE THE PROCESS?

In this Toolkit, we present accountability as a pathway. The first step on that pathway is stopping violence, or stopping it enough to be able to take the next step. It is difficult for someone to take responsibility in the middle of violence or in the middle of a cycle of violence that keeps continuing over and over again. It is difficult to ask for change and expect change to be lasting within a pattern or cycle of violence.

This Toolkit encourages us to take resistance into account. As we will repeat, we need to create systems flexible enough to allow for the expected process of dodging and delaying accountability and strong enough to withstand and diminish these tactics over time.

We actually expect that people confronted for their patterns or acts of harm will try to avoid accountability. Think about times that you may have been accused of something. Even if you did what you were accused of doing, you may have been resentful that someone brought it up. You may have tried to make excuses. This is not to underestimate the damage that the lack of accountability can do or to say that minor harms are the same as serious types of violence that people may have committed. This is to help us understand and anticipate very likely forms of resistance so that we can be prepared and we can improve our process. In this Toolkit, we have no sure way of ensuring accountability. In fact, we are only beginning to understand this process and have included all of our knowledge so that others can benefit from what we learned and can build upon it. Our general viewpoint is that we must build processes that both expect resistance and can contain and reduce it over time.

The flip side of this is to build processes that can connect to the perspectives and well-being of the person doing harm. How can we connect to their values? How can we connect to what they care about? Can we imagine keeping people doing harm in our communities without excusing or minimizing whatever harm they have done? What would it take?

See Section 4.F. Taking Accountability for more concrete information on accountability processes.

FAQ #18: I HEAR A LOT ABOUT RESTORATIVE JUSTICE AND TRANSFORMATIVE JUSTICE. IS THIS THE SAME THING?

Many people are beginning to talk about alternative types of interventions to violence. Terms such as restorative justice, community accountability, community-based responses to violence and transformative justice have many overlapping principles and sometimes refer to the same types of processes. Restorative Justice, in particular, has been around since about the 1970s and has been developed as a way to approach many different types of harms – especially in New Zealand, Australia, and Canada. It has been used less in looking at domestic violence or sexual assault although it has been used in some cases. Restorative Justice has often been developed in collaboration with the criminal justice system. This Toolkit and many others who are talking about these types of alternatives are smaller scale and do not connect with the criminal justice system. Many are also opposed to the criminal justice system because that system is not "just," is violent, itself, and/or takes away the possibility for processes based on connection and care – instead, relying more upon punishment.

Many people using this Toolkit may be comfortable with the term Transformative Justice that has been used more frequently in social justice spaces. This Toolkit is well aligned with the principles of Transformative Justice.

In general, this Toolkit is more practical in nature and does not get into a lot of discussion about different forms of justice. However, Creative Interventions has been generally very involved in promoting these alternatives in part because of its concern regarding social justice and the harms of the criminal justice system.

See the Creative Interventions website at www.creative-interventions.org for more information and links to other organizations carrying out these discussions.

2 SOME BASICS EVERYONE SHOULD KNOW

2.0 Introduction

2.1 What is the Community-Based Intervention to Interpersonal Violence?

2.2 Interpersonal Violence: Some Basics Everyone Should Know

2.3 Violence Intervention: Some Important Lessons

2.0. INTRODUCTION

Section 2: *The Basics Everyone Should Know* has some basic information that it is important to know as you think about what you want to do about violence and consider using this Toolkit.

No matter what your familiarity is with the topic of interpersonal violence, including domestic violence or sexual assault, you may find it useful to read through the Basics section. The information we present here is different from the kind of basic domestic violence or sexual assault information offered in other books, websites and community education materials.

This Section includes:

2.1. What Is the Community-Based Intervention to Interpersonal Violence? This explains in more detail the approach used in this Toolkit that is introduced in Section 1: *Introduction & FAQ.*

2.2. Interpersonal Violence: Some Basics Everyone Should Know. Our society continues to feed us misinformation about interpersonal violence. This section gives an overview of some important things that you and others should know about interpersonal violence in order to better understand its dynamics and to create a more effective response to it.

2.3. Violence Intervention: Some Important Lessons. In this section, we offer some basic lessons that Creative Interventions learned about violence intervention over the 3 years of our project. It also builds upon the many lessons shared among other groups who have been creating similar responses to violence, many of which are listed in the *Preface* and *Acknowledgements: A Community Effort.*

2.1. WHAT IS THE COMMUNITY-BASED INTERVENTION TO INTERPERSONAL VIOLENCE?

COMMUNITY-BASED INTERVENTION TO INTERPERSONAL VIOLENCE

Brief Definition

In brief, the CI definition of community-based interventions to interpersonal violence is:

- An attempt to address, end, reduce, or prevent interpersonal violence (or what we call *intervention*)
- Using community resources rather than relying on the criminal legal system or social services
- That directly involve friends, family, co-workers, neighbors, or community members (what we mean by *community*)
- With the possibility of directly dealing with (or engaging) the person or people doing harm

Making It Through Confusing Language

You may also see language that refers more generally to *community-based responses* or a *community-based approach.*

We sometimes say community *accountability* because this is language commonly used by others.

Many of our partner organizations have found the term transformative justice useful to refer to many of these same ideas. We do not use this language or refer to "justice" generally speaking. And we find that many people using the term restorative justice still look at types of interventions that involve the police or criminal justice system, so we do not use this language either. (For a good explanation of transformative justice, see Generation Five's *Toward Transformative Justice: A Liberatory Approach to Child Sexual Abuse and other forms of Intimate and Community Violence* downloadable at http://www.generationfive.org/downloads/G5_Toward_Transformative_Justice.pdf)

In this section, we will try to clarify what CI means (and does not mean) by these sometimes confusing terms.

WHAT DO WE MEAN BY INTERPERSONAL VIOLENCE?

COMMUNITY-BASED INTERVENTION

- *Domestic violence or intimate partner violence* that takes place within an intimate relationship such as marriage, domestic partnership, dating relationship, former relationship.
- *Family violence* that can include domestic violence but can also extend to children, parents, grandchildren, grandparents, other family members and others who may be very close to family like family friends, guardians or caretakers.
- *Sexual violence* that includes unwanted sexual attitudes, touch or actions such as *sexual assault, rape, sexual harassment, molestation, child sexual abuse.*
- *Child* abuse that is any kind of abuse against children.
- *Elder abuse* that is any kind of abuse against elderly people.

While CI focuses on the types of violence just listed above, this Toolkit may also be useful for those experiencing violence in other settings such as within neighborhoods, schools, organizations, workplaces, other employment situations and so on – these forms of violence can also be considered interpersonal

The violence may be physical, emotional, sexual, economic, or may take some other form.

See Section 2.2. Interpersonal Violence: Some Basics Everyone Should Know for more important information.

WHAT DO WE MEAN BY COMMUNITY?

CI supports approaches to interpersonal violence based in the community. By community, we mean the networks of people with whom we may live, play, work, learn, organize, worship and connect to each other as community.

Since interpersonal violence generally happens in these community spaces and sometimes directly involves our fellow community members, CI believes that the answer to violence also lies in these same places, with these same people. These are the people most affected by violence, who know the most about the people involved in violence, who understand the culture and resources of the community, and who ultimately have the most to lose from violence and the most to gain from ending it.

By involving community, we can:

- Address violence where it happens.
- Take action to confront violence when and where it first shows up.
- Help people in communities gather together to address, reduce, end – and ultimately – prevent violence (violence intervention).
- Make violence intervention an everyday skill – rather than something that waits and waits until it's too late.

We also know that survivors or victims of violence usually first turn to people they know – and not crisis lines, advocates or police. Family and friends are usually the "first responders."

The problem is that they turn to us, but we do not always know what to do. And the violence "experts" tell us that we need to turn to professionals and the police to solve the problem of violence. The purpose of this Toolkit is to bring knowledge and skills back to communities – and assist communities to effectively intervene in violence.

What we DO NOT MEAN by community is: police – even if it is called "community policing," the child welfare system, the government, or even organizations that might be called "community-based" unless those organizations are directly involving everyday people in communities as the primary actors in ending violence. We also do not necessarily mean domestic violence and sexual assault agencies in the community because they currently tend to disagree with the basic assumption that everyday community members are the best people to intervene in violence.

While this Toolkit results from the collaborative work of domestic violence and sexual assault organizations, particularly those serving communities of color including immigrant and queer communities, we also recognize the gap between the model described in the Toolkit and what our own organizations generally support.

We invite domestic violence and sexual assault organizations and other service providers, counselors and others to see how to support this type of community-based approach to violence intervention. Some organizations that have been bridging the divide between traditional approaches and a community-based approach are among the organizations that we name in Preface and Acknowledgements: A Community Effort.

WHAT IS COMMUNITY ACCOUNTABILITY?

The term, *community accountability*, can be thought of as a more specific form of a *community-based response* or *approach to interpersonal violence*. The word, "community" acknowledges that it is not only individuals but also communities that are affected by violence. Interpersonal violence is not only an individual problem, but a community problem. The word, *accountability*, points to the idea of *responsibility*.

In brief, accountability is the ability to *recognize, end and take responsibility* for violence. We usually think of the person doing harm as the one to be *accountable* for violence. Community accountability also means that communities are accountable for sometimes ignoring, minimizing or even encouraging violence. Communities must also *recognize, end and take responsibility for violence* – by becoming more knowledgeable, skillful and willing to take action to intervene in violence and to support social norms and conditions that prevent violence from happening in the first place.

Accountability is the ability to recognize, end and take responsibility for violence. We usually think of the person doing harm as the one to be accountable for violence. Community accountability also means that communities are accountable for sometimes ignoring, minimizing or even encouraging violence. Communities must also recognize, end and take responsibility for violence – by becoming more knowledgeable, skillful and willing to take action to intervene in violence and to support social norms and conditions that prevent violence from happening in the first place.

This Toolkit provides more information about accountability in Section 4.E. Taking Accountability

Finally, communities are places of meaning, connection and resources for survivors or victims of violence and persons doing harm. Communities hold great potential in their ability to challenge violence and also for using meaning, connection and resources as part of the solution to violence. Community accountability can be used towards supporting the compassionate repair of harm for survivors of violence and all of those affected by violence; supporting people doing harm to take accountability for violence (that is, recognize, end and take responsibility), and changing community norms so that violence does not continue.

WHAT DO WE MEAN BY INTERVENTION?

Intervention expands beyond thinking and talking about what to do about violence – and moves into actions that can actually interrupt violence.

In this Toolkit, interventions to violence are actions to address, reduce, end or prevent violence.

While we would ideally like all forms of violence to end and never happen again, we also know that our interventions cannot always achieve this end.

We also understand that interventions are rarely one-time events. They are usually processes – involving the steps that we describe in this Toolkit's Section 4: *Tools to Mix and Match* such as Getting Clear, Staying Safe, Setting Goals, Mapping Allies and Barriers, Taking Accountability, Working Together, and Keeping on Track.

PUTTING COMMUNITY AND INTERVENTIONS TOGETHER

Breaking it down, community-based interventions to interpersonal violence are:

- **Collective.** The intervention involves the coordinated efforts of a group of people rather than just one individual.
- **Action-Oriented.** A community takes action to address, reduce, end or prevent interpersonal violence.
- **Community-Based.** The intervention is organized and carried out by friends, family, neighbors, co-workers or community members rather than social services, the police, child welfare or governmental institutions.
- **Coordinated.** The intervention links people and actions together to work together in a way that is coordinated towards the same goals – and that makes sure that our individual actions work towards a common purpose. It sees us as a team rather than individual, isolated individuals working as lone heroes or rescuers – or as separated parts, not knowing about or considering what actions others may be taking.
- **Holistic.** The intervention considers the good of everyone involved in the situation of violence – including those harmed (survivors or victims of violence), those who have caused harm, and community members affected by violence. It also builds an approach that can include anyone involved in a situation of violence as a participant in the solution to violence – even the person or people who have caused harm if this is possible.

- **Centers on Those Most Affected by Violence to Create Change.** The intervention centers those most affected by violence. It provides ways for those affected by violence and causing violence to develop new skills, insights and ways to put together a solution to violence – or to form a system that not only addresses violence but reduces the chances that violence will continue.
- **Supports the sometimes complex pathway to change and transformation.** Changing violence, repairing from violence, and creating new ways of being free from violence can take time.
- **For the survivor/victim**, the intervention relies upon consideration of the best ways to support survivors or victims of harm by sharing the responsibility for addressing, reducing, ending, or preventing violence (**breaking isolation** and **taking accountability**), without blaming the survivor/victim for their choices (without **victim blaming**), and by offering support towards what they define as their own needs and wants (supporting **self-determination**).
- **For the person doing harm**, the intervention relies upon consideration of the best ways to support people doing harm to recognize, end and be responsible for their violence (what we also call **accountability**), without giving them excuses (without **colluding**), and without denying their humanity (without **demonizing**).
- **Facilitated.** The intervention works well if someone in our communities can act as a facilitator, someone who can act as an anchor for the process of intervention, or someone who can help us to walk through different parts of this Toolkit. Therefore, we call this a *facilitated* model. The facilitator role can be taken on by more than one person or it can rotate among group members as the process continues. The facilitator does not have to be a professional or someone who is an expert on violence intervention. It simply needs to be someone who can be clear-headed, act within the values and guidelines of the group, and who has some distance from the center of violence to be clear of the chaos and confusion that is often a part of a violent situation. See more about the facilitator role in Section 4.C. *Mapping Allies and Barriers*. If one cannot find a facilitator, then at the very least, this Toolkit and the many people whose experiences it represents may help to guide us through the process of violence intervention.

HOW IS THE COMMUNITY-BASED INTERVENTION APPROACH DIFFERENT?

CI offers a community-based approach which is an alternative to most commonly available responses to violence intervention. Most commonly available resources include domestic violence or battered women's centers, shelters, sexual assault or rape crisis centers, legal assistance clinics, counseling centers, victim-witness programs, and Family Justice Centers.

Usual Violence Intervention Approach

While the usual resources can be and have been helpful to many people, especially women experiencing violence, they also tend to recommend solutions that:

1. Assume that survivors or victims want to separate from the people doing harm.
2. Tells survivors or victims that calling the police or 911 is the safest way to end violence.
3. Requires a report to child protective services if resource providers think that a child is being harmed.
4. Works primarily with only the survivor or victims of violence rather than also working together with friends, family, neighbors, co-workers and community members.
5. Deals with people doing harm through the police or criminal justice system. (Batterer intervention programs often go through the police first, rather than the community first.)

THE NEED FOR AN ALTERNATIVE: HOW IS THE COMMUNITY-BASED RESPONSE UNIQUE?

CI found that many people seeking an intervention to violence did not feel safe or comfortable with these approaches, but they did not have other options.

In response, CI sought a community-based approach that:

1. Explores options that may allow survivors or victims to stay together with the people doing harm or at least support co-existence in the same community.
2. Does not rely upon the police or systems to address, reduce, end and prevent violence (violence intervention) but rather on friends, family, neighbors, co-workers and community members (community allies).
3. Brings intervention and prevention skills and knowledge to victims or survivors, friends, family, neighbors, co-workers and community members rather than relying solely on "experts".
4. Envisions change of the person or people doing harm through connection with what is important and meaningful rather than simply through force, punishment and shaming.
5. Considers the person or people doing harm as potential allies in ending violence.
6. Changes the language of violence intervention from criminal justice terminology such as "perpetrators," "perps," "predators," and "offenders" to the language of "people doing harm", or "people who caused harm."

WHAT IF YOU ARE USING SERVICES OR SYSTEMS?

Some people who want to use a community-based approach to violence may already be involved in the criminal justice system, receive social services or are involved in more traditional violence intervention programs. As mentioned before, the model promoted in this Toolkit may actually be in conflict with these systems. For example, this Toolkit's approach allows survivors or victims of violence to consider the possibility of dealing directly with the person doing harm while taking into account one's goals and safety concerns. If someone is in a shelter, contact with the person doing harm may break shelter rules, even if the contact is made through a third party. If someone has a restraining order, this contact may violate that order. These are examples of how this model can violate the rules and assumptions of the usual types of intervention available.

This Toolkit also encourages actively working together with other people in one's family, friendship network or community. While this might not be counter to the rules of service providers or the criminal justice system, conventional or mainstream systems assume that the person is making decisions on one's own or with an advocate or professional and not with other community members. The decision-making process might conflict with the ways in which these systems expect that people will make decisions. People working in conventional or mainstream systems may even consider a group process to be strange or wrong. They may think that survivors or victims that seek a process involving more people means that they are weak or dependent, rather than finding strength through their communities. The value of collectivity is one that is different from the way that most individually-focused systems work.

People wanting to use this Toolkit should be aware of these possible conflicts in values and approaches. At the same time, it is possible to use this community-based approach with more traditional services and systems by being aware of the differences. You may want to use this Toolkit or parts of it to better define and reach your goals. If you are already involved with systems or services, this Toolkit may be used along with these systems. This Toolkit may even be helpful in managing or counteracting the harms that can result from the use of other systems.

CREATIVE INTERVENTIONS COMMUNITY-BASED INTERVENTION VALUES

Creative Interventions developed this model not only to end violence, but to lead to healthier ways of being in community with each other.

We found it important to create values to guide us in our own work. As we did our work, we returned to these values to see if our day-to-day way of doing things followed these values. We also returned to our values from time to time to see if they really reflected what we believed and to see if we were missing anything that was important to our work. These values underlie our vision and practice and are reflected throughout this Toolkit.

The following is a list of the Creative Interventions values.

CREATIVE INTERVENTIONS VALUES (LONG VERSION):

1. **Creativity.** Solutions to violence can emerge out of a creative process.

2. **Collectivity or Community Responsibility.** We believe that violence is not an individual problem and that solutions also cannot be individual. It takes all of us to end violence. The actions of a group (if done well) can be much wiser, healthier, effective and long-lasting than those carried out by an individual.

3. **Holism.** Solutions to violence can involve consideration for the health and well-being of everyone involved in and affected by violence – this includes the survivors or victims of violence; people doing harm; and friends, family and community.
We also want our solutions to keep communities whole. This does not mean that abusive relationships or families necessarily need to stay together, but this does mean that they may be able co-exist peacefully in the same community or transform to healthier, more cooperative and respectful relationships.

4. **Safety.** We are interested in creating safety in all of its forms (physical, emotional, sexual, economic, spiritual and so on).

5. **Risk-Taking.** While we prioritize safety, we also believe that it sometimes takes risks to create more safety in the long-run. Safety may require action which has the potential to increase short-term risk or danger in order to reach long-term goals.

6. Accountability. All of us have our own role and responsibility to take in ending violence. Community-based solutions to violence require that we all step up and think about the ways we may have contributed to violence, the ways we may need acknowledge and make amends for our contribution to violence, and the ways we can take action to make sure that violence does not continue and that healthy alternatives can take its place.

7. Transformation. We believe that everyone involved in violence can go through positive change. What is needed is a model for taking action which believes that healthy change is possible for all – and can also take realistic and sometimes difficult steps to create an environment in which long-term change can be supported.

8. Flexibility. Situations of violence are often complicated and so are the steps towards long-term change. We try to remain flexible so that we can make changes and create new strategies when needed.

9. Patience. Violence is built over time and so the solution to violence takes time. We ask people to step out of expectations of quick results and take the time to create thoughtful solutions to violence, solutions which will hold in the long run.

10. Building on What We Know (Organic). We believe that we all as individuals, families, friendship networks, communities and cultures have a history of creative and community-based ways to resolve violence. We want to remember, honor and build upon the positive things we have known and done throughout history.

11. Sustainability. We need to support each other to create change in ways that can last over the time it takes to successfully intervene in violence. We encourage that solutions to violence are built to last over the course of the intervention, over our lifetimes, and throughout future generations.

12. Regeneration. We can all contribute to expanding opportunities to challenge violence and contribute to liberation. Although any of us may be thinking of our own unique situation of violence when creating a community-based response to violence, our successes lead to new changes and transformations for everyone involved. And our stories can be passed on to others so they can learn from our experiences. We ask you to consider sharing your intervention stories and lessons learned through the website (www.creative-interventions.org), the StoryTelling & Organizing Project (STOP) (www.stopviolenceeveryday.org) and through other community spaces.

NOTE A brief version of Creative Intervention values is in checklist form later in this section of the Toolkit. You will also find a helpful list of values created by Communities against Rape and Abuse (CARA) in Section 5.4 that may help you think about the values that you want to guide your intervention.

2.2. INTERPERSONAL VIOLENCE: SOME BASICS EVERYONE SHOULD KNOW

Interpersonal violence is very commonly a way to gain power and control over another person. It often takes advantage of unequal power relations. This is why interpersonal forms of violence, especially domestic violence and sexual assault, are so often committed by men against women and girls, boys against girls, male-identified over female-identified, adults over youth and children, able-bodied over people with disabilities, citizens over immigrants, legal immigrants over undocumented immigrants, people with high status over people with lower status, rich over poor or those who financially depend on them, and so on.

Because we are talking about interpersonal violence, this violence can be committed by people within the same race, ethnicity, income or class, family, household, neighborhood, organization, and so on. This is not always the case and sometimes these differences become important factors in the imbalance of power.

Sometimes, people who are in a less powerful position in society use their feelings of powerlessness to justify the use of violence in their interpersonal relationships – as an excuse for their violence or a way to "make up" for the powerlessness they feel in other places in their lives.

Because we are talking about interpersonal violence, the survivor or victim and the person doing harm may also love and care about each other or move back and forth between powerful feelings of love and hate.

There are many reasons that a consideration of interpersonal violence and the end to violence are important:

1. Our interpersonal relationships (families, intimate relationships, close friendships) are often the first place we learn about violence and relationships. Those experiences can have a life-long Impact. The value of transforming lessons about violence, helplessness, and powerlessness to love, respect and shared power is immeasurable.

2. Disconnecting ideas about intimacy, families and closeness from violence and abuse can stop us from growing up and repeating relationships that find love through violence and abuse – and that repeat the cycle of violence generation after generation.

3. Learning to love and respect those within our families and communities, especially if we are from communities at the bottom of society, can strengthen and unite us to tackle larger abuses in our society – the bigger enemies of poverty, racism, homophobia, anti-immigrant discrimination, ableism and so on.

4. Changing ourselves from victims and abusers to companions, supporters and friends can release us from hate, fear and violence towards powerful positive forces for building healthy lives, relationships and communities.

In this section, we take time to share some of the basic knowledge about interpersonal violence we have gained through years of practice.

Although people hear more about domestic violence, sexual assault and other forms of interpersonal violence in our culture, interpersonal violence is still very much misunderstood including among very educated people. This lack of information leads us to blame victims, excuse people causing harm, or sometimes just turn the other way.

The following presents 10 basics about interpersonal violence that everyone should know.

BASIC ONE — Interpersonal violence usually takes place between people who know each other – sometimes making violence more complicated and confusing.

Interpersonal violence is violence that occurs between:

People in an intimate relationship (dating, marriage, live-in, domestic partner, former partner, parents of same child, etc.) – domestic violence or intimate partner violence

People in a family or family-like social network – family violence

Friends

Household Members

Neighbors

Co-Workers

Members of the same organization (e.g., church, community organization, etc.)

Acquaintances

Because these relationships of violence may also include relationships of love, companionship, friendship, loyalty and also dependence and even survival, this can make it more confusing to understand dynamics of violence and also to change them.

BASIC TWO

Interpersonal violence can look many different ways and take many different forms.

We look at interpersonal violence as any form of abuse, harm, violence, or violation taking place between two or more individuals. It can include forms of violence used to harm someone, keep someone under one's control, or get someone to do whatever one wants them to do. Examples include the following:

- **Physical Violence or Threats** – Includes using intimidating body language; pushing; slapping; hitting; beating; kicking; strangling; pulling hair; holding down; locking into a room or space; driving dangerously; keeping someone up at night – not letting them sleep; leaving someone in a dangerous location; or using a weapon.
- **Verbal and Emotional Violence** – Includes yelling; name-calling; put-downs; humiliating behavior; always being right; or making someone feel crazy.
- **Isolation** – Includes making it difficult for someone to make friends; keep up relationships; see one's family; remain connected to one's community; go to work; go to school; go outside of the home; talk to other people; look at other people; make phone calls.
- **Sexual Violence** – Includes making someone participate in sexual activities of any kind against their will; making someone do sexual acts that they do not want to do; making someone watch pornography or see pornographic images against their will; or making sexual remarks, looks, or gestures against their will; sending unwanted sexual text messages (sexting), calls or emails; threatening to or publicly revealing sexually revealing photographs of the abused person. With regard to children, sexual violence includes any form of sexual activity with a child, any exposure to sexual content, any sexual remarks or looks.
- **Economic or Financial Abuse** – Includes withholding financial information from an intimate partner; controlling income against the will of one's partner or other family member; gambling or abusive use of credit cards; leaving too little money for financial survival; coming around during the time that someone's work check or government check comes in and taking control of that money.
- **Controlling Property and Pets** – Includes destroying property, especially property that is emotionally or financially valuable to that person; controlling someone's important documents and papers such as identification, passport, immigration papers; controlling car keys and other means to get to transportation; threatening or harming pets.

- **Stalking** – Includes sending text-messages, emails or calling repeatedly; following someone at their home, workplace, school or other places where they might be; monitoring someone's emails or text-messages; taking someone's identity and getting into their bank accounts, email accounts or other private spaces; or leaving notes and messages repeatedly or in a harassing manner.

- **Using someone's vulnerability (due to prejudice/discrimination/oppression) against them** – Includes using vulnerability and forms of prejudice/discrimination/oppression to justify one's control and violence as a form of abuse (such as calling people names, using put-downs, treating someone with abuse based upon this form of prejudice/discrimination/oppression); taking advantage of society's prejudice/discrimination/oppression to control someone even more or prevent the abused person from getting help (such as threatening to call immigration authorities on someone who is an immigrant or who is undocumented) (See Figure 3: The Relationship between Prejudice/Privilege/Oppression and Interpersonal Violence).

- **Using one's own vulnerability (due to discrimination) to manipulate or control someone, or to excuse one's own use of violence** – Includes making one's lack of power in society a justification for using power and control over others at home, in the relationship, or in the workplace; includes making it one person's personal responsibility to "make up for" all social barriers or discrimination one faces; creating a contest over who is more oppressed than the other; using the excuse of "I'm more oppressed than you" to justify abuse and violence over the other person; using one's disadvantage or abuse during childhood as an excuse for violence.

- **Using things or people someone values against them** – Includes "outing" (making public) someone who is lesbian, gay, bi-sexual, transgender, queer; making trouble at someone's workplace; damaging someone's reputation; harming or threatening to harm someone's friends, family, or pets; or threatening to take someone's children or to get custody just to harm someone.

These forms of interpersonal violence are also known by other names: domestic violence or intimate partner violence; sexual assault or abuse; sexual harassment; family violence; child abuse including child sexual abuse; elder abuse; violence within friendship network or organization; and, in some cases, self-harm.

COMMON FORMS OF INTERPERSONAL VIOLENCE

TERM & WORKING DEFINITION	CAN INCLUDE:
DOMESTIC VIOLENCE OR INTIMATE PARTNER VIOLENCE Acts of abuse or harm or pattern of power and control exercised by one person over another within an intimate relationship (dating, living together, married, domestic partner, former relationship, parents of same children; heterosexual or same-gender)	Physical abuse including threats and threats to harm others or self Verbal abuse/put-downs Emotional abuse Intimidation Isolation Sexual abuse/assault Economic/financial abuse Threats or use of other systems of oppression to gain power/control such as immigration enforcement (ICE, formerly known as INS), queer outing, etc. Stalking
SEXUAL HARASSMENT Unwanted sexual/affectionate attention or creation of an unwanted sexualized environment	Sexual looks/gestures Sexual comments Sexual jokes Unwanted request for dates, sexual relations Subjecting to pornography or environment demeaning to women/girls/queer people Threats to demote, fire, harm (emotionally or physically) if sexual or dating requests are not met or if victim/survivor tells other people
SEXUAL ABUSE/ASSAULT Coerced or otherwise unwanted sexual contact (for a child, this can be any sexual exposure, behavior or contact)	Sexual touching Fondling, molesting Exposure to sexual parts/genitals of the person causing harm Oral, vaginal, anal touching or penetration by the harming person's body or object Threats to harm (emotionally or physically), demote, fire if sexual contact is not met or if victim/survivor tells other people

TERM & WORKING DEFINITION	CAN INCLUDE:
CHILD ABUSE INCLUDING CHILD SEXUAL ABUSE Acts of abuse or harm against children by adults or others in a relationship of power to a child	Physical abuse including threats Physical violence including use of physical discipline Verbal abuse – put-downs Emotional abuse Intimidation Neglect – not providing adequate food, shelter, clothing, heat, sleep, adult supervision Allowing others to abuse a child Any type of sexual exposure, behavior or contact with a child
ELDER ABUSE Acts of abuse or harm against an elderly person by another adult	Physical abuse including threats and threats to harm others or self Verbal abuse – put-downs Emotional abuse Intimidation Isolation Sexual abuse/assault/harassment Economic/financial abuse including taking social security money or other income, abusing power-of-attorney relationship
VIOLENCE WITHIN FRIENDSHIP, NETWORK, OR ORGANIZATIONS Acts of abuse or harm between members of a social network, community, organization	Physical abuse including threats and threats to harm others or self Verbal abuse – put-downs Emotional abuse Sexual abuse/assault/harassment Abuse of power in hierarchical relationship Creating a threatening or intimidating environment

NOTE

These definitions and categories are simplified for the purpose of these tables. They intentionally avoid overly legalistic terms which can be used to dismiss abuse or violence or distract from the facts of abuse. Adapted from Incite! Women of Color Against Violence. Gender Oppression, Abuse, Violence: Community Accountability in the People of Color Progressive Movement. Author, 2005 and downloadable at http://www.incite-national.org/media/docs/2406_cmty-acc-poc.pdf.

2.A. WHAT ABOUT SELF-HARM? CAN THIS BE A FORM OF VIOLENCE?

What is self-harm? Some forms of self-harm include:

- Cutting or other forms of self-injury
- Use or overdose of drugs
- Driving recklessly
- Taking reckless or dangerous action likely to cause harm or death
- Attempts to kill oneself
- Threatening suicide

What could be called **aggressive self-harm**? We consider these acts or threats to be forms of harm to others **if they are primarily meant to manipulate or control** others in the ways described above. Some ways that aggressive self-harm can be used are:

- To coerce someone to come back into a relationship.
- To pressure someone to maintain contact or communication.
- To get someone to take actions that someone would otherwise not want to take and that may hurt them.
- To distract people from looking at the abuse or violence one has taken against others.

We do not automatically consider self-harm as a form of abuse and ask for caution in the inclusion of self-harm. For example, survivors or victims of violence can also feel a desire to harm themselves or others as a defensive measure or as a sign of hopelessness and despair. Even though there may be elements of this with someone who is using self-harm aggressively, we ask that you consider what appears to be the underlying or primary motivations and intended consequences of these actions.

BASIC THREE

Interpersonal violence is often about using a pattern of power and control rather than anger, passion or loss of control.

Although violence comes in many forms and in many situations, violence is often used as a way for one person or one group to have power and control over another. We may think that violence is about anger, passion or loss-of-control. But, we find that interpersonal violence is often:

- ***One-sided*** – One person or group has a pattern of harming another person or group; one person or group is more afraid of the other person or group. Even if harm is committed on both sides, there is often a one-sided pattern of who is more harmful and who gets most harmed.

- ***Attempts to control others or get one's own way*** – Interpersonal violence is often used to try to get someone else to do what one wants – against the will or the best interests of the other. Although violence may fail to get what one wants or may seem to bring about more negative consequences, it is often used to attempt to gain power and control over another.

- ***Takes advantage of vulnerability*** – People who use violence often take advantage of or even seek out people who are vulnerable or who are in a situation where they do not have as much power or as much protection.

- ***Continues in a pattern*** – Interpersonal violence often does not take place in one act of violence but in a pattern of many subtle acts of violence in many areas.

- ***May be calculated and planned even if it does not look like it*** – Even if interpersonal violence often looks as if one is completely out of control, we often find that violence is planned and calculated. For example, some people doing harm tend to hurt those who will not tell others or who may not be believed; some people injure others in places that do not show such as hitting someone on the head or injuring someone where wounds are covered by clothes; some people wait until others are not around to see the violence occur; some people hide their violence and only show calm or respectable behavior in front of others.

- ***May follow a cycle*** – Some people experience a "cycle of violence" – 1) build up of tension; leading to 2) a violent act, outburst or series of violent acts; leading to 3) a period of relative calm which could look like apologies and remorse or perhaps just a period in which violence does not occur. The cycle can follow hours, days, months or years. Apologies and remorse can be used as a way to continue the cycle of violence rather than as a sincere sign that violence will end.

- ***May increase over time*** – Once someone uses one form of violence, it often leads to an increase in the seriousness of violence and/or the frequency of violence.

3.A. WHAT CAN MAKE SOMEONE MORE VULNERABLE TO VIOLENCE?

Violence is related to power. People who have less power can be more vulnerable to violence because they are an easier target, because they are less likely to be protected or are more likely to be blamed. They may have less places to go to get help.

People can be more vulnerable to violence depending upon:

- **Gender/sex** (especially if they are female, female-identified, transgender, or gender non-conforming)
- **Race** (especially if they are people of color or a discriminated-against race or ethnicity)
- **Class or income level** (especially if they are poor or low income)
- **Level of education** (especially if they have less formal education)
- **Immigration status** (especially if they are immigrant non-citizen or are undocumented)
- **Sexual orientation** (especially if they are lesbian, gay, bi-sexual or questioning)
- **Age** (especially if they are very young or elderly)
- **Physical or mental ability** (especially if they have some form of disability)
- **Physical appearance** (especially if they are considered unattractive in some way)
- **What country or region they're from** (especially if they are from a disfavored country or region)
- **Religion** (especially if they are from a disfavored religion)
- **Political affiliation** (especially if they are from a disfavored political affiliation)
- **Vulnerability to the criminal justice system and immigration authorities** (especially if they are from a race, class, religion, neighborhood, immigration status, choice of occupation, country of origin, gender identity, or with criminal justice history that makes them particularly targeted by or vulnerable to law enforcement, immigration authorities and/or child protective services)
- **Emotionally, financially or otherwise dependent on others for survival**

THE RELATIONSHIP BETWEEN PREJUDICE/PRIVILEGE/ OPPRESSION AND INTERPERSONAL VIOLENCE

How does your status as...

A woman, girl or female-identified person

A person of color

A person with a physical disability

A person with a mental disability

An immigrant

An undocumented immigrant

A person who doesn't speak English or who has limited English

A person from a religion that is subject to discrimination

A person who cannot read or write

A lesbian/gay/bisexual person

A transgender person

A poor person

A person whose source of income makes them vulnerable to prejudice or arrest

A person without income

A person without a home

A person considered unattractive

A person without connection to family, friends or community

A person with a felony

A person with disfavored political beliefs

An elderly person

A young person

...become used as part of the abuse?

...prevent you from knowing where to get help?

...make survival difficult or impossible if you leave the person abusing you?

...subject you to more abuse by those who are supposed to help you?

BASIC FOUR

Using violence as self-defense is not the same as using violence to gain or maintain power and control.

We may see situations in which it is difficult to tell who is committing violence against whom – who is the primary survivor and who is the primary person doing harm. There may be some cases in which violence is somewhat equal (mutual) or at least seems that way at first. However, it is more common in interpersonal violence that one person is holding power and control over another in a pattern, not two people being engaged in mutual violent fighting.

While no one outside of a relationship (whether intimate, community-based or work-place based, etc.) can know exactly what the dynamics are inside of the relationship, there are important observations and experiences that you as friends, family, and community members can draw upon as you assess situations, and then try to imagine how to intervene and support change.

4.A. QUESTIONS TO ASK WHEN IT'S HARD TO TELL WHO'S VIOLENT

If it is hard to tell who is doing the harm, it can be helpful to ask yourself (and other allies) these questions. The answers can help to unpack a complicated situation of interpersonal violence.

See if these questions are helpful.

- Who is more afraid?
- Who starts the violence?
- Who ends up getting harmed?
- Who is changing and adapting to meet another's needs or moods?
- Who is more vulnerable?
- Who is using violence for power and control (abusive violence)? Who is using violence to try to maintain safety or integrity in an already violent situation (self-defense)?
- Who always has to win?

CAUTION

This is a guide. It is not a test with absolutely right or wrong answers. Use with caution.

BASIC FIVE

Interpersonal violence is serious and common.

Interpersonal violence seriously and deeply damages individuals, communities, and societies. Bruises may disappear. Broken bones may heal. Cruel words may make invisible wounds. But the direct and ripple effects of violence including emotionally abusive and controlling behavior can be devastating.

In the U.S., one out of four women have been physically assaulted by a current or former spouse, partner, or dating partner in their lifetime. Look around you in any crowd, and you can take a good guess that one out of four women has experienced or will experience physical violence from an intimate partner.

(Source: Patricia Tjaden & Nancy Thoennes, 2000. U.S. Dep't of Just., NCJ 181867, Extent, Nature, and Consequences of Intimate Partner Violence,. Available at http://www.ojp.usdoj.gov/nij/pubs-sum/181867.htm)

On average more than three women a day are murdered by their husbands or boyfriends.

(Source: Catalano, Shannon. 2007. Intimate Partner Violence in the United States. U.S. Department of Justice, Bureau of Justice Statistics. Available at http://www.ojp.usdog.gov/bjs/intimate/ipv.htm)

Look at our children. We can expect that an average of one out of four girls and one out of six boys will experience sexual assault by the time they reach age 18.

(Source: Finkelhor, David, et al. 1990. Sexual Abuse in a Survey of Adult Men and Women: Prevalence, Characteristics and Risk Factors.)

In eight out of ten rape cases, the survivor/victim knows the perpetrator. These are mostly not rapes by strangers as we see in the media. These are committed by loved ones, people in our communities and acquaintances.

(Source: Patricia Tjaden & Nancy Thoennes, U.S. Dep't of Just., NCJ 183781, Full Report of the Prevalence, Incidence, and Consequences of Intimate Partner Violence Against Women: Findings from the National Violence Against Women Survey, at iv (2000), available at http://www.ojp.usdoj.gov/nij/pubs-sum/183781.htm.)

These are just some of the statistics to remind us of how common interpersonal violence is. This means that we are all impacted in some way by violence in our lives.

BASIC SIX

Interpersonal violence hurts all of us - in different ways.

Interpersonal violence harms in so many ways. Below are special considerations about the ways in which interpersonal violence affects certain people involved in it or close to it.

6.A. HOW VIOLENCE CAN HURT SURVIVORS/VICTIMS

For those who are being harmed (survivors/victims), violence can cause:

- Physical injury including death
- Physical disease, unwanted pregnancy, chronic conditions due to prolonged injury, abuse, and emotional stress
- Emotional damage – which some describe as deeper and more hurtful than physical harm
- Loss of self-respect, self-esteem, belief in oneself
- Feelings of shame and guilt
- Loss of sense of identity or meaning
- Feelings of hopelessness and despair
- Inability to trust
- Guilty feelings that we are disappointing our family, friends, our community and others
- Fear that we are also bring danger to others – our children, other family members, our co-workers and so on
- Loss of income, home, and financial security
- Loss of one's ability and energy to determine one's own life; take care of others; do effective work; be happy and healthy; contribute to the community; or live a healthy spiritual life
- Inability to think clearly, plan for the future, fully protect the safety of oneself and one's children or other loved ones
- Loss of love or good feelings for the person who is harming us

6.B. HOW VIOLENCE CAN HURT PEOPLE DOING HARM

In some cases violence seems to bring benefits to the person doing harm such as getting their own way or a heightened sense of power and control, but it can also cause:

- Others to fear and hate us
- Inability to be close to people and have close meaningful relationships
- Inability to trust and be trusted
- Fear that others will find out
- Fear that loved ones will leave us
- Fear that we will be alone
- Fear that we are becoming like others who were violent against us or our loved ones
- Guilt or shame for harming others
- Loss of self-respect, self-esteem, belief in oneself
- Feelings of hopelessness and despair

6.C. HOW VIOLENCE CAN HURT CHILDREN

Children are deeply harmed by witnessing/experiencing interpersonal violence especially if their parents or other family members or caretakers are involved. For children, violence can cause:

- Direct physical harm including death if they are also being harmed or if they try to intervene and stop the harm
- Direct emotional harm if they are also being harmed
- Direct sexual harm if they are also being harmed
- Physical, emotional and other developmental damage because caretakers are unable to pay attention to their needs
- Physical disease caused by prolonged stress and worry
- Emotional damage caused by seeing people they love and depend on being harmed or harming others
- Emotional damage caused by constant feelings of danger and worry
- Emotional damage caused by confusing feelings of fear and love for those doing harm

- Emotional damage caused by confusing feelings of love for, disappointment in, or disrespect for those who are being harmed
- Unfair expectation or need to overly identify with the person doing harm or the person who is harmed.
- Unfair burden to comfort and protect others – siblings, parents, or others – from harm
- Increased vulnerability to community harms including sexual abuse, community violence, substance abuse due to lack of protection
- Increased vulnerability to self-harm including cutting or other self-injury, and substance abuse
- Increased likelihood to harm others including other children and pets/animals
- Lasting lessons about family and home as an unsafe and dangerous place
- Lasting lessons about love being confused with violence and harm
- Lasting lessons about other family members or community doing nothing to stop violence
- Lasting lessons about how using violence gets you what you want
- Lasting lessons about what bad things can happen if one is vulnerable to violence or lacking in power
- Fear that they are going to lose their parents, their home, or people close to them
- Difficulty doing well in school because of their constant worry about violence
- Difficulty having healthy relationships with friends because of learning a model of violence or other feelings of guilt, shame, or depression
- Burden of secrecy about their situation because they don't want people to find out
- Guilt about feeling like they are somehow causing the violence or that they should be able to stop the violence
- Feeling that something is wrong with them

6.D. HOW VIOLENCE CAN HURT CLOSE FRIENDS, FAMILY AND COMMUNITY

For people close to the violence or people in the community, violence can cause:

- An environment taken over by the fear of violence; the fear of people involved in violence; the physical, emotional, sexual, economic and spiritual harm caused by violence
- The acceptance of violence as a community and/or family norm
- Stress and worry about the people involved in violence
- Shame about being close to or involved in violence or having friends or family members involved in violence
- Fractions and divisions in communities as conflicting loyalties and opinions about what should be done arise
- Physical danger if we are being threatened by harm either directly or indirectly
- Threat to income, security or well-being if we rely upon people involved in violence
- Guilt about not being able to do more to stop violence
- Loss of the full potential of those around us who are involved in violence including their ability to be good friends or family members, healthy members of our communities and organizations, productive co-workers, good neighbors, church members, colleagues, comrades and so on
- Feelings of hopelessness and despair

BASIC SEVEN — Interpersonal violence is often hidden, denied or ignored.

Many times, we do not recognize interpersonal violence because:

Survivors don't want to talk about it

- We as a society still consider it shameful to be a survivor/victim of interpersonal violence, and interpersonal violence is often intimate and deeply complex and painful
- People doing harm often threaten further harm if the survivor/victim tells anyone
- Survivors may not talk because they (and others) think they did something to cause it or deserve it (blaming the victim)

Community members would rather not see or challenge the violence

- We may think that violence is acceptable or okay in certain situations
- We may hope that if we ignore violence, it might go away
- We are afraid that we might ourselves get harmed if we try to intervene or challenge violence
- We may consider interpersonal violence as private business – we do not want to get involved
- We question and criticize survivors' behavior to make sense of the violence or justify doing nothing about it

Society doesn't want to recognize it

- We are unaware of violence and, therefore, do not see it
- We as a society normalize, glorify, and romanticize violence and often do not recognize it as harm
- We may see it as something that someone deserves
- We may not think that violence can be stopped or prevented
- We may think that violence is just a part of life

BASIC EIGHT

Our personal biases and experiences can influence how we understand a situation of violence – in good ways and bad.

We all come to our understanding of violence and interventions with our own perspectives and biases – influenced by our personal experiences, histories, and the ways in which situations of interpersonal violence can play out in our communities and social networks.

This can lead to confusing feelings.

Think about your own experiences about violence.
How could they influence you, in good and bad ways?

- Do you have a personal experience of violence?
- Did you experience or witness violence as a child?
- Are you angry at yourself for being a victim? Being someone who caused harm? Standing by when someone else was getting hurt?
- Are you angry at others for being a victim?
- Did your experiences of harm end well? End badly?
- What lessons did you learn about violence? How might they influence you now?

Take the time and reflect about your experiences and beliefs about violence and how they might positively or negatively influence you now.

- How can your experiences or beliefs make you especially useful or knowledgeable?
- How can your experiences or beliefs make certain roles difficult for you to take?

8.A. COMMON CONFUSING QUESTIONS

- What if I find the survivor or victim annoying or unsympathetic?
- What if I like the person doing harm better than the survivor or victim?
- What if I get angry at the survivor? What if I get angrier at the survivor than at the person doing harm?
- What if I start to feel uncomfortable that we are putting pressure or demands on the person doing harm?
- What if I wish everyone would just forgive and forget?

There may be situations in which we do not personally like the survivor of violence and find the person doing harm more appealing or sympathetic. Sometimes this is because our friendships or alliances are just that way. For example, we may be supportive of our friends or family no matter what they do. We may have less compassion for the "other side" no matter what they do.

Other times we find that the situation of violence has contributed to the survivor becoming increasingly isolated and negatively viewed while the person doing harm maintains positive standing in the community.

Survivors may "act" or "appear" negative as they get worn down by a pattern of violence. They may become tired, depressed, hopeless, nervous, anxious, jumpy, resentful or short-tempered because of violence. These characteristics are often viewed negatively by society and may lead us to blame survivors.

Survivors often feel doubt about decisions to leave someone harming them or take action to change it. Fear, guilt, self-doubt, love, and pressures from other people can easily cause survivors to change their minds back and forth about how they feel about the violence, how they view the person doing harm, or what they want to do about it. These back and forth changes are a very normal response to violence and to fears about change. And it is also understandable that these changes can be viewed with frustration by others especially if they are trying to help.

Still other times, we may feel uncomfortable about any confrontation or conflict. Our discomfort with conflict can make us feel more empathy for the person doing harm than the survivor of the harm. We may begin to feel bad for the person doing harm as they are being called out for their violence, rather than for the survivor's experience of violence and abuse.

CAUTION

These feelings are common, but our biases can lead to community interventions that may even support violence, rather than reduce it.

8.B. GET REAL ABOUT YOUR BIASES: QUESTIONS TO ASK YOURSELF

General Questions

- Do I find one individual more appealing to me as a person?
- Is one person a member of my group of friends, family, neighborhood, group, organization, church, etc. while another person is not?
- Do I relate to one person because of our similarities or something that I admire about one person over the other?
- Do I find that one person has certain qualities that make them less or more sympathetic than the other?
- Do I depend on or get benefits from one person over the other? Does that make me fear that taking action will work against me? Do I fear that I have something to lose?
- Do I have biases, big or small, obvious or subtle, against or for anyone because of any of the following qualities?
    - Gender/sex
    - Race
    - Class or income level
    - Level of education
    - Immigration status
    - Sexual orientation
    - Age
    - Physical or mental ability
    - Physical appearance or attractiveness
    - What country or region they're from
    - Religion
    - Political affiliation
    - Emotional, financial or other dependence on others for survival

Questions Related to the Survivor or Victim

- Is the survivor or victim acting with anger, meekness, manipulation or some other behavior because of repeated exposure to violence in a way that I don't like?
- Have I been hearing biased stories about the survivor or victim (this can be part of the way in which violence was/is being used against them)?
- Do I think that the survivor or victim is so unappealing that I would also want to be violent against them or can understand why someone else would?
- Does the survivor or victim remind me of someone in my past such that I feel that they deserve some sort of violence?

Questions Related to the Person Doing Harm

- Has the person doing harm been able to use some abilities to charm and influence people to excuse or cover up their violence?
- Does the person doing harm have a story of their own victimization that makes them sympathetic (or not)?
- Have I been hearing more or biased stories about the person doing harm such that I feel closer or more sympathetic to the person doing harm?
- Does the person doing harm appear in public more positively or completely differently than the way they are in private?
- Is the person doing harm so appealing to me that I want to dismiss their violence or any other bad behavior?
- Does the person doing harm remind me of someone I like so that I want to believe that they must not have committed the violence or that they had a good reason?
- Do I depend on the person doing harm in some way? Could I be harmed or compromised if I did not "take their side?"

How did it go? What did you learn?

We remind you that violence and the harm caused by it is wrong regardless of who we personally like or do not like. Ending violence even if it means stopping and confronting the person we care about can be the best way to show that we care, and that we are by their side in a meaningful way.

BASIC NINE — We can all take steps to address, end, or prevent interpersonal violence.

Change views – help stop interpersonal violence by:

- Becoming aware of common and damaging reactions to violence
- Identify denial when you notice yourself or others:
- Not noticing that violence is happening right around them
- Blocking out the fact that violence is happening
- Thinking about violence as something other than violence (for example, thinking that domestic violence is just a bad relationship or fighting, thinking that sexual assault is just about someone getting carried away in a moment of passion)
- Not believing or disregarding someone who tells you about violence
- Forgetting that violence is happening

Challenge the tendency to minimize the violence when you notice yourself or others:

- Acting like or thinking that violence is not serious
- Comparing the level of violence to other things that seem more serious, thereby making the violence seem unimportant (for example, thinking that racism is more important than sexism, therefore, violence against women is not an important issue)
- Never doing anything to acknowledge the violence or not doing anything about it
- Acting like or thinking that violence will just go away if left alone
- Thinking that violence is just something we have to accept or is part of our culture

Catch "victim blaming" when you notice yourself or others:

- Thinking that the survivor or victim of violence must have done something to cause it
- Thinking that it is the responsibility of the survivor or victim to stop violence or get out of its way
- Thinking that the survivor or victim needs to take responsibility for asking for help
- Thinking that the survivor or victim of violence does not deserve any help
- Thinking that the survivor or victim of violence contributes just as much to the situation as the person using violence to threaten and control
- Believing stories or gossip that blame the survivor or victim

BASIC TEN

It is important to share information about interpersonal violence. Many people do not know and can benefit from being more aware.

- Give this to other people who need to know – this includes survivors/victims of violence, people doing harm, friends and family, anyone who may get involved in helping to end violence.
- Think of who you might have a special connection to: for example, specific members of your family, friendship or community; organizations you belong to – and introduce them to this information.
- If this is difficult to read, if people speak/read a different language, if they do not read, or if they are too much in emotional crisis to take in this information, then consider reading this to them or finding other creative ways to share this information. Other ways can include translating this into other languages or to more accessible language, video, youtube, drama, story telling, drawing pictures and explaining this information through pictures or other visuals.
- If you create new ways to present this material, please share this with others through the website www.creative-interventions.org or www.stopviolenceeveryday.org or through other public forums.

2.3. VIOLENCE INTERVENTION: SOME IMPORTANT LESSONS

At Creative Interventions, we discovered some important lessons as we supported and witnessed many different interventions to violence. While there are undoubtedly, many more lessons to learn, we wanted to share some basic common lessons.

LESSON ONE

Keep survivors at the center of concern.

Violence interventions can start and move ahead in very different ways. Often a survivor or victim of violence comes forward to begin an intervention. Other times, people will learn about violence and try to start an intervention in order to protect the survivor or victim of violence without necessarily having the survivor or victim actually start or even be involved in the intervention.

We have seen a variety of situations over time. One concern of ours is that as interventions move forward, we can become more involved in dealing with the person who did harm than in the survivor or victim. This can lead to the survivor or victim becoming separated from the process and losing the support and care of people as everyone gets involved in other tasks. We can sometimes make survivors or victims invisible when we attempt to protect them from what is happening. We must guard against increasing survivors' sense and experience of isolation

What can we do about it?

- Understand that the survivor's perspective is unique. They are likely to understand the violence and its dynamics better than everyone else – even if they are in denial and are minimizing violence;
- Keep survivors in the loop of what is happening. Even if the survivor decides to not be actively involved in an intervention or cannot be for whatever reason, figure out ways that feel okay for them to keep informed. This can happen on a regular basis or at key events;
- Make sure that survivors are connected to friends, family or community – and not just to therapists or professionals. While having the help of therapists and professionals can be important and helpful, contact with loved ones is also important and can be healing;
- Do not make survivors always ask for help. Anticipate what they need. In this world of "do-it-yourself," people may blame survivors for not asking for every need. Survivors often already feel burdened by their experience of violence and can feel ashamed to ask for help and be reluctant to burden others. Make it easy for them to ask for what they need. Offer your help and keep it up. Get others involved to share responsibilities.

LESSON TWO **Most of us struggle with accountability. We need to create responses which take this struggle into account.**

- Read Section 4.E. *Supporting Survivors or Victims* for more specific information.

All of us have occasions when we have needed to be accountable. Even if we apologize and are accountable at first, we often want to slip out of full accountability by using a series of tactics:

- Leaving the community, relationship, organization to avoid accountability;
- Hoping people forget;
- Hoping people feel sorry for us so they leave us alone or blame others;
- Making people scared of us or scared of our anger;
- Making people depend on us so they feel too guilty or scared to challenge us;
- Creating delaying tactics;
- Creating distractions;
- Blaming others;
- Blaming our past;
- Blaming the survivor or victim;
- Blaming those who are trying to hold us accountable;
- Making the accountability process be the problem, not our own harmful attitudes, behaviors and frameworks for thinking and acting;
- Wanting our own version of accountability to be the right one – controlling the accountability process.

What can we do about it?

- Create systems flexible enough to allow for the expected process of dodging and delaying accountability and strong enough to withstand and diminish these tactics over time.
- Help to identify appropriate people and processes which can support people doing harm through the process of dodging and delaying while challenging these tactics.
- Read Section 4.F. Taking Accountability for much more information.

LESSON THREE

Most of us are either uncomfortable with conflict or are too comfortable with conflict. We need better tools and opportunities for practice so that we can address conflict in a constructive manner.

We as a society have not learned to deal well with conflict. We do not have good tools for understanding conflict or for resolving it. We frequently resort to our own familiar styles to deal with conflict – and these are often inadequate.

What can we do about it?

- Reflect on your experience dealing with conflict and be honest about your biases – do you enjoy or thrive on conflict? Do you often cause conflict? Do you minimize conflict or pretend it isn't there? Do you run away from conflict?
- Share your conflict style with the group you are working with. Let them know so people can be aware of how to work with you better and you can work with them better.
- Think about how you can change your relationship to conflict if it is unhealthy. Think about how your pattern of dealing with conflict can help situations of violence intervention or make them more or a problem.
- Use the Toolkit to find ways to use your skills in dealing with conflict or avoid your conflict problems by following some of the tools and guidelines provided.
- Be real about your conflict style and your capacity to change. You may need to find roles that take advantage of your way of dealing with conflict and avoid roles in which your conflict style may simply be too difficult.

LESSON FOUR

If we know the people involved in a situation of violence or conflict, we have our own feelings and our own agenda. Knowing the people involved can be helpful. It can also get in the way.

Unlike many other forms of violence, interpersonal violence is often committed by and against people we know. They may even be the people we care about most. They may also be our family members, our close friends, our co-workers, our religious leaders, our community leaders, our colleagues and so on. Even if we are not directly involved in violence, it is confusing to know what to do when we share other relationships with people.

What can we do about it?

- Consider how to use your unique knowledge and care for people involved in violence to take a positive role in ending violence.
- Sometimes it is helpful to take a step back from confusing relationships with people involved in violence – and think about solutions which have the possibility of maintaining relationships while also challenging violence.
- Work together with others in order to see solutions not as an individual burden but rather a shared responsibility and opportunity to create a better, healthier community.

LESSON FIVE

Building teams to work together and coordinating our efforts often requires time shared in person, conversation, and group decision-making.

Our society does not offer us strong values, knowledge and skills about collective action and collective decision-making. Society teaches us that we are on our own and should do it alone, that we are to blame for violence ourselves, or that we should get all of our help from experts or from the criminal justice system.

This Toolkit reminds us that challenging violence within our communities requires that we rebuild common goals and strengthen the ways in which we communicate and cooperate.

What can we do about it?

- Take the time to discuss, share opinions, uncover differences, and discover commonalities with those involved in the intervention.
- Make sure that important items like goals, bottom lines, communication agreements, and safety plans are shared and agreed upon with everyone involved in the intervention.
- See Section 4.G: Working Together and Section 4.H. Keeping on Track for tools to help move forward.

LESSON SIX

Because interpersonal violence is often about power and control, danger can increase when someone is about to seek safety or help.

We may find that the person doing harm (someone who uses abuse or violence) becomes even more violent when they feel like they might lose power and control. This can happen when the survivor or victim begins to seek help, when an intervention is underway, or when a survivor or victim tries to free herself or himself from the violent situation.

People who have only used threats or mild forms of violence in the past can increase their threats and potential for violence throughout various stages of an intervention.

What can we do about it?

- See this as an opportunity for thoughtful and coordinated preparation and action – not as a reason to freeze, minimize the violence or step back from doing anything;
- Seek realistic information from those who know and understand the situation and the person doing harm to imagine different scenarios of what dangers could take place and possible steps to prevent them;
- Plan for extreme, even unimaginable situations while hoping for outcomes which are more positive;
- See Section 4.B: *Staying Safe*

LESSON S[illegible] — Change is difficult. Transformation from violence takes time.

Everybody wants a quick fix, but we have found that change is not speedy. Change often takes time, goes through cycles, moves forward and backward, and can often lead situations to get worse before they get better.

People usually learn their particular patterns of violence over time – sometimes over a lifetime. We may be responding to one violent act, but this is often something that has built up over time or that has been repeated many times.

Change takes time, patience and firmness. We often want to stop trying to make change if we are discouraged in any way. On the other hand, we may want to stop working towards change if one thing seemed to work. Change often happens in those grey areas over the course of time.

What can we do about it?

- Create systems **flexible enough** to allow for the expected process of dodging and delaying accountability and **strong enough** to withstand and diminish these tactics over time;
- Create ways to build in support (people to talk to, time to vent, time to grieve, time to play, to share good food, and so on) for everyone involved in the intervention: the survivor/victim, everyone affected by violence, the person doing harm, and those working to intervene in violence – we call this "creating sustainability";
- Celebrate successes while also taking into account things which went wrong or can be improved;
- It is easy and normal to become frustrated and impatient. Support compassion for everyone.

LESSON EIGHT — Change is difficult. Little steps can be important.

Overall, change takes time, but small actions and responses can make a big difference. Think about a time when someone confronted you with a remark, a gesture, a note or letter, a phone call, or a conversation which made a difference in your life. Sometimes it's an honest confrontation or a helpful insight made by a friend or family member, a kind stranger or even someone we do not like which can get us to think differently about our own attitudes and behavior. It may even get us to change that attitude or behavior in a significant way.

We often fear taking a chance to say something which makes a difference. Saying something that speaks to violence may be scary. We might fear making someone embarrassed or angry. We may fear making things worse. Even saying something kind and heartfelt can be difficult for some of us.

What can we do about it?

We say that "safety can take risk-taking." Simply letting someone know how we honestly feel and what we know can feel like a big risk towards moving to constructive and transformative action. These messages can include some of the following:

- We know what is happening – or we have a sense that something is wrong.
- We care.
- We are concerned.
- We may feel powerless or confused.
- We may have been responsible for creating the situation or for making it worse.
- We know this can be difficult and confusing.
- This person is not alone – we are there to offer our support.
- This person's behavior is not acceptable – we will support them to change.
- We need help.

LESSON NINE **Mental illness and/or substance abuse makes violence intervention difficult but not impossible.**

Mental Illness

Mental illness is common. Many people suffer from mental illness of many different forms and levels of seriousness. It may be obvious to other people or may be more hidden. Some forms can be easily managed with treatment or medication. Others are more difficult to manage.

Mental illness can also be linked to violent behavior

Some forms of mental illness can either seriously increase levels of violence or make it difficult or impossible for people to either receive support or to engage in a process of accountability. This does not mean that community-based interventions to violence are necessarily inappropriate for people with mental illness. It may mean that expectations about reasonable goals or about abilities to be accountable for one's actions may be limited depending upon the form of, phase of and seriousness of mental illness.

People with serious mental illness may have a higher vulnerability to committing violence. Some individuals are more prone to committing violence when in a particular phase of mental illness. For those people who do commit violence, individuals with mental illness may do so during times when they are less in control of their thoughts and behaviors. Of course, there are also many individuals with serious mental illness who are not at all violent. Unfortunately, many programs for violence are separate from those that work with mental illness. It is difficult to find help that understands all of these dimensions.

Another way in which mental illness can make community-based interventions difficult is that it can impair people's ability to be in close relationships with others and, therefore, may make their actions and consequences more difficult to link. Accountability strategies can be challenging.

Mental illness can also be linked to vulnerability to victimization

People with serious mental illness may have a higher vulnerability to victimization by violence. They may be targeted by people who are violent or can be more easily placed in situations of high violence. Depending upon the form of mental illness, they may also find it difficult to ask for support. They may require a higher level of support than people in their community feel like they can provide. They may ask for and reject support in an inconsistent way, depending upon the situation of mental illness. They may feel shame about their mental illness or be in denial, making requests for support more difficult or inconsistent.

Substance Use or Abuse

Substance use and abuse is common. Many people use substances including legal and illegal drugs and alcohol.

Substance use and abuse can also be linked to violent behavior

Creative Interventions does not have a position against drug or alcohol use of any form. However, for some people, the use and abuse of substances including drugs and alcohol can increase levels of violence. It can also make it difficult or impossible for people to either receive support or to engage in a process of accountability. This does not mean that community-based interventions to violence are necessarily inappropriate for people using or abusing substances. It may mean that expectations about reasonable goals or about abilities to be accountable for one's actions may be limited especially during periods of active substance use or abuse. Of course, there are also many individuals who use and abuse substances who are not at all violent.

For those people who do commit violence, individuals who use or abuse substances may do so during times when they are less in control of their thoughts and behaviors. Domestic violence and sexual assault advocates have long said that drugs and alcohol do not lead to violence, believing that people often use drugs and alcohol as an excuse to commit violence or to say that they were not responsible for violence.

These advocates also recognize that people who quit abusive use of drugs and alcohol are often still violent.

While this may be true, there is also some link between drug and alcohol use and violence. Unfortunately, many programs for violence are separate from those that work with substance abuse. It is difficult to find help that understands all of these dimensions.

Another way in which substance use or abuse makes community-based interventions difficult is that it can impair people's ability to be in close relationships with others and, therefore, may make their actions and consequences more difficult to link. Accountability strategies can be challenging.

Mental Illness and Substance Use or Abuse

Mental illness and substance use or abuse can often go together. These connections can be complicated and cannot be generalized. For example, some people with mental illness will use or abuse substances as a form of medication for their mental illness. On the other hand, substances including alcohol can contribute to more serious levels of mental illness. Together, these may contribute to violence and/or victimization in some of the ways already discussed above. These combined issues may also make it more challenging to address violence and accountability.

What can we do about it?

- People who are supporting survivors with mental illness and/or substance abuse issues should receive basic education regarding the particular issues affecting the survivor of violence. It may be particularly useful for a group of people to be well-coordinated, keeping track of what is going on and offering each other support in what can be a particularly stressful situation. You may be able to make use of other resources that help with mental illness and/or substance abuse and may even be open to the values and approach in this Toolkit. In particular, resources with a "harm reduction" philosophy may already practice some of these techniques.
- Likewise, people who are supporting people doing harm with mental illness and/or substance abuse issues should receive basic education regarding the particular issues regarding mental illness and/or substance abuse, violence and people's ability to take responsibility for their actions. Again, resources with a "harm reduction" philosophy may be particularly helpful.
- For people doing harm who also suffer from mental illness and/or substance use or abuse, accountability can involve self-care and support for the person doing harm to get help not only for violence but also for mental illness and/or substance abuse. This approach may lead to better possible results than threats of or actual police

interventions that can aggravate violence. This approach may also be better than interventions that focus on shaming and punishment, which can trigger worsening conditions of mental illness and/or substance abuse, and are generally unhelpful in reaching the desired goals of reduced violence or increased accountability.

LESSON TEN **There is often nothing we can do to "make up" for the original harm. Interventions can bring about positive change but cannot make the original harm disappear.**

We often demand accountability hoping that will make the original harm and the damage caused disappear.

Accountability cannot make the original harm go away. It cannot do the impossible, but achieving accountability can lead to healing, repair and positive change. Think about whether you feel that the only way that accountability can be reached is if the original harm never occurred. If so, no amount of accountability or responsibility will ever feel like enough.

What can we do about it?

Think about how to accept that harm has occurred and to use accountability to acknowledge that harm and to move towards repair and change which makes sure that this harm is not repeated.

A note about forgiveness. Accountability does NOT mean that forgiveness is necessary. Forgiveness is something that is left up to an individual and community to feel in a solid and sincere way. We encourage that people explore what forgiveness means for them and what it might bring as a benefit.

We also encourage people to think about how the pressure to forgive can be another form of power and control. All steps of accountability are possible without forgiveness ever being a goal.

NOTES

3 MODEL OVERVIEW
IS IT RIGHT FOR YOU?

3.1. Reviewing the Community-Based Intervention to Interpersonal Violence

3.2. What This Model Is NOT

3.3. Building a Model on Generations of Wisdom

3.4. Values to Guide Your Intervention

3.5. What Are We Trying to Achieve: 3 Key Intervention Areas

3.6. Interventions Over Time: 4 Phases

3.7. Tools for Interventions: 8 Sets of Tools

3.8. Model at a Glance: Tools Across the 4 Phases

3.9. Tools to Use Before You Get Started

3.10. Next Steps

3.1. REVIEWING THE COMMUNITY-BASED INTERVENTION TO INTERPERSONAL VIOLENCE

THE COMMUNITY-BASED INTERVENTION: REVIEW

In Section 1: Introduction & FAQ and Section 2.1. What is the Community-Based Intervention to Interpersonal Violence, we introduced this intervention approach as one that is:

- **Collective.** The intervention involves the coordinated efforts of a group of people rather than just one individual.
- **Action-Oriented.** A community takes action to address, reduce, end or prevent interpersonal violence.
- **Community-Based.** The intervention is organized and carried out by friends, family, neighbors, co-workers or community members rather than social services, the police, child welfare or governmental institutions.
- **Coordinated.** The intervention links people and actions together to work together in a way that is coordinated towards the same goals – and that makes sure that our individual actions work towards a common purpose. It sees us as a team rather than individual, isolated individuals working as lone heroes or rescuers – or as separated parts, not knowing about or considering what actions others may be taking.
- **Holistic.** The intervention considers the good of everyone involved in the situation of violence – including those harmed (survivors or victims of violence), those who have caused harm, and community members affected by violence. It also builds an approach that can include anyone involved in a situation of violence as a participant in the solution to violence – even the person or people who have caused harm if this is possible.
- **Centers on Those Most Affected by Violence to Create Change.** The intervention centers those most affected by violence. It provides ways for those affected by violence and causing violence to develop new skills, insights and ways to put together a solution to violence – or to form a system that not only addresses violence but reduces the chances that violence will continue.

- **Supports the Sometimes Complex Pathway to Change and Transformation.** Changing violence, repairing from violence, and creating new ways of being free from violence can take time.

  For the survivor/victim, the intervention relies upon consideration of the best ways to support survivors or victims of harm by sharing the responsibility for addressing, reducing, ending, or preventing violence (breaking isolation and taking accountability), without blaming the survivor/victim for their choices (without victim blaming), and by offering support towards what they define as their own needs and wants (supporting self-determination).

  For the person doing harm, the intervention relies upon consideration of the best ways to support people doing harm to recognize, end and be responsible for their violence (what we also call accountability), without giving them excuses (without colluding), and without denying their humanity (without demonizing).

- **Facilitated.** The intervention works well if someone in our communities can act as a facilitator, someone who can act as an anchor for the process of intervention, or someone who can help us to walk through different parts of this Toolkit. Therefore, we call this a facilitated model. The facilitator role can be taken on by more than one person or it can rotate among group members as the process continues. The facilitator does not have to be a professional or someone who is an expert on violence intervention. It simply needs to be someone who can be clear-headed, act within the values and guidelines of the group, and who has some distance from the center of violence to be clear of the chaos and confusion that is often a part of a violent situation. See more about the facilitator role in Section 4.C. Mapping Allies and Barriers. If one cannot find a facilitator, then at the very least, this Toolkit and the many people whose experiences it represents may help to guide us through the process of violence intervention.

THE INTERVENTION AS A PROCESS

The community-based intervention is rarely a one-time event. It is a process, one that can take time – and one that may sometimes seem to move one step forward and two steps back. This Toolkit advises values that include long-term commitment, creativity and flexibility to be able to stay on course for the long-run as the intervention goes through its twists and turns.

An intervention to violence involves engaging people – people who may have their own individual and unique perspective about the situation of violence; people who may have different goals and outcomes; people who may have different ideas about what good process looks like; and some who may be very strongly resistant to change, at least at first – and perhaps for a long time.

An intervention can involve strong emotions. These could include excitement that people are finally going to address violence; fear that the intervention will fall apart; shame that people are getting to know the details of interpersonal violence; fear of retaliation; disappointment or frustration if things move slowly; and relief that people are working together to bring about positive change.

An intervention to violence can be unpredictable. Things change all the time – and these changes can greatly affect an intervention. People (including the survivor or victim, people involved in the intervention as allies, and people who have done harm) may change their mind and suddenly change their attitudes and course of action. New people and new events may enter the picture. Even seemingly insignificant events can completely alter the conditions under which an intervention takes place.

The tools and values in this Toolkit attempt to take these factors into account. It views the intervention as a process. An early consideration of goals helps to set a target as the group moves forward through the twists and turns of an intervention. The tools help to gather and coordinate many different people that may include survivors or victims, community members and the person or people doing harm towards a common set of goals.

MORE ON THE FACILITATED MODEL

This Creative Interventions model is best used as a facilitated model. Through our experiences working with community-based interventions, Creative Interventions developed more ideas about the role of facilitator. This Toolkit contains many of the types of information and tools that we developed through doing this work.

What Is the Role of the Facilitator?

- As we asked these questions, we found ourselves in the role of facilitator. The facilitator acts as:
- An anchor or center-point for people who are involved in what could be confusing, ever-changing and emotionally difficult situations of violence and violence intervention.
- A guide to resources including basic information, stories and tools such as those found in this Toolkit.
- A sounding board – someone who can ask the kind of questions found in Section 4. Tools to Mix and Match – questions that can give people the chance to figure out their own answers and own steps forward.
- A group coordinator – someone who can help a group communicate together, share information, make decisions and move to the next steps.
- A group leader – someone who can help move everyone move forward in the same direction towards a common set of goals.

Who Can Be a Good Facilitator?

We believe that this model works best if someone can play the role of facilitator. The facilitator role can be taken on by more than one person or it can rotate among group members as the process continues. This person does not need to be an expert or professional. A good facilitator can be someone who is:

- Trusted.
- A good communicator.
- Familiar with or connected to the community or people involved in the situation of violence.
- Not too intensely involved in the middle of the situation of violence – has some amount of distance.
- Good at working with groups of people.
- Willing to use this Toolkit and help others become familiar with it.
- Has values that can support a community-based intervention.
- Has enough time and energy to be available for this process.

A HOLISTIC MODEL: WHAT DOES THIS MEAN?

The Creative Interventions model aims to be a holistic model.

Interpersonal violence takes place within families, friendship networks, neighborhoods, organizations, workplaces and communities that are meant to be healthy places for everyone.

Interpersonal violence destroys safety, trust and health. It divides homes, neighborhoods and communities. It builds and feeds upon systems of inequality, abuse and oppression.

This model looks for solutions that do not further break communities (such as arrest, jails and prisons) – it looks for solutions that are holistic, meaning:

- Takes into account the health and well-being of everyone affected by and participating in violence – including the survivor/victim, community members, and person doing harm.
- Tries to build an intervention process that is based upon an outcome that is beneficial to everyone – including the person doing harm.
- Tries to lead change in response to violence through support, compassion and connection.
- Maintains support, respect and connection to the survivor or victim throughout the intervention.
- Even if not able to deal directly with the person doing harm, a holistic process holds a space, even if imaginary, for consideration of the accountability of and positive transformation of people doing harm.
    - For example, even if we do not have any or enough positive contact with the person doing harm, we may think about what we would do if they wanted to come forward, what resources could we offer them if we do not feel that we ourselves can meet together, what do they care about and how might they see things differently. This is useful for envisioning something transformative even if we do not reach this goal.

A HOLISTIC MODEL:

- Some may find it necessary to use a level of pressure, force or negative consequences at the beginning to get a person doing harm, at the very least, to stop their violence (See Section 4.F. Taking Accountability). Steps that may begin as forceful can be viewed as only a first step in a series of steps that can build towards a process more supportive, open and offering connection to the person doing harm – rather than relying upon negative consequences.
- A holistic process may not always be gentle every step of the way, but it holds a large space for compassion and connection.
- In a holistic process, support and accountability connect directly and honestly with people. Although they may sometimes be carried out in part through emails, calls, written letters or meetings – these cannot replace human connection and and communication of honest emotions including love, passion, disappointment, anger, fear and the range of emotions that violence and their interventions raise.

SURVIVOR	PERSON DOING HARM	COMMUNITY ALLY
Center and support survivors: self-determination, safety, healing	Engage and support people who have done harm to take responsibility (take accountability)	Transform communities to address and prevent harm, shift attitudes and support liberation

3.2. WHAT THIS MODEL IS NOT

This model and tools encourage community-based interventions that aim to put the people most affected by violence and our communities to be at the center of positive change. Despite the hopeful vision of this model, it is also important to stress what this model is NOT.

This model is NOT a recipe for violence intervention.

- This approach is not for everyone or for every situation. There are times when there are simply not enough resources to make this approach safe enough or likely enough to turn out a positive outcome. There are times when individuals or groups do not share enough common values to make this the right model.

- This approach gives guidelines based upon the limited experience of Creative Interventions. But we intend that these guidelines be adapted to the facts of the violent situation, the culture of the group or community carrying out the intervention, the unique factors that make up each situation of violence, and the events that may come up during the intervention.

2

This model is NOT a guarantee for a successful violence intervention outcome.

- There is no way to predict a positive outcome – especially for something as complex as violence. Situations change; people change; events are unpredictable. Even groups that work well together and follow this Toolkit and other helpful tools carefully may not get the outcomes they want – especially long-term change.

- This model and Toolkit are based upon the limited experiences of Creative Interventions gathered from a 3-year period. It also relies upon the wisdom and experiences of some of the other organizations named in the Preface and Acknowledgements. Although people have been doing community-based interventions to violence throughout history, it is only very recently that we have begun to actually name these types of interventions, take these interventions seriously, and to develop them into a practical approach. This Toolkit is a beginning document to be helpful towards developing this approach. It does not have all of the answers.

This model is NOT a mediation model.

- Mediation is a process by which two or more people or representatives meet together with a mediator to resolve a conflict. Although one person or party may feel violated by another, there is generally a sense that they have some equal level of power and that a single process of mediation can resolve the conflict.

- Mediation can be part of the overall process of intervention. For example, two allies may have a conflict about some part of the process. They may have relatively equal power. A mediation process might be used to get through this conflict.

- Mediation between the survivor or victim and person doing harm is not recommended. The assumption that there is equal power does not match our assumptions about the types of interpersonal violence that this Toolkit has been created to address – domestic violence and sexual assault generally take place within or create a relationship of unequal power. This model of intervention, not mediation, takes this inequality into account. Mediation has been known to equally fault the survivor or victim and potentially place them in a situation of danger.

While this model allows for the possibility of engagement with the person doing harm, it DOES NOT require that this is part of the intervention. (By engagement, we mean talking with or having some kind of communication with directly regarding the intervention – it may be in person, phone, email, letter, through other people, etc.). Nor does this model imply that NOT engaging the person doing harm affects its value or success.

- You may find that engagement is too risky or dangerous – physically, emotionally, financially, sexually or for whatever reason.
- The person doing harm may be completely unwilling to engage or completely unapproachable.
- The person doing harm may be too dangerous.
- Engaging with the person doing harm may give them information that can make them capable of even more harm.
- You may not have the right person or people to contact and connect with the person doing harm in a way that can bring about positive change.
- You may not know who the person doing harm is or where they are now.

Even if community allies decide to engage the person doing harm, this DOES NOT mean that the survivor or victim needs to have any contact with the person doing harm.

- The survivor or victim should never be pressured to make contact – reasons of guilt, duty, need to forgive, need to show toughness, need to show love and caring, need to be part of a team, etc. are never reasons enough to pressure contact for anyone – it is a choice and one that should be made carefully and with plenty of safeguards before, during and after.
- Contact between survivor and person doing harm may be too risky or dangerous by:
  - Re-exposing the survivor or victim to unnecessary memories of the harm.
  - Re-exposing the survivor or victim to direct emotional, physical, sexual, financial or other forms of harm by the person doing harm (and possibly by others who might blame the survivor or victim or who may want to harm them).
  - Exposing the survivor or victim to retaliation.
  - Exposing the whereabouts of the survivor or victim – if the whereabouts have been or need to be kept confidential or secret.
  - Exposing the survivor or victim to a process where their own truthfulness or integrity could be called into question – if safeguards are not made to ensure that the process is not set up to question or attack the survivor or victim.
- If the survivor or victim decides to have contact with the person doing harm, then the possible risks should be fully taken into account. We suggest that before considering engagement, the survivor and allies weigh risks against benefits, make safety precautions, and consider other parts of this Toolkits and other resources to help with safety concerns (See Section 4.B. Staying Safe).

6 **While this model does encourage and anticipate that the survivor will be involved in the intervention, may be a central participant, and may drive the goals that are adopted by the team, it DOES NOT require this type of survivor or victim participation. In other words, this model is not necessarily survivor/ victim-driven or survivor/victim-centered although it may be.**

- The survivor or victim may be a child – while a child should be supported to talk about their wishes, their fears, their goals – adults may have to take on the responsibility for driving the intervention, deciding the process and determining the goals. Adults are encouraged to take into consideration the perspectives and ongoing needs of the child including those resulting from the complex impact of an intervention as they move forward with the intervention.

- The process and goals may be decided collectively, meaning that the team of allies brought together and any other key people who are affected by the violence may discuss these together, coming up with a collective response. In this situation, the survivor's or victim's wishes may be those that are taken most into consideration. However, there may be room for people to raise their own wishes or concerns or raise more community-wide concerns so that they can all be taken into account when coming up with group process and goals.

- The survivor or victim (or others in the group) may choose goals that are not in line with the values of the model in this Toolkit or of the group. For example, these might include revenge, shaming for the sake of public humiliation, violence – or, on the other hand, they may include doing little or nothing. Discrepancy between survivor or victim approaches and goals and those of allies is a common issue and one that can often be resolved through openness, honesty and thoughtful discussion. See Section 4.D. Goal Setting and Section 4.E. Supporting Survivors for more details regarding differences and resolutions.

3.3. BUILDING A MODEL ON GENERATIONS OF WISDOM

Creative Interventions believes that our communities have given us generations of lessons and examples of community-based interventions to violence. Because we as a society have done little to value and pay attention these lessons, many have been lost.

Creative Interventions and the many others who are creating community-based responses to violence have been building upon a rich history of positive, creative and courageous challenges to violence.

In order to bring these lessons back to our communities and to make them practical and usable knowledge, we have taken what we have learned about community-based responses to violence and broken them down into steps, concepts and tools that we hope are helpful to you. We have listened to and recorded stories from everyday people that can provide examples for how interventions can work. Some of these stories are included in this Toolkit. And others are available through the StoryTelling & Organizing Project on the website www.stopviolenceeveryday.org.

We have also tried to use language that is general – that might fit many different communities even if it does not fit any particular one perfectly.

Although you may not follow all of these steps or you may find your own way to deal with violence as a community, we think that at least some of these may be useful to you. We also hope that you in your community will find creative ways to think about and talk about some of these same concepts as you develop your own response to violence.

3.4. VALUES TO GUIDE YOUR INTERVENTION

Creative Interventions developed this model not only to end violence, but to lead to healthier ways of being in community with each other.

We found it important to create values to guide us in our own work. As we did our work, we returned to these values to see if our day-to-day way of doing things followed these values. We also returned to our values from time to time to see if they really reflected what we believed and to see if we were missing anything that was important to our work. These values underlie our vision and practice and are reflected throughout this Toolkit.

The following is a list of the Creative Interventions values.

CREATIVE INTERVENTIONS VALUES (LONG VERSION):

1. **Creativity.** Solutions to violence can emerge out of a creative process.

2. **Collectivity or Community Responsibility.** We believe that violence is not an individual problem and that solutions also cannot be individual. It takes all of us to end violence. The actions of a group (if done well) can be much wiser, healthier, effective and long-lasting than those carried out by an individual.

3. **Holism.** Solutions to violence can involve consideration for the health and well-being of everyone involved in and affected by violence – this includes the survivors or victims of violence; people doing harm; and friends, family and community.
We also want our solutions to keep communities whole. This does not mean that abusive relationships or families necessarily need to stay together, but this does mean that they may be able co-exist peacefully in the same community or transform to healthier, more cooperative and respectful relationships.

4. **Safety.** We are interested in creating safety in all of its forms (physical, emotional, sexual, economic, spiritual and so on).

5. **Risk-Taking.** While we prioritize safety, we also believe that it sometimes takes risks to create more safety in the long-run. Safety may require action which has the potential to increase short-term risk or danger in order to reach long-term goals.

6. Accountability. All of us have our own role and responsibility to take in ending violence. Community-based solutions to violence require that we all step up and think about the ways we may have contributed to violence, the ways we may need acknowledge and make amends for our contribution to violence, and the ways we can take action to make sure that violence does not continue and that healthy alternatives can take its place.

7. Transformation. We believe that everyone involved in violence can go through positive change. What is needed is a model for taking action which believes that healthy change is possible for all – and can also take realistic and sometimes difficult steps to create an environment in which long-term change can be supported.

8. Flexibility. Situations of violence are often complicated and so are the steps towards long-term change. We try to remain flexible so that we can make changes and create new strategies when needed.

9. Patience. Violence is built over time and so the solution to violence takes time. We ask people to step out of expectations of quick results and take the time to create thoughtful solutions to violence, solutions which will hold in the long run.

10. Building on What We Know (Organic). We believe that we all as individuals, families, friendship networks, communities and cultures have a history of creative and community-based ways to resolve violence. We want to remember, honor and build upon the positive things we have known and done throughout history.

11. Sustainability. We need to support each other to create change in ways that can last over the time it takes to successfully intervene in violence. We encourage that solutions to violence are built to last over the course of the intervention, over our lifetimes, and throughout future generations.

12. Regeneration. We can all contribute to expanding opportunities to challenge violence and contribute to liberation. Although any of us may be thinking of our own unique situation of violence when creating a community-based response to violence, our successes lead to new changes and transformations for everyone involved. And our stories can be passed on to others so they can learn from our experiences. We ask you to consider sharing your intervention stories and lessons learned through the website (www.creative-interventions.org), the StoryTelling & Organizing Project (STOP) (www.stopviolenceeveryday.org) and through other community spaces.

NOTE

A brief version of Creative Intervention values appears inchecklist form later in this section of the Toolkit. You will also find a helpful list of values created by Communities against Rape and Abuse (CARA) in Section 5.4 that may help you think about the values that you want to guide your intervention.

3.5. WHAT ARE WE TRYING TO ACHIEVE? 3 KEY INTERVENTION AREAS

One way Creative Interventions talks about interventions is that it is a way to "address, reduce, end or prevent violence." But how does addressing, reducing, end and preventing happen? What does it look like? What kinds of activities does it involve – and for whom?

In general, we at Creative Interventions have seen interventions break down into 3 core intervention areas:

INTERVENTION AREA #1 SURVIVOR/VICTIM SUPPORT

Survivor or victim support focuses on providing for the emotional and physical health, safety and other needs and wants of someone who has been the survivor or victim of harm.

The needs and wants may extend to their children, family members, pets, and others particularly who rely upon the survivor or victim and whose own health and safety may be affected by the harm directly affecting the survivor/victim. It may also extend to others because if their needs are taken care of, this frees up the survivor or victim to be able to better focus on their own important needs and wants. For example, helping a survivor or victim take care of children, elderly parents, or job responsibilities may be very supportive to a survivor or victim.

Support for the survivor may not result in "healing." Healing is a deeply personal process. Healing may not be a goal or a desire of the survivor or victim, person doing harm or anybody else involved in this intervention process. Or it may be a goal that is unrelated to this intervention – but rather pursued in another way. While healing may result from any aspect of this intervention and may be chosen as a goal, Creative Interventions does not assume that healing is necessarily a result from violence intervention.

In this model, survivor or victim support works best if:

- You provide enough support to allow the survivor or victim to figure out and name what they actually need and want (even if you cannot provide all of it).
- You provide these things without the survivor or victim constantly having to ask for support or remind you for that support.
- You feel care and compassion for them – if you cannot or if something is seriously blocking you, then you can help to figure out who can provide this support, and you can take a different supportive role.
- You have others in the community that can gather together to offer support.
- Make your way through this Toolkit, paying special attention to Section 2. Some Basics Everyone Should Know and Section 4.E. Supporting Survivors or Victims. See also Section 4. Tools to Mix and Match with attention to the Special Considerations for survivors or victims piece that is within each set of tools.

If you are the survivor or victim:

- Take the time to think about your own wants and needs — get support to think these through.
- Take the time to think about your goals and separate out what may be fantasy goals from those that are more achievable (for example, you may have unrealistic but understandable goals that things will get better by themselves, that you want revenge, that you want to get even, that the person doing harm will completely change with little effort). See Section 4. D. Goal Setting for help with goals.
- Offer this Toolkit to your allies if you think it will help them know how to offer support.
- Make your way through this Toolkit, paying special attention to Section 2. Some Basics Everyone Should Know and Section 4.E. Supporting Survivors or Victims. See also Section 4. Tools to Mix and Match with attention to the Special Considerations for survivors or victims piece that is within each set of tools.

See Section 4.E. Supporting Survivors or Victims for more information.

INTERVENTION AREA #2 ACCOUNTABILITY

Accountability of the person doing harm is the act of recognizing, ending and taking responsibility for the violence and the harm one has caused, regardless of whether or that that harm is intended, and changing attitudes and behaviors so that violence will not continue.

In this model, accountability of the person doing harm works best if:

- You balance firmness and consequences with support.
- You condemn attitudes and behavior but do not demonize the person.
- You challenge excuses.
- You hold a position that change is possible at least over the long-term even if you are never able to reach this change.
- You understand that immediate change is rare and early signs of change are often followed by resistance.
- You understand that resistance to change is normal and must be taken into account in a process of accountability.
- The person doing harm has some level of care or respect for the people who are engaging them.
- The person doing harm is able to see that change is beneficial to them – not just because of avoidance of negative consequences but also the availability of positive gain.

If you are the person doing harm,

- Understand that recognizing, ending and taking responsibility for harm is an act of courage – not shame.
- Understand that the process of recognizing, ending and taking responsibility for harm can be painful and difficult – but will ultimately benefit you.
- Think of other people you trust who will challenge you and support your change – and not just make excuses for you.
- Offer this Toolkit to possible allies.
- Make your way through this Toolkit, paying special attention to Section 4.F. Taking Accountability. See also other parts of Section 4. Tools to Mix and Match with attention to the Special Considerations for people doing harm that is within each set of tools.

See Section 4.F. Taking Accountability for more information.

INTERVENTION AREA #3 COMMUNITY ACCOUNTABILITY OR SOCIAL CHANGE

The term community accountability can be thought of as a more specific form of a community-based response or approach to interpersonal violence. The word "community" acknowledges that it is not only individuals but also communities that are affected by violence. Interpersonal violence is not only an individual problem, but a community problem. The word, accountability, points to the idea of responsibility.

The community might be a neighborhood where violence took place; it may be an organization or workplace in which violence against its members occurred; it may be an extended family that allowed violence to go on unchallenged. We usually think of the person doing harm as the one to be accountable for violence. Community accountability also means that communities are accountable for sometimes ignoring, minimizing or even encouraging violence. Communities must also recognize, end and take responsibility for violence – by becoming more knowledgeable, skillful and willing to take action to intervene in violence and to support social norms and conditions that prevent violence from happening in the first place.

In this model, community accountability works best if:

- The community recognizes its own participation in directly contributing to harm or letting harm happen while it also holds the person doing harm responsible.
- The community takes responsibility for the ways that it may have participated in harm. This can be done by:
  - Naming the ways in which it participated in harm.
  - Changing the conditions that led to or allowed the harm to happen.
  - Supporting the survivor or victim.
  - Offering repairs or reparations to the survivor or victim.
  - Supporting the person doing harm through the accountability process.
  - Changing attitudes and behavior and supporting these through policies, new practices, and new skills.
  - Keeping up these changes over the long run.

If you are a member of the community in which harm took place,

- Understand that recognizing, ending and taking responsibility for harm builds community health – it is not an act of shame or blame.
- Understand that the process of recognizing, ending and taking responsibility for harm can be painful and difficult – but will ultimately benefit all members of the community.
- Understand that community accountability supports the accountability process of the person doing harm – it does not take away from it.
- Understand that the public act of a community taking a role of responsibility can also serve as a positive model for individual people doing harm to take responsibility.
- Offer this Toolkit to community members.

See Section 4.F. Taking Accountability for more information.

3.6. INTERVENTIONS OVER TIME: 4 PHASES

At Creative Interventions, we have learned that every intervention to violence is unique. It is impossible to say that for every intervention, one particular step follows after another.

We think of 4 phases of intervention:

1. Getting Started
2. Planning/Preparing
3. Taking Action
4. Following-Up

THE 4 PHASES ON THE GROUND

Interventions are generally processes made up of many steps along the way. These phases can go in mini-cycles all along the course of an intervention, that is, you may get started, plan/prepare, take action and follow up many times as you move along an intervention.

You may also think about this in terms of the overall intervention. Getting started could refer to the initial step of your intervention, and following-up can refer to the steps as the intervention comes to a close.

For some of you, the nature of your intervention will be that it does look more like one very well-defined and short-term process. Your pathway may more clearly look like a single move from getting started to planning/preparing and on to taking action and following up.

For others, things will take a long and complicated course with lots of starts and stops along the way.

Some of you will plan an intervention and never feel prepared to take action.

Others will get partway through an intervention but never feel like you reached your goal. If so, following up may be necessary even if it is only to create some plans for safety or for coming back together if the situation changes in the future.

Regardless, thinking about these phases indicates that getting started can happen many ways; some amount of planning/preparation is a necessary part of a thoughtful and effective intervention; taking action may happen at some point and is an important part of this action-oriented model of intervention (although you may never reach a stage where you feel that there are enough resources, safety protections or willing people to take action); and following up is an often overlooked but very central part of a successful intervention process.

PHASE #1 GETTING STARTED

Getting Started on an intervention can happen any time in the course of a violent situation. Violence, itself, may have been a one-time event or may have been taking place for days, months or years. Violence may have taken place long ago, recently or may be happening right now.

Regardless of these differences, getting started happens as someone begins or at least begins to consider addressing, reducing, ending or prevention violence (violence intervention).

In this model, Getting Started:

- Can be initiated by anyone – the survivor or victim; a friend, family member, neighbor, co-worker or community member (community ally); or the person doing harm.
- Often involves first steps such as naming the violence (See Section 4.A. Getting Clear); mapping possible people and other resources to help (See Section 4.C. Mapping Allies and Barriers); mapping possible barriers to help (See Section 4.C. Mapping Allies and Barriers); and setting initial goals (See Section 4.D. Goal Setting).
- As in all steps, should involve thoughtful consideration of risks and ways to increase safety (See Section 4.B. Staying Safe).

Some examples of Getting Started steps include:

- Looking for help in the internet and finding this Toolkit.
- Talking to a trusted friend about the situation of violence and brainstorming about what can be done.
- Letting a family member know about a situation of violence and asking for their help.
- Thinking about a situation of violence that may have occurred long ago and deciding that something has to be done about it.
- The person doing harm may recognize that they need to seek help to address and stop their harm.

Getting started can happen at any time. A pattern of violence may just be starting to become clear and someone wants to do something about it before it gets worse; a pattern of violence may have reached such a level of danger that someone feels like something must be done; family, friends, neighbors, co-workers or community members may have found out about the violence and want to do something about it; the police or other authority may have been called, setting off a need to take action; someone may finally be out of crisis and able to think more clearly about taking action; someone may have seen this Toolkit and see that they have more support to take positive action; response to the violence may just be happening spontaneously – nobody knows the exact reason but it's starting to move forward.

People using this Toolkit may have tried interventions before – and are now trying to see if using this Toolkit may help with a new stage or type of intervention to violence.

PHASE #2 PLANNING/PREPARATION

Planning/preparation involves further work to plan and prepare the intervention in order to make a more effective response to address, reduce, end or prevent violence.

In this model, Planning/Preparation:

- Can involve bringing more people together to participate in the intervention (See Section 4.C. Mapping Allies and Barriers).
- Can involve creating and agreeing upon intervention goals (See Section 4.D: Goal Setting), creating good roles for everyone helping out (See Section 4.C. Mapping Allies and Barriers and Section 4.G: Working Together), and if accountability is one of the goals, then setting up an accountability plan (See Section 4.F: Taking Accountability).
- As in all steps, should involve thoughtful consideration of risks and ways to increase safety (See Section 4.B. Staying Safe).

Some examples of Planning/Preparation steps include:

- Figuring out who else can help with the intervention.
- Pulling together a meeting of allies who might be able to help.
- Thinking about potential risks and dangers as one takes action steps and figuring out a safety plan.
- Making a schedule of people who can stay with a survivor or victim and that person's children in order to offer support and safety.
- Thinking about who to alert about a situation of domestic violence in order to make sure that children are protected at school, friend's homes or daycare.
- Preparing an accountability plan for the person doing harm including what harms they committed, people who can support change, requests from the survivor or victim and the community, consequences if requests are not met.

PHASE #3 TAKING ACTION

Taking action happens as people make concrete moves to address, reduce, end or prevent violence. It is a central part of this action-oriented approach to violence intervention. It is also possible that you and your group may never reach a point where you have enough resources, safety protections or willing and able people to take action.

Taking action moves from planning or preparing to doing.

In this model, Taking Action:

- Is a more deliberate step or set of steps in violence intervention.
- Can be carried about by anyone – the survivor or victim; a friend, family member, neighbor, co-worker or community member (community ally); or the person doing harm.
- Can involve taking steps to support survivors or victims, to deal with or engage people doing harm, to bring together communities for support, to actively improve the understanding and response of friends, family or community members.
- As in all steps, should involve thoughtful consideration of risks and ways to increase safety (See Section 4.B. Staying Safe).

Some examples of Taking Action steps include:

- Staying with a survivor or victim at her/his/their home to offer support and safety.
- Contacting the person doing harm to request a meeting.
- Holding a meeting or series of meetings with the person doing harm.
- The person doing harm taking action steps to take accountability for the harms they have caused.
- Holding a community meeting about the violence that happened and your group's steps to address that violence.
- Going to a child's school to talk to the principal and others about a situation of domestic violence and requesting steps for the school to provide safety for the child.
- Going to the survivor or victim's mother to talk to her about the dynamics of domestic violence and how she can be a better ally to her child.

PHASE #4 FOLLOWING UP

Following-up happens as action steps have moved forward. It is a more coordinated part of the process with a purpose to make sure actions are following a positive course according to the values and goals of the intervention; tell whether or not adjustments or changes need to be made in order to improve the process; tell whether or not new events or changes have come into the picture; tell how close or far the intervention is to the goal; tell whether or not the intervention is at a stage where it may need to be put on hold, moved faster, shifted to another strategy, stopped altogether or brought to a close.

In this model, Following-Up:

- Is a more deliberate coordinated process following each action step, a particular phase of the intervention, or at the end of an intervention (See Section 4.G. Keeping on Track).
- Can involve everyone involved in the intervention or a smaller group of people.
- Is an important part of making sure that you are keeping on track (See Section 4.H. Keeping on Track).
- Can involve making plans to respond if violence happens again (See Section 4.B. Staying Safe).
- Can involve a process for checking in and seeing how things are going after an intervention comes to a close (See Section 4.E. Working Together and Section 4.H. Keeping on Track).
- Should happen even if action steps are never taken or if things go completely differently than planned.
- As in all steps, should involve thoughtful consideration of risks and ways to increase safety (See Section 4.B. Staying Safe).

Examples of Following-Up steps include:

- Checking in with people who were going to take an action step to see what happened.
- Reviewing the actions and results of a specific action step in order to see if they met the intervention values, goals and safety needs.
- Reviewing the actions and results of an entire intervention process to see if they met the intervention values, goals and safety needs.

3.7. TOOLS FOR INTERVENTIONS: 8 SETS OF TOOLS

Creative Interventions developed its approach to community-based intervention through three years of working with people seeking a different way to address, reduce, end or prevent interpersonal violence (violence intervention). Many of these tools took the form of sets of questions that we would guide people through as the considered and carried out an intervention to violence.

Some of these tools were developed after we completed our three-year project as we thought about what types of tools could have been helpful and we considered what people could look for in a Toolkit even if they did not have an organization like Creative Interventions in their local area.

We call these Tools to Mix and Match because they may all be used at the same time, they may be used repeatedly throughout an intervention and they may be pieced together in different ways as you move towards your intervention process.

The Tools to Mix and Match in Section 4 are divided into the following sets:

4.A. Getting Clear. What Is Going On?

4.B. Staying Safe. How Do We Stay Safe?

4.C. Mapping Allies and Barriers. Who Can Help?

4.D. Setting Goals. What Do We Want?

4.E. Supporting Survivors or Victims. How Can We Help?

4.F. Taking Accountability. How Do We Change Violence?

4.G. Working Together. How Do We Work Together as a Team?

4.H. Keeping on Track. How Do We Move Forward?

TOOLS, DEFINITIONS AND KEY QUESTIONS

The following is an introduction to the Tools in Section 4. Tools to Mix and Match along with brief definitions and key questions.

A. Getting Clear. What Is Going On?
Getting Clear means taking the time to look around, reflect and think about what is happening.

Key Questions are:

- What is going on?
- What kind of harm/violence/abuse is happening?
- Who is getting harmed?
- Who is doing the harming?
- What can be done?

B. Staying Safe. How Do We Stay Safe?
Staying Safe includes concerns, plans and actions all meant to minimize the current, potential and future levels of harm or increase the level of safety. It includes: 1) Risk Assessment to identify the level of danger, potential danger or harm; 2) Safety Planning to plan steps and roles to minimize this danger or harm; and 3) Safety Actions to take steps to minimize this danger or harm.

Key Questions are:

- What are risks and dangers right now?
- Risks to whom?
- What level of risk? None, Low, Medium, High, Emergency?
- What are the risks and dangers if we take no action?
- What are the risks and dangers if we take action?
- Who needs safety and protection?
- What plans can we make to provide safety and protection?
- What are the next steps?

C. Mapping Allies and Barriers. Who Can Help?
Mapping Allies and Barriers involves taking a look at who we have around us as helpers and community resources (allies). It also involves looking at who could get in the way of an intervention (barriers). It may also include looking at "swing" people – people who could be better allies with a little bit of help.

Key Questions are:

- Who can help?
- Who can get in the way?
- Who is in a good position to support the survivor or victim?
- Who is in a good position to offer support to the person or people doing harm?
- Who can become an ally or become a better ally with a little bit of help?
- What kind of help do they need and who can give it?

D. Goal Setting. What Do We Want?
Goal Setting includes the steps the individuals and group take to move towards a single outcome or set of outcomes that could result from their action.

Key Questions are:

- What do you want?
- What do you not want?
- What can you do to move towards these goals?
- Does the group share the same goals?
- What can you as a group do to move towards these goals?
- Are these goals realistic?
- How can you state these goals as concrete steps?

E. Supporting Survivors or Victims. How Can We Help?
Supporting survivors or victims focuses on providing for the health, safety and other needs and wants of someone who has been or is the survivor or victim of harm.

Key Questions are:

- What violence or abuse did the survivor or victim experience?
- What harms have resulted?
- What do they think will be helpful to them?
- Who can best offer this support?
- How are they getting ongoing support?

F. Taking Accountability. How Do We Change Violence?
Taking accountability is a process by which a person or a community comes to "recognize, end and take responsibility" for violence.

Key Questions are:

- What attitudes and behaviors led to the harms?
- Who directly caused these harms?
- Who allowed these harms to happen – even if they did not directly commit these harms?
- Who did they harm?
- What are the results or consequences of these harms – even if unintended?
- What and/or whom does the person doing harm care about?
- What people can influence and support change?
- How can we use care and connection more than negative consequences to promote change?
- What specific changes do we want to see?
- What specific repairs and to whom do we want to see?
- What are some specific ways that we will know that change has happened?
- How can we support long-lasting change?

G. Working Together. How Do We Work Together as a Team?
Working Together involves the ways in which two or more people can work positively and cooperatively towards a common goal. In this Toolkit, the goal is to address, reduce, end or prevent interpersonal violence.

Key Questions are:

- Who can work together?
- Does everyone know and agree with the goals?
- What are their roles?
- How will you communicate and coordinate?
- How will you make decisions?

H. Keeping on Track. How Do We Move Forward?
Keeping on Track includes tools to check in to make sure that the overall intervention is going well, that goals are in place, and that people are moving forward in a good direction. This process also includes tools for individuals to check in and do a self-check – to see if they are doing their best in moving an intervention along in a good way.

Key Questions are:

- Are we ready to take the next step?
- How did it go?
- What did we achieve?
- Did we celebrate our achievements (even the small ones)?
- What needs to change?
- What is the next step?

CI MODEL AT A GLANCE

On the next two pages, you will find a matrix with the CI Tools and Key Questions across the 4 Phases on the next 2 pages.

3.8. CI MODEL AT A GLANCE: TOOLS ACROSS THE 4 PHASES

1: Getting Started	2: Planning and Preparation
a. GETTING CLEAR What is going on? What kind of violence or abuse happened or is happening? Who is getting harmed? Who is doing the harming? What can be done?	**a. GETTING CLEAR** What happened since last time? What changed? What new barriers are there? What new opportunities are there? What do we need to do next?
b. STAYING SAFE/RISK ASSESSMENT What are the risks now? What are the risks if no action? What are the risks if take action? (Physical, Emotional, Sexual, Relationship, Money, Job, Housing, Immigration Status, Children, Custody, Other) None • Low • Medium • High • Emergency	**b. STAYING SAFE/RISK ASSESSMENT** What are risks now? Any new risks? What are risks with next actions? (Physical, Emotional, Sexual, Relationship, Money, Job, Housing, Immigration Status, Children, Custody, Other) None • Low • Medium • High • Emergency
b. STAYING SAFE/SAFETY PLANNING What do people need for safety now? What plans can we make for safety? Who can play what roles? Safety may be for survivor, allies, person doing harm, children, others	**b. STAYING SAFE/SAFETY PLANNING** How is safety plan working? What are new safety needs? Who can play what role? Safety may be for survivor, allies, person doing harm, children, others
c. MAPPING ALLIES AND BARRIERS Who can help? Who can get in the way? Who can support the survivor? Who can support the person doing harm? Who can be an ally or better ally with help? What kind of help and who can give it?	**c. MAPPING ALLIES AND BARRIERS** Who can help? Who will contact allies? Who has agreed? Who is in the way? Who can be an ally or better ally with help? What kind of help and who can give it?
d. GOAL SETTING What do you want? What do you not want? What would you consider a success?	**d. GOAL SETTING** Does everyone know and agree with the goals? Are you able to reach consensus on the goals? How can you state these goals as concrete steps? Are these goals realistic?
e. SUPPORTING SURVIVORS OR VICTIMS What violence or abuse did the survivor or victim experience? What harms have resulted? What do they think will be helpful to them? Who can best offer this support? How are they getting ongoing support?	**e. SUPPORTING SURVIVORS OR VICTIMS** How does the survivor or victim want to be involved in the intervention? What kind of support do they need? Who can best offer this support? How are they getting ongoing support?
e. TAKING ACCOUNTABILITY What could make the violence stop? What could prevent further violence? Who/What does the person doing harm care about?	**e. TAKING ACCOUNTABILITY** What is the goal of engagement? What reparations are requested/offered Who is offering support/connection? Who does what? When? Did you role play possible responses?
e. WORKING TOGETHER Who needs to be here? Who is willing to be here? Who will contact whom? What do they need? Who should not know that you're here?	**f. WORKING TOGETHER** Who can work together? Does everyone know and agree with the goals? What are their roles? How will you communicate and coordinate? How will you make decisions?
g. KEEPING ON TRACK Are we ready to take the next step? How did it go? What did you achieve? Did we celebrate our achievements? What is the next step?	**g. KEEPING ON TRACK** How did the last step(s) go? What did you achieve? Did you celebrate our achievements? What are the next steps? Who will do what? When? How?

3: Taking Action	4: Following Up
a. GETTING CLEAR What happened since last time? What changed? What new barriers are there? What new opportunities are there? What do we need to do next?	**a. GETTING CLEAR** What events have happened since the beginning of the intervention? What changes have resulted? Did we do what we could?
b. STAYING SAFE/RISK ASSESSMENT What are risks now? Any new risks? What are risks with next actions? (Physical, Emotional, Sexual, Relationship, Money, Job, Housing, Immigration Status, Children, Custody, Other) None • Low • Medium • High • Emergency	**b. STAYING SAFE/RISK ASSESSMENT** Is the survivor safe? Do they feel safe? Children? Allies? Person doing harm?
b. STAYING SAFE/SAFETY PLANNING How is safety plan working? What are new safety needs? Who can play what role? Safety may be for survivor, allies, person doing harm, children, others	**b. STAYING SAFE/SAFETY PLANNING** What are long-term safety plans? What other steps can be taken for safety?
c. MAPPING ALLIES AND BARRIERS Who is ready and willing to help? Are there roles to still be filled? Are there allies who can step into those roles? Have any allies become a barrier? Who can be an ally or better ally with help? What kind of help and who can give it?	**c. MAPPING ALLIES AND BARRIERS** Are there new allies for the following-up phase? For ongoing monitoring? For review? Are there barriers to look out for throughout the following-up phase?
d. GOAL SETTING Are the goals still realistic? Does everyone know and agree with the goals? What goals have you reached?	**d. GOAL SETTING** Have goals been met? What has not been met? Why not? Can anything be done to meet these goals? Can you let go of unmet goals?
e. SUPPORTING SURVIVORS OR VICTIMS How is the survivor or victim involved in the intervention? How is the intervention affecting them? What kind of support do they need? Who can best offer this support? How are they getting ongoing support?	**e. SUPPORTING SURVIVORS OR VICTIMS** Was enough support for the survivor or victim provided throughout the intervention? What kind of support was offered? What was most helpful? What kind of support is needed now? How are they getting ongoing support?
e. TAKING ACCOUNTABILITY Is the team supporting a process towards accountability? Are there people connected to the person doing harm? Did the person doing harm stop their violence? Did they acknowledge the violence? Did they acknowledge the harms caused? Are they working towards repairs? Are they shifting attitudes and actions?	**e. TAKING ACCOUNTABILITY** Has the person doing harm stopped violence – reduced it to an acceptable level? Has future violence been prevented? Does the person doing harm show a strong sense of responsibility about violence? Has the person doing harm followed up to repair the harm? Is there long-term support for continued accountability?
F. WORKING TOGETHER Is there a working system of coordination? Is there a working system of communication? Is there a working system of decision-making? Is everybody working towards the same goals? What improvements can be made?	**f. WORKING TOGETHER** Who can work together? Does everyone know and agree with the goals? What are their roles? How will you communicate and coordinate? How will you make decisions?
g. KEEPING ON TRACK How did the last step(s) go? What did you achieve? Did you celebrate your achievements? What are the next steps? Who will do what? When? How?	**g. KEEPING ON TRACK** Is further intervention needed? Can the process close? When will the next review happen? What are the next steps? Did you celebrate your achievements?

3.9. TOOLS TO USE BEFORE YOU GET STARTED

If you are facing a situation of violence (past, present or future) and are considering doing something about it, we ask you to read this Toolkit's Section 1. Introduction & FAQ, Section 2. Some Basics Everyone Should Know, and Section 3. Model Overview: Is It Right for You? After reading these sections, you can use the following tools to see if this model is right for you.

If you have not read Sections 1 and Section 2 but want a very quick guide to see if this model might be a fit for you, you can also use the following tools to see if you want to read further.

Tools in this Section:

Tool 3.1: Is This Model Right For You? Checklist
Tool 3.2: Values to Guide Your Intervention. Creative Interventions Checklist
Tool 3.3: Values to Guide Your Intervention (In Your Own Words). Guiding Questions

☑ TOOL 3.1. IS THIS MODEL RIGHT FOR YOU? CHECKLIST

The following boxes highlight some of the key points of the model in this Toolkit.

Want to address, reduce, end or prevent a situation of violence (violence intervention)

- ☐ Seek solutions within your family, friend network, neighborhood, faith community, workplace or other community group, organization or institution
- ☐ Can think of at least one other person who may be able to work with you to address this situation
- ☐ Want to find a way to support people doing harm to recognize, end and be responsible for their violence (accountability) without giving them excuses (without colluding) and without denying their humanity (without demonizing) – if possible
- ☐ Are willing to work together with others in your community
- ☐ Are willing to work over a period of time to make sure that solutions stick (last a long time)

If you checked all of the boxes, you may be ready to continue with this Toolkit. If you have hesitations or questions about any of these, we encourage you to read through related parts of this Toolkit or talk with other people to see if this approach fits your beliefs, your needs or the resources you have available

You may follow by going through the Values Checklist to see if your values are also in line with this Toolkit.

☑ TOOL 3.2. VALUES TO GUIDE YOUR INTERVENTION CHECKLIST

Creative Interventions developed this model not only to end violence, but to lead to healthier ways of being in community with each other. You can read the long version of the Creative Interventions Values in Section 3.3. Values to Guide Your Intervention. The short version is in the Checklist below.

Please see if these work for your group. You can also create your own Values guide using Tool 3.3. Values to Guide Your Intervention (In Your Own Words). Guiding Questions and Checklist if you think another set of values fits your own group better.

OUR VALUES

We ______________________________ have created the following values to guide us in our work together to address, reduce, end or prevent violence (violence intervention). We ask everyone involved to read through this list (or have someone read it to you) and think about what these values mean to you. We hope that you will agree to these values and let them guide your involvement in this intervention.

If you do not agree, consider what changes you would want and those you would find absolutely necessary. Others may want to consider whether to include these changes. Or these changes may mean a more serious disagreement which requires more discussion. Please be clear about changes you would seek and what this means in terms of your involvement.

Note: You can also see the principles of Communities against Rape and Abuse (CARA) that are found in Section 5. Other Resources for another similar approach. Either set of values works well with the model and tools found in this Toolkit.

I understand and can agree to the following values:

- ☐ Collectivity or Community Responsibility (Working together as a group)
- ☐ Holism (Taking into account potential wellbeing of all people involved)
- ☐ Safety and Risk-Taking (Recognizing that safety sometimes requires risk-taking)
- ☐ Accountability (Taking appropriate levels of responsibility for ending violence)
- ☐ Transformation (Working towards positive change for all)
- ☐ Flexibility and Creativity (Be ready and able to adjust to new challenges and new opportunities)
- ☐ Patience (Know that making change can take time and patience)
- ☐ Building on What We Know (Build on people's values, experience and strengths)
- ☐ Sustainability (Create ways to make changes that can last a long time)
- ☐ Expanding Our Work (Make changes and create lessons that can help others)
- ☐ Others: ____

TOOL 3.3. VALUES TO GUIDE YOUR INTERVENTION (IN YOUR OWN WORDS) GUIDING QUESTIONS

We at Creative Interventions do not expect that your values and our values will be a complete match. We were often thinking about ourselves as a group dealing with lots of interventions to violence. You may think of yourself as just dealing with one – and that can be plenty. You may also find different words or language that makes more sense to you and your group.

Use this space to reflect on your own values (individual and/or group) that might help guide your future planning, preparation and actions to deal with violence. Some guiding questions:

1. What is important to you?

2. At times that you have tried to change your own behavior, what has been helpful? What has made it hard?

3. What are some guiding principles that have helped you in your own life?

4. What are some values that you would like to hold even if they have been difficult or challenging to keep up?

5. What values do you think will lead to lasting positive change?

You can write a set of values using Tool 3.4. Values to Guide Your Intervention (In Your Own Words). Checklist. If helpful, compare them to the Creative Interventions list or the CARA list Section 5. Other Resources. See which ones you would like to keep.

TOOL 3.4. VALUES TO GUIDE YOUR INTERVENTION (IN YOUR OWN WORDS) GUIDING QUESTIONS

OUR VALUES

We ______________________________ have created the following values to guide us in our work together to address, reduce, end or prevent violence (violence intervention). We ask everyone involved to read through this list (or have someone read it to you) and think about what these values mean to you. We hope that you will agree to these values and let them guide your involvement in this intervention.

If you do not agree, consider what changes you would want and those you would find absolutely necessary. Others may want to consider whether to include these changes. Or these changes may mean a more serious disagreement which requires more discussion. Please be clear about changes you would seek and what this means in terms of your involvement.

OUR VALUES

_______________: ____

(Description)

_______________: ____

(Description)

_______________: ____

(Description)

_______________: ____

(Description)

_______________: ____

(Description)

3.10. NEXT STEPS

If you took time to fill out Tool 3.1. Is This Model Right for You? Checklist and either Tool 3.2: Values to Guide Your Intervention. Creative Interventions Checklist or Tool 3.3: Values to Guide Your Intervention (In Your Own Words). Guiding Questions and Tool 3.4. Values to Guide Your Intervention (In Your Own Words). Checklist, then you may want to go back and read the previous sections including:

Section 1. Introduction & FAQ

Section 2. Some Basics Everyone Should Know

You might also be ready to turn to the tools in Section 4. Tools to Mix and Match. A good place to start is Section 4. Introduction where you will get an overview of the tools and follow with the first set of tools, Section 4.A. Getting Clear, which can help you get clear about what your situation of violence or harm is and how to move forward from there.

The complete set of tools among those to Mix and Match include:

A. Getting Clear

B. Staying Safe

C. Mapping Allies and Barriers

D. Setting Goals

E. Supporting Survivors or Victims

F. Taking Accountability

G. Working Together

H. Keeping on Track

4 TOOLS TO MIX AND MATCH

4.A. Getting Clear. What Is Going On?

4.B. Staying Safe. How Do We Stay Safe?

4.C. Mapping Allies and Barriers. Who Can Help?

4.D. Setting Goals. What Do We Want?

4.E. Supporting Survivors or Victims. How Can We Help?

4.F. Taking Accountability. How Do We Change Violence?

4.G. Working Together. How Do We Work Together as a Team?

4.H. Keeping on Track. How Do We Move Forward?

HOW EACH SET IS ORGANIZED

Each set of tools also has the following information:

1. What Is It?
- Definitions
- Why it is important
- Using the tools in this section
- Further key questions

2. Tool Across the 4 Phases
- Describes some questions or concerns likely to come up when using this set of tools depending on whether one is at the phase of 1) Getting Started, 2) Planning/ Preparing, 3) Taking Action, or 4) Following Up (See Section 3.6. Interventions over Time: 4 Phases for more about the 4 phases)
- Relates this category with other categories with which it might connect

3. Tips
- Special things to watch out for or to be aware of

4. Special Considerations
- Things that might be particularly important to think about from the perspective of:
    - Survivor or victim of violence;
    - Community allies or people intervening in violence; and
    - Person doing harm

5. Facilitator Notes
- Tips and suggestions for the facilitator

6. Real Life Stories and Examples
- Brief real-life stories that illustrate situations where these tools might be useful

7. Tools
- Snapshots or short question guides to begin the process
- Worksheets or longer question guides meant for more thoughtful and thorough reflection and exploration
- Charts used to organize what can become complicated information
- Checklists that can more rapidly move individuals or groups through a process for thinking about next steps

MIXING AND MATCHING THE TOOLS

Flexibility in Stage of Intervention

Interventions often do not take a straight course from beginning to end. They may involve many people with different interests and agendas. They need to be flexible to accommodate people's changing schedules and varying availability. They must deal with human changes in mood, in willingness to go along with a plan, and with what can be very unexpected and surprising changes as people react emotionally to violence and to challenges to violence.

Most of what you may think of as these categories returned to again and again as groups make their way through interventions to violence. These eight categories are reminders of things that your group should consider and reconsider as you move through an intervention. They also contain tools that groups might find helpful to coordinate and make sense of what can be confusing and emotional situations of violence and intervention.

Individual versus Group Use of Tools

Some of these tools can be used for individuals to think through steps along the way. Some of them are more effectively used for groups. At times, individuals can think about these questions for themselves, and then bring them to compare with others in the group. In that way, they can be useful guides for group discussions and agreements that might involve compromise. They may also lead times where groups may recognize disagreement, even to a point that compromise is not possible.

Tools Take Different Amounts of Time

Snapshots or checklists typically take the shortest amount of time. Worksheets and charts take more time. However, it is difficult to predict how long each step of the process will take, depending upon the situation, the complexity and the level of emotion involved, and the number of people.

NOTES

4A GETTING CLEAR
WHAT IS GOING ON?

A.1. What Is Getting Clear?

A.2. Getting Clear Across the 4 Phases

A.3. Getting Clear Tips

A.4. Special Considerations

A.5. Facilitator Notes

A.6. Real Life Stories and Examples

A.7. Getting Clear Tools

A.1. WHAT IS *GETTING CLEAR?*

Getting Clear: Key Questions

- What is going on?
- What kind of violence or abuse has happened or is happening?
- Who is getting harmed?
- Who is doing the harming?
- What can be done?

What Is It?

Getting Clear means taking the time to look around, reflect and think about what is happening. It can be a quick snapshot taken at a single moment. What is going on – right now? Or it can be a more thoughtful, broad view of the big picture. What is going on – looking from many angles? How did we get there? Where are we going?

Why Is It Important?

Getting clear is especially important when you are in crisis and are confused. Having a clear understanding of the situation is helpful when you are first starting an intervention and a clear starting point from which to take action is needed. As things change, it may be necessary to continue to reassess the situation, taking snapshots along the way and noting changes as they unfold.

Piecing Together the Big Picture

Getting Clear often involves thinking about what you already know about the situation and learning from what others have seen or experienced in the situation.

Sharing information can create a fuller picture of what is going on. It is like the story of a group of people, each looking at an elephant from only one angle. One person only sees the trunk, someone else the tail, someone else the rough hide of the elephant. However, only together can the group have a more accurate picture of the elephant. In the same way each of you may describe and understand the situation in an entirely different way. Only with each other can you put the pieces together and understand that you are seeing different angles of one larger reality.

Highlighting the Important Points

Interpersonal violence can be especially confusing. These stories can be complicated because they involve close and sometimes long-term relationships, mixed emotions, the involvement of many people and dynamics of violence that unfold in multiple ways. Figuring out what is going on can thus be very difficult. Sometimes the process of Getting Clear requires us to sort through a whole set of details. It may be important to lay out all of the pieces first before figuring out what are the most critical points, and the patterns that are the most important to try to change.

Sharing Information without Constant Repetition or Rehashing

Getting Clear is helpful because it allows others to help. Taking collective action towards change often involves having other people's input on the process of Getting Clear. It may also involve sharing some details about the violent situation with the people you are asking for help. While not everyone needs to know every detail of the situation, out of concern for privacy, confidentiality or safety issues, many will want some basic information in order to decide if and how they want to get involved. Good information will also help everyone to make better decisions about what actions to take.

Finding a good way to write down, record or otherwise remember these details without making someone repeat the story over and over again is useful. It prevents those telling the story, especially the survivor or victim, from having to repeat and re-live the situation. It also keeps track of important details that can be lost as people get tired repeating the story or assume that everyone already knows the details.

USING THE TOOLS IN THIS SECTION

The Getting Clear section offers basic information and tools to help you get clear and figure out what is happening at any given moment. If you need simpler, shorter tools to help when you are in immediate crisis or have less time, refer to Tool A1. Getting Clear Snapshot/Quick Question Guide. If you need to do a full assessment at the beginning of an intervention, or when you have more time or more people involved, refer to Tool A2. Getting Clear Worksheet. You can also use these tools as you move across through different stages of what might be a long process.

Tool A3. Naming the Harms Chart and Tool A.4. Harms Statement Worksheet can help you get specific about what harms happened or what is happening and figure out how specific and what details are important for what purpose.

Tool A.5. Getting Clear Intervention Factors-at-a-Glance gives you more in-depth information about what type of violence situation you are dealing with, thoughts on communicating about the situation with others who may get involved, figuring out what strengths and weaknesses you have in terms of moving towards a successful intervention, and other factors that might be important as you move forward.

A.2. *GETTING CLEAR* ACROSS THE 4 PHASES

In Section 3.6. Interventions Over Time: 4 Phases, the Toolkit introduced the idea of 4 possible phases of interventions: 1) Getting Started, 2) Planning/Preparation, 3) Taking Action, and 4) Following Up.

Figuring out what is going on or Getting Clear may look different at different phases of an intervention process.

PHASE 1: GETTING STARTED

In this Toolkit, the beginning actions to Getting Clear, may be particularly important. It may be a key opportunity to really think about what is happening and what needs to be done. Getting clear on the details – by answering the questions in Snapshot/ Quick Question Guide or Worksheets – can lead to actions that can really address the problem. Writing these details down or recording them in some way can help others understand all of the important points of the situation without having to tire everyone out by repeating the story.

PHASE 2: PLANNING/PREPARATION

Intervention rarely ends with one action. It is helpful to keep assessing or Getting Clear of the situation as it changes over time. Things might look different as small actions or reactions take place, different events or factors enter the picture, or new people get involved. You may need to do quick snapshots of the situation at various times.

PHASE 3: TAKING ACTION

As you get ready to take action, big actions or small, you may need to continue taking snapshots and Get Clear on the situation as things continue to change or you find out new information.

PHASE 4: FOLLOWING-UP

As you move through the planning and action steps of intervention or perhaps as you reach its conclusion, you can continue to do quick snapshots of Getting Clear on the situation to figure out where things are at or what may have changed in the situation of violence.

RELATED TOOLS

Tools to identify people who can help out or are connected to the situation are in Section 4.C. Mapping Allies and Barriers and Section 4.G. Working Together.

Tools to help you look at your goals or what you want to achieve are in Section 4.D. Goal Setting.

Tools to look at how ready you are for taking action including what you need to be ready are in Section 4.H. Keeping on Track.

A.3. *GETTING CLEAR* TIPS

#1 READ SOME BASICS EVERYONE SHOULD KNOW

Interpersonal violence is complicated. Although we may hear more about domestic violence or sexual assault these days, many misunderstandings still exist and many misconceptions about what it is and how to approach it. Read Section 2. Some Basics Everyone Should Know. Pay special attention to Section 2.2. Interpersonal Violence: Some Basics Everyone Should Know in order to have a clearer picture of what is going on. The Section 2.3. Violence Intervention: Some Important Lessons also shares important basics about interventions based upon the experiences of Creative Interventions.

Share this information with others who may be involved in a situation of violence and may need some resources to help them know what to do. .

#2 FOCUS ON WHAT AND HOW. BEWARE OF WHY'S

It is normal to wonder "why" something is happening. Why is the person doing harm doing what he/she is doing? Why me – why am I the victim of violence? And so on. These "why" questions are often impossible to answer. They can keep us stuck in not-knowing and not-doing. Step away from "why" questions and move more towards "what" is happening and "how" do we change the situation.

#3 LEARN FROM THE PERSPECTIVES OF OTHERS

Do your assessment with other trusted people. You may learn that you only have part of the picture. You may be able to fill others in with important information. You may be able to step away from emotions that can be confusing. You may understand how you can work better together. Or you may find out that your differences are so serious and unchanging that you cannot work with each other.

#4 LOOK OUT FOR THE DANGER SIGNS

Although all forms of violence can be dangerous, including verbal abuse and other non-physical forms of violence, there are some signs that are particularly important. These are some signs linked to higher degrees of danger:

- Availability of guns or other weapons
- Previous use or history of violence

- Threats to kill self and/or others
- Choking
- Use of alcohol and/or drugs that contribute to violence
- Person doing harm senses a loss of power and/or control (Examples: survivor/victim is about to leave or has left an abusive relationship; person doing harm senses that other people are finding out about the situation and may take action)

#5 UNDERSTAND THE UNIQUENESS OF THE SURVIVOR'S OR VICTIM'S SIDE OF VIOLENCE

It may be particularly important to ask the survivor or victim of violence to name the violence if that person is not you. Why? First, they may be the only people who actually know the extent to which violence has taken place. Much of the violence may have been committed away from other people – or may take place in very subtle forms that others do not even notice.

Someone may have been violent once, but used that violence to show what could happen in the future. This threat may still be operating even if it is a one-time action. It can be hard for others to understand how something from the past can still have the power to cause fear for a long time afterwards.

Also, the survivor or victim may have been living with violence in isolation. Or others may have not believed that violence was taking place. Denial, minimizing the violence, and blaming the victim are very common when we look at interpersonal violence.

Having the survivor or victim name the violence and having others also listen, understand and validate this naming can be an important first step in taking action to repair the harm and stop future violence from happening. This may be an important step in an intervention in and of itself.

#6 STAY FOCUSED ON THE PATTERNS OF ABUSE OR VIOLENCE

Once you begin to name the harm, it is common to begin to closely analyze everyone's behavior. This is especially common when the survivor or victim and person doing harm have been involved in a relationship (intimate, family or other) that has gone on for a long time. If you know them well, you may be able to come up with a long list of grievances under the name of each person. While people may need to brainstorm or get these thoughts and feelings out in order to clear the air, come back to the main issue which is addressing and ending violence.

This Toolkit is not meant to create perfect relationships. It is meant to address and change fundamentally unhealthy, mostly one-sided patterns of behavior that cause significant and/or repeated harm to one person, a group of people or a series of people in situations where one person after another is being harmed.

#7 AIM FOR COMMON UNDERSTANDINGS ESPECIALLY WHEN IT IS UNCLEAR WHO IS RESPONSIBLE FOR VIOLENCE AND WHAT ARE THOSE HARMS

We often find big differences in what people think about the situation of violence including who is more responsible for the harm, who did what, and who is the most harmed. In other words, the process of getting clear/assessment can reveal completely different perspectives that do not come together to form a whole. It is important to go back to Section 2.2. Interpersonal Violence: Some Basics Everyone Should Know to develop a common understanding about violence and interventions. This may help to bring these perspectives together.

One common situation is when the survivor or victim has also taken on attitudes or actions that are unhealthy or even abusive. This can cause you to look for ways in which a survivor or victim "asked for it" or contributed to the dynamics of abuse. You may want to protect the primary person doing harm by balancing the list with everything the other person did that was unhealthy. This can cause people to question who is really the survivor or victim in the situation causing divided opinions or questions about whether this is simply a bad and unhealthy relationship with equal blame on both sides. If this is the case, some questions to ask are:

- Who is more afraid?
- Who starts the violence?
- Who ends up getting harmed?
- Who is usually changing and adapting to meet another's needs or moods? (Some say: Who sets the weather in this relationship?)
- Who is more vulnerable?
- Who is using violence for power and control (abusive violence)? Who is using violence to try to maintain safety or integrity in an already violent situation (self defense)?
- Who has to win?

Also see Section 5.6. Distinguishing between Violence and Abuse, by Northwest Network of Bisexual, Trans, Lesbian and Gay Survivors of Abuse for more information.

#8 FIGURE OUT WHO NEEDS TO GET WHAT INFORMATION AND FOR WHAT PURPOSE

The process of Getting Clear is also one about gathering and recording information. It can serve different purposes for different people. As you record and share this information, you might want to think about different versions depending upon the purpose. Below is a list of possible reasons for and results from Getting Clear.

- Getting clear on the situation of violence
- Remembering details and sorting out for important information
- Getting clear on what you want to address and change
- Sharing information with those you want to help support you in an intervention
- Avoiding the tendency to deny and minimize violence
- Naming the harms as preparation for facing the person or people responsible for the harm
- Naming the harms as a way for someone doing the harm to start to take accountability

A.4. *GETTING CLEAR* SPECIAL CONSIDERATIONS

The process of Getting Clear may be different depending upon your relationship to violence and to the people most closely involved in violence. This Toolkit promotes a process that brings together different viewpoints to create a better picture of what is really going on. This can and should happen regularly throughout the intervention. It is also important to think about some special considerations depending upon the person's relationship to violence.

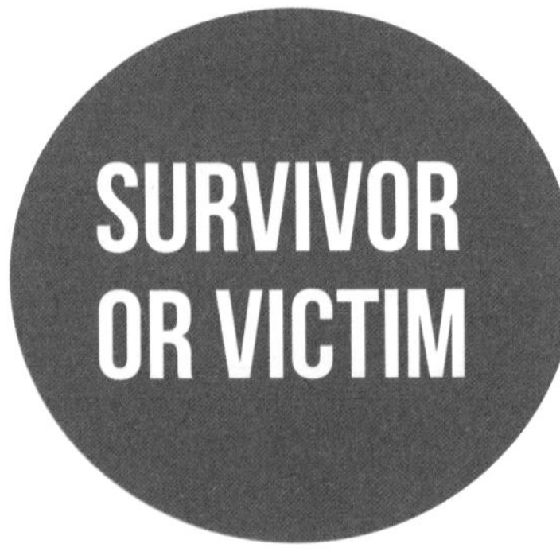

The survivor or victim is often the person who best understands the dynamics and impact of violence. She/he/they are also likely to be the person most affected by violence.Especially when we are thinking about interpersonal violence, the nature of harm can be subtle or hidden. It may have developed over a period of time, beginning with small abuses that end up becoming a pattern of abuse. It may have been one particularly violent incident that gives the message that this can always happen again.

People on the outside may not see or understand these dynamics. For example, those in domestic violence relationships can come to understand that a certain look or glance can mean that a beating could follow. To others, they might not notice that look or may dismiss it as not very harmful. They may even accuse the survivor or victim of being too sensitive or exaggerating without realizing that the survivor or victim may know very well what such looks or glances mean.

At the same time, survivors or victims can minimize or deny violence in order to protect their relationship or to fend off feelings of shame or vulnerability. Their understanding of the dynamics may change as they begin to talk about the abuse and feel some safety as they are being believed and protected by others.

The survivor or victim may also be placed in the position of having to repeat what happened to them over and over again. This can put a huge strain on this person as they remember traumatic events and as they respond to people's questions about what happened, where and why. Many times they are asked questions that can sound victim-blaming. They can get tired and give shorter and less descriptive stories, sometimes giving people incomplete information that can make the intervention harder to carry out.

The process of Getting Clear, especially at the beginning, is important. It can be an opportunity to write things down or have them recorded so that these things do not need to be repeated over and over again. The Tools in this section can help to go through this process in order to be thorough and to prevent people from having to repeat things again and again.

In this Toolkit, we do not say that the survivor's perspective is the only or always the most important perspective, although it can be. Some anti-violence and feminist organizations do say this as a part of their "survivor-centered" philosophy. We do, however, believe that the perspective of the survivor is unique and must be considered in a very serious way. In some cases, you may decide that this is the central perspective or the only one that counts. For more on "survivor-centered" decision-making, see Section 4.G. Working Together.

If you are the survivor or victim, the process of getting clear can be a difficult one. If you can, begin your part of Getting Clear by sitting down alone in a comfortable and safe place or with a trusted friend, family member, community member, counselor or advocate to get clear on the situation of violence. You can use the Tools in this section to help you make your way through the details – writing them on paper, saying them to someone else who may write them down or record your words.

Recalling details of violence and harm can take a long time and bring up memories, flashbacks, sleepless nights or nightmares. You may go back and forth about what really happened. You may feel regret and shame as you reveal the details, even to yourself. Be prepared for strong and perhaps confusing feelings. Know that this is normal.

Because this Toolkit is geared towards an intervention, this information is also meant to aid people in taking the right action at the right time. This allows for you to possibly share intimate details with people closest to you. You can then get support to figure out what other details need to be shared with other people depending on what you want to accomplish, who needs to know, and why. Possible audiences include loved ones, others affected by violence, those involved in the intervention, the person or people doing harm, and possibly a larger public audience.

The process for remembering details may be different than the process for figuring out what is most important to share and how. Questions to ask may be: What is important for right now? Who needs to know and why?

Find a way to get ongoing support during this process from people who you trust. Show them this Toolkit and other resources so that they can better offer support.

Take a breath, make your way through these Tools and find support.

The community ally (family, friend, neighbor, co-worker, community member) may also be in a position to see other important things that are going on. It may also be important for your ally to get information gathered from the process of Getting Clear to help them play a positive role in the intervention.

If you are a community ally, you may see ways in which the survivor or victim has been harmed or is endangered that may not be noticed by the person being harmed. You may notice other aspects of the situation that are important to understand what is going on or what can be done. You may also learn important things from the survivor or victim or others involved in the violence. We urge you to learn about the dynamics of violence by reading Section 2. The Basics and by looking closely at the Tips in this section which offer some lessons from others who have been involved in interventions to violence.

Take a breath, make your way through these Tools and find support.

In this Toolkit, we allow for the perspective of the person doing harm to enter the situation. This is different from many anti-violence organizations that often automatically dismiss this perspective as an attempt to manipulate the situation or blame the victim. Experience shows that people doing harm often hold a perspective that attempts to dismiss the violence through denial, minimization or victim blaming.

People doing harm have often continued and justified harm through a perspective that minimizes their role in violence, blames the victim and tries to convince others either to ignore the violence or justify it. This is especially true if the person doing harm is in a position of power in relation to the person being harmed or accused of being harmed.

While this is not necessarily the case, and the point of interventions is to try to change these tendencies over time, it may be important to keep this possibility in mind. The person doing harm may have a very different story to tell than the survivor of violence. Challenging unequal power and ending violence often prioritizes the voice of the person who has been harmed.

If you are the person doing harm or are the person accused of doing harm, we urge you to be open to the perspective of the survivor or victim of harm and to those carrying out this intervention. This openness may feel threatening at times, but a shift in your view of this situation and an understanding of the harm you may have caused can lead to positive change for you and others.

Take a breath, make your way through these Tools and find support.

FACILITATOR

This Toolkit works best with someone acting as a facilitator. This may be a friend, family member or community member. It may also be a helpful professional or someone working in an organization who is willing to work with the values and approach behind this model.

Please note again that this Toolkit contains a unique approach to dealing with violence and may be very unfamiliar to people used to working with violence. It may even be against their policies. You can share this Toolkit with people you might want to act as a facilitator and see if they are comfortable with this perspective and model.

If you are a facilitator or are willing to help out by providing a role in helping another person or a group to work through this Toolkit, then these notes are to help you.

#1 ENCOURAGE AND SUPPORT PEOPLE TO LEARN FUNDAMENTAL INFORMATION FIRST IF THEY HAVE NOT ALREADY.

This Toolkit is long and can be overwhelming. Some important parts of this Toolkit are Section 2. Some Basics Everyone Should Know. An especially important section can be Section 2.2. Interpersonal Violence: Some Basics Everyone Should Know that discusses much more about the dynamics of violence and common misunderstandings that people have.

It can be useful for you to be familiar with the different sections of this Toolkit and to read more carefully through these sections. Also encourage people to read these sections. If reading is not the best option or they cannot read English or the language that this Toolkit is in, you can help by reading this and other sections to them in a language they understand or use other formats to pass on this information.

#2 SUPPORT PEOPLE BY GOING THROUGH THESE GETTING CLEAR INFORMATION AND TOOLS THAT SEEM USEFUL.

When people are in crisis, it can especially be helpful to break down this section into manageable parts. People may be able to glance through the whole section but then begin by working through the What Is Going On? Snapshot: Quick Question Guide or What Is Going On: Worksheet. You may be able to help by knowing what is available in this section and in the overall Toolkit but help guide people to bite-size next steps.

#3 SUPPORT A COLLECTIVE OR GROUP PROCESS.

We encourage people to join together with other trusted people to carry out an intervention together. You may be collecting the information for Getting Clear by carrying out this process with a couple of people or even a small group. This may be done all together if this makes sense or by going to different people and gathering this information individually.

Be aware that any process that starts bringing together different people may also pose new risks or dangers. A group may already have formed or be an obvious group to work with. Or, you may want to read the sections on Section 4.B. Staying Safe and Section 4.C. Mapping Allies and Barriers first before expanding this group.

If you do this in a group, it can be helpful to organize this information visually on something everybody can look at. Some ways could include:

- Whiteboard or chalkboard
- Easel paper
- Post-its or cut-outs you can put on the wall
- Objects you can move on a table or on the floor

#4 FIND USEFUL AND SAFE WAYS TO DOCUMENT THIS INFORMATION SO THAT IT DOESN'T GET LOST.

It is also helpful to document/or keep in some permanent way this information so you can refer to it later, compare it with changes that occur over time, and share it with people who were not at this meeting.

Ways to document include:

- Write notes
- Draw picture
- Take pictures of notes, post-its, objects
- Roll-up and re-use easel paper notes

Again, make sure that these documents are kept in a safe way. And make sure the people most affected by violence or involved in this intervention are part of deciding who and how this happens. This may mean that even if you usually share everything that happens with your partner, your close friend, your mother, and so on, you cannot do it in this case.

Remember that emails can easily be forwarded. Written notes can be found and read by other people who may endanger the people involved, even if they don't mean to. Think about how gossip could harm a situation and try to make judgments about who is safe to share information with and how to make stronger agreements to keep information safe. On the other hand, shared information can also be part of your plan to bring more people together.

A.6. REAL LIFE STORIES AND EXAMPLES

Story A: I hear yelling in my apartment building. What is going on?

I live in a small apartment building in a city in the South near the border with Mexico. We have several immigrants from different countries living in the building. Some of us keep to ourselves and some have made friendships with the other residents. There is not a lot of fighting and violence here. But if there is, at least someone will hear – the next door neighbor or the people directly upstairs or downstairs.

I was hanging out with some of my neighbors. We don't know each other too well but we like to get together once in awhile. Sometimes our conversations turn to gossip about other people in the building. One time, one of them talked about the neighbors who live right next door to them, a couple that has been fighting. The couple has a 5-year old daughter. The husband has lived in the building for a few years – a seemingly nice guy who tends to keep to himself. He married a woman who moved in about 6 years ago. His wife mostly speaks Spanish. She's friendly but communication is usually pretty limited if you don't speak Spanish which most of us don't. I'll call them "Marcos" and "Maria" although those are not their real names. My neighbor continued with the story saying that he has heard them fighting and that the husband was yelling at his wife, Maria, "Go ahead and call the police. You don't even speak f**ing English."

I had never heard any yelling, myself. But when I heard the story, I wondered why Marcos mentioned the police. Immediately, I thought he may have hit Maria and perhaps she threatened to call the police, but I wasn't sure. When I heard about his comment about her English, I was more worried. Why is he insulting her about her English? Is he telling her she can't seek help even if she wanted to? Why is he telling her that the police won't do anything? Why is he yelling like that about the mother of his daughter who probably heard everything he said? These are all abusive and pointed to signs of more serious abuse. I also know that this type of violence doesn't usually stop one time. It was likely to continue and could get worse. I figured this story wouldn't stop here.

We wondered what was going on but didn't make any plans for action.

Later, I was talking to people who lived upstairs from them. I'll call these neighbors Tom and Grace, although these are not their real names. They could really hear the yelling, which was mostly coming from Marcos. Maria's voice was much quieter or she seemed to be crying. They thought they heard things being thrown around and were getting worried. They could hear the daughter crying during these times. I told them about what I heard from the other neighbors. Since they seemed really concerned, too, we tried to make sense from the things we knew and we had heard.

See Getting Clear Tool A1. What Is Going On? Snapshot: Quick Question Guide for how this Tool can be used in this story.

TOOLS

4.A GETTING CLEAR: WHAT IS GOING ON?

Tool A.1. Getting Clear Snapshot: Short Question Guide

Tool A.2. Getting Clear Worksheet

Tool A.3. Naming the Harm Chart

Tool A.4. Harm Statement Worksheet

Tool A.5. Getting Clear: Intervention Factors Chart & Checklist

GETTING CLEAR TOOL A1: WHAT IS GOING ON? SNAPSHOT/QUICK QUESTION GUIDE

You can use this Snapshot/Quick Question Guide to help to get started and as a way to take snapshots along the way. This just asks some possible basic questions to start getting a clearer picture of the problem.

- What is going on?
- Who is getting harmed?
- What kind of harm?
- Who is doing the harm?
- What is the impact of this harm?
- Who knows about what's going on?
- What other people or dynamics are important in positive ways?
- What other people or dynamics have been harmful or made things worse?
- Any other important things to know?
- Are there any important changes?
- What's the next step?

EXAMPLE TOOL A1: WHAT IS GOING ON? SNAPSHOT/QUICK QUESTION GUIDE

This example is from:

Story A: I hear yelling in my apartment building. What is going on?

Read Story A in Section A.6. Getting Clear Real Life Stories and Examples for the full story and background.

For this exercise, the person telling the story has filled out the quick question guide by themselves. This is also something they can go through with the two sets of neighbors who have shared their knowledge of what is going on with Marcos and Maria.

What is going on?

Marcos has lived in the building for awhile. Some of us know him but not so well. Maria moved in about 6 years ago. Nobody we know in the building knows much about her. She speaks Spanish and very little English. From the yelling and the noise reported from different neighbors, we know that there is violence happening. It seems that this has started in the last few months.

Who is getting harmed?

Maria seems to be the one getting harmed. And so is their daughter, although it is not clear if she is directly getting hit. Their daughter is being harmed just by watching this happen and hearing the yelling and insults against her mother.

What kind of harm?

There are the kind of fights where there is at least the emotional abuse of yelling. Things are being thrown, which is physically threatening. We think that this could mean that there is also physical abuse or at least something that could lead to physical abuse. The reference to the police also makes us wonder if there is physical abuse, too. There is the kind of abuse where the mother is being insulted for not speaking English. There is harm against the daughter who must witness the yelling, insults, and things being thrown around.

Who is doing the harm?

The primary person doing harm seems to be Marcos.

What is the impact of this harm?

I don't know this family well so I have to guess at some of the impact of this harm right now. I know that Maria is upset during the times that the yelling is happening. Their daughter is clearly crying and upset. I know that the impact of violence can go way beyond being upset during times of violence – it can cause a whole cycle of violence for this family.

As a neighbor, I feel upset that this family is experiencing violence. When I see Maria or their daughter, I think about the violence. I don't think that Marcos is benefiting from his violence. I feel like my own sense of peace is violated by violence in our building.

Who knows about what's going on?

So far, the next door neighbors who first talked about the yelling know. The people upstairs from Marcos and Maria know, and I know. I'm not sure who else knows.

What other people or dynamics are important in positive ways?

The neighbors who I talked to seemed at least concerned. Even though we were gossiping and not necessarily talking about doing anything about it yet, this could be positive. I don't have a strong relationship with either Marcos nor Maria but we have a friendly relationship. This could be a positive dynamic. Even though it looks like Marcos is being abusive to both his wife and at least indirectly to his daughter, he also appears to be a loving father, which is another positive dynamic. He has lived in the building a long time and probably would like to keep his home and keep a friendly relationship with his neighbors, which is another positive dynamic.

What other people or dynamics have been harmful or made things worse?

So far, we don't know much about the situation and what might be negative. But the fact that Maria seems to be a recent immigrant and we don't see other family members around makes us wonder if she is isolated. We also wonder about her immigration status, which would definitely make a difference if we decided to call the police. These days, the police might report her to immigration authorities and the results could be her arrest and her separation from her U.S. born daughter.

Any other important things to know?

There is definitely emotional abuse. And throwing things is a form of physical abuse. Is there also direct physical abuse? Has Maria been looking towards anybody for help? Is she open to get help? Is Marcos open to get help? What resources are there for them? We're not sure.

Are there any important changes?

The most important change that we know of is that some of us as neighbors have started to notice and talk about what is going on.

What's the next step?

At this point, my neighbors Tom and Grace seem to be concerned enough to take some sort of action if needed. I feel this way, as well. But we aren't sure what to do. We just let each other know that we would keep each other informed and think about next steps. We also want to try to keep it inside the building and not involve the police because that could make things worse. This is especially true because we don't know if Maria is undocumented. We think that maybe our own internal actions can stop things at an early stage and at least we have each other for support.

The next step will be to talk to Tom and Grace and share this Toolkit with them. Maybe I'll just photocopy a couple of pages so they don't get overwhelmed.

GETTING CLEAR TOOL A2: WHAT IS GOING ON? WORKSHEET

You can use this *What Is Going On? Worksheet* when you have more time or when you can do this with the support of other people if that is helpful. It can help to identify what are the key issues of violence, abuse or harm you or someone you are close to are facing.

Please take some time to think about the following.

- How can you describe the harm that is happening?
- Who is getting harmed? In what ways?
- Who is doing the harm? In what ways?
- How long has the harm been going on?
- Is it happening all of the time? Does it happen in cycles?
- Has it been getting worse? More frequent? More serious?
- What is still happening now, might be happening now or could happen in the future?
- Are there particular words or a term that best describes it?
- Are there certain people, things or circumstances that make it get worse? Or make it get better?
- Have people tried to get help before? Who? What kind of help? What happened?
- Who knows about the situation of harm?
- What are other important things to know about?
- Are there some key things you still need to find out? If so, what are some possible next steps for finding out?
- What else is important to do next?

GETTING CLEAR TOOL A3: NAMING THE HARM CHART

If you are already getting started, at least one person has likely identified that there is some sort of violence, abuse, or harm taking place. This may already be named, or there may be a more vague feeling that some problem needs to be addressed.

Can you name the harm? How would you name it? What is important in naming it?

Even if the abuse, violence or harm clearly fits into the categories of domestic violence, sexual assault or another form of abuse, one may find it more comfortable or useful to use one's own words to name the harm.

Example: "My power was taken away." "He violated my boundaries." "She violated my sense of trust – Now I can't even trust myself." "He made me feel like I was nothing – worthless." "My community was destroyed – what felt like my safe home was turned into somewhere nobody felt safe."

While some of these sentences above may have resulted in an act or pattern of violence that could also be called domestic violence or sexual assault, the survivor or victim of violence may find it more powerful and accurate to use their own words to describe what happened and what the consequences have been.

Naming the harm can be a useful first step. For some of us, it can be uncomfortable or scary to put words to abuse or violence. It can make us feel embarrassed, ashamed, guilty or vulnerable. If you are the survivor or a victim, you may fear that naming the harm will bring more harm including retaliation. If you are the person who did harm, you may not want to admit what you have done. If you are community members, friends or family, you may feel that you do not have enough information to make a judgment or that it is not our place to name the harm.

To name the harm, you can use your own words. Or you can look at the information in Section 2.2. Interpersonal Violence: Some Basics Everyone Should Know to see if this information helps you to name the harm.

The following Naming the Harm Chart is another way to think about harms. It shows that harms can take many forms: emotional; physical; sexual; economic; using family, friends, children and pets; and using people's vulnerabilities such as their immigration status. It can include threats of harm.

Harms may also come from friends, family and community members who looked away while violence was happening, blamed the victim or participated in the harm.

Below is a chart to recall the types of harms. They may be harms that have been committed in the past. They may be happening currently. Or we can use the chart to imagine what harms have been threatened or could happen in the future.

EXAMPLE A3: NAMING THE HARM CHART

This is a list of possible harms that a person may experience from the primary person doing harm.
It could answer, "I experienced these forms of violence or harm from you. You..."

EMOTIONAL

- Isolated the survivor or victim
- Kept friends or family away
- Humiliated with looks and insults
- Yelled
- Tried to control what the survivor or victim did
- Tried to control what the survivor or victim thought
- Threatened or damaged the reputation of survivor or victim
- Stalked including constant texting, phone calls
- Made survivor or victim nervous all the time causing them to "walk on eggshells"

PHYSICAL

- Physically harmed through pushing, slapping, hitting, punching, pulling hair, choking
- Threatened harm
- Physically threatened by throwing things or punching walls
- Used or threatened with weapons
- Left survivor or victim in dangerous places or situations
- Threatened or used self-harm or threats of suicide
- Didn't allow sleep
- Drove recklessly or dangerously

SEXUAL

- Made unwanted sexual looks or actions
- Created an unsafe sexual environment
- Forced sex
- Forced unwanted types of sex
- Forced to have sex with others
- Exposed to unwanted pornography

FAMILY, FRIENDS, CHILDREN & PETS

- Harmed or threatened harm to family, friends, or others
- Harmed or threatened harm to children
- Harmed others in front of children
- Caused fear in children
- Caused children to devalue or disrespect survivor or victim
- Threatened to take custody of children
- Threatened to kidnap children
- Harmed or threatened harm to pets

ECONOMIC

- Withheld money
- Took away money
- Threatened to or destroyed property or valuables
- Didn't give enough money to survive
- Threatened job
- Didn't allow to work
- Forced to work unfairly
- Gambled or used credit cards recklessly

OTHER

- Threatened to call immigration
- Refused to support immigrant papers
- Threatened to "out" someone to others for being lesbian, gay, bisexual, transgender, or questioning
- Forced to participate in unwanted acts such as stealing, violence against others, etc.

Note that the presence of weapons and threats of suicide are markers of serious levels of danger. Also note that dangers can heighten when a person doing harm senses a loss of power and/or control. Previous forms of harm can escalate into more serious types and levels of harm. While we do not automatically consider threats of suicide to be a form of harm, we also note that threats to commit suicide or harm oneself can often be used to manipulate and to control others. For more, see Section 2.2. Interpersonal Violence: Some Basics Everyone Should Know.

EXAMPLE: NAMING HARMS FROM FRIENDS, FAMILY, OR COMMUNITY

This is the list of possible harms caused by friends, family or community members. It could list how these community members should have been helpful but instead added to the harm. It could answer, "I wish I could have gotten help and support from you, but instead you..."

EMOTIONAL

- Did not believe stories of harm
- Insulted or humiliated the survivor or victim
- Blamed the survivor or victim for asking for or causing harm
- Gossiped
- Minimized the violence
- Denied that the violence was happening
- Only supported people in positions of power
- Criticized the survivor or victim for leaving or wanting to leave
- Criticized the survivor or victim for staying or wanting to stay

PHYSICAL

- Let the physical harm continue
- Pretended not to notice physical harm
- Told the person doing harm information that made things more dangerous for the survivor
- Didn't allow survivor/victim to escape or find safety
- Tried to get the survivor to minimize the harm

SEXUAL

- Allowed sexual harm to continue
- Made it seem like the survivor or victim wanted the sexual harm
- Made it seem like survivor or victim had a duty to accept sex
- Didn't want to hear about anything sexual
- Enjoyed hearing about sexual harm

FAMILY, FRIENDS, CHILDREN & PETS

- Made friends or family turn against the survivor or victim
- Didn't help yourself, friends and family to understand the dynamics of violence
- Didn't help the children with support

ECONOMIC

- Didn't help with affordable resources that may have been helpful
- Let financial reliance on person doing harm get in the way of helping

OTHER

- Threatened to call immigration
- Didn't understand how calling the police or systems could lead to further harm such as deportation

GETTING CLEAR TOOL A3: NAMING THE HARM CHART

Look at each of these categories and use it to map the types of harms done. You can use the Naming the Harm Chart (Example) on the previous page as a guide.

The columns signify different forms of harm.

The rows signify who is being harmed. This may be direct or indirect harm. This may also be either individual people or they may be thought of as workplaces, organizations, neighborhoods and so on.

WHO IS HARMED?				
	Name:________	Name:________	Name:________	Name:________
Emotional *(name calling, isolation, humiliation, threatening suicide, etc.)*				
Physical *(pushing, slapping, pulling hair, beating, threats to harm, etc..)*				
Sexual *(forced sex, unwanted sexual acts, etc..)*				
Economic *(taking money, gambling, preventing from work, etc.)*				
Family, Friends, Children, & Pets *(threatening friends, family, children, etc)*				
Other *(threatening to call immigration, threatening to "out" someone; etc.)*				

GETTING CLEAR TOOL A4: HARMS STATEMENT WORKSHEET

Once a Getting Clear Worksheet and Naming the Harm Chart is filled out, you may want to make a simpler harms statement or set of statements. These statements can serve different purposes. It can be good for one's emotional health to be clear about what harms were done. It may be to make sure this is clear and understandable to people helping to make sure that they understand what situation they are addressing. It may be useful for presenting either in writing or verbally to the person doing harm. You may be in the position of sharing this with the public.

Since there are different purposes and different audiences for harms statements, this Toolkit offers some possible categories of harm statements that might help you think about ways to write statements.

HARMS STATEMENT N CENSORED. Might include strong language, cursing, things that were done and how they hurt people.

HARMS STATEMENT TO SHARE WITH OTHERS HELPING OR POSSIBLY WITH A TEAM. Can still be strong but include more specific details about what was done, for how long, changes in frequency and other things that you may have created when thinking about "What Is Going On" (See Getting Clear Tool A3: What Is Going On? Worksheet).

HARMS STATEMENT TO SHARE WITH THE PERSON DOING HARM. Can still be strong but may include more specific, concrete details about what was done and what you want the person to be accountable for.

HARMS STATEMENT FOR A PERSON DOING HARM TO WRITE UP. As a step towards accountability, should be specific, details and include what the impact of the harm has been to different people – even if not intentional. (See Section 4.E. Taking Accountability)

HARMS STATEMENT FOR THE PUBLIC. Depending on the purpose, this may be used to let the public know about the situation of violence and the steps that have been taken to deal with the situation. It may be very detailed or general depending on what you think is the most positive way to share information with the public.

☑ *GETTING CLEAR* TOOL A5: INTERVENTION FACTORS CHECKLIST

An intervention may include a number of factors. Below are some factors that may be significant in thinking about the harm, thinking about who you might involve in an intervention, thinking about your goals or what you want to have happen, and possibilities for connecting people to the positive goals of this intervention.

Generally, challenging factors increase as you move down the list.

1. What is the relationship between people involved in the violence?

- ☐ Violence by a stranger
- ☐ Violence by a former partner or acquaintance but are not connected to now
- ☐ Violence by someone with whom we share community
- ☐ Violence in an ongoing relationship

2. What is the timeframe of violence?

- ☐ Pattern from the far past
- ☐ Isolated incident from the far past
- ☐ Isolated recent incident
- ☐ Emerging pattern of violence or abuse
- ☐ Long-standing pattern of violence
- ☐ Re-emergence or return of violent pattern

3. What is the visibility of violence?

- ☐ Public violence witnessed by one or more others (may also be situation where violence is private as well)
- ☐ Public and private violence witnessed or known about by others
- ☐ Incident of private violence with no witnesses
- ☐ Pattern of private violence with no witnesses

4. What is the level of danger?

- ☐ History and likelihood of use of weapons (guns, knives, explosives, etc. and/or other highly dangerous forms of violence)
- ☐ Threatened use of weapons and/or highly dangerous forms of violence
- ☐ Accessibility to weapons or possible highly dangerous forms of violence (even if this person has not acted in this way in the past)
- ☐ No shown willingness or ability to carry out highly dangerous forms of violence
- ☐ History of self-harm and/or suicide attempts
- ☐ Serious concerns related to substance abuse and/or mental illness
- ☐ Risk of retaliatory violence that is not necessarily life-threatening
- ☐ Low likelihood of retaliatory violence

5. What is the degree to which survivor or victim might be involved in the intervention?

- ☐ Survivor or victim is the key person leading the intervention
- ☐ Survivor or victim is leading but has input from others
- ☐ Survivor or victim has high level of involvement but with others as primary people intervening
- ☐ Survivor or victim is "in the loop" but maintaining some distance from the details of the intervention
- ☐ Survivor or victim has little or no involvement in the intervention due to choice or other factors (for example, the survivor is a child)

6. How much can we expect to engage the person doing harm?

- ☐ Has no friends or social connections
- ☐ Has issues related to substance abuse and/or mental illness that seriously gets in the way of them having meaningful social connections
- ☐ Has friends or buddies but they all collude (contribute to) violence
- ☐ Has friends or buddies but fights them or disengages if they challenge this person
- ☐ Only connection is with the survivor or victim
- ☐ Knows people who the person doing harm respects or has opinions that matter even if they may not be close friends
- ☐ Has close relationships with people whom the person doing harm respects and whose opinions matter
- ☐ Has close relationships with community members who can help support them to stop violence and use new behaviors; the person doing harm is able to talk about hard things at least with certain people

7. How likely is it that we can involve community allies in the intervention?

- ☐ No connections or community
- ☐ There are connections or community, but they will excuse or even support violence
- ☐ One or two people who are connected to at least the survivor or victim and/or the person doing harm willing to get involved in positive way
- ☐ No close community, but belong to community setting (neighborhood, city, ethnic community) that has at least some people or an organization that would be willing to get involved
- ☐ At least one or two strong leaders and a group of connected people who would be willing to get involved

8. How much do the survivor or victim, community allies, and/or person doing harm share values?

- ☐ No shared values and/or opposite values
- ☐ Some overlap of values
- ☐ Significant overlap of values
- ☐ Shared membership in a values-based community (for example, faith institution, community group, political group, etc.)

GETTING CLEAR TOOL A5: INTERVENTION FACTORS CHART

An intervention may include a number of factors. Below are some factors that may be significant in thinking about the harm, thinking about who you might involve in an intervention, thinking about your goals or what you want to have happen, and possibilities for connecting people to the positive goals of this intervention.

NOTE: CHALLENGES INCREASE AS YOU MOVE DOWN LIST

RE ATIONSHIPS BE W PEOPL N V OL CE	- Violence by a stranger - Violence by a former partner or acquaintance but are not connected to now - Violence by someone with whom we share community - Violence in an ongoing relationship
TIMEFRAME OF VIOLENCE	- Pattern from the far past - Isolated incident from the far past - Isolated recent incident - Emerging pattern of violence or abuse - Long-standing pattern of violence - Re-emergence or return of violent pattern
VISIBILITY OF VIOLENCE	- Public violence witnessed by one or more others (may also be situation where violence is private as well) - Public and private violence witnessed or known about by others - Incident of private violence with no witnesses - Pattern of private violence with no witnesses
DANGER OF VIOLENCE	- Low likelihood of retaliatory violence - No shown willingness or ability to carry out highly dangerous forms of violence - Risk of retaliatory violence that but level of harm likely low - Accessibility to weapons or possible highly dangerous forms of violence (even if this person has not acted in this way in the past) - History and likelihood of use of weapons (guns, knives, explosives, etc. and/or other highly dangerous forms of violence) - Threatened use of weapons and/or highly dangerous forms of violence - History of self-harm and/or suicide attempts - Serious concerns related to substance abuse and/or mental illness

NOTE: CHALLENGES INCREASE AS YOU MOVE DOWN LIST

SB V VOR INVOLM N T IN INTB N TION

- Survivor has little or no involvement due to choice or other factors, for example, the survivor is a child)
- Survivor is "in the loop" but maintaining some distance from the details
- Survivor has a high level of involvement but with others as primary people intervening
- Survivor is the key person intervening

LIKELIHOOD TO ENGAGE PERSON DOING HARM

- Has close relationships with community members who can help support them to stop violence and use new behaviors; the person doing harm is able to talk about hard things at least with certain people
- Has close relationships with people whom the person doing harm respects and whose opinions matter
- Has people who the person doing harm respects or has opinions that matter even if they may not be close friends
- Only connection is with the survivor or victim
- Has friends or buddies but fights them or walks away if they challenge them
- Has friends or buddies but they all collude (or contribute to) violence
- Has issues related to substance abuse and/or mental illness that seriously gets in the way of them having meaningful social connections
- Has no friends or social connections

LIKE IHOOD TO INVOLC OMMN ITY MM BBS

- At least one or two strong leaders and a group of connected people who would be willing to get involve
- No close community but community setting (neighborhood, city, ethnic, community) that has at least some people or an organization that would be willing to get involved
- One or two people who are connected to at least the survivor or victim an/ or the person doing harm willing to get involved
- No connections or community

SHARED VALUES

- Shared membership in a values-based community (for example, faith institution, community group, political group, etc.)
- Significant overlap of values
- Some overlaps of values
- No shared values and/or opposite values

4B STAYING SAFE
HOW DO WE STAY SAFE?

B.1. What Is Staying Safe?

B.2. Staying Safe Across the 4 Phases

B.3. Tips

B.4. Special Considerations

B.5. Facilitator Notes

B.6. Real Life Stories and Examples

B.7. Staying Safe Tools

B.1. WHAT IS STAYING SAFE?

Staying Safe: Key Questions

- What are risks and dangers right now?
- Risks to whom?
- What level of risk? High, Medium, Low, None, Emergency?
- What are the risks and dangers if we take no action?
- What are the risks and dangers if we take action?
- Who needs safety and protection
- What plans can we make to provide safety and protection?

What Is It?

Staying Safe includes concerns, plans and actions all meant to minimize the current, potential and future levels of harm or increase the level of safety. As you take action to address, reduce, end or prevent violence, a primary concern is staying safe.

In this Toolkit, Staying Safe has 3 parts:

1. **Risk Assessment** to identify the level of danger, potential danger or harm;
2. **Safety Planning** to plan steps and roles to minimize this danger or harm;
3. **Safety Actions** to take steps to minimize this danger or harm.

Why Is It Important?

Staying Safe is a centerpiece for most violence interventions. This model is unique in that it understands that taking action to address violence is often risky, in and of itself. This Toolkit provides many ways to ask you to consider how taking action (or not taking action) can result in harm. It also asks you to consider how an action you take may not bring harm to yourself, but could bring harm to others. The possibility of getting in the way of danger and risking retaliation to yourself and the survivor or victim (if you are not the survivor or victim) are considerations that are important every step of the way. Retaliation that might involve other loved ones such as children or other family and friends can be a real danger. And, in some situations, taking action can set off levels of harm and endangerment to the person doing harm (from themselves or from others) that should also be taken into consideration.

In this model, we know that gaining long-term safety and other goals we seek can sometimes involve short-term risks. We urge you to think carefully and thoroughly about all possible risks and dangers and safety planning and action to counteract these risks and dangers no matter what actions – large and small – you decide to take.

Safety Takes Many Forms

In the Toolkit, *Section 2.2. Interpersonal Violence: Basics Everyone Should Know*, we saw how violence can take many forms and hurt many people.

Safety may also take many forms:

- **Emotional**
  - Basic feelings of worth and integrity
  - Ability to make basic life decisions
- **Physical**
  - Safety from physical harm and neglect or threats of physical harm; having basic needs of home, food, shelter and clothing
- **Sexual**
  - Freedom from unwanted sexual looks, gestures, or touch;
  - Safety from exposure to unwanted sexualized environment including language, pictures, audio, visuals
  - Safety from pressure to be involved in unwanted sexual activity
  - For children, protection from any type of sexual look, gesture, touch or exposure
- **Economic or financial**
  - Safety that we will have basic needs of home, food, shelter, and clothing
  - Safety that we will have a decent job or source of livable income
- **Spiritual**
  - Safety to hold and express our spiritual beliefs
- **Other**
  - Other forms of safety such as safety for immigrants from detention and deportation, safety from homophobia, safety from political persecution, and more

Staying Safe Can Involve Both Planning and Action

People often think about making safety plans – for example, who to call in case of emergency or what to pack in case you need to get away. But sometimes safety requires taking higher levels of action and possible risk – for example, removing guns or other weapons to reduce the level of danger; calling friends for a meeting to figure out who can take care of children or pets in case someone has to get away; getting friends or family to keep watch at the home; or helping someone move to a safer home.

This section offers some basic information and tools for you to understand the risks as you move to action (or if you choose not to act) and to prepare for safety.

USING THE TOOLS IN THIS SECTION

Safety is never a guarantee, but this section offers tools to help increase safety or reduce risk and harm.

Tool B1. Risk Assessment Chart looks specifically at risks and dangers if one takes no action and if one takes action.

The following safety-related tools look more at how you can plan and prepare for safety. Tool B2. Safety Plan and Action Worksheet and Tool B3. Safety Plan and Action Chart provide guides to custom-made safety plans and actions depending upon your particular risks and dangers and the resources you have available to help you stay safe.

Tools also include a more conventional Tool B4. Escape Safety Checklist for those who need to prepare for situations in which escape is necessary.

Finally, Tool B5. Meeting Person Who Did Harm Safety Worksheet helps with safety planning for those of you who may consider meeting directly with the person doing harm.

B.2. *STAYING SAFE* ACROSS THE 4 PHASES

In Section 3.6. Interventions Over Time: 4 Phases, the Toolkit introduced the idea of 4 possible phases of interventions: 1) Getting Started, 2) Planning/Preparation, 3) Taking Action, and 4) Following Up.

Figuring out how to stay safe may look different at various phases or levels of crisis.

PHASE 1: GETTING STARTED

As you get started, you or someone you know may already be in a dangerous and harmful situation. You may need to think about very basic safety needs such as telling trusted people about the situation of violence. Taking care of medical or mental health needs may come first. For some, escaping from the situation of harm may become a priority.

PHASE 2: PLANNING/PREPARATION

If you are entering a phase of planning and preparation, safety concerns may be different. For example, figuring out trusted allies and how to keep information safe among them might become a key issue. Finding helpful allies who can also support the person doing harm to take responsibility might be important at an early planning stage.

PHASE 3: TAKING ACTION

As you get ready to take action, big actions or small, you may face new risks and dangers. Taking action may increase risks for those involved in the intervention or may trigger reactions that could further jeopardize safety. It may be important to use tools to assess risks and plan for safety that focuses just on the next step to be taken.

Risk assessment and safety planning may focus around next steps – with each action requiring its own risk and safety consideration.

PHASE 4: FOLLOWING-UP

As you move through the planning and action steps of intervention or perhaps as you reach its conclusion, you may be able to create systems to establish longer-term safety. You may be able to focus on maintaining and sustaining systems of safety or taking lessons learned to create wider community safety zones.

RELATED TOOLS

Tools to look closer at people who can help out with safety are in *Section 4.C. Mapping Allies and Barriers* and *Section 4.G. Working Together*. Tools to help you look at whether and how safety is a goal are in *Section 4.D. Goal Setting*. Tools to look at risks and safety when preparing to take action steps are in *Section 4.H. Keeping on Track.*

B.3. *STAYING SAFE* TIPS

#1 READ SOME BASICS EVERYONE SHOULD KNOW

Interpersonal violence is complicated. Although we may hear more about domestic violence or sexual assault these days, many misunderstandings still exist and many misconceptions about what it is and how to approach it. Read Section 2. S*ome Basics Everyone Should Know.* Pay special attention to Section 2.2. *Interpersonal Violence: Some Basics Everyone Should Know* in order to have a clearer picture of what is going on. The Section 2.3. *Violence Intervention: Some Important Lessons* also shares important basics about interventions based upon the experiences of Creative Interventions.

Share this information with others who may be involved in a situation of violence and may need some resources to help them know what to do.

#2 TAKE INTO ACCOUNT THE POSSIBILITY THAT RISKS CAN INCREASE AS YOU TAKE ACTION TO END VIOLENCE

Our model of community action recognizes that taking action to create safety can sometimes mean taking additional risks, at least in the short run. What is important is for everyone to understand what risks you are taking, who might be endangered and what precautions may ensure greater safety or minimize harm.

Interpersonal violence is often about maintaining control over others. When people take action to end violence or gain safety, violence or threats of violence can increase. In some situations, threats get more serious. Levels of violence may escalate beyond levels experienced in the past. People doing harm may also threaten to harm themselves including suicide.

Risk assessment should take into account possible reactions from the person doing harm. This could include acts of retaliation which could be provoked when the person doing harm senses loss of control, exposure through public disclosure or other negative consequences resulting from the intervention. Safety planning and safety actions need to take into account these increases in risk.

#3 THINK ABOUT SAFETY FOR EVERYONE

Safety may involve many different people – the safety of the survivor (or primary victim or target of violence), safety of others close by (children, friends, family, workplace, or community), safety for people carrying out an intervention, and safety for the people who caused or are doing harm. When possible, aim for a course of action that ensures the safety for all involved.

#4 INVOLVE OTHER TRUSTED PEOPLE IN STAYING SAFE

Because intervention actions are often taken under conditions of danger, any move to take the next step should involve at least one other person and hopefully more trusted people to help with planning, support and follow-up.

Other trusted people could help in some of the following ways:

- By acting as a sounding board
- Go through a safety plan together
- Go together with someone who is taking an action, waiting in the car or around the corner until you know someone is safe
- Being on the other end of a cell phone to receive a call that everything went okay
- Watching someone's children to make sure they are safe
- Distracting or confronting someone who may be a danger
- Even if someone is going to take some action alone, it can be helpful to have a back-up or use a buddy system – with someone who knows what they are going to do, when, and can be in communication with them either by going with them, standing close by or at least be in communication via phone or text.

#5 MAKE SAFETY CHECKS A REGULAR PART OF YOUR PLAN

The levels of risks and dangers can change constantly. Make sure you make risk assessment and safety plans a regular part of your intervention – and, if necessary, a regular part of your daily lives.

A situation can change due to a number of factors:

People have started to know about the violence and may say things or do things that cause a change – for example, they may treat the person doing harm differently

People have gathered to take action. The simple fact that people are starting to gather together and take action steps may change the situation

The survivor or victim of violence may feel more empowered to act assertively or in other ways that could shift the dynamics of power; this can cause positive change as power starts to shift; this can also increase danger if the person or people doing harm react negatively to this change.

#6 REMEMBER THE SIGNS OF INCREASED RISK

The risk of harm and level of harm is generally greatly increased if:

1. Weapons are involved – guns, knives, machetes, and others that can cause great harm;
2. Someone has a history of committing acts of violence; and
3. Someone is also threatening suicide. As mentioned above, risks can also increase as the person doing harm senses a loss of control. Violence or threats of violence can escalate in these situations.

You may need to take extra steps to assess risks and take steps to increase safety if you are facing higher levels of risk or harm.

#7 SEPARATE SAFETY FROM OTHER FEELINGS OF DISCOMFORT

For some of us, the word "unsafe" has become equivalent with "uncomfortable," "anxious," "nervous." The English language and other languages have limitations in distinguishing between these different forms of safety. Lack of safety or exposure to risks and harm are negative. However, other forms of discomfort such as anxiety, vulnerability, nervousness, embarrassment or shame may be a necessary but difficult step towards creating safety in the long term.

Exposing someone to situations that are out of their comfort zone, that may challenge their thoughts and actions that may make them feel insecure because such thoughts or actions are unfamiliar are not necessarily threats to safety, although they may make someone feel unsafe.

For example, someone who is asked to take accountability may experience this as making them feel vulnerable and, therefore, unsafe. A survivor or victim who is nervous about talking about and sharing their experience of abuse with allies may feel a sense of embarrassment or shame that makes them feel unsafe. Community allies who recognize the need to involve themselves in addressing harm that they had previously ignored may feel feelings of nervousness and uncertainty that feel unsafe.

#8 REMEMBER AND PRIORITIZE THE SAFETY OF CHILDREN AND YOUTH

Remember the sensitivity and vulnerability of children and youth to violence. If actions are taking place, they are affected by them. Actions taken for safety may be experienced as scary and threatening to young people. Careful attention may be made to think about including them in on a plan before it happens – or perhaps protecting them from that plan. Their level of maturity and ability to keep information confidential may be taken into account when considering their involvement.

Regardless of the involvement of children and youth in safety or intervention plans, special attention needs to be paid to the emotional, sexual and physical safety of children. You may consider how they can be cared for and kept safe away from the situation of harm or situations of intervention. You may consider how people they trust can spend time with them to let them express their feelings of confusion or fear, assure them that they will remain cared for and make sure they are able to continue in activities important to their well-being: time to play, attendance at school, time to do homework, regular meals, and regular sleep.

Be aware of mandated reporting laws in your state. Know that school staff, social workers, people who work regularly with youth and children, medical staff and sometimes religious leaders are required to report to authorities if they suspect physical or sexual abuse or neglect.

If children are kept safe away from parents or guardians, make sure you know the laws in terms of removal of children, escape from violence, or what is considered kidnapping. Make sure you know what school rules are in terms of who can take children from school premises. You can contact local anti-violence programs like domestic violence hotlines and shelters and sexual assault counseling centers, police or lawyers who are familiar with issues of violence, children and custody to find out. It may be possible to call without using the actual names of anybody involved to get this information without endangering yourself or these children.

Although this Toolkit is geared more for adults, youth may also be using this for violence intervention. If you are a young person reading this section, then this information is still for you.

B.3. *STAYING SAFE* SPECIAL CONSIDERATIONS

The process of Staying Safe may be different depending upon your relationship to violence and to the people most closely involved in violence. This Toolkit promotes a process that brings together different viewpoints to create a better picture of what is really going on. This can and should happen regularly throughout the intervention. We believe that bringing people together in a coordinated way can build "safety in numbers." That means that people acting together to address or end harm can create a safety net. This Toolkit promotes safety for everyone involved in violence including the survivor or victim, the community allies and the person or people who have caused harm. It also recognizes that different people in different positions may face different types of safety concerns. It uses the special roles, relationships and skills of many people to create a wider safety net.

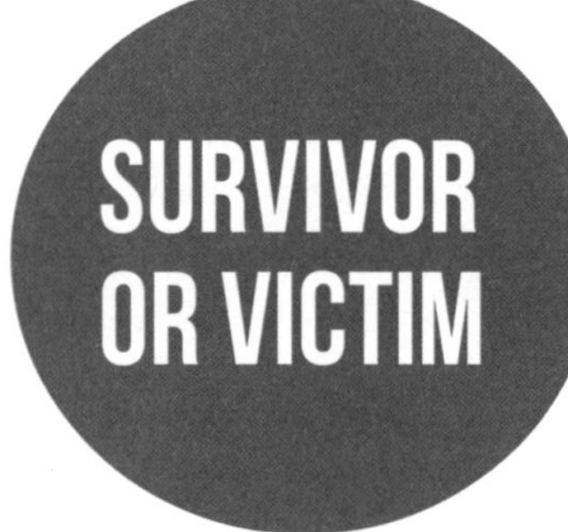

The survivor or victim is often the person who best understands the dynamics and impact of violence. That person is also likely to be the person most affected by violence. Especially when we are thinking about interpersonal violence, the nature of harm can be subtle or hidden. It may have developed over a period of time, beginning with small abuses that end up becoming a pattern of abuse. It may have been one particularly violent incident that gives the message that this can always happen again.

Likewise, the survivor or victim may have developed a keen sense of how best to stay safe under unsafe conditions. This sense can even appear to others as a strange or unwise way to keep safe. For example, survivors or victims in situations of violence are known to provoke violence as a way to control a situation that will happen regardless. People involved in a regular pattern of violence can begin to sense when tension is building. Survivors or victims or violence can sometimes react to this tension by doing something to bring on violence. For example, someone may even provoke a fight or challenge someone to, "come here and hit me" because they know that they will eventually be hit anyways. Having some control over when it happens can seem irrational to others who are not living under this fear, but can make sense in a world in which one has so little control.

This Toolkit recognizes that people who have had to live for a long time under unsafe conditions may have learned to deny or minimize the seriousness of violence for various reasons. Violence may have become a normal condition. Minimizing violence may become a coping mechanism. For others, it may seem like no other choice or escape exists – thereby making violence something to tolerate.

The primary survivors or victims of violence have already had their safety violated.

As people begin to hear about the violence and get involved, the survivors or victims may risk the judgment and blame of others as they hear the story. Many people do not understand the basics about violence and instead fall easily into victim blaming. Victim blaming can create a situation of even more danger and vulnerability. Survivors or victims who have sought safety through friends, or programs or the police may also fear retaliation for telling others. They may have been told that they will be hurt even more if they try to seek help.

If you are the survivor or victim, your direct experience with violence may make safety your first concern. As mentioned above, you may have different feelings and relationships to the idea of safety. Desire for safety may have caused you to turn to this Toolkit. Fear for your safety may also make you afraid to take action. It is also common for people to deny or minimize danger as a way to cope with an overwhelming sense of fear.

Feeling mixed and confused is normal. It is normal to wish the worst for someone who has hurt you. It is also normal to want them to be protected, especially if they are someone you have cared about. It is normal to forget about and excuse the ways that they have hurt you in one moment and think only about these things in another.

These concerns can lead to double-edged criticisms by others. You might be accused of not caring about yourself (your children, your family or others in harm's way). You might also be accused of being selfish and not caring about the person doing harm. This can be a very difficult situation.

Use of this Toolkit offers you an opportunity to think more clearly about what safety means to you and what kinds of safety you seek. It urges you to be as realistic as possible about the dangers you face and the potential dangers that you and others face as you take action. It encourages you to think realistically about risks and to make plans that take these risks into account. It reminds you that other people close to you or who get involved may also be taking risks.

The Toolkit can also help others do a better job of supporting you. You may find that during an intervention, your safety seems to become less important as people focus their energy on the person or people who have done harm. You may need to call more attention to your safety or pick out a couple of trusted people who can help you brainstorm and plan your safety and help you get others to keep their attention to safety concerns. Use these tools to get clear and to protect yourself and others as you take action.

Community allies may already be experiencing harm or threats to harm. As community allies step in to get involved in an intervention, they may expose themselves to more risk. They may be thinking about survivor or victim safety and also have to consider their risks, safety plans and safety actions.

If you are a community ally, you may already be aware that your involvement carries risks. You may be worried about a number of things. How can you make sure your actions do not lead to retaliatory violence against the survivor or victim? How can you make sure that your actions do not reveal confidential information in such a way to increase danger for the survivor or victim or others? Can you become the target of retaliation? Can you be threatened in order to reveal more information such as the whereabouts of the survivor or victim, the location of children, plans for intervention and so on?

Depending on the situation of violence and the plan for intervention, safety concerns may be relatively low. But in highly lethal situations or in situations in which the community ally is physically, emotionally or financially dependent upon the person doing harm, these threats can be high.

Be aware of your own risks and safety needs. Be honest with yourself and others about your own willingness to take these risks. Think about your own bottom-lines or boundaries regarding how much risk you are willing to take on or how much you are able to do. Let others know your limitations, and think about the best roles that you can take given these limitations.

Remember also that "safety is in numbers." Work with others to create safety plans that can rely on greater numbers of people taking advantage of their various roles, locations and skills to create a wider safety net. Use these tools to protect yourself and others as you take action.

When people take action to end violence, the safety of the person doing harm may be one of the lowest on the list of concerns. This Toolkit encourages us to think about the safety concerns of everyone. When we think about the safety of the person doing harm, this does not mean that we avoid consequences or actions that may seem negative or threatening to that person. Naming violence, asking someone to stop their violence and demanding that people take responsibility or accountability for this harm may appear threatening to that person. It may ask them to be in a position that calls attention to things that have hurt other people and may feel shameful. It may lead others to threaten or even to harm that person when they find out what they have done.

This Toolkit asks us to consider offering an intervention process that also respects the integrity of the person doing harm and that provides enough safety for that person to go through the process of taking accountability with dignity if he or she chooses to take the responsible path. Experiencing negative feelings can be a central part of the process but for some, this may even feel like a threat to safety.

This is different from intervention processes that deliberately use humiliation or forms of violence to "get even." Attempts to "get even" are not recommended in this Toolkit. However, intervention processes that result in someone feeling shame because they did something wrong, because they face the judgment of other people or because they have to step down from positions of power are often necessary steps in someone taking responsibility for their actions.

If you are a community ally, think about how standard interventions to violence such as calling the police could also threaten safety and work against the aims of intervention. Think about ways in which you can provide alternatives to support accountability without subjecting someone to the harms of arrest and imprisonment or actions that might invite other systems such as immigration control.

If you are a community ally with special ties to the survivor or victim of violence, to particular allies or to the person or people doing harm, then you can use your connections and relationships to support them in special ways. You can use your compassion and understanding to bring them out of isolation and into a more connected and collective experience of violence of intervention. Your care and support may help create a path from shame and anger towards responsibility.

If you are the person doing harm or who has been accused of doing harm, use this as an opportunity to experience the shame of doing harm, the judgment of others who may be hurt, disgusted or horrified by your actions, and the possible consequences you are asked to take. Understand how your attitudes or actions, even if unintentional, threatened the safety of others.

Find friends, allies or other supporters to help you through the painful process of admitting or reflecting on actions that led you to this process. Remember that the role of allies is not to excuse you but to support you, perhaps in ways that may be challenging. Even if you do not agree with everything, see if you can shift your perspective. See if you can carry out some of the actions of accountability and make it through uncomfortable negative feelings, a sense of vulnerability and, perhaps, what may feel like your own lack of safety. See if these actions can actually lead to a greater sense of humanity.

Ask others working with you to support you through this process. Taking responsibility to try on new attitudes and actions can be uncomfortable and may feel very threatening. Taking responsibility can also lead to new healthy relationships with yourself and with others.

For tools that can help you take responsibility and make important changes in your life ,see Section 4.F. Taking Accountability.

STAYING SAFE

Risk assessment, safety planning and safety actions are very sensitive to changing conditions. They might require constant assessment and reassessment. They may be very specific to a single step or action to be taken.

Because of this, facilitators may need to take both a broad role in looking at overall risks and safety planning and check to see if safety plans are in place as things change and as people take new actions.

If you are a facilitator or are willing to help out by providing a role in helping another person or a group to work through this Toolkit, then these notes are to help you.

#1 ENCOURAGE AND SUPPORT PEOPLE TO LEARN FUNDAMENTAL INFORMATION FIRST IF THEY HAVE NOT ALREADY.

This Toolkit is long and can be overwhelming. Some important parts of this Toolkit are Section 2. Some Basics Everyone Should Know. An especially important section can be Section 2.2. Interpersonal Violence: Some Basics Everyone Should Know that discusses much more about the dynamics of violence and common misunderstandings that people have.

It can be useful for you to be familiar with the different sections of this Toolkit and to read more carefully through these sections. Also encourage people to read these sections. If reading is not the best option or they cannot read English or the language that this Toolkit is in, you can help by reading this and other sections to them in a language they understand or use other formats to pass on this information.

#2 MAKE SURE THAT PEOPLE TAKE THE TIME TO THINK SERIOUSLY ABOUT RISKS AND SAFETY PLANNING.

This Toolkit is long and can be overwhelming. Some important parts of this Toolkit are Section 2. Some Basics Everyone Should Know. An especially important section can be Section 2.2. Interpersonal Violence: Some Basics Everyone Should Know that discusses much more about the dynamics of violence and common misunderstandings that people have.

It can be useful for you to be familiar with the different sections of this Toolkit and to read more carefully through these sections. Also encourage people to read these sections. If reading is not the best option or they cannot read English or the language that this Toolkit is in, you can help by reading this and other sections to them in a language they understand or use other formats to pass on this information.

#3 BRING PEOPLE TOGETHER TO FORM A SAFETY PLAN.

Safety is best found in numbers. Even if someone is going to take some action alone, it can be helpful for them to have a back-up or buddy system – someone who knows what they are going to do, when, and can be in communication with them either by going with them, standing close by or at least being in communication via phone or text.

#4 MAKE SURE THAT RISK ASSESSMENT SAFETY PLANNING IS A REGULAR PART OF THE INTERVENTION.

Risks and, therefore, safety plans can often change as the situation changes and as actions are taken.

Make safety planning a regular way for everyone to lower risk.

B.6. REAL LIFE STORIES AND EXAMPLES

Story B. Confronting the Person Who Raped Me

A young immigrant woman came to an immigrant rights organization seeking assistance. She had gone to a party with her former employer, the owner of a bar. That evening, he attempted to rape her. She was able to struggle and get away. However, the experience was clearly traumatizing. Outraged, the woman had decided that she wanted to confront this man. She talked to the advocate about her plan to enter the bar and directly confront him, convinced that her sense of violation could only be met by this bold move.

The advocate, moved by the courage of this woman, responded by offering to go into the bar with her, a strategy ultimately challenged by the advocate's team of co-workers. This offer went beyond the usual practices of this organization and much beyond what most anti-violence organizations would recommend. Interested in the further exploration of this woman's request, this organization wondered whether this was the right opportunity for trying out a community-based intervention. The other options didn't seem to fit. She had already gone to the police who told her she did not have a case. And she did not have money or speak English. Who would she go to for "therapy" except the organization? Besides, it seemed like she was seeking her own pathway to healing which for her meant facing him head-on.

The advocate decided not to go with her and confront this man. But she did decide to act as a supporter or facilitator to see if she could provide a supportive anchor for this woman to carry out this plan of action. Self-determination became the guiding value for the organization's workers. Safety was also foremost in their minds. How could they prioritize safety without taking away this woman's self-determination?

The staff team discussed what a facilitated community-based intervention would look like in this situation. How could the advocate ask exploratory questions without trying to convince this woman not to go or to scare her off? The advocate met again with this young woman. This time she helped her explore her goals in confronting this man. Could her goals be met in other ways? Did she think about safety? It became clear that this woman's goal was direct confrontation even after all of the questions. But she was also open to discussing safety plans and to role play this action. She appreciated the support to figure this out.

The advocate role-played possible scenarios based upon her knowledge of the dynamics of sexual assault. She presented possible dangers as well as responses of victim-blaming, denial, threats and violence. She helped the woman explore who else among her friends and family might be willing to help. The role play brought up many situations which this woman had not considered. She recognized that marching into the bar on her own or with others was too dangerous. She had not thought of the possibility of his denial or his manipulation that it was her fault or her imagination. After going through the role play, she realized that these were all possibilities and appreciated the opportunity to go through the process. She took this as useful information that helped her clarify a safer plan which still met her goals.

Since the advocate was also interested in helping this woman explore what other allies she had, she asked more about this. Although the advocate had at first been convinced to march alongside her, she thought more about this. It was dangerous. She did not "know" this man, his possible reactions, or how her presence could make the situation more dangerous. Supporting this woman to center this "intervention" within her own community made more sense. They are her first-line supporters. They know her and the situation in which she worked. And the advocate was willing to help think through their possible roles and safety as well as hers.

The woman could not identify anybody within her community to help out when this plan was first discussed. But the question seemed to make an impression. By the time she decided to go and confront the man, she had talked to a friend who agreed to stay close to her phone in case any crisis occurred.

After thinking through and role-playing the safety plan, she called her former employer to meet her at a restaurant. He agreed. When she went to prepare for the meeting, she talked to the waiter at the restaurant and asked him to keep a close watch on the situation in case anything happened. These were two allies, the friend and the waiter, that she organized to help support her safety.

The woman ended up meeting with her former employer, confronting him by naming his action and her outrage. Within a short time, he admitted his guilt and apologized without further incident. She called the organization following this confrontation with great appreciation, relief and a sense of closure.

This story illustrates the basic principles of the model of community-based intervention, the critical role of helping the survivor identify her own goals and a plan of action to meet these goals. It also highlights the importance of exploring a collective response and the opportunity it opens for a different set of options resulting from the involvement of other people. It also offers one example of engagement with the person doing harm and the transformative power of this possibility for the survivor. We can imagine that the "healing" powers of this action were deeper and more powerful than anything the police or professionals could provide.

Story adapted from Kim, M. "Alternative Interventions to Intimate Violence: Defining Political and Pragmatic Challenges." Pp. 193 – 217 in Ptacek, J. (Ed.), Feminism and Restorative Justice, (NY: Oxford Press, 2010).

TOOLS

4.B STAYING SAFE: HOW DO WE STAY SAFE

Tool B1. Risk Assessment Chart

Tool B2. Safety Plan and Action Worksheet

Tool B3. Safety Plan and Action Chart

Tool B4. Escape Safety Checklist

Tool B5. Meeting Person Who Did Harm Safety Worksheet

STAYING SAFE TOOL B1: RISK ASSESSMENT CHART

Risk Assessment: What Is It?

A risk assessment is a kind of measurement of harm, violence or danger. It takes into account what has been done in the past, what is happening now, and what could happen in the future.

Risk assessment also has to take into account changing conditions. This can include any increases in risk as people start to find out that violence has been happening or people start to find out that an intervention is being carried out. These new changes can set into motion a whole series of responses. It is important to think through all possible scenarios.

It is also important to think of the risks of harm to all people involved: the survivor or victim of violence; people close by such as family, friends, and, especially, children; and the person or people doing harm.

What Can Increase Risk?

The risk of harm is generally greatly increased if:

1. Weapons are involved – guns, knives, machetes, and others that can cause great harm;
2. Someone has a history of committing acts of violence; and
3. Someone is also threatening suicide.

Risk can also increase when people begin to confront violence. Some people leaving violent relationships have found that the level of violence or threats can actually increase during the time they are trying to get away or regain control of their lives. This does not mean that one should not leave or confront an abusive relationship. It does mean that someone may need to take extra steps to be aware of dangers and take extra action to provide safety. Safety planning and safety actions prepare people to increase safety, but it does not guarantee it.

1. Consider the full range of harms already being faced. Look at the Harms Chart filled out from the section Getting Clear: Naming the Harm Chart.
2. Review the Naming the Harm Chart to see what is still a risk now and what may be a risk later.
3. Fill in the chart's following questions to assess risk.

COLUMN 1: RISK, DANGER OR HARM

In the first column, you can name the risk, danger or harm in your own words. The following is a list that may also be useful to think of categories of harm. You can use specific words to describe the particular risk in your situation.

- Physical or threatened harm to the body or to one's life
- Physical or threatened harm to others such as children, family, friends, neighbors, co-workers
- Physical or threatened harm to self; threats of suicide
- Physical threat through use of weapon
- Physical and emotional threat through stalking or harassment using phone, text, email
- Emotional or verbal harm such as loss of reputation; "outing" or sharing unwanted information or lies to friends, family or community; isolation
- Emotional or verbal harm such as threats to harm relationships with family, friends or children
- Emotional or verbal harm through insults, threats, humiliation
- Sexual harm including rape, molestation, forced sexual acts, exposure to pornography and so on
- Financial harm through destroying property or taking away property
- Financial harm through loss of job
- Financial harm through taking money from bank account
- Financial harm through refusing to repay loans or debt or through reckless use of credit cards or gambling
- Other harms such as threats to report to immigration enforcement
- Other

COLUMN 2: WHO OR WHAT IS CAUSING THE HARM

In the second column, you can name the person or situation that may be causing the harm. Harm may be directly threatened by a person. Or the threat may come from a situation such as insecure employment, being an undocumented immigrant or something linked to a larger system of inequality.

COLUMN 3: TARGET OF RISK, DANGER OR HARM

In the third column, you can name the person or thing that is the target of risk, danger or harm. It may be the direct survivor or victim; it may be others including friends, family, or community; the threat may be to your home or to a job or to one's immigration status. The threat may be to a pet. The threat may be to those who are about to take action.

COLUMN 4: WHAT IS THE LEVEL OF DANGER

There are many ways that you might want to name levels of danger. For example, the Forest Service uses a system of:

This Toolkit suggests:

- Emergency
- High
- Moderate
- Low
- No risk now
- More information needed

You can use colors or names or symbols that suit you. The important things to think about is when it is so high that quick action is necessary (Emergency) when the danger really has disappeared for some reason (None right now) or when more information is needed (More information needed).

RISK ASSESSMENT CHART

COLUMN 1 What is the risk, danger or harm?	COLUMN 2 Who/What is the cause?	COLUMN 3 Target of risk, danger or harm?	COLUMN 4 What is the level of danger?

STAYING SAFE TOOL B2: SAFETY PLAN & ACTION WORKSHEET

What Are Safety Plans? Safety Actions?

Once the level of harm and potential risks are considered, you and your allies or team will want to think about safety plans in case of emergency and safety actions to try to gain safety now and in the future.

Safety Plans

Safety plans are often considered for "what if" situations. It requires thinking through who one can call in an emergency, signals to others that one needs help, safekeeping of items needed if one needs to escape, plans to pick up children and keep them safe.

Safety Actions

Safety actions may need to take place immediately in order to be safe, reach safety, or get people immediately out of harm's way. Safety actions are particularly necessary in situations of crisis and high danger. This does not always mean danger in terms of physical harm but also danger of emotional, sexual, financial harm. It may include taking action to remove weapons or taking action to move children to a safer place. It may mean distracting someone who is dangerous in order to de-escalate situations of violence or get them away while more plans for safety are being made. It may also mean calling friends and family to begin to involve them in providing a safety network.

Gathering Together to Make a Safety Network

Because Safety Plans and Actions are often taken under conditions of danger, any move to take a Safety Action should involve at least one other person and preferably more trusted people to give back-up planning, support and follow-up.

Therefore, Safety Plans and Actions are best done with a group of community allies whose roles may include:

1. Brainstorming risks, safety plans and actions
2. Brainstorming who best can play various roles in creating safety
3. Getting more information on who can help or what dangers might be
4. Playing an active role in the safety plan or action

HOW TO USE THE SAFETY PLAN AND ACTION WORKSHEET

1. **Get together with another person or team to come up with this Safety Plan and Action Worksheet.**
2. **Make Risk Assessment Chart or look at Risk Assessment Chart if already made. Make sure it based on up-to-date information. (See Section Keeping Safe. Risk Assessment Chart)**
3. **Think about how each risk can match up to a Safety Plan to address that risk. You may need to start with the highest emergency risks (Emergency and Very High) before being able to address the risks with lower levels of danger.**
4. **For each risk or set of risks that go together, think about a Safety Plan:**
   a. *What do we need to do to be safe (or to reduce the risk)?*

   Categories of what you can do for safety can include the following:

   - Prepare for escape
   - Tell trusted people about the situation
   - Ask trusted people to take certain roles
     (See Section 4.C. Mapping Allies and Barriers for more roles)

ROLES

- Keep a watch for danger (may be something that is in a position to check and see)

- Emergency person to call

- Help to brainstorm in times of confusion or crisis

- Be there to remember plans and details

- Check in on a regular basis through stopping by, calls, emails, texts

- Share a "special message" so that they can get emergency help when that "special message" is given

- Offer physical protection

- Offer emotional or spiritual support

- Be around to act as a "witness" to harm

- Distract or reason with person or people doing harm

- Confront person or people doing harm to prevent further harm

- Go get and take care of children or other dependents if needed

- Go get and take care of pets if needed

- Offer home, workplace, church or other location as a safe place

- Offer to keep emergency items in a safe place

- Find out about and contact appropriate resources which could include violence intervention program/organization; counselor; knowledgeable family members or friends; internet; lawyer or legal services; workplace; union; school; and so on.
- Prepare or gather things that you need to take some kind of action
- Get locks or change locks as needed
- Keep certain things in protected areas – friend's home, safety deposit box, workplace

b. Safe ways to contact people

- Think about confidentiality and making sure that information does not become public because people share computers, voice mail, and can read other people's text messages

c. Safe transportation if needed

- Safe routes to take if needed
- Safe forms of transportation
- Safe place to park car
- Back-up transportation if needed
- Pick up of other allies, family, or friends if needed

d. Safe place to meet if needed

- Think about confidentiality and making sure that people are safe to talk
- If you are contacting the person doing harm or someone who is potentially harmful, think about meeting in a public space where there are people around

e. Safe places to escape to or hide if needed

- Depending on the situation, people may need safe places to hide or public places where they might be safer

f. Communication plan detailing

- Signs or signals that things are okay – or not okay
- Follow-up communication that things are or went okay – or not okay
- Follow-up communication for next steps
- Agreement on who can know what – and who cannot

5. Think about what requires immediate action. This Toolkit refers to these as Safety Actions. These may need to be taken to ensure minimal, bottom-line levels of safety. Safety Actions may come up in a situation of emergency, high risk. On the other hand, it may come up because there is an opportunity or opening to take action more easily now than later.

Examples of situations in which you may want to take a Safety Action include:

- Someone needs to escape from immediate risk of significant harm including injury, entrapment, physical or sexual assault, kidnapping, arrest, deportation, death
- Children or youth need to be removed from risk of significant harm of any sort
- Weapons need to be removed in order to decrease high level of danger
- Emergency health or mental health concerns require immediate action
- Someone causing harm needs to be immediately removed from a situation, asked to stay away, distracted from entering a situation, locked out, banned (at least temporarily), physically restrained (if this is necessary to keep them from causing harm)

While this Toolkit encourages transparent and honest communication and action, this will not always be possible, especially at early stages of intervention, and before support towards the higher goals of violence intervention can be agreed upon. Distraction, hiding information and outright dishonesty are at times necessary particularly in situations of high danger. Safety Plans and Actions may need to take into account attempts to trick someone or may require some level of force in order to carry out this action.

This may at times mean a level of dishonesty and/or some level of threats, force or restraint upon the person doing harm.

This Toolkit recognizes that pragmatic and practical action can aim at the highest values but may need to balance safety first. As interventions are able to include all aspects of support and cooperation including from the person or people doing harm, it may be able to bring in higher levels of transparency and honesty. This honesty could include open discussions about why earlier Safety Actions were carried out in less than honest ways.

SAFETY PLAN AND ACTION WORKSHEET

THIS SAFETY PLAN IS FOR THE FOLLOWING SITUATION:

THIS SAFETY PLAN COVERS THE TIME PERIOD:

THIS SAFETY PLAN IS AS FOLLOWS. THIS MAY INCLUDE:

What are the risks and dangers? Or what can go wrong?

Who do we need to look out for? Who or what can cause risks and dangers - people, situations, systems?

Who can get hurt? How?

What can we do to stay safe?

Who is responsible for what part of the safety plan?

Do we have all the bases covered? Do we need to bring in more people?

Is there an emergency back-up plan? What is it? How will we know we should go into emergency mode? Is there a signal or code?

THE FOLLOW-UP PLAN IS AS FOLLOWS. THIS MAY INCLUDE:

How did it go?

What did we learn?

How does this affect our safety plan? Our overall intervention?

Are there any changes to be made? What are they?

Who needs to communicate and to whom?

Who can know?

Who should not know?

What are the next steps?

STAYING SAFE TOOL B3: SAFETY PLAN & ACTION CHART

If it is helpful to have the Safety Plan and Action information in chart form, you can use this tool.

COLUMN 1: RISK, DANGER, OR HARM

In the first column, you can name the risk, danger or harm in your own words. Because this Safety Plan and Action Worksheet is aimed at narrow and specific situations, you may find that it is better to be quite detailed about the risk and/or the person who might be at risk (column 3).

COLUMN 2: WHO OR WHAT IS THE CAUSE

In the second column, you can name the person or situation that may be causing the harm. Harm may be directly threatened by a person or a potential system.

COLUMN 3: TARGET OF RISK, DANGER, OR HARM

In the third column, you can name the person or thing that is the target of risk, danger or harm. Think of anyone involved who could be harmed.

COLUMN 4: WHO IS LOOKING OUT FOR SAFETY

Think about who can be responsible for watching over or dealing with a particular risk. It may mean that if the risk is to a certain person, then it is this person's job to make sure that the person in question is safe. For example, many people may be in danger in a situation of domestic violence. A child may require the special attention of someone who makes sure that his or her needs do not drop out of the picture as people deal with a larger situation of violence. If someone's particular task is to focus on that child, then it may be easier to assure that he or she does not get left out or ignored, especially in times of crisis.

COLUMN 5: WHAT SAFETY ACTION AND UNDER WHAT CIRCUMSTANCES

This may take the form of small actions such as:

- Check to see if a particular risky or dangerous person is arriving
- Make sure children are in a safe place
- Keep a particular risky or dangerous person distracted
- Stay in the car, keeping watch nearby
- Make sure to offer a particular person emotional support during and/or after a Safety Action is taken

SAFETY PLAN & ACTION CHART

THIS SAFETY PLAN IS FOR THE FOLLOWING SITUATION:

THIS SAFETY PLAN COVERS THE TIME PERIOD:

COLUMN 1 Risk, danger or harm?	COLUMN 2 Who/What is the cause?	COLUMN 3 Target of risk, danger or harm?	COLUMN 4 Who is looking out for safety?	COLUMN 5 What safety actions and under what circumstances?

CAUTION

Is there an emergency back-up plan? What is it?

How will we know we should go into emergency mode? Is there a signal or code?

THE FOLLOW-UP PLAN IS AS FOLLOWS. THIS MAY INCLUDE:

How did it go?

What did we learn?

How does this affect our safety plan? Our overall intervention?

Are there any changes to be made? What are they?

Who needs to communicate and to whom?

Who can know?

Who should not know?

What are the next steps?

☑ *STAYING SAFE* TOOL B4: ESCAPE TO SAFETY CHECKLIST

Some people may be in a situation where they need to think about escaping. For many domestic violence programs, the safety plan equals an escape plan.

While this Toolkit conceives of safety as something more than an escape plan, there are times when people may need to think about escape.

If you have children and are thinking of leaving your partner, consider how to take children with you. Once you leave, it can be difficult to regain custody if your children are left with your partner.

We are including an example of an "escape to safety" plan for those may be in this situation. This was adapted from the National Coalition Against Domestic Violence (NCADV) website at http://www.ncadv.org/protectyourself/SafetyPlan_130.html.

IF YOU ARE STILL IN THE RELATIONSHIP:

- ☐ Think of a safe place to go if an argument occurs - avoid rooms with no exits (bathroom), or rooms with weapons (kitchen)
- ☐ Think about and make a list of safe people to contact
- ☐ Keep change with you at all times
- ☐ Memorize all important numbers
- ☐ Establish a "code word" or "sign" so that family, friends, teachers or co-workers know when to call for help
- ☐ Think about what you will say to your partner if they become violent
- ☐ Other ______________________________
- ☐ Other ______________________________

REMEMBER, YOU HAVE THE RIGHT TO LIVE WITHOUT FEAR AND VIOLENCE.

IF YOU HAVE LEFT THE RELATIONSHIP:

- ☐ Change your phone number
- ☐ Screen calls
- ☐ Save and document all contacts, messages, injuries or other incidents involving the person doing harm
- ☐ Change locks, if the person doing harm has a key
- ☐ Let neighbors know about your safety needs; see if they will look out for risky or dangerous people or act as a place for you to seek emergency help
- ☐ Avoid staying alone
- ☐ Plan how to get away if confronted by an abusive partner
- ☐ If you have to meet your partner, do it in a public place
- ☐ Vary your routine
- ☐ Notify school, work or other contacts of places you go to regularly
- ☐ Call a domestic violence crisis line or shelter
- ☐ Other ______________________________
- ☐ Other ______________________________

IF YOU HAVE LEFT THE RELATIONSHIP (CONTINUED):

If you leave the relationship or are thinking of leaving, you should take important papers and documents with you to enable you to apply for benefits or take legal action. If you are planning to leave or think that you may need to, keep these items in a place that is easy to grab if you are running or keep originals or copies with a safe friend, co-worker or neighbor.

- ☐ Driver's license or other identification for you and your children
- ☐ Social security cards and birth certificates for you and your children
- ☐ Marriage license
- ☐ Birth certificates for yourself and your children
- ☐ Passport for you and your children
- ☐ Immigration papers for you and your children
- ☐ Leases or deeds in your name or both yours and your partner's names
- ☐ Medication
- ☐ Your checkbook
- ☐ Your charge/credit cards
- ☐ Bank statements and charge account statements
- ☐ Insurance policies
- ☐ Proof of income for you and your spouse or domestic partner (pay stubs or W-2's; past taxes)
- ☐ Documentation of past incidents of abuse (photos, police reports, medical records, etc.)
- ☐ Set of keys to the house and car
- ☐ Title to your vehicle
- ☐ Other ____________________
- ☐ Other ____________________

STAYING SAFE TOOL B5: MEETING WITH PERSON DOING HARM SAFETY WORKSHEET

Many domestic violence or sexual assault programs recommend that people never meet with the person doing harm, assuming that physical separation is the only safe option and that calling the police or having contact through an attorney are the only ways to have contact. They also warn others not to have contact with the person doing harm.

This may not be realistic or desired for many people in situations of violence. This Toolkit explores the possibility of contacting, communicating with and possibly working together with the person or people doing harm towards a resolution in which harm can be addressed, reduced or ended and future harm can be prevented.

The survivor or victim may still have some kind of relationship with the person or people doing harm. They may even be living together. Even if the survivor or victim and the person doing harm are no longer in contact, other people may be involved in this intervention and may be dealing with the person doing harm.

CAUTION

Depending upon the situation, such meetings can carry risks such as:

- Danger of physical or sexual violence
- Danger of emotional and verbal abuse
- Threats of various forms of violence
- Intimidation and use of fear to get the survivor or victim to come back or stop any kind of intervention
- Manipulation (intended or unintended) to get the person to go along with the desires of the person or people doing harm
- Manipulation (intended or unintended) to get the person to doubt their own beliefs
- Lies that make the person doing harm appear innocent – or make the survivor or victim or other community members look like they are to blame

If someone (survivor or victim, community ally) decides to meet with the person or people doing harm with knowledge of these risks, then some ways to stay safer include the following:

- Go through the Risk Assessment and Safety Plan and Action sections above with at least two or more people.
- Be very clear with yourself about the reason for the meeting, the expectations of outcomes, and the possibility of reaching these outcomes – think about all of the ways that this could go wrong and be clear about how you will feel or what you will gain or lose in case things go wrong.
- Understand that risk can increase when people doing harm sense a loss of control. Dangers can escalate beyond what you might have thought was possible.
- Understand that promises to be cooperative, to have one last visit, to give back belongings and so on can be insincere ways to regain control or hurt someone.
- Meet in a public place where other people are around whenever possible.
- If for some reason the meeting needs to take place in a more private space, then go with another person or have someone waiting nearby and maintain contact with the safe person. Make sure that the door or other escapes are kept within your eyesight.
- Have some kind of code or special message for the person waiting and a back-up plan if you do not come out by a certain time.
- Role play with or think about all of the possibilities with at least one other person and have that person play all possible options including the worst case scenario of what could happen – prepare for the expected and the unexpected.
- Know that you can always change your mind and not meet.
- Think about ways you can communicate through safer means such as email, letter, safe friends or family, attorney or mediator rather than a face-to-face meeting.

 MEETING WITH PERSON DOING HARM WORKSHEET

If more than one person is meeting, substitute "we" for "I" and make sure that everyone going to the meeting is in agreement about the following.

1. I am meeting with _________________ under the following circumstances:

2. I am meeting for the following reasons or to get the following results:

3. I plan to get these results through the following words or actions (make sure that each expected reason or result in #2 is matched with appropriate words or actions):

4. I will not say or do the following things because that will get in the way of my safety and/or getting my goals:

5. The safest place and time (including length of time) for us to meet is:

6. The safest way to contact ______________ is (include who will contact, form of contact, words that will be used and not used):

7. Other safety concerns to think about (such as time of day, whether that person is sober or drug-free, whether that person is likely to have a weapon, whether that person may be with someone else who can be a danger, whether that person will be with children) are:

8. Other people that would be good to have along for reasons of safety are (include their role and their level of participation – observe and witness only; speak only to certain points; or take the most active role)

9. Other people that should know or be aware that this meeting is happening are:

10. Other people who should not know that this meeting is happening are:

11. Things that _______________ may think that they could gain from this meeting are the following (these may be things that have no relation to your own reasons):

12. When I say or do the things that I plan in Question #3, the possible reactions include:

(Role play each statement if possible. Think of or get other people to think of all of the possible things that the person doing harm might say or do – including worst case scenarios. Knowledgeable people may be others who know a lot about violence or people who know the person doing harm well including his or her faults. Be prepared. Think of how you will respond. Think of what you will say and not say. Make sure that everyone that will be going to the meeting is in agreement.)

13. After this meeting is over, people could be affected in the possible ways (Think about whether or not someone else's confidence might be broken, whether there could be retaliation against yourself or other people after the meeting is over, what kind of responses ____________ could have, what kind of other reactions might follow and whether there are supports in place):

14. Follow-up communication and support for each affected person can happen in the following ways:

15. During the meeting, I will stick with the following words and actions (best to keep to 1 or 2 main points).

16. During the meeting, I will not say or do the following no matter what.

17. Emergency situations may include the following:

18. I have a plan to respond to each emergency in the following ways:

19. I need more information on the following in order to make this a safe and effective meeting.

20. My next steps in preparation for the meeting are the following (include plans to contact other people or resources, adequate support for after the meeting and more information needed).

21. I have gone through this worksheet and have:

- ☐ Read through Section 2. Some Basics Everyone Should Know section
- ☐ Read through the entire Section 4.B. Staying Safe section
- ☐ Answered every question in this worksheet thoroughly with the help of at least one other appropriate person
- ☐ Followed through with all preparations (See Question 20)
- ☐ Thought of all possible responses that ______________ could have
- ☐ Thought of my possible responses carefully
- ☐ Shared this worksheet with everyone else who will go and made sure that they agree – if they are expected to talk and act during the meeting, then they have also actively answered all questions in this worksheet
- ☐ Considered emergency worst-case scenarios and have an emergency plan for each
- ☐ Feel confident that this meeting is worth having and safety risks are worth taking
- ☐ Have someone I can trust to check in with and get support from before and after the meeting takes place

CAUTION

If you were not able to check all of these boxes, then we urge you to reconsider this meeting and take more time to see if you can get a greater level of safety before moving on.

4C MAPPING ALLIES & BARRIERS: WHO CAN HELP?

C.1. What is Mapping Allies and Barriers?

C.2. Mapping Allies and Barriers Across the Four Phases

C.3. Tips

C.4. Special Considerations

C.5. Facilitator Notes

C.6. Real Life Stories and Examples

C.7. Mapping Allies and Barriers Tools

C.1. WHAT IS *MAPPING ALLIES & BARRIERS*?

Key Questions

- Who can help?
- Who can get in the way?
- Who is in a good position to support the survivor or victim?
- Who is in a good position to offer support to the person or people doing harm?
- Who can become an ally or become a better ally with a little bit of help?
- What kind of help do they need and who can give it?

What Is It?

Mapping Allies and Barriers involves taking a look at who we have around us as helpers and community resources (allies). It also involves looking at who could get in the way of an intervention (barriers). It may also include looking at "swing" people – people who could be better allies with a little bit of help. Swing people may even be barriers who have the potential to become allies.

Community allies can play all kinds of roles in interventions to violence. They can provide support (practical, emotional, etc.) to the person who has been harmed; they can contribute to engagement, support, and accountability with the person doing harm; they can support other allies playing more involved or higher-risk roles in the intervention; and they can provide logistical or interpersonal support to the intervention team.

Why Is It Important?

This model is based on the idea that working together collectively gives us more support, power, resources and good ideas than working alone. It is also based on the idea that communities have a responsibility to come together to end violence and that we all directly benefit by creating a safer, healthier community.

Finding and mapping community allies and barriers involves looking at the people and organizations around you. Who can play a role? It may be people near and dear. Or it may be people we don't know well but who can play an important role in dealing with a particular situation of harm. They may be people who can stick around for the long-haul of an intervention, or people who can play a useful role here and there.

When we build our teams with care and consideration, we create teams that build the morale of individual members and the intervention overall. We can create teams that last.

USING THE TOOLS IN THIS SECTION

The Mapping Allies and Barriers section offers basic information and tools to help you think about who can be brought to help (allies) and who you might need to avoid or work around (barriers).

If you need simpler, shorter tools to help when you are in immediate crisis or have less time, refer to Tool C1. Mapping Allies & Barriers Snapshot/Quick Guided Questions.

When you get more time, you can go through Tool C2. Mapping Allies & Barriers Worksheet.

The checklists, Tool C3. Ally Roles Checklist and Tool C4. Good Ally Checklist can help you to brainstorm about different roles that allies can play and what characteristics make for a good ally.

Thinking about allies specifically to support the person doing harm can take special thought. Tool C5. Allies to Work with the Person Doing Harm Chart can help.

Tool C6. Barriers Checklist can help determine who or what might be getting in the way of an intervention.

When you are ready to sum up who you might have as an ally and/or a barrier, you can use Tool C7. Allies and Barriers: Summary.

And, finally, Tool C8. Invitation to Help with an Intervention helps you to think through the steps to invite other people – or to figure out what to do if they do not want to or cannot join. It gives an example of a script to use and things to think about giving them in order for them to be a better ally – even if they do not choose to join.

C.2. *MAPPING ALLIES & BARRIERS* ACROSS THE 4 PHASES

In Section 3.6. Interventions Over Time: 4 Phases, the Toolkit introduced the idea of 4 possible phases of interventions: 1) Getting Started, 2) Planning/Preparation, 3) Taking Action, and 4) Following Up.

Mapping Allies and Barriers can look different at different phases or levels of crisis. It involves team building and matching specific allies to specific roles. It can take place at all stages of an intervention because after every action we take, we assess how it went, what makes sense to do next, and who might be able to help (or might have a hard time, or might get in the way, or might need a one-on-one check-in, etc.). Mapping community allies and barriers can look one way when we first get started and build our initial team, and then look a different way once we start planning and taking different actions.

PHASE 1: GETTING STARTED

When we first start talking with each other about addressing or stopping a situation of violence, we may sit with just one other person (a close friend, family member, witness to the violence, person affected by the violence, etc.) to brainstorm who could help us and who might stand in our way.

We may initially think there is no one who can help. Or we may name one or two supportive people, and also identify a pool of people who might be able to help later, depending on what we decide to do. Sometimes it can be helpful to think about anyone (and everyone) who could possibly play a helpful role in an intervention, and to separate them into groups such as the following:

1. People who seem like they can be active members of a core team now;
2. People who can be pulled in for specific contributions later depending on what the team's goals become;
3. People who are well positioned to support and communicate with the survivor;
4. People who are well positioned to engage the person who did (or is doing) harm;
5. People who could have a good impact on the intervention but who need some guidance, encouragement, or education in order to become allies;
6. People who might sabotage the team's efforts.

PHASE 2: PLANNING/PREPARATION

We may build our initial team based on who is naturally involved in a supportive way right now, and do initial goal-setting with those few people that maps out who else to bring into the team. For example, a small initial team may form and make an immediate plan to build for allies or create a team. As the intervention progresses, it might become necessary to find new allies. Or we may find that new allies have entered the picture.

PHASE 3: TAKING ACTION

When we take action, we might be taking action to build more allies, or we might be taking action with allies to support survivors and engage people who are using violence. When we take action we may discover any or all of the following:

1. Some of the allies we mapped are not ready to be allies;
2. Someone we thought was a barrier may actually be more ready than we thought to take a positive role in the intervention;
3. A team member or ally who thought they could take the agreed upon action decides it is too hard and they can't take that kind of action again;
4. In the pressure of the moment, one or more allies does not act according to plan, or takes action on their own in a way that affects the trust of others on the team and their opinion of the person as an ally;
5. An ally playing a specific role has a positive experience and wants to join the team in an ongoing way.

PHASE 4: FOLLOWING-UP

When we follow-up on how the action went and how it affected everyone involved, we learn a lot about our map of allies and barriers.

Sometimes we learn that potential allies are not participating in the way that we'd wanted or hoped. Sometimes we need to re-assess the situation, identify and plan for the next best step toward our goal, and then map and engage a second set of potential allies who can take that next step.

RELATED TOOLS

Tools to help pass on necessary information to allies are in the section Section 4.A. Getting Clear.

Tools to help allies work better together are in Section 4.G. Working Together.

Tools to help the collective group look at your goals or what you want to achieve are in the Section 4.D. Goal Setting.

C.3. *MAPPING ALLIES & BARRIERS* TIPS

#1 READ *SOME BASICS EVERYONE SHOULD KNOW.*

Interpersonal violence is complicated. Although we may hear more about domestic violence or sexual assault these days, many misunderstandings still exist and many misconceptions about what it is and how to approach it. Read *Section 2. Some Basics Everyone Should Know.* Pay special attention to *Section 2.2. Interpersonal Violence: Some Basics Everyone Should Know* in order to have a clearer picture of what is going on. The *Section 2.3. Violence Intervention: Some Important Lessons* also shares important basics about interventions based upon the experiences of Creative Interventions.

Share this information with others who may be involved in a situation of violence andmay need some resources to help them know what to do.

#2 WATCH OUT FOR EXTREMES: "NOBODY CAN HELP" OR "EVERYONE SHOULD HELP" IN MAPPING ALLIES AND BARRIERS.

Extreme #1 can look like this: "There is absolutely no one who can help." Revisit goalsetting so that existing team members can brainstorm allies who can help with specific goals. Many more resources may appear when you focus on the intermediate steps,instead of thinking of a total transformation as the only or the immediate goal of an intervention.

Extreme #2 can look like this: "Let's make this team huge! Let's get everyone on board! Let's call a community meeting!" Be sure you have considered whether you are ready, and have clear goals and clear examples or ideas of how people can engage and contribute. Have you thought through the medium-term and long-term impact of team-building actions? Can you bring people in at different stages?

#3 BE CREATIVE IN FINDING ALLIES AMONG THOSE WHO MAY LOOK LIKE BARRIERS NOW.

Most of us are not taught how to be a good ally – especially in situations of violence. But learning the skills to become a good ally can come about through useful information and helpful support from others. Think about how your information, support and tools found in this Toolkit could turn those "swing" people who now look like barriers or poor allies into good allies. Think about who is best to deliver this information and how best to use these or other tools.

#4 PRIORITIZE SAFETY.

If there are truly no allies who are positioned to engage the person doing harm to make positive changes, or if the risk for the survivor(s) or victims or for the people involved in the intervention is too high, pause and pay attention. If there are no safe allies, reassess the goals and scope of your intervention. Think about whether it is safe to wait until more allies are available. Think about whether you might need to seek more traditionally available anti-violence resources that do not rely on other friends, family, or other community members.

#5 WATCH OUT FOR COMMON ALLY PROBLEM AREAS.

a. Look out for allies who have supported the survivor or victim (or perceived survivor or victim) and who come to feel so much anger, disgust, impatience, or desire to "get even" with the person doing harm that they cannot step outside of those feelings. These allies may have difficulty considering the success of the bigger picture goals of the intervention, or belittle all positive steps made by the person doing harm. Help people understand that while these are common and understandable responses, they may not be the best responses. People who cannot step out of these extreme reactions may find different roles to play or may step back for awhile.

b. Look out for allies who have supported the person doing harm and who start to: 1) protect that person from the intervention; 2) sabotage the intervention; 3) argue that the survivor(s) were equally responsible for the situation of violence and need to be held equally accountable; or 4) influence others to believe that the survivor or victim is "crazy." Ask questions to understand what is going on for the ally. Ask them to look at tools in *Section 4.E. Supporting Survivors or Victims* or *4.F. Taking Accountability* that might be helpful.

c. Look out for team members or potential allies who are or become too deeply and personally affected by the situation of violence to be able to contribute in a constructive way, or to have any separation between their own personal experiences and reactions and the way they participate in the intervention. Consider ways to integrate self-reflection into all meetings or conversations about the intervention. See Self-Reflection tools in *Section 4.G. Keeping on Track* for help.

#6 TRY TO INCLUDE AT LEAST SOME ALLIES WHO ARE NOT HEAVILY IMPACTED BY THE VIOLENCE.

It can be helpful to include people who have some distance from the violence and who can bring fresh new perspectives to the group. Don't only think of those closest to the situation as possible allies or team members. If you allow some space for creativity, you may think of people who are not obvious – but who may be a very good fit.

C.4. *MAPPING ALLIES & BARRIERS* SPECIAL CONSIDERATIONS

Allies can play many different roles for different people involved in a violence intervention. Some allies may be particularly helpful for supporting the survivor or victim. Allies can also be there to support others who are working on the situation of violence – that is, allies can be allies t o each other. It may be especially important to think about who makes sense to be an ally to the person or people doing harm. Below are questions that can be useful for thinking about who can be a good ally and how we can make good use of allies.

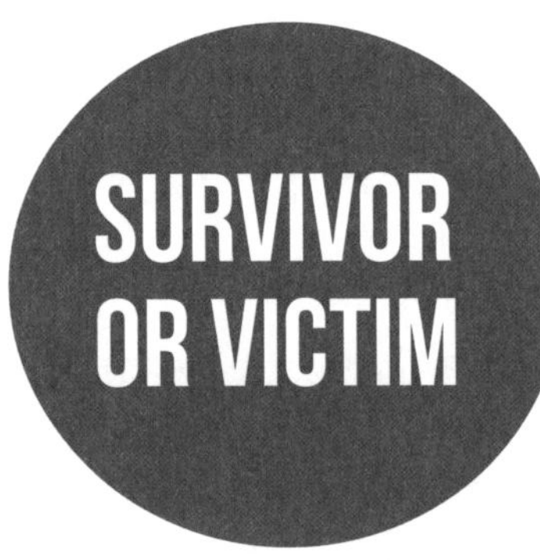

As interventions get complex and long, it is easy to isolate the survivor or victim if this person is not centrally involved, blame the survivor or victim or rely so much on the survivor or victim that they are carrying the burden of the intervention.

It is good to have people who the survivor or victim trusts to make sure that they are supported through the entire process, that their humanity and needs for compassion and healing are attended to. Interventions do not always lead to healing directly. They can leave survivors or victims raw and hurt. While this may at times be unavoidable, strong allies who not only take care of tasks but also warmth, comfort and understanding is important.

If you are the survivor or victim, you can think of some of the following questions. Who do you go to for support? Who listens to your experience? Who can help you recenter yourself during times when you start spinning into negative patterns of feelings or actions?

As more allies are brought into the team or engaged to play a specific role in the intervention, think about what personal information about your experience you want to share or not share with them? What is necessary? If it's hard on you to share that information over and over again, who else could share it for you? (See Section 4.A. Getting Clear for some tools to help you figure out what information is important and how to document it so that you do not need to keep repeating it.

When others start talking about who could be an ally to engage the person who has done harm, be prepared for what might be some hard conversations. Allies who can help support the person who has harmed you to take responsibility might not be the best people for you to consider as your personal allies. How will you prepare for those difficult conversations? Do you want to be part of all of them? Take some time to be specific about what you want to be part of and what you don't.

As this is a collective model, think about how you can respond if others disagree with what you want. Get support to help you through these difficulties.

During times when you are having a really hard time and need a break, is there an ally on the team with whom you could share your concerns and insights so that they could share it with the rest of the team or group of supporters.

Some things to think about are:

Are there specific requests you have of the allies working on the intervention?

Do you need support to voice your concerns with the group along the way? Who could support you to voice them?

What friends or supporters do you have outside of the intervention that can help you with personal healing and rebuilding that is separate from the intervention?

Use the Tools in this to help you think about allies (and barriers) and how to make good ally relations.

Community allies are generally those who provide support and play an ally role. Most of this section is focused on how to identify and get strong community allies. Allies may also need their own allies for support. Getting people who can look out for the well-being of everyone is important.

If you are the community ally, think about the following. Who do you want to build a team with? How can you contribute to building a team culture and team experience that makes you want to stay involved? How can you avoid bringing in people who do not have collaborative skills and/or easily become argumentative, antagonizing, or fixated on one approach being the only "right" one?

Use the Tools in this section to help you think about allies (and barriers) and how to make good ally relations.

Getting allies for the person doing harm is a very important part of the process. Allies are not people who will excuse violence, feel sorry for the person doing harm, and see "their side of the story." They are also not there to humiliate and punish the person doing harm to make sure that "justice is done." They are there to support accountability or that person's ability to recognize, end and take responsibility for their violence.

If you are the person doing harm or are the person accused of doing harm, think about allies as people who can support you to take responsibility or accountability for the harm – and not those who will protect you from having to take responsibility. This may be a very different way for you to think about allies or friends.

Think about who can help you feel seen and understood, without supporting you to continue the behaviors and patterns that you are trying to change. Who can you imagine going to when you mess up, fall back into an old pattern, and use violence again? How can you see their reminders of your responsibility as helpful rather than attacking or blaming?

Remember to remind yourself that someone can support the person you've harmed without becoming your enemy. Though it's easy to see people as "taking sides," try to push yourself into viewing allies as people who will help you turn away from using violence and experiencing the negative consequences of using violence.

Use the Tools in this section to help you think about allies (and barriers) and how to make good ally relations.

FACILITATOR

People are rarely 100% allies or 100% barriers. Try supporting the group to think creatively and to expand out of "black and white" and "either/or" thinking. When we think of people as 100% allies, we can overlook ways in which they are not the best fit in to certain roles. When we think of people as 100% barriers, we can miss ways in which they could be well suited to a specific task. It is possible for participants in an intervention to be allies to one goal and barriers to another.

#1 ENCOURAGE AND SUPPORT PEOPLE TO LEARN FUNDAMENTAL INFORMATION FIRST IF THEY HAVE NOT ALREADY.

This Toolkit is long and can be overwhelming. Some important parts of this Toolkit are Section 2. Some Basics Everyone Should Know. An especially important section can be Section 2.2. Interpersonal Violence: Some Basics Everyone Should Know that discusses much more about the dynamics of violence and common misunderstandings that people have.

It can be useful for you to be familiar with the different sections of this Toolkit and to read more carefully through these sections. Also encourage people to read these sections. If reading is not the best option or they cannot read English or the language that this Toolkit is in, you can help by reading this and other sections to them in a language they understand or use other formats to pass on this information.

#2 SUPPORT PEOPLE BY GOING THROUGH THESE MAPPING ALLIES AND BARRIERS INFORMATION AND TOOLS THAT SEEM USEFUL.

You may be helping people through the process of mapping allies and barriers, and then choosing allies. When supporting the group through the intervention, you may need to help the group map allies and barriers over and over again. As you do so, look out for the ways in which allies and barriers can change over time Pay special attention to the following patterns that are also described in Tips, #7.

#3 PAY SPECIAL ATTENTION TO IF YOU ARE BRINGING TOGETHER PEOPLE WHO WERE SUPPORTING THE SURVIVOR WITH PEOPLE WHO ARE FRIENDS OR SUPPORTERS OF THE PERSON DOING HARM

a. Find ways to help people focus on the goals of the intervention and of stopping violence. Steer people away from convincing each other about what version of the story is true or false, accurate or exaggerated, or what dynamics in the situation or relationship were messed up or unhealthy.

b. Help the team remember that they are not there to evaluate every last aspect of the situation or relationship. There is no way that any one of them knows the full story of what happened. They are there to reduce and stop violence, not agree on an explanation for why the violence happened. They are not there to design a therapy plan for everyone involved.

#4 MAKE SURE NEW ALLIES BROUGHT INTO THE PROCESS ARE GIVEN THE NECESSARY INFORMATION. MAKE GOOD USE OF THE HARMS CHART OR HARMS STATEMENT DESCRIBED IN THE *SECTION 4.A. GETTING CLEAR*.

a. Find ways to help people focus on the goals of the intervention and of stopping violence. Steer people away from convincing each other about what version of the story is true or false, accurate or exaggerated, or what dynamics in the situation or relationship were messed up or unhealthy.

b. Help the team remember that they are not there to evaluate every last aspect of the situation or relationship. There is no way that any one of them knows the full story of what happened. They are there to reduce and stop violence, not agree on an explanation for why the violence happened. They are not there to design a therapy plan for everyone involved.

C.4. *MAPPING ALLIES & BARRIERS* REAL LIFE STORIES & EXAMPLES

Story C. My Husband Is Hitting Our Daughter: Who Can Help?

My husband's abuse toward our first daughter started even before she was barely a year old. He clearly had lots of problem managing his own frustration and didn't seem to know how to discipline kids appropriately. He often yelled at her and spanked her when she was little. This sort of violence continued until my daughter was in sixth grade.

One incident that comes to my mind is when my daughter was about five or six years old. On the living room couch, my husband was trying to pull out one of her teeth which was shaking badly. My daughter was obviously scared and didn't want to do it. Although I knew he was getting impatient with her, I decided not to intervene at that moment since it usually made things worse. I heard my daughter crying and my husband's frustrated voice. And suddenly my daughter started to cry even louder. I remained in my bedroom. My husband went out shortly afterwards, so I came out to see if my daughter was okay. When I asked her what happened, she simply said, "Dad hit me." "Where?" I asked. She pointed her finger to her face. When I saw the mark of his hand across her face, I became furious.

The pattern was always the same. He would tell our daughter to do something or bring him something. If she didn't do it immediately, he would get upset. Then, he would shout and tell her again. If she complained or tried to explain why she couldn't do it, he got angry and accused her of talking back to him. Then he hit her. It tended to get worse if I tried to intervene or if my daughter even looked at me.

One evening, my husband and I were having an argument about the time he hit her when he was trying to pull her tooth. We were arguing in the car on the way back from church. He kept insisting that he didn't hit her at all. I became so angry that I got out of the car and walked away. I later called my friend to come and pick me up. In the meantime, I later found out that he told my oldest daughter that everything was her fault. He blamed her for my leaving the family that evening. This had a serious impact on my daughter; she still remembers his exact words years later.

I returned home that night and again got into an argument with my husband who shouted that he didn't hit her. I thought about next step, and I started to break things in the kitchen. The next day, I cut all of his shoes with scissors.

I then decided to call my father, my husband's older sister, and one of a mutual good friend/mentor. I called my father and my husband's older sister in order to reach out to the person in authority on each side of the family. They called him separately and confronted him. This was my attempt to make him somehow accountable for his behavior. I also called our mutual friend/mentor whom he respects, hoping that this might have an impact on him in the long run.

My father called my husband and told him that it was wrong to hit a child and that it shouldn't happen again. When our friend/mentor heard what had happened, he came over to our home right away. He saw my daughter's face and confronted my husband about his hitting. My husband was clearly upset and embarrassed to the person in authority on each side of the family. They called him separately and confronted him. This was my attempt to make him somehow accountable for his behavior. I also called our mutual friend/mentor whom he respects, hoping that this might have an impact on him in the long run.

My father called my husband and told him that it was wrong to hit a child and that it shouldn't happen again. When our friend/mentor heard what had happened, he came over to our home right away. He saw my daughter's face and confronted my husband about his hitting. My husband was clearly upset and embarrassed.

In the meantime, I told my daughter that it wasn't her fault and told her and my son not to worry if they hear loud voices. My goal that night was really making him feel sorry for what he did so that any future abuse can be prevented or greatly reduced.

It wasn't like I had a plan for that sort of situation. I had to think hard and fast to do all the things I could so that his behavior would stop. Although the people I called were supportive and did what they can to let him know how wrong it was to hit a child, I doubted that it would have a long lasting effect on him. I acted on my instincts and attempted to involve more people. What I was thinking all along, however, was that it is necessary for him to experience a more profound change within him to really change.

When my father, his sister, and our friend/mentor called, my husband initially denied hitting our daughter. He was angry with me for telling other people. He said I was "making a big deal out of nothing." As they continued to confront him, his denial slowly disappeared. He was upset at the fact that I had contacted several people, but became more embarrassed over time.

The intervention helped. He did stop hitting our daughter after that time, but the profound changes didn't come until later. Two things seemed to make the deepest impact. First, one of his friends shared his own story about how his grown up daughter wants to maintain distance with him because of his verbal and physical abuse toward her while growing up. This personal sharing had a big impact on my husband who always wanted to have close relationships with his kids. Second, my husband experienced a spiritual breakthrough, and he began to look at different parts of his life. He has changed so much since then.

Looking back, I think that one of the major impacts of my interventions was that my oldest daughter felt more secure and safe at home knowing that I would never overlook her dad's violent behavior. Although it took many more years before my husband was able to control his temper and stop violent behavior, my husband did realize that I will not stand for it if he treats our children in an abusive way.

I think that any kind of intervention is important. It may not stop the violence from happening again, but it almost always helps children.

TOOLS

4.C MAPPING ALLIES & BARRIERS

Tool C1. Mapping Allies & Barriers: Snapshot/Quick Guided Questions

Tool C2. Mapping Allies & Barriers: Worksheet

Tool C3. Ally Roles Checklist

Tool C4. Good Ally Checklist

Tool C5. Allies to Work with the Person Doing Harm Chart

Tool C6. Barrier Checklist

Tool C7. Allies and Barriers: Summary

Tool C8. Invitation to Help with an Intervention

MAPPING ALLIES & BARRIERS TOOL C1: WHAT IS GOING ON? SNAPSHOT/QUICK QUESTION GUIDE

You can use this Snapshot/Quick Guided Questions to help to get started thinking about allies and barriers and as a way to make snapshots along the way. This just asks some possible basic questions to start thinking about who can get involved – and who should be avoided.

- Who can help (when and how, or toward which goal)?
- Who can potentially hurt the situation?
- Who is in a good position to offer support to the victim or survivor?
- Who is in a good position to offer support to the person or people doing harm?
- Who can become an ally or become a stronger ally with a little bit of help?
- What kind of help do they need and who can give it?

MAPPING ALLIES & BARRIERS TOOL C2: MAPPING ALLIES WORKSHEET

What is it and how can we use it?

Here are some exploratory questions related to mapping allies and barriers and doing initial team-building. Skim through them and answer the ones that stand out as clear and helpful to you! You do not need to get bogged down in thinking that you must answer all of them. You can get more specific later.

These are some basic questions:

- Who can help?
- Who do you usually turn to for help? Would they be helpful in this situation?
- Who can be helpful to the survivor?
- Who can be influential with and helpful to the person doing harm? Who can help support person doing harm to stop using violence, take accountability, repair harm, and/or learn new behaviors?
- Who is connected to the situation and could help out in some way?
- Who is disconnected from the situation but could still help out in some way?
- Who might seem good at first glance, but actually could pose some problems or challenges to the intervention?
- Who might be great if they had the right information and got some support?
- Who do you know who is good at working in groups or is a good team player?
- Who do you know is good at thinking through complex situations without jumping to conclusions or leaping to take action on their own?
- Who do you know who is a great communicator?
- Who do you know who is skilled at bringing together people with strong differences of opinion?
- Who do you know who can cheer people on, appreciate what others are good at or have accomplished, and build team morale?
- Who do you know who is not afraid of conflict or confrontation, or who can stay calm in stressful situations?

- Who do you know who has resources they could share—a car, a living room, flip chart paper and markers, a safe place to sleep, a temporary cell phone, etc.?
- Would these people be good allies to help in this intervention? Why? Why not?
- If not or you're not sure, is there anything that can be done to make them a better ally? What?
- What kind of role can they play?
- Can you see them being a key person on a team that meets regularly? Or for a long time?
- Would they be willing to meet together to talk about this intervention?
- What would they need to make this meeting possible?
- Would they benefit from reading any part of this Toolkit – or have someone go over it with them?
- Which parts would be important? Who could do that?

☑ *MAPPING ALLIES & BARRIERS* TOOL C3: ALLY ROLES CHECKLIST

This is a checklist that can help you focus your thinking and assessment of individual people who might be able to help out as community allies and the roles they might play. Go through the checklist. What do your responses reveal to you?

Some potential ally roles (If you are considering if you might be a good ally, then check the roles with yourself in mind):

- ☐ Act as a facilitator for the intervention
- ☐ Coordinate logistics like where are we meeting, when, what do we need
- ☐ Take notes
- ☐ Keep track of goals
- ☐ Keep track of decisions
- ☐ Keep track of timelines (including start and end times for meetings)
- ☐ Make sure next steps were followed by checking in with people
- ☐ Make sure to think about risks and safety planning (See Section Staying Safe)
- ☐ Be a good reality check
- ☐ Defuse or reduce physical conflict
- ☐ Defuse or reduce emotional conflict
- ☐ Offer useful information about the dynamics of violence – may include their own experience if they are comfortable to share
- ☐ Be emotionally supportive to the victim or survivor or other people directly affected by violence (for example, children)
- ☐ Be emotionally supportive to people taking action in the intervention
- ☐ Be emotionally supportive to the person doing harm
- ☐ Offer resources (money, food, rides, shelter, storage, etc.) to the victim or survivor or other people directly affected by violence (for example, children)
- ☐ Offer resources (money, food, rides, shelter, storage, etc.) to support people taking action in the intervention
- ☐ Offer resources (money, food, rides, shelter, storage, etc.) to the person doing harm
- ☐ Be a person who can communicate well with the survivor or people affected by violence (for example, children)
- ☐ Be a person who can communicate well with the person doing harm
- ☐ Be a person who can communicate well with others involved in the intervention
- ☐ Drive if/when necessary
- ☐ Pick up supplies if/when necessary
- ☐ Hold meetings in their home or office or other space if/when necessary
- ☐ Cook or provide food for meetings
- ☐ Provide for spiritual needs (for example, hold a prayer, bless the space, provide spiritual counseling for anyone involved in the intervention, etc.)
- ☐ Other: ______________________

☑ *MAPPING ALLIES & BARRIERS* TOOL C4: GOOD ALLY CHECKLIST

Think about a potential ally and check the box if this person: (If you are considering if you might be a good ally, then check the box with yourself in mind)

- ☐ Is a good listener
- ☐ Has a good understanding of dynamics of violence or is willing to learn
- ☐ Will not blame the survivor or victim or will be open to understanding that blaming is not helpful
- ☐ Can think about the person doing harm with compassion (even if they are outraged, angered, disgusted, etc.)
- ☐ Does not always have to be right – can be part of group decision-making
- ☐ Does not always have to be the center of attention – can be a good team player
- ☐ Is not a gossip or at least will not gossip about this situation
- ☐ Is a good communicator or is willing to learn how to be better
- ☐ Is good at follow-through or would be for this situation
- ☐ Has some time to be available for conversations, meetings, etc.

LOOKING AT THE BOXES, WOULD YOU SAY...

☐ THIS PERSON WOULD BE A GOOD ALLY:

Good qualities:

Potential roles:

Next steps:

☐ THIS PERSON COULD BE AN IMPORTANT GOOD ALLY, BUT:

They could use help with:

Good ways to provide this help are:

Good people to provide this help are:

Next steps:

☐ THIS PERSON IS MOST LIKELY NOT A GOOD ALLY AND IS EVEN A DANGER TO THE INTERVENTION (SEE MAPPING COMMUNITY BARRIERS)

☐ THIS PERSON IS MOST LIKELY NOT A GOOD ALLY BUT IS NOT A DANGER WE CAN KEEP THEM IN MIND FOR THE FUTURE

MAPPING ALLIES & BARRIERS TOOL C5: ALLIES TO WORK WITH THE PERSON DOING HARM CHART

Right from the start, you may want to think about allies whose special role is to engage the person doing harm. This is a particularly important role but one that can be a difficult role to play.

Generally speaking, it is hard to take responsibility for and to change harmful behaviors (think of the last time you were successful in meaningfully changing something about your own behavior!). It is especially hard when others openly demand it of you. It is pretty much impossible when we are left to do it alone without support and in the face of judgment, criticism, and contempt.

So when working toward goals that involve supporting a person doing harm to take accountability for violence, mapping allies and barriers is critically important.

When planning to help support accountability or make it possible, it is important to think through who in the community is best positioned to help make it possible, and who in the community might get in the way, or make accountability less likely to happen. To do so, look at the community contexts surrounding situations of violence. They can be very diverse.

1. Sometimes there is a natural community surrounding the situation. It might be neighbors, family members, witnesses in a workplace, a friend group, etc.
2. Sometimes the person doing harm has very few social relationships and/or has burned bridges (destroyed relationships) in their past, leaving no people who are willing or well-situated to provide them support.
3. Similarly, survivors can also be extremely isolated, and/or have lost friends and supporters as a situation of violence and its impact in their life has progressed.
4. In still other situations, especially those in which the interpersonal violence happened outside of any kind of ongoing relationship, there might be very little (or no) overlap between people who know the survivor and people who know the person who did harm. Mapping allies and barriers will look different in these situations.

Overall, there are a few basic trends:

1. It is often easier to engage allies to provide support to the survivor or victim, to team members, or to the intervention overall, than it is to find support for the person doing harm.
2. Unfortunately, it can also be easy to engage allies to protect the person using violence by making excuses for them, justifying their behavior or criticizing those who are trying to stop or address the violence.
3. It is harder to find and nurture allies who can and are willing to engage people who are using violence and support them to reduce, stop and transform it.

Helping your friends, family members, or acquaintances take accountability for their violence and practice new coping and communication strategies and behaviors is hard. How do can you tell who can help and who might hurt? Tips on mapping allies and barriers related to supporting accountability are below. Remember to think creatively! Sometimes people might not be who we first expected.

Accountability allies can be people who...	People who might be barriers to accountability and transformation (but who might still support the intervention in other ways) can be people who....
Matter to the person doing harm.	Have no connection or have a negative connection to the person who did harm.
Can see the person doing harm as a human being deserving of basic respect and compassion.	Feel anger, disgust, disdain, rage, or contempt to the point that their approach to the person doing harm would be overwhelmed by judgment, criticism, harshness, etc.
Understand the harmful impact(s) of the violence, even when met with anger, tears, defensiveness, or emotional collapse (etc.) from the person doing harm.	Minimize or deny the harmful impact(s) of the violence, especially when they see any sign of anger, tears, defensiveness, or emotional collapse (etc.) from the person doing harm.
Can be clear and specific in their communication.	Get thrown off easily by other people's responses, make huge generalizations or are unclear and unspecific in their communication.
Have a sense of when to back off and give someone some space or time to take in new information.	"Go for the jugular" or go for the extreme point at all costs or who push their point and do not notice when 1) the other person is unable to hear more; or 2) when their communication is having a negative impact on reaching their goal.
Can get support to sustain the hard experience of being rejected by the person doing harm, or becoming the (perhaps new) target of that person's anger or criticism.	When rejected or targeted by the person doing harm, either 1) responds with anger in a way that escalates the situation; or 2) does not get support and ends up incapable of sustaining themselves as the other person struggles against accountability; or 3) buckles to the intimidation, critique, or other form of retaliation from the person doing harm.
Can develop understanding and compassion for the person doing harm's emotions and experience, but keep that separate from condoning or supporting the person doing harm's uses of violence.	Develops understanding and compassion for the person doing harm's emotions and experience, and connects that with 1) justifying the person doing harm's uses of violence; and 2) an increased questioning and criticism of the survivor's imperfect behaviors or imperfect attempts to stop the violence.
Can help motivate the person doing harm to withstand community involvement or exposure, resist pushing everyone away, and make a positive change.	Can only "say my piece" or "tell the truth" and leave it to the person doing harm alone to figure out how to change.
Can assess that how the person doing harm behaves with them (during times of calm, with people who are not the targets of their controlling or violent behavior, etc.) is not reflective of how the person behaves in all situations.	Experience a positive connection or moment with the person doing harm and decide that their behavior can't have been "that bad" based on their own experience.
Can communicate clearly and regularly with other team members, even when there might be disagreement or conflict in the team.	Avoid conflict or disagreement by withdrawing from communication or potentially sabotaging the intervention.

☑ *MAPPING ALLIES & BARRIERS* TOOL C6: BARRIERS CHECKLIST

This tool is to help to identify people or organizations who are barriers or roadblocks to an intervention. Key questions are: Who should not know about this intervention? Who should not be involved? Can anything be done to change them to become an ally or a neutral person (and not a barrier)?

Think about potential barriers to the intervention. (If you are considering if you might be a ally, then check the box with yourself in mind.) Check the box if this person or organization:

- ☐ Will tell people who should not be told about the intervention – even if trying to be helpful (this could include person doing harm, others who will tell person doing harm, police or other authorities you do not want to get involved – at least for now, etc.).
- ☐ Benefits in a significant way from the violence or thinks that they do.
- ☐ Could suffer negative consequences by actions taken to address, reduce, end, or prevent violence.
- ☐ Believes that the violence is okay.
- ☐ Is dependent (financially, emotionally, due to immigration status, etc.) on the person doing harm.
- ☐ Is likely to feel threatened if people try to address, end or prevent violence.
- ☐ Will "blame the victim."
- ☐ Could otherwise harm the survivor or increase their vulnerability.
- ☐ Is likely to harm the person doing harm if they find out or know that others are taking action.
- ☐ Gossips in a way which will threaten the success of an intervention.
- ☐ Would try to get in the way of an intervention if they know about it.
- ☐ Not sure why – but just have a sense that they would be harmful to an intervention.

BARRIERS CHECKLIST SUMMARY

If this person or organization seems to be a potential barrier, what are next steps? Look at the following suggested steps and see whether they make sense in this situation.

1. **Make sure that they do not find out**
   - Get people to agree that they will not tell this person
   - Make sure that this person does not have access to communication (like emails, notes, able to overhear conversations, etc.)

2. **Create some distractions to decrease their chances of finding out or creating harm**

3. **Make some safety plans in case this person finds out or creates harm**
   - (See Section 4.B. Staying Safe)

☑ OTHER ROADBLOCKS TO AN INTERVENTION: CHECKLIST

It's not just people who can be barriers or roadblocks. We can think of other things such as time, resources, laws, etc.

This Tool is to help you identify other possible roadblocks and make plans to work around them.

RESOURCES

- ☐ No transportation to get to a meeting
- ☐ No place to meet that is big enough, private enough, warm enough, cool enough, etc.
- ☐ Need babysitting or childcare to be able to meet
- ☐ Financial needs so urgent that nothing else can be done
- ☐ Other:

TIME

- ☐ Timeline or deadline coming up: (for example, we need to help someone escape during the time that her partner is out of town – the partner is returning in 2 days)Benefits in a significant way from the violence or thinks that they do.
- ☐ People can't find the right overlapping time to meet.
- ☐ People don't have time to meet at all (for example, I just can't meet; email me or text me but I can't do anything else)
- ☐ People can be active but only for a short time (for example, I can be available for the next week/month but not after that)
- ☐ Other:

LAW OR SYSTEMS

- ☐ Dealing with child abuse but don't want to report -- need to think about who is a mandatory reporter to child welfare such as teachers, social workers, doctors
- ☐ Want to or need to use medical care but know that clinics are mandated to report known abuse of adults and children to police
- ☐ Someone involved is undocumented so run the risk of authorities reporting and getting someone deported
- ☐ Someone involved is in trouble with the law so run the risk of getting arrested
- ☐ Want to tell workplace but not sure what their policies are around violence or potential violence – what do they do regarding victims/survivors; what do they do regarding people doing harm/perpetrators
- ☐ Other:

MAPPING ALLIES & BARRIERS TOOL C7: ALLIES & BARRIERS SUMMARY CHART

Potential Ally	Strengths/ Possible Roles	Risks/Possible Challenges	Point of contact	Are they on board? (yes, no, need more info)

NEXT STEPS REGARDING ALLIES:

Potential Barriers: Name of Person/Situation	Why Harmful?	Strategies to Reduce Harm

NEXT STEPS REGARDING BARRIERS:

MAPPING ALLIES & BARRIERS TOOL C8:
INVITATION TO HELP OUT WITH AN INTERVENTION

(This can be handed to a potential ally or used as a "script" to talk to a potential ally)

HELLO, I WANT TO TALK TO YOU ABOUT...

(Insert brief description of the situation)

WE ARE ASKING IF YOU WOULD CONSIDER BEING PART OF OUR GROUP AS WE...

(Insert brief description of the possible intervention)

WE THINK YOU WOULD BE A GOOD PERSON FOR...

(Insert brief description of possible role or roles)

WE THOUGHT OF YOU AS A POSSIBLE PERSON TO HELP BECAUSE...

(who you know, skills, knowledge, resources, etc.)

MAPPING ALLIES & BARRIERS

WE ASK YOU TO AGREE TO RESPECT THE FOLLOWING (EVEN IF YOU DECIDE NOT TO JOIN):

Who it's okay to talk to:

Who it's not okay to talk to:

Requests made by survivor:

Special considerations regarding person doing harm:

Other considerations requested:

THINGS THAT YOUR INVOLVEMENT MIGHT INCLUDE:

NEXT STEPS FOR PARTICIPATION:

CONTACT PERSON IF YOU HAVE MORE QEST IONS.

OTHER INFORMATION TO HELP PREPARE YOU

Information about violence (Could include: Section 2.2. Interpersonal Violence: Some Basics Everyone Should Know)

Information about this approach to violence intervention: (Could include: Section 1. Introduction & FAQ; Section 2. Some Basics Everyone Should Know; and Section 3. Model Overview: Is It Right For You?)

4D SETTING GOALS
WHAT DO WE WANT?

D.1. What Is Goal Setting

D.2. Goal Setting Across the 4 Phases

D.3. Tips

D.4. Special Considerations

D.5. Facilitator Notes

D.6. Real Life Stories and Examples

D.7. Goal Setting Tools

D.1. WHAT IS *GOAL SETTING?*

Key Questions

- What do you want?
- What do you not want?
- What would you consider a success?

What Is It?

Goal Setting includes the steps the individuals and group take to move towards a single outcome or set of outcomes that could result from their action. Goal Setting is the process used to name a goal or set of goals that:

- 1. Can be agreed upon enough for everyone to move forward;
- 2. Help to guide next steps and actions;
- 3. Create ways which can help everyone measure success;
- 4. Can guide the person or people doing harm to steps and actions that would show themselves and others that they are taking responsibility to address the violence, repair the harm, and change their attitudes and behavior away from violence and towards responsibility.

Why Is It Important?

Goal Setting sets a clear direction in which you are headed. It gives a guide to lead the way during times of confusion. It also lets others who are involved in the intervention get a better picture of what they are working towards and what is expected of them. This may also include the person doing harm.

While everyone may agree that they want violence to end, we at Creative Interventions have found that agreement often stops there. What different people mean by this and how they think that should happen can be the points of conflict that make an intervention break down. The Goal Setting tools help you to understand that you as individuals may come into an intervention with different ideas about goals but that these differences can be discussed and group agreement can be reached. It also helps you turn vague goals into something more concrete – so that you can have a better idea when goals are actually met.

Goal Setting in Six Basic Steps:

Goal setting can take various steps including:

#1 Name goals. Get concrete about the outcomes an individual or group wants and does NOT want – we call these desired outcomes "goals."

#2 Name bottom lines. Get concrete about any limits that an individual or group might have, things that they will not agree to, a line they will not cross – we call these "bottom lines."

#3 Create group consensus. Come together to form a group consensus or agreement regarding their goals and bottom lines (individuals may have to make compromises in order to reach agreement).

#4 Separate short-term and long term goals. Separate immediate or short-term goals from goals that are more long-term.

#5 Prioritize most important goals. Prioritize goals by naming one or two that are the most important goals. An alternative may be to also think about the goals most easy to achieve at least at the beginning.

#7 Turn goals into action plans. Turn these goals into a plan of action – a plan that can be revised or changed over time.

Different Situations May Call for Different Types of Goals:

When setting goals, it might be helpful to also categorize the type of relationship in which the violence took place and what the relationship outcome might be. Goals may include something defining the desired relationship that you would want as an outcome of an intervention. For example, do you want to stay in close relationship with the person who did harm? Do you want to co-exist but not stay in close relationship? Do you not want to be in any kind of relationship? The different situations that violence may involve include:

#1 Violence within ongoing intimate or close relationship – have the intention to stay together.

- Goal may include staying together in a healthy relationship

#2 Violence within ongoing intimate or close relationship – have no intention to stay together.

- Goal may include separating safely
- Goal may include being able to co-exist in the same community without staying in a close relationship

#3 Violence from former relationship – have no intention to stay together or to reconnect.

- Goal may include separating safely

#4 Ongoing non-intimate relationship (coworker, friend, member of same organization) – may not stay closely connected but may still share the same community, same space or same circles.

- Goal may include co-existing peacefully in the same community

#5 Violence caused by an acquaintance in the community – not a close relationship and do not share the same space or circles.

- Relationship may not be part of goal

#6 Stranger – don't know – cannot identify the person.

- Relationship may not be part of goal

What Could Goals Look Like?

In Section 3.5. What Are We Trying to Achieve: 3 Intervention Areas, we introduced three basic areas of interventions. We could also say that this represents three types of goals:

#1 Survivor or victim support. This focuses on providing for the health, safety and other needs and wants of someone who has been the survivor or victim of harm. This may also extend to children, family members, pets, and others who rely upon the survivor or victim and their well-being.

#2 Accountability of the person doing harm. This focuses on support for the person doing harm to recognize, end and take responsibility for the harm one has caused, regarding of whether or not that harm was intended. It also includes changing attitudes and behaviors so that the violence will not continue.

If accountability or responsibility is not possible, then this may be less about accountability and more about taking steps to make sure the violence stops and will not continue.

#3 Community accountability or social change. This focuses on working with communities to recognize the ways in which they are responsible for harm and to make changes so that harm will not continue. This might refer to harm directly caused by communities or harms that were allowed by communities that did not do enough to make sure that these harms do not happen.

Goals may be organized under one, two, or all three of these areas. This may be a useful way to think about goals.

You might also want to think of goals in more specific ways that address a particular need and that more closely match your own situation – in your own words. The following is a list of some possible areas of goals. Some of these goals may overlap – goals of ending violence may overlap with safety and so on. Some of these goals may come from the survivor of violence. Others may come from friends, family, and community members of the survivor. Goals may also be defined by the person who has caused harm as some of these examples show.

#1

Goals about taking first steps in changing the situation of violence may include:

- Want to tell at least one trusted person about what is happening.
- Want to contact and find out about one crisis line I can call in case of emergency.
- Want to share this Toolkit with my close friends.
- Want to make my first intake appointment with batterer intervention program to get help ending my own violence.

#2

Goals about violence may include:

- Want the physical violence to end completely.
- Want all verbal abuse to end.
- Want my children to free from violence.
- Want to be able to argue without fearing physical violence.
- Want to be able to say "no" to sex without fear.

#3

Goals about freedom from control:

- Want to be able to go out without having to report to my partner.
- Want to be able to get a job without threats or being called a "bad mother."

#4

Goals about safety:

- Want an emergency plan and at least two people I can call in case of emergency.
- Want my children to feel safe.
- Want to be able to live without fear most days of the week.

#5

Goals about relationship:

- Want to feel like I can be in this relationship without my partner fearing me.
- Want to end this relationship completely.
- Want to end this intimate relationship but remain friends if possible.
- Want to end this relationship but be able to co-parent our children.
- Want my friends to understand the dynamics of violence and be on my side.
- Want to have some people who I can trust.

#6

Goals about the way the intervention is carried out:

- Want to meet person doing harm face-to-face.
- Do not want to meet person doing harm face-to-face.
- Want the person doing harm to be dealt with in a compassionate way.
- Do not want the police to be involved.

#7

Goals about what you want from the person who caused harm:

- Want them to stay away and stop all contact.
- Want them to stay away and stop all contact until safety is established.
- Want them to understand and admit what they have done
- Want a sincere apology.
- Want repair in the form of ______________________________.
- Want them to respect safe space by staying away from the following places: ______________________________.
- Want them to seek and follow through getting the following help ______________________________.

#8

Goals about what you want from the community (might be family, friends, an organization):

- Want the community to understand how they supported violence and admit what they have done.
- Want a sincere apology from the community.
- Want the community to adopt guidelines regarding safety and violence so this does not happen again.

WHAT ARE LIMITS OR BOTTOM LINES?

Bottom lines may be a limit that you draw for yourself in order to stay involved in the intervention. They might be personal limits such as the amount of time you can spend.

They might be limits to how the intervention takes place.

This Toolkit suggests that you think about whether you have any absolute limits to participation, and if so, that you make these clear so that other people know.

For example:

- I can be involved in this intervention, but I will not be meeting the person who did harm face-to-face.
- I can only meet about this on weekday evenings.
- I want to hear about the intervention so I don't get in the way of what they are trying to achieve – but I do not otherwise want to be involved.
- I will be involved but only as long as we do not commit acts of violence against the person doing harm.
- I will be involved but I do not want to report to the police.

USING THE TOOLS IN THIS SECTION

The tools in this section offer guides to help you as individuals and as a group to get clearer about what you want and what you hope to get from your intervention. To begin, Tool D1. Dealing with Strong Negative Feelings and Fantasy helps you sort through what you really want from what is really do-able.

Tool D2. Goal Setting Guiding Questions and Chart can be used by individuals or groups to think through that person's goals for the intervention. Once individuals come together as a group, Tool D3. Mapping Combined Goals Chart and Tool D4. Shared Collective Goals Charts can help you move forward from individual goals to group goals that you can all stand behind. Since goal setting can at times be a complicated process, especially when you are working together as a larger group, Tool D5. Collective Goals Summary Checklist and Next Steps can help you put all of these goals together into one list.

Finally, Tool D6. Turning Goals into Action in this section helps you to move from broad goals to the concrete steps to make these goals a reality.

D.2. *GOAL SETTING* ACROSS THE 4 PHASES

In Section 3.6. Interventions Over Time: 4 Phases, the Toolkit introduced the idea of 4 possible phases of interventions: 1) Getting Started, 2) Planning/Preparation, 3) Taking Action, and 4) Following Up.

Goal setting is an important step in violence intervention. Over time, goals might change. Check in regularly with your goals to make sure that they are still what you want, to see if they are realistic and to let people you are working with stay on the same page.

PHASE 1: GETTING STARTED

As you get started, your most important goals may be short-term goals, including getting immediate safety, gathering people together to help out, or finding someone to call for support.

Long-term goals can be important to set your direction and to revisit in order to see how the situation may have changed – or how your feelings about what you want may change.

If only one or two people are involved as this intervention starts, then goals may be

PHASE 2: PLANNING/PREPARATION

As you plan an intervention and possibly bring more people together, then your goals may begin to expand. You may need to get more concrete about long-term goals in order to better guide your plans. You may need to have a group process to come to consensus about goals. If you started off setting goals on your own, then the goals might expand to include the group or you may need to share your goals with others and make sure that they understand and agree with these goals.

PHASE 3: TAKING ACTION

By the time the group starts to take action, it is good to have a solid set of goals with which everyone understands, agrees and remembers.

PHASE 4: FOLLOWING-UP

As your group begins to close an intervention process or a phase of the process, you can return to goals to measure your success, to celebrate those goals you were able to achieve, and to remind yourselves of what you need to keep doing in the future.

RELATED TOOLS

The process of Section 4.A. Getting Clear may involve getting clear about what someone's goals may be.

Tools to help with decision-making including setting goals are in Section 4.G. Working Together.

Tools to link goals with ways that you expect the person or people who caused harm to take responsibility for violence are in Section 4.F. Taking Accountability.

Tools to help you take action towards meeting goals are in Section 4.H. Keeping on Track.

D.3. *GOAL SETTING* TIPS

#1 READ *SOME BASICS EVERYONE SHOULD KNOW.*

Interpersonal violence is complicated. Although we may hear more about domestic violence or sexual assault these days, many misunderstandings still exist and many misconceptions about what it is and how to approach it. Read *Section 2. Some Basics Everyone Should Know.* Pay special attention to *Section 2.2. Interpersonal Violence: Some Basics Everyone Should Know* in order to have a clearer picture of what is going on. The *Section 2.3. Violence Intervention: Some Important Lessons* also shares important basics about interventions based upon the experiences of Creative Interventions.

Share this information with others who may be involved in a situation of violence and may need some resources to help them know what to do.

#2 GOALS MAY BE STATED IN TERMS OF WHAT PEOPLE WANT AND IN TERMS OF WHAT PEOPLE DON'T WANT.

Ask both what you want and what you don't want to get a more complete picture of goals.

#3 DO NOT ASSUME THAT PEOPLE WORKING TOGETHER SHARE THE SAME GOALS. MAKE THE PROCESS OF SHARING GOALS A CONCRETE ONE.

Many people agree that they do not want violence – but may not agree on the details. It is important to make sure that people are clear on what their own goals are, what others name as their goals and how they can come together to agree on these goals.

#4 SEPARATE FANTASY GOALS FROM REALITY GOALS.

There's room for people to dream of what they would want in an ideal world, including fantasy worlds of revenge or the fantasy of a perfect ending. This may be an important step towards getting to more realistic goals, goals that will not lead to more harm, or goals more fitting with our higher values. Take time to separate fantasy goals from reality goals. See Tool D2. Dealing with Strong Negative Feelings and Fantasy During Goal Setting for help.

#5 GOALS CAN BE AND SHOULD BE REVISITED.

At some point, you want to settle on basic goals that you all agree to and remember. Even if these goals stay the same, it is good to keep checking in to make sure that they still make sense as the situation changes.

#6 REMEMBER TO SHARE GOALS WITH NEW PEOPLE AS THEY GET INVOLVED.

It is easy to forget to share goals or assume people have the same goals as new people get involved. Remember to carefully go through the sharing of goals to make sure that new people are aware of them – and agree to them.

#7 SEPARATE GOALS EXPECTED THROUGH THE INTERVENTION FROM GOALS THAT MIGHT BE MET IN ANOTHER WAY.

It is easy to forget to share goals or assume people have the same goals as new people get involved. Remember to carefully go through the sharing of goals to make sure that new people are aware of them – and agree to them.

#8 ANTICIPATE CONFLICTS IN GOALS.

While people will generally want a good outcome, specific goals and bottom lines might differ and even clash. The tools help individuals think about their own goals and to come together and see if people's goals: a) do not conflict; or b) can be agreed upon through compromise. If there is too much disagreement, it is possible that someone will decide to leave the intervention or the group may even disband. There are tools to help to work through these steps.

#9 THINK ABOUT WHAT GOALS WOULD BE "GOOD ENOUGH"

It is good to aim high in terms of goals – to think about what you really want. It may also be important to think about what is "good enough." What could you consider a success – even if you do not reach all of your goals?

D.4. *GOAL SETTING* SPECIAL CONSIDERATIONS

Goals can come from different individuals or groups involved in a situation of violence.

For example, goals may come from a:

- Survivor or victim
- Community allies
- Person or people doing harm
- A team of people made up of any of the above

Goals can also be directed towards different individuals or groups involved in a situation of violence. For example, goals may be:

- About survivor safety or well-being
- About safety of children or other vulnerable people
- About community safety or community sense of responsibility
- About person or people doing harm taking responsibility
- About person or people doing harm being supported and being safe

It can be expected that goals can be reached through the intervention. But goals may also be met through things that happen outside of the intervention.

See the Tool D1: Dealing with Strong Negative Feelings and Fantasy during Goal Setting, for ways on separating fantasy from reality. The move towards goals that are more in line with group values and that can realistically be reached.

Many interventions will base their goals on those stated by the survivor or the victim.

Many anti-violence organizations have a philosophy of being survivor-centered. This means that they believe that the survivor should be the person determining goals and what should be done to reach these goals.

This Toolkit does not assume that interventions will necessarily be survivor-led, although this is one possibility. Survivor or victim goals, however, are an important part of interventions. They need to be seriously considered because the survivor or victim often has suffered the most serious harm.

Survivors or victims often understand the dynamics of violence the most. The harm has often left survivors or victims with a loss of control of their lives, making control of the outcomes or goals of intervention an important part of the solution to violence.

It is important that the group not create a situation in which the survivor or victim becomes isolated and has her or his goals judged by a group that may have clearly distinct goals. At the same time, an environment in which communities allies can state their goals even if they are different or even conflict with that of the survivor should also be allowed in the space. Goal setting is ultimately a negotiating process. Community allies may easily and naturally come to recognize survivor-driven goals as their own. Or the process may lead to dialogue and discussion in which everyone's goals shift towards mutual agreement (or consensus) in which the group process actually creates collective goals that are actually better and more solid that those of any one individual.

If you are a survivor or victim, you may want to go through the process of thinking about your goals on your own before stating them in a group setting. You might want to ask someone to support you in that process so you can reflect on whether they really represent what you want and so you can prepare for disagreements or challenges from the group. You can think about what is very important to you and what you could open to compromise from others.

The community-based approach of this Toolkit also recognizes that communities are also harmed by violence and have a responsibility to challenge violence. Therefore, it is possible that goals defined by the survivor or victim may be understood and respected by community allies while also being balanced by community goals.

If you are a community ally, you may feel that it is most appropriate to follow the survivor or victim's goals. You may also want to think about your own personal goals and goals that might address something that is more of a community-level concern. The important piece is to be clear about what goals are important to you as an individual and be aware of how you feel about any compromises that might come about in a group process. In that way, you may be able to move forward with a good feeling about the group process and not let differences get in the way of your ability to move forward as a solid team member or part of a solid group process.

4D / SETTING GOALS

The group may also have an opportunity to support the person doing harm in a goal-setting process that may end up happening in a separate space than that with the survivor but can ultimately come together as part of the collective goals. If it is the beginning of a process, then supporting and allowing the person doing harm to name goals that may be the opposite of taking responsibility such as "having the process be quick," "wanting the survivor to take equal or greater blame," "being able to say sorry and move on" or not wanting this process at all can be stated but in a space where these lead towards more productive goals that are in line with the process that may include their accountability.

If you are a person doing harm or are accused of doing harm, the goal setting process may be challenging. Group goals including those of the survivor may at least at first feel unfair or oppressive. You may feel judged and feel that you have little control. You may be handed a list of group goals that you were not a part of creating but which may include things that you need to do. It may be a very difficult and yet important process to see how your own personal goals can change throughout this process. You may think about how you can name personal goals such as reflecting on why people perceive your attitudes or actions as harmful, thinking about its impact on others, taking responsibility, remaining connected to people you care about, or stopping your own pattern of violence as goals that you can achieve. It is useful to ask for and get support to help you in that process.

#1 THINK ABOUT HOW PEOPLE CAN REFLECT ON INDIVIDUAL GOALS IN PREPARATION FOR AGREEING ON GROUP GOALS.

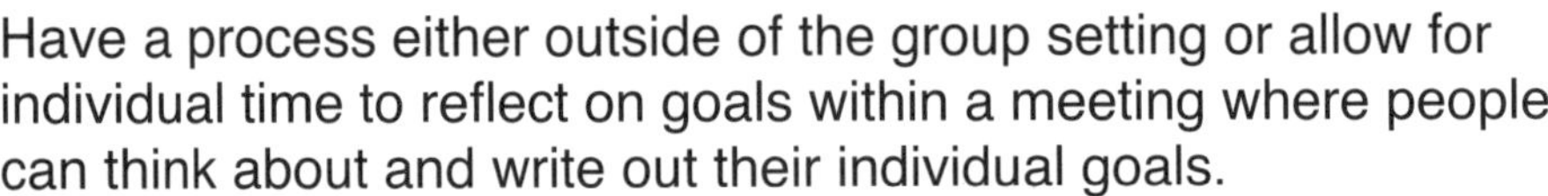

Have a process either outside of the group setting or allow for individual time to reflect on goals within a meeting where people can think about and write out their individual goals.

#2 UNDERSTAND THE UNIQUENESS OF SURVIVOR GOALS.

Special consideration of survivor goals are important in any intervention. This is true whether the survivor is leading an intervention, is at the center of an intervention, or is taking more of a back seat.

If you have a survivor-driven process or one where the survivor is actively involved, you may facilitate in such a way that the survivor's goals are first stated and written down or shared in a way that everyone can easily understand and remember what they are. Make sure that people understand what these goals are and do not have further needs for clarification.

#3 HELP PEOPLE DISTINGUISH BETWEEN FANTASY.

Coming in with fantasies about goals is normal. This can include fantasies of revenge or fantasies of a quick and perfect ending. You want to end up with things that are realistic and do not cause greater harm. See Tool D1. Dealing with Strong Negative Feelings and Fantasy during Goal Setting for help.

#4 CONSIDER A PROCESS WHERE EVERYONE CAN EXPRESS THEIR INDIVIDUAL GOALS AS A STEP TOWARDS REACHING GROUP GOALS THAT EVERYONE CAN AGREE ON.

a. A process can then follow where people reflect on their own goals and see how they go along with, add to or are maybe even in possible conflict with these goals. You can then have each person share and/or read out their goals. People can always pass if they feel uncomfortable.

b. Get all the goals together in a way that everyone can see them. You can ask each person write goals on a board or easel paper; or ask participants to write goals on post-its and put them up on the board or on the wall – you may think of other creative ways to put them up in a way that everyone can see them.

c. Help the group figure out what goals are overlapping (you can mark them with a check mark or a star).

d. Help the group identify which are individual, but not necessarily collective goals. Help identify which are non-negotiable, bottom-line goals.

e. Help the group see that individual goals and bottom-lines can be maintained without getting in the way of the overall goals (you can mark with plus).

f. Help the group see how conflicting individual goals and bottom-lines can be let go of to keep a set of goals that everyone can agree to (you can mark with question mark).

g. Help the group to identify and clarify collective group goals. Expect that there will be some changing of minds and explanations to help convince others.

h. Double check to see if the group can agree to the goals. See if there are remaining question marks and whether these can be crossed off or reworded into pluses or checks.

i. Make sure to write down these collective group goals/bottom-lines and any questions or concerns that arise. You can return to these later.

D.6. *SUPPORTING SURVIVORS OR VICTIMS* REAL LIFE STORIES & EXAMPLES

Story D: Community Responds to Domestic Violence

Two years ago, I was married to a man who I'd been with for ten years prior, and our relationship had troubles. Over the last year of our marriage, my former partner was going through training as a police officer, and at the same time, we had just relocated to a new state. We were struggling with some large issues in the marriage, and things had gotten more difficult. I just became increasingly afraid of someone that I used to feel really safe with.

I have three kids who were ten, six, and four, and they were witnessing a lot of arguments, a lot of loud screaming, a lot of doors being slammed, a lot of things that I felt were really unsafe for them to see. My home just felt more and more dangerous. I felt scared to leave the house. I felt scared to come home. I felt scared to sleep in my bed.

The last straw came one night when I had gone to a friend's house and my partner followed me in his car. And when I arrived at my friend's house, he pulled up and got out of the car and was yelling and screaming horrible things at me. I felt very afraid, but I didn't know what to do. I knew wherever I went, he would follow me. So I decided I would go to my office which was nearby, and it was night time so there wouldn't be anybody there. When I finally got inside, I waited for a few minutes and he left.

I called a friend, who came and met me at my office, and she suggested that I call another friend who had a house I could go to while we figured out what to do, so that's what I did. When we got there, everybody sat around in the living room and just reassured me that it was safe for me to be there, that they were welcoming of it, that they understood. I was at this point on the run from someone who was furious and had a gun, and I still felt bad. I felt like I was exposing people to something that I couldn't control, something I was terrified of. But I didn't know what else to do at that point, and they were saying it was where they wanted me to be.

My friends asked me if there were any people that I could gather up, that I could call, that might be support from in this time. I guess I should say that being part of this, this community organization which is committed to ending sexual violence which meant that we had a way of responding that I knew people would come together. I knew if I needed help, people would come and talk to me and we could work it out together. So it didn't feel strange to meet, to call people and say, "Hey, I need help, and this is what's going on."

And at the same time, experiencing these things in my home felt like people would see me differently; people would judge me; people would think I was a hypocrite; people would think I was weak. And I remember being really troubled by that the first few days. But I got reassurances from folks that that was exactly what the point of the organization was, and that experiencing harm is not about being strong or weak, that experiencing harm just is. It's what we choose to do about it that's important.

So we made phone calls, and asked people to come over. We had seven or eight people come over and just started talking through what to do. At that point it felt totally overwhelming. I was still on, "Is this really happening to me?" and, "What can I do to make it okay?" rather than thinking of anything beyond tomorrow, or next week.

But I think my wants were something like: I want to be in my home; I want my kids to feel safe; I think I said, "I want him to leave."

I think those were basically it at that moment, and then we just brainstormed what needs to happen right now in the next hour, in the next day, in the next week, for those wants to happen. We walked through it so if I want to be in my home, how do we make that happen? How do we make sure that that's a safe space? And, I think one of the answers to that question was, at least in the near future, having folks be there with me.

So we eventually set up a schedule. We put out an email with a schedule for the week, and blanks for people to fill in, and I was amazed that people did fill it in. And they did come by. They came by every day and they came and sat in my living room, and they brought food, and we just sat together. I was amazed at that. That was how we got home to be a safe space for me again.

When we were thinking about whether to call the police or not, I did feel like I needed some help in calming the situation down, but I didn't know what to do, because if I can't call his friends on the job, and I can't call them in…It doesn't seem right to call them in an unofficial way, because who knows what's going to happen with that. And calling them in an official way doesn't necessarily seem like it's going to produce any certain results either.

So we tried to think about who could talk to him. And we figured out some people in the community that he could talk to, if he was open to doing that. My mom talked to him, and she was willing to deal with him. He was totally raging, and for whatever reason she was not intimidated at all and just was able to talk to him really calmly.

I had people checking on me, people staying during the daytime hours, sometimes overnight for the next week, and it just felt good. It felt so good to have this full house, you know, this busy house of people coming by, and, you know, people were playing with the kids, and we were making art in the kitchen, and someone was always making tea, and it felt not alone.

In terms of talking about successes, I guess the biggest one is that I did get all three things that I wanted, that I identified as wants to happen. That my kids went through that time feeling safe; that he did leave the house; that I was able to return home; and that all that happened in a fairly short amount of time. So in terms of success, I'd say, ultimately for me as a survivor, those were the most meaningful successes.

Another success in terms of communication was that we made a phone list immediately. That was one of the first things we did so I always knew I had someone to call. And people would call and check on me. At that time, I think it was hard. I was worried about people burning out. I was worried about people feeling overwhelmed by me and my stuff.

So I didn't have to constantly, hour by hour, be reaching out for needs to be met because we'd identified them beforehand and there were enough people involved. It felt like no one was carrying all of it, or more than they could. It certainly wasn't that things didn't feel hard. It felt really bad. I think what was helpful was this wasn't an intervention where it was like, "How are we going to get him away from me? It was like, "How are we going to make sure that there's not harm happening in our community? How are we going to make sure that we've done our best to address that? The problem was consistently the harm. The problem was consistently the events or the behaviors, or the things that were harmful that were happening, but not him that was a problem – not that my choice to stay as long as I had was a problem.

That made it possible for me to feel like I could come into the space and say what I needed which at that time really included not being someone who was perpetrating harm against him by engaging the power of the state whether or not it would have benefited me in that moment. It could only have had negative effects on him.

And then I got to make a decision about what do I really need right now to do my work, to take care of my kids, to get through this day, to heal.

We need to trust people to be the experts on their own lives and to take them seriously and have faith in people to set the course for working from harm to transformation. I think that comes best from people who are experiencing harm and have a vision for themselves about what they want. And to give people time to identify what that is and be willing to sit with the discomfort of not being able to rescue somebody in a simple or quick way. I think that those values were ultimately the most healing for me.

(Adapted from the transcript from Community Responds to Domestic Violence available from StoryTelling & Organizing Project (STOP) www.stopviolenceeveryday.org. The story is also available in downloadable audio mp3 on the same website)

TOOLS

4.D GOAL SETTING: WHAT DO WE WANT?

Tool D1. Dealing with Strong Negative Feelings and Fantasy during Goal Setting

Tool D2. Goal Setting Guided Questions and Chart

Tool D3. Mapping Combined Goals Chart

Tool D4. Shared Collective Goals Chart

Tool D5. Collective Goals Summary Checklist and Next Steps

Tool D6. Turning Goals into Action

GOAL SETTING TOOL D1: DEALING WITH STRONG NEGATIVE FEELINGS AND FANTASY DURING GOAL SETTING

It is common for people to have strong negative feelings, fantasies or unrealistic expectations linked to goals about situations of harm. At some point during the goal setting phase, it is good to let a full range of feelings be expressed no matter how far fetched they may seem to you. Considering the entire range of goals generated in response to a situation of harm may help people to be able to express strong negative feelings and fantasies – as well as other goals that may be more realistic.

For example, the survivor may express goals such as:

- I wish the person doing harm were dead or experience the same harm they did to me.
- I wish the person doing harm could be publicly humiliated or hurt so that they would know they could never do this again.
- I wish this had never happened to me.
- I wish that I would feel the same as before this ever happened.

Allies may express:

- I wish the survivor would have walked away.
- I wish the survivor would cut off all contact with the person doing harm.
- I wish the survivor would just move on.
- I wish someone else would deal with this.

The person doing harm may want things like:

- I wish everyone would just forgive me and forget about this.
- I wish everyone would understand that I was under a lot of pressure and cut me some slack.
- I wish everyone would know that the survivor deserved it – anybody would have done the same thing if they were in my shoes.
- I wish this had never happened.

While extreme responses and fantasies may be normal, we ask you to think about the following in assessing whether or not you want to pursue a goal:

- Values. Does this goal fit your values?
- Risk assessment. Will pursing this goal lead to more harm to yourself or others, retaliation, and so on?
- Realistic or achievable. Is it actually possible to achieve this goal?

GOAL SETTING TOOL D2: GUIDED QUESTIONS AND CHART

These are some basic questions you can think through in moving towards goals. They can be asked individually or as a group.

If this process is survivor-driven, that is, if the process will prioritize the goals of the survivor, then this may be focused around the survivor's or victim's needs and desires. Others can also look at this and think about these questions for themselves as individuals and also focus on the needs of the survivor and the community.

GUIDED QUESTIONS

What do I want?

- For myself
- For the survivor or victim (if I am not the survivor or victim)
- For other important people (children, other family members, friends, organization, etc.)
- For the person doing harm (if I am not the person doing harm)
- For the larger community (it may be useful to name who we mean by the community)

What do I NOT want? (You can use the categories above)

What is important to me? This can be values or ways in which things will happen or people.

What are the most important wants (or goals)?

Is there anything that is an absolute "must have" or "must do"?

Do these goals fit with my values? Is there anything I would add or leave out after thinking about this?

Are some more achievable than others? Which are most achievable? Is there anything I would add or leave out after thinking about this?

Will pursing any of these goals lead to more harm to myself, the survivor or victim, the person doing harm, or others, retaliation, and so on? Is there anything I would add or leave out after thinking about this?

What goals might be fantasies? Is there anything I would add or leave out after thinking about this?

What would I consider a success?

What goals would I consider "good enough?"

Can I divide these goals into long-term and short-term? (If that makes sense, you can do that)

GOAL SETTING CHART

After answering the guided questions, see if you can write your goals in the following chart. The chart will be easier to refer to and share with others.

Goals/Wants (or don't wants) **Mark with an * if this is necessary / important.**	**For Whom?**	**Is this goal realistic?** (yes, no, maybe)	**Short-term or long-term?**	**Anything else?**
I want:				
I don't want:				
Limits or bottom lines				

REMEMBER: Limits or bottom lines may be a limit that you draw for yourself in order to stay involved in the intervention. They might be personal limits such as the amount of time you can spend. They might be limits to how the intervention takes place. (See What Is Goal Setting? for more about Bottom lines).

GOAL SETTING TOOL D3: MAPPING COMBINED GOALS CHART

After the individuals involved in the intervention have had a chance to complete their goals worksheets, this chart can be used to help compile the individual answers and help begin to develop shared goal as a group.

Goals Brainstorm list everyone's goals here	**Individuals Goals** list things that seem like an individual's goals (add name/ initials to show whose)	**Goals specific to the survivor** list goals that are specific to the survivor	**Goals specific to the person doing harm** list goals that are specific to the person doing harm	**General goals** list goals that are related to the intervention rather than a specific person
Bottom-Lines Brainstorm List things that are must-haves about the results or the process (can mark with +) or must-not-haves (can mark with -)	**Individuals Bottom-Lines** List things that seem like an individual's bottom lines (add name/initials to show whose)	**Bottom-Lines Specific to Survivor** List things that are specific to the survivor	**Bottom-Lines Specific to the Person Doing Harm** list things that are specific to the person doing harm	**General Bottom-Lines** List things that are specific to any other person, group, organization, etc.

GOAL SETTING TOOL D4: SHARED COLLECTIVE GOALS CHART

After mapping the group's goals, you can use the chart below to document the "final" goals that the group agrees to collectively for the situation of harm. This chart should be used as a reference point and should be revisited often, as changing conditions or participants may cause the initial set of goals to change over time.

Agreed-Upon Goals	
Agreed-Upon Bottom-Lines	
Goals/Bottom-Lines Conflicts/ Disagreements/ Questions	
Goals/Bottom-Lines Need More Information	

☑ *GOAL SETTING* TOOL D5: COLLECTIVE GOALS SUMMARY CHECKLIST AND NEXT STEPS

Once the group has gone through the process of coming up with collective goals, you can use this checklist to figure out next steps. The key question is: Do we agree enough to move forward?

Check the box if you as a group:

- ☐ Have enough agreement on goals to move forward
- ☐ Can live with any goals or bottom-lines that might be essentially important to one person but not to everyone in the group
- ☐ Do not have conflicts or disagreements in goals so serious that you cannot move forward
- ☐ Do not have conflicts or disagreements in bottom-lines so serious that you cannot move forward
- ☐ Do not need more information which is likely to significantly influence goals or bottom-lines

GOAL SETTING TOOL D5: GOALS NEXT STEP TIMELINE

If you check all boxes, you can move ahead and fill in next steps, who is responsible and timeline.

Next Steps	Who is Responsible	Timeline & Other Conditions

GOAL SETTING TOOL D5: SIGNIFICANT CONFLICT ON GROUP GOALS AND OPTIONS FOR MOVING FORWARD

If you DO NOT check all boxes (You do not have agreement or consensus right now), you may consider the following options:

OPTION 1. Plan another meeting (people reflect in-between):

o Yes o No

If "yes", where is the next meeting, when will it be? ______________________

Who will be able to make it? ______________________

____

Who cannot make it? ______________________

____

For those who cannot make it, how can they give their input? ______________________

____

What should everyone be thinking about before the next meeting? ______________________

____

What if anything should people bring to the next meeting? ______________________

____

OPTION 2. Plan another way to continue building agreement or consensus:

o Yes o No

If "yes", what means will you use to communicate (email, phone, in-person meetings, etc.) ?

____

Who will coordinate results? ______________________

Who will make sure everyone gets the results? ______________________

____

How will you know when you can move on? ____________________

____

____

OPTION 3. Someone with goals or bottom-lines which block full agreement decides that they can live with the group goals and bottom-lines even though they do not fully agree.

o Yes o No

If "yes", are there any requests or ideas about revisiting these disagreements later? If so, what are they? ____________________

____

____

OPTION 4. Need to get more information.

o Yes o No

If "yes", what information do you need? ____________________

____

How will you get it? ____________________

____

Who will get it? ____________________

____

How will they communicate that information back to the group? ____________________

____

What are the next steps? ____________________

____

OPTION 5. This group disbands at this point.

o Yes o No

If "yes" and you disband, will a different team be formed (may still include some of the same people)? If so, how? ____________________

____

If "yes" and you disband, agree upon ways in which people will leave the process without creating more harm. (For example, it could cause more harm to tell certain people that agreement could not be reached – this could give an impression that no one will address, stop or prevent harm. It could also could increase harm and/or increase vulnerability for the survivor or victim or others involved in the planning of this intervention)

Safety and confidentiality questions to ask:

Who can know about this process so far? ______________________________

____

____

Who cannot know about this process so far? ______________________________

____

____

Any other safety measures that should be followed? ______________________________

____

____

Any other considerations that should be followed? ______________________________

____

____

List agreements:

If "yes and you disband," acknowledge and recognize ways in which some of you may continue to address the situation independently. If so, are there ways in which you can still remain in contact and offer support? Or conditions under which you may come back together?

List ways some of you may continue to address the situation:

GOAL SETTING TOOL D6: TURNING GOALS INTO ACTION

A key to making an action plan is to turn goals into action. Take each goal which the group has agreed to. You can include goals which are more personal or individual as long as nobody disagrees with or blocks that goal (See earlier Goal Setting section for creating collective goals). Some goals may also be broken up into more than one action step.

Next Steps	Who is Responsible	Timeline & Other Conditions

NOTES

4E SUPPORTING SURVIVORS OR VICTIMS: HOW CAN WE HELP?

E.1. What Is Supporting Survivors or Victims?

E.2. Supporting Survivors or Victims Across the Four Phases

E.3. Tips

E.4. Special Considerations

E.5. Facilitator Notes

E.6. Real Life Stories and Examples

E.7. Supporting Survivor or Victims Tools

E.1. WHAT IS *SUPPORTING SURVIVORS OR VICTIMS*?

Supporting Survivors or Victims: Key Questions

- What violence or abuse did the survivor or victim experience?
- What harms have resulted?
- What do they think will be helpful to them?
- Who can best offer this support?
- How are they getting ongoing support?

What Is It?

Survivor or victim support focuses on providing for the health, safety and other needs and wants of someone who has been or is the survivor or victim of harm.

The needs and wants may extend to their children, family members, pets, and others who rely upon the survivor or victim and whose own health and safety may be affected by the harm affecting the survivor/victim. It may also extend to others because if others' needs are taken care of, this frees up the survivor or victim to be able to better focus on their own important needs and wants. For example, helping a survivor or victim take care of children, elderly parents, or job responsibilities may be very supportive to a survivor or victim. And it may also allow some relief so that they can devote some time and energy to take necessary steps to move forward.

Note: Throughout this Toolkit, we use both the words survivors and victims. Some people experiencing violence prefer to think of themselves as survivors, and others will identify as victims. Many people will simply want to be referred to by their name and not feel comfortable with either term. However, because this Toolkit needs to use some kind of language that will clarify how someone is related to the situation of violence, we have chosen to use both terms, survivors or victims, whenever possible. If space only allows for one term, we mostly use the term "survivor."

Why Is It Important?

Supporting Survivors or Victims can be the first step in addressing the harms that interpersonal violence brings. This includes physical, emotional, sexual, spiritual and financial harms. Some survivors or victims make the claim that it is the emotional harm that can hurt even more than the physical. Direct emotional harm can be brought about through constant fear, humiliation, put-downs and attempts to make someone doubt their own judgment and self-worth. This can be made even worse by isolation, shame, self-blame and blame by others that often accompany victimization by interpersonal violence.

Since interpersonal violence often involves people we know or even care deeply about, this can be confused by mixed feelings of love for the person doing harm or fear that coming forward to find help may also cause unwanted consequences to the person doing harm. We may fear that we risk losing someone close to us, that we will hurt the parent of our child, that they might end up in jail, that immigration authorities may take them away if they are undocumented, that they might lose their job, or that others will look down both on the person doing harm and on us for being victims of violence.

Even though people are generally much more aware about domestic violence, sexual assault and other forms of interpersonal violence, misunderstanding and blame of victims still run very deep.

Note: Support for the survivor may not result in "healing." Healing is a deeply personal process. Healing may not be a goal or a desire of the survivor or victim, person doing harm or anybody else involved in this intervention process. Or it may be a goal that is unrelated to this intervention, but rather pursued in another way. While healing may result from any aspect of this intervention and may be chosen as a goal, Creative Interventions does not assume that healing will necessarily result from violence intervention. Therefore, we leave it to those using this Toolkit to choose whether the term "healing" is useful to you.

What Survivor or Victim Support Can Look Like

Survivor or victim support may include such things as:

- Believing the survivor.
- Listening to the survivor's story, concerns and needs.
- Putting yourself in the survivor's shoes – empathizing.
- Holding back before telling the survivor what to do or offering your advice.
- Holding back when you feel yourself becoming judgmental or impatient or having other negative feelings.
- Offering advice or feedback if the survivor wants it and being humble enough to see that your advice or feedback may not be right.
- Being patient with repetition.
- Being a sounding board to help the survivor get clear about what they want and need.
- Being patient with and helping the survivor or victim sort through mixed feelings and confusions such as confusion about:
    - Whether one is really in danger.
    - How they about the person doing harm.
    - What they want to do about the harm.
    - Whether or not they to stay with the person doing harm (if this is someone they are in a close or intimate relationship with)

- How the survivor feels about anyone addressing or confronting the person doing harm.
- Whether they want other people to know about what happened.

- Helping think through your role in providing things like:
  - Emotional support
  - Safety
  - Companionship
  - Help going to necessary meetings or appointments
  - Help thinking of who is a safe and trusted ally
  - Help with shelter, childcare, transportation, food, money and other needs
  - Help contacting other allies
  - Help educating other allies
  - Help building a network of support
- Being an ally through other aspects of a community-based intervention such as:
  - Acting as the facilitator
  - Engaging with the person doing harm
  - Playing other roles as listed in Section 4.C. Mapping Allies and Barriers or Section 4.F. Working Together
  - Engaging with the community to organize support, educate the community or challenge dynamics that contribute to violence
- Being an ally in active and consistent ways
- Finding your own support to prevent burn-out and resentment – this can be done with other allies as you form a team
- Keeping this story only among safe people
- Stopping yourself from telling their story in a gossipy way
- Helping them use this Toolkit and other useful resources
- Making your way through this Toolkit and other useful resources

USING THE TOOLS IN THIS SECTION

The Supporting Survivors or Victims section highlights the importance of supporting survivors or victims and offers tools to think through what types of support might best meet their needs.

Every person and every situation is unique. Tool E1. What Does the Survivor or Victim Need? Checklist offers a list of possible types of support a survivor or victim might want or need. It is good for allies to see this list especially since it might include things that a survivor or victim is unable to express or afraid to ask for.

Survivors or victims can use Tool E2. What Does the Survivor or Victim Need? Guiding Questions to think more carefully about the kind of support that might be helpful to them, what they could ask for and what allies or resources might be able to offer this support.

Finally, survivors or victims may be involved in interventions at very different levels, from taking an active lead role to no involvement. This Toolkit works best with at least some level of involvement in the intervention by the survivor or victim. In fact, receiving support from allies willing to work together towards addressing, reducing, ending or prevention violence (violence intervention) can be a powerful form of support. Tool E3. Survivor or Victim Participation in an Intervention Chart helps a survivor or victim and the intervention team to better understand possible types and levels of survivor or victim participation. It also offers tips about how support can still be offered even if the survivor or victim is not at all involved in the intervention or even if they disagree with an intervention.

E.2. *SUPPORTING SURVIVORS OR VICTIMS?* ACROSS THE 4 PHASES

In Section 3.6. Interventions Over Time: 4 Phases, the Toolkit introduced the idea of 4 possible phases of interventions: 1) Getting Started, 2) Planning/Preparation, 3) Taking Action, and 4) Following Up.

Supporting Survivors or Victims will likely change throughout an intervention. It is difficult to determine how because survivors or victims have such a wide range of ways in which they are involved in interventions.

PHASE 1: GETTING STARTED

Very often, a survivor or victim of violence is the first person to initiate an intervention. This may be done in a very subtle way – he or she may hint that there is a problem of violence or they may tell someone but quickly take back the story or minimize the violence. Survivors or victims of violence often want help but may be reluctant to reach out to others because of shame, fear or prior experiences of being dismissed or blamed.

Some survivors or victims may not want to talk about the violence because of these and other reasons. An intervention may get started because other people recognize the violence and want to do something about it – even when the survivor or victim is not ready or perhaps not even aware of what is happening.

Survivors or victims may want to talk about the violence – but only if they are encouraged and feel like they might actually get sympathy and help. The risk of speaking out may be weighed against the support that someone can expect to receive.

Yet other survivors or victims may be very vocal whether or not they get support from others. It is impossible to generalize how a survivor or victim will feel, express themselves or get involved in a community-based intervention.

The phase of getting started may be a time when the survivor or victim makes beginning attempts to reach out to others or when others reach out to the survivor or victim to offer help. The model of community-based intervention presented in this Toolkit can be a way for survivors or victims to express what they have experienced and what they want in their own words. If handled with care, it can offer them some sense of control – something that is usually destroyed in the experience of interpersonal violence. Getting the solid support of people they are close to like friends, family, neighbors, co-workers or other community members may be a good first step in changing their situation of violence.

PHASE 2: PLANNING/PREPARATION

Again, it is difficult to generalize about how active a survivor or victim will be in the planning or preparation of an intervention. Survivors or victims may lead the planning and preparation. Or a group of allies may take leadership and make sure to support the survivor or victim in playing an active role in this phase.

If the survivor or victim decides to take more of a back seat or is less involved – for example, if they are a child, then it may be important to stay connected and check in with the survivor or victim regularly to make sure that they are aware of what is happening and can voice concerns, ask questions or adjust their level of involvement. It is important to keep up any and all levels of support, particularly since it may be easy to turn focus away from the survivor's or victim's needs as people get more involved in other aspects of the intervention.

PHASE 3: TAKING ACTION

Similar to the planning and preparation phase, the survivor or victim may be taking a lead or very active role in taking action. If not, it may again be important to make sure he or she is aware of what is happening and are able to voice concerns or change their level of participation. As the intervention team takes action, especially if this involves addressing, reducing, ending or preventing the violence of the person doing harm, it is easy to lose focus on support for the survivor or victim. It is important to make sure that at least some allies remain connected to and supportive of the survivor or victim throughout the intervention.

PHASE 4: FOLLOWING-UP

As the intervention moves into a phase of following-up, the survivor or victim may be in many different situations. They may have already moved on and be satisfied that an intervention took place. It is possible that a survivor or victim may feel like they can move on if the intervention was ultimately unsuccessful. For some, the fact that an attempt was made can seem like a success. The team may only be responsible for giving an update on a follow-up plan.

On the other hand, the survivor or victim may be actively involved and be the central person determining whether or not the intervention has reached the point where there is some closure. Following-up may be a phase during which period checking in regarding survivor support and safety may be planned to make sure that the intervention has long-term effect.

RELATED TOOLS

Tools to identify the dynamics of harm experienced by the survivor or victim are in *Section 4.A. Getting Clear. Section 4.C. Mapping Allies and Barriers* can be used to find the right people to help offer survivor or victim support. Tools to help coordinate support of survivors or victims with the other aspects of the intervention are in *Section 4.F. Working Together.*Tools to think more deeply about safety as a form of support are in Section 4.B. Staying Safe. Getting more specific about other ways that supporting survivors or victims might look like as an intervention goal is in *Section 4.D. Goal Setting.*

E.3. *SUPPORTING SURVIVORS OR VICTIMS* TIPS

#1 READ *SOME BASICS EVERYONE SHOULD KNOW.*

Interpersonal violence is complicated. Although we may hear more about domestic violence or sexual assault these days, many misunderstandings still exist and many misconceptions about what it is and how to approach it. Read *Section 2. Some Basics Everyone Should Know.* Pay special attention to *Section 2.2. Interpersonal Violence: Some Basics Everyone Should Know* in order to have a clearer picture of what is going on. The *Section 2.3. Violence Intervention: Some Important Lessons* also shares important basics about interventions based upon the experiences of Creative Interventions.

Share this information with others who may be involved in a situation of violence and may need some resources to help them know what to do.

#2 UNDERSTAND THE MANY BARRIERS TO SURVIVORS OR VICTIMS ASKING FOR SUPPORT.

Survivors or victims may not always be straightforward in stating their feelings or their needs. Fear of judgment from others, fear of retaliation from the person doing harm if they find out, self-blame and shame about being a victim – these and many other factors can make it difficult to talk about violence and to ask for support.

Many survivors or victims may have reached out to others for help and received a negative response or no response at all. They may be reluctant to try again or may fear that they will again get a reaction that might make them feel even more helpless and alone.

It may be easy to blame survivors or victims for not asking for what they need, for changing their minds, or for asking for too much. It is easy to think that it is the survivor's or victim's fault. We have many ways of and words for blaming the victim.

Supporting survivors or victims asks us to be patient, forgiving and non-judgmental. It asks us to have some understanding of the many barriers they face in seeking help.

#3 DO NOT PROMISE MORE THAN YOU CAN GIVE. TRY TO GIVE WHAT YOU PROMISED.

It is also easy to promise many things if or when a survivor or victim tells us their story of violence. Think about what you can do – your time, your energy, your ability, your own safety. Work with others so that together you can offer support that none of you can do alone.

If you did promise something that you cannot deliver, talk honestly with the survivor or victim and take accountability for your inability to follow through. See if you can find other ways to offer support.

If you find yourself starting to blame the survivor or victim or others for your inability to follow through with your promises or commitments, take a step back and be honest with yourself about how it feels to let somebody down. Again, it is better to be honest with yourself and with the survivor or victim rather than cover up feelings of guilt, shame or embarrassment with blame.

#4 THE TYPE OF COMMUNITY-BASED INTERVENTION INTRODUCED IN THIS TOOLKIT WORKS BEST WHEN THE SURVIVOR OR VICTIM IS INVOLVED.

Although many interventions will likely begin with and be led by a survivor or victim, this is not always the case. Survivors or victims may not want to be involved for many reasons. They may be young children or otherwise not in a position to be directly participating in an intervention. They may not recognize themselves as survivors or victims of violence. They may not want any changes to their situation. They might fear retaliation or losing their relationship. They may fear that an intervention will call attention to their victimization and associate that with shame, embarrassment or fear of judgment.

In other situations, the survivor or victim may want an intervention, but not want to be actively involved. They may think that it is the responsibility of others to finally step in and do something. They may be completely tired of and over the situation of violence and want to step away from any involvement. They may find it too emotionally difficult to be directly involved. They may simply think that the intervention would be more effective if they were not involved.

Allies may also not want the survivor or victim involved because they find that survivors or victims appear too emotionally involved or seem overly biased. They may not agree with the wishes or the perspective of the survivor or victim. They may want to protect the survivor or victim from any further involvement.

In this approach to violence intervention, Creative Interventions found that it is helpful if the survivor or victim is participating in some way in the intervention. The levels of participation may be that they are:

a) Leading the intervention;

b) Actively involved;

c) Checking in on a regular basis to get information and give feedback;

d) Getting information about what was done and how the intervention is going very infrequently; or

e) Finding out about the final outcome of an intervention only.

Any of these levels is all right as long as there is some level of discussion and agreement to this level of participation by everyone.

#5 HELP TO KEEP UP SURVIVOR OR VICTIM SUPPORT THROUGHOUT AN INTERVENTION.

It is easy to forget survivor or victim support once an active intervention moves forward, especially if people focus on the person doing harm. Make survivor or victim support a central part of the intervention plan. Make sure at least one person has a primary role to keep connected with the survivor or victim, see what the survivor or victim wants or needs. Offer a space for survivors or victims to voice fears or concerns. Make sure that survivor or victim safety is maintained, or make sure that others connected to the survivor such as children or other dependents are also supported.

#6 OFFER HONEST SUPPORT TO A SURVIVOR OR VICTIM.

You may not always agree with the values, opinions or goals of the survivor or victim. This Toolkit offers a variety of tools for people to discuss and reach consensus on the values guiding the intervention and the goals of the intervention. It offers information and tools regarding common situations in which people disagree with the survivor or victim and with each other (See Section 3.4. Values to Guide Your Intervention and Section 4.D. Setting Goals) The Toolkit also address situations in which people may be unclear about who is the survivor/victim or the person doing harm (See Section 2.2. Interpersonal Violence: Some Basics Everyone Should Know). It promotes a holistic approach that takes into account the well-being of everyone involved in violence including the person doing harm.

This Toolkit encourages people to hold back when they experience feelings of judgment, blame and frustration with regard to the survivor or victim. It encourages people to self-check on where these feelings are coming from and whether or not they are coming from a personal bias against that particular person or some other aspect of that person such as their gender (male, female or other), race or class. It also acknowledges that working with violence and accompanying feelings of anger, fear, disappointment, shame and so on can easily turn people against the survivor or victim. Once you get clearer about your own feelings, it may be easier to separate these feelings from important opinions that you may have about the intervention process. As much as possible, step back and use the tools in this Toolkit to tackle differences and reach consensus. Honesty is an important part of this process.

#7 OFFERING SUPPORT CAN BE VERY DIFFICULT. MAKE SURE YOU HAVE YOUR OWN SUPPORT.

Offering support can be difficult. It can be exhausting, frightening, and disappointing. It can bring up painful memories of our own histories of violence or other related experiences.

At times, our efforts to support may be unacknowledged and unappreciated. The survivor or victim may find that the support you offer is not they asked for or are comfortable with. You may make a mistake. You attitudes or actions may cause harm – however unintentional. You might disappoint or anger the survivor or victim.

Understand that disappointment or anger can come from the stressful situation of violence and intervention. It can also be a very real response to shortcomings in the way you offer support.

Be willing to learn from these experiences. Forgive yourself for mistakes that you may make. And rely upon other intervention allies or your own allies to support yourself. Encourage an intervention team process that allows for time to step away, reflect and offer helpful feedback and support to everyone involved in the intervention.

#8 SUPPORT FOR SURVIVORS OR VICTIMS CAN BE COMPLICATED IF YOU HAVE A RELATIONSHIP TO THE PERSON DOING HARM.

Some of us who offer support to survivors or victims will also have a relationship to the person doing harm. We can be in a particularly good position to care about the person doing harm and also support the survivor or victim. Having people who can play both of these roles can help the team act in a more holistic way.

Having a relationship with the person doing harm can also bring about conflict. We might feel that our support for the survivor or victim is betraying the person doing harm. We might feel protective of the person doing harm and interpret the intervention as unfair or overly harsh. We might question our own loyalties and wonder whose side we are on.

It might be helpful to remind ourselves that supporting survivors or victims, in the long term, can also be beneficial to the person doing harm. Thinking about how to maintain an intervention process that feels like it supports the survivor or victim and is connected to and supportive of the person doing harm can help to drive a holistic intervention.

You may also find that you can play a better role actively supporting the person doing harm while lessening your direct role in supporting the survivor or victim or vice versa. Or you may have such difficulty playing these dual roles, that you decide to step back a distance from the intervention altogether. Use the tools in this Toolkit to help you figure out a way to offer support that minimizes your sense of conflict and makes best use of the compassion that you might feel for survivor or victim and the person doing harm.

E.4. *SUPPORTING SURVIVORS OR VICTIMS* SPECIAL CONSIDERATION

Supporting Survivors or Victims may be a central part of many interventions to violence. However, the dynamics of supporting survivors or victims can vary greatly depending upon many factors.

One of those factors is the degree to which the survivor or victim is leading, participating in or agreeing with the intervention. Although many interventions will likely begin with and be led by a survivor or victim, this is not always the case. The following are some special considerations on supporting survivors or victims.

The relationship that the survivor or victim of violence has to support can be very different depending upon that person's personality, their experience in receiving help in the past, and their relationship to the person or people offering support.

Generally, most people experiencing violence will want that experience to change, whether it is addressing something from the past, ending violence in the present, or preventing violence in the future. It is also common that survivors or victims may not trust that the process leading to change will make things better. In fact, it is true that interventions to violence are not necessarily positive. They can lead to backlash.

They can lead to more violence. They can expose the survivor or victim to gossip, judgment and possibly further harm if people start to blame the survivor or victim for the violence. Aspects of the intervention that people do not agree with could further expose the survivor or victim to blame for the intervention. It is no wonder that a survivor or victim may not trust that they will get the kind of support they need.

Sensitive, consistent and non-judgmental support, on the other hand, even if distrusted or even rejected at first may be accepted if it is extended over time. Trust can take a long time to build. Patience and understanding can go a long way.

If you are the survivor or victim, you may have difficult trusting that you will receive the support you need. You may find support inconsistent and, at times, disappointing.

Because this intervention approach relies upon a community of people – even if that community is only made up of you and one other person, this Toolkit encourages you to start with at least one person you can trust. Use the information or tools in this Toolkit to think about what kind of support you most need and to identify the best people to offer at least some pieces of support. Use the Toolkit to help your friends, family or other allies to know how best to offer their support to you.

Trust your own feelings about the kind of support you are getting. Is it helpful or not? Does it make you more confused or more clear-headed? Do you feel cared for? Does it make you feel even more helpless?

Try to identify the feelings that you have regarding the support you are receiving. Use this as an opportunity to speak honestly about your feelings, make changes regarding who you are receiving support from or what kind of support you are requesting from them.

You may also find that you need to make peace with the shortcomings of others or with the reality that no amount of support feels like it is enough. This does not mean that you have to reject the support coming your way, but that you can make wise use of this support, even if it is not exactly right.

Creative Interventions also found that survivors or victims may want an intervention to happen but may not want to be involved in any way. As much as this is understandable and may be agreeable to the people involved in the intervention, it may also make it difficult for them to make an effective intervention. The situation of violence may be complicated and difficult for them to understand even if they are supportive. They may come up with an intervention that you think completely misses the point based upon what happened. While this may seem to put a burden on the survivor or victim to make too many decisions or expose you to what can be disturbing details of an intervention that does not always go well, your participation can be helpful to the overall goal.

On the other hand, people involved in the intervention may not want the survivor or victim to actively participate due to differing opinions about what should be done or a feeling that they are being too closely watched for doing the right or wrong thing.

These two extreme situations can be difficult to manage. If possible, it is best to be somewhere in the middle and able to be flexible enough to talk about and deal with any tensions that come up if the intervention moves to one side or the other.

See Tool E.3. Survivor or Victim Participation in an Intervention Chart

The community ally (family, friend, neighbor, co-worker, community member) is likely to be offering support to the survivor or victim in some way. In some interventions, supporting survivors or victims may even be the focus of all or most of the intervention, especially if for whatever reason, the intervention does not address or engage the person doing harm at all.

If you are a community ally, supporting survivors or victims can look a variety of ways. The survivor or victim may be a close family member or friend and be someone that it is easy to support. You may know exactly what this person needs. They may be a person close to you but be difficult to support. You may know them well, but not be so good about knowing how to offer support. Or this situation of violence and intervention may be bring up new challenges.

Sometimes community allies do not know the survivor or victim well but may have been brought into an intervention because they are somehow connected to them or perhaps are introduced by others on the team. At times, this can be an easy match. At others, it will take some time to figure out the best way to play a supporting role.

Supporting survivors is often a key aspect of an intervention and can be complicated. See Section 4.A.1. Supporting Survivors or Victims What Is Supporting Survivors or Victims and 4.A.3. Supporting Survivors or Victims Tips for more suggestions on how allies can help to support survivors or victims.

In this Toolkit, we allow for the perspective of the person doing harm to enter the situation. This is different from many anti-violence organizations that often automatically dismiss this perspective as an attempt to manipulate the situation or blame the victim. Creative Interventions has found that people doing harm have very different approaches to supporting survivors or victims.

On one extreme, some people doing harm wish only to continue harming the survivor or victim. An intervention may be the greatest threat and may bring on desires for retaliation in any way possible.

Other people doing harm want to support the survivor or victim because they hope that it will lead to a continued relationship. If the survivor or victim desires a continued relationship, then this can form the basis for some kind of co-existence or even closeness. If the survivor or victim does not desire a continued relationship, then support can look more like manipulation to get what the person doing harm wants.

Efforts to support survivors or victims may also be genuine. It is important to take the lead of survivors or victims to sense whether or not this is the type of support they want. It may also be important for allies to watch to make sure that efforts by the person doing harm to support survivors or victims are not used to get out of accountability or to gain access to survivors or victims in order to continue an abusive relationship. This may seem like a cynical interpretation of a positive effort. However, in the experience of Creative Interventions, such outcomes happened frequently enough to raise caution.

If you are the person doing harm or are the person accused of doing harm, the greatest support you can offer the survivor or victim may be your ability to take accountability for the harm you have caused. This includes stopping all forms of harm, acknowledging the harm, recognizing and acknowledging the consequences of harm even if you did not intend them, making repairs for harm, and changing attitudes and behaviors that have been harmful and that have contributed to your harm.

If you have been in a position of causing harm, then it is very possible that your interpretation of support may not be the same as that of the survivor or victim you have harmed. Much of accountability is about shifting from a me-centered perspective to an other-centered perspective. This is not an easy shift to make.

See Section 4.F. Taking Accountability and other parts of this Toolkit to get a better idea of how you can take accountability, offer appropriate and welcome support to the survivor or victim and others affected by your attitudes and actions, and reach outcomes that are truly beneficial to them. Be open to how taking accountability is helpful to you, as well.

People are rarely 100% allies or 100% barriers. Try supporting the group to think creatively and to expand out of "black and white" and "either/or" thinking. When we think of people as 100% allies, we can overlook ways in which they are not the best fit in to certain roles. When we think of people as 100% barriers, we can miss ways in which they could be well suited to a specific task. It is possible for participants in an intervention to be allies to one goal and barriers to another.

#1 ENCOURAGE AND SUPPORT PEOPLE TO LEARN FUNDAMENTAL INFORMATION FIRST IF THEY HAVE NOT ALREADY.

This Toolkit is long and can be overwhelming. Some important parts of this Toolkit are Section 2. Some Basics Everyone Should Know. An especially important section can be Section 2.2. Interpersonal Violence: Some Basics Everyone Should Know that discusses much more about the dynamics of violence and common misunderstandings that people have.

It can be useful for you to be familiar with the different sections of this Toolkit and to read more carefully through these sections. Also encourage people to read these sections. If reading is not the best option or they cannot read English or the language that this Toolkit is in, you can help by reading this and other sections to them in a language they understand or use other formats to pass on this information.

#2 MAKE SURE TO RETURN TO THE SURVIVOR OR VICTIM AS AN ANCHOR TO THE INTERVENTION PROCESS.

If the survivor or victim is part of or at least connected to the intervention process, then you as a facilitator may be in a good position to make sure that people are considering the perspective of the survivor or victim, their needs and wants, and their safety. This may be done by regularly checking in with the survivor or victim during a discussion to make sure the process is working for them.

If the survivor or victim is not in the room, you may help support them by reminding people that someone needs to connect with the survivor or victim, see how they are doing, see what they need, and keep them informed about the progress of the intervention. Perhaps this will be part of your own role as the facilitator.

This may be by making sure that at least one person has a role of supporting the survivor directly by staying connected to them and making sure that their needs are being met, they are staying safe, and any fears or concerns are being addressed. This support may be extended to their children, family members, friends and pets.

#3 MAKE SURE THAT SURVIVOR OR VICTIM SAFETY IS ADDRESSED.

The survivor or victim may be in an especially vulnerable position with regard to safety. Actions taken by the intervention team may lead in anticipated and unanticipated ways to retaliation against the survivor or victim as they have been a central target of violence by the person doing harm.

While the possibility of retaliation may not stop you from going ahead with the intervention, all risks must be examined and explored before moving forward. Safety plans need to be established so that the survivor or victim as well as allies or others involved in the intervention are not further harmed as a result of the intervention. This concern may also extend to other vulnerable people such as children, family members, friends, pets or anyone that is involved in or close to the intervention.

E.6. *SUPPORTING SURVIVORS OR VICTIMS* REAL LIFE STORIES & EXAMPLES

Story E. Getting Support from My Co-Workers

So we'd been married for a year and a half. We were both very involved politically. I had a new baby, I was at home. I know that I started feeling like my life was kind of slipping away.

But his world started to change. And he started to become much more community-involved and I was less and less community involved. And it led to a lot of tension in the relationship, and a lot of tension around me being at home and he being sort of out in the world. I think the arguing and the fighting and the challenging verbally started. And it just escalated. And became very contentious, you know. The relationship was very contentious.

So I remember he came home one night, and he had been out. And I remember he came home one night and we just started fighting. I picked up a glass and threw it at him and it hit him in the side of his face and that was it. He chased me in the living room. We have this brick fireplace in the living room. He chased me in the house and grabbed me, threw me on the floor and just pounded my face into the brick wall. I mean, when thinking about it now, I'm thinking, "How did I survive that?" I felt like he was going to kill me. I mean, I felt like this man has lost his mind, and I'm dead. I remember that he just kicked me, pounded my face into the brick wall, into this fireplace, and…and then he left.

The first assault was one thing. That was shocking to me. The second one was more shocking. Because the first one felt to me like he just lost it, and he just wasn't aware of what he was doing, and he just responded so violently because he lost control of himself. And that to me was not as shocking as the second time because I felt like the second time was almost more being very much more intentional. So I was much more shocked that actually happened after we got back together. I still felt like I was in a lot of shock, and I was very depressed.

You know, I was depressed after this happened. I was depressed for probably about three or four months. I was just in a deep, deep depression. And mostly because I felt like you know this was a person that I just didn't know. I just didn't see this side of him.

I couldn't go to work. My supervisors were very supportive. I mean my whole face was...I couldn't go to work because my face was so damaged that there was no way I could leave the house looking like I was looking. So my co-workers were very supportive and gave me the time I needed to be off.

I don't think we called the police. And I wasn't going to. I mean, police to me was never an option. I don't think I felt like they would have done anything at all. I wasn't necessarily opposed to the police, but I just didn't feel like I knew what their role was. So I didn't call them, but there was plenty of other support. And I don't think I ever, I don't think I felt like there was anybody who was not supportive of me. I never heard anybody say things like, "Well, you need to leave the motherf*****" or to say, "What did you do to provoke him?" I don't think I heard those kind of comments from anybody. I got a lot of support and affirmation and people wanting to be helpful.

I think the first level of support was concern for my physical well-being. And you know, really making sure that I felt safe. And where I was, was I safe? And did I feel like I needed some support to make me safe? And I don't think there was much of a sense from my friends of any sort of like domestic violence shelters or anything like that. I think it was, "Do you feel safe here in your house? He's not here, he's gone, do you feel safe? Do you feel like he'll come back? And if he comes back do you feel safe about that?" And so I think there was a lot of concern about my safety.

There was also a lot of concern about my mental health and what that meant in terms of just taking care of myself physically. People brought me food. "Are you eating?" "Do you need somebody to be here with you?" I mean, I think the fact that I was depressed was really scary for people. "Do you need us to be here to make sure you're eating?" "Make sure you're not sort of thinking about suicide or anything like that." So there was a, there was a lot of that. "Do you just need someone, do you just need someone to come and cook you some dinner or lunch or whatever." I had people that bought groceries for me, and brought food to me, and offered to come and help clean the house. And it wasn't at all patronizing. It was like, "You know what, we understand that right now you might not have the energy to do all of these things, so let us take care of you."

Even to the point where – I just, I never will forget this. We had hardwood floors at the time. And I remember one person saying, "Do you want me to come in here and paint your walls?" I mean, it was like, "We'll paint for you!" You know, I think they wanted to change the environment or create an environment where I felt comfortable. "Is there something different we can do here in your house." So I remember that a couple people came and painted my living room and dining room, and I remember getting new rugs on the floor.

So my friends were more concerned about my well-being and I had a little nine month old. They were concerned about "Was I able to take care of her and did I need some support in taking care of her?" So people were providing tangible things for me. And then, people were just willing. "You need to call us in the middle of the night, call me." I mean I just had people who were like, "Just call me." "You need to talk, just call me and talk." I felt like I was a burden, and I felt like I didn't want to impose this on my friends, but I felt like they were there. "You want to talk ad nauseum, talk ad nauseum." So I felt like there was just kind of listening, they were able to listen to me.

TOOLS

4.E SUPPORTING SURVIVORS

Tool E1. What Does the Survivor or Victim Need? Checklist

Tool E2. What Does the Survivor or Victim Need? Guiding Questions

Tool E3. Survivor or Victim Participation in an Intervention Chart

☑ *SUPPORTING SURVIVORS OR VICTIMS* TOOL E1: WHAT DOES THE SURVIVOR OR VICTIM NEED? CHECKLIST

Supporting survivors or victims can look many different ways to many different people. This tool offers ideas of possible types of support that survivors or victims have said have been helpful over time.

POSSIBLE WAYS YOU CAN SUPPORT A SURVIVOR OR VICTIM OF INTERPERSONAL VIOLENCE

- ☐ Make a human connection
- ☐ Let them know you care
- ☐ Listen to their story
- ☐ Ask them what they need
- ☐ Help them get what they need
- ☐ Let them know that interpersonal violence happens to many people
- ☐ Praise them for anything and everything they do to address their situation of harm – including talking to you
- ☐ Let them know that they are not alone
- ☐ Things you can offer:
    - ☐ Listening ear
    - ☐ Patience – through what may be their inability to make a decision, confusion, changing minds, repetition
    - ☐ Someone to lean on or hand to hold – through fear, shame, confusion, depression, embarrassment
    - ☐ Sounding board – to listen and offer feedback, not necessarily to give advice
    - ☐ Safety (See Section 4.B. Staying Safe)
    - ☐ Medical care
    - ☐ Mental health care or counseling
    - ☐ Religious or spiritual support

- ☐ Companionship
- ☐ Help supporting children or other dependents – childcare, child pick-up, activities with children, emotional support for children who may be going through hard time through violence or intervention
- ☐ Help taking care of pets or other beings or things that the survivor or victim usually cares for
- ☐ Help educating and informing others to be good allies – trusted friends, family members, neighbors, co-workers, community members
- ☐ Help protecting from people who may bring risk or harm – including those who mean to be helpful but who are not
- ☐ Help support the person doing harm to take accountability – if you are in a position to do so (See Section 4.E. Taking Accountability)
- ☐ Help finding and connecting them to resources
- ☐ Help with housing or safe shelter if needed
- ☐ Help moving, storing things, packing, unpacking
- ☐ Help with accompaniment, rides/transportation, access to telephone or internet
- ☐ Help with other necessary things – (example, clothes, food, money, bus card)
- ☐ Help figuring out how they want to talk about their situation, what they specifically need, and what they want to prioritize
- ☐ Help with translation, interpretation, for non-English or limited-English speakers or hearing or visually impaired and explaining of factors such as culture or immigration status to services providers
- ☐ Help figuring out way around "systems" such as police, criminal justice, immigration, or child welfare if these systems might present risk or harm (for example, if they are an undocumented immigrant)
- ☐ Help them use the Toolkit
- ☐ Become familiar with this Toolkit
- ☐ Introduce them to Toolkit in a way that is useful (and not overwhelming) – may include reading pieces, photocopying pages, translating useful information
- ☐ Introduce other allies to the Toolkit in a way that is useful
- ☐ Play a role as an ally as presented in this Toolkit (See Section 4.C. Mapping Allies and Barriers)

? SUPPORTING SURVIVORS OR VICTIMS TOOL E2: WHAT DOES THE SURVIVOR OR VICTIM NEED? GUIDING QUESTIONS

If you are a survivor or victim of violence and think you might want the support from others that you trust about your situation of violence, here are some questions to think about:

WHO CAN SUPPORT YOU?

1. Who are the people you usually turn to?

2. Who has been helpful – and what is it that made them helpful?

3. Who do you think could be helpful in supporting you with your situation of violence?

4. If you are not sure you want to turn to those you usually turn to, why or why not?

5. When you think about people to support you with your situation of violence, what is important to you?

6. Who are some other trusted people you might be able to talk to (if this is different than the list of people you usually turn to)?

7. If you cannot think of anybody right now, what are some types of people you could look for who might be able to help?

WHAT KIND OF SUPPORT DO YOU WANT?

1. When you think about what kind of support you want, you think of the following (make a list):

   (See the previous tool, Section 4.E. Supporting Survivors or Victims Tool E1: What Does the Survivor or Victim Need? Checklist for a list of ideas that might be helpful)

2. When you look at the list above, the most important are (or list them in order with the most important on top):

3. What are some things that you definitely do NOT want?

4. Think about how to use this exercise to ask for help. You can practice asking for these things. You can meet with someone you trust and have them help you figure out how to find more support. You can use these lists to write a letter about what you want (and what you don't want).

SUPPORTING SURVIVORS OR VICTIMS TOOL B: SURVIVOR OR VICTIM PARTICIPATION IN AN INTERVENTION CHART

While Creative Interventions encourages active survivor or victim participation, this can happen at different levels. This chart helps you sort out what level of survivor or victim participation best describes your intervention process – or – which level best describes what you would like your process to look like.

	Survivor or Victim Leadership in the Intervention	**Survivor- or Victim-Centered Intervention Goals**	**Survivor or Victim Coordination and Decision-Making**	**Communication with Survivor or Victim**
Highest Level of participation and priority	Survivor or victim is leading and directing the intervention	Survivor goals = intervention goals	Survivor is making all key decisions and coordinating individual allies or leading a group of allies	Survivor is making all decisions and so knows all information – decides what to communicate with other allies or person doing harm
Priority but consideration of others is important	Survivor or victim is leading the intervention but others may act in other important roles such as facilitator, coordinator or other key roles	Survivor or victim goals are the priority but there has been group input into and group agreement with goals	Survivor or victim is involved in all decision-making but there is also a process to get input from others	Survivor or victim knows all information and is involved in all decision-making but there is active involvement of a group that also has significant information
Important but consideration weighed with others	A group has agreed to some process of shared leadership – even if survivor may have actively started the process – or if there is a main facilitator or coordinator	Survivor or victim goals are central but they have also been taken into consideration with key input from others including ally or community goals – group consensus has been reached	A group is coordinating decision-making that includes the survivor or victim as a key contributor	There is a group process for shared information and communication with everyone including the survivor or victim
Important but role is mostly to give feedback	Survivor or victim has some distance from the intervention – agrees to a process to give feedback	Survivor or victim has participated in and agrees with the overall goals – may or may not be involved in changes in goals depending on prior agreement	Survivor or victim has some distance but has agreed to a process for giving feedback that is given special consideration	Survivor or victim has some distance but there is an agreed upon process and timing for giving information and receiving feedback
Survivor or victim agrees but is not involved*	Survivor or victim agrees generally with the intervention but will not be involved	Survivor or victim may have participated in and agree with the overall goals – may or may not be involved if goals change depending on prior agreement	Survivor or victim is not involved in coordination or decision-making	Survivor or victim may or may not be given information at some agreed-upon timing or perhaps at the end of the intervention

Survivor or victim disagrees and is not involved*	Survivor or victim disagrees with the intervention and is not involved	Survivor or victim disagrees but group considers known or likely survivor goals including safety	Survivor or victim is not involved in coordination or decision-making	Survivor or victim disagrees and may or may not be given at least some information to let them know what is happening with the intervention
Survivor or victim is not at all involved*	For some reason, survivor or victim is completely unavailable	Group considers known or likely survivor or victim goals including safety	Survivor or victim is not involved in coordination or decision-making	Survivor or victim if known or reachable may or may not be given information to let them know what is happening with the intervention

WHAT IF THE SURVIVOR OR VICTIM IS NOT INVOLVED?

The last three rows show a situation in which the survivor or victim is not involved in the intervention process. Again, Creative Interventions has found that survivor participation is best. However, it may be possible to carry out a community-based intervention that minimally involves the survivor or victim or does not involve them at all.

For example, this may happen in cases where an organization or a community group has a policy to always deal with known situations of violence that happen within the organization or among its members. In this case, the organization or community group may have come to know about a situation of violence and even have been told by the survivor or victim. It is possible that the survivor or victim would request that nothing be done about it. An organization or community group might have a policy that is more "survivor-centered," meaning that it would go along with whatever the survivor or victim requested. In this case, a request to do nothing may be followed even if the organization or community group wanted to take action.

On the other hand, the organization or community group could have a policy that they will take some type of action whenever they learn about a situation of violence or abuse, perhaps depending upon the level of abuse or the type. They may let the survivor or victim know that it is their policy and their responsibility to address the violence, preferably with the participation of the survivor or victim.

The survivor or victim may then decide to become involved even though they were hesitant at first. They may become involved at various levels of participation such as those outlined in the chart above. Or it is possible that they will still disagree with this decision, may ask not to be involved, or may even be actively against an intervention.

If the survivor or victim does not agree with the intervention or does not want to participate, then the organization still has the responsibility to support the survivor or victim as best as it can given the circumstances. In a holistic intervention, the well-being of all is taken into consideration – even among those who are not participating or willing to participate. While this usually refers to the person doing harm, this can also include the survivor or victim.

If the survivor or victim is not participating, then a community-based intervention still has the responsibility to support the survivor or victim as best as it can. This can include:

- Leaving an open door to the participation of the survivor or victim and process by which they can check in
- Finding a way to include their known goals or their likely goals into the intervention goals
- Offering support through the many options listed in Section 4.E. Supporting Survivors or Victims Tool E1: What Does the Survivor or Victim Need? Checklist.
- Offering an occasional update on the intervention which can include:
    - Requests made of the person doing harm and/or the community that did or allowed harm
    - What kind of follow up that the person or community doing harm has committed to and completed
    - Results of the intervention at some certain points of the intervention (for example, weekly, monthly, after certain key meetings or events or at the end/ closure of an intervention)

In other situations, the survivor or victim may be completely unknown or unavailable. They may be in safe hiding and may need or request complete confidentiality. They may be too young to actively participate. They may be too injured or ill. They may not be alive. In these cases, a known person who can represent them such as a partner, a parent or guardian, a family member, or a close friend may serve as someone to connect to this person or to represent them as best as they can.

4F TAKING ACCOUNTABILITY
HOW DO WE CHANGE VIOLENCE?

F.1. What Is Taking Accountability?

F.2. Taking Accountability Across the 4 Phases

F.3. Tips

F.4. Special Considerations

F.5. Facilitator Notes

F.6. Real Life Stories and Examples

F.7. Taking Accountability Tools

F.1. WHAT IS *TAKING ACCOUNTABILITY?*

Taking Accountability: Key Questions

- What could make the violence stop?
- What could prevent further violence?
- Who/What does the person doing harm care about?

What is Accountability?

In brief, accountability is the ability to recognize, end and take responsibility for violence. We usually think of the person doing harm as the one to be accountable for violence. Community accountability also means that communities are accountable for sometimes ignoring, minimizing or even encouraging violence. Communities must also recognize, end and take responsibility for violence by becoming more knowledgeable, skillful and willing to take action to intervene in violence and to support social norms and conditions that prevent violence from happening in the first place.

Note that this Toolkit and this section focuses primarily on the accountability of the person doing harm. However, this information and these tools can also apply to communities that have directly caused harm and/or communities that have allowed harm to happen.

Also note that a beginning step of accountability may be getting violence to stop. Depending upon the willingness and openness of the person doing harm to take accountability, the ability of the survivor or victim or the allies to push for these changes, and such factors as how serious the level of violence, the step of stopping violence may be the result of pressure or even force. This Toolkit encourages a process of accountability that relies upon changes that the person doing harm (or the community) actively participates in making. The level of participation and willingness of the person doing harm to take accountability, however, may change significantly as the intervention process moves along. And the direction of change, positive or negative, can differ widely and shift dramatically over time, even within a single intervention and with a single individual.

Accountability Means Many Things

Accountability involves listening, learning, taking responsibility, and changing. It involves conscientiously creating opportunities in our families and communities for direct communication, understanding and repairing of harm, readjustment of power toward empowerment and equal sharing of power, and rebuilding of relationships and communities toward safety, respect, and happiness.

While it would certainly be a simpler world if accountability were one concept and one conversation, the reality of accountability is complex. Many different people have different ideas about what accountability is and what it looks like. Accountability is a many-sided word. What we mean by accountability shifts depending on whether we are looking at the short term, the long term, how we take accountability ourselves, and how we support others to take accountability.

The word "accountability" can also bring up all kinds of images and feelings for different people at different times. Often, we think of accountability as linked to punishment, "paying" for what someone did, or even going to prison.

For Creative Interventions, we are trying to have a different way of thinking about accountability – one that is more positive, that is tied to responsibility and change, but not to punishment and revenge. One that can be driven by connection and care rather than fear and anger alone. This is not to take away from the fact that violence and abuse cause fear, anger and outrage. It does. And such emotions have their place.

But the change from violence to compassion, safety, respect and health also needs to come from the values that we want to see even if these might be difficult to feel when we are facing violence.

Interpersonal violence primarily takes place within our families, friendship networks, neighborhoods and communities. They happen among people we know and sometimes among those we are closest to. Therefore, we are promoting accountability as a way to 1) stop violence; 2) acknowledge violence; 3) acknowledge the harms resulting from violence – even if unintended; 4) repair those harms; and 5) fundamentally change those attitudes and actions responsible for the violence.

We are promoting accountability as a way to keep our communities whole, safe and healthy, rather than a way to punish, separate and send away.

This does NOT mean that survivors or victims need to forgive the people who do harm, or that we simply ask for an apology and everything is fine, or that relationships and families need to stay together. None of these fit the definition of accountability, although it is possible that forgiveness, apologies and even staying together may be part of what some people decide that they want and may even be able to reach.

A person's choice to make a change is key. Toward that goal, "taking responsibility" or even "taking accountability" work better as approaches and phrases than "holding someone accountable." When we say 'people need to be held accountable,' we are likely to come across sounding punitive and controlling. The person who is expected to be accountable is not ever going to choose to want to be held accountable. Who would choose that? Anyone would struggle against it. And if we want success, we need that person, someplace in themselves, to want to make a change. They have to be and feel active.

It can just mean supporting someone to learn something new and change out of old patterns.

ACCOUNTABILITY AS A PROCESS

We can think of accountability in several ways.

1. ACCOUNTABILITY CAN HAPPEN OVER A CONTINUUM OF TIME.

Accountability is something someone can take in the short term. We might:

- Stop using violence.
- Slow down and listen to understand how our actions have impacted those around us.
- Take action to repair the harm that our actions have caused others.
- Identify and try out new ways of thinking and behaving.
- Get support and encouragement for our efforts and successes.
- Taking accountability or accountability is also a long-term and life-long process. We might:
- Grow our confidence to face our imperfections and turn away from patterns that harm others (and ultimately ourselves).
- Grow our ability to feel our emotions without acting them out.
- Practice and promote behaviors that honor ourselves and others.
- Humbly support others around us to do the same.
- Learn from and move beyond mistakes and set-backs.
- Practice self-awareness and self-reflection to build mutually supportive and enjoyable relationships.

2. ACCOUNTABILITY CAN HAPPEN ALONG A CONTINUUM OF DEPTH.

Any of the following can be thought of as elements of accountability:

- Being confronted at all, even just once about the violence that was done.

- Experiencing and understanding that violence has natural negative consequences (for example, recognizing that one's violence caused their friends to be shocked and scared – finding that friends began to avoid them).

- Stopping or reducing violence – even if doing so is a response to social pressures from friends or community, or to a threat of losing relationships due to continued use of violence – and not because of deep change.

- Listening to the person who was harmed talk about their experience of violence – without being defensive, interrupting or reacting against this story.
- Acknowledging the reality of the experience for the person who was harmed – even if this is not at all what was intended.
- Acknowledging that the use of violence was ultimately a choice – not something caused by someone else.
- Expressing sincere apology, taking responsibility, and showing care to the person who was harmed.
- Giving financial repairs (or reparations) to the person harmed.
- Giving other significant repairs, perhaps in the form of service, replacement of property, and so on, to the person harmed.
- Agreeing and taking every step possible to assure that these harms will not be committed again.
- Knowing and agreeing that any future acts of harm will result in certain negative consequences.
- Telling others about one's own uses of violence not in order to gain followers or sympathizers, but to stop hiding private interpersonal violence.
- Telling others about one's own uses of violence to ask for support in changing.
- Telling others about one's own uses of violence to show that taking accountability can be an act of honor and courage.
- Making it one's own choice, commitment and goal to address root causes of violence, to learn new skills, and to deeply transform violent behaviors.
- Showing actual changes in thinking and behavior in good times.
- Showing actual changes to thinking and behavior in hard and stressful times.
- Supporting others who have used or are using violence to take steps to take accountability.

ACCOUNTABILITY AS A PATHWAY

In this Toolkit, we talk about accountability as a pathway. You can start one step at a time, and you can measure progress each step of the way.

Although we use this pathway to show steps towards accountability and a vision of positive and transformative change, an intervention may never reach any of these steps. Intervention goals may only anticipate reaching Step 1 as a measure of success.

And, rather than walking up the pathway one step at a time, one might consider the progression as more of a dance -- one may be dealing with more than one step at a time and at times may move from one step to another and back again.

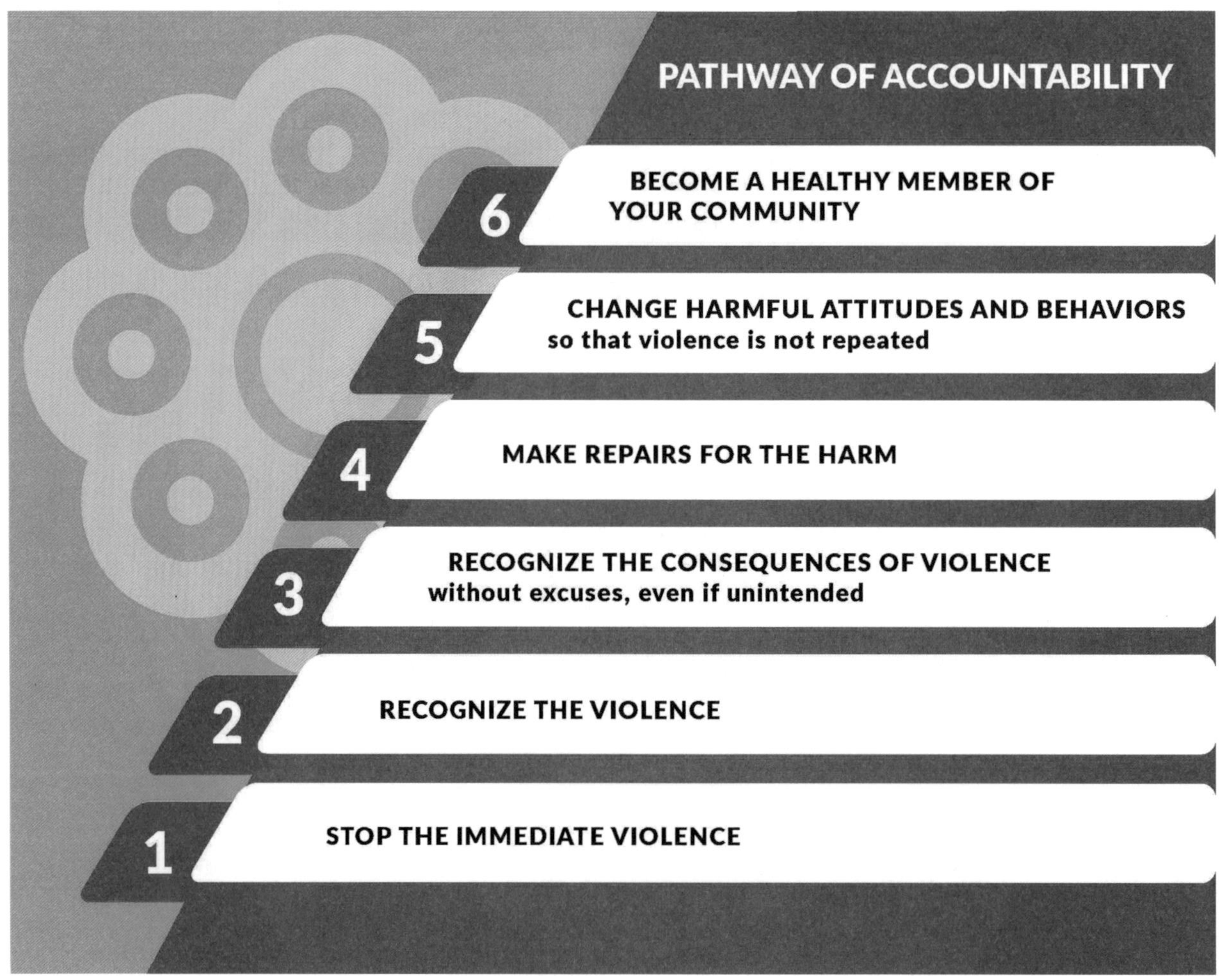
PATHWAY OF ACCOUNTABILITY
6 BECOME A HEALTHY MEMBER OF YOUR COMMUNITY
5 CHANGE HARMFUL ATTITUDES AND BEHAVIORS so that violence is not repeated
4 MAKE REPAIRS FOR THE HARM
3 RECOGNIZE THE CONSEQUENCES OF VIOLENCE without excuses, even if unintended
2 RECOGNIZE THE VIOLENCE
1 STOP THE IMMEDIATE VIOLENCE

Accountability Looks Different With Each Situation

There is no blueprint for accountability. People are different. Situations and types of violence or risk are different. Some processes do well with lots of time and intense involvement. Other processes work best when they are short, to the point, and are allowed to show their impact over time.

Accountability does not have to be punitive, painful, terrifying, or retaliatory. We can make it clear, encouraging, firm, and practical. We can make aspects of it feel like a relief. Accountability can help us be seen and understood by those around us. It can help us not be and feel so alone, and can help us develop the kinds of relationships we want in our lives.

At the same time, accountability does not make sense as a primary goal for every violent situation or intervention. Sometimes a community does not have the resources, time, or opportunity to engage a person to take accountability for their violence. Sometimes people doing harm are not ready or willing to make any acknowledgement of or effort to change their viewpoints and violence. Sometimes the violence committed is so morally heinous to us or so progressed and long-standing that we feel hatred, anger, and disgust, and cannot find anyone who might engage the person doing harm with intent free of aggression or vengeance. Sometimes the most thoughtful, open, non-penalizing, and supportive invitation to accountability from a friend, community member or leader does not result in most of the levels of accountability listed earlier. And sometimes people doing harm show that any confrontation or request for accountability results only in escalating their harmful behaviors.

But these efforts are something.

Though resulting positive changes might not be immediate, visible, "enough" or lasting, these efforts to intervene in violence are a big deal. They rise above silence, passivity, and inaction, and make peace and wellness in our families and communities something we work, not wait for.

Why Is It Important?

This Toolkit is based upon the belief that communities working together can overcome violence, and the vision that each of us as individuals are capable of meaningful change towards that end. Our vision of accountability as a process or as a pathway of change means that we value any step leading towards the end of or reduction of violence and that we also see each small step as one that can lead to our bigger vision of community well-being and, ultimately, liberation.

USING TOOLS IN THIS SECTION

This section has lengthy tools to use for the process of Taking Accountability. Tool F1. Pathway of Change introduces the concept of accountability as a process. It offers a way for you to see your own situation through the lens of these steps and allows for you to adapt them to your particular circumstances.

Tool F2. Level of Participation for Survivors or Victims Chart acknowledges that survivors or victims may have very different levels of involvement in a process of taking accountability. It breaks these possibilities down so that you can more clearly keep in mind how survivors or victims have chosen to stay involved and what kind of communication you will need to keep up. Tool F3. Self-Reflection and Guiding Questions for Survivors or Victims and Allies offers special tools for survivors or victims to think about their involvement in the accountability process.

Allies also have special needs regarding their involvement in the accountability process. Tool F4. Self-Reflection and Practice for Allies. Practice Questions offers some practical guiding questions and statements to help with what can be a difficult process.

Taking Accountability can be particularly challenging for people doing harm. Tool F5. Breaking through Defensiveness. Guiding Questions for the Person Doing Harm and Tool F6. Preparing for Direct Communication. Affirmations and Guided Questions for the Person Doing Harm offer some constructive support for people doing harm as they deal with the common pattern of defensiveness.

F.2. *TAKING ACCOUNTABILITY* ACROSS THE 4 PHASES

In Section 3.6. Interventions Over Time: 4 Phases, the Toolkit introduced the idea of 4 possible phases of interventions: 1) Getting Started, 2) Planning/Preparation, 3) Taking Action, and 4) Following Up.

Taking Accountability can look very different depending upon the phase of intervention.

PHASE 1: GETTING STARTED

Interventions generally begin with some need to address, reduce, end or prevent violence. Interventions will likely follow along one, two, or all three of the following areas (See Section 3.5. What Are We Trying to Achieve: 3 Key Intervention Areas):

1. Supporting survivors or victims (See Section 4.E. Supporting Survivors or Victims).
2. Accountability of person doing harm,
3. Community accountability or social change.

Accountability of the person doing harm or of a community that was responsible for allowing harm may never be part of an intervention. It may seem to too dangerous: the person doing harm may not be known, or people may simply be unable to think of any way in which they could possibly participate in a process of change. On the other hand, accountability may be a primary goal from the very beginning. It is even possible that an intervention begins with the person doing harm wanting to change and starting a process of taking responsibility for that change.

While it is impossible to generalize about how taking accountability might factor into an intervention at the beginning stages, it is likely that taking accountability, if pursued at all, will begin with some kind of difficult communication with the person doing harm. This may look like energetic resistance to violence, a confrontation, a challenging conversation. Even if this initial communication takes place with love, compassion and support, it is likely to be a difficult connection with perhaps uncertain results. It may be met with resistance, denial, minimization, victim blaming, or even violence. It may be welcomed, only to be denied later on. The process of taking accountability, in most cases, is a difficult one. We need a process that takes into account this difficulty while staying firm enough to support increasing levels of responsibility or accountability.

PHASE 2: PLANNING/PREPARATION

If taking accountability is part of the intervention, then there may be a period of planning and preparation to effectively communicate with and work together with the person doing harm. Some of this planning and preparation may involve deciding what are your goals that you expect from the intervention, what specific harms you want to address, what specific things you expect the person doing harm to do, and what will be the consequences if the expectations are not met. It may help to identify the person who is best to directly deal with the person doing harm , who has enough confidence to handle what may be a very difficult process; who does the person doing harm respect; how can the process be safe for the people intervening, the survivor or victim, and the person doing harm; what is the best process for talking with and supporting the person doing harm.

PHASE 3: TAKING ACTION

Taking action may refer to time spent with the person doing harm; discussions regarding the intervention, the expectations, and the possible outcomes; support for the person doing harm to move through a process of change; connection with helpful resources; and a process to give feedback to the person doing harm regarding these changes.

PHASE 4: FOLLOWING UP

If the intervention reaches a point of closure because goals have been met, then taking accountability may move towards a process of maintaining the positive changes reached and checking in to make sure that there is not a return to violent attitudes or behaviors. Systems may be set up to check in regularly.

It is also possible to bring closure even if goals are not met. The group may run out of resources to continue, the survivor or victim may move on and choose another pathway or strategy, or the person doing harm may resist involvement. In all of these situations, the intervention may still be considered a success in some way. Closure in this case may include some process where people can identify the areas of success and what aspects of the intervention may need following up. Plans can be made on how to make those steps happen.

RELATED TOOLS

A process of taking accountability is often accompanied by or a part of supporting survivors or victims. See *Section 4.E. Supporting Survivors and Victims* for information and tools. *Section 4.B. Staying Safe* has tools to help determine risks and plan for safety. These may be important steps to make when working with a person doing harm throughout an intervention. In order to think through which people or organizations may be helpful in directly communicating with and supporting a person doing harm, see *Section 4.C. Mapping Allies and Barriers.* These tools can be helpful in thinking about which people might be particularly good to positively communicate with and work with a person doing harm. This section may also identify who is likely to continue to support or excuse their violence and who, therefore, may be barriers to an intervention.

F.3. *TAKING ACCOUNTBILITY* TIPS

#1 ACCOUNTABILITY IS A PROCESS; IT MAY TAKE MANY TYPES OF STRATEGIES ALONG THE WAY.

In this Toolkit, we present accountability as a staircase. The first step on that staircase is stopping violence – or stopping it enough to be able to take the next step. It is difficult for someone to take responsibility in the middle of violence or in the middle of a cycle of violence that keeps continuing over and over again. It is difficult to ask for change and expect change to be lasting within a pattern or cycle of violence.

This Toolkit encourages us to take resistance to accountability into account. As we will repeat, we need to create systems flexible enough to allow for the expected process of dodging and delaying accountability and strong enough to withstand and diminish these tactics over time.

Strategies may include:

a. Communicating and showing connection and care.

b. Gathering people and power to widen the community net, shift community norms, increase leverage, and increase caring connection and support.

c. Using some measure of pressure, threats, force or coercion if no other means are possible or if necessary to prevent further violence. By this we do not mean the use of physical violence, but acts such as asking someone to stay away or leave, letting someone know that there will be consequences if violence continues, or physically restraining someone from acting out violently at that moment.

No matter what the strategy or level of resistance, create options and leave an open door to the possibility of someone becoming a "participant" in an intervention, and not just a "target."

There are times that violence must simply be stopped before any other meaningful action can take place. There are times that violence must be stopped immediately to prevent any further harm, injury or even death. There are times that taking accountability does not begin as a voluntary act. Sometimes, it begins with force.

But we urge caution. If force or any of these acts are used as punishment, vengeance, a way to get even, to let them know how it feels, to hurt them for the sake of making them feel the pain, then this may not be a justifiable form of force. However, if some level of force is the only reasonable and available way to get someone to stop their violence and to try to prevent further violence, then this can be considered a form of self-defense.

In some cases, people doing harm may be ready and willing, from the beginning, to take responsibility for their actions and change their behavior. This, however, is not often the case. More commonly, change and accountability are resisted, at least at first, and often over time.

Orienting attitudes, values, and options towards compassion and connection rather than punishment and revenge can help to keep an open pathway to a holistic solution — one that takes into account the wellbeing and participation of the survivor or victim, the community allies and the person doing harm.

#2 REMEMBER CONTEXT; IT MATTERS.

It is important to think about the relationship context of the violence through the lens of accountability. Remember to ask yourself: What kind of violent situation are you addressing?

In our experience, we have seen 4 common contexts for relationships. They are listed below. As you think with others about how to support a survivor, engage a person using violence to take responsibility, and/or involve a community in increasing safety and reducing or ending violence, remember always to bear in mind the context of your situation and how it impacts your approach and your goals.

4 Common Types of Relationship Contexts

a. The survivor or victim and the person doing harm are in an intimate or close relationship and are both trying to stay in a relationship which has been and may continue to be violent. Changing violence and shifting power dynamics over time might be the primary goal. A goal may also be that they live peacefully, or peacefully enough, with each other.

b. The survivor or victim and the person doing harm are not in an intimate or close relationship but do live in close shared community. They need to build understanding, responsibility, and repair to a degree that allows both to function in shared community, but not in the context of an ongoing intimate or close relationship. A goal may be that they co-exist in the same shared community without conflict.

c. The survivor or victim and the person doing harm are not living in shared community and/or are no longer in an intimate or close relationship. The violence happened a while ago and there is no intention to rebuild a relationship, or need to find a way to function well in shared community spaces. A goal may not include anything about their ongoing relationship – or may just want to put closure on a previous relationship.

d. A stranger or distant acquaintance commits an act of interpersonal violence. Perhaps neighbors or community members saw and did not intervene or create safety and support for the person harmed, or worsened some dynamics of interpersonal violence in their treatment of the harmed person after the violence. A goal may be that the community takes accountability for not doing enough to provide safety, for not taking action to stop the harm or to take responsibility to make sure that kind of harm does not happen again.

#3 MAKE SURE TO KEEP PEOPLE CONNECTED TO THE PERSON DOING HARM

If the intervention seriously takes on the process of taking accountability, then it is important to keep connected to the person doing harm. Because people are often uncomfortable dealing directly with the person doing harm, that person can be kept out of the loop and left hanging. Because people may be unsure about how to handle accountability, things can move slowly.

People can easily forget to update them on what's going on and can want to handle communication through the least personal forms of communication – like email. The person doing harm who is willing to participate can begin to build up anxiety especially if no communication is made or the only communication is vague and seemingly impersonal.

Keep connected. You may need to choose someone whose role is to keep the person doing harm informed, to keep connected to them, and to let them know that while stopping violence is important – supporting the person doing harm towards long-term change is also important.

#4 KEEP AN EYE ON SAFETY.

If the group is working with the person doing harm, then safety may be a major concern. The person doing harm could react with violence to a process of accountability. This could be directly when being pressed to make changes. This could also happen behind the scenes. For example, they could be trying to turn other people against the survivor or victim in retaliation; they could be trying to damage the reputations of the people working on the intervention; they could be getting their own supporters to do some kind of damage.

In some situations, these safety concerns may be minimal. In others, even if the person seems to be cooperating with the process or has not shown a high level of violence in the past, they may still be capable of significant harm.

It is easy to be too concerned about safety – so concerned that no action is taken. It is also easy to forget that safety is an issue – and act carelessly, perhaps exposing oneself and the survivor or victim to harm.

Harm may also be an issue for the person who has caused harm. Others may be out to get them, hoping that the process of accountability will be hurtful and punishing – or thinking that it is not punishing enough. People may be targeting the person doing harm for punishment or revenge.

#5 REMEMBER THAT COMMUNITIES ARE ALSO RESPONSIBLE FOR VIOLENCE. PAY ATTENTION TO THE COMMUNITY'S RESPONSIBILITY.

Community accountability reminds us that interpersonal violence is a community problem, not just an individual problem. It reminds us that communities have the responsibility to address, reduce, end and prevent violence, and that they have both the responsibility and the power to change violence.

It also reminds us that communities (including those who are actively working on this intervention) have had a role to play in allowing violence to happen.

Holding a process of accountability for a community to recognize the ways we have caused violence or allowed violence to happen, to recognize consequences even if unintended, to take steps to repair the harm, and to change community attitudes and actions is an important part of taking accountability.

This process of community accountability can serve as an important model of accountability for the person doing harm. And it can show the broader community (this may be at the level of family, friendship networks, organization, local community and so on) the big changes that communities need to make in order to prevent violence in the future.

#6 FOCUS ON ACCOUNTABILITY FOR VIOLENCE, NOT FOR EVERYTHING I DIDN'T LIKE OR JUDGE NOW AS A PROBLEM.

When working to make accountability and movement away from violence possible, remember that we are encouraging a community standard around violence, not dictating or micro-managing people's lives and relationships. There may be tons of things you don't like about the person doing harm, or that you don't like about the other person's or people's responses in the situation. There may be numerous actions or behaviors that you find frustrating, unhelpful or problematic in the person doing harm. You may also feel this way about the survivor or victim of violence.

If you find yourself or other involved people starting to list out all of the things you don't approve of or can't stand or want to look different, find a way to step back from being self-righteous; remember humility; and refocus on intervention goals.

Expecting people to change their core personalities as a result of a single community intervention is unwise and unrealistic. Expecting people to relate to other people in radically different ways after one conversation is very unlikely. Remember that there are thousands of different ways to be in relationship with other people that are not violent, but might not be a perfect model of clear communication, conflict resolution, love, and equality. We as community members do not need to "answer" to each other for our differences. We have to answer to our community about the violence we use, and then continue on our journey of learning how to relate to others in respectful, responsible, fulfilling, and sustaining ways.

#7 SEEK OUT THE MIDDLE GROUND.

When working to support people in taking responsibility, it can be easy to move toward the extremes: to have either extremely high (unrealistic, rigid, etc.) demands for accountability or to have very minimal expectations and to think that the smallest of actions show that they must have changed. It is helpful to check in with oneself and whoever else is involved, so as not to expect too much or too little about the response we want to see from a person doing harm.

#8 ACCOUNTABILITY GOALS; CONSIDER MAKING THEM ABOUT WHAT YOU CAN DO.

Sometimes we get so focused on other people and what we want them to do or stop doing, we forget that the accountability goals we can be sure to achieve are the ones that involve what we will do to make accountability and change possible. When working toward engaging people to stop violence, take responsibility, and make new choices, stay away from making all of your goals reflect how you'd like other people to respond to you and your requests. Avoid thinking of success as only what you get the other person to stop doing or start doing or change. You can never guarantee someone else's response. And you can never monitor someone's every move. Remember that you can make some of your intervention's accountability goals reflect your own efforts to make accountability and responsibility possible. These can have positive ripple effects across your community.

#9 ACCOUNTABILITY GOALS; BIGGER IS NOT USUALLY BETTER.

If our accountability goals are small or contained, it is not because we are weak, not demanding enough, not fierce enough, or not allowing room for transformation. It is because we are matching our actions to fit the situation. It is because we are not basing a plan on magical thinking. Small change that really happens is transformational! In community-based interventions that include efforts at accountability, we want to take thoughtful risks that allow for the possibility of lasting change—not take wild risks (for the sake of risk-taking or for the glory of quick, righteous action) that might open our intervention and the people involved in it to serious vulnerability and danger.

If we set a giant or all-inclusive goal that we can't realistically achieve, we risk losing our sense of accomplishment, direction, and hope. If we set a small goal and achieve it, we can set a next one, and then a next one after that. Our momentum grows.

#10 BE PREPARED; FIGURING OUT WHO IS THE SURVIVOR OR VICTIM AND WHO IS THE PERSON DOING HARM CAN BE COMPLICATED.

Sometimes violent dynamics are very clear and obvious. Being able to tell who is the primary person using violence and who is being harmed can be pretty obvious. Of course, we know from Section 2.2. Interpersonal Violence: Some Basics Everyone Should Know that even when it is obvious, some people still choose to deny the violence or blame the victim – this is still true even though people are much more aware about domestic violence and sexual assault.

Other times the dynamics of violence can be confusing and cause intense debate. Two (or more) people can tell their sides of the story to their friends and community and get two sides to be in opposition to each other on their behalf. Both sides might be crying out that they are the victim of the other person's wrongdoing and that the other person needs "to be held accountable." Especially in domestic violence situations, sometimes the person loudly calling the community together for support is actually the person doing harm. Sometimes they are doing this to make sure that the survivor or victim of their violence does not have access to any community support or resources. Sometimes they are calling for a huge response to an act of violence or resistance that their partner finally used in self-defense, in retaliation, or to finally say "no" to the violence by using violence as self-defense.

Often times, it is easy to tell who is responsible for the violence in the beginning when people come together to support their friend or family member who has told them about their experience of interpersonal violence. But later when those same people think about engaging (communicating with) the person who used the violence to take responsibility or accountability, they might decide to bring in other allies who may develop another perspective.

For example, bringing in an ally who can make a positive, influential connection to the person doing harm can be helpful to the intervention. However, once this ally talks with the person doing harm, they may hear another story – perhaps a story that the person doing harm is making up or exaggerating in order to blame the victim or get out of accountability. This is very common.

The community member might then have a different opinion than the other people who started the intervention or who invited them. They might think that the intervention is unfair or is even targeting the wrong person. Sometimes that is when assessment gets more complicated—when people tell another side to the story.

A list of some possible scenarios is below:

a. People carrying out an intervention are clear about who is the survivor or victim and who is the person doing harm. Even though others in the community might argue especially if they do not have an understanding about interpersonal violence, the key people doing the intervention are clear and agree upon how they view the basic dynamics of violence and who is responsible for accountability.

b. It is clear who is the survivor or victim and who is the person doing harm. However, people also have questions about or problems with the survivor or victim. They are not the "perfect" victim. They may have behaved in ways that are annoying or even seem abusive. Perhaps they carried out an intervention in a way that people disagree with. Even so, people are still clear about who is the survivor or victim and who is the person doing harm.

c. The group is split. Some people think there is a clear pattern of violence and a clear survivor or victim and person doing harm. Others think that both people or parties are significantly or equally accountable for the violent situation.

Because it is unclear, people use the questions in Section 2.2. Interpersonal Violence: Some Basics Everyone Should Know:

- Who is more afraid?
- Who starts the violence?
- Who ends up getting harmed?
- Who is changing and adapting to meet another's needs or moods?
- Who is more vulnerable?
- Who is using violence for power and control (abusive violence)? Who is using violence to try to maintain safety or integrity in an already violent situation (self-defense)?
- Who always has to win?

This can play out in the following ways:

- After more discussion (and re-reading Section 2.2. Interpersonal Violence: Some Basics Everyone Should Know), the group sorts through victim blaming and concludes that the violence is or was being used by one person against the other.
- The group reaches the conclusion that the situation really does involve a pattern of unhealthy behavior in which both people have significant patterns of using intimidation, control, manipulation, and/or use violence against each other.
- Sometimes the situation will be too hard to figure out. Sometimes you'll make a mistake that you'll learn about later, as you encounter more information about the situation or the people involved.

If you're trying to help everybody learn not to use violence and control tactics in their interpersonal relationships, what will you do if both people are using violence against each other? You may end up working with two or more people. Maybe you'll be supporting one person to address and repair from violence in ways that do not involve the use of retaliation. Maybe you'll be supporting another person to realize that they cannot use controlling or abusive attitudes and behavior against others in order to deal with their feelings of insecurity or need to feel powerful and in control.

Just be prepared to discover that figuring out or agreeing on who is the survivor or victim and who is the person doing harm is not always simple. This can add to complications when you need to find allies who can engage the person or people using violence.

#11 REMEMBER, IMPERFECT BEHAVIOR BY THE SURVIVOR OR VICTIM DOES NOT EXCUSE VIOLENCE.

Even though it's possible that both (if this directly involves two) people could be using violence as a control tactic against each other, this is not the norm. In relationships that involve violence and abuse, there is usually a pattern in which one person does this more than the other; one person starts abusive behavior more than the other; one person has to win or be right; the other person feels more afraid.

It is common that the survivor or victim also acts aggressively, seems manipulative or does not appear like a completely "innocent victim." We cannot expect survivors or victims to look like pure, innocent victims like puppy dogs or helpless children on TV. Even so,they may still be survivors or victims of interpersonal violence, deserving support and interventions to violence that primarily ask the person harming them to be the one to take accountability. (See Section 2.2. Interpersonal Violence: Some Basics Everyone Should Know).

#12 BEWARE OF CALLS FOR ACCOUNTABILITY AS A WAY TO AVOID DIRECT COMMUNICATION.

What we have also found is that in communities in which the ideas about community accountability have become common or popular, community accountability and processes for accountability sometimes become a substitute for direct communication. We live in a world where we are regularly insensitive, where we make mistakes, where we are unaware of our impact over others. While some of these attitudes and behaviors calls for the types of interventions we are talking about in this Toolkit, there are times when people can begin with direct communication. They can think about the attitudes or behaviors that were hurtful and speak directly to the person who caused harm. They can get help and support to think more clearly about what they want to say in order to prepare for this communication. They can bring somebody with them to stand by in order to support them and to make sure that someone else is there to hear and see the other person's response – or to provide for emotional or physical safety. They can state the harm, talk about how they felt, and ask that the other person listen without excuses, interruptions, or arguments. They can ask the other person to think about what was said and come back at another time for continued discussion.

This may be an intervention on a small scale. And in some cases, this is a good starting place. Even with these small-scale interventions, getting allies to help support you to carry it out, make sure you think about safety, and make sure that this is an appropriate way to move forward are important steps to take. Looking through and using tools in this Taking Accountability section, may be helpful and appropriate.

You may want to see Section 2.B. Seeking Safety to find tools to figure out whether direct communication is a reasonable and safe enough approach to take and to take precautions just in case. Staying safe is reasonable and wise. However, in some situations, nervousness about doing something difficult and discomfort with conflict may not be so much about safety. It may call for us to move beyond our comfort zone and take healthy risks that can lead to positive change – and live with the real possibility that the changes we want from other people may not result.

#13 MINDSET MATTERS; NOT ALL PEOPLE DOING HARM ARE THE SAME.

Strategies to create accountability are more successful when they meet the people doing harm "where they are at." Though it is common that people can use surprisingly similar tactics to hurt, control or manipulate the people they choose to harm, people who use violence are not all the same. Some differences matter more than others, and examining them can help us make our efforts at engaging people doing harm to unlearn violence more likely to succeed.

The statements below are examples of general mindsets or starting points for a person doing harm. They reflect possible points of "where they are at" with regard to relating to others and to their own violent attitudes, values, and behaviors.

- "My closest friends, my community and I find my violence acceptable and normal. I see no problem with my violence but see a problem with someone who challenges it."
- "I find my violence acceptable and normal. Maybe others don't, but I don't care about them or what they think."
- "I do not have enough emotional capacity or level of maturity to acknowledge or handle feelings of discomfort or healthy shame without self-destruction and/or violent destruction of others. Because of this, I will destroy you before you have a chance to hurt me."
- "I blame my violence on other people. Although somewhere deep inside, I may feel embarrassed and know that my violence is not okay, I will never admit this or show this to anyone. I have never done so and will not do it now – even if sometimes I wish I could."
- "I always or almost always blame my violence on other people, although I have at rare times expressed embarrassment or shame about my use of it. Even though I blame others, I sometimes wonder if it is my fault, but I would never admit this to others."
- "I usually blame my violence on other people. But sometimes I can see that it is my fault and can even admit it. But I hate that feeling of it being my fault and really hate it when somebody else starts blaming me – so sooner or later, I blame other people again. I only change for a short while and, over time, never really change."
- "I have a fundamental belief that violence is not a good thing. I take some responsibility for my violent actions but am quick to get defensive. I want to change but the thought of what it might take to change makes me uncomfortable."
- "I don't want to have a harmful impact on others, and I have some healthy shame around what is happening (or I would if I understood it just a bit better). I need some help, but I don't know how to get it or don't believe that anyone knows the right way to help me."
- "I realize that my behavior has a cost that is higher than I'd like to pay. I'd like to change."
- "I have done things that I never thought were possible – and are against my values. I may be afraid of change, but I am willing to take the challenge and do whatever I need to do to make that change."

Looking at patterns of mindsets such as these can help us decide whether or how to engage someone using violence. They can impact how we think about what short term change can look like, what steps we can plan, and how we can ground our discussions and expectations about accountability in reality. It can also help us understand what might be important to the person doing harm and what might be most effective in reaching out to them.

#14 FIGURE OUT THE LEVEL OF "ENGAGE-ABILITY": HOW LIKELY IS IT THAT YOU CAN MAKE A POSITIVE AND EFFECTIVE CONNECTION WITH THE PERSON DOING HARM.

Remember that community interventions should engage (communicate with, work with, and support) the person doing harm to the degree that makes sense based on the situation you have to work with. While this model values engagement of the person doing harm, it is NOT a requirement. In some cases, it will simply be too dangerous; the person may be too unwilling or too difficult to reach; or we may not have the right people or right conditions to be able to connect with and engage with the person doing harm.

The level of violence that the person doing harm has committed in the past may or may not affect their ability to change. Their level of danger is obviously influenced by this but is not always equivalent to their level of danger. For example, someone who has used weapons or used a high level of violence against someone in the past can reasonably be considered capable of a high level of danger. However, this does not necessarily mean that that person is less capable of change. Situations vary greatly, and one's values and the quality of one's social connections can say a lot about one's "engage-ability."

As you assess "engage-ability" in your own situation, consider the presence or absence of the following factors.

Factors Related to the Engage-ability of the Person Doing Harm

- The person doing harm has no friends or social connections – engage-ability may be low.
- Issues related to substance abuse and/or mental illness impair the person doing harm's ability to have meaningful social connections – and/or make them unable to figure out and follow through with positive change – engage-ability may be low or may change depending upon their state of mental illness or substance use.
- The person doing harm has some friends but they all collude with the violence by directly supporting it or encouraging it, or by excusing it or doing nothing about it – engage-ability may be low.
- The person doing harm has some friends but disengages with anyone who challenges them – they turn against or cut off from any person who challenges them – engage-ability may be low.

- The person doing harm's only connection is with the survivor or victim of harm and not with anybody else. This may be positive if their care and connection for the survivor or victim becomes a motivation for change. But it also can simply mean that their connection is also based upon the dynamic of violence. This may put survivors or victims in an impossible situation of being responsible for changing the violence that they never caused in the first place – engage-ability may be low.
- There are people who support accountability who are not necessarily the close friends of the person doing harm, but whom the person respects and whose opinions matter – engage-ability may be moderate or high.
- The person doing harm has close relationships with community members who are willing and able to engage the person doing harm to stop using violence and use new behaviors; the person doing harm has the ability to talk about difficult things and to be vulnerable with people – engage-ability may be moderate or high.

The more interpersonal connections the person doing harm has and cares about, the more likely you are to find a point of access or leverage for using community to support a person to change. Usually when people have nothing to lose, they have no motivation to change.

#15 BE THOUGHTFUL ABOUT FINDING THE BEST PEOPLE TO ENGAGE WITH THE PERSON DOING HARM TO TAKE ACCOUNTABILITY.

In this model of violence intervention, it is easier to take accountability with the support of others. Who can support the person doing harm to make choices toward accountability for violence and change? This may be a very different set of people than those more directly supporting survivors or victims.

Taking accountability is challenging. It may take changes of the most fundamental ways that people think about things, make decisions, and take actions. People may be asked to take accountability in a situation where emotions are heated. People may be angry or fearful. They may feel disgust or even contempt for people who have caused harm.

And the person doing harm may feel cornered, ashamed and exposed. It may remind this person of other situations that may have felt threatening. Or this may be the first time that someone has ever faced a situation in which they have been named as someone causing harm which can also feel threatening.

It may be important to make sure that we look deeper for opportunities (and people) to engage the person doing harm to learn and change, and not back away when accountability gets hard.

See Section 4.C. Mapping Allies and Barriers, Tool C.5. Allies to Work with the Person Doing Harm Chart for tips on finding allies to work with the person doing harm.

#16 EXPECT THAT PEOPLE OFTEN RESIST TAKING ACCOUNTABILITY. CREATE SYSTEMS FLEXIBLE ENOUGH TO ALLOW FOR THE EXPECTED PROCESS OF DODGING AND DELAYING ACCOUNTABILITY AND STRONG ENOUGH TO WITHSTAND AND DIMINISH THESE TACTICS OVER TIME.

Most of us struggle with accountability and experience it as a rejection, a threat, and an unjust imposition. We need to create responses that take this struggle into account.

All of us have experienced occasions when we have needed to be accountable. Even if we apologize and are accountable at first, we often want to slip out of full accountability using a series of tactics such as the following:

- Leaving the community, relationship, organization to avoid accountability
- Showing change early on in hopes to get people to stop holding us accountable – then going back to old behavior when there's less pressure
- Hoping people forget
- Hoping people feel sorry for us so they leave us alone or blame others
- Making people scared of us or scared of our anger
- Making people depend on us so that they feel too guilty or scared to challenge us
- Creating delaying tactics
- Creating distractions
- Blaming others
- Blaming our past
- Blaming the survivor or victim
- Blaming those who are trying to hold us accountable
- Making the accountability process be the problem, not our own harmful attitudes, behaviors and frameworks for thinking and acting
- Wanting our own version of accountability to be the right one – controlling the accountability process

It is unrealistic and a recipe for frustration and failure if we expect change to happen with one conversation or one meeting; if we expect a pattern of attitudes and behavior to change quickly; or if we believe that positive changes early on mean that changes will be long-lasting. While this is not impossible, this is rarely the case.

Instead, we need to create systems flexible enough to allow for the expected process of dodging and delaying accountability and strong enough to withstand and diminish these tactics over time.

We need to rely upon ourselves and the support of others who understand interpersonal violence and who understand the nature of accountability (which can be helped through this Toolkit) to keep up a system that can support change over time.

#17 IT'S OKAY TO REMIND SOMEONE OF COMMUNITY CONSEQUENCES TO USING VIOLENCE.

To guide someone toward taking responsibility for violence, it is sometimes necessary to point to or allow for the consequences of violence. While this Toolkit does not support the use of punishment, revenge and humiliation as a way to support accountability, it does recognize that violence can lead to negative consequences.

This can involve the loss of respect, the loss of status, the loss of trust, the loss of a position of responsibility, and the loss of relationships and friends. In some cases, this can lead to the loss of a home and community. Even if we do not support punishment and revenge, we also cannot force others to continue to like us and respect us. We may never gain someone's trust even if we change. These are some of the possible consequences that we may have to realize are the costs of our harmful attitudes and behaviors.

Pointing out social or community consequences of using violence is not the same as holding a threat over someone's head. Sometimes people doing harm are in denial or just plain unaware of the consequences of their violence. Sometimes they might blame the consequences on everyone else (the survivor, the survivor's family members, the other people in the community, people involved in the intervention, etc.). Sometimes they believe people will just forget or care less about the violence over time. Sometimes they have convinced themselves (seriously) that they are invincible – and unlike ordinary human beings, are not subject to repercussions or consequences.

And oftentimes communities will protect people using violence from ever experiencing community consequences of their actions. People cannot take responsibility for their violence and make new choices if they are protected from the consequences of their own behavior. It is important to help them make the connection that they risk losing others' respect, compassion, trust, favors, relationships, friendships, their job, etc. when they hurt people with violence. When their violence causes them to lose something, it is important not to protect them from ever having to feel regret, sadness, fear, or loss. Again, these are not necessarily punishments. These are the possible human costs for causing harm and suffering.

For some people, facing these possible consequences of violence may make them feel like change is not worth it. If they lose everything, then why bother? They may only try to change because they think that there will be certain rewards that they will be able to keep relationships, trust, a job, or respect. While these things may be possible for some people, there is simply no guarantee that this will be the case.

When taking accountability, one must eventually accept those losses that one cannot control and try to create new attitudes and behaviors that will lead to self-respect, trust in oneself and the potential for new, meaningful relationships.

#18 LOOK OUT FOR SHIFTING TARGETS: WHEN AN ALLY BECOMES THE NEW ENEMY.

Be prepared that after being engaged by an ally to take responsibility for violence, the person doing harm might shift their anger toward that ally and away from the survivor or victim. Look out for attempts to make the ally the new "enemy" and to re-make the relationship or history with the survivor or victim as if it is problem-free, or not the real problem. Plan for how to support allies and create safety for them after they engage the person doing harm.

For the survivor or victim, be aware of your vulnerability to also make someone else the problem if this dynamic comes about. A shift from yourself to another person as the target can be a huge relief and bring about positive feelings that you may have experienced in the past with the person doing harm. Think about how long this experience of closeness or relief will last – and how your alliance with the person doing harm may eventually cost you your own allies. Even if you take a moment to benefit from a period of relief, beware of accepting this as a new reality and take care to get real about the pattern of violence or harms that you experienced in the past.

#19 REMEMBER THAT WE CAN ONLY CONTROL OURSELVES.

We cannot control or guarantee anyone else's response. Our intervention may have specific goals concerning the types of attitudes and behaviors we expect from the person doing harm. However, attempts to tightly control someone else or demand very exact verbal or behavioral responses may be unrealistic. In community-based interventions and especially in conversations inviting someone to self-reflect and take responsibility, we have to be persistent and patient to help someone take small steps in the right direction.

If you are the survivor or victim and are trying to maintain a relationship with the person doing harm, then it is important to be aware of the basic types of attitudes and behaviors you expect and deserve. Expressing this and being specific about this with the person doing harm as a part of accountability is important. It can be difficult to tell the difference between being patient and letting someone cross the line. Get help from your allies to keep you on the right track regarding your goals and whether or not they are being met.

#20 STAY SPECIFIC. THEN GIVE IT TIME.

Community interventions that include efforts to invite someone to take responsibility and make positive changes can be exhausting, and it is important to make every effort to stay specific, focus on behaviors that we want to address and behaviors that we want to see in the future, and then give things time. Take care of yourself and your loved ones! A 100% focus on the intensity of pain that violence causes, the stress of confrontation, the distress of rejection, the hardship that comes when we see things differently within our communities is unsustainable for any person or group. When you encounter moments, hours, and days that feel unbearable, know that they will change with time. Persistently seek out opportunities to remind yourself of the good things—the strengths, the opportunities, the fun, the resilience, and every other bit of joy in life. They are as important a part of community interventions as any other effort.

F.4. *TAKING ACCOUNTABILITY* SPECIAL CONSIDERATIONS

The process of taking accountability is a difficult one. It can be a long and complicated process. It can move forward and backward and can easily confuse and wear people down. It can also look very different depending upon the position you have to the situation of violence.

No matter who you are in relationship to accountability, it is useful to read this entire section on taking accountability in order to get information that might be particularly useful to you.

Again, the process of taking accountability is not a one-time event. It often requires creating systems flexible enough to allow for the expected process of dodging and delaying accountability and strong enough to withstand and diminish these tactics over time.

This system involves supporting a person doing harm through a process of accountability that may begin with elements of force and coercion that move towards self-reflection and deep levels of change.

This system supports the survivor or victim to address and begin to repair the harms committed against them – to take collective action and break from the isolation of victimization – and to participate in and benefit from a process that may support a process of accountability from the person doing harm.

This system supports the community to take a more active role in recognizing individual and interpersonal levels of violence as a community problem. It organizes community power to support survivors or victims and actively support people doing harm to become agents of positive change rather than perpetrators of harm.

Again, an intervention may not have taking accountability as a goal. But if it does, then these are some special considerations.

The survivor or victim may be in very different positions regarding taking accountability. One factor to look at is the relationship of the survivor or victim to the person doing harm. If this is an intimate or close relationship, the survivor or victim may wish to stay in relationship with the person doing harm. The survivor or victim and the person doing harm may never have been in a relationship and may even be strangers. They may have once been in relationship but are no longer connected in any way, They may be sharing community even if not in relationship, thereby making some form of co-existence without conflict a goal (See F.3. Taking Accountability Tips).

The survivor or victim may have very different positions regarding his or her level of participation in the intervention. He or she may be taking a lead role in every aspect of the intervention; the victim or survivor's goals and directions may be prioritized over all others but with the input of others. The victim or survivor may have a high level of participation but with goals and directions shared with others. Other times, the survivor or victim may take a back seat and only give feedback, may not be involved at all,or may even disagree with the intervention (See Section 4.E. Supporting Survivors or Victims).

In all of these cases, the Toolkit encourages the intervention to give special consideration to the goals and safety of the survivor or victim. Even if they are strangers or are no longer in relationship, the intervention and steps towards a process of accountability could provoke resistance, retaliation or other forms of harm from the person doing harm and others who may not agree with the intervention. It can also involve strong emotions that can impact the survivor or victim and affect their well-being and ability to concentrate or deal with their daily lives. Because each situation is different and each survivor or victim will experience their intervention in different ways, the impact on and necessary support for the survivor or victim needs to be considered throughout the intervention.

For example, if the survivor or victim is in a current relationship with the person doing harm, then taking accountability can be complicated by strong emotions tied to the experience of violence and harm and emotions regarding the promise of change. It can be common to feel anger and fear about the violence or the memory of violence. It can also be common to feel guilt about putting someone through a process of accountability. Failures to follow through with accountability or perhaps return to abusive attitudes and behaviors – all common events– can bring about feelings of anger, frustration and fear. Often the person doing harm is keenly aware of the survivor or victim's emotions and vulnerabilities. It is easy for them to take advantage of these emotions and use them to get their way or to dodge accountability, even if they are not completely aware that they are doing so.

This is to say that there can be powerful and confusing emotions for a survivor or victim who is also interested in the changes that accountability promises to bring. Having no hope for change or not caring about change can, in fact, at least protect one's emotions from the ups and downs that can go along with emotional ties to change. If one's safety and survival depend on positive change, then what one has to gain or lose can be even more serious.

It can be difficult to tell whether one is expecting too much, expecting changes that are unreasonable in a short amount of time or for any human being to possibly achieve – or if one is expecting too little, seeing every small positive change as proof of transformation or excusing every set-back or returning act of violence as something that will eventually change.

If you are the survivor or victim, you may consider some steps to help you stay steady and not tie your present and your future to every up and down that the person doing harm may take in the accountability process.

If you are still closely connected (physically and/or emotionally) to the person doing harm, the process of taking accountability can be particularly confusing. Some steps you can take are:

1. Setting your goals and your bottom-lines in a process with allies and separate from the person doing harm (See Section 4.D. Goal Setting).
2. Writing these goals and bottom-lines down and returning to them on a regular basis with the support of an ally or group of allies.
3. Working on including other important people or activities separate from the person doing harm in your life.
4. Making sure not take on the responsibility or burden of accountability for the person doing harm. Make sure that their process of taking accountability is supported by people other than you and a process outside your direct involvement even if you are somewhat involved.
5. Getting support so that you can work through confusing feelings that can include cycles of hope, fear, anger, guilt, and disappointment.
6. Watching out for a situation in which the intervention process and/or allies in the intervention process become the new enemy shared by you and the person doing harm. This is a common dynamic that can bring about relief, shared perspectives and even pleasure as you and the person doing harm find a common enemy. But this can also jeopardize their process of accountability and your safety. If you cannot resist, then see if you can take this relief in a small dose, enjoy the brief sense of rest or pleasure it may bring, and then get real quickly – most importantly, with yourself. If you know you are doing this, then ultimately, this is your dynamic to control. Do not rely upon the person taking accountability to do this for you. Resistance and testing on their part is in some ways to be expected. Part of the accountability process for the person doing harm is to recognize resistance tactics and to stop using them. But it is also your responsibility not to give in to these dynamics – once you understand them for what they are.

Of course, it is also possible that you really disagree with the intervention process, and you are starting to see them as the enemy. If so, think about the following: 1) Are you frustrated that change is not happening quickly and so you are taking it out on the intervention? 2) Are you frustrated that the person doing harm is not being accountable and so you are taking it out on the intervention? 3) If you are really having problems with the accountability process, can you meet with the group or a particular trusted person or support people to make these issues known? Can you give this as feedback to the process – to let the intervention team know what's working and what's not?

In this intervention approach, community allies may be very actively communicating with and working together with the person doing harm to support their process of accountability. In particular, the survivor or victim may take a less active role in face-to-face communication because it may be unsafe. They may not be able to feel or express any level of positive connection to the person doing harm, or it may well be the community's responsibility to take on this aspect of an intervention.

Supporting a process of accountability works best if it includes a person or people who have the respect of the person doing harm – who can both apply the "push" of community pressure and also the "pull" of positive role-modeling and community connection. They may know the person doing harm and understand the personal experiences and values that might make it easier to connect accountability to what this person thinks is important – what the person doing harm could gain and strengthen by taking accountability and also what they could lose if they do not.

It is important for the people working together to support accountability to share goals and values, or at least agree enough to not work at cross purposes. It is important for them to share some level of care and even respect for the person doing harm – even if what this person has done offends them greatly.

And it is important for those working most closely in direct communication with the person doing harm to actually be connected to them and to have a long-term commitment to supporting their change, whether or not they are able to achieve this change.

If you are a community ally, you may be taking a very important role in supporting the process of taking accountability. This can be a very difficult role. The process of taking accountability can be long. It can move forward and then backwards. It can get you very emotionally involved in hoping for change, being frustrated, trusting and not trusting the person doing harm, or perhaps feeling frustrated with the survivor or victim or other allies.

As community allies supporting the process of accountability, you may need to form systems of support for each other, including ways to prepare and then debrief after meeting with the person doing harm, and ways to check in during difficult times, so that you can keep steady and stay healthy.

If you are actively participating in the process of taking accountability, you may think about the following:

1. Return to the goals and values of the intervention and use them to guide the process of taking accountability. If these goals or values do not seem to fit or seem to steer you in ways that do not feel right, then go back to the group and request that you as a group look at these goals and/or values again.

2. Do not do this alone. At times, we seek a lone hero to confront the person doing harm and make things right. Even if there may be times that you meet with the person doing harm or take on some aspect of the intervention yourself, make sure that you have the support of the group, some people within the group or other useful resources for preparation and check-in as you move forward.

3. Think about safety for the survivor or victim, yourself, other allies, and for the person doing harm. This may include immediate physical safety, things that could jeopardize the safety of the survivor or victim and feed into acts of retaliation, or things that could throw off the intervention. Think about what information you will share, what should remain confidential, and back-up support for safety. Make sure that your ideas regarding these points are consistent with other people who are involved in this intervention. See Section 4.B. Staying Safe and use the safety tools for help.

4. Remember that support does not always look like you are "taking the side" of the person doing harm. It may mean that you are challenging their sense of reality, calling them out if they lie, or checking to see if they followed up with demands or what they said that they would do. Supporting someone to take accountability rests on the belief that stopping violence and harm is, in the long run, beneficial not only to the survivors or victims or the community, but also to the person doing harm.

5. Watch out if you find the process of Taking Accountability splitting off from the process of Supporting Survivors or Victims. It is easy for the process of taking accountability to begin to take a life of its own. It can become the full focus of an intervention, sometimes leaving the survivor or victim isolated and alone – without any active support or with support that is completely unconnected with the rest of the intervention. It can begin to take on different goals than a holistic intervention that would also prioritize or take into account the needs and goals of the survivor or victim.

People working directly with the person doing harm may begin to hear their "side of the story." They may start feeling more sympathy for the person doing harm than for the survivor or victim. They may hear new stories that seem to present a different picture than the one they had. They may begin to feel like they're on the "team" of the person doing harm and start working for them rather than working on behalf of the entire intervention.

The terms for engagement may start to be set by the person doing harm who may use pressure, coercion or emotional pulls such as crying, pleas for sympathy, telling the worst stories about the survivor or victim to get allies to go easy on them, throw them off, or even begin to view the person doing harm as the survivor or victim rather than the other way around. They may completely believe this story. It may reflect their sense of truth. They may be completely manipulative – using anything possible to get out of accountability and "get back" at the survivor or victim.

These dynamics are very common aspects of interventions to interpersonal violence. They should be anticipated and become part of the process of intervention and taking accountability – as much as is possible. And if these come up along the way, these are the very points that community allies should look at, reflect upon, and share with others in order to keep on the path to accountability and keep systems flexible enough to allow for the expected process of dodging and delaying accountability and strong enough to withstand and diminish these tactics over time.

6. Prepare and make space for reflection and follow-up with each step of taking accountability. The process of accountability is usually a winding road. Figuring out what has moved forward, what are barriers and possible ways to move forward can be an important part of reaching your long-term goals. Use tools in this Section 4.F. Taking Accountability and Section 4.H. Keeping on Track for help.

Concerns that the person doing harm raises or concerns that you yourself have may simply be part of the normal "dodging and delaying" tactics around accountability. But they may also reflect real concerns.

Listen to these concerns if they are raised by the person doing harm, and watch out not to show reactions that may look like you agree with them. Note these concerns and share them with the group. Use tools in the Toolkit and other resources to see if any of them can help you respond to these.

You can bring these concerns back to your team which may include the survivor or victim for reflection and responses. They can be used to figure out how far someone is in the accountability process; they can help you better respond to the person doing harm. They can be used to reshape an intervention.

7. Be prepared for how personal relationships with the person doing harm affect the intervention and vice versa. Sometimes close friends are the best people to engage with a person doing harm. They may care the most about change, may know the person and their values best, and may be respected by the person doing harm.

At the same time, an intervention process, particularly one that goes on for a long time can seriously affect a friendship. Does your friendship turn into a series of accountability meetings? Do you find yourself liking this person less and less? Or hating the intervention more and more?

Sometimes, finding out about violence committed by someone you care about makes you question the friendship. If you question your friendship but can find a way to continue your care through participating in this intervention, it can be a true act of friendship. Find support to help you figure out feelings of confusion, anger, disappointment, and sadness that may accompany this process.

If you simply cannot continue your relationship with this person (including being part of the intervention), figure out if you can express your feelings about why. This may end up being helpful information for the person doing harm – even if may be difficult to say and to hear.

If you cannot continue your friendship but can still be involved in the intervention, think about an appropriate role for you to participate in so that the strong feelings that accompany the end of a friendship (on your side and theirs) do not become a barrier to the intervention.

In this Toolkit, we allow for the perspective of the person doing harm to enter the situation. This is different from many anti-violence organizations that often automatically dismiss this perspective as an attempt to manipulate the situation or blame the victim. Creative Interventions has found that people doing harm have very different approaches to supporting survivors or victims.

In this approach to intervention, we aim to include the person doing harm as a positive participant in an intervention to violence. We also recognize that this may take a series of steps – and that in some cases, this may be a goal that we never reach.

Because we are talking about interpersonal violence, the survivor or victim and the person doing harm may also love and care about each other or move back and forth between powerful feelings of love and hate.

The person doing harm is not simply and exclusively someone who is violent. This is why this Toolkit does not use labels such as batterer, rapist, perpetrator, perp, abuser, predator, offender or other words usually used by the criminal justice system. They are people who are part of our families, friendship networks and communities.

At the same time, we take interpersonal violence seriously and believe that this is not simply a problem among individuals, or an unimportant problem that we can ignore. Interpersonal violence is a serious problem. Violence committed among those we care about can be extremely damaging, causing injuries at the deepest levels of our being.

This Toolkit invites the person doing harm to participate in change. It also recognizes that change is difficult – it is a long-term process. Change requires the person doing harm to accept change as a goal. Because we are not isolated individuals (although we may feel like it at times), but are people in relationship with family, friends, co-workers, acquaintances, and neighbors, we need the support of others to help us reach long-term change.

If you are the person doing harm or are accused of it, this Section 4.F. Taking Accountability offers a lot of information and tools for you and others to use in this process.

If you are reading this or someone is giving you this information, then we hope that you have others to support you to change.

We also know that support can be difficult to find. We ask that you at least use the tools in this Toolkit (also found at www.creative-interventions.org) to help you reflect on and figure out a process towards change. If someone is already asking you to change or is offering support, then you can use this Toolkit along with that support to take accountability and transform yourself.

If no local help is available, then refer to this Toolkit and use the tools to help guide you. Go to a local library and look up books on violence and changing violence to get whatever help you can find.

If you are able to find other people who may be having the same problem, or local spiritual leaders or community leaders, you can let them know about this Toolkit in order to give them some basic information to guide them to help you better. They can become a "facilitator" – another person that serves as an anchor – to help move this process along.

Changing your violence may not bring back relationships you have lost. You may never be forgiven for your actions – at least, not by the people you may have harmed. You may never regain their trust.

However, you may be able to make deep changes as someone who has the ability to honor and respect yourself and others – and to contribute to your community.

For the facilitator, the process of Taking Accountability can be particularly challenging. The process can be long and consuming. It can become the focus of everyone's attention and energy, perhaps leaving the survivor or victim isolated and without adequate support. And resistance by the person doing harm is commonplace, making the process of taking accountability confusing and frustrating.

As the facilitator, you may be taking the role of keeping things on track and making sure that people do not start working at cross purposes.

If your intervention includes the process of taking accountability, some of these tips may be helpful:

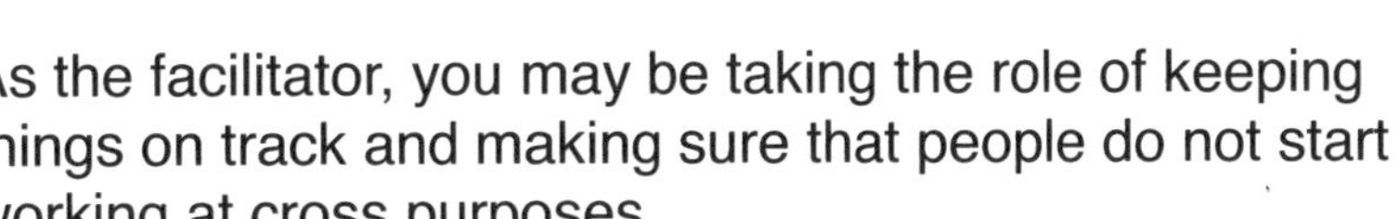

#1 READ THIS SECTION 4.F. TAKING ACCOUNTABILITY CAREFULLY AND OFFER INFORMATION OR TOOLS THAT MIGHT HELP THE PROCESS.

Taking accountability is a very difficult process. People most involved in supporting this process (including the allies, survivor or victim, and the person doing harm) can easily become confused along the way. You may be in a good position to notice when questions or problems come up that could be helped with the information or tools in this

#2 KEEP AN EYE ON SAFETY.

The process of taking accountability can appear threatening to the person doing harm. Depending on their "mind set," they may see admitting a wrong and making a change as something to be challenged. Shows of cooperation can go along with plans to threaten survivors or victims, intimidate allies, or undermine the entire accountability process.

See Section 4.B. Staying Safe for more tools that people can use to increase safety as they move forward in the process.

#3 REMIND PEOPLE OF THE GOALS AND VALUES AND MAKE SURE THEY GUIDE THE PROCESS.

The process of taking accountability can take many twists and turns along the way. The progress of the person doing harm to take accountability is ultimately not in the control of any single person or group of people. Things can change dramatically along the way, making a return to simple guidelines helpful. See Section 4.D. Goal Setting for more information.

As facilitator, you may be able to remind people of the goals and values that guide the intervention. If the goals or values are no longer helpful or no longer fit, then you might help the group come back to reconsider what goals and values may make better sense.

#4 MAKE SURE THAT SUPPORT IS AT THE CENTER.

The process of taking accountability can be difficult and energy-draining. A supportive environment for everyone is necessary if the process is going to continue for the long time that may be necessary for it to stick.

Help people find support through their own loved ones and through each other. Help create a positive environment so that people can counter frustration with appreciation. And make sure that the survivor or victim does not get forgotten as the group begins to put energy into the process of accountability.

#5 KEEP A HOLISTIC PROCESS.

The process of taking accountability can become the focus of the whole intervention. It can be easier for this process to split off from the process of providing support for the survivor or victim and to find the people working on one aspect of the intervention separated from those working on another. It is easy to forget about the needs of the survivor or victim or to leave them out of the process of accountability. It is easy to put all attention on the person doing harm and forget to pay attention to the community context.

As the facilitator, you may be able to see the bigger picture and make sure that people are communicating with and connected to each other. You may need to think about what aspects of the intervention are being forgotten and make sure that these pieces are picked up.

F.6. *TAKING ACCOUNTABILITY* REAL LIFE STORIES & EXAMPLES

Story F.1. A Cultural Organization Deals with Sexual Assault

In the summer of 2006, a drumming teacher from South Korea was invited to teach a week-long drumming workshop at a Korean cultural community center in Oakland, California. After an evening of singing, storytelling and drinking, several students stayed the night to rest and recover for the next day. For over two decades, the cultural center had developed a safe space for the teaching of Korean drumming and dance, community performance and cultural and political exchange. That night, safety was shattered when the drumming teacher sexually assaulted one of the students.

People staying at the center immediately heard what had happened, and center leaders quickly pulled together a direct confrontation involving the members and their community-led board. The next day, members and board members gathered at the center to denounce the sexual assault and support the victim. In this situation, the victim refused to name herself as a "survivor" – finding "victim" a better description of her experience of violence.

Liz, the president of the Oakland cultural center at that time, recollects the next day's meeting. "When we got there, the teacher got on his knees and knelt in front of us which is the deepest sign of respect. And then he asked us, begged us, not to tell his organization back home. We said we couldn't do that. 'We're not here for your apology. We're here to tell you what happened, what we're going to do, and that's it.' He made a big sign of remorse, taking his drumming stick and breaking it. He put it on the ground like 'I'll give up drumming for this.' Most of us were disgusted."

What followed was a series of actions, including a set of sexual assault awareness workshops for the center members and members of other local drumming groups. The board made an immediate telephone call to the head of the drumming center in Korea. Their leader expressed his profound shock and unconditional apology. This call was followed by a letter with a list of demands. The Oakland organization demanded that the Korean institution establish sexual assault awareness trainings for their entire membership ranging from college students to elder farmers in the village, a commitment to send at least one woman teacher in their future exchanges to the U.S., and a request that the teacher step down from his leadership position for an initial period of 6 months and attend feminist therapy sessions directly addressing the assault. Even though it was culturally difficult for the Korean American group to make demands of their elders in Korea, everyone decided this was what needed to be done. The group in Korea also did not question these demands. They respected them and did not make any complaints.

The Korean American organization also made contact with a sister drumming group in Korea, one that had dealt with their own experience of sexual assault in the past. That organization had organized their one hundred members to address a sexual assault that had occurred among their membership. In that situation, the person who had committed the assault went through an extensive process with the leaders and members of the group, leaving the organization but following through with a public apology posted on their website and retained relationships with drumming group members.

Inspired by this story of community accountability, the fact that it had been made public and a process in which the person doing harm took responsibility and offered a public apology, the Oakland organization followed with a series of events that reversed the usual silence and victim-blaming accompanying sexual assault. The annual October festival was dedicated to the theme of healing from sexual violence. Facts regarding the incident were printed in the program and shared as a part of the evening's festival, not as a shaming act although it may have indeed shamed the teacher, but as a challenge to the community to take collective responsibility for ending the conditions perpetuating violence including collusion through silence.

This story reveals other painful lessons about community violence and the limitations of our community-led processes. The Korean cultural center came together with a unified response to violence but grew divided as the process continued. What became a long drawn-out period of institutional reflection and engagement sapped the energy and spirit of the organization and the friendships that had held it together. The victim never returned. The continued presence of the teacher at community festivities in South Korea were viewed with resentment and suspicion by Korean American visitors who participated in drumming events in Korea. His eventual removal from the institution did not necessarily lead to the sense of justice that people desired.

Liz, the center's president, reflected on this set of events and the uncertainties accompanying the process of community accountability.
"Some people asked us later why we didn't call the police. It was not even a thought in anybody's mind. I know that a couple folks, her close friends, tried to break in, to kick his ass, but they couldn't find him. Luckily they didn't. Luckily for him and the organization, too, because I think if they did that we would have just been in a whole

world of fucking mess. Well, I don't want to say luckily because the victim even felt at some point, 'maybe we should've just kicked his ass. Now, I feel like I've got nothing. I don't have the police report. We didn't throw him into jail. We didn't kick his ass. We didn't do nothing.'

We talked to her and said, 'We didn't move forward on anything without your consent.' We asked, 'What else can we offer you?' We offered her to go to counseling and therapy. We offered her whatever we could do at the time. In retrospect, I wish we could have spent more time to just embrace her and bring her in closer."

The story further explores the role of force and violence in our response to violence. Frustration over a long and complex process of accountability spurred discussions among the members of the Oakland organization over the potential benefits of violence. Liz reflected on a member's remark as they considered retaliation. "That's what the teacher wanted. He wanted that. When he was making that apology, he wasn't necessarily saying 'beat me up,' But he was saying, 'do anything you want to me, I deserve it.' That way, once you do, he can walk away and say, 'Okay, now I'm done, wipe my hands and walk away. They've done everything they can already.'" While some may most fear a violent response, some could also welcome a quick but symbolic pay back. "Kicking ass," can also substitute for a process of repair and change.

(Adapted from Kim, M. (2012). "Moving beyond critique: Creative Interventions and reconstructions of community accountability." Social Justice 37(4). For audio and transcript of Liz's Story, visit www.stopviolenceeveryday.org)

Story F.2. Women Come Together to Confront Our Community Leaders

I got a story for you, and it's about community accountability. This Hmong woman in Wausau – she was killed by her husband and then he killed himself. He shot her boyfriend, too, and now he's in the hospital in critical condition.

The reason a lot of Hmong women don't leave violent relationships or go back and forth is because when you're married, you belong to your husband's clan in the spirit world. When you die, they bury you and you have a place to go. If you're in-between places, then nobody's gonna bury you, nobody's gonna pay for a funeral, and you have no place to go in the spirit world. That's why so many women stay or don't do anything.

So this woman, her husband's clan wouldn't bury her because they said she's a "slut." Then her boyfriend's clan said, "she doesn't belong to us so we're not going bury her." And her parent's family said, "if she listened to us, this wouldn't have happened." So they wouldn't bury her either. So nobody's claiming her and nobody's going to bury her or pay for the burial. This is three weeks later.

So this woman's been working with an advocate from Women's Community in Wausau up there. She's been working with this woman who was killed, and she calls me. We'd been talking with the advocates up there for awhile trying to figure out what to do. I'd already been planning to go there to talk about domestic violence and community accountability to a big group of Hmong people at a conference they were planning.

So I say, go back to that clan and say that if they don't bury her and pay for the funeral, we're going to publicly shame them. They have until Wednesday, and if they don't do it, then we're going to go out nationally and write an article and tell everyone that we don't even bury our dead. We'll go to all the women's organizations and shame the community. We'll let them know that there's eighteen clans up there, and nobody buried her.

I said, we always gotta go back to the problem which is that this is why women don't leave or go back and forth – because they're afraid they're going be left with nobody to bury them when they die. You bury him first, and he's the one who killed her. And you leave her and say that she died because she's a slut. She didn't die because she's a slut, she died because this guy was abusing her and you all knew that. She died because the Hmong considered her somebody's property, and now she gets killed and can't even get buried. She's not a slut. Hmong men go out with other women all the time, and nobody dies.

Everybody knew that she was getting treated like s*** by this guy. If they don't do something about this, then we're gonna go out and tell everybody and shame the whole community.

So one of the advocates working with the clan leader – she told them this, and you know what? They got the money together and buried her. Her husband's clan took responsibility for her and buried her. That's community accountability.

Story F.3. Stopping Violence as a First Step

I was in a relationship with Karen for 3 years. Even though I started seeing the warning signs, I agreed to live with her. Our fighting started getting worse and more regular. It got so every day I would wake up worried that my day would begin with a fight. I did everything to avoid her getting mad, but everything I did seemed to get her upset.

After every argument or fight, she and I would process about how she handled frustration. She had thrown a cup against the wall so hard that the plastic split and shattered. She had gotten out of the car that I was sitting in and slammed her hands on the roof of the car as hard as she could. She had hit her head against the bathroom wall and slammed the sink top with her hands. She had thrashed her legs around under the covers in bed and kneed the wall when she was mad that I hadn't brushed my teeth. She would yell, curse, and literally sprint away during a disagreement or argument.

We had processed and processed about it and had moments of shared understanding about why she experienced things and behaved in the ways she did, how she had learned it, what she was reacting to, etc. She came to understand that although she never physically hurt me and wasn't a "batterer" using threatening or controlling behaviors against me, her behavior made me anxious, uncomfortable, and eventually full of contempt.

She learned that it was hurting the relationship. But all of the talking did not result in actual change. Finally, a couple years later, after one incident, I told her that I would assuredly leave her if she did not change this aspect of her behavior. I asked her what she thought would work—what would make her change her behavior, since talking together about it wasn't working. We had long passed the point where talking had any chance of stopping her from escalating her anger.

She didn't want me to leave and knew that I was serious. She came up with something herself, and we agreed upon a rule. If she began to get upset, she would try to use calming, self-soothing practices for herself. And if she expressed her anger and frustration with physical violence even once – including throwing things against the wall or pounding on things without necessarily touching me – she would arrange for herself to stay in a motel that night, and cover the costs and transportation on her own. She would take a cab and not walk to a motel at night (even if she wanted to walk), because putting her as a queer woman on the street alone at night was not going to be part of the plan. She could get hurt. And even if she didn't, I would worry so much that I would get no rest. She agreed that she would take the cab so that she would be safe and I wouldn't have to worry. The whole decision around these consequences seemed like such a small thing, but it made a big difference in her behavior.

We eventually broke up. Her agreement to stop her abuse, and her plans to take steps to avoid further abuse made a difference. I think it also helped her understand that she really could take steps to control her abuse. It took years of me explaining to her how I felt and years of tolerating what I now find to be an intolerable situation. But she did finally admit that what she was doing was wrong or at least wrong to me. And she finally took steps to change her behavior. She stopped the most immediate violence and took responsibility to make plans to make sure that she would either stop or at least remove herself from our home if she couldn't make herself stop in any other way. This was a first step and an important one. She could finally recognize with my insistence over and over again that her abusive behavior was wrong. We were for able to take a break from the continued cycle of violence for a while.

But she chose to go no further. She would not change her underlying attitudes and behaviors. She refused to admit how deep these problems were and how simply stopping the most immediate behaviors would not be enough for me to trust her and relax enough to enjoy our relationship together. We had a moment of relief, but without deeper changes, I knew it would be just a matter of time before her abuse would start again.

Stopping violence takes many steps. Changing violence and becoming someone who can truly enjoy human connection, love without control, communicate without having to make every conversation into an argument or a contest, and be open, curious and appreciative about one's partner are things that I now seek.

Story F.4. Surviving and Doing Sexual Harm: A Story of Accountability and Healing

Introduction to Surviving and Doing Sexual Harm

The following is a story from the perspective of a person doing harm, a person who has also survived harm. In his story, these two dynamics are intimately interlinked. Because there are so few stories from the perspective of the person doing harm, we have included many details occurring over many years of struggle, believing that certain pieces may be important for people doing harm, survivors and allies to better understand the dynamics of accountability.

At this point in time, the public stories of people who have done harm and who are taking accountability seriously remain rare. This is only one story told in some detail. This person's feelings and process may or may not be similar to those of other people doing harm. This person's ability to find resources, political groups doing accountability with values that are non-punishing and non-criminalizing, may not be there for everyone although our goal is that these resources will become more and more commonly available.

Note that this story is shared by someone whose name remains anonymous. This is not only to protect confidentiality but also to make sure that this story does not become a means for this person to receive public recognition or a sense of heroism for his accountability. It is common for people doing harm who have made some movement towards change to be elevated above people who have survived harm – especially if they are men. The story teller has specifically asked to not receive recognition for any contributions they have made towards this project or Toolkit. Humbleness and humility are core parts of the accountability process. From the story, we can see that the process of accountability, itself, has been long and difficult. But, ultimately, it is accountability to oneself and to others that has made this person's healing and transformation possible.

The story teller also asks that if people are able to recognize him or other identities through the details included in this story, that you please have compassion about who you share these identities with. If you recognize him, he asks that you please talk with him about this story, even if only to acknowledge that you know this part of his history; he does not want this story to be an unspoken secret among those that know him.

Surviving and Doing Sexual Harm
Why I Am Telling My Story

In all of my years trying to find resources, I've only come across three stories of people who've done harm and only one of them had enough information, enough of the person's real story, to actually be helpful to me. I want to tell my story to help people who are trying to work on their sh** and also to help people who are supporting that process or who are mentors to have some idea of what might be going on for that person who still doesn't understand themselves – to help folks be better support for accountability processes.

Naming the Harm
You know, for most of the harm that I've done, I've never really been called out for it, so I don't really have other people's names for it, just my own names. I consider myself to have sexually assaulted people, also crossed people's boundaries in sexual ways that aren't sexual assault, and just generally had patriarchal behavior. And then the last thing that's always a little more difficult for me to talk about is that I also molested a relative of mine when I was young.

Accountability and Its Early Beginnings
My accountability process started in my early 20's. The violence and harm I had been doing wasn't just a one-time thing where I just messed up once, it was like an ongoing pattern that was chronic, and happening over and over again in my life. There were a couple of moments when I was able to stop myself in the moment when I was doing harm, like when I hurt someone I cared about very much, seeing her weep when I pushed her sexual boundaries, what I see as sexual assault, I said, "Sh**. I need to stop right now." But even then, that kind of like horror wasn't enough to let me intervene in the big, chronic patterns. It took a lot more before I could start changing, even when I was recognizing chronic patterns of harm I was doing in my life and hated that I was doing those things.

By that point in my life, I was a total wreck. For years and years of my life, my mind had been filled almost with nothing but images of doing gruesome violence to myself. I was having trouble just keeping my life together. I was just under huge amounts of stress, having total breakdowns on a fairly regular basis, and was just being ripped apart inside by everything. And also, being ripped apart by trying to keep myself from the knowledge of what I'd done. It was too much for me to even look at. At the same time, I really wanted to talk with people about it. I was just so scared to do it because of the particular sorts of thing that I had done. You know, like, people who sexually abuse are the most evil of all the monsters in our cultural mythology. And everybody is basically on board with doing nothing but straight up violence to them. And so much of my life had been organized around just trying to keep myself safe that it wasn't a risk I could take. It wasn't even a question of choice. It just wasn't a possibility, even though wanted nothing more.

At some point, I started spending more time around people involved in radical politics and feminist politics. And so one person that I knew, I'll call him Griffin (not his real name), one of their friends had been sexually assaulted. So I just happened to be at a table when Griffin was having a conversation about what people were going to do about it. And that was the first time that I had ever heard of Philly Stands Up. Where I was living at the time was really far away from Philly, so it was just basically a name and an idea. But, you know, that one tiny seed of an idea was enough to make me realize that it was possible. That there were people that I could talk to that weren't going to destroy me.

It was a few months later. There was just a lot of stuff going on in my life where my history of doing violence to people and my history of surviving violence, they were coming up over and over and over in my life. But I still refused to acknowledge either of them. And it wasn't like a conscious thing. I don't know exactly what it was, but I hadn't gained the moment of insight yet into understanding that that is my history. I ended up talking with that same friend, Griffin, who had mentioned Philly Stands Up, and just in this one conversation, my whole history came out. It was the first time I talked with anybody about either my history of being raped or my history of doing sexual violence to other people. That was a moment when I stopped running from my past. Those two things in my life, surviving violence and doing violence, are inseparable. I started coming to terms with both of them in the exact same moment. That was the first time I ever broke my own silence. And that's when I started trying to find some way of doing accountability.

Part of what made this possible was the particular relationship with one of the people I had harmed, June (not her real name), a person that I loved tremendously, and somebody who, even though I haven't seen her for years and probably won't see her again in my life, I still love tremendously. And so the pain of hurting somebody that I love that much was part of it. And then I think part of it was that I had had someone to talk to. I'd never been able to communicate with people about anything in my life before. And part of it was that things got so bad at one point that I didn't have the choice anymore of not seeking support. I had a breakdown where somebody came into my life and listened to me, and I couldn't hold it in any more. And so I had started learning how to communicate from that. And then Griffin, the person I had the conversation with, really started off my own accountability process. I think for me, it was about that friend. I didn't feel threatened by them. I had a trust with them that if I talked to them, they would still care about me and see me as a person. But it's all part of this much larger context. It wasn't just something about that one particular friendship that made the difference; it was like this whole arc of all these huge things that were happening in my life, all of these breakdowns and changes and new commitments and new understandings that were all developing together that brought me to that point.

Actually, now that I think about it, there was a moment a couple of years before that was really the first time I'd ever broken my silence, but in a very different way. For a few years before that moment, I'd started being exposed to feminist politics and things like that. And for the first time I knew that someone that I loved and cared about was a survivor of rape. I was in kind of a tailspin for awhile trying to figure out how to respond to that. I started seeking out more information about how to support survivors of sexual violence, but it hadn't really been connected to my own life, really. I started to understand the importance of having the violence that was done to you being acknowledged and decided that I needed to step up in my own life. So the real first time that I ever broke my own silence about the harm that I had done was when I talked to the person who I had molested. I approached them and said, "Hey, I did this."

But I didn't have the capacity yet to actually engage with it. And so I talked about it with that person and totally broke down and put that person in a position where they were having to worry about caretaking for me, you know, the way that it happens so stereotypically. I gave them some resources, like a rape crisis number to call and things like that. That person asked me if they could tell a particular adult in their life, and I told them, "You can tell whoever you want." But I didn't have the capacity in my life yet to really work through everything that meant, and so I just brought the shutters down and the walls and everything else and cut that part off from my life again. After that, I shut down and I became totally numb, totally blank, for months.

By this point a couple of years later, I had two friends that I ended up talking with, disclosing this to, Griffin and my friend, Stephen (not his real name). And I didn't tell anyone more than that because I was scared, I was scared of everything that would happen. The only thing before Griffin who had mentioned to me about Philly Stands Up, the only thing I'd ever heard in the scene that I was part of there was that all perpetrators should be ridden out of town on a rail. Just like that, along with my own fear of violence that I'd carried for at least a decade by that point, made me really scared to talk about it with anyone else. It was just Griffin and Stephen. Those two were the only ones that I had talked about any of this with for like a year.

The Accountability Process: A Difficult Beginning
Over the course of that year, I ended up finding out that I crossed two more people's boundaries, even though I was committed to doing everything that I needed to do to make sure that I didn't cross people's boundaries. Like the first time it happened, I thought that I was asking for consent, but I wasn't. Or I wasn't able to communicate enough in order to actually have real consent. And so that person, when I crossed that person's boundaries, they confronted me on the spot about it. They were like, "Was that sexual for you?" And I was like "oh damn," but I was like, "Yeah. yeah, it was." And they were like, "I didn't consent to that, and that was a really difficult thing for me because of this and this and this." And then later on, it happened again, when I thought I was doing everything that I needed to have consent.

Part of what was going on at that point, was that I still had a huge amount of guilt and shame and traumatic reactions to being vulnerable. But after the second time that I crossed someone's boundaries, I realized what I was doing wasn't working and I needed to take accountability a step further. I decided to do all of these disclosures to people in my life. When I was doing these disclosures, I wasn't able to be present at all. I was forcing myself to do it, over and over again, and was just like totally emotionally overwhelmed and burnt out. I didn't think about how I was doing them and how that would impact other people. Because I wanted to be 100% sure that I wasn't going to cross anybody's boundaries, I dropped out of everything and just socially isolated myself.

It also seemed like everyone was totally happy to let me become totally isolated and let me drop out of everything. Nobody reached out to me, or as far as I know, people didn't really talk amongst each other or anything. I think it was just like people didn't know what to do with the information, so they didn't do anything. Griffin and Stephen had moved out of town, so they weren't there to support me any more. In that period, the only two people who did reach out to me were people whose boundaries I had crossed. And they were offering support, but I was just like, "No, I can't put you in the situation where you're taking care of me." Because by that point – during the year when I'd just been keeping quiet about things and trying to deal with it by myself, I started reading a lot of zines about survivor support, stories of survivors doing truthtelling and that kind of thing. By that point I'd learned enough to know that there is the pattern of survivors having to emotionally caretake for the people who had done harm to them. So I put up the boundary and I was like, "Thank you, but I can't accept your support."

I was doing all this stuff that was self-punishing, having no compassion for myself – just this combination of a desire to be 100% certain that I wasn't going to be crossing anybody's boundaries and this destructiveness that came out of intense self-hatred. And then it kept going, but I left town. I got way beyond burnt out; I wasn't even running on fumes any more, just willpower. But, I didn't cross anybody's boundaries!

Accountability: My Stages of Change

What were the stages of change for me? The first stage, which isn't one that I would really recommend that people generally include in accountability processes, was the self-destructive one where I would just step back from things. A component of this could be good, but not in a self-punishing, destructive way. But that was really the first step, isolating myself from everything. And then, doing some research and selfeducation at the same time. I was also going to therapy and was coming to understand my own history better, was able to articulate for myself that really what I needed to do was containment – figure out the boundaries that I needed to assert for myself to make sure that I wasn't going to hurt anybody. It took me a while to understand that because of the ways that people who are socialized male in this society, they're never expected to assert any boundaries on their own sexuality. Both in terms of, "I don't want to do this," but also in terms of actively seeking other people's boundaries, seeking out to understand what other people's boundaries are. So basically that whole first period was just tracking myself, figuring out in what sorts of emotional states I was most likely to cross somebody's boundaries and what it felt like when I was getting there; what sorts of situations were likely to trigger it and also in day-to-day interactions, what kinds of boundaries I needed to be asserting for myself to make sure I wasn't getting close to any of those things.

Then once I had that containment figured out and had the space where I was trusting myself not to be crossing people's boundaries, then there was room in my life to be able to go inwards and start working on self-transformation and healing. Part of that, too, was that I was still crossing people's boundaries on a regular basis. Every time it would happen it would be a crisis for me. Sometimes I would get suicidal.Sometimes I would just be freaking out and paranoid and have huge flare-ups of guilt and shame. So when I was crossing people's boundaries, there wasn't emotional room for that type of transformation and healing to take place. I needed to create this sort of containment not just for the worthy goal of not doing harm but also to make sure that I had the capacity, the emotional space, to be able to work on that healing and transformation. So that was the second phase, when I was working with an accountability group that I sought out for myself. There was a lot of healing and selftransformation.

Now at this point, I feel like I've gotten enough of that worked out that I feel like I'm getting to a place where it becomes an ethical possibility for me to start reaching back outwards again, and starting to work on getting involved in organizing or perhaps have relationships. Because for this whole time I've had a strict rule for myself around abstinence and celibacy, just not getting involved in people because – because I know that any time that would happen, that all these things that I haven't dealt with would come up. And once all that unresolved trauma flares up, then the game is basically lost for me. So now, the potential for having intimate or sexual relationships starts to become more of a reality for me and at this point I feel like I've learned enough about where all that's coming from, and I've healed enough that I can communicate about it enough to understand my limits and boundaries and to reach out at the same time.

Another shift that's been happening, too, is that towards the beginning it was basically like I couldn't have people in my life that I wasn't able to disclose to. There were some people that were either an acquaintance or some sort of person that had power over me that were in my life that I didn't really disclose to. But basically, every person that I was becoming friends with, at some point I'm gonna need to tell them, just as part of the process of being friends. When I decided that I wanted to be friends with them, I would have to tell them. At this point, as I'm getting to the point where I'm putting people less at risk, I feel like I'm gaining back more of the privilege of retaining my anonymity. It's still really important for me to disclose with people, and there are some situations in which I'm probably always going to be disclosing to people really early on. For example, any time I want to get involved in anti-violence work, that's going to be a conversation I have at the outset, before I get involved. But I feel like I'm regaining some of that privilege of anonymity now, too.

Accountability and Healing: Moving through Guilt, Shame and a Traumatic Response to Vulnerability

Now it's been years of seeking support through political groups working on accountability and therapy and staying committed to the process. The things I now understand about healing, in the wholeness of my experience, as both a survivor and a perpetrator, look very different than the ones that I've read about or that people have talked to me about, where it's healing only from surviving abuse or violence.

I think that the three biggest emotions that I've had to contend with in that healing and transformation – and this is something that I've only articulated in the last, like, month of my life – I think the three biggest things that I've had to contend with are guilt, shame and a traumatic response to being vulnerable.

I think those three things – in myself at least – are the sources for the self-hate. It took me a long time trying to figure out even what guilt and shame are. What the emotions are, what they feel like. I would just read those words a lot, but without being able to identify the feeling. One of the things someone told me was that it seems like a lot of my actions are motivated by guilt. And that was strange to me because I never thought that I had felt guilt before. I thought, "Oh, well, I feel remorse but I don't feel guilt." It was years of pondering that before I even understood what guilt was or what it felt like in myself. Once I did, I was like, "Well damn! That's actually just about everything I feel." I just hadn't understood what it felt like before, so I didn't know how to identify it.

Now my understanding of guilt is that it's the feeling of being worthy of punishment. That guiltiness crops up when I become aware of the harm that I've done. I might engage in minimization, trying to make that harm go away, so that I don't feel that guiltiness for it any more, so that I don't feel worthy of being punished. I might try denying it – same sort of thing. Maybe I'm going to try to numb myself so that I don't feel that – so that I don't have that feeling any more. Or maybe I'm going to make that punishment come to me – just being in that place where there's this feeling that the other boot is gonna drop all the time, and that it should drop, trying to bring about a sense of resolution to that sense of impending harm by harming myself.

And another thing that I can see in myself is trying to get out of that sense that harm is gonna come to me by dedicating my life to amending the harm. But the thing is that it's different from compassion, trying to right wrongs because of guilt instead of because of compassion. Doing it through guilt, I notice that I can't assert any boundaries with myself. It's like a compulsion, and it leads me to burnout, Because any time that I stop, that feeling comes back, and it's like, the harm is gonna come. I'm learning how to stay present with that difficult feeling and breathe through it. It helps me a lot.

And then, as far as the shame goes, my understanding of shame is it's like the feeling that I am someone who I cannot stand to be. I was at this workshop where somebody was talking about their experiences with addiction and said, "My whole life, when I was in the middle of this addiction, I had this combination of grandiosity and an inferiority complex." You know, like this sense that I was better than everyone else and that I was the worst scum of the earth. I think when that's the manifestation of shame – that this is who I should be and this is who I really am. When I've seen myself in that kind of place, then usually I'm reacting to the shame either by trying to drown out that awareness of the side of me that's scum, and one of the primary ways that I did that was through finding ways of getting sexual rushes or something like that. And the other thing that I've seen myself do is trying to eradicate that part of me that's the scum. And mostly that happened through fantasies of doing violence to myself, targeted at that part of myself that I hated, that part of myself that I couldn't stand to be, and trying to rip myself into two. I think that's a lot of what was fueling my desire for suicide, too.

One of the things that happened with the accountability process is that once I started talking to people about the things I was most ashamed about, and making it public, then that grandiosity went away. And instead I had to come to terms with this other understanding of myself that wasn't as caught up in illusions of grandeur and instead was this forced humbleness. Like, I'm a person and I'm no better than anybody else. I'm a person and I can also change. So through talking about the things that I'm most ashamed of, that shame became transformative for me. That was a really big aspect of healing for me. And it required a lot of grieving, a lot of loss. And that's something that I was going through during that first year when I was talking with people about it.

As I was talking with other people about it, all these possibilities were closing off in my life. I'll never be able to do this thing now. I'll never be able to have this type of relationship now. The world was less open to me. Like, I can't think of myself in the same way any more. A lot of times I didn't really have the capacity to really face it. But in the moments of insight I had, where I was coming to terms with it, I was really grieving, weeping, over the things that I was losing because of the accountability. That was a big part of healing for me, finding and connecting with and expressing the grief. And also the grief over everything that I had done.

There are still some things that I probably will have to let go of but that I haven't allowed myself to grieve yet, some possibilities that I'm still clinging to. I've found that a lot of time when I get on a power trip and find myself in this controlling sort of attitude, one of the things that resolves that is if I can find a way to grieve. The power trips, the controlling attitudes, tend to happen when I'm trying to control things that are changing. If I can just accept the change and grieve ways that possibilities are changing, then that brings me back. I mean, I've come to terms with a lot of the things that I was grieving when I first started talking with people about it. I'm starting to be able to find ways in my life now of different paths to some of the same things that I wanted for my life, but just paths that have a lot more humility in them. And I think that's one of the really valuable things that accountability has given me. Any time I start that thinking big about myself, then I bring it back to this accountability that I'm doing and It's helped me a lot in just like helping me find ways to stay connected to humility. That's something that I really appreciate about it.

The third one's a traumatic response to vulnerability. And this is one that I still don't understand that well because I'm just now starting to have some understanding of it. But like I was saying before, because of the violence that I've experienced in my own life, a huge portion of my life has been dedicated to keeping me safe. And for me, those behaviors have been enforced in myself through that same type of self-hate and violence. So if I leave an opening where I'm vulnerable, then that self-hate comes to close it down. If I ever mess up in a way that left me vulnerable, then I find that I start having all these fantasies of doing violence to myself. It's a way of enforcing in myself to never let that happen again. I don't really understand it that well. One of the things that I've been working on more recently is learning how to be open to vulnerability. And that's the last part of self-hate that I've healed the least.

One thing that my history of surviving violence has created is a huge dedication in my life to making sure that I never allow myself to be vulnerable. In the past, it's been utterly impossible for me to allow people to see that I'm any sort of sexual being and has also made it impossible to talk about any sort of like emotions of importance. Or just asking for consent, there's a sort of vulnerability that's involved with that. So this created this wall that set me up to make it really, really hard for me to have consensual sexual interactions with anybody. In my family, we had no communication about anything whatsoever. I didn't have any models around communication. Now that I'm in a world where communication is possible, it's hard for me to convey to people what it's like to be in a world where that's not possible. For a huge portion of my life, there wasn't even a glimmer of possibility. These things that I was feeling, they weren't in the realm of talkability. It meant that I couldn't ever be present enough with the emotions to learn how to intervene. Any time they would come up, I would just try to eradicate them with all this violent self-imagery, without even realizing what I was doing.

Accountability as a Gift

I have a friend that's been involved in a lot of accountability work, and he's insisted to me that what I'm doing isn't accountability because there's not survivors somewhere who are issuing a list of demands or that kind of thing. But for me, that's only one aspect of accountability. There's another aspect that's being accountable to myself, making sure that I'm living the values that are important to me in the world. Ultimately, accountability for me is a commitment to do what I need to do to make sure that I don't repeat those patterns, that they stop with me. Part of that has been the work around creating boundaries for myself. Part of that has been the healing and transformation. And part of it is also engaging with the world, to not see it as an individual thing, but to see myself as part of a social struggle. I need to be engaged with the world to be part of ending all of this sexual violence that's everywhere.

The accountability has this gift of humility. One of the things that is really valuable for me about that humility is the amount of compassion that it's allowed me to have for other people. I still have superiority complexes, but nowhere near like I did. At this point in my life, I'm able to understand myself as being the same kind of human as so many other people. I don't put myself on a different level from them. And so I feel like I have a much greater ability to understand people's struggle and pain, and to learn from it, and to love people, coming out of that compassion and shared struggle.

That ability for real, authentic love is something I never had. I thought that love was this obsessive thing. And when I realized that I needed to stop that, I had this moment of grieving and loss and doubt, because I thought, "Well, if I stop this, will I ever feel love again?" It required this huge shift. Once it quieted down, once I stopped it, then the whole landscape was just silent. It took me awhile to re-tune my hearing so that it wasn't just the roar of this obsession, but that I could hear the birds, and the insects, and the breezes. From there, learn a sort of love that's based in resilience, and shared commitment, and sacrifice. So that's been a real gift that it's given me.

Another thing too, is that I can bear to live with myself. I never could before. Most of the time I'm okay being in my own skin. It's been huge – even though I went through some extremely dark and difficult periods where the basin of depression that I'd lived in for so long in my life dropped into an abyss, Coming out of that abyss, through a continuing commitment to accountability, it's like the first time in my life when I'm starting to feel I'm free of this sort of depression and this crippling anxiety and paranoia. I have emotional capacity now; like I can feel things. I'm still not in a place where joy is a big part of my life, but it seems possible now. Through all this grieving and everything that I've done, I've also had a couple moments of clarity and lightness that I'd never experienced before in my life.

I think something else that has been a real gift for me, in terms of accountability, is the possibility for having lasting intimate relationships with people, whether sexually or not sexually. And having some capacity for pleasure – sexual pleasure, even, because before it was so caught up in shame and guilt and feeling triggered that I only ever felt horrible. Now I don't feel like I'm consigned to that for the rest of my life. I feel that there's a possibility of being liberated from it.

(This story is available at the StoryTelling & Organizing Project (STOP) website at www.stopviolenceeveryday.org.)

TOOLS

4.F TAKING ACCOUNTABILITY

Tool F1. Staircase of Change

Tool F2. Level of Participation of Survivors or Victims Chart

Tool F3. Self-Reflection for Survivors or Victims and Allies

Tool F4. Self-Reflection and Practice Questions for Allies

Tool F5. Guiding Questions for Person Doing Harm

Tool F6. Preparing for Direct Communication, Affirmations, and Guided Questions for Person Doing harm

TAKING ACCOUNTABILITY TOOL F1: PATHWAY OF CHANGE

Our vision of accountability is one that:

- Believes that transformational change is possible even for those who commit the most serious acts of violence.
- Focuses on responsibility rather than punishment.
- Understands that it is not only individuals that are responsible for change – it is our communities.
- Sees accountability as a process of change.

Process of Change as a Pathway. This Toolkit refers to one way of understanding the process of change as a pathway. The image of a pathway tells us that:

- Change may come one step a time
- Each step is significant
- We can aim for the top of the pathway, but we may not be able to reach it
- For every situation, each step will mean different actions and different changes
- Any one of us may not be able to see the next step until the step just below is reached

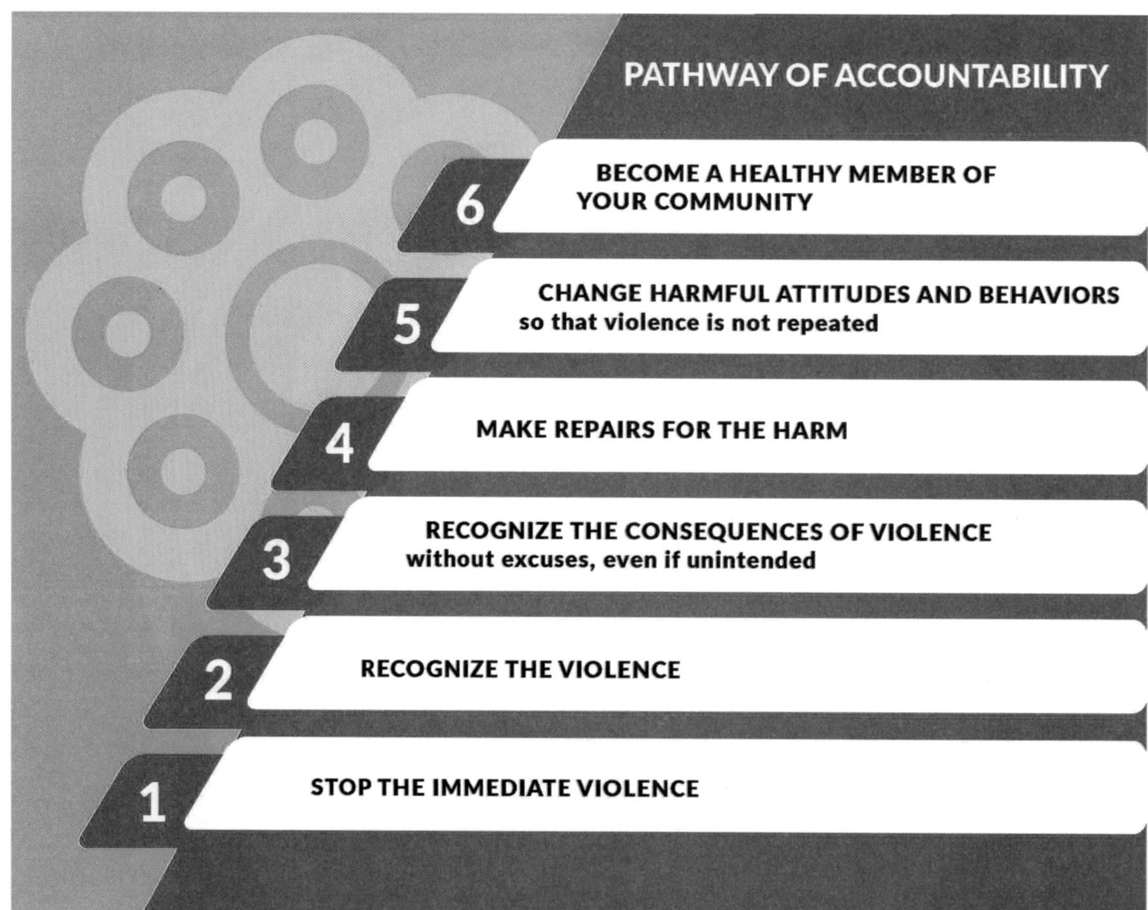
PATHWAY OF ACCOUNTABILITY
6 BECOME A HEALTHY MEMBER OF YOUR COMMUNITY
5 CHANGE HARMFUL ATTITUDES AND BEHAVIORS so that violence is not repeated
4 MAKE REPAIRS FOR THE HARM
3 RECOGNIZE THE CONSEQUENCES OF VIOLENCE without excuses, even if unintended
2 RECOGNIZE THE VIOLENCE
1 STOP THE IMMEDIATE VIOLENCE

STEP #1: STOP IMMEDIATE VIOLENCE

For some interventions, Step 1: Stop immediate violence may be the ultimate goal of the intervention. The approach in this Toolkit aims for intervention results that may transform the person doing harm and/or a community that may have done harm or allowed harm to happen. However, Step 1 may be the first step necessary to reach these larger aims.

Step 1 can mean many things and can be reached a number of ways.

Sometimes the first step of accountability is stopping a specific act of violence from happening or stopping violence enough so that we can even discuss what the next step might be. (See Story F3. Stopping Violence as the First Step)

Although we have grander visions of accountability and change – leading to equality, mutual respect, and shared power – the pragmatic steps may begin with something very simple. Stop violence.

Sometimes we cannot reach any type of agreement from the person doing harm that violence should stop. Sometimes we need to use some manner of pressure, threats, force or coercion to make sure it does (See Section 4.F.3. Taking Accountability Tips for more about the use of force). By this we do not mean the use of physical violence, but acts such as asking someone to stay away or leave, letting someone know that there will be consequences if violence continues, or physically restraining someone from acting out violently at that moment.

We may need to act immediately. We may be facing a situation of serious harm, injury or even death. We may be protecting children. We may not be able to get any form of agreement from the person doing harm to stop – or may not have time to see if this is possible.

Sometimes stopping violence means that we need to get out of harm's way. For some, escape from the person doing harm may be the only way to stop violence – at least in the short term.

STEP # 2: RECOGNIZE THE VIOLENCE

Step 2 is to recognize the violence.

For some people who have caused harm, this step can be significant. They may not want to admit the things that they did. They may not even be aware that they were violent. They may be aware but deny or minimize the fact that these actions had ever happened.

Recognizing the violence means to say, "Yes, I did do these things." (See Section 4.A. Getting Clear for a section on naming the harms).

"Yes, I did hit you."

"Yes, it's true. I didn't let you go to work."

STEP #3: RECOGNIZE THE CONSEQUENCES WITHOUT EXCUSES -- EVEN IF UNINTENDED

Step 3 moves from recognizing violence to recognizing the results or consequences of violence – without excuses. This includes consequences that were not intended by the person doing harm.

The person (or community) doing harm that reaches Step 3 has stepped back and thought about what they've done. They've listened to other people share their experience of the violence and are starting to understand the full impact of their attitudes and actions on others, and perhaps on themselves.

They've stopped making excuses or stopped asking for us to make excuses for them. They can now accept the violence and abuse as their fault and their responsibility.

They've stopped getting angry when confronted with what they've done. They've stopped going to other people to get their sympathy and to tell their side of the story.

They've started feeling sorry for what they've done – feeling remorse. They are starting to deal with whatever difficulties they may have regarding feelings of regret, embarrassment, and shame. They have begun to accept these feelings without fighting against it, making excuses, being self-destructive or destroying other people because they can't handle being wrong or having to show their faults.

They are starting to understand that there are consequences to what they've done. They may have lost trust, relationships and more. They don't blame others for losing these things – they see that it is the result of their own attitudes and actions.

The following are some examples of how someone may begin to take accountability.

- "Yes, I did hit you. I hit you with my fist and tried to hit you in a place where nobody would see the mark. I kept saying and thinking it was your fault, but I now see that I had a choice. It is my fault – not yours.
- I see that by hitting you, I caused fear. I caused you to hate me, to not trust me – maybe never to trust me again. I caused you physical pain, but most of all I can now see how much I hurt you at your very core.
- Now that I can admit what I did, I can remember the look in your eyes – how afraid you were, confused and then how angry. You had to hide your bruises so nobody would see them. We pretended like nothing happened. I wouldn't let you bring it up, threatening to hit you again if you did. Sometimes I didn't use the words, but gave you a look so that you would know that you'd better watch it or else."

- "Yes, I called you names in front of the kids. I knew it would hurt you and humiliate you. Thinking back now, that's why I did it. I felt angry and took it out on you. I didn't care if the kids were around. In fact, maybe I wanted them to think you were a bad mother and turn against you.

- I didn't see how much this hurt my kids. I didn't care. I can now see how our son acts like me – terrorizing his sister and calling you a b****, just like I did. Now I can see how our daughter hates me. She won't even look at me. I blamed it all on her or you or anybody but me. I never wanted to admit that it was my fault – even to myself. I was proud that my son didn't take s*** from you and stood by my side. But now I see that he's scared of me, too."

STEP #4: MAKE REPAIRS FOR THE HARM

With Step 4, the person doing harm makes sincere attempts to repair the harm – these repairs are not just the ones they can do cheaply and quickly. They are repairs that are requested by the people that have been hurt or by the community. These may also be repairs that they have considered themselves after deep reflection about the harm they have caused.

These repairs may never be able to make up for the harm done. Often they cannot – nothing can. But they are real and symbolic attempts to do something significant to make the lives of those who have been harmed better.

These repairs may be:

- Sincere apologies:
    - With specific and full details of the harm (Step 1 and 2)
    - Without excuses (Step 2)
    - With full acknowledgment of the negative consequences they created for individuals and the community (Step 2)
    - With the intended repairs (Step 3)
    - With a commitment never to repeat these harms to the survivor or victim or any other people again (See Step 5)
    - With knowledge that repeating these harms will lead to negative consequences (See Step 5)
    - Without making this for the purposes of making oneself look like a hero or a martyr or any other form of self-gain except the gains of making repairs for harms done
    - In other forms such as: video conference or zoom (if transportation is an issue); written letter, letter published on a website, and so on
    - Without making this for the purposes of making oneself look like a hero or a martyr or any other form of self gain except the gains of making repairs for harms done

- Services such as: help fixing things that are broken; cooking; cleaning; making something useful; providing other valued services for the survivor or victim, the community or other people or organizations that are agreed upon
- Financial repairs such as: money for the needs of the people harmed; money for damages; money to pay for something valued by the people harmed; return of funds stolen, taken, gambled or spent carelessly; taking over credit card payments, mortgages, IRS payments or other forms of debt; money so that the people harmed can receive medical care or go to counseling; money so that the people harmed can enjoy themselves.
- A commitment to stop violence now and in the future -- and action to back it up.

EXAMPLE OF AN ACCOUNTABILITY LETTER

"I am letting L, her family and our friends know about my previous actions against her. Although she asked me to write this, I also agree that sharing this with all of you is my responsibility. This is just one step in being accountable for how much I had hurt her and in doing so, hurt all of you as well.

As you know, L and I met 8 years ago. I loved her and respected her and respect her to this day. But I acted in ways that were the opposite of loving and respectful.

My abuse began with my jealousy. I was jealous whenever she looked at anybody else. I was even jealous when she was with her friends. I began to control her behavior – making her feel uncomfortable whenever she went out without me. I questioned what she did, who she talked to, how she felt. I knew it was wrong, but I justified it in my mind – that this was my being a loving person or that I couldn't lose her so I had to watch her all the time.

When she wouldn't answer the way I wanted or she went out anyways or did what she wanted, I began to lose my temper. At first I yelled. Then I began to throw things and hit things near her. One time, I hit her, leaving the mark of my hand on her face. I begged her not to tell anyone and I promised never to do it again. She stayed home from work for a couple of days – and I did stop for awhile.

But it didn't stop there. The next time I knew not to hit her where anyone would see the mark. I started to hit her on her head or body where people wouldn't see. This happened about every 6 months at first. But it started to get worse, and I would hit her or threaten to every couple of months. I apologized every time and begged her to forgive me. I promised to change and go to counseling. But I never followed through. I never found any help and hoped that she would forget. I hoped I would just stop or things would change. I told myself that I didn't hit her so hard – that it was understandable because she kept doing things I asked her not to do. I always made excuses for my behavior or blamed her.

She tried to talk to me about it, but I would never let this be the subject. I didn't want to talk about it and would either threaten her or walk out of the house or tell her that she was crazy every time.

I didn't think about how this affected her. I only thought about how I felt – about how everything and anything affected me.

She finally threatened to leave me and this time I believed it. I hit her and broke the things that were most important to her. I got so I didn't even apologize any more. I would just leave the house and come back later hoping that everything would be forgotten.

Some of you came to me then. I know that I lied at that time. I said it only happened a couple of times. I said that she was crazy and exaggerating things. I didn't want to face up to what I had done. I felt incredibly ashamed and still blamed her for telling other people about our business.

This past few months have been my biggest challenge. But I also have to thank you for stopping me. I'm not sure what I would have done next.

You didn't back down, and L, you didn't back down even though I wanted you to. I now know that if you hadn't stepped in – especially L's sister and her husband, I would not have stopped. Somehow, I just didn't know what to do and just kept doing the same thing over and over again.

I am hoping that L and I can continue our relationship. But I also know that it might be too late. I have come to accept that I cannot control our relationship but only control myself. I am going to counseling every week now and am starting to discover what it means to be an adult and take responsibility for my behaviors.

I am deeply sorry. I apologize to all of you. L, I apologize to you and know that I hurt you so many times in so many ways. I do hope that you will be able to trust people again and will heal from everything I have done to you. I know that trust is something I must earn and that it may take a very long time. I accept that responsibility and hope that I can honor that no matter what happens – even if you decide that you can no longer stay in this relationship. If that is the case, please know that I will not do anything to stop you or to hurt you. This is your choice.

I apologize to your family. I hurt your daughter. I made your sister suffer. I know that I have caused so much pain and suffering as you worried about L's safety and dignity. I know that you saw her change from a loving person with confidence to someone living in constant fear. I also know that nothing can make up for that loss.

I have talked with all of you and as you know, I promise to do the following:

I will treat L with respect and kindness.

I will never ever threaten L with harm. I will not throw anything, hit anything. I will not touch her in any harmful or unwanted way. I will never insult her or call her names. I will not tell her what she can do or not do, who she can see or not see. I will communicate with her and discuss what she wants and needs. I will listen and not interrupt.

I will continue to seek help in order to change my attitudes and behaviors. I have a better understanding now than ever in my life and for that, I am grateful. And I know that change takes time. I will not stop getting help. I have found a group that has a program for people who are violent. I started going and will continue to attend through to the very end.

I will support L. to get what she needs in order to recover and have agreed to make sure that I pay for her counseling.

I will also talk about other things with L – how we share work around the house, decisions about what we do together, decisions about our finances. These are things that I know now that we must share together.

I believe I am a changed person and thank L and all of you for helping me stop my violence. And I know I have a long way to go."

STEP #5: CHANGE HARMFUL ATTITUDES AND BEHAVIORS SO THAT VIOLENCE IS NOT REPEATED

Step 5 brings the person doing harm to a deeper level of change. It moves beyond the specific harms to go to the deeper causes for violence. It makes one truly responsible not only for past harms but for future behavior, free from violence.

Changing harmful attitudes and behaviors involves a deep look at oneself and the types of attitudes and behaviors that are related to violence. This will be different for different people, but this could include fundamental changes such as:

- Shifting a sense of superiority over others to one of equality and humility.
- Shifting an expectation that one is to get whatever one wants to an expectation of shared giving and receiving.
- Dealing with issues of insecurity and low self worth to healthy self-confidence.
- Seeking support to change unhealthy relationships to alcohol and drugs that lead to abuse of self and others.
- Seeking support for problems of gambling or careless spending.
- Seeking support to deal with personal experiences with abuse such as child sexual abuse or physical abuse to look at their connection to violence.
- Letting go of controlling behaviors and opening to relationships of give and take, spontaneity and curiosity.
- Seeing other people as partners and companions, not as objects.
- Seeking community as a space for sharing and reciprocity.

STEP #6: CREATE A HEALTHIER COMMUNITY

Steps 1 – 5 are stages towards being a healthy member of one's community. At some point, efforts to stay accountable may shift towards ease and confidence in one's ability to be a healthy and respectful partner, family member, friend, co-worker, neighbor and fellow community member.

Someone who has been able to take accountability and go up the pathway of change may be in a position to help someone else who is causing harm and who could benefit from the support of another who has been through the same thing.

Finally, as a healthy member of one's community, one may be a part of changing the process of taking accountability from one associated with shame to one of honor and courage. This is the task of all of us no matter what position we have in relationship to violence.

YOUR PATHWAY OF CHANGE: WHAT DOES IT LOOK LIKE?

This tool can be used for anyone to think about what a pathway of change would look like for this specific situation. What specific steps would show that someone is moving up and making progress with the process of taking accountability?

For the survivor or victim and allies, you can use this tool to figure out what specific things you can ask the person doing harm (or the community) to do. Remember that Step 1 is significant and may be as far as you get in an intervention. You may think that your goal with regard to accountability would be just getting to Step 1.

You may want to go further. You may set goals that include Step 2, that the person doing harm (or the community) need to specifically name the harms and recognize the specific attitudes and actions that were harmful.

You may want to go further to Step 3 and set an expectation that the person doing harm (or the community) fully account for all of the consequences of that harm without making any excuses, whether or not these harms were intended.

Step 4 may be an expectation, as well. You may want the person doing harm (or the community) to take action or provide resources or services that actually contribute to repairing the harm.

Processes of accountability as an expectation may stop with Step 4. It is easier to come up with concrete things that people can do to meet these steps.

Step 5 and 6 are important but harder to make specific measures. You may be able to tell, but explaining what that looks like is harder to do.

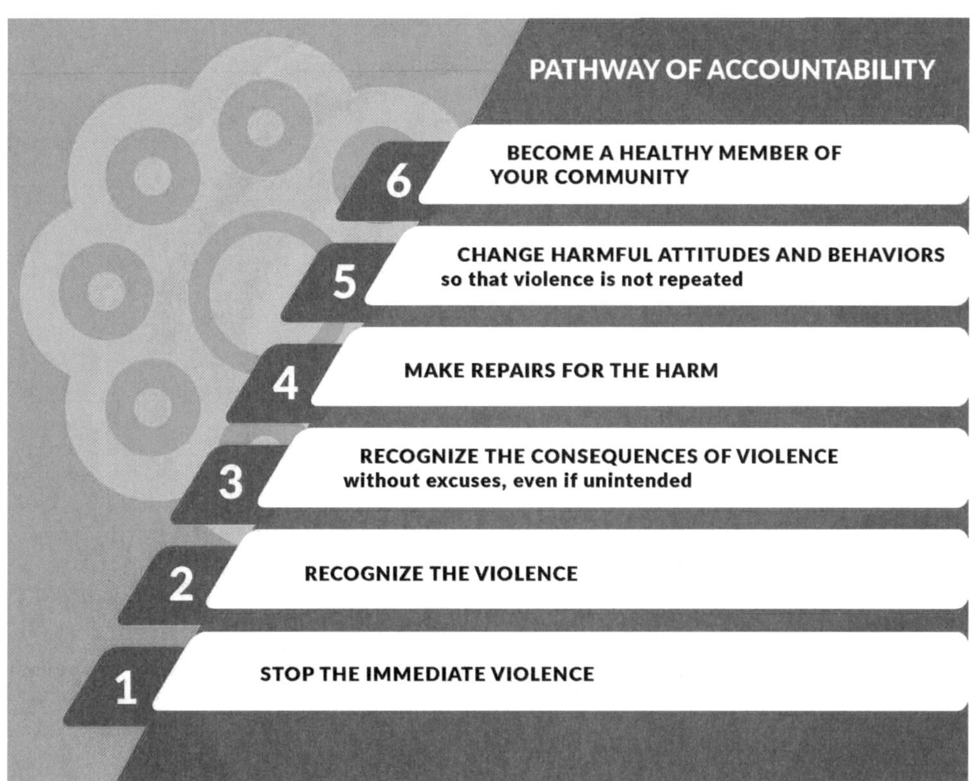
PATHWAY OF ACCOUNTABILITY
6 BECOME A HEALTHY MEMBER OF YOUR COMMUNITY
5 CHANGE HARMFUL ATTITUDES AND BEHAVIORS so that violence is not repeated
4 MAKE REPAIRS FOR THE HARM
3 RECOGNIZE THE CONSEQUENCES OF VIOLENCE without excuses, even if unintended
2 RECOGNIZE THE VIOLENCE
1 STOP THE IMMEDIATE VIOLENCE

STEP #1: STOP IMMEDIATE VIOLENCE

What specific harmful, abusive or violent actions should stop? (See Section 2.2. Interpersonal Violence: Some Basics Everyone Should Know and Section 4.A. Getting Clear)

Are there some that are absolutes or bottom-lines?

Are there priorities?

Are there some forms of harm, abuse or violence that are less priorities to stop – or that you could even let go of? Or come back to at a later time when things progress?

To what level do you expect these particular types of harms or violence to stop?

STEP #2 RECOGNIZE THE VIOLENCE

What specific harmful, abusive or violent actions do you want the person doing harm (or community) to name and recognize?

Are there some that are absolutes or bottom-lines?

Are there priorities?

Are there some forms of harm, abuse or violence that are less important to name – or that you could even let go of? Or come back to at a later time when things progress?

STEP #3 RECOGNICE THE CONSEQUENCES - WITHOUT EXCUSES - EVEN IF UNINTENDED

What are the consequences of violence? (See Section 2.2. Interpersonal Violence: Some Basics Everyone Should Know)

To whom – what individuals, families, groups or organizations have been hurt or negatively affected by the violence?

What were immediate consequences, for example, injuries, fear, lost days from work?

What are more long-term consequences, for example, inability to trust, nervousness, nightmares, flashbacks, loss of self-confidence, lost relationships with children, incarceration?

STEP #4: MAKE REPAIRS FOR THE HARM

What can be done to repair the harm? (understanding that there may be nothing that can repair it?) Financial repair? Services? Apologies? Public apologies or other responses?

To whom?

For how long?

STEP #5: CHANGE HARMFUL ATTITUDES AND BEHAVIORS SO THAT VIOLENCE IS NOT REPEATED

What underlying or deep attitudes and behaviors have contributed to the violence?

What underlying or deep changes in attitude or behavior need to be made?

STEP #6: CREATE A HEALTHIER COMMUNITY

How can you contribute to a healthier, less violent community overall?

What are situations of violence in my community that I have witnessed or have been aware of but where I was unable to intervene?

What are some of the social or community dynamics that helped me to intervene? Or that were a barrier to intervening?

Who are other people in my community that could benefit from having a staircase of their own, and how can I support them?

PATHWAY OF CHANGE

Use your own words to describe what your steps to change or accountability look like.

Step 6	
Step 5	
Step 4	
Step 3	
Step 2	
Step 1	

TAKING ACCOUNTABILITY TOOL F2: LEVEL OF PARTICIPATION FOR SURVIVORS OR VICTIMS CHART

If you are the survivor or the victim, you can choose how you want to be involved in the process of taking accountability.

You may already have a clear view of what you want from the process of goal setting. See Section 4.D. Goal Setting. As you move through an intervention, however, you may have different ideas of how you think about accountability or what specific things you want.

Taking Accountability and the Person Doing Harm

In this Toolkit, the process of taking accountability usually involves some level of connection with the person doing harm. This Toolkit offers the Pathway of Change as a framework for thinking about accountability as a series of steps, a process. It also relies upon the idea that accountability can best come about not through punishment or revenge, but from compassion, connection and support for the person doing harm. It aims to support an understanding that change can be a benefit not only to you and the community – but to the person doing harm, as well. This is not just so they can make some kind of calculated gains – getting status, getting out of punishment or prison, looking like a hero or a martyr. What we mean by benefit is that they can have better and more meaningful relationships, they can live better lives, they can create respect and healthiness rather than abuse and harm.

If you do not believe in this form of accountability, then you might consider a different approach to intervention – perhaps one that is not in this Toolkit but that may be found in other types of domestic violence or sexual assault programs. See Section 3. Getting Started: Is This Model Right For You?

How involved will you be – or how will you be involved?

This approach to violence intervention works best with the participation of the survivor or victim. However, the levels of participation can be very different depending on the situation and what the survivor or victim wants. For possible levels of participation in the intervention over all, see Section 4.E. Supporting Survivors or Victims, Tool E3: Survivor or Victim Participation in an Intervention. Chart.

The process of Taking Accountability require some special consideration since this process is primarily involved in engaging the person doing harm. Exposure to danger, potential manipulation and a repetition of the dynamics of abuse and violence that bring us to this intervention in the first place can easily be played out in the process of Taking Accountability. For this reason, it may be important for the survivor or victim to consider how they can best be involved or not involved in this process. Their level of participation could be different in this aspect of the intervention than in others.

The following is a chart that marks out the possible levels of involvement and participation of the survivor or victim in the process of Taking Accountability. Please note also that these may be different depending upon where we are in the Pathway of Change. For example, a survivor or victim may want to be very involved in naming the violence and the consequences of that violence. But they may want the person doing harm to take the steps to figure out what repairs are most appropriate and give feedback once these are proposed.

They may want to be involved in guiding goals and thinking about repairs, but want the allies to be the ones who put the most energy into this process.

Again, the Pathway of Change in this Toolkit is:

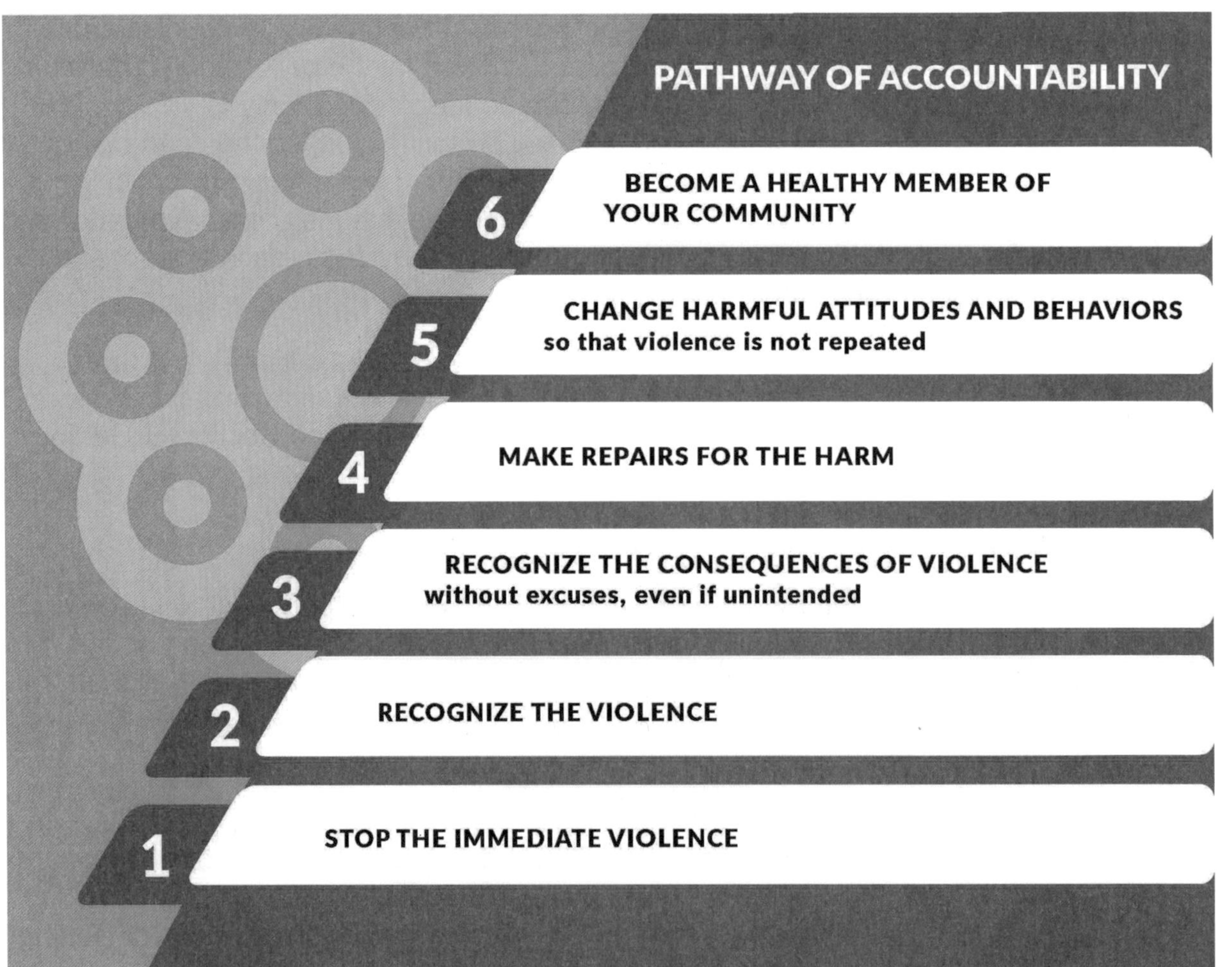
PATHWAY OF ACCOUNTABILITY
6 BECOME A HEALTHY MEMBER OF YOUR COMMUNITY
5 CHANGE HARMFUL ATTITUDES AND BEHAVIORS so that violence is not repeated
4 MAKE REPAIRS FOR THE HARM
3 RECOGNIZE THE CONSEQUENCES OF VIOLENCE without excuses, even if unintended
2 RECOGNIZE THE VIOLENCE
1 STOP THE IMMEDIATE VIOLENCE

Think about each step (if this is useful to you) and think about how you want to participate.

There are a number of components to an intervention; remember, your participation can be high in one component of the intervention and low in another. The factors to consider are:

1. **Physical Presence**. Do you want to be there in person in any stage of engaging the person doing harm? Is there a particular time or way in which you (or the intervention) would benefit from you being there in person? If so, how? What is important in terms of your own safety – physical, emotional and other? If not, what other options are available?

2. **Leading or Directing.** How much do you want to be leading or directing? How much are you setting the terms? How much do you want to work with your allies to set the terms – or how much should you work with them even if it is uncomfortable? How much can you expect the person doing harm to actively participate in setting the terms?

3. **Engagement with the Person Doing Harm.** This approach has as part of its vision the idea that the person doing harm would have some level of initiation and participation in the steps towards accountability at least at some point in the process. At the same time, this may be an uneven path. We anticipate that there will be resistance. Our motto is that we are creating systems flexible enough to allow for the expected process of dodging and delaying accountability and strong enough to withstand and diminish these tactics over time. Even if an intervention necessarily begins with an act that involves pressure, force, or coercion, make space for compassion and connection with the person doing harm. This may lead to further steps that can bring in the person doing harm as a participant of an intervention, and not just a target.

4. **Information and Communication.** The final component we present with this tool is that of information and communication. This is especially important as the participation of the survivor or victim may become less direct and physically present. What kind of information and communication does the survivor or victim expect, want and need? This column offers a variety of options to consider.

TAKING ACCOUNTABILITY TOOL F2 : LEVEL OF PARTICIPATION BY THE SURVIVOR OR VICTIM IN THE PROCESS OF ACCOUNTABILITY

While Creative Interventions encourages active survivor or victim participation, this can happen at different levels. This chart helps you sort out what level of survivor or victim participation best describes your intervention process – or – which level best describes what you would like your process to look like.

Level	Physical Presence	Leading or Directing	Engagement with Person doing Harm	Information and Communication
Highest	I want to be there in person and actively involved as the main actor.	I want to be leading, directing and setting the terms.	I want my input and participation to be the most visible and prioritized. I want the person doing harm to listen and follow – but not make any decisions.	I want to decide and to know everything.
High	I want to be there in person and prioritized with special consideration but not necessarily the main actor.	I want to be in a primary role and I want my perspective to be the priority. I do not always need to be leading.	I want my input and participation to be the most visible and prioritized. And the person doing harm can make suggestions and comments that may be taken into account.	I want to know everything but I will not always be deciding.
Middle	I want to be there in person but at a level similar to other people.	I want to be participating in a similar way to others.	I want my input and participation to be high, and I expect to have significant participation and input by the person doing harm. We can have some back and forth.	I want to know the most important pieces of information
Low	I want to be there but I would like to be in a protected position.	I want to give input and feedback but I don't want to actively participate.	I want the person doing harm and their allies to make a proposal for an accountability process and I will make comments and changes.	I want information at key moments or at some regular timing – but don't need to know everything that's going on.
Minimal	I want to be there but via something like another room or communicating through phone, skype or other method of communication..	I want to give my input and feedback but then step away from any involvement.	I am leaving this to my allies to work together with the person doing harm to figure out how accountability will happen. I want to know what is going on and will give feedback.	Let me know what happens at the end or if there are significant changes. Otherwise, I don't want to know.
None - but you have approval	I don't want to be there.	I trust the group. I don't want to be involved.	I am leaving this to my allies to work together with the person doing harm to figure out how accountability will happen. I am stepping away.	I don't need any further information.
None - the survivor or victim disagree	Not there or there but disagreeing.	May be uninvolved or actively disagreeing or countering the intervention.	May be uninvolved; carrying out another intervention in a different way; working together with the person doing harm to counter the intervention.	May not be in communication; in communication in order to have more control over a process that I disagree with

ⓘ *TAKING ACCOUNTABILITY* TOOL F3: SELF-REFLECTION AND GUIDING QUESTIONS FOR SURVIVORS OR VICTIMS AND ALLIES

The process of Taking Accountability can be particularly challenging for the survivor or victim of violence. Since this involves some level of engagement (communication, working with, supporting) the person doing harm, there is lots of opportunity for re-living the dynamics of abuse and violence that led the survivor or victim to this intervention.

If we consider the process of taking accountability as one that can lead to deep and transformational change, then it can be a long and difficult process with anticipated resistance from the person doing harm.

Again, we are creating systems flexible enough to allow for the expected process of dodging and delaying accountability and strong enough to withstand and diminish these tactics over time. Along the way, we can expect resistance in many forms that can be dangerous to or threatening to the survivor or victim, as well as others vulnerable to violence including anybody participating in the intervention.

This Toolkit attempts to reverse the kind of dynamics that feed interpersonal violence. It also attempts to provide more effective measures for communities to make meaningful change – and not simply rely upon escape and punishment as a means towards resolving violence. The alternative we offer, however, is still in its early stages of formulation. As we say in Section 3.2. What This Model Is NOT, this is not a guarantee of success.

For the survivor or victim, this approach offers promises. It allows you to name your goals, find your way towards them, and offers tools for you to bring together your allies to make this a possibility. At the same time, this approach has its risks and does not offer guarantees. It asks you, in particular, to take the risk of possibly participating in engaging the person doing harm if taking accountability is one thing you work towards.

This section offers some tools to help the survivor or victim, allies and the person doing harm to take the courageous and challenging set of steps leading to transformation and change. We offer some guiding questions for you to ask yourself and your allies in order to prepare you for some level of participation in the process of taking accountability.

If you do not feel prepared enough or have enough support to participate in this or to even propose it as an area of your intervention, then we ask that you reconsider this arena of the intervention. We have found that even asking yourself that question can be a powerful step towards gaining a sense of power and control in your own life.

YOUR SPECIAL ROLE AS A SURVIVOR OR VICTIM

If you are the survivor or victim of violence, you may be in very different relationships to the violence and to the person who has done harm. What you consider goals in relation to the violence and the person may differ depending on your relationship to each of them. For example, is this someone you are together with as a partner, and do you want to stay together? Is this someone you do not want to stay with? Is this someone you are separated from, and that you want to remain separated from? Is this someone with whom you may still need to share community? (See Section 4.D. Goal Setting for more support around these questions.

If you are reading this Toolkit, then it is possible that you considering a high level of participation in the intervention or are already participating at a high level. If you are the survivor or victim, you can play a very powerful role in driving this process. You may know best what happened, the nature of violence, the harms that have resulted from that violence and what needs to be done. Others may have some understanding of the situation but may not be able to formulate all of the strategies necessary to change the situation nor know all of the details that could come under question if and when they meet with the person doing harm.

At the same time, this puts a great burden on you to be the survivor or victim of violence and the person in a position of great responsibility to address it. This is a difficult position and one that you may choose not to take.

Working together with allies can lighten this burden and help you come up with better ideas and strategies than you would alone. This tool can help you get more specific about what you expect from the accountability process and how to best prepare.

This does not take away from your responsibility to weigh the costs and the benefits of your involvement, made even more difficult when you don't know what the outcome will be. Keep this in mind as you make your way through this tool and through the intervention.

OVERALL QUESTIONS

- What are your goals? What do you want?
- How is any step in the accountability or any step in the Pathway of Change linked to your goals?
- What could bring about change in the person doing harm?
- What do they care about? This could be positive things such as care for other people or questionable things like their reputation. Anything could count but the strategies would need to change depending upon what these are.
- Have you seen their potential for change?
    - If so, could these moments of change be part of a cycle in which change including apologies or remorse seem to be simply parts of a cycle that includes a return to violence?
    - Are these moments of change including apologies or remorse a tool to get what this person wants such as your return to the relationship, control over the situation, sympathy from others, a belief in change from you?
- Even if things they care about are self-centered, are they things that could at least help you reach your goals?
- If so, what kind of strategies could use these points as anchors or leverage for you to reach your goals?
- Is there anything that the person doing harm could say or do that can jeopardize your credibility, your side of the story?
    - Is there important information that you have not shared with others in the intervention – things that the person doing harm could share?
    - Can you anticipate all of the accusations the person doing harm could make against you? Are you ready to handle these?
- Is there anything that someone else, including allies or potential allies, could say or do that can jeopardize your credibility, your side of the story?
- What can be the worst result of this request for accountability?
- How can you protect yourself from the worst results? Can you live with the worst results?

DO YOU WANT TO GO AHEAD?

There are many further ways to approach these questions. In this following section, we will go through the Pathway of Change and ask questions that accompany each step.

QUESTIONS USING THE PATHWAY OF CHANGE

STEP 1: STOP IMMEDIATE VIOLENCE OR STOP IT ENOUGH TO GO TO NEXT STEP

As we have said, Step 1 may be the ultimate goal of the intervention. Stopping immediate violence can be a challenging step in and of itself. It may be the best some of us could hope to achieve. For others, this step may be one that is no longer meaningful. The violence may be long over. What we want now is a response.

By force or coercion, we do not necessarily mean an act of violence. But this may look like a demand that someone stop, yelling at somebody to stop, bringing a group of people to tell someone forcefully to stop, a threat that continuing violence could result in leaving a relationship, telling others about the violence, threats of retaliatory violence, threats of some unknown consequence that would be serious, and threats to call the police.

Stopping violence with force may look like: the confiscation of a gun, throwing someone out of the house, banning someone from being near or visiting children they had harmed, putting them on suspension at work, or grabbing someone who is beating their partner. It may be leaving a partner or a person doing harm, changing locks so they cannot re-enter the house, or preventing them from coming near you.

The goal of stopping violence may be straightforward or very complicated. It could deal with the person doing harm at the highest level of risk. They may never have been challenged before. They may be favored by people in your social circle, including those whom you might bring into an intervention.

An intervention that is able to accomplish Step 1 may be considered a success. For many, this will be the end goal. Moving beyond this step may simply not be possible at this time with the amount of resources you have. Moving beyond this step may come years later. Or it may not come at all.

Step 1 is a significant step on the staircase. The power of this first step should not be underestimated.

QUESTIONS

- What specific forms of their violence do you want to address, reduce, stop or prevent?
- Do you want to address it, reduce it, stop it or prevent it? What makes most sense?
- What could bring this about?
- How can this be brought about with the participation and agreement of the person doing harm? Is this possible?
- What kinds of pressure or force might be necessary? What would this look like?
- Is this pressure or force a punishment, revenge or pay-back? If pressure or force is necessary, can you imagine it without the elements of punishment, revenge or pay-back? What would it look like then?
- What does your role need to be in order to make this happen or at least to attempt it?
- Should you take this role? What are the benefits? What are the drawbacks?
- What are the particular dangers to you if you are physically present? How will you stay safe? (See Section 4.B. Staying Safe)
- What are your goals and bottom-lines in terms of stopping the violence? (See Section 4.D. Goal Setting)
- Could you consider reaching Step 1 and only Step 1 a success?
- How will you feel if you are not able to reach Step 1?
- Will there be consequences carried out by you and others affecting the person doing harm if they do not reach Step 1?
- What would these consequences be? Would you communicate these consequences to them? By whom and how would this communication be delivered? How could this communication be done most safely and effectively? Would you in reality carry out these consequences? What are possible effects of these consequences if you carry them out? What are possible effects if you do not carry out these consequences?
- What would be other concerns if Step 1 were not reached? Think of safety, possible increases in their violence or ability to carry out violence, other possible results? How can you safeguard yourself and others? (See Section 4.B. Staying Safe).

STEP 2: RECOGNIZE THE VIOLENCE

In this step of accountability, the person doing harm (or the community) needs to recognize and admit that they are responsible for a particular act or pattern of violence.

QUESTIONS

- What specific forms of their violence do you want to you want the person doing harm to specifically take responsibility for?
- What words do you use to describe this?
- What words do you expect the person doing harm to use to describe this? Do they need to be the same as the words you use?
- How important is it to you that the person doing harm be able to think about what these are on their own (or with an ally or supporter)? Is it okay if they accept your version of the harm and your words?
- What is the bottom-line in terms of what you would want the person doing harm to name?
- Could you consider reaching Step 1 and Step 2 a success if you got no further?
- How will you feel if you are unable to accomplish Step 2?
- What could possibly result from the failure to reach Step 2?
- Would you and others carry out consequences affecting the person doing harm if they do not reach Step 2?
- What would these consequences be? Would you communicate these consequences to them? By whom and how would this communication be delivered? How could this communication be done most safely and effectively? Would you in reality carry out these consequences? What are possible effects of these consequences if you carry them out? What are possible effects if you do not carry out these consequences?
- What would be other concerns if Step 2 were not reached? Think of safety, possible increases in their violence or ability to carry out violence, other possible results? How can you safeguard yourself and others? (See Section 4.B. Staying Safe).

STEP 3: RECOGNIZE THE CONSEQUENCES OF VIOLENCE - WITHOUT EXCUSES - EVEN IF UNINTENDED

This is a much higher level of responsibility in which the person is able to identify all of the different people and groups that the act of or pattern of violence has affected and how it has affected them – in the short term and long term.

QUESTIONS

- Who has experienced those harms that have resulted from the acts of or patterns of violence caused by the person doing harm?
- What are the harms? Short-term and long-term?
- What words do you and others who experienced harm use to describe this?
- What words do you expect the person doing harm to use to describe this? Do they need to be the same as the words you and others use?
- What kinds of excuses has the person doing harm used – and which they need to stop using?
- What is the bottom-line in terms of what you would want the person doing harm to name as the consequences of their violence?
- Could you consider reaching Step 1, Step 2 and Step 3 a success if you got no further?
- How will you feel if you are unable to accomplish Step 3?
- What could possibly result from the failure to reach Step 3?
- Would you and others carry out consequences affecting the person doing harm if they do not reach Step 3?
- What would these consequences be? Would you communicate these consequences to them? Who and how would this communication be delivered? How could this communication be done most safely and effectively? Would you in reality carry out these consequences? What are possible effects of these consequences if you carry them out? What are possible effects if you do not carry out these consequences?
- What would be other concerns if Step 3 were not reached? Think of safety, possible increases in their violence or ability to carry out violence, other possible results? How can you safeguard yourself and others? (See Section 4.B. Staying Safe).

STEP 4: MAKE REPAIRS FOR THE HARM

Making repairs is offering money, services and other things that contribute to repairing the harm. Repairs are sincere and take effort. They are not only ones that can be done cheaply and quickly. See the previous Section 4. Taking Accountability, Tool 4.1. The Pathway of Change for examples of repairs.

These repairs may never be able to make up for the harm done. Often they cannot – nothing can. But they are real and symbolic attempts to do something significant to make the lives of those who have been harmed better.

For many interventions and attempts to get accountability from the person doing harm (or the community), you may only reasonably be able to reach Step 4. Step 5 and 6 are more abstract and life-long processes that are more difficult to name as specific requests.

QUESTIONS

- Think about the harms that you, others and the community have experienced. What could the person doing harm do to have some sense of repair? (Money, services, apologies)
- Look at the list of repairs in Section 4. Taking Accountability, Tool 4.1. The Staircase of Harm. Which seem to fit your situation and what could possibly be offered?
- How important is it to you that the person doing harm (and their allies or support) be the ones to come up with the repairs?
- Would you prefer that they respond to your request for specific repairs? Would you prefer to respond to their offer of specific repairs? Would you prefer a process in which you make a request and they make an offer that you then try to agree to together?
- Are any parts of the repairs to be made public? For example, would one of the repairs be a public accountability statement or apology? If so, what aspects would be important for you to make public? Who is that public?
- It may be impossible to force someone to be sincere. Would a response that tries to meet your request but is not completely sincere be okay with you?

- What is the minimal form of repair that would seem like a successful outcome to you? Be specific about what this would look like – for example, how much, for how long.
- What is the bottom-line in terms of what you would want the person doing harm to offer in terms of repairs?
- How will you feel if you are unable to accomplish Step 4?
- What could possibly result from the failure to reach Step 4?
- Would you and others carry out consequences affecting the person doing harm if they do not reach Step 4?
- What would these consequences be? Would you communicate these consequences to them? By whom and how would this communication be delivered? How could this communication be done most safely and effectively? Would you in reality carry out these consequences? What are possible effects of these consequences if you carry them out? What are possible effects if you do not carry out these consequences?
- What would be other concerns if Step 4 were not reached? Think of safety, possible increases in their violence or ability to carry out violence, other possible results? How can you safeguard yourself and others? (See Section 4.B. Staying Safe).

STEP 5: CHANGE HARMFUL ATTITUDES AND BEHAVIORS SO THAT VIOLENCE IS NOT REPEATED

It may be more difficult to make specific requests beyond Step 4. The changes in Step 5 and Step 6 require the person to have the motivation, long term commitment and necessary support that are fundamental for higher levels of change.

If you do not know the person doing harm well and are not planning to remain connected with them except perhaps as someone who will co-exist in the same community, then you may consider stopping at Step 4.

If you are in an intimate or close relationship with the person doing harm, thinking about Step 5 may be more important to you. This may be because you care more about and are more connected to the person doing harm. This may also be because these steps will be important in making sure that violence is not repeated and that this person is capable of a healthy, respectful relationship with themselves and with you and others close to you.

QUESTIONS

- What attitudes and behaviors do you want changed? These may be the same that you listed in Step 1.
- What would new, positive attitudes and behaviors be?
- How can you say this in specifics? Note that it is hard to know what it means if the request is, "You will be a kind person." Rather, kindness may look like specific things such as, "You will never insult me – call me names like (you can come up with your own)."
- How would you know if someone reached Step 5?
- How will you feel if the person doing harm is unable to reach Step 5?
- Would you and/or others carry out consequences affecting the person doing harm if they do not reach Step 5?
- What would these consequences be? Would you communicate these consequences to them? By whom and how would this communication be delivered? How could this communication be done most safely and effectively? Would you in reality carry out these consequences? What are possible effects of these consequences if you carry them out? What are possible effects if you do not carry out these consequences?
- What would be other concerns if Step 2 were not reached? Think of safety, possible increases in their violence or ability to carry out violence, other possible results? How can you safeguard yourself and others? (See Section 4.B. Staying Safe).

STEP 6: BECOME A HEALTHY MEMBER OF THE COMMUNITY

Creative Interventions believes not only in healthy individuals but healthy communities. Therefore, we include Step 6 as a possible high aim towards accountability. Each step along the way (1 – 5) already move in this direction.

At some point, efforts to stay accountable may shift towards ease and confidence in one's ability to be a healthy and respectful partner, family member, friend, co-worker, neighbor and fellow community member.

Someone who has been able to take accountability and go up the pathway of change may be in a position to help someone else who is causing harm and who could benefit from the support of another who has been through the same thing.

It may be unrealistic for other people to ask for this level of accountability from the person doing harm. This may become a personal goal for this person, one that they set along with their allies. It could be one that they choose to reach in dialogue with the survivor or victim. It may be one that every member of one's community set as a goal for themselves.

QUESTIONS

- How can Step 6 be a healthy goal for everyone involved in the intervention – not only the person doing harm, but the survivor or victim, allies, and other community members?
- What does this mean? What does it look like?
- What are things you can do now that move towards this goal?
- How can the things you have learned and accomplished in moving from Step 1 to Step 5 and beyond be used to help others in the community to also move through this process of accountability?
- Can you share your story of success with others so you can be an example? For example, you can share your story through www.creative-interventions.org or www.stopviolenceeveryday.org.

TAKING ACCOUNTABILITY TOOL F4: SELF-REFLECTION AND PRACTISE FOR ALLIES PRACTICE QUESTIONS

Being an ally that supports the process of taking accountability can be challenging. This section includes self-reflection tools that may be helpful for allies.

Self-Reflection 1: How can I deal with my discomfort with conflict?

We all know of times when we have not wanted to speak up, to intervene, or to directly address painful realities—whether they involve people harming us or people harming someone else. We don't want to get involved, or we just want to move on and tell ourselves things will get better on their own. We know that harm is being done, but out of discomfort, lack of confidence, and/or conflict avoidance, we say to ourselves things like the following:

- Who am I to judge?
- We haven't heard the other side.
- It's not that big of a deal.
- I don't know all of the details, so I can't really say anything about the situation.
- I think they'll just work it out in their own time.
- The person doing harm won't be able to handle the confrontation. I don't think he's ready. I think he needs a lot of support before he'll be ready.
- You already talked with the person doing harm— I don't see how bringing it up again will make a difference.
- Maybe this isn't a good time.
- It was just a moment of crisis — it's not a pattern. It's not my place to say anything
- I'm too busy and tired to deal with this. People need to sort their own lives out.

If you notice these thoughts in yourself, you can ask yourself if:

- I am uncomfortable with conflict and could be thinking these thoughts because I am avoiding conflict. If so, be aware of your way of dealing with conflict and see if you can make a change.
- I am stressed out and need to step back a moment and take a rest. If so, take a moment to reflect, step out and catch a breath, or find support to help you take care of yourself. If your stress level requires more than a brief step out, then let the group know.

- I still have questions about what happened and would feel better if I have answers. If so, let the group know or see if you can talk to someone else in the group or the facilitator to see if you can get the answers. Other people may have similar questions, or you may find that you just have to feel comfortable with a situation in which there are still unanswered questions.
- I have so many conflicts with this situation and my role that I cannot play it in a good way. If so, let the group know or see if you can talk to someone else in the group and get support to figure out a better role.

Self-Reflection 2: How can I separate compassion from collusion – or making excuses?

This approach to violence intervention asks us to seek change through compassion. Anger, disgust, sadness and fear are commonplace reactions to violence and can motivate us to get involved in an intervention.

However, support for accountability requires compassion, understanding and a willingness to make a connection to the person doing harm.

There can be a difficult balance between compassion and understanding and colluding or making excuses for violence. We can think that supporting the person doing harm means that we can listen to their pain, their fear and perhaps even their blame of others, and try to see their side of the story.

Being able to see challenges to violence as a part of compassion can be difficult. The following questions can help by identifying positive parts of the person doing harm with possibilities of change.

- What positive connection do we have?
- How is my support in this process of taking accountability a gift to the person doing harm – even if it is challenging and difficult?
- How is this opportunity a gift to me – even if it is challenging and difficult?
- What kind of signs of health can I see in the person doing harm?
- What values have they shown that connect to their ability to change?

PRACTICE: WHAT DO I SAY TO THE PERSON DOING HARM?

Whether we are working together with just one person or a group of people, we can practice saying simple phrases to each other to help get comfortable in our role and help move beyond some of the frozen, tongue-tied experiences that we fear.

Face another ally or team member or involved person in your situation. Have one person read from this list, and have each person in the pair repeat the sentence aloud, while looking at the other person. Ask people to just use a normal speaking voice. We're not angry, bored, threatened, or anything else when doing this exercise. You can come up with your own sentences that are helpful in your situation. There are shared as examples.

1. I care about you.
2. I'm not rejecting you.
3. I want you to have good relationships in your life.
4. I want to understand how you are feeling.
5. I want to support you to change your violence.
6. I want to support you to try new responses that might work better in your situation.
7. I want to understand what this is like for you.
8. How are you doing?
9. I think you're blaming the process right now so that you don't have to talk about what's really hard. Is it possible that that's true?
10. I don't think this kind of violence is ever acceptable. How could you express what is important to you in a non-violent way?
11. I know it can be hard to say what is really going on for you.
12. Please lower your voice.
13. Do you need to take a break?
14. I'm sorry this is so hard.
15. I'm sure things can get better even though they're hard now.
16. Let's slow down.
17. What might that be like for ________ (the other person)?
18. Why do you want to make a different choice next time?
19. What are you scared of losing?
20. I hear you focusing on the other person and their faults again.
21. What are you responsible for in this situation?
22. How do you want me to share my thoughts and observations with you?
23. I need a break.
24. What is one thing you can do this week that feels like a move in a good direction?
25. Let's hang out again. / Let's talk again.

? *TAKING ACCOUNTABILITY* TOOL F5: BREAKING THROUGH DEFENSIVENESS. GUIDING QUESTIONS FOR THE PERSON DOING HARM

If you are the person being asked to take accountability, we know this process can be difficult. You are likely facing people who feel angry. You may feel all alone – in a sea of accusation.

It is easy to feel defensive – to try to protect ourselves by thinking things like:

- It's none of their business.
- They weren't there and have no idea what they're talking about.
- Who are they to judge?
- What about my side of the story? I think I'm the victim.
- I can't handle being blamed. I'm going to do whatever I can to get out of this.
- This is all ____'s (not my) fault!

We might get really defensive and attack them with words or actions. We might feel furious when we find out that people are talking behind our back, or that our friends or loved ones did not keep private what we think they should have kept private. We might want to withdraw from them entirely, build our own camp of supporters, or use violence to get back at them before they hurt us more.

Plus, this may all be an unknown. Taking accountability – using ways that don't mean punishing us or locking us up – is just not usually done. We may not have any idea about what's going to happen next. Fear, confusion, anger and defensiveness are understandable.

It takes courage and effort to slow down, realize that we are not going to die or be destroyed.

These questions are for self-reflection. They are meant to break through defensiveness so that you might actually be able to face this challenge, learn from it, and gain some new skills. See how answering these questions might help you.

This might be a good time to get together with someone who is supportive of you – but isn't just supportive by agreeing that you were right and excusing your violence. Find someone who can support you and challenge you at the same time. See Section 4.C. Mapping Allies and Barriers for more help on how to find a good support person or ally for yourself.

TRY ASKING YOURSELF THESE QUESTIONS:

1. When I'm feeling angry or defensive, I tell myself this story about why these people are talking to me or confronting me about violence…
2. Is there a more positive story I can tell myself (about why they are talking with me about this)? What is it?
3. Can I imagine myself as someone who can listen to what is being said without being defensive? What is that person like? When are times that I have been like this?
4. When I imagine or remember what it's like for _______ (the person who was harmed) to be receiving my violent behaviors and actions, I see…
5. What can I share with the people confronting me so that they know me better, and can help me feel connected to them – instead of rejected? What can I share that isn't making and excuse for myself or putting blame on other people?

ⓘ *TAKING ACCOUNTABILITY* TOOL F6: PREPARING FOR DIRECT COMMUNICATION AFFIRMATIONS AND GUIDED QUESTIONS FOR THE PERSON DOING HARM

This tool can help prepare the person who caused harm and who is being asked to take accountability for a direct meeting with the survivor or victim, or their representatives, or the community allies that may be communicating the kinds of changes that they are requesting.

It offers affirmations that can help to ground the person who caused harm to be in a more position. And it offers guiding questions that can also help the person doing harm to prepare.

The tool involves moving through 4 steps that can be repeated over time and can be done separately depending upon what discussions are coming up next. You can add or substitute your own words to make this more meaningful for yourself.

STEP 1: I BELIEVE

I will remind myself of the following messages. Thinking about these messages can bring me some sense of calm and peace – as I enter into a challenging situation.

1. I am a good person.
2. Like everyone, I am imperfect. I make mistakes.
3. I am stronger when I acknowledge both my strengths and my imperfections to myself.
4. I have the strength to listen to how I impact people (even when that impact is not what I intended) – without interrupting.
5. I have the strength to open my mind to another person's way of thinking.
6. My mistakes do not define me. They only have power if I refuse to acknowledge them.
7. I know that (even when they are upset with me) others see some of my strengths and good intentions.
8. I am strong enough to understand others even if they are different from myself and to receive understanding from others.
9. I trust that I will be strong enough to let you tell your story and understand that that story is real to you.
10. I trust that I will be strong enough to stay calm even if my own story is not accepted or is questioned.

Question: Which three of these statements resonate most with me? How do they help me be more calm and more open minded? Are there other words that work better for me and still are in line with these statements?

STEP 2: I CAN LISTEN

1. I can listen with the intention to understand. If I find myself finding fault, wanting to defend myself or wanting to attack, I will remind myself to stop and listen.
2. Even if I have heard all of the things said before, I will listen with a new openness and see if I hear anything different.
3. I will relax and see what happens if I let what is being said enter into my own picture of what happened. This will not erase what I think or believe. It will add to it.
4. After I listen, I can take time to reflect and think about what was said. I can ask for support to help me to do this. I can use these questions to help me:
   - How has my understanding of the ________'s experience of me changed my own story or feeling about what happened?
   - From what I have heard, what is it that has affected ________ the most?
   - What 1-2 things are most important to _______________?
   - What struck me as most "real" in what _______________ said?

STEP 3: MAKE TRUE ATTEMPTS AT REPAIR

1. I am strong enough to admit the harm I have caused to others.
2. I am wise enough to see the impact of my harm, and understand who it hurt and how even if I did not intend it.
3. I am honorable enough to apologize for everything I have done without making any excuses.

4. I can offer my apology as a gift, expecting nothing in return.
5. I understand that repairs will take my energy and efforts. Apologies are important and are the first step in making repairs.
6. I will take time and get help from my allies if I need it to think of things I can do to offer repairs.
7. I understand that my idea of repairs and the requests from __________ may be different. We will be able to find a solution.
8. I understand that nothing I do can fully make up for the harm. Things were taken away that can not be given back.
9. Taking the step to make repairs is an important step to healthy change.

Question: When being honest with myself, what are three things I can acknowledge about my role in this situation?

STEP 4: CHANGE MY ATTITUDES AND BEHAVIORS OVER TIME

1. I commit to deep changes in my attitudes and behaviors so that I will not repeat my harmful behaviors.
2. I will stay connected to people, things, places and activities that support these changes. These include the following:

   People:
   Things:
   Places:
   Activities:
   Other:

3. I commit to reflecting on my attitudes based on what I heard from ______________________________and seeing what attitudes I need to question and change.
4. I commit to reflecting on my behaviors and actions based on what I hard from ______________________________ and seeing what I need to question and change.
5. If I am finding it difficult to change or have set-backs, I will do the following things:
6. If I commit harm again, I will do the following things:
7. If I commit harm again, I expect the following consequences:

Question: What are 2-3 things I do (currently or in the past) during stress or conflict that the ______________________________ has found challenging (or that are challenging to the situation overall)?

What is one strategy for handling this in the future that I think I can do?

If you are staying connected to each other, you can ask yourself this question.

What are two things I'd like us to commit to as bottom lines for how we behave toward each other during future situations of stress and conflict?

4G WORKING TOGETHER
HOW DO WE WORK TOGETHER AS A TEAM?

G.1. What Is Working Together?

G.2. Working Together Across the 4 Phases

G.3. Tips

G.4. Special Considerations

G.5. Facilitator Notes

G.6. Real Life Stories and Examples

G.1. WHAT IS *WORKING TOGETHER*

Key Questions

- Who can work together?
- Does everyone know and agree with the goals?
- What are their roles?
- How will you communicate and coordinate?
- How will you make decisions?

What Is it?

Working Together involves the ways in which two or more people can work positively and cooperatively towards a common goal. In this Toolkit, the goal is to address, reduce, end or prevent interpersonal violence.

Working together rests on the belief that interpersonal violence is not just an individual problem, but is a community problem requiring a community level solution. For some of us, the community we can bring together is small, perhaps just a couple of people. For others, a community may be much larger.

This Toolkit offers some ways to think about working together as a group or a team and gives some tools to help us do it better. Working together consists of finding a good group or team, agreeing on goals, making group decisions, communicating well and keeping regular check-ins to make sure that everyone is taking action that is in cooperation with others.

This section attempts to correct tendencies to do nothing or to just do one's own thing without regard for how this affects the bigger picture. It calls on us to be compassionate and patient with ourselves and others while doing the difficult work required to address, end, reduce and prevent violence.

Why Is It Important?

Working together – rather than alone or separately – can offer:

- Support for those most affected by the violence.
- Support for those involved in the intervention.
- Support for each other – counteracting the way that violence divides and hurts everyone in the community.

- More people with a larger set of skills and resources.
- More wisdom and knowledge about the situation of violence and opportunities for change.
- More people with various relationships of care and concern to the survivor or victim, person or people doing harm and others.
- A collective approach reduces isolation.
- More leverage for supporting positive change.
- Fewer gaps in the community for people to slip out of responsibility and accountability.
- Build a collective or community with new experience, skills and practices that may prevent violence in the future.

USING TOOLS IN THIS SECTION

These tools are to be used along with Section 4.C. Mapping Allies and Barriers, which may be helpful with starting a process of thinking about who allies may be.

Although you and your allies may never reach the size of a "team" and may be as few as just a couple of people, this section may help you think of the types of roles you may find yourself playing and help clarify other areas of working together such as communication and decision-making.

For an introduction to teams and a quick list of questions you might ask about how your team (big or small) functions, see Tool G1: Working Together. Snapshot: Short Question Guide.

Tool G2: Team Roles. Checklist names some typical team roles such as instigator, facilitator, nurturer, cheerleader and so on and what types of personalities might suit those roles well. It includes a checklist to help you sort out who might play these roles with the understanding that people will often play multiple roles.

Tool G3: Agreements for Sustaining over Time offers some basic agreements that can help move your group forward and can help when things get stuck.

Good communication is important for people to work well together. Tool G4: Communication Worksheet has a list of guiding questions to help you think through your communication guidelines to make sure that everybody gets the information they need.

Tool G5: Decision-Making Types and Models clarifies different ways a group can make decisions, so that you can choose what makes sense for your group, or you can clarify how your group is already making decisions. It gives a few suggestions about models of decision-making such as voting and consensus that may be unfamiliar to your group but may be helpful especially if your group is large.

G.2. *WORKING TOGETHER* ACROSS THE 4 PHASES

In Section 3.6. Interventions Over Time: 4 Phases, the Toolkit introduced the idea of 4 possible phases of interventions: 1) Getting Started, 2) Planning/Preparation, 3) Taking Action, and 4) Following Up.

Figuring out how to work together may look different at different phases or levels of crisis.

PHASE 1: GETTING STARTED

An intervention to violence might start with just one person, or a couple of people who identify a situation of interpersonal violence and feel that something should be done. It could start with the survivor or victim of violence. It could start with someone related to a situation of violence – the survivor or victim, a friend, family member, co-worker or neighbor or what we call "community ally." It may be that the person or people doing harm begin to see that they want to change and need some support to make that happen.

PHASE 2: PLANNING/PREPARATION

This Toolkit encourages the people who may first start thinking about taking action to look around and see if there are other people who can take a role in the intervention to violence. The team may get larger. People may take on particular roles that suit them. They may think of others that can join. As the group or team begins to plan and prepare to move forward, the team may need to begin to work more closely together – going through the other steps in this Toolkit, identifying allies, creating common goals, and coming up with action plans. Groups or teams may meet frequently or for longer periods of time as they create a stronger working relationship, struggle through differences that they might have and work towards a more common understanding.

PHASE 3: TAKING ACTION

Taking Action builds upon the plans and preparations that the group or team worked on together. As goals turn into actions, different members of the group or team may take more active roles. Some may take more supportive or advisory roles. Team meetings may turn from getting clear towards taking next steps. As the group or team takes action, it may become clear that others need to join or that you need to go back and look through this section or other sections to work better. It may be that people who were resistant at first, including those who caused harm will get on board as the intervention moves forward. The actions of the larger group or team may begin to bring them in to work together in a more cooperative way. As once-resistant people, such as the person or people doing harm, begin to understand the benefits of working together, they may begin to move into more active and cooperative roles.

PHASE 4: FOLLOWING UP

With success, there will be a time when the intervention moves towards closure or following up. The group or team or some smaller set may decide to keep meeting on a regular basis to follow up and make sure that change stays on a long-term basis. The team may stay together. Or they might decide that their active role is over and they can disband or change the nature of their group.

RELATED TOOLS

A group or team may start with the tools in Section 4.A. Getting Clear just to figure out what is going on and to make sure that they are on the same page.

A group or team may have started using the section Section 4.C. Mapping Allies and Barriers and build more allies using this same section.

Section 4.B. Staying Safe is always important, but a growing number of people involved in an intervention may raise other safety concerns. In this case, making sure that people cooperate and have a common understanding regarding things like confidentiality and safety planning may be necessary.

A key to Working Together well is having the group or team work through the process of Section 4.D. Goal Setting. Differences of opinion within a group can be identified and worked out so that everyone can agree on common goals and cooperative ways to reach those goals.

G.3. *WORKING TOGETHER* TIPS

#1 READ *SOME BASICS EVERYONE SHOULD KNOW.*

Interpersonal violence is complicated. Although we may hear more about domestic violence or sexual assault these days, many misunderstandings still exist and many misconceptions about what it is and how to approach it. Read Section 2. Some Basics Everyone Should Know. Pay special attention to Section 2.2. Interpersonal Violence: Some Basics Everyone Should Know in order to have a clearer picture of what is going on. The Section 2.3. Violence Intervention: Some Important Lessons also shares important basics about interventions based upon the experiences of Creative Interventions.

Share this information with others who may be involved in a situation of violence and may need some resources to help them know what to do.

This dialogue can offer a chance for you to see how the group works together, offering an entry point to thinking, listening and learning together.

#2 TAKE THE TIME TO MEET IN PERSON.

Building a team takes in-person time. Most people are not taught how to respond to violence. There are few common understandings about how to do this well. It is useful to find out what people's unique priorities might be, what they are concerned about, or what are their bottom-lines. Sometimes, these differences can only emerge when everyone is in the room, hearing what others are saying, and sharing their own opinions.

This is also useful for building group trust and relationships. This can be especially important when things go wrong and when it becomes easy to blame others or leave the group in frustration or anger. Things will likely go wrong. Trusting and understanding other people's unique perspectives can go a long way in helping a group withstand the challenges of interventions.

We understand that you may have team members or people working together who may live far away but who play a very important role. Make sure that you communicate well with them. See Tool G4. Communication Worksheet for guiding questions that may help you decide what information will be particularly helpful to share with people who may not be able to meet in person. Creative solutions such as using Chat, or Skype or social networking programs can be one way to include people in meetings and processes. Think through confidentiality when using social networking tools.

#3 TAKE THE TIME TO MEET ALL TOGETHER ESPECIALLY WHEN IMPORTANT INFORMATION IS SHARED AND IMPORTANT DECISIONS NEED TO BE MADE.

If the intervention seriously takes on the process of taking accountability, then it is important to keep connected to the person doing harm. Because people are often uncomfortable dealing directly with the person doing harm, that person can be kept out of the loop and left hanging. Because people may be unsure about how to handle accountability, things can move slowly.

People can easily forget to update them on what's going on and can want to handle communication through the least personal forms of communication – like email. The person doing harm who is willing to participate can begin to build up anxiety especially if no communication is made or the only communication is vague and seemingly impersonal.

Keep connected. You may need to choose someone whose role is to keep the person doing harm informed, to keep connected to them, and to let them know that while stopping violence is important – supporting the person doing harm towards long-term change is also important.

#4 EXPECT DIFFERENCES, TAKE THEM SERIOUSLY AND DO THE HARD WORK TO FIND COMMON GROUND.

Addressing, reducing, ending and preventing violence is an important and challenging task. The dynamics of violence are complex and often hidden. Reactions to violence are often emotional. And people's responses to violence can be very different.

Even if everyone has the same opinion about what happened and who is responsible, they often differ on what is to be done and how to get there. If these differences are not recognized, taken seriously and worked through to a common decision that everyone can agree with, they can cause mistakes and misunderstandings that can be not only be frustrating but also dangerous.

#5 WORKING TOGETHER SOMETIMES REQUIRES MAJOR COMPROMISES.

Finding common ground can mean deciding what is most important to move towards the group goal. It may require people to let go of points of disagreement for the common good. It is rare for everyone to feel 100% good about an intervention. People working together may need to find a common ground and decide whether they can live with the compromises. This section offers different models of decision-making that can help the group figure out how to make these difficult decisions.

#6 PEOPLE CAN BE INVOLVED AT DIFFERENT LEVELS. SOME PEOPLE CAN PLAY A SMALL AND SPECIFIC ROLE.

This Toolkit encourages in-person meetings that at times of information-sharing and decision-making need the participation of everyone actively involved. There are situations, however, when people can be brought in for a brief, specific role that just needs them to know enough to play that role well. For example, they may provide transportation, provide a meeting space or share specific information and just need to know enough to keep safety and whatever confidentiality is necessary.

#7 NOT EVERYONE MAKES A GOOD TEAM MEMBER.

Make use of the section Mapping Allies and Barriers to see who makes a good team member. You may find surprising allies where you would least expect it and may sometimes need to keep closer friends and family in smaller roles or out of the team entirely. People may also find that they cannot agree enough with your goals to stay on your team. They may need to step away.

#8 BE READY TO HOLD MULTIPLE ROLES.

This section highlights different roles that make a team run well. Most teams will not have the luxury of having the perfect person to play each of these roles. It is likely that people hold multiple roles, switch roles and jump in to play a role as it is needed.

#9 IF AN ORGANIZATION IS INVOLVED, THINK ABOUT WHO NEEDS TO KNOW ABOUT THE INTERVENTION OR THE DETAILS OF THE INTERVENTION AND WHO NEEDS TO BE PART OF A TEAM.

This Toolkit encourages creative thinking about who might be on a team. However, when violence occurs within an organization, the organizational rules and culture might affect how a team gets put together. For example, it may be expected that the team is the board of directors or management or the human resources division or maybe the whole organization. It may be a group of church elders. If this happens within a collective, there may be another type of group that makes sense to work on an intervention. Often, however, an organization has not thought about how it will deal with violence or abuse. It may struggle to figure out what its role is.

This Toolkit encourages creative thinking about who might be on a team. However, when violence occurs within an organization, the organizational rules and culture might affect how a team gets put together. For example, it may be expected that the team is the board of directors or management or the human resources division or maybe the whole organization. It may be a group of church elders. If this happens within a collective, there may be another type of group that makes sense to work on an intervention. Often, however, an organization has not thought about how it will deal with violence or abuse. It may struggle to figure out what its role is.

We encourage organizations to take a look at this Toolkit and see how it can be useful in figuring out what members within the organization can best form a team. Organizations might also think about how to include other people from outside of the organization – such as friends and family of the survivor or victim or of the person doing harm.

It is also possible that people outside of an organization are coordinating their own intervention. It may be useful to coordinate to make sure that both are working towards the same goals, or at least are not in conflict with each other.

#10 BUILD CARE, FUN AND SUSTAINABILITY INTO THE PROCESS OF WORKING TOGETHER.

Interventions to violence involve hard work and difficult emotions.

In order to move towards the positive transformations we wish to make, it is important to build care, fun and sustainability into this work. These can be little things such as:

- Checking in at the beginnings and ends of meetings.
- Making room for spiritual practices that are meaningful to the group.
- Greeting people as they enter and leave discussions, making sure that new people are greeted and made welcome.
- Making sure there's food and drink available to "break bread," fill empty stomachs and bring another element of enjoyment to the meeting.
- Guarding against the overwhelming feelings of bitterness and disappointment. Laugh at oneself, recall larger goals and values, bring compassion and humor to the mistakes that everyone will make along the way.
- Noticing when people are burning out or have personal issues or crises to which they must attend. Acknowledging this and giving permission for people to take care of themselves when needed.
- Celebrating achievements, large and small.

G.4. *WORKING TOGETHER* SPECIAL CONSIDERATIONS

Throughout history, people have been involved in violence intervention. However, this involvement is too often based on misinformation on the dynamics of violence. People often take actions as individuals, without taking into account the opinions and actions of other people involved. Many people mean well, but lack of coordination and cooperation can lead to mixed messages, confusion and, at times, further harm.

Working Together tries to coordinate well-intentioned efforts into a system of more effective teamwork. This involves roles that suit the person, a good process for communicating and decision-making and matching these roles with well-thought out actions.

The survivor or victim is often the first or one of the first people to begin an intervention to violence. They often seek help – and in doing so, create the first steps towards working together and forming a group or team. This help-seeking may not look as obvious as some of the steps in this Toolkit. But it is these small first steps that, with some help, can lead to a process of Getting Clear, Mapping Allies and Barriers, Goal Setting and so on.

Unlike many other domestic violence or sexual assault program approaches, this Toolkit does not assume that the survivor or victim will be directly involved in the intervention. There may be other reasons that a community ally begins an intervention – sometimes without the knowledge or consent of the survivor or victim. If we think about the abuse of children, this may be the case. Children experiencing violence need help and support, but adults might need to take all of the responsibility in finding a solution to the violence children experience.

Survivors or victims may also begin an intervention but may choose to take a different, less active role once the intervention develops. They may already feel like they've carried the burden of violence and want others to take a more active role in making change. They may have left the situation and be unavailable for involvement. Or, in some cases, victims may be left unable to take an active role because of injury or even death.

Survivors or victims may choose to take active roles during some part of the intervention and not others. They may want to be active in some part of information sharing or decision making and not others. This Toolkit offers some guidance in making these decisions and working together with these special considerations in mind.

This Toolkit does not assume a survivor-centered or survivor-determined model, although this is one possible approach or path. It does, however, prioritize the consideration of the experience, knowledge and decision-making of the survivor and understands that the survivor or victim is often the person most impacted by violence. It also acknowledges that the impact of violence and the responsibility to address violence extends to other members of the community. This means that the process of Working Together may sometimes involve differences and even conflicts among the different people involved that need to be worked out towards common goals. Unlike the kind of survivor-centered model that is usually promoted within sexual assault or domestic violence programs, it does mean that while the survivor or victim's needs and desires need to be taken very seriously and may even be at the center, they may also be taken into a larger set of considerations.

If you are the survivor or victim, you may have conflicting feelings about your involvement in the intervention and the decisions made among the group or team working together. Because this is a group model, you may sometimes be asked to share information that can be uncomfortable and repetitive. You can be creative about how you feel most comfortable sharing this knowledge. You may hear questions and responses from your allies that can be hurtful. You may not always get full agreement on what you think should or should not be done. This Toolkit offers different tools to make this process thoughtful and respectful of your experience, needs and desires.

If you are someone who wants to be in full control of the intervention process, you may find that other people's considerations make you feel ignored or left out of the process.

If you are someone who wants others to take full responsibility, you may find that people are still making requests of you to tell them what happened, what you want or what they should do next.

Although you may be able to find a good match between what makes you feel comfortable and what others working together are doing, it is also likely that you will at least at times feel at odds with the process.

It may be difficult, at times, to tell the difference between a process that has gone wrong and a process that considers the needs of the community and even of the person or people doing harm. You may find it helpful to ask yourself whether the process seems to be moving towards a goal of greater change, over all.

Use the tools in this Toolkit, get support from trusted allies and see if you can express your needs and work through what may at times feel uncomfortable and even painful. Also know that you can choose to contact more mainstream or traditional domestic violence or sexual assault programs for resources that are available for survivors. You can call or visit them and ask them questions about their services if you think that you prefer this over the community-based intervention approach supported by this Toolkit. They might also be another source of support as you go through a more community-based intervention.

Unlike most other models or approaches to interpersonal violence, the community ally has an active role in Working Together. Whereas other domestic violence or sexual assault programs will usually only work directly with the survivor or victim of violence, this community-based approach assumes that the most effective intervention brings together at least some friends, family, neighbors, co-workers or other community members to work together with the survivor or victim and possibly the person or people doing harm.

This may mean bringing your knowledge, skills or actions towards helping this process. It may include regular in-person meetings to make sure that you are playing a role based on solid information and actions that are in cooperation with the rest of the group or team.

If you are a community ally, you may offer to help with or have been asked to be part of a community-based intervention process. You may even be the first person or among the first to take action to address a situation of violence and be using this Toolkit to bring others together to help out.

Use these tools including those in Mapping Allies and Barriers and in this section to determine some possible best roles and to work cooperatively with others.

It is possible that the person or people doing harm are the first to work actively to make positive change. They may have found this Toolkit or been given this Toolkit as a way to begin a process to take responsibility to address and end their violence and prevent further violence. Working Together may provide guidance towards creating a team to support a healthy process towards change.

It is also possible that the person or people doing harm are currently in no position to work as part of the team. They may be actively harmful and entirely resistant to change. A large part of this intervention may be in taking action to address and end their violence with or without their voluntary cooperation.

The aim of this Toolkit is to work together as a community in order to gain the cooperation of the person or people doing harm and to support a process of accountability and long-term change. The person or people doing harm may be resistant to working with the team at first or even for quite awhile. It is possible that they never cooperate or that their level of cooperation shifts back and forth. In Section 2.3. Violence Intervention: Some Important Lessons and In Section 4.F. Taking Accountability we state that most of us struggle with accountability. We urge you to create responses which take this struggle into account. We also know even with the good work of a team, accountability of those doing harm may not always be possible.

With this Toolkit, we approach the person or people doing harm with the intention of gaining their support and cooperation, but with the knowledge that this is very difficult and, in some cases, not possible. In Section 4.F. Taking Accountability, we describe an accountability process that creates a pathway to working together towards the common goal of ending, preventing and repairing violence. At the same time, we understand that we may not reach this goal. Reducing harm may be the best we are able to achieve.

If you are the person doing harm or are the person accused of doing harm, we urge you to consider how you can work together with this process. Even if you are the person starting this process or joined this process early on, you may find yourself in a position of being told what to do. You may have received a list of demands or feel forced into a position that does not feel like one where you are working together. You may not agree with what you are being asked to do or how it is communicated to you.

Working together may take a high degree of humility, something that may feel shameful or scary or may make you feel vulnerable, angry, and perhaps even victimized.

Your attitudes and/or acts of violence may have brought a great deal of distrust. Your may need to work hard and for a long time in order to get people to accept your change. The ways in which you harmed others may have been unintentional. The lists of harms may not totally fit what you think you have done. However, accountability may require you to consider another point of view or accept difficult compromises.

Working together is largely about working toward a common good and accepting compromises. Your compromises may be the highest in this process – in part because this process addresses harms that you imposed upon others – even if you did not mean to or did not realize their impact. Being responsible, taking accountability and making change may require big shifts of power in which your sense of individual power is greatly reduced. This may be completely uncomfortable, even devastating, and require a long period of reflection and acceptance. It may also bring relief and allow you to find compassion for yourself as well as those who were harmed. We ask you to work together to make that change.

See Section 4.F. Taking Accountability for tools to help you take accountability.

FACILITATOR

This Toolkit is long and can be overwhelming. Some important parts of this Toolkit are Section 2. Some Basics Everyone Should Know. An especially important section can be Section 2.2. Interpersonal Violence: Some Basics Everyone Should Know that discusses much more about the dynamics of violence and common misunderstandings that people have.

#1 ENCOURAGE AND SUPPORT PEOPLE TO LEARN FUNDAMENTAL INFORMATION FIRST IF THEY HAVE NOT ALREADY.

This Toolkit is long and can be overwhelming. Some important parts of this Toolkit are Section 2. Some Basics Everyone Should Know. An especially important section can be Section 2.2. Interpersonal Violence: Some Basics Everyone Should Know that discusses much more about the dynamics of violence and common misunderstandings that people have.

It can be useful for you to be familiar with the different sections of this Toolkit and to read more carefully through these sections. Also encourage people to read these sections. If reading is not the best option or they cannot read English or the language that this Toolkit is in, you can help by reading this and other sections to them in a language they understand or use other formats to pass on this information.

#2 FIGURE OUT OR GET HELP FIGURING OUT THE EXTENT OF YOUR FACILITATOR ROLE.

This Toolkit understands that the fundamental role of the facilitator is to help guide the process to support people to use the tools in this Toolkit, and to make sure that everyone is getting the right information, is checking in with each other, and is working together in a coordinated way.

There are several other roles that might belong to you. You may also find yourself initiating the intervention (initiator), leading it (leader), writing everything down (note taker), being a primary supporter to someone else. There may only be a couple of you working on this intervention, meaning that you find yourself playing multiple roles.

If you have other people working together who can play these various roles, then you will more likely be a kind of bottom-line person, returning people to the tools in this Toolkit as needed, noticing what is not getting done and making sure that people work together to fill in these gaps.

If there are not enough people and you find yourself playing multiple roles that seem overwhelming, you may be able to pause the process and figure out what other allies can be recruited to play these roles.

#3 MAKE SURE THAT PEOPLE ARE OPEN TO EXPRESS THEMSELVES.

The process of taking accountability can appear threatening to the person doing harm. Depending on their "mind set," they may see admitting a wrong and making a change as something to be challenged. Shows of cooperation can go along with plans to threaten survivors or victims, intimidate allies, or undermine the entire accountability process.

See Section 4.B. Staying Safe for more tools that people can use to increase safety as they move forward in the process.

#4 SUPPORT PEOPLE TO WORK THROUGH THE TOOLS IN *WORKING TOGETHER*.

The facilitator will likely play a major role in figuring out the key roles that others can play, the decision-making process that makes the most sense for this group, and the communication process.

You may have people who have not worked in a coordinated way before. They may have a hard time understanding some of these group processes.

Note who is having a hard time and help support them to learn these processes and get more familiar with them. If someone simply is not and cannot become a team person even with support, then you and the team may have to find a way to ask this person to play a different role that does not require them to work within a team or to step off of the team if that is not possible.

G.6. *WORKING TOGETHER* REAL LIFE STORIES & EXAMPLES

Story G. *A Small Story (He Korero Iti)*

We live in a town, but many of my husband's extended family (whanau) live in the valley where he grew up about 40 kilometres away. My husband and his brother are renowned for a number of things – one being how they extend the life of their cars and vans using highly technical items like string and wire – another how they share these vehicles for a variety of tasks such as moving furniture or transporting relatives, building materials, tractor parts, traditional herbal medicines (rongoa), eels, vegetables, dogs, and pigs (dead or alive).They are renowned for being people of the people, the ones to call on in times of trouble and death, the ones who will solve the problem and make the plan. They travel to and from town, to the coast to dive for sea food, to endless meetings, to visit extended family (whanau) - along the many kilometres of dirt roads in and around the valley, through flood or dust depending on the season in those patched up, beat up, prized cars.

There are a number of things to know about the valley - one is that the last 33 children in the world of their small sub-tribe (hapu ririki) to grow up and be educated on their own lands go to school here, despite government efforts to close the school. Another is that the valley is known to outsiders and insiders as 'patu wahine' – literally meaning to 'beat women' and this is not said as a joke. The mountain for this valley is named as the doorway spirits pass through on their way to their final departure from this life. This valley is also the valley where my husband and his siblings were beaten at school for speaking their first language. It is the valley their mother sent them to so they would be safe from their father – back to her people. It is where they milked cows, pulled a plough, fed pigs but often went hungry, and were stock whipped, beaten and worse.

My brother-in-law still lives in the valley, in a group of houses next to the school. So it's no surprise that one of our cars would be parked by these houses – right by where the children play. Perhaps also not a surprise that while playing that time old international game of rock throwing our eight year old nephew shattered the back window of the car. If I'd been listening I probably would have heard the 'oh' and 'ah' of the other children that accompanied the sound of glass breaking from town, and if I'd been really tuned in I would have heard the rapid, frightened heart beat of 'that boy' as well.

His mother is my husband's cousin – and she was on the phone to us right away. She was anxious to assure us 'that boy' would get it when his father came home. His father is a big man with a pig hunter's hands who hoists his pigs onto a meat hook unaided.

He is man of movement and action, not a man for talking. Those hands would carry all the force of proving that he was a man who knew how to keep his children in their place. Beating 'that boy' would be his way of telling us that he had also learned his own childhood lessons well.

So before he got home we burned up the phone lines – sister to sister, cousin to cousin, brother-in-law to sister-in-law, wife to husband, brother to brother. This was because my husband and his brother know that there are some lessons you are taught as a child that should not be passed on. The sound of calloused hand on tender flesh, the whimpers of watching sisters, the smell of your own fear, the taste of your own blood and sweat as you lie in the dust – useless, useless, better not born. This is a curriculum like no other. A set of lessons destined to repeat unless you are granted the grace of insight and choose to embrace new learning.

So when the father of 'that boy' came home and heard the story of the window 'that boy' was protected by our combined love (aroha) and good humor, by the presence of a senior uncle, by invitations to decide how to get the window fixed in the shortest time for the least money. Once again phone calls were exchanged with an agreement being made on appropriate restitution. How a barrel of diesel turns into a car window is a story for another time.

Next time my husband drove into the valley it was to pick up the car, and 'that boy' was an anxious witness to his arrival. My husband also has very big hands, hands that belong to a man who has spent most of his life outdoors. These were the hands that reached out to 'that boy' to hug not hurt.

A lot of bad things still happen in the valley, but more and more they are being named and resisted. Many adults who learned their early lessons there will never return. For people of the land (tangata whenua) this is profound loss – our first identifiers on meeting are not our own names but those of our mountains, rivers, subtribe (hapu) and tribe (iwi). To be totally separate from these is a dislocation of spirit for the already wounded. This is only a small story that took place in an unknown valley, not marked on many maps. When these small stories are told and repeated so our lives join and connect, when we choose to embrace new learning and use our 'bigness' to heal not hurt then we are growing grace and wisdom on the earth.

Di Grennell

Whangarei, Aotearoa-New Zealand

TOOLS

4.G HOW DO WE WORK TOGETHER AS A TEAM?

Tool G1. Working Together Snapshot: Short Question Guide

Tool G2. Team Roles: Checklist

Tool G3. Agreements for Sustaining a Team over Time

Tool G4. Communication Worksheet

Tool G5. Decision-Making Types and Models

? *WORKING TOGETHER* TOOL G1: WORKING TOGETHER AS A TEAM BASICS & GUIDING QUESTIONS

This Toolkit uses the language of building a team, but you may think of other ways of describing the creation of a group of people to work cooperatively towards common goals.

Some basic questions are: How will the team remain a team? How often will it meet? How do they meet? Where? Do they have to meet in one group or can meetings happen in pairs, over the phone, over email?

Teams can be different sizes:

- Just me and the Toolkit for now – looking for more allies/team members
- A couple of us helping each other out
- Some helpful members of our family
- A group of friends
- Some people from our apartment building, neighborhood
- Our organization, church, workplace
- A group of us connected across cities
- A bunch of people connecting in different ways

Teams can take different shapes or forms or structures:

- We meet regularly and work together on everything.
- One person coordinates the team to make sure we are part of the same plan – the rest of the team does their part but usually independently from the rest.
- We have a lot of people working on this, but a small core group of us meets together regularly to coordinate.
- We have a team working together – but we also have other people who we trust to play special roles.

Why and when is it helpful to have a big group meeting?

The steps of Getting Clear, Staying Safe and Goal Setting may take the biggest group of people who are affected by and who will take part in the intervention.

These steps often work better when there is a high degree of common knowledge such as Getting Clear and a high degree of consensus such as Goal Setting.

Times it may be critical to have a big group in-person meeting:

1. Getting Clear (Section 4.A.)
2. Staying Safe (Section 4.B.)
3. Goal Setting (Section 4.D.)
4. Regular or semi-regular big meetings to update, review goals and actions, and offer support and feedback to one another – either by time period, for example, monthly, or after an important milestone or event.
5. Special meetings necessitated by any big changes, emergencies or opportunities.
6. Closure meeting either set by time period or after a significant portion or all of the action steps and results have been met.

Maintaining the group between big group meetings:

It may be that carrying out an action plan can be best carried out with smaller core committee meetings or by smaller one-on-ones. People carrying out the action or people who are most affected by the intervention should always have regular support people to meet with and check in with even if the larger group does not meet for awhile.

WORKING TOGETHER TOOL G1: SNAPSHOT/QUICK QUESTION GUIDE

This list is to help you figure out what kind of team you are, who's in your team, and how often you expect people to meet.

1. Who's on your team (or other word you may want to use instead)?
2. How often do you expect to meet?
3. Who needs to be part of that regular meeting?
4. Is there a smaller core group that meets more frequently? Who? How often? Where? What is their role?
5. Are there other key supporters – people who you can count on but who may not meet regularly?
6. Where do you meet?
7. What do you need at the meeting – can be supplies, food, beverages, spiritual supplies?
8. How is an agenda made for the meeting? By whom?
9. What are types of discussions or decisions that require everyone to meet together?

☑ *WORKING TOGETHER* TOOL G2: TEAM ROLES CHECKLIST

When thinking about teams, we are matching team roles with people who have the skills, knowledge and resources to play that role well.

Working Together well requires:

- ☐ Ideas about what are good roles to fill.
- ☐ Thought and reflection about the qualities you and your community allies have.
- ☐ Identifying gaps of what else is needed and who could fill that role.
- ☐ Invitation of other possible people and organizations.
- ☐ Coordination of all team members either in group meetings or coordinating separate conversations.

Some Basic Team Roles:

The following are some roles into which people naturally fall. Think about whether someone is already playing this role, if they are right for the role, and if someone needs to be recruited to play this role.

Instigator – The One Who Gets Things Started

If you are reading this now, you may be the Instigator or someone may have already gotten things started. The Instigator may be the primary survivor or victim or may have been the first person motivated to start a process.

The Instigator may only have this role at the beginning – they may only kick things off but may take on a different role as things move forward.

Good people for Instigator:

- ☐ If you kicked this process off, then you are likely a natural Instigator

Facilitator – The One Who Holds the Process

The facilitator is a key role in this Toolkit. Some may prefer to call this role the "holder" because the facilitator keeps things going by "holding" the process and making sure that the people working on the intervention can be supported by and guided by the tools in this Toolkit.

Good people for Facilitator:

- ☐ Trusted person
- ☐ Not too involved in the situation of violence – but knowledgeable
- ☐ Level-headed person
- ☐ Able to see the big picture and keep details moving along
- ☐ Has a somewhat good memory or a good way of recording things

Coordinator – The Glue

There may be a coordinator in this process, not necessarily making all of the decisions but making sure that everyone on the team is on board, working well together, getting the right information and playing their role effectively. This may also be a role taken on by the Facilitator.

Good person for Coordinator:

- ☐ Trusted person
- ☐ Able to see big picture and keep things moving along
- ☐ Sensitive to others
- ☐ Good at being inclusive and not leaving people out
- ☐ Good at working with different types of people and personalities

Logistics Person – Dealing with the details of time and place

There may be one person who makes sure there's a place to meet, there's food and drink at the meeting, there's paper, kleenex, and other supplies as needed.

Good person for Logistics Person:

- Responsible
- Detail oriented
- Organized

Notetaker – Keeping the details

As an intervention moves along, it will be useful to have some notes or other ways to keep track of important points such as:

- ☐ Basic information about what happened (see Getting Clear)
- ☐ Goals
- ☐ Safety Plan
- ☐ Important communication sent to or received from survivor, person doing harm or others involved in the intervention
- ☐ Key steps along the way

Good person for Notetaker:

- ☐ Detail oriented
- ☐ Good memory
- ☐ Able to keep notes in an organized way and in a safe place

Nurturer – Keeps people feeling good

Violence intervention is difficult and exhausting work. The Nurturer keeps people in a caring, compassionate environment and encourages people to make sure that they are considering not only tasks to be done but the compassionate spirit underlying the task

Good person for Nurturer:

- ☐ Trusted person
- ☐ Compassionate and caring

Reality Checker – Makes sure we are doing things that are realistic

It is easy to set up ambitious goals and ambitious timelines. The Reality Checker thinks about what is likely to happen and tries to prevent unrealistic expectations that could lead to frustration and burn-out.

Good person for Reality Checker:

- ☐ Has good understanding of the people and the situation
- ☐ Can bring people back to reality without losing the higher aims
- ☐ Gets real without wallowing in negativity

Communicator – Make sure we are listening to each other, checking in and following up

The Communicator is similar to the Coordinator or the Facilitator but the focus is on communication – verbal, written, email, etc. The Communicator makes sure that people share the right information, within a reasonable amount of time, and have good follow-up.

Good person for Communicator:

- ☐ Trusted person
- ☐ Understands that different people give and receive information differently
- ☐ Has good follow-up

Vision-Keeper – Helps us keep to the loftier parts of our goals

The Vision-Keeper keeps an eye to loftier goals and reminds people when morale sinks or when people begin to driven by hate, revenge or other negative motivations.

Good person for Vision-Keeper:

- ☐ Visionary
- ☐ High ideals

Cheerleader – Keeps people energized and positive

The Cheerleader can keep people energized and positive. The Cheerleader keeps a positive team spirit.

Good person for Cheerleader:

- ☐ Enthusiastic
- ☐ Inspirational
- ☐ Fun

Supporter – Supports, stands by and advocates for the key people within the group

A healthy team has people who are able to act as supporters for the survivor or victim, other vulnerable people such as children, an organization that may be suffering under the weight of violence and the process of intervention, the person or people doing harm, and other people on the team who may have a particularly stressful or difficult role.

The Supporter will be looking out for that person or organization, take special notice of their needs, and help to advocate for them when others are not paying enough attention. They can make sure that information is being adequately communicated, that they are participating in decision-making and that their emotional needs are being addressed.

Good person for supporter:

- ☐ Trusted person
- ☐ Compassionate
- ☐ Able to balance needs of one person within the needs of the whole group
- ☐ Supports certain individuals without adding to divisions within the group – works towards a healthy whole

Roles Checklist:

Do you have someone to play these roles? (Someone may play more than one role). If not, can you work together well without it? Do you need to find someone to fill in the gaps?

- ☐ Facilitator ______________________________
- ☐ Coordinator ______________________________
- ☐ Logistics Person ______________________________
- ☐ Notetaker ______________________________
- ☐ Nurturer ______________________________
- ☐ Reality Checker ______________________________
- ☐ Communicator ______________________________
- ☐ Vision Keeper ______________________________
- ☐ Cheerleader ______________________________
- ☐ Supporter for survivor or victim ______________________________
- ☐ Supporter for children ______________________________
- ☐ Supporter for person doing harm ______________________________
- ☐ Supporter for other ______________________________

Add your own:

- ☐ ______________________________
- ☐ ______________________________
- ☐ ______________________________

WORKING TOGETHER TOOL G3: AGREEMENTS FOR SUSTAINING OVER TIME

Keeping teams together is difficult work. These are some basic agreements that others have used that may be helpful.

1. Check in to see what everyone is thinking and feeling about the situation you are working on – make room for confusion, doubts, and questioning
2. When in doubt, ask a question
3. Take notes – you won't remember and things get more confusing over time (You may want to assign a Notetaker)
4. Review and clarify decisions – make sure you all agree on what you decided
5. Praise efforts and celebrate achievements – celebrating even the small things can take you a long way
6. When absent, follow up with someone
7. Forgive each other, cut each other slack – and – at the same time, find a way to get necessary steps done
8. Make sure steps and goals match the team's capacity or what's possible
9. Make criticisms specific and constructive
10. Move towards resolution. Move away from gossip.

Add your own:

WORKING TOGETHER TOOL G4: COMMUNICATION WORKSHEET

One of the most important things about teams is to keep up communication. Communication helps the process of an intervention to go more smoothly. People can be reminded of goals and action plans. They can be informed to take a different course of action or to meet again as a team especially if things do not go as planned.

Communication can be particularly challenging when dealing with violence because the details of intervention are often confidential and teamwork is informal. Facebook may not be appropriate for communication because of privacy concerns. In-person meetings might be difficult because everyone is busy or lives in different places.

Emergencies can come up, or so can new opportunities. There may be key pieces of information that others need to make sure that they take action that fits the situation.

These are some guiding questions to create sound systems of communication:

1. **Is there a key person to direct communications or to check in to make sure that people know what is going on?**

   - You may think about the facilitator, a communications person, a notetaker

   - You may want to think about someone who has good communication skills

     - Direct and diplomatic
     - Careful and thorough
     - Has good judgment
     - Has enough time and access to resources like phone, email, etc. to keep up a good flow of communication
     - Has a good memory for details or can take notes
     - Has a solid understanding of the values, goals, bottom-lines and action plan well enough
     - Will inform but not gossip

2. Who gets to know what types of knowledge?

- Think about key people or roles to consider. What can they know? What should they know? Are there things they should not know?

  - Faciliator
  - Survivor(s) or victim(s)
  - Person or people doing harm
  - Parents or guardians particularly if this involves a child
  - Everyone involved on this intervention
  - Regular team members but not necessarily other allies who are also helping
    - Sub-group, core group or steering committee
    - Everyone in the community

3. What are the key things to communicate?

- Goals, bottom lines and updates

- Action plan and updates

- Action steps taken and results of those actions

- New, unexpected changes arising such as:

  - Risk and safety concerns
  - New opportunities to take action or to add people as team members or allies
  - Major changes in people's feelings about the intervention or steps planned – time to reflect and change course of action
  - Major changes in people's ability to carry out the intervention or steps planned – time to speed up, delay or change course of action

4. What are the safety considerations and how does this affect communication? (See Section 4.B. Staying Safe)

- Can there be risks or dangers to anybody if certain people find out?

    - See risks and danger chart in Section 4.B. Staying Safe

- Can there be risks or dangers to the intervention – will it be jeopardized or ruined if certain people find out?

- Are there risks and dangers if the "system" finds out? Police, schools, mandated reporters, child protective services, ICE (immigration authorities)?

5. What are the best methods for communication among those who need to know?

- Think about convenience, accuracy of information and need for forms of communication that promote trust and team-building. There can be different methods for different people and situations.

    - In-person one-on-one?
    - In-person meetings?
    - Phone calls? Conference calls?
    - Written notes? If these need to be private, how can you insure that they do not get into the hands of people who might pose a risk or danger?
    - Emails? List serves? Do these need to be private and protected?
    - Blogs? Do these need to be private and protected?

- Is there a communication system to pass along information that will work with your group? Here are some alternatives:

    - Everyone communicates to everyone (easier if there are very few people)
    - One person communicates to everyone and oversees that everyone gets the information they need?
    - People on the team divide up who they communicate to – it may be based on how often they see certain people, how close they are to them, and so on

- Special considerations. Unless the survivor or victim and/or person doing harm have a key or leading role in the intervention, it can be easy to drop them out of the communication loop. They can start to feel isolated or anxious as they have to fill in the blank of non-communication with their imagination. You may want to make sure that someone they are comfortable with plays a special role in making sure that they get the information they need and want.

- Survivor or victim: Do you have agreements on what information gets communicated to the survivor or victim, who communicates, how often and through what format?
- Person doing harm: Do you have agreements on what information gets communicated to the person doing harm? Who communicates, how often and through what format?

WORKING TOGETHER TOOL G5: DECISION-MAKING TYPES AND MODELS

Who gets to make decisions? How are they made? Are there key decisions made collectively while others can be made by certain individuals? Are there decisions made along the way that need to be brought back to others in the group?

Decision-making is closely linked to communication. Groups with good communication should also communicate about what kind of decision-making that it will follow. Even if it is decided that someone in the group has more authority to make certain decisions.

DECISION

Types of Decision-Making

1. Collective consensus
2. Executive Committee or Steering Committee
3. Authority-led (with collective input)
    a. Survivor-led or survivor-centered
    b. Group leader agreed upon by everyone because they are trusted, can be more neutral, or have leadership skills
    c. Group leader due to agreed-upon leadership role in that group or institution
        i. For example, in a family, it may be a parent, a grandparent, or an elder
        ii. In a faith-based institution, it may be the clergy or a church elder

Different decision-making styles:

Note: The different ways of getting collective involvement listed at the end of this section: 1) Five fingers; 2) Voting; and 3) Round Robin can all be used with any kind of decision-making method.

CONSENSUS

Consensus decision-making means that everyone at least in the primary team is participating in a shared and equal manner to make decisions. This type of decision-making requires a trusting relationship among everyone or the need to work closely together to build a trusting relationship. Collective consensus can be helped by using the guides in this Toolkit which clarifies some of the considerations that should be made and some processes through which the whole group can work together towards collective decisions.

Sometimes this is also called modified consensus because there may be times that the group will let go of everyone feeling 100% good about a decision. See the Five Finger consensus tool below to see how groups can come to consensus without always reaching full agreement.

KEC UTIVE COMMITTEE OR STEERING COMMITTEE

Sometimes a large group can come together and make certain key decisions such as goals, allies and barriers, action plans. It may be more efficient for a smaller team to make decisions along the way, including the decision to bring a particular issue back to the larger group. The large group can determine which decisions must be brought back to the big group and which can be handled by the smaller committee.

GROUP LEADER

Oftentimes groups have an official or unofficial leader, somone who weighs in more strongly on decision-making. Although groups can also have a leader who simply makes all of the decisions without much consideration of the group, this type of leadership does not work well with the community-based model. If this is a collective process, then even if one authority has more leadership and weighs in more strongly on decision-making, there must still be significant input and feedback from the collective group.

Some groups may choose a leader or a leader may naturally emerge. The leader should not simply be the loudest voice, the most outraged person, or the most aggressive or assertive person. The leader also does not have to be the traditional authority in the group. For example, even though many families traditionally have fathers or male elders as leaders, the leader may be someone who is well-respected but not necessarily the traditional head of a household. Or, even though churches often have the clergy as a leader, an intervention taking place within a church or being helped by church members, the intervention leader may be a trusted person who is not traditionally a church leader.

SOME CONSIDERATIONS FOR LEADERS

Good leadership skills and characteristics. A leader should be trusted, have good judgment, and consider well the opinions and concerns of everyone who is affected by the violence and by the intervention. The leader should be attuned to all of the opinions held within the team.

The leader should either have a good understanding of interpersonal violence or take time to learn more about violence by talking to the survivor who usually has expertise on the violence they have faced. The leader can also look on the internet for information or talk to someone at a local resource center. We strongly suggest that the leader and all key people participating in the intervention read the entire Section 2. The Basics.

Some groups may consider a "survivor-centered" or "survivor-led" process in which the group has decided that they feel most comfortable with the survivor driving the decision-making. This is often a political decision made for various reasons: 1) Since it is usually the case that violence has most impacted the survivor, it may be politically important for the survivor or victim to take primary leadership in the intervention. 2) The nature of interpersonal violence is often to leave the survivor or victim in a powerless position. Taking leadership and power in the intervention can be considered a key turn towards reversing this relationship of power. 3) The group may consider the survivor's or victim's leadership and self-determination as a primary goal of the intervention.

FIVE FINGERS

A useful tool for collective consensus is the five-finger approach. Following discussion of some aspect of the intervention, if a decision needs to be made, the facilitator can ask for consensus.

Using five fingers, everyone in the group can see how people weigh in on a decision, even if they've been silent. This helps decision-making to be clear and transparent rather than relying on someone's impression of what others think. It helps to prevent people with strong opinions from dominating the decision even if they have dominated the discussion. It helps quiet people express their opinions even if they did not speak up.

Five fingers also helps get a group move more quickly through decisions. It reduces the need for everyone to repeat how they feel. While sometimes this is helpful and necessary, it may take up valuable time if this has to happen every step along the way.

Five fingers is preferable to voting since "majority rules" can mask huge disagreements – disagreements which may show up later on through dissatisfaction with action steps taken, splits within the group, breaking confidentiality and so on.

HOW TO USE FIVE FINGERS:

Make sure everyone understands the five finger consensus. It may feel awkward, but after getting used to it, it can really make decision-making quicker while still making it fair. After discussion of the situation that needs to be decided on, the facilitator or someone can ask for a consensus vote – you can use your own words for this procedure. For example, ask "are we ready to make a decision? Can we see if we have a consensus?"

Everyone has to hold up their hand and show their opinion. If the facilitator is not just a neutral outsider but is a part of the decision-making team, then they also need to show their opinion.

1. One finger (index finger) – I strongly agree
2. Two fingers (index and middle finger) – I agree
3. Three fingers (index, middle, and fourth finger) – I have some reservations, but I can go with it
4. Four fingers (Index, middle, fourth finger, and pinkie) – I don't like it, but I'll go along with it – I won't stop the process by blocking
5. Five fingers (whole hand open) – I feel strongly enough about this to block this decision
6. Six fingers (whole hand plus index finger of other hand) – Wait, I have questions or need clarification

If everyone has one to four fingers up, then consensus is reached. If you feel comfortable with a stronger level of consensus (ones and twos), you could ask the threes and fours why they hesitated. This could lead to more discussion until a stronger consensus is reached or the request for some alternatives which could lead to a stronger consensus.

If someone has a five, consensus is blocked. This is a pretty strong stand to take, and it should be understood that fives are saying that they feel so strongly that they are willing to block decision-making. More discussion needs to follow until the person or people blocking can shift. If blocking happens often, the facilitator can help the group figure out if there is another dynamic going on. Is the team just moving forward without considering some important conflicting opinions? Are there certain people who simply cannot work within this team structure?

If someone has a six, consensus is halted until that person's questions are answered. If your group often gets sixes, then it is likely that not enough discussion is taking place and decisions are being rushed.

VOTING

For voting, people are asked to raise their hands if they agree. Votes are counted, and generally a "majority rules" (more than half raise their hands) moves that decision forward.

This collective intervention does not favor voting because voting can overlook significant conflicts within the group. If certain people do not agree with a decision, this can lead to factions breaking off, which may take a different or conflicting set of actions. It can lead to people breaking confidentiality to tell others what this group has decided because they are unhappy with the decisions. It can cause people to leave the group or drop off because they have serious disagreements.

Sometimes, a well-functioning collective simply cannot come to consensus on a certain decision and will agree that a vote is the only way to move forward. If the group has tried consensus and at least can come to consensus that they feel okay about resorting to a vote, then voting can make sense in these limited situations.

ROUND ROBIN

There may be certain times in discussion and decision-making where it is useful to get everyone's opinion on a certain situation. Round-Robin is a way to ask everyone to share their unique opinion, concerns or questions. This can be a way to get a big picture of where everyone is at, to see where there are key commonalities and differences, and to uncover certain important points which others may not have even considered.

Round-Robin may be useful as the group is getting to know each other or may just be getting familiar with the situation of violence they are addressing. This is especially true during the goal-setting phase where it is important to make sure that everyone is in touch with their own ideas about what should be done and that they also understand other people's perspectives.

NOTES

KEEPING ON TRACK
HOW DO WE MOVE FORWARD?

H.1. What Is Keeping on Track?

H.2. Keeping on Track Across the 4 Phases

H.3. Tips

H.4. Special Considerations

H.5. Facilitator Notes

H.6. Real Life Stories and Examples

H.7. Keeping on Track Tools

H.1. WHAT IS *KEEPING ON TRACK?*

Key Questions:

- Are we ready to take the next step?
- How did it go?
- What did we achieve?
- Did we celebrate our achievements (even the small ones)?
- What needs to change?
- What is the next step?

What Is It?

A process of violence intervention is likely to be made up of many moments when decisions need to be made, actions are taken and next steps are planned and reviewed. Keeping on Track makes sure that the overall intervention is going well, that goals are in place, and that the process is moving forward in a good direction. It includes self-checks both for groups and for individuals to make sure that everyone is moving towards the goals. It gives opportunities for adjustments to be made as actions are taken along the way and as situations change.

In short, Keeping on Track helps us to figure out:

1. Are we ready to take the next step?
2. How did it go?
3. What is the next step after this?

These steps can continue in cycles as in intervention process moves forward. So we can expect that these questions will be asked repeatedly along the way.

Why Is It Important?

Because the dynamics of interpersonal violence and those of interventions are complicated and often ever-changing, even the best initial plans require some degree of monitoring and evaluation. Having a regular way to continually check in can help us make the appropriate changes in our course as we move along.

USING TOOLS IN THIS SECTION

The tools in this section are organized around typical situations in which we might need to take a look around: 1) at the beginning or end of a meeting; and 2) before and after taking an action.

Oftentimes, a meeting about an intervention will end with next steps. Making sure that these are clear and having a plan for these to be carried out is an important part of keeping on track and moving forward. Tool H1: How Are We doing? End of Meeting: Guiding Questions can help to make sure that these next steps will happen.

To figure out next steps in general, use Tool H2. What Are Next Steps: Guiding Questions. As you are about to take these next steps, then you can use Tool H3. Are We Ready for the Next Steps: Guiding Questions.

After you take the next step, then Tool H4. How did we do? Reflecting on an Action: Guiding Questions can be useful in reflecting on how it went. Some people refer to this as an evaluation.

It may be useful for individuals or groups to occasionally step back and see how they have been doing as a group. Tool H5. How Are We Doing? Individual Self-Check: Guiding Questions can be a useful tool for individuals to think about the process and see how they are contributing. For groups, this can be done with Tool H6. How Are We Doing? Group Self-Check: Guiding Questions.

Finally, the group will come to a time when the intervention comes to a close and moves into a phase of following-up. This might be because goals have been reached. Or it may be a time to step even if goals have not been reached. Tool H7. How are we doing? Closing an Intervention: Guiding Questions can help your group move through this step.

H.2. *KEEPING ON TRACK* ACROSS THE 4 PHASES

In Section 3.6. Interventions Over Time: 4 Phases, the Toolkit introduced the idea of 4 possible phases of interventions: 1) Getting Started, 2) Planning/Preparation, 3) Taking Action, and 4) Following Up.

Keeping on Track includes tools that can be used at any stage of the intervention.

PHASE 1: GETTING STARTED

As you get started, you may start putting the pieces together that will form the foundation of your intervention. Although things can change dramatically along the way, you may want to use the tools in this Section to return to the basics and make sure that you are following a steady course of action.

PHASE 2: PLANNING/PREPARATION

As you plan and prepare your set of actions, these tools can serve as good check points to move along. If you are primarily involved in planning meetings during this stage, the tools can help you make sure that you have clarified next steps at the end of each meeting.

PHASE 3: TAKING ACTION

This section also contains tools that are focused on preparing yourself for taking action. It has simple checklists and guiding questions that can help you get clear and prepared right before you are ready to take your next step. Once you take the next step, it can help you to determine whether that last action went well or if changes need to be made.

PHASE 4: FOLLOWING UP

These tools can help you to see what follow up work you may need to do as you move towards the end of an intervention, or if you decide that you can no longer move forward.

RELATED TOOLS

Tools to help teams or coordinated efforts are included in the Section 4.G. Working Together.

Tools to determine safety concerns before taking next steps are included in the Section 4.B. Staying Safe.

H.3. *KEEPING ON TRACK* TIPS

#1 READ SOME BASICS EVERYONE SHOULD KNOW.

Interpersonal violence is complicated. Although we may hear more about domestic violence or sexual assault these days, many misunderstandings still exist and many misconceptions about what it is and how to approach it. Read Section 2. Some Basics Everyone Should Know. Pay special attention to Section 2.2. Interpersonal Violence: Some Basics Everyone Should Know in order to have a clearer picture of what is going on. The Section 2.3. Violence Intervention: Some Important Lessons also shares important basics about interventions based upon the experiences of Creative Interventions.

Share this information with others who may be involved in a situation of violence and may need some resources to help them know what to do.

#2 AS MORE ACTIONS TAKE PLACE, IT CAN BE USEFUL TO USE THE TOOLS IN THIS SECTION AS "CHEATSHEETS" OR A QUICK REFERENCE AS YOU PREPARE TO TAKE ACTION.

Even if you have a good understanding of your overall goals and direction, each action taken can have specific narrower concerns on which to focus, especially if actions might involve safety risks. These Tools can be used as a quick list to make sure that you enter an action situation with clearly defined do's, don'ts and emergency back-up plans.

#3 AFTER TAKING ACTION, IT CAN BE USEFUL TO LOOK BACK TO SEE HOW YOU DID, WHAT YOU LEARNED AND HOW YOU CAN IMPROVE.

Interventions rarely take place exactly as planned. They often involve many unknowns about how people will react, how well teams prepare and communicate with each other, and emotional reactions that one might have when actually taking action. The tools to help look back and learn lessons are helpful in making sure that adjustments can be made.

#4 CELEBRATE YOUR ACHIEVEMENTS.

Interventions are difficult. They can be painful, slow-moving and frustrating. There may be many interventions that do not result in the goals that were set out at the beginning.

This does not mean that there is nothing to celebrate. There is!

Simply calling together a meeting can call for celebration. Making a list of goals can be a reason to celebrate. Staying safe for a day, a week is cause for celebration. Stopping violence for one more month and noticing the change is worth celebrating.

For some people celebrating will be easy and natural. For others, this will be unfamiliar territory – criticism and negativity or silence may be a more common way to get through something difficult.

Even if you do not feel comfortable with celebration, try celebrating a little. Try praising someone else for something achieved. Praise yourself. Clap. Sing a song. Do a little dance. Or simply say, "good job."

Celebrating achievements is a necessary step towards keeping on track and moving forward.

H.4. *KEEPING ON TRACK* SPECIAL CONSIDERATIONS

While the process of Keeping on Track may be different depending upon your relationship to the violence, these tools are the most general set of tools within this Toolkit.

They are useful for determining next steps whether you are the survivor or victim of violence, the people primarily intervening or the person who has done harm. There are no special considerations for these tools. They can be used by anyone for any part of the process of intervention.

This Toolkit is long and can be overwhelming. Some important parts of this Toolkit are Section 2. Some Basics Everyone Should Know. An especially important section can be Section 2.2. Interpersonal Violence: Some Basics Everyone Should Know that discusses much more about the dynamics of violence and common misunderstandings that people have.

#1 KEEP THE GOALS IN MIND AND USE THE TOOLS IN KEEPING TRACK TO MOVE TOWARDS THE GOALS.

If an intervention goes for a long time, it can be easy to lose track of where you are going. These tools help you to move along to the next step. Keeping these tools in mind as you work towards the goals can be a useful way to stay on a path to progress.

#2 KEEP THESE TOOLS ON HAND AT EVERY MEETING OR EVERY STEP.

These tools can help you figure out the next steps after a meeting, after an action or just along the way. They can be used for an individual or for a group. You can think about how to use the questions to move you along as you facilitate a meeting. Or you can remind everyone that these tools are there to help each individual to keep on track.

#3 REMEMBER TO CELEBRATE THE ACHIEVEMENTS.

You will likely find that an intervention to interpersonal violence is hard work. It is easy to feel confused, disappointed and wonder if anything will move forward. These tools help to figure out how you are doing and how to move to the next step. However, an important step will be to notice the small successes, however small, like the little steps forward, things somebody did well or led to some kind of positive feeling. Celebrating small and big steps along the way will be important in moving towards bigger goals.

It is possible that in an intervention, there will only be the small achievements. We at Creative Interventions have come to see each step and each gain as important. We urge you to do the same.

H.6. *KEEPING ON TRACK* REAL LIFE STORIES & EXAMPLES

Put your story here.

TOOLS

4.H HOW DO WE MOVE FORWARD?

Tool H1. How Are We Doing? End of Meeting: Guiding Questions

Tool H2. What Are Next Steps: Guiding Questions

Tool H3. Are We Ready for the Next Step: Guiding Questions

Tool H4. How Did We Do? Reflecting on an Action: Guiding Questions

Tool H5. How Are We Doing? Individual Self-Check: Guiding Questions

Tool H6. How Are We Doing? Group Self-Check: Guiding Questions

Tool H7. How Are We Doing? Closing an Intervention: Guiding Questions

? *KEEPING ON TRACK* TOOL H1: WHAT ARE NEXT STEPS? GUIDING QUESTIONS

At the end of each meeting or phone call, email discussion, or other form of communication, you will have next steps. Various next steps may come up throughout the call, email discussion or meeting. It can be useful to summarize these at the end to make sure that you: 1) remember the next steps; 2) agree on the steps; and 3) have a clear plan to tackle each one.

To organize next steps, you can follow these guided questions:

TIP: If some steps are only for certain people, write their name or initials after that step.

1. **Will you meet again or talk again? When? Where?**

2. **Will you communicate before the next meeting?**
   - What will you communicate?
   - How will you communicate?
   - Who will initiate communication?
   - By when will you communicate?

3. **What other "homework" or actions will happen before the next meeting?**

What Tasks/Actions?	By Whom?	**Notes** *(timeline, type of follow-up, etc.)*

KEEPING ON TRACK TOOL H2: ARE WE READY FOR THE NEXT STEP? GUIDING QUESTIONS

Sometimes it is useful to take a moment and make sure you are prepared for the next step in your plan. These are some questions you can ask yourself as you are about to take the next step.

1. **Are we clear about what the next step is?**
   a. What is it that we are about to do?
   b. What concrete steps does it involve?
   c. Who is going to do what?
2. **Are we clear about the reason or reasons we are doing this?**
   a. Why are we taking this next step?
   b. What do we hope to achieve?
   c. What larger goal is this linked to?
3. **Are we clear about how we want to do the next step?**
   a. How are we taking the next step?
   b. Are there any clear "do's" or "don'ts" about how we take the next step?
4. **Are we clear about who is responsible for taking the next step?**
   a. Who will is responsible overall?
   b. Who will initiate it or get it started?
   c. Who else is involved and what are their roles?
   d. Who will serve as back-up if other people cannot do their part?
5. **Are we clear about when the next step should happen?**
   a. When are we starting the next step?
   b. Are there phases to the next step? If so, when do they start?
   c. Is there a time by which we want or need the next step to be completed?
6. **Are we clear about follow-up after the next step?**
   a. When the next step is completed, what is to happen? And who is responsible?
7. **When we complete the next step, what happens after that? What is the next step or steps?**
8. **Is there anything else that is important?**

ⓘ *KEEPING ON TRACK* TOOL H3:
HOW ARE WE DOING? END OF MEETING GUIDING QUESTIONS

These are good questions to ask at the end of a meeting. They can help improve your meetings as you go along so that they are productive, constructive and move you towards your goals.

1. Did we meet the goals of the meeting?
2. Did the meeting have a good feeling overall?
3. Were there disagreements or conflicts? If so, what were they about? (For example, different perspectives, different values, different communication styles, conflicting personalities?)
4. If there were disagreements or conflicts, were we able to reach a place to move forward?
5. Was there anybody who was taking up too much space? Too little space? What can we do about it?
6. Did we make sure to address any special needs of the survivor, person doing harm, or others?
7. Was the meeting well-facilitated? Did it move along smoothly?
8. Does anything need to change? If so, what needs to change? What is our system or plan for change?
9. What were the achievements (including small ones)? Did we celebrate the achievement?
10. Did we end up with clear next steps? What are the next steps?

KEEPING ON TRACK TOOL H4: HOW ARE WE DOING? INDIVIDUAL SELF-CHECK GUIDING QUESTIONS

Evaluation of the process is important at each step of the way. The following is a list of guiding questions to ask ourselves as individuals as we are working on an intervention.

1. **How does this process relate to what is important to me?**
2. **What do I bring to this process?**
   a. Things that I value or care about
   b. Things that I know or people that I know
   c. Things I have to offer – can include things like transportation, cooking, good listener, spaces to meet, etc.
   d. Other?
3. **What are some negatives I need to watch out for?**
   a. Attitudes (for example, negativity, impatience, tendency to gossip, tendency to fight or put people down, tendency to stay silent and not say what I think)
   b. Ways of communicating that put people off
   c. Ways of being in a group that can get in the way
4. **This is about ending violence. Did I fully go through Section 2: Some Basics Everyone Should Know? How can I look through this thoroughly or have someone share it with me?**
5. **Do I know about the collective goals and action plan? If I do not, how can I ask for them?**
6. **This is a team or collective process. How is this for me?**
   a. What feels good and supportive?
   b. What is difficult?
   c. How am I helping?
   d. What am I doing to get in the way?
   e. How can I make things better?
7. **How have I contributed to the group process or to moving towards the goals?**
8. **What else can I do to contribute?**

9. **Is there anything I have a problem with or disagree with that I need to share with the group (and haven't so far)? Are there any secrets or things people don't know about that I need to share?**
   a. What is it?
   b. Is there any difficulty in sharing this? Why?
   c. Does this need to be shared? If so, how can I do it in the best way?
   d. Who can I go to for support?
10. **Is there anything else that is important?**

? KEEPING ON TRACK TOOL H5: HOW ARE WE DOING? GROUP CHECK GUIDING QUESTIONS

These are general questions to ask along the way to help make sure things are working smoothly.

1. **Do we have clear goals and bottom lines? What are they?**
2. **Are we guided by clear values? What are they?**
3. **Do we all seem to be on the same page? If not, who is on the same page? Who is not? What can we do to get everybody on the same page?**
4. **Are we working through disagreements or conflicts in a good way?**
5. **Are we all getting enough support?**
6. **Are we offering enough support?**
7. **Are we keeping connected to and supporting the survivor?**
8. **Are we keeping connected to and supporting the person doing harm?**
9. **Are we taking care of people who are vulnerable or need our extra care? (for example children, etc.)**
10. **Are we regularly doing risk assessment and safety planning?**
11. **Are we moving towards or do we have a clear action plan with the right people taking responsible for each piece, specific tasks or expectations, reasonable timelines?**
12. **Are we flexible enough to consider new opportunities or unanticipated roadblocks?**
13. **Are there things we need to change? What are they?**
14. **Do we have a good system or plan for change? If not, what changes need to be made?**
15. **What are the next steps?**

? *KEEPING ON TRACK* TOOL H6:
HOW DID WE DO? REFLECTING ON AN ACTION GROUP CHECK GUIDING QUESTIONS

An intervention will involve actions along the way. It is helpful to take a look back at an action to see how it went, what we can learn from that action, and what we should do in the future.

These questions guide us through helpful questions regarding an action.

1. **Was the action well-planned?**
    a. Specific enough?
    b. Did it involve the right people?
    c. Did it involve the right number of people? Too many? Too few?
    d. Did everyone work together well?
        i. If so, what made it go well?
        ii. If not, why?
        iii. What can be improved?
    e. Was the action appropriate for its goal?

2. **Were the possible risks and safety planning taken into account?**

3. **Did the action go as planned? If not, assess:**
    a. Why not? Could this be improved if you did it again? Or for the future?
    b. Were we able to make moves to correct for this?

4. **Did the action do what it was supposed to do?**
    a. Yes, no, maybe?
    b. How do you know?
    c. Do we need to get more information? What?

5. **What did we learn?**
    a. Positives
    b. Negatives

6. **Does anything need to change? If so, do we have a good system or plan for change?**

7. Does the action change anything significant in other parts of the intervention? What?

8. What do we need to communicate back to others? To whom?

9. What are the next steps?

ⓘ *KEEPING ON TRACK* TOOL H7: HOW ARE WE DOING? CLOSING AN INTERVENTION GUIDING QUESTIONS

At some point, you may come to the end of an intervention. This may be because the intervention went well and your goals were reached. It may also be because you need to end the intervention – even if you did not reach all of your goals.

These are some questions to ask yourself regarding the intervention as a whole.

1. **How did the intervention go as a whole?**
2. **How did the group or team work together?**
3. **Have overall goals been met? If not all, which ones?**
4. **Have people's individual goals been met? If not all, which ones?**
5. **Has the intervention process been guided by the team values and bottom-lines? Which were particularly followed? Which were not?**
6. **Did the team work well together?**
   a. Was there enough/appropriate support?
   b. How was the communication?
   c. How was the decision-making process?
   d. Is the group sustainable or able to keep together for long enough to reach the group's goals?
7. **What changes have happened for the group or community? What is positive? What is unchanged? What is negative?**
   a. How is the level of trust?
   b. How is the sense of community affected?
   c. How was the safety of the community affected? More safe? Less safe?
   d. Would we be able to do this again if necessary?
   e. Are we able to share these lessons with others?
   f. Anything else?

8. **What changes have happened for the survivor or victim? What is positive? What is unchanged? What is negative?**
    a. How is the level of trust for others?
    b. How did this affect one's sense of safety?
    c. How did this affect one's health (physical, emotional, spiritual, etc.)?
    d. Did this lead to a sense of repair from the harm?
    e. Did this person feel supported – feel a sense of community?
    f. Are we able to share these lessons with others?
    g. Anything else?
9. **What changes have happened for the person doing harm? What is positive? What is unchanged? What is negative?**
    a. How is the level of trust for others? How is the level of trust from others for the person doing harm?
    b. How is the sense of this person's safety? How is this person now affecting the safety of others?
    c. How did this affect the health (physical, emotional, spiritual, etc.) of the person doing harm? And how did this affect the health of others who were impacted by the harm?
    d. How does this person now understand the harm that they caused and the impact of that harm to others – and to themselves?
    e. How did this change this person's harmful attitudes?
    f. How did this change this person's harmful behaviors?
    g. Did the person doing harm receive support for these changes – a sense of community?
    h. Are we able to share these lessons with others?
    i. Anything else?

10. **What changes have happened for others ________________________? What is positive? What is unchanged? What is negative?**
    a. How is the level of trust for others?
    b. How did this affect one's sense of safety?
    c. How did this affect one's health (physical, emotional, spiritual, etc.)?
    d. Did this lead to a sense of repair from the harm?
    e. Did people feel supported – feel a sense of community?
    f. Are we able to share these lessons with others?
    g. Anything else?
11. **Would you consider this intervention a success?**
    a. What was successful?
    b. What wasn't successful?
    c. Is it overall a success?
12. **Congratulations! Can you share your story (successes and limitations) with others? Think about sharing your story with the StoryTelling & Organizing Project (www.stopviolenceeveryday.org).**

NOTES

5 OTHER RESOURCES

5.1. Key Words – Definitions: Words We Use and What They Mean to Creative Interventions

5.2. Real Life Stories and Examples from the Toolkit

5.3. Creative Interventions Anti-Oppression Policy (Anti-Discrimination/Anti-Harassment)

5.4. Community-Based Responses to Interpersonal Violence Workshop

5.5. Taking Risks: Implementing Grassroots Community Accountability Strategies, by Communities Against Rape and Abuse (CARA).

5.6. Distinguishing between Violence and Abuse, by Connie Burk, Northwest Network of Bisexual, Trans, Lesbian and Gay Survivors of Abuse

5.7. Portrait of Praxis: An Anatomy of Accountability, by Esteban Kelly and Jenna Peters-Golden of Philly Stands Up (PSU)

5.8. Confronting Sexual Assault: Transformative Justice on the Ground in Philadelphia, by Bench Ansfield and Timothy Colman of Philly Stands Up (PSU)

5.9. Shame, Realisation and Restoration: The Ethics of Restorative Practice, by Alan Jenkins

5.10. Tips for Seeking a Therapist [for People Who Have Done Sexual Harm], by Anonymous.

5.1. *KEYWORDS & DEFINITIONS:*

Words We Use and What They Mean to Creative Interventions

Ableism: Attitudes, actions, or structures that belittle or put down a person(s) because of actual or perceived physical, developmental or mental impairment.

Abuser (See Person Doing Harm)

Accountable, Accountability: For people involved, thinking about the ways they may have contributed to violence, recognizing their roles, acknowledging the ways they may need to make amends for their actions and make changes toward ensuring that violence does not continue and that healthy alternatives can take its place.

Ageism: Attitudes, actions, or structures that belittle or put down a person(s) because of their youth or actual or perceived lack of lived experience.

Ally (See Community Ally):

Bisexual: Being attracted to two sexes or two genders, but not necessarily simultaneously or equally.

Bystander: Someone not directly involved in a situation of harm, but who may have witnessed the harm and who may be called on to address the situation of harm or prevent future harm from happening. Creative Interventions tends to use the term allies rather than bystanders since the term bystanders sometimes seems like someone who just happens to be in the area of where the violence happened rather than someone who may have significant relationships with the people involved in violence – what we refer to as allies or community allies.

Collective: An approach relying on collaboration including shared capacity, resources and decision-making.

Collusion, Collude, Colluding: Acting on behalf of the person(s), groups or institutions perpetrating harm through supporting their violence, denying it, minimizing it, excusing it, or by blaming the survivor or victim.

Community: A grouping of people based on some common experience including geography, interests or values, identities, or interests. When we use this term we do not assume complete agreement within the group nor do we assume it to have only positive dynamics.

Community Accountability: A process in which a community such as family, friends, neighbors, co-workers or community members work together to transform situations of harm. This can also describe a process in which the community recognizes that they are impacted by violence even if it is primarily between individuals, that they may have participated in allowing the violence to happen or even causing the violence, and are responsible for resolving the violence.

Community Ally: Someone from one's community (either close-in community member or someone from within a larger community) who may become involved as an active participant in an intervention – and who brings their energy, skills or other resources to help bring about positive change.

Community-Based: Approaches that build on and promote community knowledge, skills, values and resources especially those of oppressed communities.

Criminal Legal System: Another name for the criminal justice system but one which emphasizes that this system may actually not be connected to real justice. It may also take into account the civil system of law such as that governing divorce, child custody, property ownership and lawsuits.

Criminal Justice System: The system controlled by the state or the government which produces people who are considered illegal, laws that determine who is criminal and who is not, the system under which people are determined to be criminal or not, the system of punishments and the actual carrying out of the punishment, itself, most notably including incarceration, parole and probation, and the death penalty.

Criminalization: The process through which actions (most often directly associated with people oppressed communities) become illegal.

Culture: A shared system of learned values, beliefs, and practices of a group of people.

Engagement: Meaningful communication with someone including their involvement or participation in an intervention.

Gay: Term often used to describe male-identified people who are attracted to other male-identified people. Sometimes used as an umbrella term for all queer identities.

Gender: Social constructions applied to behaviors, expectations, roles, representations used to delineate people as men, women, and transgender or gender-variant. Different from sex or sexuality.

Gender-Based Violence: A phrase used to describe violence targeting specific individuals or groups on the basis of their gender.

Gender Queer or Gender Non-Conforming: Demonstrating gender behaviors and traits not associated with a person's biological sex as typically dictated by dominant society.

Gendered Violence: A phrase often used instead of gender-based violence to describe violence that targets individuals or group on the basis of their gender or through ideas and actions that force certain ideas about gender through the use of violence.

Harm: Some form of injury to a person, group or community. This injury can be of many types: physical, financial, emotional, sexual, spiritual, environmental and so on.

Harm Reduction: A set of practical strategies that reduce negative consequences of drug use that meet drug users "where they're at," addressing conditions of use along with the use itself while engaging users in deciding the best course of action. Recently, harm reduction principles have been applied to a range of situations including interpersonal violence to advocate for approaches that involve those people closest in to the situation of harm to reduce as many harmful factors as possible while acknowledging that complete separation may not be possible or favorable.

Heteronormativity: A system that assumes that heterosexuality is "normal"—thereby marginalizing people who do not identify as heterosexual and carrying out the activities and institutions of everyday life as if everyone is and should be heterosexual.

Heterosexism: A system privileging heterosexuality above all other sexual orientations and marginalizing people who do not identify as heterosexual.

Hir: A gender neutral pronoun that can be used instead of his/hers.

Holistic: Holding all parts including survivor(s), allies/community, person(s) doing harm to possibilities of positive change.

Homophobia: The irrational fear and intolerance of people who are homosexual or of homosexual feelings. It is generally due to one's internal fear of those feelings in oneself but instead directed to other people.

Interpersonal Violence: Harm occurring between people in non-intimate relationships, usually in workplaces, community networks or institutions, or other collective formations.

Intervention: Action(s) taken to address, end, significantly reduce, or prevent violence.

Intimate Violence: A phrase used to describe actions including physical, emotional, and sexual abuse of children, elders, and people with disabilities by people known to them. It also includes intimate partner abuse, sexual violence committed in the context of a relationship, marital rape.

Lesbian: Term often used to describe female-identified people who are attracted to other female-identified people.

Liberation: To be freed from oppression, confinement, or control.

Liberatory Approach: An approach for addressing harm that does not rely on rely upon the state or other oppressive systems, but instead look to communities to end harm as central to a group's liberation.

Male Supremacy: A system of power that privileges male-identified people as well as their actions, ideas, and beliefs, that is maintained through the exploitation and repression of people who do not identify as male.

Nativism: The policy and practice of favoring the people already living in a place (usually a country or nation) over immigrants.

Oppression: Exercise of power and authority over another person(s).

Organic: An approach that builds from what people and communities already know and value.

Outing: Making public an identity or behavior someone wants to keep private. While usually used in terms of gender or sexuality outing can also include disclosing health conditions, immigration status, age, etc.

Patriarchy: A system in which male-identified people exercise power and privilege over female-identified or other people and justify their dominance to what they consider to be "natural" differences between men and women.

People of Color: African, Asian, Pacific Islander, Latino or Latino, Arab, Middle Eastern, Indigenous, and mixed and biracial persons of these ethnicities, races, or cultures who identify themselves in resistance to white supremacy in a collective and cultural community.

Perpetrator (See Person Doing Harm)

Person Doing Harm: The primary person committing or perpetrating harm or the people directly committing or perpetrating harm in a situation of interpersonal violence. Other people may also be involved as people doing harm, perhaps in a less direct way, by encouraging or tolerating harm or by discouraging efforts to address, stop or prevent harm.

Prison Industrial Complex: A term recognizing prisons and jails as a part of a broad system that ties together the state or the government; industries such as those building jails and prisons, those that benefit from prison labor, and those that are in the business of determining who is criminal and who is not; and ruling the way that the public thinks about "crime" as a way to not think about the ways that people who are named as criminals are actually a product of a larger capitalist system that feeds upon the poverty, oppression and exploitation of certain people at the expense of others – often based upon race, class, gender, sexuality, ethnicity, religion, national origin and other forms of discrimination.

Queer: Although some people still reject this term as only being a slur, "queer" has increasingly come to be an umbrella term to describe sexual orientations or gender identities that reject heteronormativity.

Racism: A system that uses the concept of race as the basis for maintaining inequality in society.

Regenerative: Create solutions that expand healthy change to more people and more communities.

Restorative Justice: A model that aims to repair harm by engaging community members and restoring community balance by calling on shared values, principles, and practices of accountability.

Self-Determination: A concept describing the ability and practice of communities to determine their own dealings without being controlled or restrained by outside or governmental forces. This is sometimes also used to describe the ability and practice of individuals, especially those usually oppressed, to be able to carry out their thoughts and activities without restraint or control by others (usually those who would oppress them) or governmental forces.

State: Set of people and interests that determine the laws, policies, and practices of a predetermined area. Also known as the government – federal, state, and local.

State Violence: Violence perpetrated at the hands of or on the behalf of state. This can include police violence, military violence, the types of punishments and uses of control by schools and so on.

Survivor: Person(s) harmed. The word survivor is often used as a more positive way to think of someone who has been harmed. Sometimes this word is used interchangeably with the word victim.

Sustainable: Able to be maintained or carried out over the long-term or over a long time without running down the energy and resources of the people carrying out the activity or process.

Team: A group of people involved in ending, significantly reducing, or preventing violence. Their roles can include supporting safety and healing, serving as a facilitators, providing resources, etc.

Transformative Justice: Phrase used to describe an approach to and processes for addressing harm that seeks to not only address the specific situation of harm in question, but to transform the conditions and social forces that made such harm possible. Sometimes used interchangeably with community accountability.

Transgender: A term referring to a gender identity not falling within, or actively rejecting traditional gender identities of male and female including people who reject their socially assigned gender or select a unique gender identity, people who prefer to express ambiguous gender identities, or no gender identity at all.

Transphobia: The irrational fear or hatred of transgender people.

Two Spirit: Two Spirit people are those who fulfill one of many mixed gender roles found traditionally among Native Americans, Inuit and other indigenous groups expressing itself through the presence of masculine and feminine spirits living in the same body.

Victim (see Survivor): may be applied in cases in which the person does not survive harm. Some people who have been harmed prefer the term victim to survivor.

Violence: Use of physical, economic, structural, emotional, sexual or psychological force exerted for the purpose of coercing, violating, damaging, or abusing.

Violence: Use of physical, economic, structural, emotional, sexual or psychological force exerted for the purpose of coercing, violating, damaging, or abusing.

Violence against women: A phrase used to describe a range of acts generally committed against people who identify as women based on their gender identity. These forms of violence are usually thought to include domestic violence, sexual assault, stalking and human trafficking specific to women and girls.

White Supremacy: A system of power that privileges people of European descent as well as their actions, ideas, beliefs, that is maintained through the exploitation and repression people of color. This is similar to racism but makes specific that this system upholds the privilege and power of white people.

Witness: Person who observes or experiences harm happening but may not be directly surviving that harm. The impacts of witnessing violence can be very severe in themselves.

Zie (also spelled ze): A gender neutral pronoun that can be used instead of he/she.

5.2. REAL LIFE STORIES & EXAMPLES FROM THE TOOLKIT

The following real life stories and examples are from Section 4. Tools to Mix and Match.

We have put them here in one place so that you can see stories and examples that you can use to think about your situation of interpersonal violence and violence intervention.

They are short pieces from what are often long and complicated interventions to violence. But they represent diverse situations and various types of strategies that people have taken to address, reduce, end or prevent interpersonal violence. They also highlight some of the tools presented in Section 4. Tools to Mix and Match.

Story A: I hear yelling in my apartment building. What is going on?

I live in a small apartment building in a city in the South near the border with Mexico. We have several immigrants from different countries living in the building. Some of us keep to ourselves and some have made friendships with the other residents. There is not a lot of fighting and violence here. But if there is, at least someone will hear – the next door neighbor or the people directly upstairs or downstairs.

I was hanging out with some of my neighbors. We don't know each other too well but we like to get together once in awhile. Sometimes our conversations turn to gossip about other people in the building. One time, one of them talked about the neighbors who live right next door to them, a couple that has been fighting. The couple has a 5-year old daughter. The husband has lived in the building for a few years – a seemingly nice guy who tends to keep to himself. He married a woman who moved in about 6 years ago. His wife mostly speaks Spanish. She's friendly but communication is usually pretty limited if you don't speak Spanish which most of us don't. I'll call them "Marcos" and "Maria" although those are not their real names. My neighbor continued with the story saying that he has heard them fighting and that the husband was yelling at his wife, Maria, "Go ahead and call the police. You don't even speak f**ing English."

I had never heard any yelling, myself. But when I heard the story, I wondered why Marcos mentioned the police. Immediately, I thought he may have hit Maria and perhaps she threatened to call the police, but I wasn't sure. When I heard about his comment about her English, I was more worried. Why is he insulting her about her English? Is he telling her she can't seek help even if she wanted to? Why is he telling her that the police won't do anything? Why is he yelling like that about the mother of his daughter who probably heard everything he said? These are all abusive and pointed to signs of more serious abuse. I also know that this type of violence doesn't usually stop one time. It was likely to continue and could get worse. I figured this story wouldn't stop here.

We wondered what was going on but didn't make any plans for action.

Later, I was talking to people who lived upstairs from them. I'll call these neighbors Tom and Grace, although these are not their real names. They could really hear the yelling, which was mostly coming from Marcos. Maria's voice was much quieter or she seemed to be crying. They thought they heard things being thrown around and were getting worried. They could hear the daughter crying during these times. I told them about what I heard from the other neighbors. Since they seemed really concerned, too, we tried to make sense from the things we knew and we had heard.

See Getting Clear Tool A1. What Is Going On? Snapshot: Quick Question Guide for how this Tool can be used in this story.

Story B. Confronting the Person Who Raped Me

A young immigrant woman came to an immigrant rights organization seeking assistance. She had gone to a party with her former employer, the owner of a bar. That evening, he attempted to rape her. She was able to struggle and get away. However, the experience was clearly traumatizing. Outraged, the woman had decided that she wanted to confront this man. She talked to the advocate about her plan to enter the bar and directly confront him, convinced that her sense of violation could only be met by this bold move.

The advocate, moved by the courage of this woman, responded by offering to go into the bar with her, a strategy ultimately challenged by the advocate's team of co-workers. This offer went beyond the usual practices of this organization and much beyond what most anti-violence organizations would recommend. Interested in the further exploration of this woman's request, this organization wondered whether this was the right opportunity for trying out a community-based intervention. The other options didn't seem to fit. She had already gone to the police who told her she did not have a case. And she did not have money or speak English. Who would she go to for "therapy" except the organization? Besides, it seemed like she was seeking her own pathway to healing which for her meant facing him head-on.

The advocate decided not to go with her and confront this man. But she did decide to act as a supporter or facilitator to see if she could provide a supportive anchor for this woman to carry out this plan of action. Self-determination became the guiding value for the organization's workers. Safety was also foremost in their minds. How could they prioritize safety without taking away this woman's self-determination?

The staff team discussed what a facilitated community-based intervention would look like in this situation. How could the advocate ask exploratory questions without trying to convince this woman not to go or to scare her off? The advocate met again with this young woman. This time she helped her explore her goals in confronting this man. Could her goals be met in other ways? Did she think about safety? It became clear that this woman's goal was direct confrontation even after all of the questions. But she was also open to discussing safety plans and to role play this action. She appreciated the support to figure this out.

The advocate role-played possible scenarios based upon her knowledge of the dynamics of sexual assault. She presented possible dangers as well as responses of victim-blaming, denial, threats and violence. She helped the woman explore who else among her friends and family might be willing to help. The role play brought up many situations which this woman had not considered. She recognized that marching into the bar on her own or with others was too dangerous. She had not thought of the possibility of his denial or his manipulation that it was her fault or her imagination. After going through the role play, she realized that these were all possibilities and appreciated the opportunity to go through the process. She took this as useful information that helped her clarify a safer plan which still met her goals.

Since the advocate was also interested in helping this woman explore what other allies she had, she asked more about this. Although the advocate had at first been convinced to march alongside her, she thought more about this. It was dangerous. She did not "know" this man, his possible reactions, or how her presence could make the situation more dangerous. Supporting this woman to center this "intervention" within her own community made more sense. They are her first-line supporters. They know her and the situation in which she worked. And the advocate was willing to help think through their possible roles and safety as well as hers.

The woman could not identify anybody within her community to help out when this plan was first discussed. But the question seemed to make an impression. By the time she decided to go and confront the man, she had talked to a friend who agreed to stay close to her phone in case any crisis occurred.

After thinking through and role-playing the safety plan, she called her former employer to meet her at a restaurant. He agreed. When she went to prepare for the meeting, she talked to the waiter at the restaurant and asked him to keep a close watch on the situation in case anything happened. These were two allies, the friend and the waiter, that she organized to help support her safety.

The woman ended up meeting with her former employer, confronting him by naming his action and her outrage. Within a short time, he admitted his guilt and apologized without further incident. She called the organization following this confrontation with great appreciation, relief and a sense of closure.

This story illustrates the basic principles of the model of community-based intervention, the critical role of helping the survivor identify her own goals and a plan of action to meet these goals. It also highlights the importance of exploring a collective response and the opportunity it opens for a different set of options resulting from the involvement of other people. It also offers one example of engagement with the person doing harm and the transformative power of this possibility for the survivor. We can imagine that the "healing" powers of this action were deeper and more powerful than anything the police or professionals could provide.

Story adapted from Kim, M. "Alternative Interventions to Intimate Violence: Defining Political and Pragmatic Challenges." Pp. 193 – 217 in Ptacek, J. (Ed.), Feminism and Restorative Justice, (NY: Oxford Press, 2010).

Story C. My Husband Is Hitting Our Daughter: Who Can Help?

My husband's abuse toward our first daughter started even before she was barely a year old. He clearly had lots of problem managing his own frustration and didn't seem to know how to discipline kids appropriately. He often yelled at her and spanked her when she was little. This sort of violence continued until my daughter was in sixth grade.

One incident that comes to my mind is when my daughter was about five or six years old. On the living room couch, my husband was trying to pull out one of her teeth which was shaking badly. My daughter was obviously scared and didn't want to do it. Although I knew he was getting impatient with her, I decided not to intervene at that moment since it usually made things worse. I heard my daughter crying and my husband's frustrated voice. And suddenly my daughter started to cry even louder. I remained in my bedroom. My husband went out shortly afterwards, so I came out to see if my daughter was okay. When I asked her what happened, she simply said, "Dad hit me." "Where?" I asked. She pointed her finger to her face. When I saw the mark of his hand across her face, I became furious.

The pattern was always the same. He would tell our daughter to do something or bring him something. If she didn't do it immediately, he would get upset. Then, he would shout and tell her again. If she complained or tried to explain why she couldn't do it, he got angry and accused her of talking back to him. Then he hit her. It tended to get worse if I tried to intervene or if my daughter even looked at me.

One evening, my husband and I were having an argument about the time he hit her when he was trying to pull her tooth. We were arguing in the car on the way back from church. He kept insisting that he didn't hit her at all. I became so angry that I got out of the car and walked away. I later called my friend to come and pick me up. In the meantime, I later found out that he told my oldest daughter that everything was her fault. He blamed her for my leaving the family that evening. This had a serious impact on my daughter; she still remembers his exact words years later.

I returned home that night and again got into an argument with my husband who shouted that he didn't hit her. I thought about next step, and I started to break things in the kitchen. The next day, I cut all of his shoes with scissors.

I then decided to call my father, my husband's older sister, and one of a mutual good friend/mentor. I called my father and my husband's older sister in order to reach out to the person in authority on each side of the family. They called him separately and confronted him. This was my attempt to make him somehow accountable for his behavior. I also called our mutual friend/mentor whom he respects, hoping that this might have an impact on him in the long run.

My father called my husband and told him that it was wrong to hit a child and that it shouldn't happen again. When our friend/mentor heard what had happened, he came over to our home right away. He saw my daughter's face and confronted my husband about his hitting. My husband was clearly upset and embarrassed to the person in authority on each side of the family.

In the meantime, I told my daughter that it wasn't her fault and told her and my son not to worry if they hear loud voices. My goal that night was really making him feel sorry for what he did so that any future abuse can be prevented or greatly reduced.

It wasn't like I had a plan for that sort of situation. I had to think hard and fast to do all the things I could so that his behavior would stop. Although the people I called were supportive and did what they can to let him know how wrong it was to hit a child, I doubted that it would have a long lasting effect on him. I acted on my instincts and attempted to involve more people. What I was thinking all along, however, was that it is necessary for him to experience a more profound change within him to really change.

When my father, his sister, and our friend/mentor called, my husband initially denied hitting our daughter. He was angry with me for telling other people. He said I was "making a big deal out of nothing." As they continued to confront him, his denial slowly disappeared. He was upset at the fact that I had contacted several people, but became more embarrassed over time.

The intervention helped. He did stop hitting our daughter after that time, but the profound changes didn't come until later. Two things seemed to make the deepest impact. First, one of his friends shared his own story about how his grown up daughter wants to maintain distance with him because of his verbal and physical abuse toward her while growing up. This personal sharing had a big impact on my husband who always wanted to have close relationships with his kids. Second, my husband experienced a spiritual breakthrough, and he began to look at different parts of his life. He has changed so much since then.

Looking back, I think that one of the major impacts of my interventions was that my oldest daughter felt more secure and safe at home knowing that I would never overlook her dad's violent behavior. Although it took many more years before my husband was able to control his temper and stop violent behavior, my husband did realize that I will not stand for it if he treats our children in an abusive way.

I think that any kind of intervention is important. It may not stop the violence from happening again, but it almost always helps children.

Story D: Community Responds to Domestic Violence

Two years ago, I was married to a man who I'd been with for ten years prior, and our relationship had troubles. Over the last year of our marriage, my former partner was going through training as a police officer, and at the same time, we had just relocated to a new state. We were struggling with some large issues in the marriage, and things had gotten more difficult. I just became increasingly afraid of someone that I used to feel really safe with.

I have three kids who were ten, six, and four, and they were witnessing a lot of arguments, a lot of loud screaming, a lot of doors being slammed, a lot of things that I felt were really unsafe for them to see. My home just felt more and more dangerous. I felt scared to leave the house. I felt scared to come home. I felt scared to sleep in my bed.

The last straw came one night when I had gone to a friend's house and my partner followed me in his car. And when I arrived at my friend's house, he pulled up and got out of the car and was yelling and screaming horrible things at me. I felt very afraid, but I didn't know what to do. I knew wherever I went, he would follow me. So I decided I would go to my office which was nearby, and it was night time so there wouldn't be anybody there. When I finally got inside, I waited for a few minutes and he left.

I called a friend, who came and met me at my office, and she suggested that I call another friend who had a house I could go to while we figured out what to do, so that's what I did. When we got there, everybody sat around in the living room and just reassured me that it was safe for me to be there, that they were welcoming of it, that they understood. I was at this point on the run from someone who was furious and had a gun, and I still felt bad. I felt like I was exposing people to something that I couldn't control, something I was terrified of. But I didn't know what else to do at that point, and they were saying it was where they wanted me to be.

My friends asked me if there were any people that I could gather up, that I could call, that might be support from in this time. I guess I should say that being part of this, this community organization which is committed to ending sexual violence which meant that we had a way of responding that I knew people would come together. I knew if I needed help, people would come and talk to me and we could work it out together. So it didn't feel strange to meet, to call people and say, "Hey, I need help, and this is what's going on."

And at the same time, experiencing these things in my home felt like people would see me differently; people would judge me; people would think I was a hypocrite; people would think I was weak. And I remember being really troubled by that the first few days. But I got reassurances from folks that that was exactly what the point of the organization was, and that experiencing harm is not about being strong or weak, that experiencing harm just is. It's what we choose to do about it that's important.

So we made phone calls, and asked people to come over. We had seven or eight people come over and just started talking through what to do. At that point it felt totally overwhelming. I was still on, "Is this really happening to me?" and, "What can I do to make it okay?" rather than thinking of anything beyond tomorrow, or next week.

But I think my wants were something like: I want to be in my home; I want my kids to feel safe; I think I said, "I want him to leave."

I think those were basically it at that moment, and then we just brainstormed what needs to happen right now in the next hour, in the next day, in the next week, for those wants to happen. We walked through it so if I want to be in my home, how do we make that happen? How do we make sure that that's a safe space? And, I think one of the answers to that question was, at least in the near future, having folks be there with me.

So we eventually set up a schedule. We put out an email with a schedule for the week, and blanks for people to fill in, and I was amazed that people did fill it in. And they did come by. They came by every day and they came and sat in my living room, and they brought food, and we just sat together. I was amazed at that. That was how we got home to be a safe space for me again.

When we were thinking about whether to call the police or not, I did feel like I needed some help in calming the situation down, but I didn't know what to do, because if I can't call his friends on the job, and I can't call them in…It doesn't seem right to call them in an unofficial way, because who knows what's going to happen with that. And calling them in an official way doesn't necessarily seem like it's going to produce any certain results either.

So we tried to think about who could talk to him. And we figured out some people in the community that he could talk to, if he was open to doing that. My mom talked to him, and she was willing to deal with him. He was totally raging, and for whatever reason she was not intimidated at all and just was able to talk to him really calmly.

I had people checking on me, people staying during the daytime hours, sometimes overnight for the next week, and it just felt good. It felt so good to have this full house, you know, this busy house of people coming by, and, you know, people were playing with the kids, and we were making art in the kitchen, and someone was always making tea, and it felt not alone.

In terms of talking about successes, I guess the biggest one is that I did get all three things that I wanted, that I identified as wants to happen. That my kids went through that time feeling safe; that he did leave the house; that I was able to return home; and that all that happened in a fairly short amount of time. So in terms of success, I'd say, ultimately for me as a survivor, those were the most meaningful successes.

Another success in terms of communication was that we made a phone list immediately. That was one of the first things we did so I always knew I had someone to call. And people would call and check on me. At that time, I think it was hard. I was worried about people burning out. I was worried about people feeling overwhelmed by me and my stuff.

So I didn't have to constantly, hour by hour, be reaching out for needs to be met because we'd identified them beforehand and there were enough people involved. It felt like no one was carrying all of it, or more than they could. It certainly wasn't that things didn't feel hard. It felt really bad. I think what was helpful was this wasn't an intervention where it was like, "How are we going to get him away from me? It was like, "How are we going to make sure that there's not harm happening in our community? How are we going to make sure that we've done our best to address that? The problem was consistently the harm. The problem was consistently the events or the behaviors, or the things that were harmful that were happening, but not him that was a problem – not that my choice to stay as long as I had was a problem.

That made it possible for me to feel like I could come into the space and say what I needed which at that time really included not being someone who was perpetrating harm against him by engaging the power of the state whether or not it would have benefited me in that moment. It could only have had negative effects on him.

And then I got to make a decision about what do I really need right now to do my work, to take care of my kids, to get through this day, to heal.

We need to trust people to be the experts on their own lives and to take them seriously and have faith in people to set the course for working from harm to transformation. I think that comes best from people who are experiencing harm and have a vision for themselves about what they want. And to give people time to identify what that is and be willing to sit with the discomfort of not being able to rescue somebody in a simple or quick way. I think that those values were ultimately the most healing for me.

(Adapted from the transcript from Community Responds to Domestic Violence available from StoryTelling & Organizing Project (STOP) www.stopviolenceeveryday.org. The story is also available in downloadable audio mp3 on the same website)

Story E. Getting Support from My Co-Workers

So we'd been married for a year and a half. We were both very involved politically. I had a new baby, I was at home. I know that I started feeling like my life was kind of slipping away.

But his world started to change. And he started to become much more community-involved and I was less and less community involved. And it led to a lot of tension in the relationship, and a lot of tension around me being at home and he being sort of out in the world. I think the arguing and the fighting and the challenging verbally started. And it just escalated. And became very contentious, you know. The relationship was very contentious.

So I remember he came home one night, and he had been out. And I remember he came home one night and we just started fighting. I picked up a glass and threw it at him and it hit him in the side of his face and that was it. He chased me in the living room. We have this brick fireplace in the living room. He chased me in the house and grabbed me, threw me on the floor and just pounded my face into the brick wall. I mean, when thinking about it now, I'm thinking, "How did I survive that?" I felt like he was going to kill me. I mean, I felt like this man has lost his mind, and I'm dead. I remember that he just kicked me, pounded my face into the brick wall, into this fireplace, and…and then he left.

The first assault was one thing. That was shocking to me. The second one was more shocking. Because the first one felt to me like he just lost it, and he just wasn't aware of what he was doing, and he just responded so violently because he lost control of himself. And that to me was not as shocking as the second time because I felt like the second time was almost more being very much more intentional. So I was much more shocked that actually happened after we got back together. I still felt like I was in a lot of shock, and I was very depressed.

You know, I was depressed after this happened. I was depressed for probably about three or four months. I was just in a deep, deep depression. And mostly because I felt like you know this was a person that I just didn't know. I just didn't see this side of him.

I couldn't go to work. My supervisors were very supportive. I mean my whole face was...I couldn't go to work because my face was so damaged that there was no way I could leave the house looking like I was looking. So my co-workers were very supportive and gave me the time I needed to be off.

I don't think we called the police. And I wasn't going to. I mean, police to me was never an option. I don't think I felt like they would have done anything at all. I wasn't necessarily opposed to the police, but I just didn't feel like I knew what their role was. So I didn't call them, but there was plenty of other support. And I don't think I ever, I don't think I felt like there was anybody who was not supportive of me. I never heard anybody say things like, "Well, you need to leave the motherf*****" or to say, "What did you do to provoke him?" I don't think I heard those kind of comments from anybody. I got a lot of support and affirmation and people wanting to be helpful.

I think the first level of support was concern for my physical well-being. And you know, really making sure that I felt safe. And where I was, was I safe? And did I feel like I needed some support to make me safe? And I don't think there was much of a sense from my friends of any sort of like domestic violence shelters or anything like that. I think it was, "Do you feel safe here in your house? He's not here, he's gone, do you feel safe? Do you feel like he'll come back? And if he comes back do you feel safe about that?" And so I think there was a lot of concern about my safety.

There was also a lot of concern about my mental health and what that meant in terms of just taking care of myself physically. People brought me food. "Are you eating?" "Do you need somebody to be here with you?" I mean, I think the fact that I was depressed was really scary for people. "Do you need us to be here to make sure you're eating?" "Make sure you're not sort of thinking about suicide or anything like that." So there was a, there was a lot of that. "Do you just need someone, do you just need someone to come and cook you some dinner or lunch or whatever." I had people that bought groceries for me, and brought food to me, and offered to come and help clean the house. And it wasn't at all patronizing. It was like, "You know what, we understand that right now you might not have the energy to do all of these things, so let us take care of you."

Even to the point where – I just, I never will forget this. We had hardwood floors at the time. And I remember one person saying, "Do you want me to come in here and paint your walls?" I mean, it was like, "We'll paint for you!" You know, I think they wanted to change the environment or create an environment where I felt comfortable. "Is there something different we can do here in your house." So I remember that a couple people came and painted my living room and dining room, and I remember getting new rugs on the floor.

So my friends were more concerned about my well-being and I had a little nine month old. They were concerned about "Was I able to take care of her and did I need some support in taking care of her?" So people were providing tangible things for me. And then, people were just willing. "You need to call us in the middle of the night, call me." I mean I just had people who were like, "Just call me." "You need to talk, just call me and talk." I felt like I was a burden, and I felt like I didn't want to impose this on my friends, but I felt like they were there. "You want to talk ad nauseum, talk ad nauseum." So I felt like there was just kind of listening, they were able to listen to me.

Story F.1. A Cultural Organization Deals With Sexual Assault

In the summer of 2006, a drumming teacher from South Korea was invited to teach a week-long drumming workshop at a Korean cultural community center in Oakland, California. After an evening of singing, storytelling and drinking, several students stayed the night to rest and recover for the next day. For over two decades, the cultural center had developed a safe space for the teaching of Korean drumming and dance, community performance and cultural and political exchange. That night, safety was shattered when the drumming teacher sexually assaulted one of the students.

People staying at the center immediately heard what had happened, and center leaders quickly pulled together a direct confrontation involving the members and their community-led board. The next day, members and board members gathered at the center to denounce the sexual assault and support the victim. In this situation, the victim refused to name herself as a "survivor" – finding "victim" a better description of her experience of violence.

Liz, the president of the Oakland cultural center at that time, recollects the next day's meeting. "When we got there, the teacher got on his knees and knelt in front of us which is the deepest sign of respect. And then he asked us, begged us, not to tell his organization back home. We said we couldn't do that. 'We're not here for your apology. We're here to tell you what happened, what we're going to do, and that's it.' He made a big sign of remorse, taking his drumming stick and breaking it. He put it on the ground like 'I'll give up drumming for this.' Most of us were disgusted."

What followed was a series of actions, a set of sexual assault awareness workshops for the center members and members of other local drumming groups. The board made an immediate telephone call to the head of the drumming center in Korean. Their leader expressed his profound shock and unconditional apology. This call was followed by a letter with a list of demands. The Oakland organization demanded that the Korean institution establish sexual assault awareness trainings for their entire membership which ranged from college students to elder farmers in the village, a commitment to send at least one woman teacher in their future exchanges to the U.S., and a request that the teacher step down from his leadership position for an initial period of 6 months and attend feminist therapy sessions directly addressing the assault. Even though it was culturally difficult for the Korean American group to make demands of their elders in Korea, everyone decided this was what needed to be done. The group in Korea also did not question these demands. They respected them and did not make any complaints.

The Korean American organization also made contact with a sister drumming group in Korea, one that had dealt with their own experience of sexual assault in the past. That organization had organized their one hundred members to address a sexual assault that had occurred among their membership. In that situation, the person who had committed the assault went through an extensive process with the leaders and members of the group, leaving the organization but following through with a public apology posted on their website and retained relationships with drumming group members.

Inspired by this story of community accountability, the fact that it had been made public and a process in which the person doing harm took responsibility and offered a public apology, the Oakland organization followed with a series of events that reversed the usual silence and victim-blaming accompanying sexual assault. The annual October festival was dedicated to the theme of healing from sexual violence. Facts regarding the incident were printed in the program and shared as a part of the evening's festival, not as a shaming act although it may have indeed shamed the teacher, but as a challenge to the community to take collective responsibility for ending the conditions perpetuating violence including collusion through silence.

This story reveals other painful lessons about community violence and the limitations of our community-led processes. The Korean cultural center came together with a unified response to violence but grew divided as the process continued. What became a long drawn-out period of institutional reflection and engagement sapped the energy and spirit of the organization and the friendships that had held it together. The victim never returned. The continued presence of the teacher at community festivities in South Korea were viewed with resentment and suspicion by Korean American visitors who participated in drumming events in Korea. His eventual removal from the institution did not necessarily lead to the sense of justice that people desired.

Liz, the center's president, reflected on this set of events and the uncertainties accompanying the process of community accountability.

"Some people asked us later why we didn't call the police. It was not even a thought in anybody's mind. I know that a couple folks, her close friends, tried to break in, to kick his ass, but they couldn't find him. Luckily they didn't. Luckily for him and the organization, too, because I think if they did that we would have just been in a whole world of fucking mess. Well, I don't want to say luckily because the victim even felt at some point, 'maybe we should've just kicked his ass. Now, I feel like I've got nothing. I don't have the police report. We didn't throw him into jail. We didn't kick his ass. We didn't do nothing.'

We talked to her and said, 'We didn't move forward on anything without your consent.' We asked, 'What else can we offer you?' We offered her to go to counseling and therapy. We offered her whatever we could do at the time. In retrospect, I wish we could have spent more time to just embrace her and bring her in closer."

The story further explores the role of force and violence in our response to violence. Frustration over a long and complex process of accountability spurred discussions among the members of the Oakland organization over the potential benefits of violence. Liz reflected on a member's remark as they considered retaliation. "That's what the teacher wanted. He wanted that. When he was making that apology, he wasn't necessarily saying 'beat me up,' But he was saying, 'do anything you want to me, I deserve it.' That way, once you do, he can walk away and say, 'Okay, now I'm done, wipe my hands and walk away. They've done everything they can already.'" While some may most fear a violent response, some could also welcome a quick but symbolic pay back. "Kicking ass," can also substitute for a process of repair and change.

(This story is in Section 4.F. Taking Accountability to show how one community organization dealt with the person doing harm to address his violence; how they turned to the organization that he represented to ask them to take on a process of accountability with their community; and how they turned to a sister organization to learn from them about how they had dealt with a similar situation of sexual assault within their organization.)

(Adapted from Kim, M. [In press]. "Moving beyond critique: Creative Interventions and reconstructions of community accountability." Social Justice 37(4). For Liz's Story audio and transcript, see Liz's Story at www.stopviolenceeveryday.org)

Story F.2. Women Come Together to Confront Our Community Leaders

I got a story for you, and it's about community accountability. This Hmong woman in Wausau – she was killed by her husband and then he killed himself. He shot her boyfriend, too, and now he's in the hospital in critical condition.

The reason a lot of Hmong women don't leave violent relationships or go back and forth is because when you're married, you belong to your husband's clan in the spirit world. When you die, they bury you and you have a place to go. If you're in-between places, then nobody's gonna bury you, nobody's gonna pay for a funeral, and you have no place to go in the spirit world. That's why so many women stay or don't do anything.

So this woman, her husband's clan wouldn't bury her because they said she's a "slut." Then her boyfriend's clan said, "she doesn't belong to us so we're not going bury her." And her parent's family said, "if she listened to us, this wouldn't have happened." So they wouldn't bury her either. So nobody's claiming her and nobody's going bury her or pay for the burial. This is 3 weeks later.

So this woman's been working with an advocate from Women's Community in Wausau up there. She's been working with this woman who was killed, and she calls me. We'd been talking with the advocates up there for awhile trying to figure out what to do. I'd already been planning to go there to talk about domestic violence and community accountability to a big group of Hmong people at a conference they were planning.

So I say, go back to that clan and say that if they don't bury her and pay for the funeral, we're going to publicly shame them. They have until Wednesday, and if they don't do it, then we're going to go out nationally and write an article and tell everyone that we don't even bury our dead. We'll go to all the women's organizations and shame the community. We'll let them know that there's 18 clans up there, and nobody buried her.

I said, we always gotta go back to the problem which is that this is why women don't leave or go back and forth – because they're afraid they're going be left with nobody to bury them when they die. You bury him first, and he's the one who killed her. And you leave her and say that she died because she's a slut. She didn't die because she's a slut, she died because this guy was abusing her and you all knew that. She died because the Hmong considered her somebody's property, and now she gets killed and can't even get buried. She's not a slut. Hmong men go out with other women all the time, and nobody dies.

Everybody knew that she was getting treated like s*** by this guy. If they don't do something about this, then we're gonna go out and tell everybody and shame the whole community.

So one of the advocates working with the clan leader – she told them this, and you know what? They got the money together and buried her. Her husband's clan took responsibility for her and buried her. That's community accountability.

(This story is in Section 4.F. Taking Accountability to show how women in a community came together to challenge their community's leaders to do the right thing and to honor the death of a woman who was killed by her husband in an act of domestic violence. Even though they were not able to save this woman's life, they came together to challenge the woman's family and community leaders to make an important statement and demand for respect.)

Story F.3. Stopping Violence As A First Step

I was in a relationship with Karen for 3 years. Even though I started seeing the warning signs, I agreed to live with her. Our fighting started getting worse and more regular. It got so every day I would wake up worried that my day would begin with a fight. I did everything to avoid her getting mad, but everything I did seemed to get her upset.

After every argument or fight, she and I would process about how she handled frustration. She had thrown a cup against the wall so hard that the plastic split and shattered. She had gotten out of the car that I was sitting in and slammed her hands on the roof of the car as hard as she could. She had hit her head against the bathroom wall and slammed the sink top with her hands. She had thrashed her legs around under the covers in bed and kneed the wall when she was mad that I hadn't brushed my teeth. She would yell, curse, and literally sprint away during a disagreement or argument.

We had processed and processed about it and had moments of shared understanding about why she experienced things and behaved in the ways she did, how she had learned it, what she was reacting to, etc. She came to understand that although she never physically hurt me and wasn't a "batterer" using threatening or controlling behaviors against me, her behavior made me anxious, uncomfortable, and eventually full of contempt.

She learned that it was hurting the relationship. But all of the talking did not result in actual change. Finally, a couple years later, after one incident, I told her that I would assuredly leave her if she did not change this aspect of her behavior. I asked her what she thought would work—what would make her change her behavior, since talking together about it wasn't working. We had long passed the point where talking had any chance of stopping her from escalating her anger.

She didn't want me to leave and knew that I was serious. She came up with something herself, and we agreed upon a rule. If she began to get upset, she would try to use calming, self-soothing practices for herself. And if she expressed her anger and frustration with physical violence even once – including throwing things against the wall or pounding on things without necessarily touching me – she would arrange for herself to stay in a motel that night, and cover the costs and transportation on her own. She would take a cab and not walk to a motel at night (even if she wanted to walk), because putting her as a queer woman on the street alone at night was not going to be part of the plan. She could get hurt. And even if she didn't, I would worry so much that I would get no rest. She agreed that she would take the cab so that she would be safe and I wouldn't have to worry. The whole decision around these consequences seemed like such a small thing, but it made a big difference in her behavior.

We eventually broke up. Her agreement to stop her abuse, and her plans to take steps to avoid further abuse made a difference. I think it also helped her understand that she really could take steps to control her abuse. It took years of me explaining to her how I felt and years of tolerating what I now find to be an intolerable situation. But she did finally admit that what she was doing was wrong or at least wrong to me. And she finally took steps to change her behavior. She stopped the most immediate violence and took responsibility to make plans to make sure that she would either stop or at least remove herself from our home if she couldn't make herself stop in any other way.

This was a first step and an important one. She could finally recognize with my insistence over and over again that her abusive behavior was wrong. We were for awhile able to take a break from the continued cycle of violence.

But she chose to go no further. She would not change her underlying attitudes and behaviors. She refused to admit how deep these problems were and how simply stopping the most immediate behaviors would not be enough for me to trust her and relax enough to enjoy our relationship together. We had a moment of relief, but without deeper changes, I knew it would be just a matter of time before her abuse would start again.

Stopping violence takes many steps. Changing violence and becoming someone who can truly enjoy human connection, love without control, communicate without having to make every conversation into an argument or a contest, and be open, curious and appreciative about one's partner are things that I now seek.

(This story is in Section 4.F. Taking Accountability to show how one woman and her abusive partner came to an agreement about how she will stop her violence in the future.)

Story F.4. Surviving & Doing Sexual Harm: A Story of Accountability & Healing

Introduction to Surviving and Doing Sexual Harm: A Story of Accountability and Healing

The following is a story from the perspective of a person doing harm, a person who has also survived harm. In his story, these two dynamics are intimately interlinked. Because there are so few stories from the perspective of the person doing harm, we have included many details occurring over many years of struggle, believing that certain pieces may be important for people doing harm, survivors and allies to better understand the dynamics of accountability.

At this point in time, the public stories of people who have done harm and who are taking accountability seriously remain rare. This is only one story told in some detail. This person's feelings and process may or may not be similar to those of other people doing harm. This person's ability to find resources, political groups doing accountability with values that are non-punishing and non-criminalizing, may not be there for everyone although our goal is that these resources will become more and more commonly available.

Note that this story is shared by someone whose name remains anonymous. This is not only to protect confidentiality but also to make sure that this story does not become a means for this person to receive public recognition or a sense of heroism for his accountability. It is common for people doing harm who have made some movement towards change to be elevated above people who have survived harm – especially if they are men. The story teller has specifically asked to not receive recognition for any contributions they have made towards this project or Toolkit. Humbleness and humility are core parts of the accountability process. From the story, we can see that the process of accountability, itself, has been long and difficult. But, ultimately, it is accountability to oneself and to others that has made this person's healing and transformation possible.

The story teller also asks that if people are able to recognize him or other identities through the details included in this story, that you please have compassion about who you share these identities with. If you recognize him, he asks that you please talk with him about this story, even if only to acknowledge that you know this part of his history; he does not want this story to be an unspoken secret among those that know him.

Surviving and Doing Sexual Harm: A Story of Accountability and Healing

Why I am Telling My Story

In all of my years trying to find resources, I've only come across three stories of people who've done harm and only one of them had enough information, enough of the person's real story, to actually be helpful to me. I want to tell my story to help people who are trying to work on their sh** and also to help people who are supporting that process or who are mentors to have some idea of what might be going on for that person who still doesn't understand themselves – to help folks be better support for accountability processes.

Naming the Harm

You know, for most of the harm that I've done, I've never really been called out for it, so I don't really have other people's names for it, just my own names. I consider myself to have sexually assaulted people, also crossed people's boundaries in sexual ways that aren't sexual assault, and just generally had patriarchal behavior. And then the last thing that's always a little more difficult for me to talk about is that I also molested a relative of mine when I was young.

Accountability and Its Early Beginnings

My accountability process started in my early 20's. The violence and harm I had been doing wasn't just a one-time thing where I just messed up once, it was like an ongoing pattern that was chronic, and happening over and over again in my life. There were a couple of moments when I was able to stop myself in the moment when I was doing harm, like when I hurt someone I cared about very much, seeing her weep when I pushed her sexual boundaries, what I see as sexual assault, I said, "Sh**. I need to stop right now." But even then, that kind of like horror wasn't enough to let me intervene in the big, chronic patterns. It took a lot more before I could start changing, even when I was recognizing chronic patterns of harm I was doing in my life and hated that I was doing those things.

By that point in my life, I was a total wreck. For years and years of my life, my mind had been filled almost with nothing but images of doing gruesome violence to myself. I was having trouble just keeping my life together. I was just under huge amounts of stress, having total breakdowns on a fairly regular basis, and was just being ripped apart inside by everything. And also, being ripped apart by trying to keep myself from the knowledge of what I'd done. It was too much for me to even look at. At the same time, I really wanted to talk with people about it. I was just so scared to do it because of the particular sorts of thing that I had done. You know, like, people who sexually abuse are the most evil of all the monsters in our cultural mythology. And everybody is basically on board with doing nothing but straight up violence to them. And so much of my life had been organized around just trying to keep myself safe that it wasn't a risk I could take. It wasn't even a question of choice. It just wasn't a possibility, even though wanted nothing more.

At some point, I started spending more time around people involved in radical politics and feminist politics. And so one person that I knew, I'll call him Griffin (not his real name), one of their friends had been sexually assaulted. So I just happened to be at a table when Griffin was having a conversation about what people were going to do about it. And that was the first time that I had ever heard of Philly Stands Up. Where I was living at the time was really far away from Philly, so it was just basically a name and an idea. But, you know, that one tiny seed of an idea was enough to make me realize that it was possible. That there were people that I could talk to that weren't going to destroy me.

It was a few months later. There was just a lot of stuff going on in my life where my history of doing violence to people and my history of surviving violence, they were coming up over and over and over in my life. But I still refused to acknowledge either of them. And it wasn't like a conscious thing. I don't know exactly what it was, but I hadn't gained the moment of insight yet into understanding that that is my history. I ended up talking with that same friend, Griffin, who had mentioned Philly Stands Up, and just in this one conversation, my whole history came out. It was the first time I talked with anybody about either my history of being raped or my history of doing sexual violence to other people. That was a moment when I stopped running from my past. Those two things in my life, surviving violence and doing violence, are inseparable. I started coming to terms with both of them in the exact same moment. That was the first time I ever broke my own silence. And that's when I started trying to find some way of doing accountability.

Part of what made this possible was the particular relationship with one of the people I had harmed, June (not her real name), a person that I loved tremendously, and somebody who, even though I haven't seen her for years and probably won't see her again in my life, I still love tremendously. And so the pain of hurting somebody that I love that much was part of it. And then I think part of it was that I had had someone to talk to. I'd never been able to communicate with people about anything in my life before. And part of it was that things got so bad at one point that I didn't have the choice anymore of not seeking support. I had a breakdown where somebody came into my life and listened to me, and I couldn't hold it in any more. And so I had started learning how to communicate from that. And then Griffin, the person I had the conversation with, really started off my own accountability process. I think for me, it was about that friend. I didn't feel threatened by them. I had a trust with them that if I talked to them, they would still care about me and see me as a person. But it's all part of this much larger context. It wasn't just something about that one particular friendship that made the difference; it was like this whole arc of all these huge things that were happening in my life, all of these breakdowns and changes and new commitments and new understandings that were all developing together that brought me to that point.

Actually, now that I think about it, there was a moment a couple of years before that was really the first time I'd ever broken my silence, but in a very different way. For a few years before that moment, I'd started being exposed to feminist politics and things like that. And for the first time I knew that someone that I loved and cared about was a survivor of rape. I was in kind of a tailspin for awhile trying to figure out how to respond to that. I started seeking out more information about how to support survivors of sexual violence, but it hadn't really been connected to my own life, really. I started to understand the importance of having the violence that was done to you being acknowledged and decided that I needed to step up in my own life. So the real first time that I ever broke my own silence about the harm that I had done was when I talked to the person who I had molested. I approached them and said, "Hey, I did this." But I didn't have the capacity yet to actually engage with it. And so I talked about it with that person and totally broke down and put that person in a position where they were having to worry about caretaking for me, you know, the way that it happens so stereotypically. I gave them some resources, like a rape crisis number to call and things like that. That person asked me if they could tell a particular adult in their life, and I told them, "You can tell whoever you want." But I didn't have the capacity in my life yet to really work through everything that meant, and so I just brought the shutters down and the walls and everything else and cut that part off from my life again. After that, I shut down and I became totally numb, totally blank, for months.

By this point a couple of years later, I had two friends that I ended up talking with, disclosing this to, Griffin and my friend, Stephen (not his real name). And I didn't tell anyone more than that because I was scared, I was scared of everything that would happen. The only thing before Griffin who had mentioned to me about Philly Stands Up, the only thing I'd ever heard in the scene that I was part of there was that all perpetrators should be ridden out of town on a rail. Just like that, along with my own fear of violence that I'd carried for at least a decade by that point, made me really scared to talk about it with anyone else. It was just Griffin and Stephen. Those two were the only ones that I had talked about any of this with for like a year.

The Accountability Process: A Difficult Beginning

Over the course of that year, I ended up finding out that I crossed two more people's boundaries, even though I was committed to doing everything that I needed to do to make sure that I didn't cross people's boundaries. Like the first time it happened, I thought that I was asking for consent, but I wasn't. Or I wasn't able to communicate enough in order to actually have real consent. And so that person, when I crossed that person's boundaries, they confronted me on the spot about it. They were like, "Was that sexual for you?" And I was like "oh damn," but I was like, "Yeah. yeah, it was." And they were like, "I didn't consent to that, and that was a really difficult thing for me because of this and this and this." And then later on, it happened again, when I thought I was doing everything that I needed to have consent.

Part of what was going on at that point, was that I still had a huge amount of guilt and shame and traumatic reactions to being vulnerable. But after the second time that I crossed someone's boundaries, I realized what I was doing wasn't working and I needed to take accountability a step further. I decided to do all of these disclosures to people in my life. When I was doing these disclosures, I wasn't able to be present at all. I was forcing myself to do it, over and over again, and was just like totally emotionally overwhelmed and burnt out. I didn't think about how I was doing them and how that would impact other people. Because I wanted to be 100% sure that I wasn't going to cross anybody's boundaries, I dropped out of everything and just socially isolated myself.

let me drop out of everything. Nobody reached out to me, or as far as I know, people didn't really talk amongst each other or anything. I think it was just like people didn't know what to do with the information, so they didn't do anything. Griffin and Stephen had moved out of town, so they weren't there to support me any more. In that period, the only two people who did reach out to me were people whose boundaries I had crossed. And they were offering support, but I was just like, "No, I can't put you in the situation where you're taking care of me." Because by that point – during the year when I'd just been keeping quiet about things and trying to deal with it by myself, I started reading a lot of zines about survivor support, stories of survivors doing truth-telling and that kind of thing. By that point I'd learned enough to know that there is the pattern of survivors having to emotionally caretake for the people who had done harm to them. So I put up the boundary and I was like, "Thank you, but I can't accept your support."

I was doing all this stuff that was self-punishing, having no compassion for myself – just this combination of a desire to be 100% certain that I wasn't going to be crossing anybody's boundaries and this destructiveness that came out of intense self-hatred. And then it kept going, but I left town. I got way beyond burnt out; I wasn't even running on fumes any more, just willpower. But, I didn't cross anybody's boundaries!

Accountability: My Stages of Change

What were the stages of change for me? The first stage, which isn't one that I would really recommend that people generally include in accountability processes, was the self-destructive one where I would just step back from things. A component of this could be good, but not in a self-punishing, destructive way. But that was really the first step, isolating myself from everything. And then, doing some research and self-education at the same time. I was also going to therapy and was coming to understand my own history better, was able to articulate for myself that really what I needed to do was containment – figure out the boundaries that I needed to assert for myself to make sure that I wasn't going to hurt anybody. It took me a while to understand that because of the ways that people who are socialized male in this society, they're never expected to assert any boundaries on their own sexuality. Both in terms of, "I don't want to do this," but also in terms of actively seeking other people's boundaries, seeking out to understand what other people's boundaries are. So basically that whole first period was just tracking myself, figuring out in what sorts of emotional states I was most likely to cross somebody's boundaries and what it felt like when I was getting there; what sorts of situations were likely to trigger it and also in day-to-day interactions, what kinds of boundaries I needed to be asserting for myself to make sure I wasn't getting close to any of those things.

Then once I had that containment figured out and had the space where I was trusting myself not to be crossing people's boundaries, then there was room in my life to be able to go inwards and start working on self-transformation and healing. Part of that, too, was that I was still crossing people's boundaries on a regular basis. Every time it would happen it would be a crisis for me. Sometimes I would get suicidal. Sometimes I would just be freaking out and paranoid and have huge flare-ups of guilt and shame. So when I was crossing people's boundaries, there wasn't emotional room for that type of transformation and healing to take place. I needed to create this sort of containment not just for the worthy goal of not doing harm but also to make sure that I had the capacity, the emotional space, to be able to work on that healing and transformation. So that was the second phase, when I was working with an accountability group that I sought out for myself. There was a lot of healing and self-transformation.

Now at this point, I feel like I've gotten enough of that worked out that I feel like I'm getting to a place where it becomes an ethical possibility for me to start reaching back outwards again, and starting to work on getting involved in organizing or perhaps have relationships. Because for this whole time I've had a strict rule for myself around abstinence and celibacy, just not getting involved in people because – because I know that any time that would happen, that all these things that I haven't dealt with would come up. And once all that unresolved trauma flares up, then the game is basically lost for me. So now, the potential for having intimate or sexual relationships starts to become more of a reality for me and at this point I feel like I've learned enough about where all that's coming from, and I've healed enough that I can communicate about it enough to understand my limits and boundaries and to reach out at the same time.

Another shift that's been happening, too, is that towards the beginning it was basically like I couldn't have people in my life that I wasn't able to disclose to. There were some people that were either an acquaintance or some sort of person that had power over me that were in my life that I didn't really disclose to. But basically, every person that I was becoming friends with, at some point I'm gonna need to tell them, just as part of the process of being friends. When I decided that I wanted to be friends with them, I would have to tell them. At this point, as I'm getting to the point where I'm putting people less at risk, I feel like I'm gaining back more of the privilege of retaining my anonymity. It's still really important for me to disclose with people, and there are some situations in which I'm probably always going to be disclosing to people really early on. For example, any time I want to get involved in anti-violence work, that's going to be a conversation I have at the outset, before I get involved. But I feel like I'm regaining some of that privilege of anonymity now, too.

Accountability and Healing: Moving through Guilt, Shame and a Traumatic Response to Vulnerability

Now it's been years of seeking support through political groups working on accountability and therapy and staying committed to the process. The things I now understand about healing, in the wholeness of my experience, as both a survivor and a perpetrator, look very different than the ones that I've read about or that people have talked to me about, where it's healing only from surviving abuse or violence.

I think that the three biggest emotions that I've had to contend with in that healing and transformation – and this is something that I've only articulated in the last, like, month of my life – I think the three biggest things that I've had to contend with are guilt, shame and a traumatic response to being vulnerable.

I think those three things – in myself at least – are the sources for the self-hate. It took me a long time trying to figure out even what guilt and shame are. What the emotions are, what they feel like. I would just read those words a lot, but without being able to identify the feeling. One of the things someone told me was that it seems like a lot of my actions are motivated by guilt. And that was strange to me because I never thought that I had felt guilt before. I thought, "Oh, well, I feel remorse but I don't feel guilt." It was years of pondering that before I even understood what guilt was or what it felt like in myself. Once I did, I was like, "Well damn! That's actually just about everything I feel." I just hadn't understood what it felt like before, so I didn't know how to identify it.

Now my understanding of guilt is that it's the feeling of being worthy of punishment. That guiltiness crops up when I become aware of the harm that I've done. I might engage in minimization, trying to make that harm go away, so that I don't feel that guiltiness for it any more, so that I don't feel worthy of being punished. I might try denying it – same sort of thing. Maybe I'm going to try to numb myself so that I don't feel that – so that I don't have that feeling any more. Or maybe I'm going to make that punishment come to me – just being in that place where there's this feeling that the other boot is gonna drop all the time, and that it should drop, trying to bring about a sense of resolution to that sense of impending harm by harming myself.

And another thing that I can see in myself is trying to get out of that sense that harm is gonna come to me by dedicating my life to amending the harm. But the thing is that it's different from compassion, trying to right wrongs because of guilt instead of because of compassion. Doing it through guilt, I notice that I can't assert any boundaries with myself. It's like a compulsion, and it leads me to burnout, Because any time that I stop, that feeling comes back, and it's like, the harm is gonna come. I'm learning how to stay present with that difficult feeling and breathe through it. It helps me a lot.

And then, as far as the shame goes, my understanding of shame is it's like the feeling that I am someone who I cannot stand to be. I was at this workshop where somebody was talking about their experiences with addiction and said, "My whole life, when I was in the middle of this addiction, I had this combination of grandiosity and an inferiority complex." You know, like this sense that I was better than everyone else and that I was the worst scum of the earth. I think when that's the manifestation of shame – that this is who I should be and this is who I really am. When I've seen myself in that kind of place, then usually I'm reacting to the shame either by trying to drown out that awareness of the side of me that's scum, and one of the primary ways that I did that was through finding ways of getting sexual rushes or something like that. And the other thing that I've seen myself do is trying to eradicate that part of me that's the scum. And mostly that happened through fantasies of doing violence to myself, targeted at that part of myself that I hated, that part of myself that I couldn't stand to be, and trying to rip myself into two. I think that's a lot of what was fueling my desire for suicide, too.

One of the things that happened with the accountability process is that once I started talking to people about the things I was most ashamed about, and making it public, then that grandiosity went away. And instead I had to come to terms with this other understanding of myself that wasn't as caught up in illusions of grandeur and instead was this forced humbleness. Like, I'm a person and I'm no better than anybody else. I'm a person and I can also change. So through talking about the things that I'm most ashamed of, that shame became transformative for me. That was a really big aspect of healing for me. And it required a lot of grieving, a lot of loss. And that's something that I was going through during that first year when I was talking with people about it.

As I was talking with other people about it, all these possibilities were closing off in my life. I'll never be able to do this thing now. I'll never be able to have this type of relationship now. The world was less open to me. Like, I can't think of myself in the same way any more. A lot of times I didn't really have the capacity to really face it. But in the moments of insight I had, where I was coming to terms with it, I was really grieving, weeping, over the things that I was losing because of the accountability. That was a big part of healing for me, finding and connecting with and expressing the grief. And also the grief over everything that I had done.

There are still some things that I probably will have to let go of but that I haven't allowed myself to grieve yet, some possibilities that I'm still clinging to. I've found that a lot of time when I get on a power trip and find myself in this controlling sort of attitude, one of the things that resolves that is if I can find a way to grieve. The power trips, the controlling attitudes, tend to happen when I'm trying to control things that are changing. If I can just accept the change and grieve ways that possibilities are changing, then that brings me back. I mean, I've come to terms with a lot of the things that I was grieving when I first started talking with people about it. I'm starting to be able to find ways in my life now of different paths to some of the same things that I wanted for my life, but just paths that have a lot more humility in them. And I think that's one of the really valuable things that accountability has given me. Any time I start that thinking big about myself, then I bring it back to this accountability that I'm doing and It's helped me a lot in just like helping me find ways to stay connected to humility. That's something that I really appreciate about it.

understand that well because I'm just now starting to have some understanding of it. But like I was saying before, because of the violence that I've experienced in my own life, a huge portion of my life has been dedicated to keeping me safe. And for me, those behaviors have been enforced in myself through that same type of self-hate and violence. So if I leave an opening where I'm vulnerable, then that self-hate comes to close it down. If I ever mess up in a way that left me vulnerable, then I find that I start having all these fantasies of doing violence to myself. It's a way of enforcing in myself to never let that happen again. I don't really understand it that well. One of the things that I've been working on more recently is learning how to be open to vulnerability. And that's the last part of self-hate that I've healed the least.

One thing that my history of surviving violence has created is a huge dedication in my life to making sure that I never allow myself to be vulnerable. In the past, it's been utterly impossible for me to allow people to see that I'm any sort of sexual being and has also made it impossible to talk about any sort of like emotions of importance. Or just asking for consent, there's a sort of vulnerability that's involved with that. So this created this wall that set me up to make it really, really hard for me to have consensual sexual interactions with anybody. In my family, we had no communication about anything whatsoever. I didn't have any models around communication. Now that I'm in a world where communication is possible, it's hard for me to convey to people what it's like to be in a world where that's not possible. For a huge portion of my life, there wasn't even a glimmer of possibility. These things that I was feeling, they weren't in the realm of talkability. It meant that I couldn't ever be present enough with the emotions to learn how to intervene. Any time they would come up, I would just try to eradicate them with all this violent self-imagery, without even realizing what I was doing.

Accountability as a Gift

I have a friend that's been involved in a lot of accountability work, and he's insisted to me that what I'm doing isn't accountability because there's not survivors somewhere who are issuing a list of demands or that kind of thing. But for me, that's only one aspect of accountability. There's another aspect that's being accountable to myself, making sure that I'm living the values that are important to me in the world. Ultimately, accountability for me is a commitment to do what I need to do to make sure that I don't repeat those patterns, that they stop with me. Part of that has been the work around creating boundaries for myself. Part of that has been the healing and transformation. And part of it is also engaging with the world, to not see it as an individual thing, but to see myself as part of a social struggle. I need to be engaged with the world to be part of ending all of this sexual violence that's everywhere.

The accountability has this gift of humility. One of the things that is really valuable for me about that humility is the amount of compassion that it's allowed me to have for other people. I still have superiority complexes, but nowhere near like I did. At this point in my life, I'm able to understand myself as being the same kind of human as so many other people. I don't put myself on a different level from them. And so I feel like I have a much greater ability to understand people's struggle and pain, and to learn from it, and to love people, coming out of that compassion and shared struggle.

That ability for real, authentic love is something I never had. I thought that love was this obsessive thing. And when I realized that I needed to stop that, I had this moment of grieving and loss and doubt, because I thought, "Well, if I stop this, will I ever feel love again?" It required this huge shift. Once it quieted down, once I stopped it, then the whole landscape was just silent. It took me awhile to re-tune my hearing so that it wasn't just the roar of this obsession, but that I could hear the birds, and the insects, and the breezes. From there, learn a sort of love that's based in resilience, and shared commitment, and sacrifice. So that's been a real gift that it's given me.

Another thing too, is that I can bear to live with myself. I never could before. Most of the time I'm okay being in my own skin. It's been huge – even though I went through some extremely dark and difficult periods where the basin of depression that I'd lived in for so long in my life dropped into an abyss, Coming out of that abyss, through a continuing commitment to accountability, it's like the first time in my life when I'm starting to feel I'm free of this sort of depression and this crippling anxiety and paranoia. I have emotional capacity now; like I can feel things. I'm still not in a place where joy is a big part of my life, but it seems possible now. Through all this grieving and everything that I've done, I've also had a couple moments of clarity and lightness that I'd never experienced before in my life.

I think something else that has been a real gift for me, in terms of accountability, is the possibility for having lasting intimate relationships with people, whether sexually or not sexually. And having some capacity for pleasure – sexual pleasure, even, because before it was so caught up in shame and guilt and feeling triggered that I only ever felt horrible. Now I don't feel like I'm consigned to that for the rest of my life. I feel that there's a possibility of being liberated from it.

(This story is in Section 4.F. Taking Accountability to show one person's experience of coming to terms with both surviving and doing sexual harm and the process of accountability and healing.)

(This story is available at the StoryTelling & Organizing Project (STOP) website at www.stopviolenceeveryday.org.)

Story G. A Small Story (*He Korero Iti*)

We live in a town, but many of my husband's extended family (whanau) live in the valley where he grew up about 40 kilometres away. My husband and his brother are renowned for a number of things – one being how they extend the life of their cars and vans using highly technical items like string and wire – another how they share these vehicles for a variety of tasks such as moving furniture or transporting relatives, building materials, tractor parts, traditional herbal medicines (rongoa), eels, vegetables, dogs, and pigs (dead or alive).They are renowned for being people of the people, the ones to call on in times of trouble and death, the ones who will solve the problem and make the plan. They travel to and from town, to the coast to dive for sea food, to endless meetings, to visit extended family (whanau) - along the many kilometres of dirt roads in and around the valley, through flood or dust depending on the season in those patched up, beat up, prized cars.

There are a number of things to know about the valley - one is that the last 33 children in the world of their small sub-tribe (hapu ririki) to grow up and be educated on their own lands go to school here, despite government efforts to close the school. Another is that the valley is known to outsiders and insiders as 'patu wahine' – literally meaning to 'beat women' and this is not said as a joke. The mountain for this valley is named as the doorway spirits pass through on their way to their final departure from this life. This valley is also the valley where my husband and his siblings were beaten at school for speaking their first language. It is the valley their mother sent them to so they would be safe from their father – back to her people. It is where they milked cows, pulled a plough, fed pigs but often went hungry, and were stock whipped, beaten and worse.

My brother-in-law still lives in the valley, in a group of houses next to the school. So it's no surprise that one of our cars would be parked by these houses – right by where the children play. Perhaps also not a surprise that while playing that time old international game of rock throwing our eight year old nephew shattered the back window of the car. If I'd been listening I probably would have heard the 'oh' and 'ah' of the other children that accompanied the sound of glass breaking from town, and if I'd been really tuned in I would have heard the rapid, frightened heart beat of 'that boy' as well.

His mother is my husband's cousin – and she was on the phone to us right away. She was anxious to assure us 'that boy' would get it when his father came home. His father is a big man with a pig hunter's hands who hoists his pigs onto a meat hook unaided. He is man of movement and action, not a man for talking. Those hands would carry all the force of proving that he was a man who knew how to keep his children in their place. Beating 'that boy' would be his way of telling us that he had also learned his own childhood lessons well.

So before he got home we burned up the phone lines – sister to sister, cousin to cousin, brother –in-law to sister-in-law, wife to husband, brother to brother. This was because my husband and his brother know that there are some lessons you are taught as a child that should not be passed on. The sound of calloused hand on tender flesh, the whimpers of watching sisters, the smell of your own fear, the taste of your own blood and sweat as you lie in the dust – useless, useless, better not born. This is a curriculum like no other. A set of lessons destined to repeat unless you are granted the grace of insight and choose to embrace new learning.

So when the father of 'that boy' came home and heard the story of the window 'that boy' was protected by our combined love (aroha) and good humor, by the presence of a senior uncle, by invitations to decide how to get the window fixed in the shortest time for the least money. Once again phone calls were exchanged with an agreement being made on appropriate restitution. How a barrel of diesel turns into a car window is a story for another time.

Next time my husband drove into the valley it was to pick up the car, and 'that boy' was an anxious witness to his arrival. My husband also has very big hands, hands that belong to a man who has spent most of his life outdoors. These were the hands that reached out to 'that boy' to hug not hurt.

A lot of bad things still happen in the valley, but more and more they are being named and resisted. Many adults who learned their early lessons there will never return. For people of the land (tangata whenua) this is profound loss – our first identifiers on meeting are not our own names but those of our mountains, rivers, subtribe (hapu) and tribe (iwi). To be totally separate from these is a dislocation of spirit for the already wounded. This is only a small story that took place in an unknown valley, not marked on many maps. When these small stories are told and repeated so our lives join and connect, when we choose to embrace new learning and use our 'bigness' to heal not hurt then we are growing grace and wisdom on the earth.

Di Grennell

Whangarei, Aotearoa-New Zealand

(This story in both versions is in Section 4.G. Working Together to show how a whole family pulls together to protect a young boy from a beating by his father.)

Glossary

Whanau – extended family group

Rongoa – traditional herbal medicines

Hapu ririki – small sub-tribe

Patu – hit, strike, ill treat, subdue

Wahine – woman/women

Aroha – love, concern for

Tangata whenua – people of the land

Hapu – subtribe

Iwi -tribe

5.3. CREATIVE INTERVENTIONS ANTI-OPPRESSION POLICY (ANTI-DISCRIMINATION/ANTI-HARASSMENT)

The following is the Anti-Oppression Policy used by Creative Interventions to help to create an organizational culture that supports accountability. This includes expectations that people disclose histories of violence and do no further harm. It also creates expectations that harm that does take place within the organization or by people that are affiliated with the organization will be addressed using the kind of accountability values and processes that are in this Toolkit.

We found that many organizations have no policies in place to deal with situations of violence or harm -- or that policies are there in paper only with little thought given to how this can help strengthen organizational cultures.

We encourage organizations, groups, families, friendship networks think about what kind of environment you want to uphold regarding harm and violence and that you discuss together what values and practices you want to have. We also encourage you to think about processes that do not necessarily jump to banning, punishment or criminal justice without thinking about how you can rather encourage disclosure and can provide support to survivors and support accountability for people doing harm.

This is just one example that may be helpful in creating an environment challenging violence and supporting accountability.

CREATIVE INTERVENTIONS ANTI-OPPRESSION POLICY (ANTI-DISCRIMINATION/ANTI-HARASSMENT)

Commitment to Social Justice and Equality

Creative Interventions is an organization promoting social justice and equality on the basis of gender, race, ethnicity, class, immigration status, education, national origin, religion, age and physical ability.

Freedom from Oppressive, Demeaning, Degrading, Discriminating, Harassing, Sexualized Attitudes/Behavior

As such, Creative Interventions and its personnel agree that as an organization and as individuals, we are committed to the following policies:

1. Non-oppressive work/organizational conditions due to gender, race, ethnicity, class, immigration status, education, national origin, religion, age and physical ability including:
    a. Freedom from demeaning or degrading gesture, look, talk or touch within the work/ organizational environment;
    b. Freedom from sexual or otherwise inappropriately intimate gesture, look, talk or touch within the work/organizational environment;
    c. Freedom from assignment to demeaning or degrading tasks due to gender, race, ethnicity, class, immigration status, education, national origin, religion, age and physical ability.
2. Commitment to deal collectively and positively with any violations of these freedoms if they occur including:
    a. Organizational process supported by the Executive Director and/or Board of Directors in line with the recommendations of the Incite! Gender Oppression, Abuse, Violence: Community Accountability within the Progressive People of Color Movement Document (Incite!, July 2005), Taking Risks: Implementing Grassroots Community Accountability Strategies and the Creative Interventions Toolkit: A Practical Guide to Stop Interpersonal Violence.
3. Commitment to the development of education to promote respectful attitudes and behavior throughout the organization and the prevention of violation of these expectations.

Process for Addressing Violations of Anti-Oppression Policy

If any individual or group of individuals feels that this anti-oppression policy has been violated, they have the right and responsibility to address this to the Executive Director and/or Board of Directors in verbal or written form and should expect a response as to next steps within two (2) weeks of the issue being raised.

I have read and agree to the above:

Signature	Date
Printed Name	CI Person Signature

Community-Based Responses to Interpersonal Violence

Day One: Understanding Interpersonal Violence

OVERVIEW:

— PRIMARY USE —

This workshop is designed to provide participants with (Day 1) information about interpersonal violence and state violence, and (Day 2) tools/principles for practicing community based approaches to interpersonal violence

— GOALS —

- Participants will draw clear understanding of the different types of interpersonal violence and state violence
- Participants will develop analysis about intersections of state and interpersonal violence in order to understand set the framework for practicing community based responses to violence.

— AUDIENCE —

Anyone open to learning the basics of community based responses to interpersonal violence.

GETTING STARTED:

— AGENDA —

1. Welcome and Review Agenda & Objectives & Housekeeping	10 mins
2. Introductions/Ice Breaker	10 mins
3. What is Violence?	10 mins
4. What is Interpersonal Violence?	15 mins
5. Examples of Interpersonal Violence	20 mins
6. Interpersonal Violence is related Power	40 mins
7. LUNCH	45 mins
8. Statistics Game with State Violence	45 mins
9. Small Group Discussion	15 mins
10. Large Group Discussion	20 mins
11. Resources	5 mins
12. Closing and Evals	5 mins
Total Time	**4hrs**

— MATERIALS NEEDED —

Group agreements on easel paper (unless they will be created with group)
Pens and markers
Blank easel papers
Slips of State Violence Statistics (pg. 7-8)

Charts with list of questions (Types of Interpersonal Violence, small and large group questions)
Power and Control Wheel handout
Blank Index Cards and Evaluation Symbol Chart
Tape

Facilitator Tips

Prepare flip charts with list before you begin. Prepare Statistic Slips on pg. 7-9 and keep an answer sheet for accuracy. Prepare Evaluation Symbol Chart.

DIRECTIONS:

1. Welcome and Review Agenda & Objectives

10 mins

Welcome
Logistics: Housekeeping (the gender neutral restrooms, lunch, interpreter ethics, and a note on pronouns, scent sensitivity, accessibility for people with disabilities etc.)
Group Expectations/Group Agreements with Participants
Review Agenda and Goals
Take care of yourself: The topic of violence is very close to many of us, today we will be speaking in detail about interpersonal violence and if for whatever reason you feel like you'd like to take a break please feel free to do so at anytime during the presentation.

2. Icebreaker/Team Building

10 mins

Do a go-around and ask participants to:

1.) **Write their name vertically on a piece of paper**
2.) **With each letter in your name, write the reason why knowledge about interpersonal violence is important to you**
3.) **Have participants move around the room introducing themselves to at least 3 people and have them share their responses**

Example:
seXual abuse is prevalent in my community
Although there are services available, I want to be able to support my friends
Not only has sexual and domestic violence been a part of my current community, I am a survivor
Demanding longer prison sentences for people who cause harm is not working
Responding in a way that nurtures the well being of queer people of color is important to me
Ally to grassroots political approaches to ending violence

3. Defining Violence

10 mins

Ask Participants to define violence. If participants have trouble give examples to get them started.

What is violence?

Facilitator Note: Keep this list up somewhere in the room so you can continue to reference this definition. This definition can include internalized violence, academic violence, state violence, ideological violence, etc.

4. Defining Interpersonal Violence

15 mins

Facilitators should ask question jot down answers and share the CI Toolkit's types of Interpersonal Violence.

What is interpersonal violence?

In addition to the participant's definition, share the below list:

Types of Interpersonal Violence

- Most often takes place within a relationship, intimate partner, family, dating, friendship, acquaintances, co-workers, neighbors, members of organizations
- Domestic violence or Intimate partner violence that takes place within an intimate relationship such as marriage, domestic partnership, dating relationship, former relationship
- Family Violence that can include domestic violence but can also extend to children, parents, grandchildren, grandparents, other family members and others who may be very close to family like family friends, guardian, caretakers, and so on
- Sexual violence that includes unwanted sexual attitudes, touch or actions such as sexual assault, rape, sexual harassment, molestation, child sexual abuse,
- Child abuse any kind of abuse against children
- Elder abuse any kind of abuse against elderly people

Are there any others we didn't name?

5. Examples of Interpersonal VIolence

20 mins

Because these relationships of violence may also include relationships of love, companionship, friendship, loyalty and also dependence and even survival, this can make it more confusing to understand dynamics of violence and also to change them. We look at interpersonal violence as any form of abuse, harm, violence, or violation taking place between two or more individuals. It can include forms of violence used to harm someone, keep someone under one's control, or get someone to do whatever one wants them to do. The violence can be:

(Have this already written up and share the following)
The Violence can be:

- **Physical, emotional, sexual, economic, or may take some other form**
- **Isolation, stalking, using someone's vulnerability due to discrimination against them**
- **Using someone's vulnerability against them**

•Using one's own vulnerability to manipulate or control someone or excuse one's own use of violence
•Using things someone values against them- outing of sexuality or work in order to damage someone's reputation at work in community or relationships or threat of harming others or pets

You can highlight any of the examples above by asking the participants or sharing some examples. Some examples are listed below.

What are some examples of using one's own vulnerability to manipulate or excuse one's own use of violence?

Some examples include (only state those that you think may be helpful): Physical (pushing, slapping, hitting, beating, kicking, pulling hair, holding down, locking into a room or space, weapons), Emotional (name calling, put downs, humiliation, always being right, or crazy making), sexual ((includes making someone participate in sexual activities of any kind against their will or without their acknowledgment), Economic (withholding financial info from partner, controlling income against will of partner, gambling, abuse of credit cards, destroying one's property), Isolation (making it difficult for someone to make friends, keep up relationships, see one's family, go to work, go outside the home, talk to other people, or make phone calls), Stalking (sending/monitoring text messages, emails, or calling repeatedly, following someone home, workplace, school or other locations, leaving notes/messages in a harassing manner), Vulnerability (theatening to call immigration enforcement authorities, taking advantage based on the person's gender, sexual orientation, race, class or economic situation, age, education, ability to speak English, physical or mental ability or disability), Vulnerability (uses one's own lack of power in society as a justification for power and control of others, sometimes using one's own abuse during childhood as an excuse for violence, sometimes using self-harm suicide, driving recklessly, overdose, cutting),

---

6. Interpersonal Violence is related to Power

40 mins

Although we know violence can come in many forms and look different, violence is often used in a way that makes one person have power and control over another. Sometimes we may think that violence as anger, passion, or loss of control. But we find that interpersonal violence is often used to maintain power and control over their partners.

Hand out Power and Control Wheel and discuss as a group the below list of patterns of power and control:
One sided
Attempts to control/dominate/coerce
Takes advantage of vulnerability
Exists in a pattern
Calculated and planned
Exists in a cycle
May increase over time
Isolation

Often we think of mutual abuse, but what we have to rememeber is that this is a myth and after observing patterns in a relationship we can see that someone's life is always getting smaller and resources (friends, money, family etc) are always becoming more and more limited and controlled.

Some things we may want to recognize is how interpersonal violence uses vulnerabilities to abuse. What are some of these?

Write these down as the group dictates them to you and offer the additional list if necessary.

–Gender/sex

-Race
-Class/income level
-Level of education
-Immigration status
-Sexual orientation
-Age
-Physical of mental disability
-Occupation (in underground economies)
-Religion
-Political affiliation
-Emotionally, financially or otherwise dependent on others for survival
-What country or region they are from (especially if under current or historical colonial control)

Facilitator Transition: *Many people live at the intersections of many of these categories/oppressions. For example: Women of color live at the dangerous intersections of sexism, racism and other oppressions. In this case, interpersonal violence is not simple a tool of patriarchal control, but it is also a tool of racism and colonialism. That is, colonial relationships are themselves gendered and sexualized and are most often exercised through the state. After lunch, we will participate in an activity that will show us, through statistics, how the state contributes to further marginalize survivors and people who abuse within the context of interpersonal violence.*

6. LUNCH Break

45mins

7. Statistics Mix and Match

45 mins

In this section, you will need to have prepared the statistics slips on pg. 7-9. You will find that each statistic has a partial statement and answer. Cut them separately and when passing them out make sure that the answer and partial statement are somewhere among the group. Each participant will be asked to roam the room looking for the "match" to their partial statistic. You, as the facilitator, should have an answer sheet with the correct answers so that you can check for accuracy.

Pass out statistics slips and give the participants enough time for each one to find their match. Once this is completed. Have each duo/match share their statistic with the group. While each duo/match shares their statistic, make sure they are in fact correct with your answer sheet and ask if there are any comments or questions.

Facilitator's Transition: *We are not sharing these statistics to bring you down or make you feel hopeless, these statistics are vital to our understanding of the intersections of state and interpersonal violence. These intersections help us understand just how important it is for us to develop creative interventions to interpersonal violence that do not prioritize 911, criminalization or prisons. For a few minutes lets discuss in small groups the impacts of this violence on our communities, survivors, and people who cause harm.*

8. SMALL GROUP DISCUSSION about impact of violence

15 mins

Break up into small groups and ask each group to answer the following questions:

(These questions should be written up)
- **How might interpersonal/state violence hurt/impact close friends, family and community?**
- **How might the interpersonal/state violence hurt/impact the survivor?**
- **How might the interpersonal/state violence hurt/impact the person doing harm?**

If difficult for groups to answer, give participants a simple scenario. After a 10 minutes of this discussion in small groups ask them to move back to the large group and ask for informal report back of a few of these questions.

9. LARGE GROUP DISCUSSION

20 mins

Even as we recognize the impact of interpersonal/state violence it's still difficult for us to recognize interpersonal violence or state violence because we sometimes don't want to deal with it//face it. But by looking at our personal biases we can be more responsive in our lives to interpersonal violence. Here a few questions I'd like for us to loosely discuss before we close the workshop today.

- **How might our personal biases and experiences influence how we understand violence?**
- **How does your discipline and the institution you are a part of strengthen/uphold violence?**
- **How might we be more responsive in our positions/lives to the needs of people who cause harm, survivors, communities who experience interpersonal violence?**

10. Resources

5 mins

Share local resources for dv/sa and other online resources for learning more in depth about interpersonal violence.

Facilitator's Transition: *Great. We'll we are at the end of our workshop session. We hope you enjoyed it and that you will join us for DAY TWO of this workshop. Today's workshop helps to lay the framework for using community based responses to violence.*

11. Short Eval and Closing

5 mins

Put up evaluation symbol chart and pass out index cards.

Before you leave today please fill out an index card with the following symbols and your responses. THANK YOU and see you for the next session of WORK IT OUT!

AND

Pass out index cards and ask participants to write their thoughts within the following four categories:

 **(a key learning)**

 **(change/improvement to session)**

 **(any question)**

 **(something you liked)**

Pick up Index Cards and Close.

Statistics Mix and Match

You will find that each statistic has a partial statement and answer. Cut them separately and when passing them out make sure that the answer and partial statement are somewhere among the group. Each participant will be asked to roam the room looking for the "match" to their partial statistic. You, as the facilitator, should have an answer sheet with the correct answers so that you can check for accuracy.

Pass out statistics slips and give the participants enough time for each one to find their match. Once this is completed. Have each duo/match share their statistic with the group. While each duo/match shares their statistic, make sure they are in fact correct with your answer sheet and ask if there are any comments or questions.

Note: Read the statistics and choose enough for your group and the ones you feel are more relevant or find relevant statistics to substitute the ones below.

Border Statistics

1. Latinos and Black people compromise 43% of those searched through customs even though they compromise ______________________________.

they compromise 24% of the population (Bhattacharjee 2001).

2. American Friends Service Committee documented over 346 reports of gender violence ______________________________.

on the US Mexico border by Border Patrol from 1993-5 and this is just the report of one agency.

3. Immigration officials often rape and sexually violate immigrant women in exchange for ______________________________.

crossing into the U.S. and for green cards.

4. Policies like Secure Communities (S-Comm) increase the collaboration between federal immigration law enforcement and local police and this endangers immigrant survivors ______________________________.

because they are less likely to call police for fear of deportation.

5. Queer people of color crossing the borders experience heightened levels of scrutiny and violence if they are gender non-conforming. Until 1990, ______________________.

queer and LGBT immigrants were not allowed into the U.S. This has significantly impacted how "deviant sexuality" is policed today on the border.

6.An undocumented woman from Tucson calls the police for help in domestic violence situation. Under current mandatory arrest laws, ______________________________.

the police must arrest someone on a domestic violence call. Because the police cannot find the batterer they arrest her and have her deported.

Criminalization of Women of Color and Queers

7. A Black homeless woman calls the police because she has been a victim of group rape ______________________________.

and the police arrest her for prostitution (Chicago)

8. A Black woman calls the police when her husband who is battering her accidentally sets fire to their apartment. ______________________________.

She is arrested for the fire (NYC).

9. Over 40% of women are generally in prison as a direct or indirect result of ______________________________.

gender violence. (Jurik & Winn 1990)

10.When police are called to intervene in queer or LGBT relationship violence, police often use sexist and homophobic stereotypes to determine to who arrest and sometimes arrest both parties under the "mutual combat" theory. They often believe "women cannot be abusers and men cannot be abused." ______________________________.

Reports of mis-arrests rose by 120 % in Los Angeles. (NCAVP, 2008)

11.Gender non-conforming people "consistently report experiencing extreme disrespect when attempting
________________________.

to access legal services, having their cases rejected or ignored by the agencies they turn to, and feeling so unwelcome and humiliated that they often do not return for services." (Attorney Dean Spade, 22)

Welfare

12. In New Orleans and now in more than 17 states, there has been an increase in legislative attacks on women,
________________________.

who are often survivors of interpersonal violence, seeking state support must consent to drug testing in order to be eligible for TANF/ state assistance.

13. Welfare reform policies contribute to rising levels of housing insecurity and homelessness. This causes many survivors of interpersonal violence to ________________________.

stay with their abusive partners in order to generate more income.

14.The state has forced families to face the impossible choice of ________________________.

"choosing" shelter/feeding/childcare or being safe from their abusive partners.

15. Approximately 37% of women and 28% of men in prison had ________________.

monthly incomes of less than $600 prior to their arrest.

Incarceration

16. The War on Drugs has incarcerated ________________________.

thousands of survivors of rape and abuse.

17. Since 1980 the number of people in women's prison ________________________.

rose almost twice as fast as the growth of the number of men imprisoned.

18. Many women, men and children are raped and sexually exploited by prison guards as well as other inmates while in prison. ________________________.
The number of assaults is 3 to 4 times higher than the number outside prison walls.

19. One study of 6 male prisons in California in 2007 found that 67% of the respondents who identified as LGBT reported having been sexually assaulted by another inmate during their imprisonment,
________________________.

a rate that is 15 times higher than the rest of the prison population. (Journal of Interpersonal Violence 21, no. 12 2006)

20. 30% of women prisoners are African American and 16% are Latinas. Black women
________________________.

are incarcerated 4 times the rate that white women are.

21. More than half of the women in state prisons have been abused, ______________________________.

47% physically abused and 39% sexually abused (with many being survivors of both types of abuse)

22. In California alone, there are 600 women in prison for killing ______________________________.

their abusers in self-defense. (Prison Activist Resource Center) Average prison terms are twice as long for killing husbands as for killing wives.

5.5 CARA TAKING RISKS: IMPLEMENTING GRASSROOTS COMMUNITY ACCOUNTABILITY STRATEGIES

The following is a piece written by a collective of women of color from Communities Against Rape and Abuse (CARA): Alisa Bierria, Onion Carrillo, Eboni Colbert, Xandra Ibarra, Theryn Kigvamasud'Vashti, and Shale Maulana. This gives principles and case studies based upon years of CARA's experience organizing against sexual violence and against state violence.

CARA TAKING RISKS: IMPLEMENTING GRASSROOTS COMMUNITY ACCOUNTABILITY STRATEGIES

Sexual violence is often treated as a hyper-delicate issue that can only be addressed by trained professionals such as law enforcement or medical staff. Survivors are considered "damaged," pathologized beyond repair. Aggressors are perceived of as "animals," unable to be redeemed or transformed.[1] These extreme attitudes alienate every-day community members – friends and family of survivors and[2] aggressors – from participating in the critical process of supporting survivors and holding aggressors accountable for abusive behavior. Ironically, survivors overwhelmingly turn to friends and family for support, safety, and options for accountability strategies.

Communities Against Rape and Abuse (CARA), a grassroots anti-rape organizing project in Seattle, has worked with diverse groups who have experienced sexual

1 For the purposes of this article, we use the word "aggressor" to refer to a person who has committed an act of sexual violence (rape, sexual harassment, coercion, etc.) on another person. Our use of the word "aggressor" is not an attempt to weaken the severity of rape. In our work of defining accountability outside of the criminal system, we try not to use criminal-based vocabulary such as "perpetrator," "rapist," or "sex predator." We also use pronouns interchangeably throughout the article.

2 Golding, Jacqueline M., et al. "Social Support Sources Following Assault," Journal of Community Psychology, 17:92-107, January 1989. This paper is just one example of research showing that survivors are much more likely to access friends and family for support than they are to access police or rape crisis centers. Golding's research reveals that 59% of survivors surveyed reported that they disclosed their assault to friends and relatives, while 10.5% reported to police and 1.9% reported to rape crisis centers. Interestingly, Golding's research also asserts that survivors rated rape crisis centers as most helpful and law enforcement as least helpful. She suggests that, since friends or relatives are the most frequent contact for rape victim disclosure, efforts should focus on enhancing and supporting this informal intervention.

violence within their communities to better understand the nature of sexual violence and rape culture, identify and nurture community values that are inconsistent with rape and abuse, and develop community-based strategies for safety, support, and accountability. Using some general guidelines as the bones for each community-based process, we work with survivors and their communities to identify their own unique goals, values, and actions that add flesh to their distinct safety/accountability model. In the following paper, we discuss these community accountability guidelines and provide three illustrative examples of real community-based models developed by activists here in Seattle.

Because social networks can vary widely on the basis of values, politics, cultures, and attitudes, we have found that having a one-size-fits-all community accountability model is not a realistic or respectful way to approach an accountability process. However, we have also learned that there are some important organizing principles that help to maximize the safety and integrity of everyone involved – including the survivor, the aggressor, and other community members. An accountability model must be creative and flexible enough to be a good fit for the uniqueness of each community's needs, while also being disciplined enough to incorporate some critical guidelines as the framework for its strategy.1 Below is a list of ten guidelines that we have found important and useful to consider:

CARA'S ACCOUNTABILITY PRINCIPLES

1. Recognize the humanity of everyone involved. It is imperative that the folks who organize the accountability process are clear about recognizing the humanity of all people involved including the survivor, the person(s) who has committed the sexual assault, and the community involved. This can be easier said than done! It is natural, and even healthy, to feel rage at the aggressor for assaulting another person, especially a person that we care about. However, it is critical that we are grounded in a value of recognizing the complexity of each person, including ourselves. Given the needs and values of a particular community, an accountability process for the aggressor can be confrontational, even angry, but it should not be de-humanizing.

   Dehumanization of aggressors also contributes to a larger context of oppression

---

1 Borrowing from philosopher Cornel West, we can call this approach of simultaneous improvisation and structure a "jazzy approach." Much like jazz music, a community accountability process can incorporate many different and diverse components that allow for the complexity of addressing sexual violence while also respecting the need for some stability and careful planning. Also, like jazz music, an accountability process is not an end point or a finite thing, but a living thing that continues to be created. Our understanding of community accountability ultimately transcends the idea of simply holding an abusive community member responsible for his or her actions, but also includes the vision of the community itself being accountable for supporting a culture that allows for sexual violence. This latter accountability process truly necessitates active and constant re-creating and re-affirming a community that values liberation for everyone.

for everyone. For example, alienation and dehumanization of the offending person increases a community's vulnerability to repeatedly being targeted for disproportional criminal justice oppression through heightening the "monster-ness" of another community member. This is especially true for marginalized communities (such as people of color, people with disabilities, poor people, and queer people) who are already targeted by the criminal system because of their "other-ness." When one person in our community is identified as a "monster," that "monsterization" is often generalized to everyone in the community. This generalization can even take place by other members of the marginalized community because of internalized oppression.[1]

Also, dehumanizing the aggressor undermines the process of accountability for the whole community. If we separate ourselves from aggressors by stigmatizing them as monsters then we fail to see how any of us could become or have been aggressors of violence or how we have contributed to a context that allows such violence to happen. By not seeing the humanity of the aggressor, as well as the aggressor's support network, we miss how the community may have played a role in not creating a sustainable measure of support and accountability that may reduce future acts of violence.

2 Prioritize the self-determination of the survivor. Self-determination is the ability to make decisions according to one's own free will and self-guidance without outside pressure or coercion. When a person is sexually assaulted, his sense of self-determination has been profoundly undermined. Therefore, the survivor's values and needs should be prioritized, recognized and respected. The survivor should not be objectified or minimized as a symbol of an idea instead of an actual person. (Remember, respect the humanity of everyone.) It is critical to take into account the survivor's vision for accountability which can be the foundation for the implementation and vision for when, why, where and how the aggressor will be held accountable. It is also important to recognize that the survivor may not want to lead or orchestrate the plan. The survivor must have the right to choose to lead and convey the plan or choose not to be part of the organizing at all. The survivor should also have the opportunity to identify who will be involved in this process. Some survivors may find it helpful for friends or someone from outside of the community to help assess the process and help facilitate the accountability process with their community. To promote explicit shared responsibility, the survivor and his community can also negotiate and communicate boundaries and limits around what roles each person is willing to play and ensure that others perform their roles in accordance with clear expectations and goals.

---

1 We define "internalized oppression," as the process of a person that belongs to a marginalized and oppressed group accepting, promoting, and justifying beliefs of inferiority and lack of value about her group and, perhaps, herself.

3. Identify a simultaneous plan for safety and support for the survivor as well as others in the community. Safety is complex and goes far beyond keeping your doors locked, walking in well-lit areas, and carrying a weapon or a cell phone. Remember that the "plan" in "safety plan" should be a verb, not a noun, and requires us to continue thinking critically about how our accountability process will impact our physical and emotional well being[1]. Consider questions such as these: How will the aggressor react when he is confronted about his abusive behavior? How can we work together to de-mechanize the aggressor's strategies? Remember, one does not have control over the aggressor's violence, but you do have control over how you can prepare and respond to it.

   Violence can escalate when an aggressor is confronted about her behavior. Threats of revenge, suicide, stalking, threats to out you about personal information or threats to create barriers for you to work, eat, sleep, or simply keep your life private may occur. The aggressor may also use intimidation to frighten the survivor and others. She may use privilege such as class, race, age, or socio-political status to hinder your group from organizing. While planning your offense, organizers must also prepare to implement a defense in case of aggressor retaliation. If your situation allows you to do so, organizers can also alert other members of the community about your plan and prepare them for how the abuser may react.

   Organizers must also plan for supporting the survivor and themselves. It is easy to become so distracted with the accountability process that we forget that someone was assaulted and needs our emotional support. It is likely that there is more than one survivor of sexual assault and/or domestic violence in any one community of people. Other survivors within the organizing group may be triggered during the community accountability process. Organizing for accountability should not be just about the business of developing a strategy to address the aggressor's behavior, but also about creating a loving space for community building and real care for others. Organizers should also try to be self aware about their own triggers and create a plan for support for themselves as well. Sometimes it's helpful to have a separate group of friends that can function as a support system for the survivor as well as for the organizers.

4. Carefully consider the potential consequences of your strategy. Before acting on any plan, always make sure that your group has tried to anticipate all of the potential outcomes of your strategy. Holding someone accountable for abuse is difficult and the potential responses from the aggressor are numerous. For example, if you choose to use the media to publicize the aggressor's behavior, you might think

---

1 Thank you to the Northwest Network of Bisexual, Trans, Lesbian, and Gay Survivors of Abuse for asserting the verb in "safety plan" and sharing that important distinction with the rest of us!

of the consequences of the safety and privacy of the survivor and the organizers involved. But you will also have to consider the chances of the media spinning the story in a way that is not supportive to your values, or the possibility that the story outrages another person outside of your community so much that he decides to respond by physically threatening the aggressor, or the chance that the media will give the aggressor a forum to justify his abusive behavior. This need to "what-if" an accountability strategy is not meant to discourage the process, but to make sure that organizers are careful to plan for possible outcomes. Your first plan may need to be shifted, modified, and tweaked as you go. You may find that you are working to hold this person accountable for a longer period of time than you expected. There may be a split in your community because of the silence surrounding abuse, especially sexual and domestic violence. You may feel that you are further isolating the survivor and yourselves from the community. Think of the realistic outcomes of your process to hold someone accountable in your community. Your process may not be fully successful or it may yield prosperous results. Whatever your outcome you may find that you are more prepared and skilled to facilitate a process of holding others in your community or circle of friends accountable in the future.

5. Organize collectively. It is not impossible to organize an accountability process by one's self, but it is so much more difficult. There are many reasons why organizing collectively with a group of community members is usually a better strategy. A group of people is more likely to do a better job of thinking critically about strategies because there are more perspectives and experiences at work. Organizers are less likely to burn out quickly if more than one or two people can share the work as well as emotionally support one another. It is much harder to be targeted by backlash when there is a group of people acting in solidarity with one another. A group of people can hold each other accountable to staying true to the group's shared values. Also, collective organizing facilitates strong community building which undermines isolation and helps to prevent future sexual violence.

6. Make sure everyone in the accountability-seeking group is on the same page with their political analysis of sexual violence. Sometimes members of a group that is organizing for accountability are not working with the same definition of "rape," the same understanding of concepts like "consent" or "credibility," or the same assumption that rape is a manifestation of oppression. In order for the group's process to be sustainable and successful, organizers must have a collective understanding of what rape is and how rape functions in our culture. For example, what if the aggressor and his supporters respond to the organizers' call for accountability by demanding that the survivor provide proof that she was indeed assaulted or else they will consider her a liar, guilty of slander? Because of our legal structure that is based on the idea of "innocent until proven guilty,"

rape culture that doubts the credibility of women in general, it is a common tactic to lay the burden of proof on the survivor.[1] If the group had a feminist, politicized understanding of rape, they might be able to anticipate this move as part of a larger cultural phenomenon of discrediting women when they assert that violence has been done to them.

This process pushes people to identify rape as a political issue and articulate a political analysis of sexual violence. A shared political analysis of sexual violence opens the door for people to make connections of moments of rape to the larger culture in which rape occurs. A consciousness of rape culture prepares us for the need to organize beyond the accountability of an individual aggressor. We also realize we must organize for accountability and transformation of institutions that perpetuate rape culture such as the military, prisons, and the media.

Lastly, when the aggressor is a progressive activist, a rigorous analysis of rape culture can be connected to that individual's own political interests. A political analysis of rape culture can become the vehicle that connects the aggressor's act of violence to the machinations of oppression in general and even to his own political agenda. Sharing this analysis may also help gain support from the aggressor's activist community when they understand their own political work as connected to the abolition of rape culture and, of course, rape.

7 Be clear about what your group wants from the aggressor in terms of accountability. When your group calls for accountability, it's important to make sure that "accountability" is not simply an elusive concept that folks in the group are ultimately unclear about. Does accountability mean counseling for the aggressor? An admission of guilt? A public or private apology? Or is it specific behavior changes? Here are some examples of specific behavior changes: You can organize in our community, but you cannot be alone with young people. You can come to our parties, but you will not be allowed to drink. You can attend our church, but you must check in with a specific group of people every week so that they can determine your progress in your process of reform.

Determining the specific thing that the group is demanding from the aggressor pushes the group to be accountable to its own process. It is very easy to slip into a perpetual rage that wants the aggressor to suffer in general, rather than be grounded in a planning process that identifies specific steps for the aggressor to take. And why not? We are talking about rape, after all, and rage is a perfectly

---

1 We do not mean to simply imply that the principle of "innocent until proven guilty" should be completely discarded. However, we also recognize that this particular goal is actually often disregarded in a criminal system that is entrenched with institutional racism and oppression. Our goal is to create values that are independent from a criminal justice-based approach to accountability, including thinking critically about ideas such as "innocent until proven guilty" from the perspective of how these ideas actually impact oppressed people.

natural and good response. However, though we should make an intentional space to honor rage, it's important for the purposes of an accountability process to have a vision for specific steps the aggressor needs to take in order to give her a chance for redemption. Remember, the community we are working to build is not one where a person is forever stigmatized as a "monster" no matter what she does to transform, but a community where a person has the opportunity to provide restoration for the damage she has done.

8. Let the aggressor know your analysis and your demands. This guideline may seem obvious, but we have found that this step is often forgotten! For a number of reasons, including being distracted by the other parts of the accountability process, the aggressor building distance between himself and the organizers, or the desire for the organizers to be anonymous for fear of backlash, we sometimes do not make a plan to relay the specific steps for accountability to the aggressor. Publicly asserting that the person raped another, insisting that he must be accountable for the act, and convincing others in the community to be allies to your process may all be important aspects of the accountability plan – but they are only the beginning of any plan. Public shaming may be a tool that makes sense for your group, but it is not an end for an accountability process. An aggressor can be shamed, but remain unaccountable for his behavior. Organizers must be grounded in the potential of their own collective power, confident about their specific demands as well as the fact that they are entitled to make demands, and then use their influence to compel the aggressor to follow through with their demands.

9. Consider help from the aggressor's friends, family, and people close to her. Family and friends can be indispensable when figuring out an accountability plan. Organizers may hesitate to engage the aggressor's close people; assuming that friends and family may be more likely to defend the aggressor against reports that he has done such a horrible thing. This is a reasonable assumption – it's hard to believe that a person we care about is capable of violently attacking another – but it is worth the time to see if you have allies in the aggressor's close community. They have more credibility with the aggressor, it is harder for her to deny accountability if she is receiving the demand for accountability from people she cares about, it strengthens your group's united front, and, maybe most interestingly, it may compel the aggressor's community to critically reflect on their own values and cultural norms that may be supporting people to violate others. For example, this may be a community of people that does not tolerate rape, but enjoys misogynist humor or music. Engaging friends and family in the accountability process may encourage them to consider their own roles in sustaining rape culture.

Also, the participation of the aggressor's close people ensures long-term follow through with the accountability plan. Friends can check in with him to make sure he is attending counseling, for example. Also, the aggressor may need his own support system. What if the intervention causes the aggressor to fall into a deep suicidal depression? The organizers may not have the desire or the patience to support the aggressor, nor should they need to. However, the aggressor's family and friends can play an important role of supporting the aggressor to take the necessary steps of accountability in a way that is sustainable for everyone.

10 Prepare to be engaged in the process for the long haul. Accountability is a process, not a destination, and it will probably take some time. The reasons why people rape are complicated and it takes time to shift the behavior. Furthermore, community members who want to protect the aggressor may slow down or frustrate organizing efforts. Even after the aggressor takes the necessary steps that your group has identified for him to be accountable, it is important to arrange for long term follow through to decrease the chances of future relapse. In the meantime, it's important for the organizers to integrate strategies into their work that make the process more sustainable for them. For example, when was the last time the group hung out together and didn't talk about the aggressor, rape, or rape culture, but just had fun? Weave celebration and fun into your community, it is also a reflection of the world we want to build.

Also, the change that the organizing group is making is not just the transformation of the particular aggressor, but also the transformation of our culture. If the aggressor's friends and family disparage the group, it doesn't mean that the group is doing anything wrong, it's just a manifestation of the larger problem of rape culture. Every group of people that is working to build a community accountability process must understand that they are not working in isolation, but in the company of an on-going vast and rich global movement for liberation.

Again, these principles are merely bones to be used as a framework for a complex, three-dimensional accountability process. Each community is responsible for adding its own distinctive fleshy details to make the body of the accountability process its own. Below is a review of three very different scenarios of community groups struggling with sexual violence and mapping out an accountability plan. These scenarios occurred before the folks at CARA crafted the list of principles above, but were important experiences that gave us the tools we needed to identify critical components of accountability work.

ACCOUNTABILITY SCENARIOS

Scenario One:

Dan is a Black man in an urban area who is active in the movement to end racial profiling and police brutality.[1] He is also active in working with young people to organize against institutional racism at an organization called Youth Empowered. He is well known by progressives and people of color in the area and popular in the community. Over the course of three years, four young Black women (ages 21 and younger) who were being mentored by Dan approached CARA staff with concerns about on-going sexual harassment within their activist community. Sexual harassment tactics reported by the young women included bringing young people that he mentored to strip clubs, approaching intoxicated young women who he mentored to have sex with them, and having conversations in the organizing space about the size of women's genitals as it relates to their ethnicity. The young women also asserted that institutional sexism within the space was a serious problem at Youth Empowered. Young women received fewer chances for leadership opportunities and their ideas were dismissed.

Organizers at CARA met with Dan in an effort to share with him our concerns and begin an accountability process, but he was resistant. Women of color who were Dan's friends, who did not want to believe that Dan was capable of this behavior, chose to protect Dan from being confronted with the information. Instead, several young women was surprised by unscheduled meetings within the Youth Empowered, facilitated by an older woman of color, where they were bullied into "squashing" their concerns about Dan. They were accused of spreading lies and were told that they should be grateful for the organizing opportunities afforded to them by Dan. In one of these meetings, a young woman was shown a letter from the police department that criticized Dan about organizing a rally. This was an attempt to make her critique of Dan's behavior seem divisive to the movement against police brutality. After these meetings, each young woman felt completely demoralized and severed all ties with Youth Empowered.

Black activists have struggled with the tension of patriarchy within our social justice movements since the movement to abolish slavery. Women who identify the problem and try to organize against sexism and sexual violence within our movements are often labeled as divisive, and even FBI informants. Their work is discredited and they are often traumatized from the experience. They often do not want to engage in an accountability process, especially when they are not getting support from people they thought were their comrades, including other women of color.

Over the first two years, CARA made several attempts to hold Dan accountable and each effort was a struggle. An attempt to connect with women of color who organized with him only strained the relationship between our organizations. We also realized that our staff was not on the same page with how to address young women who were aggravated with

---

1 All names of people and organizations have been changed for the purposes of this article, not because we are concerned about the legal ramifications of slander or because we have a blanket rule about confidentiality, but because we try to be intentional about when and for what reason we publicly identify aggressors.

one organization discussing the problem at our organization. How did that impact our ability to build strategic coalitions with Youth Empowered? How were we going to support the young women to tell their truth without the story descending into a feeling of hopelessness? Was this a problem about Dan or was this a problem with the organizational culture within Youth Empowered?

We realized that it was not enough to recognize Dan's behavior as problematic and try to appeal to the conscience of the people around him. We needed a thoughtful plan supported by everyone in our organization and we needed to identify folks within CARA who would take the necessary leadership to map out the plan for all of us. We decided that the women of color would meet separately from the general CARA membership to develop an analysis and strategy and the rest of CARA would follow their lead. The women of color decided that our struggle with Dan and his behavior had now become an organizational issue rather than just a community issue, and we identified it as such. We named Dan as a person who had on-going chronic issues with sexual harassment. Surprisingly, this intentional defining of the problem had not yet happened among our staff. We talked about his behavior as problematic, unaccountable, manipulative, but we had not collectively and specifically named it as a form of sexualized violence.

Importantly, we decided that our analysis of his behavior was not secret information. If people in the community asked us about our opinion about Dan or disclosed that they were being sexually harassed at Youth Empowered, we decided that our analysis would not be confidential but would be shared in the spirit of sharing information about destructive behavior. In the past we struggled with whether or not sharing this information would be useless and counterproductive gossip. We knew the risk of telling others that a well-known Black man who organized against police violence was exhibiting sexualized violence. But we decided that it was safer for our community if we did not allow ourselves to be silenced. It was also safer for Dan if we supported our community to move along in its process of struggling with his behavior and eventually demanding accountability. If our community didn't hold him accountable and compel him to reform his behavior, we worried that he would step over the line with a young white woman who may not hesitate to report him to the police, giving the police the ammunition they needed to completely discredit Dan as well as our movement against police violence. Therefore, we made a decision to tell people the information if they came to us with concerns.

We decided that instead of meeting with all the women of color in Dan's ranks, we would choose one Black woman from CARA to invite one Black woman from Youth Empowered to have a solid, low-drama, conversation. We also asked another Black woman familiar and friendly with both groups and strong in her analysis of sexual violence within Black communities to facilitate the conversation. The woman from Youth Empowered had positive experiences organizing with CARA in the past and, though our earlier conversations about Dan were frustrated with tension and defensiveness, she was willing to connect with us. The participation of the third woman as a friendly facilitator also helped us to be more relaxed in our conversation. The first meetings with these women went very well. The CARA representative was clear that her organization's analysis was that Dan had a serious problem with sexual harassment and we were specifically concerned about the fact that he was working with young people. The Youth Empowered representative received the information with very little defensiveness and was eager to have more conversation about the reality of Dan's behavior. This one-on-one strategy seemed to loosen the intensity of two progressive organizations warring with one another and instead became three sistas trying to figure out the problem of misogyny in our community.

Rape Crisis Centers should tend to have information available about which therapists offer sliding scale fees. They should also generally refer people to therapists who are competent, ethical, and helpful. In the U.S., you can locate the nearest rape crisis center by going to RAINN's listing at http://centers.rainn.org/

Another useful resource for finding therapists near you is the Psychology Today Find a Therapist function. If you go to Psychology Today's website at http://www.psychologytoday.org and click on "Find a Therapist" on the bar near the top of the page, you can search and sort their extensive listing of therapists. Using an advanced search, you can find therapists according to things like average session cost, age specialty, ethnicity, sexual orientation, and language spoken.

If you can't find any sliding-scale therapists through the above avenues, you may also try calling the local Social Services office. They should have information on any county- or state-sponsored mental health clinics in the area. In the county where I used to live, there was a county-sponsored mental health clinic that offered therapy sessions for as low as $5 apiece. The therapists who worked there were almost universally highly recommended by the therapist I was seeing at the time. So, all in all, that's not too shabby.

If none of this works, try the Yellow Pages looking for therapists.

The recommendations of any friends who have seen therapists in the area are solid gold for finding a helpful therapist, too, in general (though friends' therapists won't necessarily have experience working with sexual violence issues).

The Interview

SO, now you've found the names of SOME therapists... How to choose which one? How do you know which therapist will be a for-real ally, and how do you find out which therapist is bound to become an unhelpful bugbear in your life?

The answer to this question is the therapist interview. Even if you get a great recommendation from someone, saying that Therapist A is radical and experienced, it's still crucial to give them an interview. This vets them for personality, approach, and compatibility, and it empowers you to be more active during the therapy itself. Interview a number of candidates before picking one. Therapists usually (and should) provide an opportunity for you to interview them, without charging anything. I found defensiveness, she was willing to connect with us. The participation of the third woman as a friendly facilitator also helped us to be more relaxed in our conversation. The first meetings with these women went very well. The CARA representative was clear that her organization's analysis was that Dan had a serious problem with sexual harassment and we were specifically concerned about the fact that he was working with young people. The Youth Empowered representative received the information with very little defensiveness and was eager to have more conversation about the reality of Dan's behavior. This one-on-one strategy seemed to loosen the intensity of two progressive organizations warring with one another and instead became three sistas trying to figure out the problem of misogyny in our community.

The outcome of these meetings was the healing of the strategic relationship of our organizations, which was important for movement building, but we still had not moved to a place where we could hold Dan accountable. We struggled with the specific thing we wanted to see happen. The women who he sexually harassed were not asking for anything in particular, they understandably just wanted to be left alone. We decided that we did not want him ejected from the activist community, but it was not safe for him to mentor young people. It was at this time that a young 17 year old Black woman, Keisha, connected to us through Rashad, a young 17 year old Black man who was organizing both with CARA and with Youth Empowered. (Rashad was referred to CARA through Youth Empowered because the rift between the two groups had significantly healed. If we had not accomplished this, Keisha may not have found CARA.) Keisha was an intern at Youth Empowered and had written a four-page letter of resignation that detailed Dan's sexist behavior. The women at CARA listened to Keisha's story, read her letter, and decided to share with her our collective analysis of Dan's behavior. Because Dan is so deeply supported at Youth Empowered, this information helped her feel affirmed and validated. CARA's organizers helped Keisha strategize about sharing the letter at Youth Empowered by asking her what she wanted to achieve, how she wanted to be supported, and what she wanted her next steps to be after the meeting.

Keisha read her letter aloud to Youth Empowered members that night, with Rashad acting as her ally. She received some support from some women in the community, but she was also told that her letter was very "high school" and immature by a Black woman within the organization who was also a mentor. Dan pulled Rashad aside after Keisha read her letter and told him that he was making a mistake by organizing with CARA because "those women hate Black men." It was a very painful event, and yet both Keisha and Rashad felt positive about the fact that they followed through with their plan and publicly revealed the same problems that other young Black women before Keisha had named but privately struggled with.

The Black woman from Youth Empowered who had been engaging with CARA was stunned by Keisha's letter and quickly organized a meeting with Dan, Keisha, Rashad, her CARA contact, and other Youth Empowered organizers, along with the same Black woman as a facilitator. Keisha and CARA organizers prepared for tactics that Dan and his supporters would use to discredit Keisha. Though each organizer admitted that there was a problem with institutional sexism within Youth Empowered, they belittled the conflict as if it were a misunderstanding between Keisha and Dan. They said she was "acting white" for putting her thoughts on paper and for wanting to resign her internship. Keisha, being the youngest person at the meeting, was mostly intimidated and silenced by these hurtful tactics. The CARA organizer who was there, however, carefully challenged each attempt to discredit Keisha. We continued to support Keisha during and after this meeting.

Keisha's letter, however, had a strong rippling effect that continued to impact Youth Empowered. The Youth Empowered organizer who had been talking with CARA was moved by Keisha's letter and committed to figuring out an accountability plan for Dan that made sense for her organization. She began to organize discussions to clarify the issues that included organizers from CARA, Dan, and organizers from Youth Empowered. These conversations were much different than when we had started two years ago. We no longer had to convince folks that institutional sexism existed in the organization, or that Dan's behavior was a form of sexualized violence. Because of the pressure created by Keisha's letter and CARA's stronger connections with women of color at Youth Empowered, Dan resigned from his mentorship position at the organization. With his absence, the new leadership at Youth Empowered began to more confidently address the institutional sexism issues within the organization.

Although we think that this work has created a safer environment at Youth Empowered, Dan still has not been accountable for his behavior. That is to say, he has not admitted that what he did was wrong or taken steps to reconcile with the people who he targeted at Youth Empowered. However, at the time of this writing, we expect that he'll continue to go to these meetings where these conversations about sexual violence (including his own) will be discussed in the context of building a liberation movement for all Black people.

Working The Principles: In the above scenario, CARA organizers utilized many of the community accountability principles discussed above. We were sure to respect the autonomy of the young women. They needed distance from the situation, so we did not pressure them to participate in the often-grueling process. However, we did regularly update them on our progress, keeping the door open if they changed their minds about what they wanted their role to be. In the meantime, we set up support systems for them, making sure we made space for Black women to just relax and talk about our lives instead of spending all of our time processing Dan.

Because the issue was complicated, we planned together as a group, running strategies by one another so that many perspectives and ideas could help improve our work. We also learned from our mistakes and learned to consider more carefully the consequences of strategies such as calling a big meeting rather than strategically working with individuals. Also working with the Black woman from Youth Empowered, a friend and comrade of Dan's, was really critical in bringing Dan closer to the possibility of accountability. Her participation brought important credibility to the questions we were asking.

However, the most important principle that we exercised in this process was taking a step back and making sure we were all on the same page with our analysis of what we were dealing with. Our frustration with Dan was a little sloppy at first – we weren't sure what the problem was. For example, there was a question about whether or not he raped someone, but we had not spoken to this person directly and, therefore, had no real reason to think this was true other than the fact that he was exhibiting other problematic behavior. We had to decide that the behavior that we were sure about was enough for which to demand accountability. The power of naming the problem cannot be underestimated in this particular scenario. Because the behavior was not intensely violent, such as sexual assault, we were searching for the right to name it as sexualized violence. Sexual harassment often presents this problem. There is no assault, but there are elusive and destructive forms of violence at play including power manipulation, verbal misogynist remarks, and the humiliation of young people.[1] Once we reached consensus in our analysis, we were prepared to receive the opportunity that Keisha's letter and work offered and use it to push the accountability process further along.

Scenario Two:

Kevin is a member of the alternative punk music community in an urban area. His community is predominantly young, white, multi-gendered, and includes a significant number of queer folks. Kevin and his close-knit community, which includes his band and their friends, were told by two women that they had been sexually assaulted at recent parties. The aggressor, Lou, was active and well-known in the music community, and he was employed at a popular club. Lou had encouraged the women to get drunk and then forced them to have sex against their will.

One of the survivors and her friends did a brief intervention with Lou, confronting him in person with the information. She reports that at first he was humbled and apologetic, but, after leaving them, reversed his behavior and began to justify his actions again.

Frustrated with Lou's lack of accountability and with sexual violence in the music community in general, Kevin's group began to meet and discuss the situation. They not only reflected on the survivors' experiences, but also how the local culture supported bad behavior. For example, they discussed how a local weekly newspaper, popular in the alternative music community, glamorized the massive amount of drinking that was always prevalent in Lou's parties. Kevin's group decided that there was a real lack of consciousness about the issue of sexual violence and the community needed to be woken up. To that end, they designed fliers that announced Lou's behavior and his identity, asserted the need for Lou's accountability as directed by the survivors, included a critique of the newspaper, and suggested boycotting Lou's club. With the survivors' consent, the group then passed the fliers out at places where members of their community usually congregated.

---

1 We can't say enough how much of a debt we owe Anita Hill for giving us the voice to call out sexual harassment as violence, particularly in a context of Black folks working with one another. While not going into the complete complexity of the Hill-Thomas hearings, we do respectfully want to give props to that sista for helping to create the opportunity for other women, especially Black women, to name sexual harassment for what it is.

A couple of weeks later, the newspaper published an article defending Lou by implying that, since the women that he allegedly assaulted had not pressed criminal charges, the allegations could not be that credible. Kevin's group realized that they needed to do a lot of re-education about sexual violence within the music community. At the same time, they were being pressured by Lou with threats to sue for libel. The group had not planned for this possible outcome, but instead of backing off, they re-grouped and used anonymous e-mail and the Internet to protect their identities.[1]

They proceeded to write a powerful document that shared the survivors' experiences (written by the survivors), defined sexual violence, and addressed issues of consent and victim-blaming. Using a mixture of statistics and analysis, they challenged the criminal legal system as an effective source for justice, thereby undermining the newspaper's absurd assertion that sexual violence can only be taken seriously if the survivor reports it to the police. Most importantly, the group clearly articulated what they meant by community accountability. By permission, we have reprinted their definition of accountability below:

> We expect that the sexual perpetrator be held accountable for their actions and prevented from shifting blame onto the survivor. We expect that the perpetrator own their assaultive behavior and understand the full ramifications their actions have and will continue to have on the survivor and the community. The perpetrator must illustrate their compliance by making a public apology and, with the help of their peers, seek counseling from a sexual assault specialist. It is equally important that they inform future partners and friends that they have a problem and ask for their support in the healing process. If the perpetrator moves to a new community, they must continue to comply with the community guidelines set forth above. We believe that by working with the perpetrator in the healing process, we can truly succeed in making our community safer.2

They released their full statement to the press and also posted it to a website. The statement made an important impact. A reporter from the popular newspaper contacted them and admitted that the statement compelled her to rethink some of her ideas about sexual violence. It also kindled a conversation in the larger music community about sexual violence and accountability.

---

1 Those of us working on community accountability should have a talk about aggressors' threats of suing for slander and libel. These threats happen often, especially if the aggressor is well-known and has a reputation to defend. However, the individual who sues for slander or libel has the burden of proof and must be able to demonstrate that the allegations are false. It's very hard to prove that something is false, especially when it's, in fact, true. Still, the threat of a lawsuit can understandably be frightening and it would be helpful to have more conversations about what the actual danger is and perhaps develop some best practices when considering using public disclosure as a tool to reach accountability.

2 Press Release, January 25, 2003

Besides sending lawsuit threats to the group, Lou mostly ignored the group until the boycott of the club where he worked started to gain steam. Soon, bands from out of town also began to intentionally avoid playing at the club. This pressure compelled Lou to engage in a series of e-mail discussions with Kevin with the goal of negotiating a face-to-face meeting. Engaging through e-mail was a difficult and frustrating process. Lou was consistently defensive and wanted "mediation." Kevin was clear about his group's analysis and goals and wanted accountability. Eventually, they gave up on setting a meeting because they couldn't agree on terms.

Throughout this process, Kevin's group experienced a great deal of exhaustion and frustration. During the periodic meetings that CARA staff had with Kevin for support and advice, he often expressed feeling really tired of the project of engaging with Lou at all. Slowly, Kevin and his group switched tactics and focused more on community building, education, and prevention. It's a critical shift to decide to use your resources to build the community you want rather than expend all of your resources by fighting the problem you want to eliminate. They began a process of learning more about sexual violence, safety, and accountability. They hosted benefits for CARA and other anti-violence organizations. They prepared themselves to facilitate their own safety and accountability workshops. They did all of this with the faith that they could transform their music community to reach a set of values that were consistent with being fun, sexy, and liberatory and explicitly anti-rape and anti-oppression.

Working the Principles: Similarly to the first scenario, this community engaged in some trial and error and learned a lot about different strategies. They were careful to check in with survivors about each of their strategies. It's important to note that one survivor changed her role as the process continued. At first, she was the main person who drove the initial confrontation with Lou. As the group pressured Lou more indirectly, she chose to stay on the sideline. The group did a good job of being flexible with her shifting role.

The fact that the group worked collectively was also very critical. We had the impression that sometimes their work was more collectively driven and sometimes only one or two people were the main organizers. When only one or two people were doing the work, it was clear that the process lost some sustainability. However, we must also reflect a lot of compassion on the reality that some folks who initially began to organize realized down the line that they needed stronger boundaries between themselves and the process. In terms of planning, it may be helpful to do on-going self-checks to note how the work may be triggering one's own experience of surviving violence or to determine if one just generally has a low capacity for doing this kind of accountability work. Perhaps a specific type of strategy is not a good match for the culture of the group. As this group moved into a different direction that focused more on raising consciousness and building stronger community connections, we noticed a significant revival in the energy of the organizers.

Finally, we think that the most important principle that made a difference in this community's work was when they presented a critical analysis of sexual violence and rape culture to the larger community of rock musicians and alternative artists. It seemed important to sap the arrogance of the newspaper's uncritical defense of Lou given how much influence the newspaper has within the larger community. We also think that creating and sharing the statement was important in light of the group's flyering strategy. There's very little one can say on a flyer and sexual violence can be very complicated. Their statement did a great job of demonstrating the full dimension of sexual violence by weaving in the survivors' voices in their own words, using statistical information to show why people do not believe survivors, and presenting a liberatory vision of accountability and justice.

Some members of the community may regret that they were ultimately unable to compel Lou to follow their demands. However, CARA feels that it's not unreasonable to think that their work did have a significant impact on Lou. After experiencing the full force of collective organizing which asserted that his behavior was unacceptable, we venture to guess that Lou might be less likely to act in manipulative and abusive ways. In any case, we think their work may have also compelled other members of the community to think critically about the way in which consent operates in their sexual encounters, which is important work in preventing future sexual violence. Also, it's important to remember that this community did in fact stay with their accountability process for the long-haul – they now simply have their sights set higher than Lou.

Scenario Three:

Marisol is a young, radical Chicana activist who organizes with CARA as well as the local chapter of a national Chicano activist group, Unido. While attending an overnight, out-of-town conference with Unido, a young man, John, sexually assaulted her. When she returned home, she shared her experience with organizers at CARA. She told us how hurt and confused she felt as a result of the assault, especially since it happened in the context of organizing at Unido. The organizers validated her feelings and supported her to engage in a healing process. We then began to talk with her more about Unido to get a better grasp on the culture of the organization as a whole and if they had the tools to address sexual violence as a problem in their community.

Marisol realized that she needed to discuss the problem with other young women at Unido. Through conversations with them, she learned that John had an on-going pattern of sexually assaulting other young women organizing with Unido. She found three other women who had had similar experiences with the same activist. This information led Marisol to organize an emergency meeting with the women of Unido to discuss the problem. At this meeting, she learned that this behavior had been happening for years and women before her tried to address it and demand that John be ejected from the position of power he possessed within the organization. However, though Unido's leadership had talked to the John about his behavior, there was no real follow-up and no consequences.

The young Chicana women of Unido decided to devise a plan to confront Unido's largely male leadership about the problem of sexual violence in general and John's behavior specifically. Identifying the criminal system as a real problem in their community, they did not want to pursue law enforcement. Also, Marisol did not want the episode to end with Unido simply isolating the aggressor without resolving John's abusive behavior. The young women decided that they wanted John to be held responsible for his actions and for his behavior to change. Their plan included demanding that John step down from leadership positions in Unido, that he pursue counseling and that his friends supported him to go to appropriate counseling, and that Unido pursue intensive educational work on sexual violence.

The women's collective strength and demands were so powerful, that Unido's leadership agreed to remove John from Unido's ranks and to sponsor trainings on sexual violence not just within Unido's local chapter, but prioritize the issue throughout Unido's national agenda. The workshop curriculum focused on the connection between liberation for Mexicans and Chicanos and the work of ending sexual violence.

Also, because of the help of his friends and community, John was supported to go to culturally-specific counseling addressing power and control issues, particularly for aggressors of sexual violence. Marisol also worked to build a strong community of support for herself and other survivors within Unido. Eventually she decided it was better for her health to create a boundary between herself and this particular chapter of Unido, but after a year's break, she is organizing with another chapter of Unido. There, she is incorporating a consciousness sexual violence and misogyny into the local chapter's political agenda.

Working the Principles: Compared to the other two scenarios, this scenario had a pretty short timeline. While the first scenario has taken over two years (so far!), the second scenario has been happening for a little over a year, the third lasted for a mere two months. One reason is the ease in which a strong accountability process can be facilitated when the community is a specific group of people rather than an unstructured and informal group. If there is a system of accountability within the community that is already set up, organizers can maximize that tool to facilitate an accountability process for sexual violence.

Interestingly, organizers at Unido previously attempted to hold the aggressor accountable using the same means, but their demands were not taken seriously. We think the attempt led by Marisol was more successful for two reasons. First, survivors were backed up by a collective of people instead of just a few folks. This lent credibility and power to the group of organizers as they approached Unido's leadership. Second, the organizers were clearer about what they wanted to see happen with John as well as with Unido. Instead of a vague call for accountability, the women asserted specific steps that they wanted John and Unido to take. This clarity of instruction helped pressure Unido to meet the challenge by complying with the specific demands that the women called for.

Also, the fact that John's friends agreed to support him to attend counseling was a great success. Support from friends and family is perhaps one of the most effective ways to ensure that aggressors attend counseling if that is the goal. They can be more compassionate because they love the person, they are more integrated in the person's life, and they have more credibility with the person. Support from the aggressor's friends and family can be a precious resource in securing an aggressor's follow through with an accountability process.

5.6. DISTINGUISHING BETWEEN ABUSE & VIOLENCE

Adapted from a speech given by Connie Burk, Northwest Network of Bisexual, Trans, Lesbian and Gay Survivors of Abuse titled Intimate Partner Violence: Are We Measuring What Matters? Dec 2nd & 3rd, 2008, Washington, D.C.

Domestic abuse is in many ways not a question of violence at all, but a question of agency.

Domestic violence, at its core, is a process where one person systematically undermines the agency of another person in a relationship. Agents are people who are in charge of themselves. Another word for "agent" is "subject," a person who can do something, experience reasonable consequences, reflect on those consequences, learn and then act again.

In the simplest terms, domestic violence objectifies survivors.

That is to say, folks who batter attempt to change subjects into objects, people into things. People who batter attempt to change self-determining subjects, people who can act, experience reasonable consequences, reflect and act again, into objects, into things that do not act but are acted upon.

If you think back to 7th grade English and diagramming sentences, it looks something like this:

Mike kicks the ball.

Mike kicks Andrea.

This process of objectification has been called "power and control". An abusive person attempts to systematically assume power and control over their partner. They may control their partner's access to friends and family, money, clothing choices, food, spiritual and religious practices, shelter and medical services. People who batter often use physical violence to reinforce their tactics of control and to demonstrate that there are irrational and frightening consequences for resisting that control.

People who batter also exploit their partners' resources, displaying a profound sense of entitlement to their partners' body, mind and spirit. This exploitation has been such a prominent experience for LGBT people that, at the NW Network, we generally talk about "Power, control & exploitation". Survivors may find themselves working several jobs to make ends meet, attempting to support their abusive partner to deal with a drug addiction, a history of sexual abuse, discrimination at work, financial troubles or depression. A person experiencing this exploitation can find their personal, physical, spiritual, economic and mental resources drained in an attempt to meet the needs of their abusive partner. This process, again, attempts to turn a subject into an object: to turn a person who is the center of their own life into a person whose primary purpose is to serve another person's needs and wishes.

Abuse or domestic violence, therefore, refers not just to a specific violent or cruel incident—or even a series of violent or cruel incidents—but to the totality of attitudes, behaviors and contexts that enable one person to objectify another.

My partner directs the Washington State Domestic Violence Fatality Review. Over the past decade, they have reviewed almost 100 of the nearly 500 domestic violence related fatalities in Washington State since 1999. As the data from our domestic violence fatality review, and the data from reviews from around the country can attest, batterers can overwhelm a survivor's struggle for agency and literally turn a subject into an object; a living, breathing person into a still, lifeless body. When a batterer kills their partner, it is the twisted yet logical endpoint of objectification uninterrupted. Even one domestic violence murder is too many, and we know that hundreds of people are killed by their batterers every year.

But, given the thousands and thousands of abusive relationships in our communities, relatively few batterers actually achieve this logical endpoint of objectification. There have been 500 domestic violence related fatalities in Washington State in the past 10 years, but thousands and thousands of partners have been battered. Why is that?

It is because survivors survive. Not as objects only acted upon but as subjects. As actors acting. Survivors learn and adapt, they provoke and fight back, they reach out and get help, they toil in obscurity, they quietly save money and plan to flee, they scream, they accommodate and placate, they plot and manipulate, they defend their children, they lie and misdirect, they find a way where there is no way and they resist objectification. They try to make sense out of their experience and they survive.

"Surviving" refers to all the things a person does to resist objectification and attempt to take back power in one's own life. Some of the things that people do while surviving are noble and beautiful and consistent with the story of how a survivor should act. They make great United Way copy. Many of the things that people do to survive are complicated and feel shameful, scary or confusing to survivors and to outside observers. As advocates, we may find ourselves cheering survivors' actions that resonate with us and avoiding the ones that trouble us, but all of it matters. All of it is part of the messy process of survival and all of it merits our thoughtful and compassionate attention.

But, When it comes to being fully open to the entire span of survivors experiences—of the choices and actions survivors take within the context of surviving abuse—the anti-violence movement—from across the spectrum of response—has fallen short. We center people who batter as the "actors" in abusive relationships and we can describe in detail the actions they take to establish abusive systems of power, control and exploitation, but we really speak very little about what survivors do to survive. We are constrained by the need to convince the larger community to support survivors—to prove that survivors are good and therefore worthy of care and regard.

We are constrained by an ironically sexist applied domestic abuse analysis that centers batterers, people understood to be men, as the only people whose actions "matter". (We are deeply concerned about what happens to survivors, but we are less interested in understanding what survivors do themselves.)

We are constrained by our over-reliance on the criminal legal system in our response to domestic violence. And we are constrained by our own pain and discomfort when confronted with the complex realities of survivors' (even our own) experiences.

We may be reluctant to talk about or help make sense of the complex, confusing choices that survivors make in the context of surviving abuse—but I can assure you that people who batter are not. People who batter say: You are just as bad as me. If those people knew what you did, they would never help you. You deserve this. You are the abuser, not me. Our confusion and reluctance colludes with batterers' goals.

Our ambivalence lingers on and, in the meanwhile, our movement to end violence looses credibility with survivors, and community members and institutions—because women act violently AND because survivors use violence to survive.

We know this. We have observed it in the actions of our mothers and ourselves and the women in shelter. And everyone who lives in the world long enough will have the opportunity to observe this for themselves. Women use violence—that is straightforward.

The question is: Who will assign meaning to this information and what meaning will be assigned?

Since 1997, I have been working in my diverse lesbian, bisexual, trans and gay community in a queer specific anti-violence context. Almost all of the trans and female survivors and most of the male survivors we work with want to avoid the criminal legal system. Since we work in a context of same-sex abuse, we cannot rely on gender to determine if a person is establishing a pattern of abusive power and control, resisting objectification or doing something else altogether. We have developed a very useful assessment process to understand if and how power, control & exploitation may be working in a relationship. We have also had to meet squarely the facts that women batter women and men, men batter women and men, & survivors use violence to resist objectification.

I think this helps us hold the various tensions involved in our discussions with a lot of compassion.

I know women use violence. I am not saying that the recent spate of research on gender symmetry in IPV is accurate. Actually, I am highly skeptical of data suggesting that, in intimate relationships, women use physical force as often or more often than men do. The E.R's and the morgues just don't back that up. BUT I am saying that it would not challenge my analysis of domestic violence if those dubious claims were true.

This is because:

1. Men's power over women is privileged in our society.
2. Batterer's control relies on gender disparities and other systems of inequality in our society.

   and

3. Assessment of context, intent & effect is needed to understand the <u>meaning</u> of a given action.

It is not a coincidence that in heterosexual relationships, men overwhelmingly batter women.

In fact, if you only could have one piece of information about a person in an abusive heterosexual relationship, what piece of information would be most predictive of whether a person was a survivor or a batterer? Gender.

This is not because women are biologically nicer, or that women are socially constructed to be non-violent, or that women are incapable of exploitation. Thousands of kids can tell us that women can be violent; thousands of undocumented domestic workers can tell us that women are capable of exploitation; and thousands of lovers can tell us that women can be abusive.

My mother was a smart, outgoing, talented, generous woman who would gladly knock us from here to kingdom-come, I learned early that there was nothing inherently non-violent about women.

In heterosexual relationships, women are more likely to be battered because sexism privileges men's power over women in our society.

In Kansas, at the shelter where I worked, women would come to the shelter and we would take them to the bank to get their money, out of a joint bank account under their name, and they would be told something like—"No, problem, Sally, just get your husband, Sam, to co-sign and we will give you this money." The Banker was operating completely independently of Sam. They had not coordinated their control. Sam was not holding a gun to the Banker's head, or promising him a reward if he thwarted Sally's attempts to leave him. The Banker didn't know anything about Sam and Sally as such. Sexism, in this case, the sexist assumption that women aren't to be trusted with the family's money (that is to say, their own money) completely independently backed up her husband's control.

Men's power over women in our society is asserted in ways we register as wonderful, and ways we register as benign and ways we register as sinister. Women are taught to defer to this power and men are taught to assume this authority in a thousand little moments. Girls wait to be asked to the big dance, and wives take their husband's names, and women walk on eggshells, and sometimes they get hit.

Almost all of these moments are legal, and a very very good many of them are celebrated as some of the most precious and valuable experiences a heterosexual person can ever have. These moments establish a baseline of authority in relationships and in the larger world that is different for women than for men.

Of course, the categories of "women" and "men" are not stable. And like every other binary construction used to categorize human experience, there is more diversity within than between these two groups and many people fall outside the categories altogether.

But in the dominant culture, the expectations surrounding the notion of "man" and the notion of "woman" are rigid and remain relatively strictly produced and enforced. In case folks think I'm reaching into the irrelevant past, there is a new One-a-Day vitamin campaign for teens—using cutting edge science they created different vitamins to meet the specific health needs for growing teen boys and teen girls. The commercials promise moms that the girl vitamins will help nourish beautiful skin and the boy vitamins will build strong muscles.

Women's experience is not a monolith. My mother was a mixed race woman raised to be a matriarch of matriarchs who would die by the age of 53. My partner's mother was a young white woman and wife with three children as the second wave of feminism broke. She would come out as a lesbian and eventually live away from her sons on women's land. My partner's step mother was a young white unwed mother trying to establish a career who accepted the task of raising three more children and would eventually rise to incredible success in her profession. Three women with wildly different experiences all living within a few miles of one another in Kansas.

Despite their differences, our mothers' actions, like other women's actions in heterosexual relationships took place with a backdrop of undermined authority, little social support for establishing authority over male partners, a dominant culture default of paternalism both for the survival of the family (undergirded by unequal pay for equal work and the persistent burden of childrearing and homemaking) and protection from men's violence in the larger world (undergirded by women's experience of many types of objectification over the course of their lifetimes). Our mothers' experience of gender disparity was compounded by the consequences of racism and homophobia and poverty and other manifestations of institutional inequality. And so it goes. In religious practice, women are constituted as helpmeet to men and are exhorted to be subject to men in every Western tradition. While egalitarian movements within Judaism, Christianity and Islam re-vision this frame, these are not the fastest growing branches of any of these faiths.

Women, religious and secular, conservative and liberal, are taught to heedfully notice their men's priorities and to take them seriously at a minimum, and internalize them as their own whenever possible. When they don't, they will pay a lonesome price. From the institutional to the personal, women's agency is constituted with vulnerabilities shot through.

Even in the most egalitarian contexts, women are cautioned to be vigilant not to claim their power in a manner that threatens men's.

So, this is the backdrop of women's actions. Men's actions are taking place with this backdrop in relief.

These backdrops, though related to one another, set opposite stages—and the meaning of the action on those stages cannot be the same.

Men walk onto the stage with almost all the set pieces in place to establish and maintain coercive control. Most men do not choose to use violence or batter even then. They may experience certain irritating benefits in their relationship based on their privileged power, they may do less housework even though their partner is employed as well, but they do not overstep into violence or into battery.

However, given the abundance of social and institutional supports for men's accepted power over women, it's difficult for a man NOT to establish a credible framework for abusive control over a female partner when he uses petulant, mean, scary or violent behaviors.

The meaning one man's violence against his female partner is formed in the larger context of male violence and male privilege. Even with the absence of "intention" to batter, even when a man is acting out of remedial skills and a lack of emotional competence—those times when a man is just being a asshole but has no intention to turn a subject into an object—his scary actions will more easily be coercive. Like it or not, those actions carry to weight of the history of men's coercive control of women. At the same time, when a man has even the slightest will to batter—the conditions of sexism in the world around him will power-boost his attempts at abusive control.

With few exceptions, women's petulant, mean, scary and violent behaviors against male partners lack a backstory of "women's violence" in society—as warriors, or serial rapists, or whathave you. Women's actions often lack the credibility to leverage institutional supports to establish authority over men. Women can set the stage for coercive control in heterosexual relationships, but it takes a disproportionate degree of determination to do so.

Still, in many, many conversations, survivors of abuse express feeling trapped in abusive relationships by the guilt and shame and confusion over their own petulant, mean, scary and violent behaviors. Even those behaviors that they used to directly resist abuse.

We can all agree that such behaviors matter when they are used to batter someone. But do women's petulant, mean, scary and violent behaviors matter even if they do not have the consequence of coercive control? Or if they are only used to survive abuse? I say yes.

We must understand that there is a distinction between "violence" and "abuse". Not all violence is abusive. Some violence is resistant—it is used to resist objectification, to resist abuse.

These actions are not abuse AND they matter AND their meaning must be understood in context.

In order to attempt to meet survivors unflinchingly in their full experience, we have to be able to accept survivors as agents--as people who act, not things only acted upon. We must agree that, as people, it matters what survivors do. Even when the choices of survivors are viciously limited, when survivors are between a rock and a hard place, when the toll of threats and crazymaking turn one's understanding of the world upside down, what a person does as a survivor matters. It matters because one's humanity—one's "person-ness"—matters. When advocates are unable to meet survivors in the full, messy, broken, heroic, petty realness of the actual choices that survivors have made—we reinforce the silence and shame that often haunt survivors of violence.

So, I say "Yes!" it matters—because what women do matters and what survivors do matters—to them, to their humanity, to their children, to their partners, to our community, to me! But many in the field say, "No."

I believe this is because the only current location we have for "mattering" is a punitive response from the criminal legal system—a system that is particularly ill-suited to understand or respond helpfully to survivors' actions. Right now, we have not looked carefully at these actions as they are used by survivors to survive. They only exist in our discussions as actions used by batterers to batter. And our only real response to batterers is a criminal legal response, and we know that such a response for survivors is harmful. We don't know how to sort out the meaning of a given behavior. Is it abusive? Is is resistance? And we get stuck. And we've stayed stuck.

Which brings us to the importance of assessment.

In our trainings, we do an exercise where specific behaviors are passed around to the participants. Things like: Reads partner's mail. Hits wall next to partner's head. Pressures partner to have sex. In dyads, people answer the question: how might a person who batters use this behavior to establish or maintain a pattern of power, control or exploitation?

Next they are asked to describe how a person surviving abusive power & control might use the same behavior.

In the debrief, folks are able to think of reasons a survivor might use each behavior to resist abusive power & control. Sometimes the reasons imagined are self-defensive, or retaliatory, or provoking, or testing. But they are all very credible and, surprisingly to most folks, by their own experience very common. In the first moments after being asked why a survivor might pressure their partner to have sex, there is often a pause. But, even then, people can offer a variety of contexts, intents & hoped consequences that reconcile the behavior with the experience of surviving. Survivors might pressure their partner to have sex to head off the threat of more lethal physical violence, to prove to a partner that s/he is still sexually interested in them, to distract a partner from violence against children/or leaving to drive drunk/or escalating accusations, to "earn" money or privileges that commonly are given only in exchange for sex, to try to reconnect with some tender aspect of the relationship.

In our same-sex abuse assessments: We can't use gender to make an assessment of who is abusing. And we can't use a list of behaviors. We know from talking to people that any behavior—from the power and control wheel or the conflict tactic scale or any list of behaviors—can be used to establish a pattern of power & control or to resist a pattern of power & control. Any specific behavior can be used to abuse OR to survive.

"Assessment", in this context, refers to an intentional process to learn as much about what is happening in a person's life as needed in order to 1) identify if & how coercive power, control & exploitation is working in a relationship and 2) to connect that person with the best possible resource.

So, here's a little quantum physics for you. Our process conceptualizes domestic abuse as a system, not a machine. With a machine, no matter how complicated, one could eventually identify and catalogue all it's parts. One could identify which parts were broken and had to be repaired for the machine to work or which parts would have to be removed to prevent it from functioning. If domestic abuse was like machine, assessment would be much simpler and lists of behaviors would suffice. But a system, unlike a machine, is fractal, self-referencing and adaptive. It can incorporate new information and change—you don't care if I trash you anymore, so, what happens if I trash your sister? In our assessment, we aren't looking for a specific behavior or condition or even sets of behaviors or conditions, we are attending to whether or not a system of power, control and exploitation will emerge in our conversations.

To understand context, intent & effect, we may talk about money & resources, anger and coolness, sex, staying and leaving, leveraging institutional privilege, identities, connection & isolation, sharing information and lying, blame, guilt & entitlement, cultural & religious practices and expectations, use of physical & sexual violence & force. We are less interested in the content of people's agreements (such as whether they seem to us to express sexist or egalitarian views) than in how those agreements were arrived at, how they can be renegotiated and if the consequences are reasonable if agreements are breached.

We listen for a range of things that don't appear on the power and control wheel, things like dread and using vulnerabilities:

- Violent incidents can be chaotic and careening and anyone involved may experience fear, dread tends to reflect the 24/7 and the cumulative effect of coercion.
- People who batter often use their own vulnerabilities (drug use, illness, experiences with oppression, past abuse) to insist that their partner prioritize their needs over the partner's own. A survivor might be expected to work two jobs to make ends meet because their partner's past arrest record means getting a job is difficult, or to stay still during the night so as not to trigger a partner's ptsd from war trauma or childhood sexual abuse.

And, as you might imagine, the assessment process was how we first came to hear so much about things survivors had done that they regretted, or still could not comprehend or that they feared would mean that no one would help them or that they wouldn't deserve help.

Once you talk to someone about the violence that they have used to resist abuse and they express their ambivalence and confusion and—at times—how trapped they feel by their actions, you have to start to deal with it. You can't say: "Great News, We've assessed that you're a survivor so never mind about all that violence—you had to do it!" And you wouldn't want to.

So what does that mean for folks who are responding to domestic violence?

Some of the facts that are confounding to advocates and policy makers and law enforcement and researchers and friends & family, include:

- some women use violence
- some women use violence in intimate relationships
- some women abuse men
- some survivors use violence against abusers

I believe that these facts do not challenge a feminist, advocacy-focused analysis of domestic abuse that understands domestic violence has a form of objectification and that recognizes the real experience of surviving. They are entirely reconcilable with this understanding of domestic violence. Not all violence is abusive. Violence must be understood in context.

However, the observations are not reconcilable to a criminal legal framework. Victim and perpetrator – as legal categories – are mutually exclusive.

Advocacy Model Language	Criminal Legal System Language
Survivor – A person who experiences a pattern of power and control by another. ***Abuser/Batterer*** – A person who establishes a pattern of power and control over another.	***Victim*** – A person against whom a crime of battery has been committed. ***Perpetrator*** – A person who has been convicted of committing a crime of battery.
The advocacy model understands that people who abuse their partners may: • Establish a pattern of control that occurs 24-7, • Control/exploit their partner over time, • use a number of tactics—some of which are illegal, **most of which are legal,** • rely on systems of oppression and social inequalities to maintain their control over their partner.	***Meanwhile, the criminal legal system:*** • is designed to address specific incidents and determine if they are legal or illegal, • Evaluates "moments in time", not patterns of abusive control, • Ignores bias and treats everyone as 'agents under the law'—regardless of institutional inequalities.

The criminal legal system is incapable of acknowledging and integrating sociopolitical differences among people—it understands everyone to be 'equal agents under the law'—it can't deal with race or gender or sexuality in meaningful ways and yet we know that institutional inequality is a big deal here.

The criminal legal system is not able to address survivors' use of violence in the context of surviving abuse. And it's not able to adequately address the different meanings of the same actions given different social positions, histories or contexts.

So, why do we care so much if the criminal legal system can't handle it? After all, domestic abuse is not a criminal experience; it's a human experience that may include criminal acts. And, the anti-violence movement is not a criminal legal movement, but a human rights movement.

We have to care because domestic violence interventions and domestic violence advocacy are immersed in a criminal legal paradigm.

The collapse between a criminal legal paradigm based on the understanding of domestic battery as essentially being a criminal legal category of behaviors and actions involving "perpetrators" and "victims" with an anti-violence paradigm based on the understanding of domestic abuse as essentially being a question of agency has created great confusion.

Survivors' actions don't make sense from a strictly criminal legal lens. They cannot be understood or even clearly named or explained. "Victim" and "Perpetrator" are mutually exclusive terms, but "Survivor" of abuse and "Perpetrator" of an illegal act are not.

Tillie Black Bear and Dr. Beth Richie and countless other advocates and organizers warned us about the narrow slice of women's experience that we were attending to when we focused on the criminal legal system to the virtual exclusion of everything else. They warned us that poor women, women of color, undocumented women, queer women would be the most vulnerable to the worst consequences of this approach. We didn't change course, even after these women and others demonstrated the importance of economic justice, and racial justice and reproductive justice and other critical paths that would fortify survivors' agency and make them less vulnerable to objectification—by their lovers, by the state.

Rather than understanding criminal legal consequences for battering as one project within a global and holistic effort to repair the damage to women and men caused by sexism, to create loving and equitable relationship and to prevent abuse--rather than understanding criminal justice as a small bit of the global arc of justice that could include economic, racial, reproductive etc justice--our anti-violence interventions, policy priorities and research have been thoroughly absorbed into a broad criminal legal project.

I think it is this—not the facts that women can abuse or survivors resist abuse with violence—that is so hard to deal with and keep the issue of survivors' use of violence so confounding.

And it is this that we will have to repair if we are going to truly, fully advocate for all survivors.

PHILLY STANDS UP PORTRAIT OF PRAXIS:

AN ANATOMY OF ACCOUNTABILITY

by Esteban Lance Kelly & Jenna Peters-Golden of *Philly Stands Up!*

The alchemy of our accountability work is a serendipitous mixture; part art, part science. To be sure, the skill and complexity involved in working on accountability processes is difficult to finesse. Nevertheless, we affirm that average people, regular folks in communities all across North America develop and exercise their own processes for making justice in sexual assault situations internal to their communities. In doing so, average people will meet more success, by any measure, than the State ever has in addressing the chaos of issues stirred up by incidents of sexualized violence.

What we now know, we learned through trial and quite a bit of error. Our missteps enabled, and in some cases exacerbated pain for which we are both responsible and repentant. Very few of us in the history of Philly Stands Up came to the group with formal prior experience working on sexual assault issues, let alone doing work with people who have caused harm. We are average people, figuring out how to do thorny work and our achievements stem from being committed to our values and purpose. We believe that people who have caused harm can change, and that we can play a crucial role in catalyzing that shift.

In recognition of contemporary peers and historical generations of people who have figured out and passed along lessons such as these, it is with a great sense of humility, that we share some logistical guts of what we've devised for our process and practices in working on sexual assault situations.

When we say that we work to hold people who have perpetrated sexual assault accountable[1] for the harm they have done, what this means is that we strive for them to:

1. Recognize the harm they have done, even if it wasn't intentional.
2. Acknowledge that harm's impact on individuals and the community
3. Make appropriate restitution to the individual and community.
4. Develop solid skills towards transforming attitudes and behavior to prevent further harm and make contributions toward liberation.

[1] Our working definition is based on Generation Five's articulation of accountability in their document, Toward Transformative Justice.

We conceptualize roughly five phases to an accountability process: the Beginning, Designing the Structure, Life Process, Tools We Use, and Closing a Process.

Phase 1. The Beginning:

People find us in many ways: we are known from leading educational workshops, contributing to zines and also through word of mouth, the internet, or through personal connections with individual members in PSU.

Sometimes a person who has caused harm gets in touch with us and says something like, "I really messed up and the person I hurt told me I need to work with you guys." Sometimes they say: "A few years ago I was abusive/ I sexually assaulted someone/ and I wasn't really ready to deal with it until now." In our workshops, people are often surprised to hear about those situations. The reality is that people who have caused harm are a complicated variety of people, and as they grow, many folks reflect on past behavior and see problems that they need to resolve.

Another approach is that someone might say, "I was sexually assaulted by *so-and-so*, and I want to hold them accountable." They would then task us with tracking down *so-and-so*, and attempting to instigate an accountability process. Beyond these cases, there are always the instances where someone who is neither the survivor nor the person who caused harm gets in touch with us on behalf of either party.

In any event, once we have touched base with the person who has caused harm, we vaguely sketch out the situation and discuss it as a group. We first find out if two collective members are able to take on this situation (we learned early on to always strive to work in pairs). If so, we discuss what we know about the situation and we honestly assess if we are equipped to handle it. There is always the possibility that there are pieces of this situation that we can't handle. Sometimes we are not qualified for one reason or another and by trying to work on it we could cause more harm than good. Sometimes PSU members decline engaging a situation because of elements that feel emotionally triggering.

After we have assessed the situation, we schedule a meet-up with the person who has caused harm. We typically meet in places that are public but run a low risk of encounters with people we know; examples include parks, train stations, hotel lobbies, food courts or outdoor cafés.

Phase 2. Designing the Process:

Next we try to design a process based on what the situation warrants. Often, we have a document listing "demands." Demands are actions the survivor needs from the community or the person who caused harm in order to be safe and to heal. Below is a sample list of common demands:

* "Pay for my STI testing/ abortion/ doctors appointment"
* "Deal with your drug/ alcohol problem"
* "If you see me out somewhere, it's your responsibility to leave the premises"
* "Don't talk to me or contact me"
* "Don't go to 'such and such group' meetings for now" (typically an organization in which both the survivor and person who has caused harm participate)
* "Disclose to all the people you are sleeping with or dating, that you sexually assaulted someone and are in an accountability process"
* "Write me a sincere letter of apology"

Demands are the central document in our accountability process. In situations where we have a list of demands, they fundamentally drive the design for our process. Our goals as facilitators of the process are to meet the demands laid out by the survivor- and in some cases the community at large- both in letter and in spirit. In designing a particular process, we bear several principles in mind:

Firstly, we try to involve the person we are working with into the design of the process. If they help make the plans, timelines, goals and help to brainstorm the things we can do together, then they feel more invested in everything. They are reluctant to bail on things because they do not see themselves as walking out on an externally imposed program.

Secondly, in order to engage them, we figure out methods that specifically work for the other person. If it is a visually-oriented person, we make drawings or word maps to describe what we are talking about in a meeting. If they hate to read, we might record a reading for them. If they have ability needs that make it hard for them to sit down for meetings, we might plan walks around the block while we talk. In our engagement efforts, we have even arranged meetings consisting of street skating and board games. Be accommodating and creative!

Another important practice of ours is that we use the meetings as an opportunity to model the behavior we are trying to build in the person with whom we are working. Some examples of how we demonstrate preferred behavior include: articulating and maintaining discrete social/ physical boundaries, striving for clear communication, practicing empathy, showing respect (which is perceptibly appreciated among people who have been ostracized in the aftermath of sexual assault), and exemplifying utter honesty. If the person we are working with misses a meeting or arrives late, we will discuss how they needed to communicate this better, and help them understand how the ways in which it was inconsiderate. Together, we lay down ground rules for how we want to communicate with one another, which gives us concrete agreements for holding folks accountable. We use their progress in adhering to agreements to create positive momentum; an endorsement for their capacity to grow and change- to be their better selves.

Phase 3. Life Structure:

When it is needed, we often put a lot of emphasis into fostering balance and creating structure in the person's life. If they are unstable then it is becomes difficult for them to be present in the work we are doing together. In such situations, it becomes crucial for us to account for the fuller context of challenges in their lives. The more grounded one is, the better their chances are of following through on their accountability process.

Toward that end, we create space for them to have a personal "check-in" at the beginning of each meeting. This is a moment for them to share anything they wish about their daily lives, emotional state, or logistical hurdles. The check-in allows us to hear, for example, about their progress in finding a therapist or stable housing, or about job interviews or family visits. At times, we have actively passed along jobs prospects, accompanied people in looking for viable housing, and given people rides to therapy appointments. This humbling and more fundamentally 'human' work has helped us to see what it truly means to acknowledge that we are all in community together; that a politics of trust depends on everyday support and interdependence, and that nobody rests outside of that in a just society.

Phase 4. Tools we use:

Each process is unique. Most meetings consist primarily of talking. We talk about stories, the instances of assault that took place, relationship patterns and countless connected issues. We employ several general tools as guides in the meeting space:

- Story telling- We ask to hear stories, encourage discussion about dynamics or emerging themes, and use these didactically, sometimes revisiting their stories.
- Writing- Giving "homework" is a good way to maintain continuity between meetings. Sometimes people write down recollections of an instance of abuse, record what certain words mean to them, keep a log of times they felt frustration or anger (those are common emotions we work with), and maintain a journal about how the accountability process is going for them.
- Role Playing- Taking a cue from Augusto Boal's Theatre of the Oppressed, we sometimes try to act out interactions that have occurred or that could occur. Role Playing is great for building skills of perception and empathy, and is a safe way for people to try out new behaviors and understand past ones.
- Reading/ Listening/ Watching- Most situations that we come across call for educational development. There are countless helpful texts, films, lectures, podcasts etc that help to explain everything from patriarchy, to substance abuse, internalized oppression and dynamics of power, privilege, and oppression. Here, our role is to tailor any resources for the person we are working with.

Phase 5. Closing a Process:

Improving upon ourselves is lifelong work for everyone and certainly for folks who have a history of perpetrating violence. Most of our accountability processes last between nine months and two years, and could usually continue ad infinitum. This begs the question, "when is it time to wrap up a situation?" Much like therapy, there is no objective answer to this, but here are some indicators for when it might be appropriate to wind things down.

One obvious moment to close out a process is when both the letter and the spirit of the demands have been met. If a demand is "write me a letter of apology," it won't do for the person who has caused harm to draft a letter within the first few months of their process. Composing an apology may be the technical letter of the demand, but writing it to convey sincere contriteness is the true spirit of the demand. This penitence can only be declared once hard work and requisite time have gone into understanding one's role in the harm of the assault, and once they have gained a sense of empathy for how it affected the survivor(s) and the community.

If a demand calls for sobriety or a reduction in the use of illicit substances, then fulfilling the true spirit of the demand would require both cutting back substance use and moving toward a true understanding of how the survivor (or community) came to this demand. What we would look for is recognition by the person who caused harm that in their case, drinking or using creates conditions for their judgment to be impaired and how this traces to their abusive behavior. Making that connection and changing their relationship to that substance would therefore be true fulfillment of the demand.

Another indicator for transitioning out of a formal process is that the person who has caused harm has identified ways to change the behavior that has led to sexual assault and has demonstrated their capacity to navigate through "gray zones". Here, it is important to see how they have practiced this shift in their everyday life and to feel confident as a guide in the process that this change is profound and lasting.

Often we would be hesitant to wind down an accountability process unless we are confident that whomever we are working with has developed responsible and sustainable systems of support in their life. We look for clues that they have not one or two, but plenty of upstanding friends, with whom they can talk to about matters of consequence. This can include housemates or family members who they can trust for support when challenges come up, particularly with issues related to this work. We also work to ensure that they are familiar with the resources available to them around the city that can serve their needs.

Usually "ending" a process looks more like phasing it out. Over time we go from meeting each week, to twice a month, to once a month, until finally we are only meeting to check-in periodically. After an accountability process, the people with whom we have worked know that we are here for them whenever they need us.

This piece is forthcoming in *Social Justice*, Vol. 37, No. 4.

ROAD ★ MAP OF AN ACCOUNTABILITY PROCESS

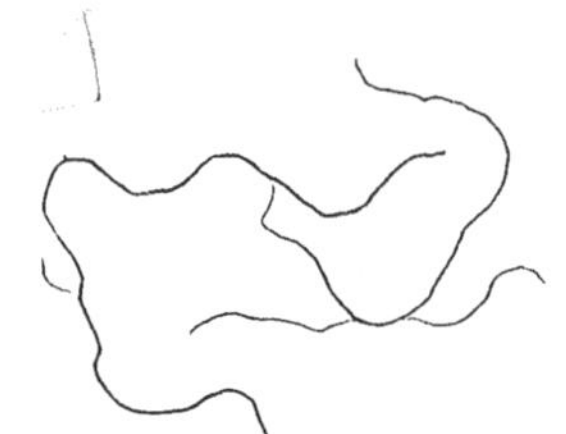

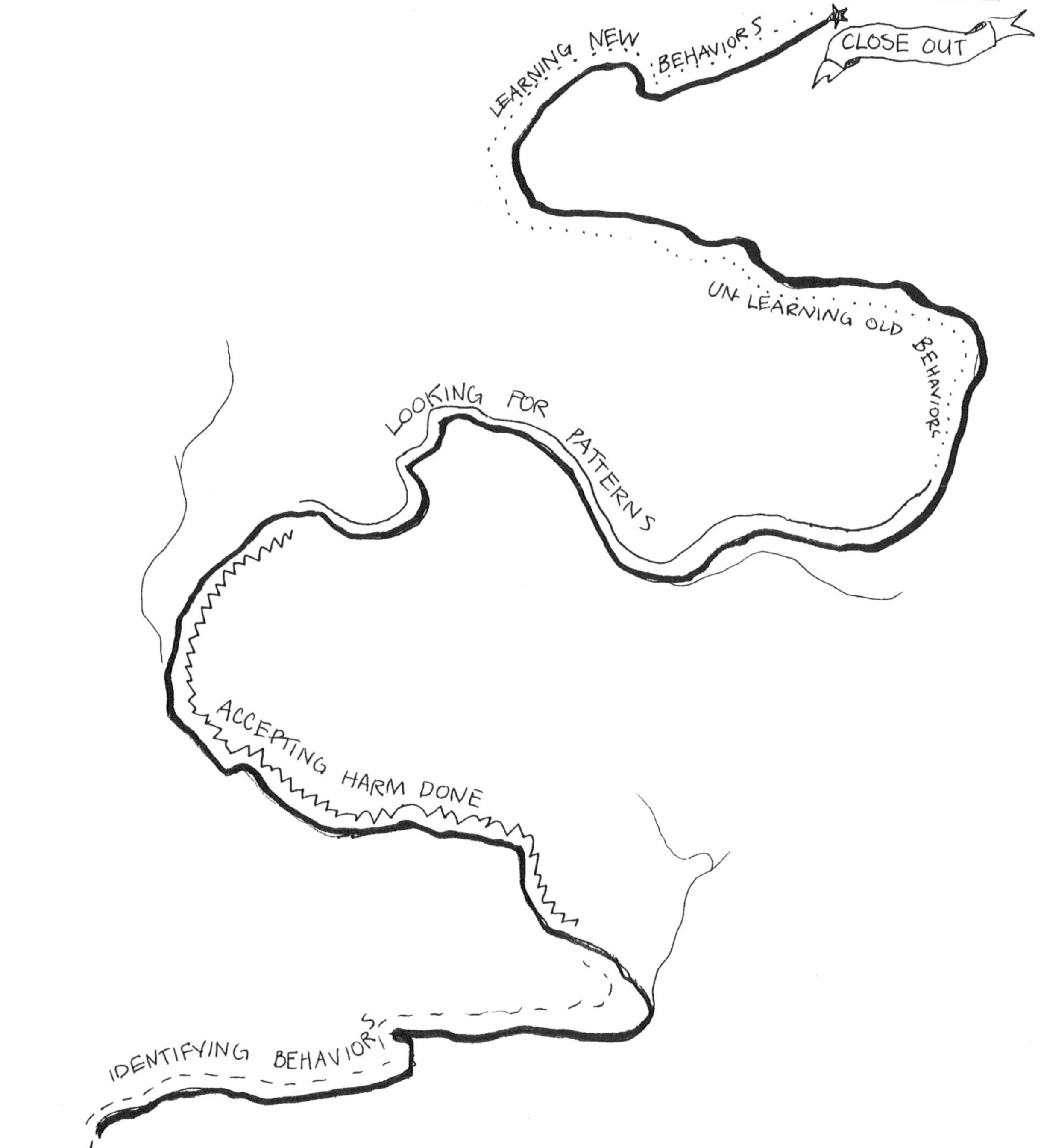

Road Map of an Accountability Process

An Accountability Road Map sketches out a process to give it structure while clarifying intentions, goals, and allowing you to get a sense of the trajectory and the big picture. Because accountability processes are never linear or clear cut, we use a road map instead of an agenda; Road Maps have ample room for construction, road blocks and detours. They help you maintain a sense of your over all goals, while remaining flexible and open to re-routing paths and re-imagining the journey once you've started.

The Five Major Phases of Accountability Processes

There are endless ways to map out phases of an accountability process, but here are the five most common phases we have charted in our work and experience:

Identifying Behaviors

The first step in a process is that a person must have an awareness and understanding of the actions and behaviors for which they are being called out. This is foundational and can sometimes take longer to accomplish than you might imagine.

Accepting Harm Done

Building on the understanding of what specific behaviors led them to this accountability process, the next step is to acknowledge in what ways these behaviors were harmful -- even if harm wasn't their intention. This is the seed of one of most frequent goals in a process: building empathy.

Looking for Patterns

Making comprehensive change to prevent future assault requires broadening the focus beyond the isolated incident(s) that precipitated this process. This means identifying and naming the person's history of abusive/ harmful actions and contextualizing these behaviors in their underlying assumptions and socialization.

Unlearning Old Behaviors

The process of breaking habits starts with identifying harmful dynamics and then deepens beyond naming to analysis and understanding. Gaining an awareness and determining the kinds of situations that trigger or enable abusive or harmful behaviors and then having clear strategies to avoid and diffuse the potential path for harm.

Learning New Behaviors

Building new positive/healing patterns of behavior goes hand in hand with breaking down the old harmful patterns. One of the tools in this stage is role play, where a person can rehearse their consent practices, graceful acceptance of criticism, disclosure strategies, etc. Also important is becoming familiar with their resources to support positive and new behavior [affordable therapy, sites to find jobs, a clearly defined network of supportive friends, membership to the gym, etc]. This phase is very much about understanding the *ways* to build new behaviors so this skill becomes sustainable and fueled by self reliance.

Blueprint for Doing the Work

Three of the most consistent and challenging barriers people going through accountability processes run up against are:

1. inability to recognize and name the emotions they commonly feel
2. lack of empathy for others (specifically the survivor[s])
3. getting lost in the sea of dynamics, feelings, and memories they are being asked to consider, talk about and revisit.

The Blueprint is a tool we came up with to help move past all three of these sticking points. It is a structure that can sometimes be conceptual and confusing to get the hang of, but it has endless possibilities for how you can use it and the potential to help ground them in what is often a confusing and overwhelming process.

Floors

In the Blueprint, each floor is assigned to represent one person or group of people. The first floor is often the Person Who Has Perpetrated Harm's floor. The 2nd floor is the Survivor's floor. There is no limit to how many floors you can add.

Rooms

Each floor is made up of rooms. One room holds one emotional state like, "anger", "feeling misunderstood", "embarrassed", "joyful", "irritated", "anxious", "rational" and on and on and on. You can fill in the rooms of your blueprint as you get to know each other. Together you can all build the rooms based on what themes or commonly experienced emotions the person you are working with feels. It is helpful and feels productive to say, "I've noticed that when you are telling stories about times you've lost your temper or gotten upset, you often feel frustrated at the beginning and end of the interaction. Would you say that *Frustration* is a room we should build on the first floor?" The process of building rooms together is a great way to have all of you meaningfully participate in the hard work of the process. **Building rooms is also a key way to identify patterns of behavior.** Where you place specific rooms can also help see the connection between two or three emotions, i.e. if "feeling misunderstood" often results in "anger" or "being mean" it is helpful to build those rooms next to each other, so you can all see how they interact with one another.

How to Use Your Blueprint

While the act of building it is ongoing [you can always add more rooms, closets, relabel rooms], once you have some things labeled and constructed, there are lots of ways to use the blueprint. Often, we have it sitting on the table while the person we are working with is telling us a story from their week or discussing an instance of assault that we are working through in our process. If they get confused, are getting off track or losing focus, we can say "Where were you on the first floor when he said that to you?" They can take a minute to reground and work to notice what emotional state they were in.

You can use the model of a "house" as realistically or creatively as you want. Often, we use the “hallways” as actions and opportunities for making decisions; “When that conflict was happening, you were walking down this hallway and you turned in to the “manipulative” room. What would happen if you had turned in to a different room?” or “What would it take for you to have gotten up out of “anxiety” room and walked down the hallway to the “spiritual centered” room? What route would you have taken?” The hallways are key. They remind the person you are working with that there are decisions and actions before, during and after conflict or conditions that lead to harm. Pointing out how they have choice in which rooms they walk in to is a way to point out responsibility -- it is also a way to talk about the real challenges of and default ways they get to a specific emotional state.

The distinction of floors can be confusing. The struggle of “learning empathy” often looks like the person who has caused harm having a difficult time seeing anything from a point of view that is different than theirs. This can come off as egotistical and narrow. If the person you are working with is spinning around and around in their version and experience of the story and you want them to move or see it from a different vantage point, it's hard (and probably not helpful) to say, “you are being completely self -involved. Look at it from the survivor's point of view!.” It is possible, though (and maybe more helpful) to say, “you are stuck on the first floor. I want you to try and get to the stairs and walk up to the second floor for a little while.” The second floor usually won't have any rooms labeled because you (probably) don't know the emotional states of the survivor. Being “on the second floor” is symbolically important because it signifies a separation from the person who has caused harm's story and rooms. When they are on the second floor it is an exercise in imagining and trying to understand how someone could have interpreted or experienced their actions differently than they might think.

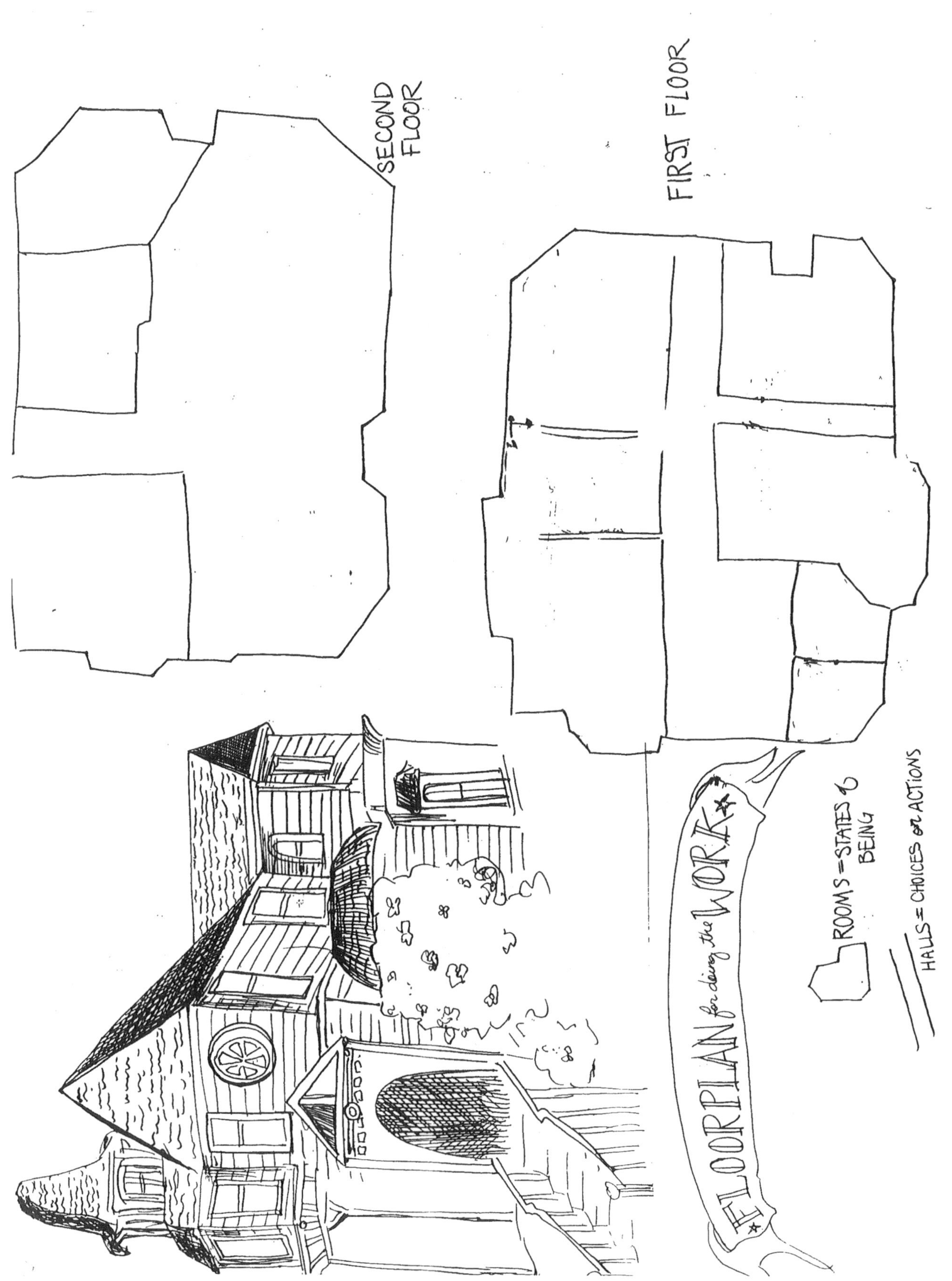
SECOND FLOOR
FIRST FLOOR
FLOORPLAN for doing the WORK
ROOMS = STATES of BEING
HALLS = CHOICES or ACTIONS

5.8. CONFRONTING SEXUAL ASSAULT: TRANSFORMATIVE JUSTICE ON THE GROUND IN PHILADELPHIA

The following is an article written by Bench Ansfield and Timothy Colman describing a situation of sexual violence in the Philadelphia community and PSU's vision of transformative justice.

CONFRONTING SEXUAL ASSAULT: TRANSFORMATIVE JUSTICE ON THE GROUND IN PHILADELPHIA

by Bench Ansfield and Timothy Colman

An earlier version of this piece appeared in Volume 27, Issue 1 of Tikkun (www.tikkun.org), a quarterly interfaith critique of politics, culture, and society published by Duke University Press.

Lee was all too familiar with the impact sexual assault can have on lives, communities, and social justice organizing. After being sexually assaulted by a prominent anti-poverty organizer, Lee felt confused and betrayed. He stepped back from the campaign the two of them had been working on together and began to avoid the organizer as much as possible. It was months before he told anyone about the assault.

Eventually, he joined a support group for survivors of sexual violence, and began to work through some of the numbness, shame and fear that had developed after the assault. As he began to confront these feelings, what emerged from within him was a deep well of grief and anger. It became more and more difficult to see the organizer at community meetings or friends' parties. He started getting angry with his housemates for inviting the organizer to events at the house, even though they had no knowledge of the assault. Much of his anger stemmed from the lack of repercussions facing the organizer, as well as the lack of power he had to protect himself from the organizer's ongoing presence in his life.

Lee knew that he did not want to report the sexual assault to the police, for a whole long list of reasons. He would lose control of his story if he reported it; he would be forced to tell the details of what happened to the police and to testify in court; a number of painful details about his own life and history might emerge; and he would almost definitely lose the case. But more importantly, the idea of pressing charges felt like its own tragedy. He had become politicized in the anti-police brutality movement and was now involved in prison abolition organizing. Lee's sense of justice, what would make him feel like the anti-poverty organizer had faced his due, had nothing to do with courts or cops or prisons. Finally, no matter the verdict, he didn't believe a court case would make the organizer change. Lee wanted him to somehow understand the harm he had done, take responsibility for it, and transform whatever it was inside him that had made him do it. But Lee didn't want to be the one to push the organizer to change—he couldn't even bear to be in the same room with him. And so he just tried to forget the incident had ever happened.

Lee's story—which we are sharing with his permission, having changed his name and identifying details—evokes the frustratingly limited options available to survivors of sexual assault in most U.S. cities and the urgency of creating new systems. This is a helpful starting point to begin discussing transformative justice approaches for addressing sexual assault.

What would happen if our responses to sexual assault came from a vision of the world we want to live in? A scattering of groups, including UBUNTU in Durham, Safe OUTside the System Collective in Brooklyn, Young Women's Empowerment Project in Chicago, Community United Against Violence in San Francisco, and others across the United States and Canada, are working to create community accountability and support networks based not on the punitive and coercive methods of the criminal justice system but rather on principles of care and harm reduction.

In Pennsylvania, two organizations involved in this work are Philly Stands Up and the Philly Survivor Support Collective, groups that trace their roots back to 2004, when a group called Philly's Pissed formed out of a burning rage at the lack of options for survivors of sexual assault in their communities. Based in West Philadelphia, both groups work in collaboration to shift cultural responses to sexual assault, bring healing and accountability to the fore, and challenge the punitive response of the state. Faced with a criminal legal system that routinely disempowers survivors and an exploding U.S. prison population, it is clear that we are in desperate need of alternatives to prevent, confront, and heal from sexual assault and intimate partner violence.

One way to move away from the punitive methods of the criminal legal system is to turn toward the idea of community accountability. Our work is about realizing the potential carried by our families, communities, and networks to address violence without relying upon the police, courts, prisons, or other state and nonprofit systems. We did not invent this strategy; many of our guiding principles have been made possible by indigenous communities' responses to violence, both historically and contemporaneously, as well as INCITE! Women of Color Against Violence's groundbreaking efforts to document community accountability models.

Instead of interrogating and victim-blaming the survivor, then punishing and demonizing the person who perpetrated assault, we envision and construct systems of community accountability that are grounded in safety, self-determination, healing, and the human potential to change. Central to this generative project is an understanding that instances of sexual violence occur within larger systems of structural violence and oppression. We must confront each individual act of sexual violence within its systemic context. At the same time, we must build alliances with movements both in Philadelphia and beyond to end all forms of interpersonal and state violence. We call this work transformative justice, and we practice it as part of an inspiring movement that is germinating throughout North America.

Forging Paths to Safety, Justice, and Healing

Applying a transformative justice approach to the issue of sexual assault means working to support individual survivors while building real options for safety, justice, and healing outside of punitive and disciplinary state systems. Efforts to create alternative systems such as this are underway from North Carolina to California. Here in Pennsylvania, the Philly Survivor Support Collective is working to create and maintain systems of support and accountability wholly outside the framework of the criminal legal system.

Our commitment to transformative justice comes out of a recognition that the criminal legal system dehumanizes and disempowers all survivors, in addition to increasing the amount of violence in all of our lives. This negative impact is most acute for survivors and communities who are already disproportionately targeted by state violence, including communities of color and indigenous communities, and survivors who are sex workers, incarcerated, and/or transgender. We believe that efforts to transform our communities must be grounded both in the present moment—in the form of ensuring survivor safety and prioritizing survivors' self-directed healing—as well as in the long haul: working toward a vision of the world we want. In order for the movement to end sexual assault to be led by those most directly affected, we must build our capacity to support each other's healing, ensuring that as survivors, we are able to bring the fullness of our wisdom and experience to the work.

For many people, it is difficult to even conceive of a way of responding to violence—whether sexual assault or other kinds—that does not rely on the courts, police, or prisons. We are eager to share a description of our work in Philly with the hope that it will encourage others to join in the growing movement to create alternative approaches to addressing harm.

On an individual level, our work is always directed by the survivor. Our role is to listen to them, meet them where they're at, offer emotional support and resources, and create solutions together. We ask survivors if they have initial priorities that they want to focus on as a first step; after they identify these, we creatively plan together how to address them. These often include immediate health or safety needs, such as emotional support, medical care, counseling, strategizing to engage the support of people close them, acupuncture, child care, safety planning, travel to get away from a harmful situation or to be near loved ones or concrete resources, or any number of other needs.

After these urgent needs are met, we stay present with survivors as they begin to explore options for accountability, justice, and healing. Transformative justice offers a lens through which survivors can examine the underlying conditions where the violence occurred, and identify what change they might want from the person who harmed them, their community, or the broader world. Survivors might pursue individual or collective paths to healing, might make demands for accountability or transformation from the communities or organizations where the assault occurred, and might make demands of the person who harmed them or leave that person aside altogether. During this process, we work to transform the community, people, or institutions that surround the survivor, increasing the capacity of the community to be responsive to the survivor's needs.

Each situation we take on offers its own challenges, which are also possibilities for growth and transformation. If a survivor chooses to make demands for accountability from the person who caused harm, we may assist the survivor in engaging the support of friends or community members to communicate these demands, or in facilitating an accountability process with Philly Stands Up. If the person who caused the harm is still in the survivor's life or community, we can work with the survivor to create a safety plan or ask for certain shared-space policies.

Safety planning is a tool often used by survivors who are in a relationship with an abusive partner, to minimize potential harm and to have a plan to draw upon quickly if they need to leave. Shared-space policies are commitments made by loved ones, community members, or organizations to take certain actions, as determined by the survivor, in the event that the survivor is put in the position of sharing space with a person who has harmed them. These policies can act as one alternative to a restraining order. The action requested by the survivor might be to ask a person who has caused harm to leave spaces where the survivor is present until that person has demonstrated a behavior change, or to have support teams on hand that can offer solidarity, support and safety to the survivor when the person who caused harm is present. Another option survivors might pursue is identifying harmful practices or attitudes endemic within their community or the larger culture that contributed to instances of sexual violence, such as victim-blaming, silencing, sexism, racism, transphobia, transmisogyny, classism, ableism, criminalization of sex work, and many others, and calling upon people to work collectively to eradicate these attitudes.

It is important not to place the burden for ending sexual assault on survivors. We must fight the idea that the survivor of a sexual assault is responsible for transforming the person who harmed them or preventing that person from sexually assaulting someone else. Our work is founded in the transformative justice principle that we are all responsible for addressing the root causes of sexual assault, and that together, we hold the power to transform our communities.

Toward a Non-Punitive Accountability

It can be a harrowing process to let ourselves open up to the hope that someone who has perpetrated assault can truly be accountable, especially given the shortage of models of justice that are not entrenched in retribution, dehumanization, and incarceration. Transformative justice processes—like those that Philly Stands Up facilitates with people who have perpetrated assault—are fundamentally about altering our ideas about what seems possible, reminding us that we can no longer afford to dismiss people who harm others as inescapably violent. Our accountability processes are inspired by our faith that we really can dream up and practice methods for confronting sexual violence that move us toward safer, more self-determined communities, as well as gnaw at the structural underpinnings fostering cultures of violence.

Our interventions are rooted in the safety, healing, and demands of the survivor, but often go beyond these foundations to ask how we can identify and transform the patterns of behavior that enabled the assault in the first place. As we work to shift accountability away from the survivor and onto the person who perpetrated assault, we have to define what accountability means in each unique situation. The contours of each process look quite different from one another, but they share the same core objectives. Over the course of weeks, months, or years, our weekly meetings strive to push the person who perpetrated assault to recognize the harm they have done (regardless of their intentions), acknowledge the harm's impact, make appropriate restitution, and develop skills for transforming attitudes and behaviors that are harmful to self or others.

Whenever possible, an intervention treats as its grounding document a list of demands from the survivor that have been shared with us by the survivor directly or through the survivor support collective. These demands can range from "do not share space with the survivor" to "compose a letter of apology" to "disclose to your current and all future partners." The demand list guides us throughout an intervention and offers a tangible checklist we can use to measure our progress.

Frequently, though, our processes are forced to reckon with issues unprompted by a survivor's demands. When a person who has just been called out for sexual assault first comes to us—either on their own volition or due to community pressure—their life is often in shambles. Before we can start recounting specific violent incidents or reading over a demand list, we have to make sure that they have secure housing, a decent job, and a steady diet. It is not unusual for us help them obtain a suitable therapist or assist them in reaching out to their loved ones for support and guidance. These tasks are critical for most any transformative justice process, as they enable the capacity for change by collaboratively cultivating tools for finding balance and grounding. Through this methodology, we not only build trust and model interdependence, we also work toward eliminating a mainspring of sexual assault—instability and insecurity.

Often the most difficult challenge facing an intervention is earning "buy in" from the person who perpetrated assault. Because we reject the forceful violence intrinsic to the criminal legal system's interventions into sexual assault—such as forced "rehabilitation," incarceration, or, so frequently, inaction—we are forced to devise creative techniques to consensually pull someone into a process. Although we sometimes have to rely upon the use of community leverage to persuade someone to work with us, we make every effort to draw someone in by helping them acknowledge their own call to change.

It is critical to tailor an accountability process in such a way as to make the person we are working with understand that they need the process. Of course, this acknowledgement can only arise in a trusting atmosphere. For this reason we keep our meetings small and intimate, with two members present for each intervention. Often we meet in public spaces like a park or a train station so as to avoid making the person who perpetrated assault feel cornered or attacked. And we collaboratively design a process around their needs and abilities. During one intervention, any given meeting might have involved visual activities like sketching and mapping, breathing exercises, or poetry. These strategies reflect an ongoing balancing act as we strive to make the person who perpetrated assault feel safe enough to respect the process and be vulnerable, while still being open to the challenges we are posing.

As an accountability process slowly gains traction, we begin to identify harmful patterns of behavior as potential sites of transformation. Facilitating the recognition of deep-seated and destructive cycles of behavior can be one of the most trying elements of an intervention. Most often, this requires naming and unpacking the ways that various privileges and internalized oppressions play out in relationships. For instance, we may have to unravel how ableism was at work in an able-bodied person's repeated coercion of her partner to have sex during flare-ups from an autoimmune disorder. Or we may have to map out how a cisgendered man's patriarchal socialization contributed to a general imbalance of control in a heterosexual relationship. In a similar fashion, our interventions frequently scrutinize how oppressive race and class dynamics contribute to a relationship atmosphere ripe for sexual assault. As facilitators, this is often the most hazardous ground to cross. Acting as both witness and mentor to a transformative justice process is alternately frustrating and enlivening, appalling and regenerative.

It is critical to note that our work is not about "curing" the person who perpetrated assault. A lifelong and cross-generational project rooted not in that person's rehabilitation, nor in the restoration of the community that existed pre-assault, transformative justice is, rather, a consistent movement toward community safety and individual/collective transformation.

By way of illustration, our intervention with Jesse (again, a pseudonym) lasted two years, and continues with occasional check-ins. At the beginning of his process, Jesse showed up to meetings recalcitrant and invulnerable. Certain that he had done nothing harmful, he argued that his ex-partner—the survivor in this situation—was getting revenge on him by "misrepresenting" as assault an incident that was in actuality a simple issue of poor communication. In order to sustain the process and keep him coming to meetings, we put the assault in question on the back burner for the first six months, dedicating our time together to building trust and helping him secure a new home. Slowly, as facilitators, we began to identify his harmful patterns of behavior—including pent-up anger, narcissism, and an inability to communicate his needs. Correspondingly, we set about cultivating relevant tools, such as empathy-building, anger management, communicating in stressful contexts, and establishing consent during sex. By the time Jesse was amenable to discussing the specific incidents of assault, we had already developed an arsenal of tools for empathizing with the experience of the survivor, identifying his destructive actions, and practicing a different course of action in a similar context. Many months later, when Jesse had met the survivor's demands, indicated his capacity for healthy relationships, and demonstrated a command over his own damaging behavior, we began transitioning out of the process. Yet even now, with the intervention no longer active, our check-ins with Jesse confirm that he is pressing on with the critical work of self-transformation, effectively

Seven years out, it still feels as though we are reaching through the dark nearly as often as we are coming up against familiar scenarios. As one small piece of a growing movement, we know it is only through our risks and mistakes that we can collectively forge creative responses to violence.

Bench Ansfield is an organizer with Philly Stands Up and Philly BDS. Timothy Colman is an organizer with the Philly Survivor Support Collective, a former member of Philly's Pissed, and a contributor to The Revolution Starts at Home: Confronting Intimate Violence Within Activist Communities (South End Press, 2011). If you are interested in learning more or donating to support our work, please visit: http://phillysupportstands.wordpress.com.

Shame, Realisation and Restitution: The Ethics of Restorative Practice

Alan Jenkins

In this article, I want to highlight the ethics of restorative practice in therapeutic intervention with men who have abused family members. The term *restorative action* is commonly evoked in the aftermath of abuse, especially in the context of attempts to re-establish respectful relationships between family members. I will critique popular ideas concerning remorse, forgiveness, pardoning and reconciliation, and pose possibilities for ethical practices of restorative action.

Key Words: Shame, Apology, Forgiveness, Restorative Action

Restorative action is commonly regarded, in accordance with dictionary definitions of restoration, as an attempt to rebuild, repair or return to a former state. Such meanings tend to promote a nostalgia or homesickness for what was. Nostalgia is often evident when a man who has abused his partner longs to return to the comfort of earlier times in a relationship, when he could rely on his partner to be tolerant and to defer to him in issues of concern. Such nostalgia invokes *a time when we didn't argue, a time when things were simple and uncomplicated.*

A similar nostalgic concept of restorative action, at a broader societal level, is apparent in our Prime Minister John Howard's invitation for us to reclaim the 'relaxed and comfortable' lifestyle of the 1950s. This was a time, he proposes, when mateship and family values were paramount; a time unfettered by the interference of political correctness. His nostalgia neglects to acknowledge the hegemony inherent in the White Australia Policy, Native Protection Act and criminal codes, which safeguarded the 'values' in question through actively suppressing diversity in the community.

Both men might be seen to possess a similar longing for past times when things seemed easier or less complicated for those with privilege, where acknowledging diversity and difference could be seen as unacceptable and threatening to corrupt a 'decent' way of life.

When we think of restorative action, it is perhaps helpful to consider:

- To restore what?
- For whom?
- For what purpose?
- And, in whose interests?

One alternative meaning of *restorative* caught my eye in the dictionary entry, one that seemed conspicuously different: *the tendency to give new strength or vigour.* This interpretation points to something new, something better and healthier, suggesting a revitalisation, or new possibilities that might develop. In this context, *restorative* suggests something creative and productive.

I would like to consider this expansive concept of restorative action from an ethical perspective. What possibilities might such a concept open up in work with men who have abused family members?

Responses to Sexual Assault in a School Community

Some time back, I was telephoned by a school counsellor who wanted to refer a 14 year-old boy who had 'sexually harassed' on the school oval a girl from his year group. I enquired about what had taken place and was told by the school counsellor that the boy had initially wanted the girl to go out with him. At first she agreed to his request but later decided not to. Following her decision, the boy and his friends followed the girl around the schoolyard for two days, making offensive and derogatory comments. This harassment finally culminated in the boy 'molesting' the girl.

Alan Jenkins has becoming increasingly intrigued with possibilities for the discovery of ethical and respectful ways of relating in his work with people who have abused and members of their communities. This paper is an abridged version of the keynote address delivered at 26th Australian Family Therapy Conference, October 2005. **Contact address:** NADA Consultants, PO Box 773, Stirling SA 5152; alanjenkins@ozemail.com.au

I discovered that the counsellor's descriptions of the boy's behaviour were seriously understated. The boy forcibly pinned the girl to the ground, removed her clothing and raped her with his fingers. His friends watched this assault. On reflection, the school counsellor agreed that this behaviour constituted sexual assault.

I enquired about how the school had responded to this incident. I was informed that the assault had been reported to police who were apparently uninterested, because the girl had initially agreed to go out with the boy, albeit briefly. The counsellor had sought counselling help for the girl, which she and her family declined. They apparently did not want police involvement, and the girl ceased attending school. The school had suspended the boy for two weeks and was seeking counselling for him with the hope that he might soon be ready to attend a re-entry meeting and return to school.

The counsellor agreed that the suspension was perhaps inadequate, and that the boy's conduct made it questionable whether he should return to the school community. However, he pointed out that the school would face difficulties in taking a stand because the education authority and the boy's parents would most likely be concerned about depriving him of his 'right to an education'.

I enquired about how the school response to this incident might impact on the girl, *her* right to an education, and *her* decision to leave the school. The counsellor agreed that the girl might feel extremely unsafe, intimidated and humiliated. These experiences might affect her ability to return to the school, particularly with the prospect of the boy's imminent return. She might feel uncertain about the attitude of the staff and students of the school towards her. The counsellor acknowledged that perhaps the girl's entitlement to receive an education at this school should have some priority over the boy's, in these circumstances. However, he did not think that the school and education bureaucracies would support this priority, particularly in light of the fact that the police had decided not to charge the boy.

I enquired about what the school had done about the boy's friends, who had watched the assault but had taken no action.

I noted that the school's motto included the words 'respect' and 'consideration', and asked the following questions to the school hierarchy:

- How had this incident impacted on young people feeling safe at school?
- What had it meant for boys and girls' sense of being emotionally secure at the school?
- What might have been lost or damaged in the school community as a result of this incident?
- What action did the school intend to take to address these issues?

It rapidly became apparent that the initial views of restorative action at the school were based on nostalgic considerations. The school's proposed actions comprised:

- Send the girl off for 'counselling' and hope that she soon feels safe to come back to the school.
- Provide 'counselling' for the boy to ensure he understands that his behaviour is unacceptable and have him return to school as soon as possible.
- Arrange mediation between the boy and girl with the hope that an apology will lead to forgiveness and the re-establishment of cordial relations.

Little consideration had been given to the impact of this incident upon the school community or the need to address the experience and behaviour of the boys who witnessed the assault. The school's responses would constitute a reactionary form of restorative action which focuses on a few individuals and the hope that everything can go back to the way it was, as though the incident could be quickly left behind or forgotten.

Fortunately, the counsellor agreed to organise meetings with student leaders, staff and members of the parent council, to discuss the nature and effects of the incident and consider how the school might respond with the individuals concerned and to address the impact upon the school as a whole. These forums enabled deeper consideration, with a focus on restorative action involving the whole school community. In this way, the incident could be seen as provoking a creative renewal within the school.

Taking an ethical focus, the counsellor urged the audience at these forums to consider:

- What does this school stand for?
- How might we establish a respectful, safe, protective and considerate school culture?
- Having established such a culture, how do we maintain it?
- How do we reach out to provide safety and protection to the girl who was assaulted?
- What would it mean if the boy's right to an education at that school were privileged over the girl's?

- How do we establish expectations and consequences for a student who has hurt another student and thereby caused harm to the whole community?
- How do we establish expectations and consequences for those bystanders who took no action?
- How do we assess and address the effects of this abuse on our community?
- How do we raise awareness and educate about sexual assault, abuse and violence in the school community?

The school community's collaborative approach focused on ethical behaviour, and agreed to strive to restore fairness and justice for all involved in the incident. Further, the school community examined school culture, and recommended strategies to prevent future abuse.

The Nature of Apology

I now want to consider the ethics of restorative action from the perspective of work with men who have abused. The concept of apology has become increasingly popular, even pivotal, in restorative action within therapeutic, criminal justice and social justice practices. However, we need to consider when, how and in what circumstances an apology might be likely to be restorative, in the expansive as opposed to the nostalgic sense. The caricature apology in the film *A Fish Called Wanda*, which is delivered at gunpoint to a terrified and unwilling recipient, might strongly resonate with survivors of abuse who have felt further harmed or insulted by ill-considered attempts at apology.

When apology is an instrumental act designed to achieve a specific goal, it can result in further abuse of a person who may already feel humiliated and vulnerable.

I witnessed such an apology. An eight-year-old child had been sexually assaulted by her older brother, and had been left feeling culpable and ashamed as a result. During his apology, the young man burst into intense sobbing. His expression of emotion inadvertently privileged his feelings, in a context that had been intended to support the little girl. She appeared distressed and overwhelmed and interrupted his apology to deliver her own apology to him, perhaps for causing him so much distress or perhaps to end this distressing ritual.

A Judaeo-Christian tradition links the concept of atonement, which may be expressed through apology, with the concept of forgiveness. Dominant and popular concepts of forgiveness tend to emphasise the achievement of three major components (Jenkins, Hall & Joy, 2002):

- Relinquishment by the offended person of suffering or resentment
- Pardoning the person at fault, or the offensive act
- Reconciliation or re-establishment of a relationship, or significant connection

"When apology becomes regarded as an externally prescribed moral obligation, its nature tends to become corrupted."

These represent separate *possibilities*, each of which may be considered by a person who has been subjected to abuse. However, if possibilities become *requirements*, notions of apology and forgiveness become subject to expectations and move into the realm of moral obligations. A demand for apology; 'What you did is terrible — you go over and apologise right away', can in turn lead to a demand for forgiveness by the wronged individual. This provides little opportunity for anyone to realise the nature of abusive acts or their potential impact upon others. The kind of apology that results tends to be based on a sense of appeasing the demands of others or a self-centred desire to be released from guilt and responsibility for one's actions; for a 'quick fix' of forgiveness and forgetting. Such apologies can even be followed with moralising outrage by the abusing person, when the persons suffering from the abuse are unwilling to forgive.

Stephen had sexually assaulted his granddaughter, Ava, but became increasingly preoccupied with his daughter Monica's distress, outrage and reluctance to have contact with him. Following his apology, he self-righteously complained, 'She can't forgive'; 'Her anger is eating her up and destroying what we have as a family'; 'She must learn to put it all behind her and move on — for her own good'.

When apology becomes regarded as an externally prescribed moral obligation, its nature tends to become corrupted. The vital importance of acknowledging the exploitative nature and effects of abusive behaviour upon others becomes obscured.

Our Prime Minister's refusal to apologise, on behalf of white Australians, to Indigenous Australians for past injustices perpetrated, appears to mirror Stephen's lack of recognition of the effects of injustice. Aboriginal leaders and many Australians have requested or demanded such an apology, as a symbolic basis for reconciliation and reparation. The Prime Minister has stubbornly refused, questioning the patriotism of 'black armband' historians. A government policy based on a watered down 'statement of regret' and misleading notions of 'practical reconciliation', reflects a belief that Aboriginal–White Australian reconciliation can and should take place without appreciation and acknowledgment of previous injustice and harm.

Media coverage of political and cultural events frequently highlights corrupted notions of apology. The politician who recently made gratuitous and opportunistic references to a previous party leader's resignation in disgrace and subsequent suicide attempt, was interviewed by a journalist about his dishonourable comments. The interviewer clearly expected that an apology might be due. The politician declined, stating, 'I'm not the most sensitive man'. He appeared to invite us to excuse his actions as those of a person perhaps incapable of considering their harmful effects. He then reluctantly added, 'If it makes people feel better, I'll apologise'. The notion 'If I have offended anyone, then I am sorry', is frequently trotted out by politicians, spin bowlers and any number of public figures, in circumstances where they have behaved offensively. This kind of apology clearly means little more than a desire for others to relinquish resentment and bad feelings. Such apologies reflect nostalgic views of restorative action.

The major Christian churches have established 'healing' protocols, which can involve apologies to those who have been sexually assaulted by clergy. However, these protocols and apologies generally fail to acknowledge that the abuses took place in the name of the church and that the church breached a duty of care in taking no action to prevent them. Perhaps this failure to acknowledge responsibility stems from a lack of understanding of the nature of abuse and the experiences of those who suffered it, or perhaps it is driven by priorities of financial risk management. Whatever the reason, many people are outraged and feel further abused when they participate in these 'healing' processes.

The concept of apology is perhaps most destructive when linked with the expectation that an apology should automatically lead to the proffering of forgiveness.

Such expectations are apparent in the demands of a man who had physically, verbally and sexually abused his marriage partner over a period of 10 years: 'I have owned up to it. I am coming to counselling. I have said I am sorry. She should forgive me. What more is she expecting? Why can't we get back together?'

The Nature of Restitution

Rather than 'apology', which has become corrupted by misunderstandings, I have found the concept of *restitution* to be more helpful in restorative practice. Restitution involves a process of expanding one's understanding through acknowledging the abuse of power inherent in the original harmful action, and consideration of the feelings and experiences of the other(s) whom one has harmed. Restitution is informed by remorse, which is centred on the experience of those who have been hurt by the abuse, rather than the sense of personal distress and loss felt by the person who has abused. Restitution moves towards renewal, whereas apology frequently invokes nostalgia.

> David had abused his partner, Amy, and terrified his children, who witnessed some of this abuse, over a period of several years. David wrote the following passage in an attempt to apologise for his actions. 'I am really sorry. I will never treat any of you like this again. I think we can make it work if you just give me another chance. We can put this behind us and have the family we have always dreamed of.'
>
> David genuinely felt sorry, and was committed to ceasing abusive behaviour. However, his statement reflects a self-centred preoccupation with a desire for Amy to relinquish her angry and hurt feelings, pardon him, and reconcile with him.
>
> Only when David was invited to consider closely the profound effects of his abusive actions upon family members, alongside recollections of his father's hollow apologies to his mother in similar circumstances, did he begin to recognise the offensive and reactionary nature of his apology. This led him to embark on a patient journey towards a restorative understanding of his family's experiences and needs.

Acts of restitution require acceptance of the abused person's entitlement to make his/her own judgments about whether or not to relinquish feelings, pardon or reconcile. There can be no strings attached. The person who has abused is prepared to accept whatever decision is taken by the other. There can be no expectation or requirement for forgiveness.

Derrida in his essay 'On Forgiveness' invites us to examine and elevate the concept of forgiveness beyond the popular and banal. He examines the concept of reparation in the context of attempts by nation states to address crimes against humanity, and notes that forgiveness is often sought or offered 'in the service of a finality' where it 'aims to re-establish a normality' (Derrida, 2001: 31). He goes on:

> Forgiveness is not, it *should not be*, normal, normative, normalising. It *should* remain exceptional, extraordinary, in the face of the impossible: as if it interrupted the ordinary course of historical temporality (ibid: page 32).

Derrida highlights a paradox; 'There is the unforgivable. Is this not in truth, the only thing to forgive?' (ibid: 32). He continues, 'If one is only prepared to forgive what appears forgivable, what the church calls "venial sin", then the very idea of forgiveness would disappear'. When we consider that 'forgiveness forgives only the unforgivable', we face an aporia or paradox which opens up remarkable possibilities in forgiveness but which highlights the consideration that forgiveness cannot be conditional and 'should never amount to a therapy of reconciliation'.

The Politics of Atonement

It is in this light that I want to consider the nature of the journey that a man might take towards restitution; a journey of atonement. This journey involves a shift from a self-centred to an other-centred focus, through:

- Political realisation about the nature and effects of abuse
- Restitution and reparation for the harm caused
- Resolution, through accepting the preferred outcomes of those that have been hurt.

This concept of atonement departs from the Judeo-Christian tradition that appears to link apology to forgiveness and reconciliation (Isaiah 43.25; Ephesians 1.7–8; Leviticus 16.6–30).

This is a political journey towards becoming ethical. Its reference point is the man's own ethics; his preferences for his own ways of living and relating with others. His ethics concern the kind of man, partner or father that he wants to become.

In order to assist the man discover and clarify his ethics, we as therapists are required to take a parallel ethical journey which calls for us to be open to the possibility that there may be more to this man than violence, minimisation of responsibility and self-centred demands for forgiveness and forgetting. The parallel journey requires openness to the possibility that this man might value qualities such as partnership, caring, compassion, mutual respect and equity, yet be pursuing them in extremely misguided and destructive ways. He may be attempting to pursue ethical goals, using cultural blueprints that inadvertently promote controlling behaviour, disrespect and violence.

When the man acts from a sense of exaggerated entitlement and abdicates responsibility for his actions, he will be used to relying upon others to take action on his behalf, in regard to his abusive behaviours. He may not be wilfully cruel or nasty, but he may never have taken the time or trouble to think about his partner's experience. He may be used to relying upon her to tolerate his abusive behaviour, worry about it, try to prevent it, walk on eggshells around it, and take responsibility for coping with its consequences (Jenkins, 1990).

A journey towards becoming ethical involves being accountable to the experiences and needs of those who have been subjected to abuse:

- Who is doing the work to address the effects of abusive behaviour?
- Who thinks most about the impact of abuse?
- Whose job should it be to think about it?

Ethical preferences and investments are discovered when we explore the flux that exists between practices of complicity and practices of resistance which characterise all power relations (Ransom, 1997).

> Rob had a long history of police intervention for violence and had just completed a prison sentence for vengefully assaulting his uncle (who had sexually assaulted him as a child). Rob had been diagnosed by prison psychologists as a man with 'empathy deficits' and 'poor impulse control'. However, he was able to relate an alternative history which involved caring, protectiveness and courage as a child, when he tried, albeit unsuccessfully, to protect his younger sister from his uncle's abuse.
>
> When Rob was again taunted by his uncle, he managed to stop himself from committing another assault. He reported that he 'felt like killing' his uncle, so I enquired as to how he had managed to prevent further assault under these provocative circumstances. He explained that he was on parole and that he did not want to go back to prison. I enquired about why this was important to him. At first he appeared surprised at my question, imagining the answer to be self-evident. However, he stopped and thought for a moment and responded, 'Gemma (his three year-old daughter) needs a dad'. I continued to enquire about why this was important to him, and he began to think deeply. He responded with tearful eyes, 'I don't want to put her through what I went through'.
>
> In subsequent conversation, Rob appeared to rediscover ethics of care and concern, with a strong desire to protect and provide for his daughter. These were ethics that he previously appeared to have lost sight of, having resigned himself to

accept, in accordance with other's judgements and assessments, that perhaps he was selfish, 'mean' and 'out of control'.

Ethics, Morality and Love

The work of philosophers like Deleuze and Nietzsche can help us to understand the importance of considering ethics which are immanent rather than transcendent. This concept of ethics is not concerned with judging modes of existence according to external moral standards, that is, whether Rob's behaviour is 'good or bad' or 'right or wrong', whether his thinking and actions conform to our own or someone else's moral standards. Rather, this concept of ethics focuses on the extent to which Rob's thinking and actions enable him to *move towards actualising* his ethics and preferences.

According to Deleuze, who elaborated concepts originally proposed by Nietzsche and Spinoza, ethics that are in the process of emerging can either affirm or detract from desire and life. They can be productive, creative, expansive, opening up possibilities and embracing difference, or alternatively, restrictive, repressive and reductive of options (Deleuze, 1981; Nietzsche, 1990; Smith, 1997; Colebrook, 2002a, 2002b; Protevi, 2003).

A Deleuzian notion of love departs from common *domestic* understandings by regarding love as 'an encounter with another that opens up to a possible new world'. Such a notion of love refers to a power to move beyond what we know and experience directly; to reach into and imagine the world of the other. Love requires extending oneself through creative and novel connections, which point to new possibilities that may be expansive, and creative. Love entails reaching out and embracing differences. Deleuzian love stands in stark contrast to *domestic* forms of love, which reflect a kind of capture by dominant cultural interests. These concepts of domestic love prescribe requirements for commonality and sameness, along with the suppression of difference. ('If you love me you will think the same as I do and I can feel entitled to challenge and suppress any differences you express, in the name of love.') Domestic love is not always repressive but can prescribe ownership and a sense of entitlement to correct the other and enforce sameness. From this perspective, violence is commonly enacted in the name of love (Jones, 2003).

The Deleuzian concept of love fits with restitution and with the expansive concept of atonement and restorative action I have proposed. Love supports non-violative and respectful relationships, which privilege fairness and accountability.

Our own parallel journeys as therapists require us to act from a similarly expansive sense of love when working with men who have abused. We are required to reach out and become open to understanding ethical possibilities in the man's preferences. Ethically, we can only enable the man to express his own preferences, we cannot impose our own concepts of what is right or wrong.

Over many years, I have struggled to hold my practice accountable to this concept of love. When a man attempts to justify shockingly abusive behaviour and appears to show indifference, even contempt, for those he has harassed and terrified, I find it difficult to be respectful and open to possibilities. I must make it my business to try to understand what family members have experienced as a result of being subjected to his abuse. If I failed to experience outrage and grief, I would become part of the problem. Yet I must find ways to act from love rather than from states of judgemental tyranny, when working with such a man. I rely upon my community of colleagues and their love, for critique and support in this challenging endeavour.

The Concept of Remorse

I have found Raimond Gaita's work to be extremely helpful in clarifying ethics in restorative action. Gaita regards the experiences of *love* and *remorse* as fundamental in understanding ethical practice. Through these experiences, we come to appreciate 'the full humanity', 'inalienable dignity' and the 'unique and irreplaceable nature' of others (Gaita, 1991: page xxii).

Gaita highlights the experience of *remorse* as 'a pained, bewildered realisation of what it (really) means to wrong someone' (ibid: page xiv). We ask ourselves:

- 'My God what have I done?'
- 'How could I have done it?'

The experience of remorse is 'an awakened sense of the reality of another ... through the shock of wrongdoing the other' (ibid: 52).

This sense of remorse is clearly vital in meaningful restorative action.

Gaita also highlights the importance of an 'ethic of renunciation'; an ethic which requires that we

> keep fully amongst us:
>
> - those who suffer severe, ineradicable and degrading afflictions
> - (and) those who have committed the most terrible deeds and whose character seems to fully match them (ibid: xxxii).

In a similar vein, Iris Murdoch highlights an ethical task whereby expressions of love enable us 'to see the world as it is' (Murdoch, 1970: 40). Through expressions of love, compassion and justice, we can come to appreciate the reality of another person. This task has utmost ethical priority in consideration of how we might live.

In this context, restorative action requires ethical realisation which enables both:

- Restitution to those specifically hurt and to the community.
- Reclamation of integrity and a sense of self-respect.

Gaita's concept of ethics stands in stark contrast to currently popular ethical theories such as those of Peter Singer, whose 'practical ethics' appears to concern the weighing up of relative consequences, in a utilitarian consideration of the 'greater good'. Relative, utilitarian considerations can be used to justify any number of injustices in the name of the greater good, including the indefinite detention of refugees, marginalisation of indigenous communities and lying by politicians.

The Nature of Shame

It is not possible to embark upon a restorative journey without facing shame. The experience of shame is a sense of disgrace which unavoidably accompanies deeper realisations about the nature and impact of dishonourable and destructive actions. However, this experience of shame seems highly restraining and disabling for men who have abused family members — the shame often feeling toxic to the point of annihilation. Shame and disgrace tend to motivate desperate attempts to run and hide from their presence.

Here we must recognise a distinction between *shaming* and *facing shame*. When a man faces shame, he comes to his own realisations through recognising a contradiction between his ethics and his actions. By contrast, shaming others is a political act, an attempt to coerce or compel.

Our work cannot be ethical if it employs shaming. Our job is to provide *safe passage* to assist the man to discover and face the inevitable sense of shame which will accompany his own realisations about the nature and effects of his abusive practices (Jenkins, 2005).

Shame has tended to receive bad press in popular literature, where it is regarded as restrictive; something to be overthrown along with all oppressive structures; an obstacle to enlightenment and liberation of the self. However, Schneider invites us to consider the creative potential of shame and to situate self-development in the context of community. He asserts 'Shame is not a disease ... it is a mark of our humanity'. Shame can be valued as 'a pointer of value awareness', whose 'very occurrence arises from that fact that we are valuing animals' (1992: xviii–xviv). Schneider regards shame as vital in social relations because it is 'aroused by phenomena that would violate the organism and its integrity' (ibid: xxii). Shame offers us a warning regarding potential violation and can help protect privacy. 'To avoid the witness of shame' is regarded by Schneider as akin to removing the brakes on a motor vehicle because they slow it down.

In the context of Indigenous–White reconciliation, Gaita stresses that 'national pride and national shame ... are two sides of the same coin'. 'They are two ways of acknowledging that we are sometimes collectively responsible for the deeds of others' (Gaita, 2004: 8).

As Gaita points out, our Prime Minister asserted 'We settled the land, fought the fires and withstood the droughts. We fought at Gallipoli and later stood against murderous tyranny in Europe'; but refused to acknowledge that 'We took the traditional lands and smashed the traditional way of life. We bought the disasters, the alcohol. We committed the murders. We took the children from their mothers' (ibid: 7).

Gaita contends

> The wish to be proud without sometimes acknowledging the need to be ashamed is that corrupt attachment to country — I will not call it love — that we call jingoism'. The sense of national shame is really nothing other than the plain, humbled acknowledgment of the wrongs in which we have become implicated because of the deeds of our political ancestors and which a faithful love of country requires of us (ibid: 8).

Such an experience of shame does not require debasement or wallowing in self-loathing, as our Prime Minister alleges in his critique of the 'black armband' approach. Indeed, this would constitute a corrupt or self-indulgent expression of shame. Facing shame is crucial to restorative action.

Windows to Shame

> Jack had been physically and emotionally abusive to his partner Sue, over six years. This abusive behaviour had terrified his four-year-old son, Paul who had witnessed his father's violence, possessive interrogations and attempts to restrict his mother's freedom. Jack was engaged in a therapeutic program to address this abusive behaviour and over time, made significant realisations about his actions and their effects. Jack's realisations were followed by some respectful reconnection with Sue and Paul.

I will specifically refer to two vital moments in therapeutic intervention with Jack, when he experienced forms of remorse which fit with those described by Gaita. This remorse enabled Jack to *look shame in the eye*; to *see his abusive behaviour like it really was.*

In the early stages of work with Jack, I quickly discovered that, despite his initial hostile and minimising presentation, he wanted a sense of connection and belonging within his family and a relationship with his son that was very different to the one he had experienced with his own father. We had detailed conversations about Jack's ethical preferences for family relationships, especially in regard to the kind of father he wanted to be.

One of Jack's first strong connections with remorse was experienced when a 'window to shame' opened, as he was describing an incident in which he had assaulted Sue whilst she was holding their son, Paul. At first, when he began recall this incident, Jack started to become caught up in righteous indignation about Sue's 'unreasonable' and 'provocative' behaviour. I interrupted his flow and enquired, 'Where was Paul when you grabbed Sue?' Jack immediately averted his eyes downwards and looked somewhat shaken. I commented, 'You look like you don't feel proud about what you did?' I enquired, 'What are you realising?' Jack told me that he could see Paul and that Paul was 'terrified'. I enquired about how Jack knew this. He responded that he could see Paul cowering on the floor and he could tell by 'the look in his eyes'.

Here was an image with the capacity to haunt Jack; its shocking nature evoking intense shame through the contradiction represented in its violation of certain ethics that were precious to him. Such a recognition had enormous potential to connect Jack with his own ethics and motivate him to take action. Jack had grown up in extreme disadvantage and was subjected to abuse as a child. When Paul was born he was delighted and considered 'all the things I want to give to my son; a family for the first time'. It had been important for Jack to provide something for his son that was different to what he had received himself as a child. Yet Jack had been described as a man with 'empathy deficits'. To work with Jack, we must recognise that empathy and compassion are not fixed 'traits' but highly context-specific. Like many men, when placed in a relevant context, Jack was able to feel intense remorse.

Much later on in therapeutic intervention, Jack had begun to reconnect with Sue and Paul. Jack was demonstrating respect for Sue, who was beginning to feel safe and entitled to 'be her own person' in their relationship. At one point, when Jack was feeling close to Sue, he attempted to reinitiate their sexual relationship. Sue did not feel able to respond and declined his invitation. Jack then felt hurt and became critical of her. His response was characterised by a re-emergence of self-centred notions, that he had previously been challenging; 'What more do I have to do? She should trust me by now'. Sue began to feel guilty and thought that she should want to be intimate with him. However, she also felt angry about Jack's 'pushy' behaviour.

Such a re-emergence of self-centred feelings and ideas should not lead us to discount the work that Jack had already done. It provided a further opportunity to invite him to re-connect with his ethical preferences and imagine more about Sue's experience.

I invited Jack to consider what his sexual initiative might have meant to Sue, and why he thought Sue might not be ready to start having sex again. When I asked Jack about his knowledge of Sue's experience of sex and trust, Jack's eyes averted. He stuttered and looked ashamed. Here was another window to shame. I said, 'You look like there is something you don't feel proud about? What are you realising?' Jack's eyes became tearful as he described an incident that had taken place after he had physically abused Sue. He had felt 'bad' about his actions and had tried to 'make up' by initiating sex. She felt outraged and told him to 'fuck off'. He responded by sexually assaulting her. I enquired, 'What are you seeing?' Jack responded 'Sue frozen with fear and hatred'.

At this moment, Jack was feeling intense disgrace as he faced a haunting image of Sue feeling violated and humiliated. He acknowledged that she had also been sexually assaulted as a child by her older brother and that this abuse had had a huge impact on how safe she felt about sex. Such realisations generally promote avoidance; doing anything to avoid experiencing the sense of disgrace that accompanies seeing them clearly. Our job is to reposition shame so that it can become enabling rather than disabling.

I enquired further:

Have you spoken out about this before?

What does it do to you to look at it so closely?

What does it do to you to see it like it really is?

How does it affect you to speak out about it like this?

Jack named his actions as 'rape'. I commented on his preparedness to *call it what it really is*:

You are trying to see with your eyes wide open what you did to Sue.

What difference does this make (to what you are now able to see)?

What is it taking?

How does it affect you (make you feel)?

In reflecting on the fact that he had added to Sue's experiences of sexual assault Jack replied that he had never felt so low. He recalled the devastating impact of his own experience of being sexually assaulted by his uncle and lamented that he had 'put this on to Sue'. Jack appeared to be experiencing a point of remorse, as described by Gaita: an awakening realisation about Sue's humanity.

In attempting to help Jack reposition his shame and provide safe passage for him to experience it, I enquired:

What would it say about you if you could think about what you did as rape, if you could see Sue frozen with fear and hatred, and you didn't feel ashamed? What does it say about you that you are thinking and feeling; that you are not running away?

Through the process of *talking about talking about it*, Jack could be assisted to connect his realisations and experience of shame with his ethics.

Is this the right direction for you?

What do you respect most; facing it or running away from it?

What path fits with the person you are becoming?

How will this help you?

What is it taking?

Will it make you stronger or weaker as a person?

How does it fit with the man/partner/father you want to be?

Do you think your Dad ever stopped and thought like this?

What difference would it have made if he had?

Over time, I invited Jack to consider:

You have made apologies before, but have you ever looked this closely at what you have done?

What would an apology mean without this level of realisation?

Later on, Jack could be invited to consider:

Who has carried the hurt and humiliation of this incident, in the past?

Who needs to carry it? Whose job is it?

How will you do this?

Will it make you stronger or weaker as a person?

Are you ready to take this further?

In this way, Jack was invited to consider his readiness to make restitution and reparation; to avoid the temptation to wallow in corrupt or counterfeit forms of shame.

"Restitution requires realisations and actions that reach out towards the experiences of others. However, restitution does not always involve expressing those realisations to those that have been hurt."

We are inviting a man to embark upon a painful journey, which requires a readiness to carry the shame on his own shoulders. Such a journey inevitably requires entering a sense of disgrace which initially involves a negative judgment of self, but recognising that atonement lies in these realisations, and taking steps to own and express them. These steps inform restitution and make it possible to reclaim the man's own immanent ethics and thus gain or regain a sense of honour and integrity. In the light of courageous and honourable steps, shame gradually ceases to mean disgrace to self (judging oneself as dishonourable) and becomes a discretionary principle for motivation. The realisation that *I committed terrible acts but I am not a terrible person*, can only be earned through embarking upon this painful journey. We do not assist our clients in any way if we encourage them to avoid or bypass shame or attempt to draw the distinction between disgrace and the shameful actions prematurely (Jenkins, 2005).

Restitution requires realisations and actions that reach out towards the experiences of others. However, restitution does not always involve expressing those realisations to those that have been hurt. Restorative action can involve *staying away* from those who have been hurt and offended by abusive conduct. Such forms of restitution may involve the recognition that, in abusing an individual, you destroy something or damage something within a community. Acts of abuse by one person towards another generally harm the integrity of whole communities by threatening their ethical foundations for trust, connection and interdependence. It is possible to make restitution by putting something back into the community that does not necessarily require direct contact with the individual person whom you have hurt.

Any form of ethical restoration requires our commitment to a parallel ethical journey that must be entered from a state of love; a position of hospitality and accountability. We must recognise our potential to inadvertently act in abusive ways, in the name of love, justice or protection. We must be prepared to face shame ourselves in these instances and to take similar restorative action in the direction of creative new possibilities for our own lives.

I recall instances in which I have acted abusively, in the name of *child protection* or some other *noble* cause. I once engaged in a form of *good cop, bad cop* with a colleague when we both felt frustrated with a young man who denied his sexual assaults on several children who had been in Family Day Care with his family. One of us verbally attacked, shamed and humiliated the young man while the other acted *kindly* at any sign of his resistance wearing down. He eventually acknowledged one of the assaults, probably to get us off his back, but continued to deny any other allegations. His acknowledgment carried no sense of ethical realisation. It was an accommodating response to our assaults. I am haunted by the image of this young man who became increasingly lost and marginalised as a result of our work with him. It is these experiences of shame, which we are also obliged to face and address, in order to develop ethical practices which express love and have integrity.

When we work towards enabling restorative action and supporting our client's journeys towards atonement, we are brought face to face with the paradox of forgiveness; forgiving the unforgivable, whilst maintaining the notion that forgiveness is exceptional and extraordinary and never something that can be invoked as a means to an end.

References

Colebrook, C., 2002a. *Understanding Deleuze*, Crows Nest, NSW, Allen & Unwin.

Colebrook, C., 2002b. *Gilles Deleuze*, London, Routledge.

Deleuze, G., 1981. *Nietzsche and Philosophy*, NY, Columbia University Press.

Derrida, J., 2001. *On Cosmopolitanism and Forgiveness*, London, Routledge. Originally published as *Cosmipolites de tous les pays, encore un effort!* Paris, Editions Galilee, 1977.

Gaita, R., 1991. *Good and Evil*, London, Routledge.

Gaita, R., 2004. Breach of Trust: Truth, Morality and Politics, *Quarterly Essay*: 16.

Jenkins, A., 1990. *Invitations to Responsibility: The Therapeutic Engagement of Men who are Violent and Abusive*, Adelaide, Dulwich.

Jenkins, A., 2005. Knocking On Shame's Door: Facing Shame Without Shaming Disadvantaged Young People Who Have Abused. In M. C. Calder (Ed.), *Children and Young People Who Sexually Abuse; New Theory, Research and Practice Developments*, London, Russell House.

Jenkins, A., Hall, R. & Joy, M., 2002. Forgiveness in Child Sexual Abuse: A Matrix of Meanings, *International Journal of Narrative Therapy and Community Work*, 1: 35–51.

Jones, D., 2003. Personal communication.

Murdoch, I., 1970. *The Sovereignty of Good*, London, Routledge.

Nietzsche, F., 1990. *Beyond Good and Evil*, London, Penguin. Originally published 1886.

Protevi, J., 2003. Love. In P. Patton & J. Protevi, *Between Deleuze and Derrida*, London, Continuum.

Ransom, J. S., 1997. *Foucault's Discipline*, Durham, Duke University Press.

Schneider, C. D., 1992. *Shame, Exposure and Privacy*, NY, Norton.

Smith, D. W., 1997. Introduction: 'A Life of Pure Immanence': Deleuze's 'Critique et Clinique' Project. In *G. Deleuze, Essays Critical and Clinical*, Minneapolis, University of Minnesota Press.

5.10. HOW TO FIND A HELPFUL THERAPIST (FOR PEOPLE WHO HAVE DONE SEXUAL HARM)

The following is some tips for finding a therapist written by someone who at the time of this writing was two years into their accountability process for sexual harm. Written by a perpetrator who is a couple years into an accountability process for sexual violence:

In all the zines I've read and all the stories I've heard, when a survivor calls out a perpetrator and makes a list of demands, it seems like one of the most common – and most commonly not observed – demands is for the perpetrator to see a therapist. I can't say for sure why this is the case, though I have some ideas.

There were a number of things that made me hesitant about seeking therapy.

Many, but not all, forms of sexual assault are technically illegal acts (regardless of how often, or how infrequently, they're brought to court or prosecuted). When I decided to look for a therapist, I was scared because I wanted help around things that I was afraid could bring the coercive hand of the state into my life – around sexual assault that is illegal. I was afraid to talk to therapists about what I needed help with when I interviewed them because I didn't have any understanding of how therapists interact with the legal and court systems. I didn't, and don't, want to be locked in a cage in jail, though I do want help. I was afraid that telling a therapist about my problems would mean that the therapist would report me; then I would have to make a choice between either denying my own actions (which accomplishes nothing but further harm) in order to stay out of jail, or be truthful and suffer the consequences of the state's free license to dole out violence with no accountability. Fortunately, my fears didn't reflect the realities of therapy; I was able to receive help without putting myself in danger. (More on this later.)

I was ashamed about what I have done, and had a lot of fear and anxiety about talking openly about it; this gave me anxiety about seeking a therapist, and also made it harder to be honest with therapists about what help I needed.

Before I decided to seek a therapist, I had a lot of negative feelings about therapy: I didn't want to deal with the stigmatization that comes with needing help or having psychological problems that are beyond my ability to deal with alone. I felt shame and confusion about my own behavior, and I felt intense fear and anxiety at the prospect of speaking about it. Because of these, I found it impossible to communicate with anyone about it for a long time – so therapy wasn't even on my worldmap as a possibility. Later on, when I found ways to talk about my actions, it was still hard to open about – which made it hard to talk to therapists about the things I most needed help with.

I was scared of the power that therapists can have – the power to diagnose behaviors or attitudes as pathological, to coercively medicate or institutionalize people. I was offended by a sense of patronization and lack of understanding I'd gotten from the couple psychologists and psychiatrists I'd had casual interactions with. I didn't get a sense from those first impressions that therapists would be capable of, or were interested in, real empathetic support. This was amplified because I don't believe in the individualized theory of mental health, that psychological and emotional problems are signs that there is something inherently wrong with a particular person; rather, I see harmful or problematic behaviors mostly as symptoms of living in a fucked-up world, and I believe that personal transformation is inseparable from social transformation. I also come from the perspective that medicalized "pathologies" of the psyche aren't necessarily "diseases" or "sicknesses;" like the folks at the Icarus Project, I feel that some of them are dangerous gifts – valuable but potentially harmful abilities and states of being. I felt all of these perspectives were completely blown off by those psychiatrists and psychologists I had interacted with, and I didn't trust the institution of psychology worth shit.

Then there's the simple fact that therapy costs money – sometimes lots of money – and I've never had expendable income; furthermore, because of other emotional problems I found it hard to hold down even a part-time job. On top of that, I come from a middle-class family, but my political sense of the world gives me a sense of guilt and shame about that privilege. I held a certain degree of hatred for therapy because I saw it as a rich people's indulgence, a sign of bourgeois decadence and yuppie lifestyle.

On top of all of that, going to therapy – even if I didn't have all these other reservations and emotions – meant I would also have to rearrange my routine, maybe cut back on or drop out of some activities that I enjoyed in order to create enough time in my schedule for weekly sessions. Besides that, I would have to find some way to get access to non-monetary resources, like a car, in order to make therapy a realistic possibility.

If other people's experiences are anything like mine, it's no wonder people don't go to therapy. It's easy for me to understand why someone would have a tremendous resistance to going – or would simply find it easier to do nothing, rather than deal with all of these huge problems. I have been through about a year and a half of therapy, however, and I would like to start up therapy again when I'm able. I know that it has been unquestionably useful in my process of understanding myself, dealing with my shit, sorting out all my emotional problems, and changing. So I want to talk about how therapy can help, and more particularly about how to find a helpful therapist – because it is completely true that there are manipulative, power-hungry, non-validating, dogmatic, and controlling therapists out there. Fortunately, I have found those aren't all therapists.

WHY THERAPY?

So how can therapy be useful?

Pattrice Jones, in her book called Aftershock, about trauma and activism, provides a good description of some of the benefits of therapy. "The great thing about talking with a therapist is that, besides being an expert in the problems in living faced by traumatized people, the therapist's sole role in the relationship is to be helpful. The conflicts of interest and personal dynamics that can prevent friends and comrades from being helpful don't get in the way." And "because the therapist will, as a matter of professional ethics, have her own source of emotional support," someone seeing a therapist "doesn't have to worry about offering reciprocal care. You can express yourself freely in the safety of the consulting room, without worrying that your memories or emotions will be too difficult for the listener to bear."

Therapists are professionals. While in almost every other circumstance, in anti-capitalist circles at least, this tends to leave a bad taste in the mouth, here it has an upside, too. For one, it means that good therapists are, well, "professional." They don't gossip, they don't hang out with your friends, you don't have any particular social obligation to make small talk with them at the grocery store. Everybody, I wager, has things they're ashamed of, or afraid of, to the point where they can't hardly squeak out a word to anyone about those things. I imagine this is even more the case for someone who is going through an accountability process for sexual violence, abuse, or boundary crossing. But a lot of times, these same issues that are surrounded by shame and fear are also the persistent, nagging issues that form the cornerstone for a whole host of other problems. These shame-silenced memories can also provide hints about other areas, maybe areas you haven't explored before, that might prove fruitful in helping you understand your own life and behavior. Airing the issues that are immerse in shame and processing them can – and in my personal experience, does – make a big difference in transformation and healing, and it can reveal all sorts of insights about the feelings that underlie larger negative patterns. Having an outlet to talk about the things I'm most ashamed of has done wonders to improve my daily A helpful therapist will listen, and be able to stay present with whatever it is you're talking about. Sometimes friends just can't handle it when somebody brings up a particularly intense topic or one that hits home for them. Sometimes friends are dealing with their own issues – which might lead them to feel overwhelmed listening to problems that other people are working through. Sometimes friends are afraid to talk about certain issues, or don't know what to say, so they change the topic or don't bring it up. Sometimes friends are just distracted. Co-counseling with people close to you is good, and it's part of a process of healing and finding support. But it's not always enough; there are times, or topics, when it can be great to have somebody who's not in the thick of their own healing process, just like you. Somebody who's not going to be triggered by what you say, or be distracted by their own need for support. (In situations of accountability, it may also plain and simple be inappropriate to talk to some of your friends about some of the things you need to talk about. If you need to talk details of something you've done, for example, in order to process it – your friends may not be able to listen, without rage, a desire for punishment, or other complicating emotions, especially if it was something done to other people they know and care about.)

On top of that, a helpful therapist will be able to bring some solid experience to the table. A helpful therapist will have experience, theoretical training, and an extensive exposure that comes from study, so they can help you identify patterns you may not see. A helpful therapist will often have a long professional history, with clients who have had problems similar to yours. They can provide little tricks that they've learned along the way for breaking out of thought cycles; they can provide forecasts for how the road may look ahead, and whether you'll turn out all right. These things can make all the difference; someone without the clinical experience may be stumbling along in the twilight next to you, looking just as desperately for some message from the future. It can be reassuring to hear someone speak from experience, not just hope and conjecture.

THE CANDIDATES

But all of these things depend on having a HELPFUL therapist. There are still a fair number of folks out there that, despite their Ph.D.s, are less useful than the rot falling off an old shoe. So the question remains: how to find a helpful therapist?

And how to find one on the cheap?

And how to find one that will be able to help you if you're looking to stop crossing boundaries?

What follows are some tips and resources I've come across, in order to help answer these very questions. Let's start with the general.

If you're looking for therapists who have experience working with people who want to stop crossing boundaries, there are a couple of organizations that keep directories and make referrals. If you need low-cost therapy, it's worth asking all of these referral services about therapists who offer sliding scale fees. (I used these referral services to find one of the therapists I saw.)

In the U.S., there's the Sex Abuser Treatment Referral Line, which is a national referral service operated by the Safer Society Foundation, Inc. for anyone interested in locating a treatment provider for an individual with sexual behavior problems. You can get in touch with the referral line

By phone: (802) 247-3132 Monday-Friday, 9am-4:30pm EST
By fax: (802) 247-4233
Or by email: tammyk@sover.net

All telephone referrals are done anonymously. For more information on the Safer Society Foundation, check out their website at http://www.safersociety.org

Then there's the Society for the Advancement of Sexual Health, which is a nonprofit organization "dedicated to promoting public and professional awareness and understanding of addictive/compulsive sexual behavior and its associated negative consequences." They also talk specifically about "out of control sexual behavior:" sexual addiction, sexual compulsivity, and sexual offending. For a mainstream organization, their analysis isn't half bad. Among other things, they offer referrals. For more information, check:

The Society for the Advancement of Sexual Health
PO Box 725544
Atlanta, GA 31139
(770) 541-9912
Email: sash@sash.net
Web: http://www.sash.net

Then there's the Sex Abuse Treatment Alliance, which is a nonprofit organization to prevent sexual abuse. They work both with those who have been abused and those who have abused. Among other things, they provide referrals for abusers and abused, they promote the use of restorative justice methods for the abused and their abusers, they "provide a network of support for abusers who are currently in treatment," and they provide information/support/letters for people in prison who want help.

Sex Abuse Treatment Alliance (SATA)
http://www.satasort.org
Phone: (517) 482-2085 or (517) 372-8207
Email: help@satasort.org

Then there's Stop It Now!, which is a public health based organization working to "prevent and ultimately eradicate child sexual abuse," and they "challenge abusers and people at risk for abusing to stop abusive behaviors and to reach out for help." Among other things, they produce informational pamphlets to educate adults on prevention of child sexual abuse. They also run a helpline, which is a toll-free number for adults who are at risk for sexually abusing a child, for friends and family of sexual abusers and/or victims, and for parents of children with sexual behavior problems. All calls are confidential and will be answered by a trained staff member; they encourage people calling to report any abuse to law enforcement, but they themselves will not report anyone. The website and helpline both offer referrals.

Stop It Now!
http://www.stopitnow.org
351 Pleasant Street, Suite B319
Northampton, MA 01060
Phone: (413) 587-3500
Helpline: 1-888-PREVENT (1-888-773-8368), Monday-Friday 9:00am-6:00pm EST
Fax: (413) 587-3505
Email: info@stopitnow.org

So those are some mainstream, sex-offender specific referral services.

If you want to find a therapist who has experience specifically around helping people to stop crossing sexual boundaries, another place you might go – though it seems counter-intuitive and frightening – is to your local Rape Crisis Center. This option might make even more sense if you're someone who has survived sexual violence yourself. It makes more sense than you might think – lots of survivors have problems with boundaries, and want to stop crossing people's boundaries in sexual ways. This is where the grey-zone of consent comes in; probably most survivors, if they do have problems with crossing boundaries, never go into that nebulous area called "assault." I actually found the therapist I saw for a number of months through the local Rape Crisis Center, and she was really helpful.

I was up front with her that I was seeking therapy because I wanted to stop crossing people's boundaries; that's when she told me what I repeated above, that lots of survivors have problems with boundaries. She mentioned it to reassure me that she does have experience in this arena. Usually, though, it wasn't the primary focus of her clients' therapy, so we had to shift her customary focus around a bit. But it worked well, once she understood that I wanted the focus to be solidly, and before everything else, on my problem crossing people's boundaries. I would suggest that you take care specifically here to be up front when interviewing therapists from Rape Crisis Centers. Some therapists who work at Rape Crisis Centers may not be prepared to counsel this process to be really helpful. More on how to conduct interviews with therapists in just a second.

But first, another quick word from pattrice jones, giving her recommendations: "How do you know whether or not a therapist is right for you? Ask questions. Make sure you feel comfortable with this therapist's way of thinking about people and their problems in living. But don't worry too much about theories. Some research indicates, and I believe, that the empathic 'match' between client and therapist is the most important factor in whether or not a course of therapy will be helpful. Make sure you feel comfortable with this person. Trust yourself. If you feel safe with this person, trust that and give it a go. But also trust your misgivings. Some people are not trustworthy. You don't want to hurt yourself further by becoming vulnerable to one of them. If you feel unsafe, you'll need to figure out whether this is because of the person or because of your own fear about talking about your trauma. How can you tell? Shop around. Have test sessions or preliminary meetings with a few prospective therapists. Whatever you feel with all of them is probably due to you. Any differences in how you feel are probably due to the differences among them."

Now, some recommendations for interviewing therapists. The first time I went looking for a therapist, I dreaded the initial contact. I felt like I would have to make myself extremely vulnerable – it's not easy to tell a total stranger who you don't trust and who has power over you the story of the sexual violence you have committed. Seeking my first therapist, I just sucked it up and did something that felt extremely unsafe to me. It ended up working out well, but that same fear and dread led me to seriously drag my heels the second time I went looking for a therapist. I didn't want to have to put myself through that kind of an emotional wringer, even to find help. Fortunately, after a couple months of dragging my feet, I met someone with some experience facilitating radical accountability processes, and he gave me a couple concise sentences that summed up what I was looking for – in therapists' own language – so that I didn't have to explain the long way by making myself extremely emotionally vulnerable with a stranger. Those couple sentences go something like this: "I'm looking for a therapist in the <your city> area to work with a noncriminal self-referral. Specifically, I'm looking for someone with expertise working with <your demographic> who have sexually offended, for an opportunity with potential for ongoing therapy, and for someone with interest in or experience with transformational healing and/or restorative justice." Having those two sentences saved me untold amounts of anxiety an apprehension. They were also useful in providing a quick filter to tell me which therapists were worth setting up an interview with.

When I was preparing to interview therapists, I made a list of questions covering all my concerns and needs prior to scheduling any interview appointments. I actually wrote all of the questions down on a sheet of paper in order to make sure I didn't accidentally leave out any important topics. I'll share some of the types of questions I asked.

First of all, probably one of the most important – in terms of allaying my fears and building a foundation for trust – comes the issue of confidentiality. As I was saying above, I was scared to talk to a therapist because I have crossed people's boundaries in ways that are illegal. It was important to me to ease some of those fears, and so I asked the therapists about confidentiality and reporting to law enforcement. I have since learned a little more about therapy and confidentiality, which lays many of my fears to rest.

According to pattrice jones, professional therapists "ethically must not and legally cannot be forced to break confidentiality about past actions." In the case of abuse and other things, however, this does not hold if the abuse is ongoing in the present. It also does not hold if the therapy client has plans to do some such action in the future. (Commonly, therapists will tell you that the only time they will report is, for example, when there seems to be a threat to the safety of either the client or someone else, in the present or the future – for example, if there is current domestic violence, if the client has a plan to commit suicide, or if the client plans to injure someone else. In cases where there is current abuse or neglect of a child or vulnerable adult, I believe therapists are actually required by law to report the abuse.) It is still important to have a frank conversation about confidentiality, however, before disclosing anything. If think you might have legal trouble at some point in the future, and you want to make sure someone like police or the FBI don't get their hands on your files, jones says "you may wish to ask the therapist with whom you work to keep only the most vague and cursory notes, so that your privacy is protected even if authorities do manage to breach confidentiality." You might want to ask potential therapists when they would report you without your consent, when they would recommend you report yourself (but not report you themselves), whether they have reported other clients in the past (and what the situation was like), and so on. You might also want to ask them about their relationship with and opinion of law enforcement – do they feel prison is rehabilitating? Do they feel the legal system is just? And so on.

It can also be wise to ask lots of questions about confidentiality if someone else – parents, boss, the government – is paying for the therapy. Be sure you're clear what the therapist will and won't tell such people. What sort of information will they have access to, and what will the therapist share with them? What sort of relationship will the therapist have with these people? What sort of power do they have over the therapist?

After this, I was up-front about what I was seeking therapy for more specifically – that I want to stop crossing people's sexual boundaries, stop engaging in sexual violence, etc. – and I asked how (or if) they feel they would be able to help. I also asked what kinds of diagnosis they would use for people coming to them with these sorts of desires. One of the therapists I saw, for example, had experience working with people with sexual behavior problems, and he said he usually diagnoses people with "adjustment disorders with depressive (or anxious, etc.) mood." (Basically: "everything is generally okay in this person's life, but they're having some problems with a particular aspect of their life and have some depressive/anxious/etc. tendencies." It's an all-purpose, vague diagnosis.) He understood that there is an incredible stigma attached to being diagnosed with a sexual behavior problem, and worked to make the therapy experience less frightening for the people he worked with.

It is a good idea to ask about the therapists' understanding of queer/trans issues, racism, specific cultural concerns, any political or religious beliefs, and so on. If they don't seem to have a good understanding of something important to your life, ask if they would be willing to educate themselves on their own time in order to become better informed and a more sensitive therapist.

I asked questions regarding the therapists' feelings about herbal medicine and their approach to pharmaceuticals (and if they'd want me to take some), and about their ability to respect things (like spiritual experiences) that might be commonly written off as crazy. If I tell them something is a problem, I asked whether they'll believe me and accept it as a problem; similarly, I wanted to know when they would and wouldn't challenge me (or simply overrule me) if there's something they see as a problem that I don't actually see as a problem. If you want to know about the therapists' particular methods, the interview is a good time to ask about the therapeutic approach different therapists take, as well.

One of therapists I saw recommended another couple questions to ask during interviews in the future: How much experience does someone have as a therapist? How much therapy/healing have they done for themselves? How much experience do they have with clients working through x or y issue? (My therapist recommended the second question as a way of gauging how present a therapist can be while they listen to what you're saying – if they'll still be working out things from their own past when you talk to them about your life, and how present they will be if you show intense emotion, or start sobbing, or whatever.)

These interviews helped me feel more empowered and assertive in the therapy, and more able to ask for what I wanted. They helped me feel comfortable saying so if I wanted to stop talking for a while and get feedback or education from the therapist, or if I wanted to stop the therapist when they were talking and go in a different direction. The ability to do this was a great gift. I felt more able to direct the therapy towards where I actually wanted to go, instead of where the therapist thought I wanted to go. Overall, the therapist interviews were invaluable to making therapy something worthwhile and something that tangibly benefited me.

CLOSING COMMENTS

In my last session with one therapist I saw, I talked with her about how the therapy had been and gave her feedback on my experience. One of the interesting things I learned from her was that it took her a handful of sessions before she was able to learn how to respond to me, and understood what I wanted her to respond to and focus on. When I first started the therapy, I was pretty uncertain about the whole thing (and whether it would even help), but I kept coming and eventually – as she adapted to where I was coming from – the therapy became really helpful. I didn't realize that even experienced therapists go through a learning curve to adjust to new clients.

In my experience with seeing therapists as part of an accountability process, I have also noticed a couple patterns worth mentioning. The first one is that therapy alone wasn't enough to give me the tools I needed for transformation. My own healing and change process has also required (and still does require) conversations with friends, conversations with people who have experience with radical conceptions of consent, reading and self-education, and a lot of personal and group work outside the context of the therapy office. The second issue that's important to bring up involves a typical therapist's understanding of radical politics and community accountability. One of my therapists – who had experience working with people with sexual behavior problems – would pretty frequently express skepticism about the accountability process I was involved in and often seemed somewhat dismissive of the things I was defining as sexual violence. It was only through constant intervention on my part – stopping him and explaining why it was important for me to value disclosure, explaining why it was that some particular things were abusive on my part, or whatever – that I was able to create the kind of therapeutic environment that helped me engage with my accountability process. I have heard, repeatedly, of other cases of people going to therapy as part of an accountability process and the therapist dismissing the need for an accountability process and minimizing the harm caused to the survivor. Because therapists are supposed to be "experts," and are widely given the authority that comes from the term, it can be easy to allow a therapist to let you off the hook. Instead, however, I would challenge you to consider the impact that letting yourself off the hook will have on the particular survivor in your situation, on the webs of trust that have been ruptured in your scenes or communities, on your own future relationships.

I would challenge you to consider: the possibility you might end up harming people you really care about in the future; and the ways you might feel boxed in, tense, stunted, defensive or closed because of any feelings you might have (like always needing to be in control). I would challenge you to start reading and believing accounts written by survivors of abuse and sexual violence. I would challenge you to educate yourself first and then start asking: What will be the greater impact of my actions if I allow myself to be let off the hook? Who will I harm, what will be made less possible, why do I want to get off the hook? For transformation and healing to happen, you have to be able to challenge an expert who's giving you an easy way out. In fact, you have to be committed to it.

Pattrice Jones also has a couple of recommendations of things to do to compliment therapy. She says while talking to others is essential, there are also things you can and should do to take care of yourself. She recommends that people make a list of these things, then refer to the list when they're feeling bad and don't know what to do. She counsels people to make themselves do things on the list until they feel better. She especially recommends making a list of "oases," activities that give you a break from trauma and intense feelings by allowing you to absorb yourself in something else. Reading and TV, for example, she doesn't consider oases; your mind can easily drift back to trauma while doing these things. Oases keep your attention by requiring you to do something. In contrast, she says bowling, gardening, and tinkering can be oases – any of these activities (and plenty of others) can be both distracting and soothing. She counsels people to make a list of what works for them, and then turn to the list when they need a break. Similarly, she talks about "anchors;" an anchor is a person, place, activity or thing that gives physical feelings of relaxation, safety, or well-being. Again, she suggests that people make a list of anchors and then go to or even just thing about an anchor when they need to experience a positive feeling for change. Self-care is an essential part of healing and transformation; healing and transformation can only happen through love, and self-care goes hand-in-hand with the kind of self-love required for positive, sustained change.

These are some of my thoughts, experiences, and collected pearls of knowledge. I hope they prove useful and help guide you on your path towards accountability. Even though I'm an anonymous ghost living behind a veil of paper and words, I care. I want you to find peace, love, and healing. The work is worth it; I know because I am doing it. Things get better and things change, and as hard as accountability can be, it is worth it.

Don't give up.

5.11. RESOURCE LIST

COMMUNITY-BASED INTERVENTIONS, COMMUNITY ACCOUNTABILITY, TRANSFORMATIVE JUSTICE & RESTORATIVE JUSTICE RESOURCES

This is a brief list of resources first gathered in 2012 available on community-based interventions to interpersonal violence, community accountability and tranformative justice. It also includes some articles and zines that can be helpful in particular to survivors of violence and people doing harm. **For ongoing updates, please see batjc.wordpress.com and transformharm.org.**

The Revolution Starts at Home
(booklet format -- has the content of the zine version, not the book version) Also available as a book published by South End Press and reprinted by AK Press.

https://incite-national.org/wp-content/uploads/2018/08/revolution-starts-at-home-zine.pdf

The Revolution Starts at Home (book)
https://www.akpress.org/revolutionstartsathome.html

Beyond Survival: Strategies and Stories from the Transformative Justice Movement, edited by Ejeris Dixon and Leah Lakshmi Piepzna-Samarasinha

https://www.akpress.org/beyond-survival.html

Fumbling Towards Repair: A Workbook for Community Accountability Facilitators

https://www.akpress.org/fumbling-towards-repair.html

Special Issue of Social Justice, 37(4), 2012. Community Accountability: Emerging Movements to Transform Violence
http://communityaccountability.wordpress.com/

INCITE! Community Accountability Within People of Color Progressive Movements

https://incite-national.org/wp-content/uploads/2018/08/cmty-acc-poc.pdf

INCITE! and Critical Resistance: Statement on Gender Violence and the Prison Industrial Complex
https://incite-national.org/incite-critical-resistance-statement/

Philly Stands Up/Philly's Pissed articles (about their organizing models)
http://phillyspissed.net/taxonomy/term/1

A Stand Up Start Up [Philly Stands Up organizing zine]
https://kloncke.files.wordpress.com/2011/04/a-stand-up-start-up.pdf

Taking Risks: Implementing Community Accountability Strategies (which is also in the Rev @ Home zine, but not the book)

http://www.transformativejustice.eu/wp-content/uploads/2010/11/Taking-Risks.-CARA.pdf

INCITE! Women of Color Against Violence Community Accountability Working Document
http://www.incite-national.org/index.php?s=93

Ending Child Sexual Abuse: A Transformative Justice Handbook
http://www.generationfive.org/wp-content/uploads/2017/06/Transformative-Justice-Handbook.pdf

Let's Talk: Adults Talking to Adults about Child Sexual Abuse https://www.stopitnow.org/sites/default/files/documents/files/lets_talk.pdf

Fight Rape: Dealing With Our Shit
https://toleratedindividuality.files.wordpress.com/2015/02/dealing-with-our-shit-six-years-of-mens-group-and-accountability-work.pdf

Protection Without Police: North American Community Responses to Violence in

http://uppingtheanti.org/journal/uta/number-12

Alternatives to Police
https://rosecitycopwatch.files.wordpress.com/2010/03/alternatives-to-police-draft.pdf

Revolution in Conflict: Anti-Authoritarian Approaches to Resolving and Transforming Conflict and Harm [audio and text versions] https://toleratedindividuality.files.wordpress.com/2015/02/revolution-in-conflict-anti-authoritarian-approaches-to-resolving-and-transforming-conflict-and-harm.pdf

World Without Sexual Assault: For A Community Response to Sexual Assault https://toleratedindividuality.files.wordpress.com/2015/02/world-without-sexual-assault-for-a-community-response-to-sexual-assault.pdft

Hollow Water [film] http://www.onf-nfb.gc.ca/eng/collection/film/?id=50027

The Interrupters [film]
https://kartemquin.com/films/the-interrupters/about

Restorative Justice and Violence Against Women, edited by James Ptacek
https://global.oup.com/ushe/product/restorative-justice-and-violence-against-women-9780195335484?cc=us&lang=en&

Survivor Support

Support
http://phillyspissed.net/node/18

Apoyo (spanish-language version of Support): http://microcosmpublishing.com/catalog/zines/2420/

Supporting a Survivor of Sexual Assault (10 Steps) http://brokenbeautifuldowloads.wordpress.com/

No! The Rape Documentary [film]
http://notherapedocumentary.org/

Male Survivor
http://www.malesurvivor.org

Trans and Intersex Survivors of Domestic Violence
https://vawnet.org/sc/serving-trans-and-non-binary-survivors-domestic-and-sexual-violence/violence-against-trans-and

Resources for Accountability

As If They Were Human: A Different Take on Perpetrator Accountability [three Tod Augusta-Scott articles in booklet form] http://relationshipanarchy.com/wp-content/uploads/augusta-scott-comp-zine-imposed_singlepage.pdf

What is the opposite of accountability (section from Community Accountability Within People of Color Progressive Movements by INCITE!) https://incite-national.org/wp-content/uploads/2018/08/cmty-acc-poc.pdf

Taking the First Step (zine form) https://ia802608.us.archive.org/19/items/TakingTheFirstStepSuggestionsToPeopleCalledOutForAbusiveBehavior/taking_the_first_step.pdf

What to do when you've been called out https://toleratedindividuality.files.wordpress.com/2015/02/what-to-do-when-youve-been-called-out.pdf

For Men/Male Identified People Working against Domestic and Sexual Violence

Why Misognyists Make Great Informants (zine form) https://ia802605.us.archive.org/17/items/WhyMisogynistsMakeGreatInformants/misogynists_great_informants.pdf

Philly Dudes Collective Year One (and a half) http://www.microcosmpublishing.com/catalog/zines/1791/

On the Road to Healing https://ia800902.us.archive.org/2/items/OnTheRoadToHealing1/on_the_road_to_healing_1.pdf

Experiments in Transformative Justice by the Challenging Male Supremacy Project http://zapagringo.blogspot.com/2010/06/challenging-male-supremacy-project.html

Anti-sexism for Men of Color http://colours.mahost.org/org/notenough.html

Positive Sexuality

Learning Good Consent http://phillyspissed.net/node/32

How to Put Together Your Own Consent Workshop http://nwbreakthesilence.wordpress.com/zine-project/

My Body My Limits My Pleasure My Choice http://phillyspissed.net/node/9

Abuse is Not S/M and S/M is Not Abuse https://www.indybay.org/uploads/2010/09/24/abuse_is_not_sm_and_sm_is_not_abuse_-_a_checklist.pdf

Trauma

Emotional Trauma First Aid Handout
http://www.ncmhr.org/downloads/trauma_first_aid_fact_sheet12-08.pdf

Trauma Stewardship: An Everyday Guide to Caring for Self While Caring for Others
http://traumastewardship.com/the-book/inside-the-book/

Survivor's Guide to Sex/Healing Sex [The newer Healing Sex publication of the book has an Introduction about somatics]
http://www.cleispress.com/book_page.php?book_id=218

Trauma and Recovery, book by Judith Herman Lewis

Thriving in the Wake of Trauma: A Multicultural Guide by Thema Bryant-Davis

The Body Remembers: The Psychophysiology of Trauma and Trauma Treatment by Babette Rothschild
Waking the Tiger, book by Peter Levine

National Phone Numbers

Stop It Now! Helpline

1-888-PREVENT (1-888-773-8368) (Monday to Friday, 12:00PM to 6:00PM EST) http://www.stopitnow.org

This is a toll-free number for adults who are at risk for sexually abusing a child, for friends and family members of sexual abusers and/or victims, and for parents of children with sexual behavior problems. All calls are confidential and will be answered by a trained staff member. (They encourage people to report to the legal system, but they will not report anyone themselves.) If you need someone to talk to, but you're afraid to start the conversations, calling the helpline may be a good first step.

National Domestic Violence Hotline

1-800-799-SAFE (7233)
1-800-787-3223 (TTY)
http://www.ndvh.org/

This is a 24-hour hotline that operates 365 days a year, and not only offers support to survivors of domestic violence, but also to perpetrators of domestic violence. Their website also has a variety of resources about domestic violence and abuse.

Gay Men's Domestic Violence Project

800-832-1901
http://gmdvp.org/gmdvp/
This website contains information on the similarities and differences between domestic violence in gay and heterosexual relationships. There are a few survivor stories from gay men abused by other gay men, myth-debunking about intimate partner abuse in gay relationships, and information about why men (and gay men in particular) stay in such abusive relationships.

NOTES